Marriages, Families, and Relationships:

Making Choices in a Diverse Society

Special 11th Edition for Iowa State University

Teresa Downing-Matibag

Mary Ann Lamanna | Agnes Riedmann

Australia • Brazil • Japan • Korea • Mexico • Singapore • Spain • United Kingdom • United States

Marriages, Families, and Relationships: Making Choices in a Diverse Society; Special 11th Edition for Iowa State University; Teresa Downing-Matibag

Executive Editors:
Maureen Staudt
Michael Stranz

Senior Project Development Manager:
Linda deStefano

Marketing Specialist:
Courtney Sheldon

Senior Production/Manufacturing Manager:
Donna M. Brown

PreMedia Manager:
Joel Brennecke

Sr. Rights Acquisition Account Manager:
Todd Osborne

Cover Image:
Getty Images*

*Unless otherwise noted, all cover images used by Custom Solutions, a part of Cengage Learning, have been supplied courtesy of Getty Images with the exception of the Earthview cover image, which has been supplied by the National Aeronautics and Space Administration (NASA).

Marriages, Families, and Relationships: Making Choices in a Diverse Society; 11 e
Mary Ann Lamanna | Agnes Riedmann

ISBN-13: 978-1-133-15209-5

ISBN-10: 1-133-15209-0

Cengage Learning
5191 Natorp Boulevard
Mason, Ohio 45040
USA

Cengage Learning is a leading provider of customized learning solutions with office locations around the globe, including Singapore, the United Kingdom, Australia, Mexico, Brazil, and Japan. Locate your local office at: **international.cengage.com/region.**

Cengage Learning products are represented in Canada by Nelson Education, Ltd.
For your lifelong learning solutions, visit **www.cengage.com /custom.**
Visit our corporate website at **www.cengage.com.**

Printed in the United States of America

MARRIAGES, FAMILIES, AND RELATIONSHIPS:

MAKING CHOICES IN A DIVERSE SOCIETY

CUSTOM TABLE OF CONTENTS

1

Marriage, Relationships, and Family Commitments: Making Choices in a Changing Society

Ariel Skelley/Getty Images

Defining *Family*

Issues for Thought: Which of These Is a Family?

Family Functions

Structural Family Definitions

Postmodern: There Is No Typical Family

Adapting Family Definitions to the Postmodern Family

Facts about Families: American Families Today

Relaxed Institutional Control over Relationship Choices—"Family Decline" or "Family Change"?

Facts about Families: Focus on Children

Three Societal Trends That Impact Families

Advancing Communication and Reproductive Technologies

The New Faces of America's Families: Fewer Non-Hispanic Whites, More People of Color

Economic Uncertainty

The Freedom and Pressures of Choosing

Personal Troubles, Societal Influences, and Family Policy

How Social Factors Influence Personal Choices

Making Choices

Choosing by Default

Choosing Knowledgeably

A Family of Individuals

Families as a Place to Belong

Familistic (Communal) Values and Individualistic (Self-Fulfillment) Values

Partners as Individuals and Family Members

Marriages and Families: Four Themes

This text is different from others you may read. It isn't intended to prepare you for a particular occupation. Instead, it has three other goals: to help you to (1) appreciate the variety and diversity among families today; (2) understand your past and present family situations and anticipate future possibilities; and (3) be more conscious of the personal decisions you must make throughout your life and of the societal influences that affect those decisions.

Families are central to society and to our everyday lives. Families undertake the pivotal tasks of raising children and providing members with intimacy, affection, and companionship. In recent times, what we think of as "family" has changed dramatically. Indeed, today's is "not your grandmother's" family.

In this chapter, we'll look at the difficulty of defining the family today, partly because the word *family* is a "nice" term—one with which almost everyone wants to be associated (Popenoe 1993, p. 529). We'll explore some definitions of the family. After that, we will discuss three broad social trends that affect our relationships and family life.

Later in this chapter, we'll note that when maintaining committed relationships and families, people need the ability to make knowledgeable decisions. The theme of knowledge plus commitment is an integral part of this book. We begin this chapter with a working definition of *family*—one that we can keep in mind throughout the course.

Defining *Family*

When asked to list their family members, some college students include their pets. Are dogs and cats family members? Some individuals who were conceived by artificial insemination with donor sperm are tracking down their "donor siblings"—half brothers and sisters who were conceived using the same man's sperm. They may define their "donor relatives" as family (Shapiro 2009). People make a variety of assumptions about what families are or should be. Indeed, there are many definitions given for the family today, not only among laypeople but also among family scientists themselves (Weigel 2008). To begin to think more about your own definition, you might examine "Issues for Thought: Which of These Is a Family?"

We, your authors, have chosen to define **family** as follows: A family is any sexually expressive, parent–child, or other kin relationship in which people—usually related by ancestry, marriage, or adoption—(1) form an economic and/or otherwise practical unit and care for any children or other dependents, (2) consider their identity to be significantly attached to the group, and (3) commit to maintaining that group over time.

How did we come to this definition? First, caring for children or other dependents suggests a function that the family is expected to perform. Definitions of many things have both *functional* and *structural* components. Functional definitions point to the purpose(s) for which a thing exists—i.e., what it *does*. For example, a functional definition of an iPhone would emphasize that it allows you to make and receive calls, take pictures, connect to the Internet, and access media. Structural definitions emphasize the form that a thing takes—what it actually *is*. To define an iPhone structurally, we might say that it is an electronic device, small enough to be handheld, with a multimedia screen, and whose components allow for sophisticated satellite communication.

© Bill Aron/ PhotoEdit

© Ron Chapple/Getty Images

An indirect indicator of the centrality of the family to American life is the degree to which family themes are used as advertising motifs. In the first photo, a family splashing happily in the ocean fronts an ad for "Hottest Hotels," while the text of the second photo from another ad describes the family life of the father and the child pictured.

Issues for Thought

Which of These Is a Family?

A husband and wife and their offspring.

A single woman and her three young children.

A fifty-two-year-old woman and her adoptive mother.

A man, his daughter, and the daughter's son.

An eighty-four-year-old widow and her dog, Fido.

A man and all of his ancestors back to Adam and Eve.

The 1979 World Champion Pittsburgh Pirates (theme song: "We Are Family").

Three adult sisters living together.

Two lesbians in an intimate relationship and their children from a previous marriage of one woman and a previous relationship of the other woman with a male friend.

Two children, their divorced parents, the current spouses of their divorced parents, and the children from previous marriages of their stepparents.

A child, his stepfather, and the stepfather's wife subsequent to his divorce from the child's mother.

Two adult male cousins living together.

A seventy-seven-year-old man and his lifelong best friend.

A childless husband and wife who live one thousand miles apart.

A widow and her former husband's grandfather's sister's granddaughter.

A divorced man, his girlfriend, and her child.

Both sets of parents of a deceased married couple.

A married couple, one son and his wife, and the latter couple's children, all living together.

Six adults and their twelve young children, all living together in a communal fashion.

Critical Thinking

Which of these do you consider a family? What is it that makes them "family" or "not family"?

Source: From *Family Theories: An Introduction*, by James K. White and David M. Klein, p. 22.

Concepts of the family comprise both functional and structural aspects (Weigel 2008). We'll look now at how the family can be recognized by its functions, and then we'll discuss structural definitions of the family.

Family Functions

Social scientists usually list three major functions filled by today's families: raising children responsibly, providing members with economic and other practical support, and offering emotional security.

Family Function 1: Raising Children Responsibly If a society is to persist beyond one generation, it is necessary that adults not only bear children but also feed, clothe, and shelter them during their long years of dependency. Furthermore, a society needs new members who are properly trained in the ways of the culture and who will be dependable members of the group. These goals require children to be responsibly raised. Virtually every society assigns this essential task to families.

A related family function has traditionally been to control its members' sexual activity. Although there are several reasons for the social control of sexual activity, the most important one is to ensure that reproduction takes place under circumstances that help to guarantee the responsible care and socialization of children. The universally approved locus of reproduction remains the married-couple family. "Marriage remains the most common living arrangement for raising children. At any one time, most American children are being raised by two parents" (Cherlin 2005, p. 37). Still, in the United States and other industrialized countries today, the child-rearing function is often performed by divorced, separated, never-married, and/or cohabiting parents, and sometimes by grandparents.

Family Function 2: Providing Economic and Other Practical Support A second family function involves providing economic support. Throughout much of our history, the family was primarily a practical, economic unit rather than an emotional one (Shorter 1975; Stone 1980). Although the modern family is no longer a self-sufficient economic unit, virtually every family engages in activities aimed at providing for such practical needs as food, clothing, and shelter.

Family economic functions now consist of earning a living outside the home, pooling resources, and making consumption decisions together. In assisting one another economically, family members create some sense of material security. For example, spouses and partners offer each other a kind of unemployment insurance. Family members also care for one another in other practical ways, such as nursing and transportation during an illness.

Family Function 3: Offering Emotional Security Although historically the family was a pragmatic institution involving material maintenance, in today's world the family has grown increasingly important as a source of emotional security (Cherlin 2008; Coontz 2005b).

Many people who own pets think of them as part of the family. Do you think it is appropriate to broaden the definition of *family* to include other than humans? What changes in the family may have encouraged changes in our attitudes about pets and family membership?

This is not to say that families can solve all our longings for affection, companionship, and intimacy. Sometimes, in fact, the family situation itself is a source of stress, as discussed in Chapters 12 and 13. But families and committed relationships are meant to offer important emotional support to adults and children. Family may mean having a place where you can be yourself, even sometimes your worst self, and still belong.

Defining a family by its functions is informative and can bc insightful. For cxamplc, Laura Dawn, in her book of stories about people who took in survivors of Hurricane Katrina, describes "how strangers became family" (Dawn 2006). But defining a family only by its functions would be too vague and misleading. For instance, neighbors or roommates might help with childcare, provide for economic and other practical needs, or offer emotional support. But we still might not think of them as family. An effective definition of family needs to incorporate its structural elements as well.

Structural Family Definitions

Traditionally, both legal and social sciences have specified that the family consists of people related by blood, marriage, or adoption. In their classic work *The Family: From Institution to Companionship*, Ernest Burgess and Harvey Locke (1953 [1945]) specified that family members must "constitute a household," or reside together. Some definitions of the family have gone even further to include economic interdependency and sexual–reproductive relations (Murdock 1949).

The U.S. Census Bureau defines a family as "a group of two or more persons related by blood, marriage, or adoption and residing together in a household" (U.S. Census Bureau 2010b, p. 6). It is important to note here that the Census Bureau uses the term **household** for any group of people residing together. Not all households are families by the Census Bureau definition—that is, persons sharing a household must *also* be related by blood, marriage, or adoption to be considered a family.

Family structure, or the form a family takes, varies according to the society in which it is embedded. In preindustrial or *traditional* societies, the family structure involved whole kinship groups. The **extended family** of parents, children, grandparents, and other relatives performed most societal functions, including economic production (e.g., the family farm), protection of family members, vocational training, and maintaining social order. In industrial or *modern* societies, the typical family structure often became the **nuclear family** (husband,

Blend Images/Getty Images

The extended family—grandparents, aunts, and uncles—is often an important source of security. Extended families meet most needs in a traditional society—economic and material needs and child care, for example—and they have strong bonds. In urban societies, specialized institutions such as factories, schools, and public agencies often meet practical needs. But extended families may also help one another materially in urban society, especially during crises.

wife, children). Until about fifty years ago, social attitudes, religious beliefs, and law converged into a fairly common expectation about what form the American family should take: breadwinner husband, homemaker wife, and children living together in an independent household—the *nuclear family model.* Nevertheless, the *extended* family continues to play an important role in many cases, especially among recent immigrants and race/ethnic minorities.[1]

Today, family members are not necessarily bound to one another by legal marriage, blood, or adoption. The term *family* can identify relationships beyond spouses, parents, children, and extended kin. Individuals fashion and experience intimate relationships and families in many forms. As social scientists take into account this structural variability, it is not uncommon to find them referring to the family as *postmodern* (Stacey 1990).

[1] The *nuclear* family has lost many functions formerly performed by the traditional extended family (Goode 1963). Economic production now primarily involves working for a nonfamily employer. Police and fire departments, the military, juvenile authorities, and mental health services provide protection and maintain social order. Schools, technical institutes, and universities educate and train the upcoming generation.

Postmodern: There Is No Typical Family

Today, only 7 percent of families fit the 1950s nuclear family ideal of married couple and children, with a husband-breadwinner and wife-homemaker (U.S. Census Bureau 2009e, Tables F1, FG8). Two-earner families are common, and there are reversed-role relationships (working wife, househusband). The past several decades have witnessed a proliferation of relationship and family forms: single-parent families, stepfamilies, cohabitating heterosexual couples, gay and lesbian marriages and families, three-generation families, and communal households, among others. It appears that individuals can construct a myriad of social forms in order to address family functions. The term **postmodern family** came into use in order to acknowledge the fact that families today exhibit a multiplicity of forms and that new or altered family forms continue to emerge and develop.

Figure 1.1 displays the types of households in which Americans live. Just 21.5 percent of households are nuclear families of husband, wife, and children, as compared with 44 percent in 1960 (Casper and Bianchi 2002, p. 8; U.S. Census Bureau 2010b, Tables 59, 63). The most common household type today is that of married couples *without* children, where the children have grown up and left or where the couple has not yet had children or doesn't plan to.

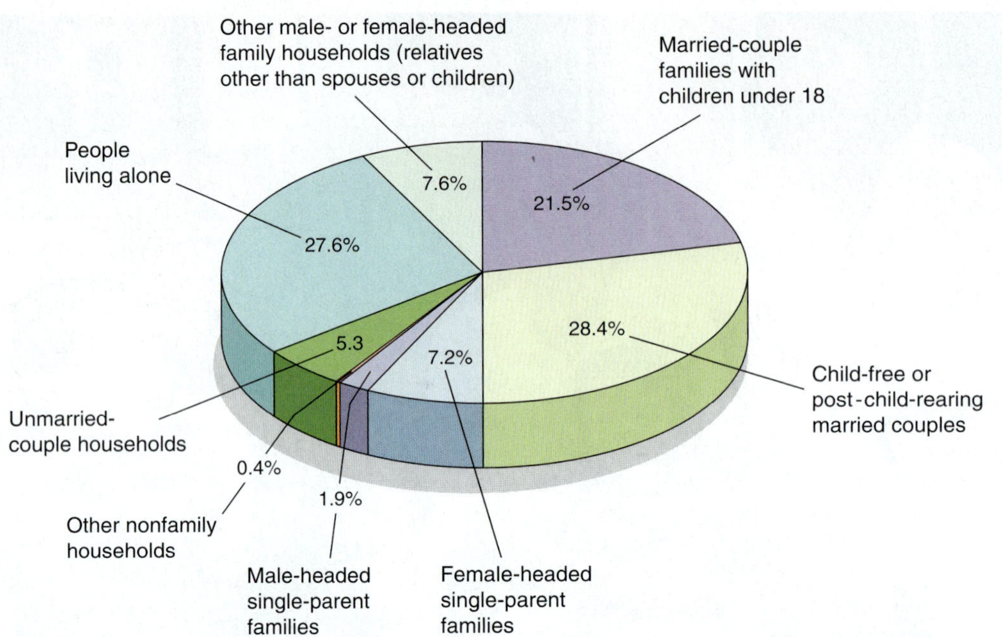

Figure 1.1 The many kinds of American households, 2008.[a] A household is a person or a group of people who occupy a dwelling unit. This figure displays both family and nonfamily households.[b]

Source: U.S. Census Bureau 2010b, Tables 59, 63.

[a]This is the most recent year for which all of the data for this figure are available.

[b]Unmarried-couple households may be composed of two male partners (5.7 percent); two female partners (6.4 percent); or a heterosexual couple (87.9 percent). The Census Bureau classifies unmarried-couple households as "nonfamily households."

More households today (27.6 percent) are maintained by individuals living alone than by married couples with children (U.S. Census Bureau 2008a). There are also female-headed (7.2 percent) and male-headed (1.9 percent) single-parent households, unmarried-couple households (5.3 percent), and family households containing relatives other than spouses or children (7.6 percent). "Facts about Families: American Families Today" presents additional information about other families. Today we see historically unprecedented diversity in family composition, or form.

As one result of this diversity, law, government agencies, and private bureaucracies such as insurance companies must now make decisions about what they once could take for granted—that is, what a family is. If zoning laws, rent policies, employee benefit packages, and insurance policies cover families, decisions need to be made about what relationships or groups of people are to be defined as family. The September 11th Victim Compensation Fund of 2001 struggled with this issue in allocating compensation to victims' survivors. New York State law was amended to allow awards to unmarried gay and heterosexual partners (Gross 2002). President George W. Bush subsequently signed a federal bill extending benefits to domestic partners of firefighters and police officers who lose their lives in the line of duty (Allen 2002).[2]

Adapting Family Definitions to the Postmodern Family

As family forms have grown increasingly variable, social scientists have proposed—and often struggled with—new, more flexible definitions for the family. Sociologist David Popenoe (1993) defines today's family as "a group of people in which people typically live together in a household and function as a cooperative unit, particularly through the sharing of economic resources, in the pursuit of domestic activities" (1993, p. 528). Sociologist Frank Furstenberg writes as follows: "My definition of 'family' includes membership related by blood, legal ties, adoption, and informal ties including *fictive* or socially agreed upon kinship" (2005, p. 810, italics in original).

Legal definitions of family have become more flexible as well. In the past few decades, judges, when

[2]A *domestic partnership* is a legal or policy-defined relationship between two individuals who live together and share a domestic life but are not married. Domestic partnership laws and policies generally apply to both same-sex and heterosexual couples.

Facts about Families

American Families Today[a]

What do U.S. families look like today? Statistics can't tell the whole story, but they are an important beginning. As you read this box, it's important to remember that the demographic data presented here are generalizations and do not allow for differences among various sectors of society. Chapter 3 explores social diversity, but for now let's look at these overall statistics.

1. Marriage is important to Americans. About 90 percent of American adults are or have been married, or say that they want to marry (Bergman 2006a; Saad 2006b).
2. Fewer people are married today. Fifty-eight percent of adults were married in 2008, compared to 61 percent in 1990. Twenty-six percent have never married; 10 percent are divorced, and 6 percent widowed (U.S. Census Bureau 2010b, Table 56).
3. People are postponing marriage. In 2009, the median age at first marriage was 25.9 for women and 28.1 for men, as compared with 20.8 for women and 23.2 for men in 1970 (U.S. Census Bureau 2010a, Table MS-2).
4. Cohabitation is an emergent family form as well as a transitional lifestyle choice. The number of cohabitating adults has increased more than tenfold since 1970 (U.S. Census Bureau 2009e, Table UC-1). Nearly 40 percent of cohabiting couples lived with children under eighteen in 2008—either their own or from a previous relationship or marriage. Unmarried-couple families are only 5 percent of households at any one time, but more than 50 percent of first marriages are preceded by cohabitation (Fields 2004; Smock and Gupta 2002; U.S. Census Bureau 2009e, Table UC-1).
5. Fertility has declined. After a high of 3.6 in 1957, the total fertility rate—the average number of births that a woman will have during her lifetime—has been at about 2 over the past twenty years (Dye 2008; U.S. Census Bureau 2010b, Table 83). One-fifth of women ages 40–44 are childless—a fraction that is twice as high as thirty years ago (Dye 2008).
6. Parenthood is often postponed. About 19 percent of women reach their forties without bearing a child (Dye 2008).
7. The nonmarital birth rate has risen over the past sixty years. Compared to 4 percent in 1950, more than one-third (38 percent) of all U.S. births today are to unmarried mothers (U.S. Census Bureau 2010b, Tables 80, 85). Between one quarter and one half of nonmarital births today occur to cohabitating couples (Carter 2009; Dye 2008).
8. Same-sex couples—some of them legally married—are increasingly visible. About 565,000 same-sex couple households existed in 2008 (Gates 2009b). It's estimated that about one-fifth of male same-sex partner households and one-third of female same-sex households include children (Rosenfeld and Byung-Soo 2005).[b]
9. The divorce rate is high. The divorce rate doubled from 1965 to 1980. Then it dropped, having fallen more than 30 percent since 1980 (U.S. Census Bureau 2006c, Tables 72, 117; 2009e, Table 123). Still, it is estimated that between 40 and 50 percent of recent first marriages will end in divorce (Cherlin 2009a; U.S. Census Bureau 2007b, Table 2).
10. The remarriage rate has declined in recent decades but remains significant. Among the divorced, about 52 percent of men and 44 percent of women remarry. In 2004, 12 percent of all adult men and 13 percent of women had been married twice. Three percent of men and of women had married three or more times (Edwards 2007).
11. There are more families with members over age sixty-five today than in the past. The proportion of Americans over age 65 is about 13 percent, and that figure is projected to reach 20 percent by 2050 (U.S. Census Bureau 2010b, Table 8).

Critical Thinking

What do these statistics tell you about the strengths and weaknesses of the contemporary American family and about family change?

a. Figures differ depending on whether *household* or *family* is the unit of analysis. For example, married-couple family households are about 61 percent of all *households*, but about 82 percent of all *families* (U.S. Census Bureau 2010b, Table 59).

b. It is difficult to accurately estimate the number of same-sex-couple households in the United States (O'Connell and Lofquist 2009). See the discussion on this topic in Chapter 8, with attention to footnotes 5 and 6 in Chapter 8.

defining the family in cases that come before them, have used the more intangible qualities of stability and commitment along with the more traditional criteria of common residence and economic interdependency (*Dunphy v. Gregor* 1994). From this point of view, the definition of family "is the totality of the relationship as evidenced by the dedication, caring and self-sacrifice of the parties" (Judge Vito Titone in *Braschi v. Stahl Associates Company* 1989).

Many employers have redefined *family* with respect to employee benefit packages. Just over half of the Fortune 500 companies, as well as many state and local governments, offer domestic partner benefits. In 2009, legislation was introduced in Congress that may extend domestic partner benefits to all federal civilian employees, and President Obama signed an executive order granting federal employees and their domestic partners some of the rights enjoyed by married couples (Human Rights Campaign 2009; Phillips 2009). Federal practices permit low-income unmarried couples to qualify as families and live in public housing. Several states allow same-sex marriage, and several others provide some spousal rights to same-sex couples. Same-sex marriage is discussed further in Chapter 8.

We, your authors, began this section with our definition of *family*. Our definition integrates important elements of the definitions described previously. We recognize the diversity of postmodern families, while paying heed to the essential functions that families are expected to fill. Our definition combines some structural criteria with a more social–psychological sense of family identity. We include the commitment to maintaining a relationship or group over time as a component of our definition because we believe that such a commitment is necessary in fulfilling basic family functions. It also helps to differentiate the family from casual relationships, such as roommates, or groups that easily come and go.

We have worked to balance an appreciation for flexibility and diversity in family structure and relations—and for freedom of choice—with the increased concern of many social scientists about the family's ongoing functional obligations. We hope that our definition will stimulate your thoughts about what a family is. Ultimately, because society exercises diminished control over what form a family should take, there is no one correct answer to the question, "What is a family?"

Relaxed Institutional Control over Relationship Choices—"Family Decline" or "Family Change"?

Historically, the family has been understood as a **social institution**. Social institutions are patterned and largely predictable ways of thinking and behaving—beliefs, values, attitudes, and norms—that are organized around vital aspects of group life and serve essential social functions. Social institutions are meant to meet people's basic needs and enable the society to survive. Earlier in this chapter, we described three basic family functions. Because social institutions prescribe socially accepted beliefs, values, attitudes, and behaviors, they exert considerable social control over individuals.

Since the 1960s, however, family formation has become less and less predictable. As young people began to postpone marriage and more couples divorced, the proportion of the adult population that was married decreased. Cohabitation and single-mother families increased. In the 1990s, "the number of same-sex cohabitating couples recorded in the U.S. census rose sharply" (Rosenfeld and Byung-Soo 2005, p. 541). More recently, same-sex marriage has emerged and is now legally available in about 10 percent of states. Combined with increased longevity and lower fertility rates, these changes have meant that a smaller portion of adulthood is spent in traditionally institutionalized marriages and families (Cherlin 2004, 2008).

"Beginning in the late 1950's, Americans began to change their ideas about the individual's obligations to family and society.... [T]his change was away from an ethic of obligation to others and toward an obligation to self" (Whitehead 1997, p. 4). Put another way, we are witnessing an ongoing social trend that involves increasingly relaxed institutional control over relationship choices. Whether this diminished institutional control is harmful or beneficial is a matter of debate among social scientists, policy makers, talk radio hosts, and many of the rest of us.

Critics have described the relaxation of institutional control over relationships and families as "family decline" or "breakdown." Those with a **family decline perspective** claim that a cultural change toward excessive individualism and self-indulgence has led to high divorce rates and could undermine responsible parenting (Whitehead and Popenoe 2006):

> According to a marital decline perspective ... because people no longer wish to be hampered with obligations to others, commitment to traditional institutions that require these obligations, such as marriage, has eroded. As a result, people no longer are willing to remain married through the difficult times, for better or for worse. Instead, marital commitment lasts only as long as people are happy and feel that their own needs are being met. (Amato 2004, p. 960)

Moreover, fewer family households contain children. According to the family decline perspective, this situation "has reduced the child centeredness of our nation and contributed to the weakening of the institution of marriage" (Popenoe and Whitehead 2005, p. 23). "Facts about Families: Focus on Children" provides some statistical indicators about the families of contemporary children.

Not everyone concurs that the family is in decline: family change, yes, but not decline. "Marriage has been in a constant state of evolution since the dawn of the Stone Age.... But although the institution of marriage is undergoing a powerful revolution, there is no marriage crisis," declares historian Stephanie Coontz (2005a, p. A17).

Advocates with a **family change perspective** argue that we need to view the family from an historical standpoint. In the nineteenth and early twentieth centuries, American families were often broken up by illness and death, and children were sent to orphanages, foster homes, or already burdened relatives. Single mothers, as well as wives in lower-class, working-class, and immigrant families, did not stay home with children but went out to labor in factories, workshops, or domestic service. The proportion of children living only with their fathers in 1990 wasn't much different from that of a century ago (Kreider and Fields 2005, p. 12).

Facts about Families

Focus on Children

In many places throughout this text, we focus particularly on children in families. As with our population as a whole, the number of children in the United States is growing. Today there are approximately 84 million children under age eighteen living in the United States. However, the proportion of children under eighteen today—about 24 percent—represents a substantial drop from the 1960s, when more than one-third of Americans were children (U.S. Census Bureau 2010b, Table 8; U.S. Federal Interagency Forum on Child and Family Statistics 2006). Here we look at five statistical indicators regarding U.S. children's living arrangements and overall economic well-being.

1. *At any given time, a majority of children live in two-parent households.* In 2008, 70 percent of children under eighteen lived with two parents—and 68 percent, with two *married* parents. Twenty-six percent of children lived with only one parent (23 percent with mother; 4 percent with father), and another 4 percent did not live with either parent (U.S. Census Bureau 2008a, Table SO901; U.S. Census Bureau 2009c, Table CH-1).
2. *Even in two-parent households, there is considerable variation in children's living arrangements.* A 2001 study on the living arrangements of children in two-parent households found 88 percent of children living with their biological parents (3 percent unmarried), 6 percent with biological mother and stepfather, 1 percent with biological father and stepmother, and smaller numbers with an adoptive parent or stepparent (Kreider and Fields 2005, Table 1).
3. *Individuals experience a variety of living arrangements throughout childhood.* A child may live in an intact two-parent family, a single-parent household, with a cohabitating parent, and in a remarried family in sequence (Raley and Wildsmith 2004). About half of all American children are expected to live in a single-parent household at some point in their lives, most likely in a single-mother household (U.S. Federal Interagency Forum 2005, p. 8, Figure POP6-A).[a]
4. *Children are more likely to live with a grandparent today than in the recent past.* In 1970, 3 percent of children lived in a household containing a grandparent, but by 2008 that rate had more than doubled, to 9 percent. In about a quarter of the cases, grandparents had sole responsibility for raising the child, but many households containing grandparents are extended family households that include other relatives as well (Edwards 2009; Kreider and Fields 2005, Tables 7, 8, 10).
5. *Although most parents are employed, children are more likely than the general population to be living in poverty.* The poverty rate of children has stood at about 18 percent over the past ten years, whereas that of the general adult population is about 12 percent and that of the elderly, about 10 percent. The child poverty rate is lower now than its peak of 22.3 percent in 1983, but higher than in 1970 (U.S. Census Bureau 2009g, Tables 690, 691; 2010b, Table 697). About 13.3 million American children live in poverty, and about 5.8 million of those live in extreme poverty (Children's Defense Fund 2009, p. 14; U.S. Census Bureau 2010b, Table 697).

Critical Thinking

Perhaps the greatest concern Americans have about contemporary family change is its impact on children. What do these family data tell us about the family lives of children today?

a. The census category "single-parent family household" obscures the fact that there may be other adults present in that household, such as grandparents. It is also the case that some households defined by the Census Bureau as single-parent households are actually two-parent households. In about 20 percent of "single-father" households and 10 percent of "single-mother" households there is a cohabitating partner (U.S. Federal Interagency Forum 2005, p. 9). The Census Bureau assumes that such a partner functions as a second parent (Fields 2003, pp. 4–5).

Family change scholars posit that today's family forms need to be seen as historically expected adjustments to changing conditions in the wider society, including the decline in manufacturing jobs that used to provide solid economic support for working-class families, the related need for more education, the entry of women into the labor force, and the increased insecurity of middle- and even upper-class jobs. These economic trends have shaped marital timing and fertility rates, as well as the ability of lower-income individuals to enter into marriage (Edin and Kefalas 2005; McLanahan, Donahue, and Haskins 2005).

Furthermore, "Accompanying…the economic changes was a broad cultural shift among Americans that eroded norms both of marriage before childbearing and of stable lifelong bonds after marriage" (Cherlin 2005, p. 46). These social scientists attribute family changes to economic developments as much as to cultural change, but they do not ignore the difficulties that divorce and nonmarital parenthood present to families and children. However, they view the family as "an adaptable institution" (Amato et al. 2003, p. 21) and argue that it makes more sense to provide support to families as they exist today rather than to attempt to turn back the clock to an idealized past (Cherlin 2009a).

Today's families struggle with new economic and time pressures that affect their ability to realize their family values. Family change scholars "believe that at least part of the increase in divorce, living together, and single parenting has less to do with changing values than with inadequate

Courtesy of Mitchell Gold and Trone Advertising

He left me. Good riddance.

He never picked up his socks. He thought I was his mother. He didn't make me laugh anymore.

He's gone. Who cares... All I wanted was the sofa and the dogs.

sofa by montauk

calgary 1327 9th ave s e 403-265-6777 vancouver 1062 homer st 604-331-2363 toronto 220 king st e 416-361-0331 montreal 4404 st laurent blvd 514-845-8285 new york 51 mercer st 212-274-1552 chicago 223 west erie 312-951-5688 san francisco 581 hayes 415-552-0930 los angeles 8163 melrose 323-655-2235 Boston 52 Boylston St. 617-338-8400

www.montauksofa.com

Courtesy of MONTAUKSOFA

One advertisement portrays a happy gay family, making the statement that this is a home like any other. Advertisers have departed from the safe image of the nuclear family to portray nontraditional family forms, as well as family crises such as divorce, as we see in the accompanying photo. The second photo goes so far as to take a rather lighthearted view of divorce. Advertisers say that they are trying to accurately reflect their customers, many of whom "do not fit into the nuclear-family tableau often seen in commercials" (Bosman 2006; see also Lauro 2000).

support for families in the U.S., especially compared to other advanced industrial countries" (Yorburg 2002, p. 33). Many European countries, for example, have paid family leave policies that enable parents to take time off from work to be with young children and that provide more generous economic support for families in crisis.

Some argue further that broad cultural values of individualism and collectivism have not changed all that much. For instance, data from the Longitudinal Study of Generations suggest that an earlier upward trend in individualism may have reversed since the early 1970s and that now the "historical trend is toward greater collectivism" (Bengston, Biblarz, and Roberts 2002, p. 119).

Then, too, most of us wouldn't want to return to an era in which marriage served primarily practical ends while minimizing in importance the happiness of a couple's relationship. Researchers Arland Thornton and Linda Young-DeMarco, who studied attitudes toward the family in the second part of the twentieth century, conclude that "Americans increasingly value freedom and equality in their personal and family lives while at the same time maintaining their commitment to the ideas of marriage, family, and children" (2001, p. 1031).

Scholars, family advocates, and the public continue "this crucial national conversation among Americans struggling to interpret and make sense of the place of marriage and family in today's society" (Nock 2005, p. 13). We return to this debate in Chapter 7. The diversity that we see among families today is the cumulative result of many individuals who have over the years made personal choices about family living. Next, we explore three societal trends that also influence our options as we make choices about relationships and families.

Three Societal Trends That Impact Families

In addition to relaxed institutional control over the family today, three other society-wide trends have already dramatically changed American family life and will continue to do so. These trends are (1) new communication and reproductive technologies, (2) changes in America's race/ethnic composition, and (3) economic uncertainty.

Advancing Communication and Reproductive Technologies

The pace of technological change has never been faster; new technologies will continue to alter not only family relationships but how we define families as well. Here we highlight two recent technologies that have dramatically impacted families: communication and reproductive technologies.

Communication Technologies What are some ways in which communication technology has impacted families? For one thing, it's only fairly recently that parents and children can be readily reached by cell phone. Today we can video record family events such as a birthday party or a bris (the ritual circumcision of a Jewish son) on our cell phones, then send them to family members around the world ("Family Ties" 2008). Then too, with calls and text messaging, parents can monitor teens who aren't home. Technologies installed in family automobiles allow parents to monitor their children's driving speeds, and Global Positioning Systems (GPS) can tell parents where their children have driven.

Developments such as e-mail, websites, webcams, blogs, Facebook, Skype, and Twitter facilitate communication in ways that we would never have dreamed possible thirty years ago. Sixty-two percent of American households have computers at home, and another 10 percent of Americans access computers elsewhere (U.S. Census Bureau 2010b, Table 1118). Many relationships now begin in cyberspace, minimizing the need for geographical proximity at first meeting. Grandparents and other extended family members stay in contact on Facebook (Grossman 2009). Internet access is changing power relations in some families, as tech-savvy youth become information experts for their families, a skill that can enhance their power relative to other family members (Belch, Krentler, and Willis-Flurry 2005).

Home access to the Internet makes family boundaries more permeable. Types of information that would not have been possible before now come into and leave the home (Turow 2001). Social support for a myriad of personal and family challenges, from infertility to living in stepfamilies to caring for someone with a chronic illness, can be found on the Internet. The Internet also offers access to a wealth of information on physical and mental health, as well as opportunities for online therapy.

However, just as the Internet has been a boon for those seeking social support, it has been the source of conflict and concern for some families who have dealt with greater access to pornography and/or with infidelity initiated on the Internet. Social networking sites such as Facebook have made breaking up or divorce potentially more hurtful as partners publish details on their pages (Luscombe 2009). Moreover, communication technology results in a *digital divide* between those who have access to and use computers and the 29 percent of Americans who don't and therefore cannot access the benefits of computer use ("Digital Divide. . ." nd.). Impacts of communication technologies on family life are further explored throughout this text.

Reproductive Technologies "Mommy, Mommy, when I grow up, I want to be a mommy just like you. I want to go to the sperm bank just like you and get some sperm and have a baby just like me" (six-year-old, quoted in Ehrensaft 2005, p. 1).

"Mom?... What was the year that you and Dad met our donor?" (Orenstein 2007, p. 35).

Technology has affected pregnancy as modern science continues to develop new techniques to enable couples or individuals to have biological children. The more common infertility interventions involve prescription drugs and microscopic surgical procedures to repair a female's fallopian tubes or a male's sperm ducts (Ehrenfeld 2002). More widely publicized assisted reproductive technology (ART) offers increasingly successful reproductive options (U.S. Centers for Disease Control and Prevention 2008).

In general, ART involves the manipulation of sperm and/or egg in the absence of sexual intercourse, often in a laboratory, and may involve third parties. ART procedures include artificial insemination (male sperm introduced to a female egg without sexual intercourse); donor insemination (artificial insemination with sperm from a donor rather than from the man who will be involved in raising the child); in vitro fertilization (sperm fertilizes egg in a laboratory rather than in the woman's body); surrogacy (one woman gestates and delivers a baby for another individual who intends to raise the child); egg sale or donation (by means of a surgical procedure, a woman relinquishes some of her eggs for use by others); and embryo transfers (a laboratory-fertilized embryo is placed into a woman's womb for gestation and delivery).

Beside allowing otherwise infertile heterosexual couples to have biological children, how do fertility technologies affect family options? For one thing, artificial insemination by donor allows single individuals, as well as lesbian and gay couples, to become biological parents. There are now commercial sperm banks oriented to a lesbian clientele (Mundy 2007). The ability to freeze eggs, sperm, or fertilized embryos enables individuals to become biological parents later in life, after careers are launched, after undergoing medical treatments that will leave them infertile, or even after death. In the last decade, men deployed to Iraq have banked sperm before their departure, anticipating either contact with hazardous materials or death. At least one baby has been conceived by a father who was killed in Iraq prior to his child's conception (Lehmann-Haupt 2009; Oppenheim 2007).

Although ART procedures allow biological parenthood in ways that were unimaginable thirty years ago, these medical advancements do raise family and ethical issues. Embryo transfer and surrogacy create situations in which a child could have as many as three mothers—the genetic mother who donates or sells her egg, the gestational mother who carries and delivers the child, and the social mother who will raise the child—as well as two fathers, a genetic father and a social father (Schwartz 2003). Many states have laws by which sperm donors, with the exception of the husband, have no parental rights, but this barrier between sperm donors and their biological children is gradually being broken. Some sperm donors are sought out by their "children" as they enter adolescence or young adulthood (Harmon 2007b).

Embryo screening—a technology for examining fertilized eggs before implantation to choose or eliminate certain ones—is a boon for prospective parents whose family heritage includes disabling genetic conditions (Harmon 2006). But it also raises the possibility of selection for sex or other traits (Grady 2007; Marchione and Tanner 2006). Those who use sperm banks may choose donor traits they would like to see in their children (Almeling 2007). Especially marketable are eggs and sperm from donors with certain characteristics such as high intelligence, physical attractiveness, athletic ability, or musical talent. Philosophers ponder the implications for parents and children when children are made to order.

Fertilized embryos may be frozen for later implantation in the event that a parent experiences a desire for more children. However, this process raises the issue of what to do with excess frozen embryos. Opponents of abortion argue that to destroy them is murder, but how long can they be saved, and where? (Excess frozen human embryos are sometimes donated to infertile couples.) ART procedures in which several fertilized embryos are implanted into the uterus, in the hope that one will successfully develop into a baby, often involve early abortion of excess developing embryos. When such abortion procedures are not followed, multiple live births—as many as eight—can be the result (Archibold 2009). Multiple births can occur after the use of fertility drugs or after embryo implantation if a woman refuses to undergo abortion of excess developing fetuses on moral grounds.

Reproductive technologies also raise inequality issues. ART is usually not affordable by those with low incomes. Then too, egg donation is an invasive procedure involving some medical risk. Yet selling of eggs offers some women a way to make money. Interestingly, we have seen more selling of eggs in this latest recession (English 2009).

Other issues involve questions about the child's identity if reproductive sperm or eggs are genetically different from those of the social parents. For example, Judaism is traditionally passed down through the mother's genetic line. Therefore, using an egg from a donor who is not Jewish can raise questions about the child's religio-cultural identity (Orenstein 2007). These issues are further explored in Chapter 9.

Like changing technology, another American social trend affecting families is an increasing racial and ethnic diversity.

The New Faces of America's Families: Fewer Non-Hispanic Whites, More People of Color

In 1965, the United States saw the first indications of fertility decline among non-Hispanic white, native-born women. That same year, the United States opened its doors wider to immigrants, the majority of whom are people of color (Mather 2009). Over the subsequent forty-five years, relatively low fertility rates among non-Hispanic whites (compared to higher rates among racial and ethnic minorities) and immigration have combined to "put the United States on a new demographic path" (Mather 2009).

Across the nation, the faces of America's families, particularly America's children, provide evidence of increasing ethnic diversity. Forty-one million African Americans, including those who identify themselves as mixed race, constitute about 14 percent of the U.S. population and are expected to reach 15 percent by 2050 (U.S. Census Bureau 2009c). Although the number of black immigrants is relatively small compared with those arriving from Latin America and Asia, black migration from Africa and the Caribbean has increased in recent years (Kent 2007; Mather 2009). Making up about one-third of the U.S. population today, racial and ethnic minorities are projected to reach 50 percent of the total population by about 2042. Mostly due to rapid growth in Latino families, the population under age eighteen is projected to reach this point by 2023 (Mather 2009).

Recent immigration rates are not climbing as quickly as they did during the 1990s and early 2000s. Still, the United States admitted approximately one million legal immigrants annually in recent decades. Asia and Latin America are the major sending regions. In addition to legal immigrants, an estimated 11 million unauthorized immigrants reside in the United States, the vast majority from Mexico, Central America, and the Caribbean (Mather and Pollard 2009).

Although immigrants were previously concentrated in a few states, now they are much more geographically dispersed. Many U.S. counties have now reached "majority-minority" status, with more than half of their residents identified as a race other than non-Hispanic white (Mather and Pollard 2009). Many refugees (persons outside the country of their nationality who cannot return to their home country due to threats of violence against a social category or group to which they belong) have spread out across the United States to areas that previously had little recent immigration. Nebraska, for example, is home not only to Mexicans and Central Americans who have come to work in meat-packing plants, but also to clusters of Afghani, Cuban, Hmong, Serbian, Somali, Sudanese, Soviet Jewish, and Vietnamese refugees.

Some immigrants are highly educated professionals who could not find suitable employment in their home countries. For the most part, however, immigrants leave a poorer country for a richer one in hopes of bettering their family's economic situation. In the current recession, many immigrants are facing the decision whether to remain in the United States or return to their country of origin (Schuman 2009). Nevertheless, as immigrants establish themselves, they typically begin to send for relatives as ethnic kin and community networks develop here. In fact, the majority of legal immigrants enter the United States through family sponsorship (Martin and Midgley 2006).

As a result, more and more Americans maintain **transnational families** whose members bridge and maintain relationships across national borders. They may experience back-and-forth changes of residence, frequent family visits, business dealings, money transfers to family, placement of children with relatives in the other country, or the search for a marriage partner in the home country. Also, many immigrant families are **binational**, with nuclear family members having different legal statuses. For instance, one partner may be a legal resident, the other not. Children born in the United States are automatically citizens, while one or both parents may be undocumented (illegal) residents. Problematically, the undocumented, or unauthorized immigrant, parents of many native-born, American children in binational families face deportation (Capps et al. 2007). Transnational and binational families are discussed in several places throughout this text, particularly in Chapter 3.

Children born to interracial and inter-ethnic unions further add to America's diversity. Although the growth in race/ethnic intermarriage *rates* for Asians and Hispanics has declined somewhat since the 1990s, their *numbers* continued to rise. Interracial and inter-ethnic marriage and cohabitation rates involving African Americans have continued to increase significantly (Qian and Lichter 2007). As a result, the proportion of interracial children is significant (Rosenfeld and Byung-Soo 2005, p. 541).

Perhaps nothing better symbolizes American families' changing faces than does our First Family. Race/ethnic inequalities and discrimination assuredly persist (Davis and Bali 2008; Jimenez 2008; Pager, Bonikowski, and Western 2009). However, the 2008 U.S. presidential election of the son of a white mother and a Kenyan father indicates that a majority of voting Americans have grown fairly comfortable with America's changing family faces (Carroll 2007a; Jimenez 2008). President Obama's overall messages are of pride in one's racial heritage and hope for the future (2006, 2007 [1995]). Having appeared on the cover of *Time Magazine* in 2009, First Lady Michelle Obama further symbolizes the accomplishment and potential of diverse American families.

To multiracial children, President Obama's victory was also one for them (Gillman 2008). According to Rice University sociologist Jenifer Bratter, President Obama "embodies the possibility of being welcomed by both

Alex Wong/Getty Images

Along with her husband, First Lady Michelle Obama symbolizes pride in one's racial/ethnic heritage and hope for one's future. Shortly after President Obama's election, she visited a Washington, DC, high school where she encouraged students to embrace whatever opportunities avail themselves. She recalled that, sadly, she had lived close to the University of Chicago as a child but never ventured inside. "It was a fancy college, and it didn't have anything to do with me...There are so many kids like that...who are living inches away from power and prestige and fame and fortune, and they don't even know that it exists" (Michelle Obama, in Gibbs and Scherer 2009, p. 24). In this photo, First Lady Obama is having lunch with Head Start students.

sides of the divide that modern interracial families are constantly contesting with" (Bratter, in Gillman 2008). As the U.S. population changes, policy makers need to recognize the complexity and diversity of the growing minority population (Mather 2009, p. 13). We return to issues of racial and ethnic diversity in Chapter 3 and throughout this textbook. Here, we turn to a third society-wide trend that affects families today—economic uncertainty.

Economic Uncertainty

"Recession means worry—all too tangible worry" (Bazelton 2009). Incomes grew little for the middle and working classes even prior to the recession that began in 2008. And although the U.S. economy was good for many Americans during the 1990s, others experienced job insecurity, loss of benefits, longer workdays, and more part-time and temporary work (Teachman, Tedrow, and Crowder 2000). Nonetheless, the recession that began in 2008 has increased unemployment and caused uncertainty and change in virtually all families (Ramo 2009). The following are some implications for relationships and families in today's economy:

- Because many put off marriage until they can earn enough to support a family, more marriages may be delayed or foregone entirely (Gibson-Davis 2009; Roberts 2009; Wang and Morin 2009).
- Fertility decisions will change. Because some individuals are not purchasing contraceptives due to the cost, more unintended pregnancies may be the result (Roan 2009b). On the other hand, bearing and raising children is expensive, so the birth rate could decline at least temporarily (Belkin 2009; Haub 2009; Wang and Morin 2009).
- Although more individuals are selling their eggs or sperm, fertility treatments are down in number (English 2009; Roan 2009a).
- Fewer parents will send their children to costly afterschool lessons and other activities.
- Fewer families will send their children to college, and fewer upper-middle-class families will send their children to exclusive universities.
- Young adults' difficulties in finding jobs mean more "boomerang kids" as they return to live in their parents' homes (Trumbull 2009; Wang and Morin 2009).
- Home foreclosures and apartment evictions mean more homeless families, as well as more extended family and intergenerational households as adult children move in with their parents (Palmer 2008; Sard 2008; Spratling 2009).
- Job losses and stock market declines mean more intergenerational households as older parents move into the homes of their adult children (Brandon 2008; Haas 2009).
- Unemployment is expected to raise psychological depression rates, particularly among men (O'Reilly 2009; "Recession Depression ..." 2009).
- Although this was already the case for poverty- and near-poverty-level parents, many more families cut back on paid daycare. Instead, they put together a combination of childcare measures, including an unemployed parent, other relatives, and/or alternating work schedules, to care for their children (Chen 2009).
- More families may relocate as they follow potential job opportunities or choose to be nearer to extended kin (Allen 2009).
- With less money for paid domestic services that previously freed many middle- and upper-class women from household chores, couples may renegotiate housework and childcare duties (Bazelton 2009).
- Because states faced with depleted budgets have cut social services, more families struggle to meet health care and other needs.
- Lost or diminished pensions means that some individuals delay retirement, whereas already retired, geographically distant grandparents make fewer trips to visit grandchildren.
- Children's and grandchildren's inheritances will decline in value ("As Recession Erodes..." 2009).
- Because stress is a causal factor in domestic violence, child and partner abuse has increased, and the consequences for some could be more serious as money for shelters and related services dries up (Lauby and Else 2008; "U.S. Recession Causing..." 2009).
- The divorce rate may drop, at least temporarily. "[F]ewer unhappy couples will risk starting separate households. Furthermore, the housing market meltdown will make it more difficult for them to finance their separations by selling their homes" (Cherlin 2009b; see also Schultz 2008; Wilcox 2009).
- Because financial, social, and psychological resources help families to cope with stress and crises, those with better finances and higher education will better weather recession-related family challenges.
- Families may find new ways to interact together with activities that don't cost money. As one middle-class mother said, "We have more time now. We talk. We may not go anywhere but at least we're all home together"(in Stetler 2009).
- Dating interest is up. Both online and offline matchmakers attribute the jump to the recession: "At a time when money is scarce or uncertain, when people are assessing their priorities, they don't want to go through it alone" (Dr. Pepper Schwartz in Ellin 2009).

This is by no means an exhaustive list. Furthermore, we don't know what the economic future will bring. Can you think of more economy-related implications

"Looks like we invested in a dysfunctional family of funds."

www.CartoonStock.com

for relationships and families? For most of us, living in a uncertain and problematic economy involves making hard choices. We'll explore the process of making choices next.

The Freedom and Pressures of Choosing

As families have become less rigidly structured, people have made fewer choices "once and for all." Of course, previous decisions do have consequences, and they represent commitments that limit later choices. Nevertheless, many people reexamine their decisions about family—and face new choices—throughout the course of their lives. Thus, choice is an important emphasis of this book.

The best way to make decisions about our personal lives is to make them knowledgeably. It helps to know something about all the alternatives; it also helps to know what kinds of social pressures affect our decisions. As we'll see, people are influenced by the beliefs and values of their society. There are **structural constraints**, economic and social forces, that limit personal choices. In a very real way, we and our personal decisions and attitudes are products of our environment.

But in just as real a way, people can influence society. Individuals create social change by continually offering new insights to their groups. Sometimes social change occurs because of conversation with others. Sometimes it requires becoming active in organizations that address issues such as racial equality, immigrant rights, gay rights, or stepfamily supports, for example. Sometimes influencing society involves many people living their lives according to their values even when these differ from more generally accepted group or cultural norms.

We can apply this view to the phenomenon of "living together," or cohabitation. Fifty years ago, it was widely believed that cohabiting couples were immoral. But in the 1970s, some college students openly challenged university restrictions on cohabitation, and subsequently many more people than before—students and nonstudents, young and old—chose to live together. As cohabitation rates increased, societal attitudes became more favorable. Over time, cohabitation became "mainstream" (Smock and Gupta 2002). Although some religions and individuals continue to object to living together outside marriage, it is now significantly easier for people to choose this option. We are influenced by the society around us, but we are also free to influence it and we do that every time we make a choice.

Personal Troubles, Societal Influences, and Family Policy

People's private lives are affected by what is happening in the society around them. In his book *The Sociological Imagination* (2000 [1959]), sociologist C. Wright Mills developed the principle that personal troubles are connected to events and patterns in the larger social world. Many times what seem to be personal troubles are shared by others, and these troubles often reflect societal influences. For example, when a family breadwinner is laid off or cannot find work, the cause may not lie in his or her lack of ambition but rather in the economy's inability to provide employment. The difficulty of juggling work and family is not usually just a personal question of individual time management skills but of society-wide influences—the totality of time required for employment, commuting, and family care in a society that provides limited support for working families.

This text assumes that people need to understand themselves and their problems in the context of the larger society. Individuals' choices depend largely on the alternatives that exist in their social environment and on cultural values and attitudes toward those alternatives. Moreover, if people are to shape the kinds of families they want, they must not limit their attention just to their own relationships and families. This is a principal reason why we explore social policy issues in various chapters throughout this text.

Family Policy **Family policy** involves all the procedures, regulations, attitudes, and goals of government, religious institutions, and the workplace that affect families.

The federal government and states have developed programs to encourage and support marriage, to encourage father involvement in fragile families, to discourage teen sexual activity, and to move single mothers from welfare to work.[3] Recently, researchers have explored how policy decisions affect foster parents and grandparent caregivers (McWey, Henderson, and Alexander 2008; Letiecq, Bailey, and Porterfield 2008).

Poverty has been a major focus of policy scholars. American families worry about making ends meet: how we will support ourselves, find comfortable housing, educate our children, get affordable health care, finance our old age. Poverty is a real problem for many U.S. families, and research suggests that deep poverty in early childhood affects outcomes for children (Wagmiller et al. 2006). The United States provides fewer services to families than does any other industrialized nation, while Western Europe offers many examples of a successful partnership between government and families in the interests of family support.

One way to view family policy is to recognize that "laws place some families in the margins of society while privileging others" (Henderson 2008, p. 983). Although this is changing, family policy has privileged heterosexual relationships by defining them as the only acceptable norm while placing same-sex unions in society's margins by defining them as not-marriage. The debates over legal marriage for same-sex families, various legislation, and court rulings all work to create family policy regarding same-sex unions. Issues regarding same-sex couples' separation, divorce, and child custody, as well as determining the legal status for lesbian parents who used ART, are all social policy matters (Hare and Skinner 2008; Oswald and Kuvalanka 2008).

Given the social and political diversity of American society, all parents or political actors are unlikely to agree on the best courses of action. Not only are Americans not in agreement on the role government should play vis-à-vis families, but they are divided on what "family" means in a policy sense. Some argue that only heterosexual, married families should be encouraged, whereas others believe in supporting a variety of families—single-parent, cohabiting heterosexual, or gay and lesbian families, for example (Bogenschneider 2006; Waite 2001). Indeed, the diversity of family lifestyles in the United States makes it extremely difficult to develop family policies that would satisfy all, or even most, of us.

Then, too, more government help to families would be costly. Yet the estimated costs of *not* having family programs might be higher. For instance, disadvantaged children whose adult lives take a bad turn could eventually cost society more in unemployment compensation and incarceration expenses than would preventive investments that help to support these children and their families (Eckholm 2007). Although no social policy can guarantee ideal families, such policies could contribute to a good foundation for family life.

Making knowledgeable family decisions can mean getting involved in national and local political debates and campaigns. One's role as family member, as much as one's role as citizen, has come to require participation in society-wide decisions to create a desirable context for family life and family choices. Concern has arisen about the degree to which Americans do actively participate in attempts to influence neighborhood, community, regional, state, or federal policy. Research indicates that—perhaps with the exception of the 2007–8 presidential campaign—the number of people with whom Americans discuss "important matters" has declined, especially among educated middle-class individuals. The authors speculate that American involvement in community and neighborhood has declined due to longer working hours, the movement of women into the labor force, commuting patterns, more heterogeneous neighborhoods, and the tendency to rely on technological tools for interpersonal contact (McPherson and Smith-Lovin 2006).

But another sociologist argues that Americans have simply changed the form of their community engagement. They are less dependent on the neighborhood and more likely to become involved in professional associations, volunteer in advocacy and service organizations, and participate in self-help groups and religious organizations (Wuthnow 2002).

How Social Factors Influence Personal Choices

Social factors influence people's personal choices in three ways. First, it is usually easier to make the common choice. In the 1950s and early 1960s, when people tended to marry earlier than they do now, it felt awkward to remain unmarried past one's mid-twenties. Now, staying single longer is a more comfortable choice. Similarly, when divorce and nonmarital parenthood were highly stigmatized, it was less common to make these decisions than it is today. As another example, contemporary families usually include fewer children than historical families did, making the choice to raise a large family more difficult than in the past (Zernike 2009).

A second way that social factors can influence personal choices is by expanding people's options. For example, the availability of effective contraceptives makes limiting one's family size easier than in the past, and it enables deferral of marriage with less risk that a sexual relationship will lead to pregnancy. Then too,

[3] Space does not permit a comprehensive review of current and proposed family policies and programs and their effectiveness. However, see, for example, Amato 2005; Capps et al. 2007; Children's Defense Fund 2008, 2009; Dion 2005; Duncan and Chase-Lansdale 2004; Offner 2005; and Ooms 2005.

as we have seen, new forms of reproductive technology provide unprecedented options for becoming a parent.

However, social factors can also limit people's options. For example, American society has never allowed polygamy (more than one spouse) as a legal option. Those who would like to form plural marriages risk prosecution (Janofsky 2001). Until the 1967 *Loving v. Virginia* Supreme Court decision, a number of states prohibited racial intermarriage. As discussed in Chapter 8, the possibility of same-sex marriage is presently being contested in various courts throughout the United States, and outcomes will either expand or limit couples' options. More broadly, economic changes of the last thirty-five years, which make well-paid employment more problematic, have limited some individuals' marital options (Sassler and Goldscheider 2004).

Making Choices

By taking a course in marriage and the family, you may become more aware of your choices, when they are available, and how a decision may be related to subsequent options and choices. All people make choices, even when they are not conscious of it. Let's look more closely at two forms of decision making—choosing by default and choosing knowledgeably—along with the consequences of each.

Choosing by Default

Unconscious decisions are called **choosing by default**. Choices made by default are ones that people make when they are not aware of all the alternatives or when they pursue the proverbial path of least resistance. If you're taking this class but you're unaware that a class in modern dance, which you would have preferred, is meeting at the same time, you have chosen not to take the class in modern dance. But you have done so by default because you didn't find out about all the alternatives before you registered.

Another type of decision by default occurs when people pursue a course of action primarily because it seems the easiest thing to do. Sometimes college students choose even their majors by default. They try to register, only to find that the classes they had planned to take are closed. So they register for something they hadn't planned on, do well enough, and continue in that program of study.

Many decisions concerning relationships and families are also made by default. For example, partners may focus on career success to the neglect of their relationship simply because this is what society seems to require. For these career-oriented partners, the goal of spending more time together or with family may be on the horizon, but it is never reached because it is not consciously planned for.

Although most of us have made at least some decisions by default, almost everyone can recall having the opposite experience: choosing knowledgeably. Figure 1.2, "The Cycle of Knowledgeable Decision Making," maps this process. You may want to look back at this figure as you go through the course and think about the decisions to be made at various life stages.

Choosing Knowledgeably

Our society offers many options. People can stay single, cohabitate, or marry. They can form communal living groups or family-like ties with others. They can decide

© Mark Romaine/Stock Connection

Families are composed of individuals, each seeking self-fulfillment and a unique identity, but individuals can find a place to learn and express togetherness, stability, and loyalty within the family. Families also perform a special archival function: Events, rituals, and histories are created and preserved, and, in turn, become intrinsic parts of each individual. These sisters are sharing memories recorded in family photos.

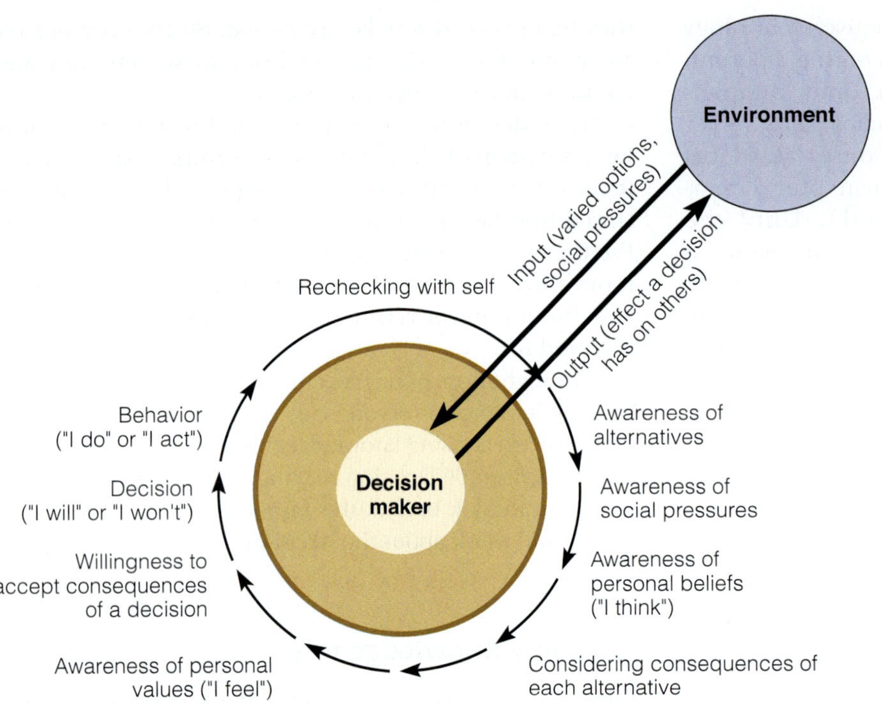

Figure 1.2 The cycle of knowledgeable decision making.

Source: Adapted from *Shifting Gears*, by Nena O'Neill and George O'Neill, p. 157, 1974. Copyright 1974 by Nena O'Neill and George O'Neill. Reprinted by permission of the publisher, M. Evans and Company, New York, NY.

to separate or stay together. They can have children with the aid of reproductive technology. They can parent stepchildren or foster children. One important component of **choosing knowledgeably** is recognizing as many options as possible (Meyer 2007). In part, this text is designed to help you do that.

A second component in making knowledgeable choices is recognizing the social pressures that may influence personal choices. Some of these pressures are economic, whereas others relate to cultural norms that are typically taken for granted. Sometimes people decide that they agree with socially accepted or prescribed behavior. They concur in the teachings of their religion, for example. Other times, people decide that they strongly disagree with socially prescribed beliefs, values, and standards. Whether they agree with such standards or not, once people recognize the force of social pressures, they can choose whether to act in accordance with them.

An important aspect of making knowledgeable choices is considering the consequences of each alternative rather than just gravitating toward the one that initially seems most attractive. For example, a considerable number of young adults live with their parents. Of those between ages 25 and 34, about 15 percent of men and 10 percent of women live with parents (U.S. Census Bureau 2009e, Table AD-1). Someone deciding whether to move back into his or her parents' home may want to list the consequences. In the positive column, moving home might mean being able to save money that would have otherwise gone for rent, utilities, food, and perhaps childcare. In the negative column, returning to one's parental home might involve giving up some independence, creating a more cramped family space, and risking increased family conflict. Listing positive and negative consequences of alternatives—either mentally or on paper—helps one see the larger picture and thus make a more knowledgeable decision.

Part of this process requires becoming aware of your values and choosing to act consistently with them. Contradictory sets of values exist in American society. For instance, standards regarding nonmarital sex range from abstinence to sex in committed relationships to sex for recreation only. Contradictory values can cause people to feel ambivalent about what they want for themselves.

Clarifying one's values involves cutting through this ambivalence in order to decide which of several standards are more strongly valued. It is important to respect the so-called gut factor—the emotional dimension of decision making. Besides rationally considering alternatives, people have subjective (often almost visceral) feelings about what for them is right or wrong, good or bad. Respecting one's feelings is an important part of making the right decision. Following one's feelings can mean grounding one's decisions in a religious or spiritual tradition or in one's cultural heritage, for these have a great deal of emotional power and often represent deep commitments.

Another important component of decision making is rechecking. Once a choice is made and a person acts on it, the process is not necessarily complete. As Figure 1.2 suggests, people constantly recheck their decisions throughout the entire decision-making cycle, testing these decisions against their experiences and against any changes in the social environment.

Underlying this discussion is the assumption that individuals cannot have everything. Every time people make an important decision or commitment, they rule out alternatives—for the time being and perhaps permanently. People cannot simultaneously have the relative freedom of a child-free union and the gratification that often accompanies parenthood.

It is true, however, that people can focus on some goals and values during one part of their lives, then turn their attention to different ones at other times. Fifty years ago we thought of adults as people who entered adulthood in their early twenties, found work, married, had children, and continued on the same track until the end of the life course. That view has changed. Today we view adulthood as a time with potential for continued personal development, growth, and change.

In a family setting, development and change involve more than one individual. Multiple life courses must be coordinated, and if one member changes, that affects the values and choices of other members of the family. Moreover, life in American families reflects a cultural tension between family solidarity and individual freedom (Amato 2004; Cherlin 2009a).

A Family of Individuals

Americans place a high value on family. It is hardly surprising that a vast majority of Americans report family is extremely important to them (Carroll 2007b, "Marriage" 2008). Why?

Families as a Place to Belong

Families create a place to belong, serving as a repository or archive of family memories and traditions (Cieraad 2006). **Family identity**—ideas and feelings about the uniqueness and value of one's family unit—emerge via traditions and rituals: family dinnertime, birthday and holiday celebrations, vacation trips, and perhaps family hobbies like working together in the garden. Family identities typically include members' cultural heritage. For example, all the children in one family may be given Irish, Hispanic, Asian Indian, or Russian names.

Families provide a setting for the development of an individual's **self-concept**—basic feelings people have about themselves, their abilities, characteristics, and worth. Arising initially in a family setting, self-concept and identity are influenced by significant figures in a young child's life, particularly those in the parent role, together with siblings and other relatives.

How family members and others interact with and respond to us continues to impact self-concept and identity throughout life (Cooley 1902, 1909; Mead 1934; Yeung and Martin 2003). A child who is loved comes to think he or she is a valuable and loving person. A child who is given some tasks and encouraged to do things comes to think of him- or herself as competent.

Early childhood also marks the onset of learning social roles. Children connect certain behaviors to the different roles of mother, father, grandmother, grandfather, sister, brother, and so on. Much of young children's play consists of imitating these roles. *Role-taking*, or playing out the expected behavior associated with a social position, is how children begin to learn behavior appropriate to the roles they may play in adult life. Behavior and attitudes associated with roles become *internalized*, or incorporated into the self.

Meanwhile, expressing our individuality within the context of a family requires us to negotiate innumerable day-to-day issues. How much privacy can each person have at home? What family activities should be scheduled, how often, and when? What outside friendships and activities can a family member sustain?

© Curtis Willocks/Brooklyn Image Group

Midlife changes can be both exhilarating and intimidating, as these college students have probably discovered. Certainly the decision of a middle-aged adult to earn a college degree involves many emotional and practical changes. But by making knowledgeable choices—by weighing alternatives, considering consequences, clarifying values and goals, and continually rechecking—personal decisions and changes can be both positive and dynamic.

Familistic (Communal) Values and Individualistic (Self-Fulfillment) Values

Familistic values such as family togetherness, stability, and loyalty focus on the family as a whole. They are *communal* or *collective values*; that is, they emphasize the needs, goals, and identity of the group. Many of us have an image of the ideal family in which members spend considerable time together, enjoying one another's company. Furthermore, the family is a major source of stability. We believe that the family is the group most deserving of our loyalty (Connor 2007). Those of us who marry vow publicly to stay with our partners as long as we live. We expect our partners, parents, children, and even our more distant relatives to remain loyal to the family unit.

But just as family values permeate American society, so do **individualistic** *(self-fulfillment)* **values**. These values encourage people to think in terms of personal happiness and goals and the development of a distinct individual identity. An individualistic orientation gives more weight to the expression of individual preferences and the maximization of individual talents and options.

The contradictory pull of both familistic and individualistic values creates tension in society (Amato 2004, Cherlin 2009a)—and tension within ourselves that we must resolve. "It is within the family...that the paradox of continuity and change, the problem of balancing individuality and allegiance, is most immediate" (Bengston, Biblarz, and Roberts 2007, p. 323).

American society has never had a remarkably strong tradition of *familism*, the virtual sacrifice of individual family members' needs and goals for the sake of the larger kin group (Sirjamaki 1948; Lugo Steidel and Contreras 2003). Our national cultural heritage prizes individuality, individual rights, and personal freedom. But on the other hand, an overly individualistic orientation puts stress on relationships when there is little emphasis on contributing to other family members' happiness or postponing personal satisfactions in order to attain family goals.

Partners as Individuals and Family Members

The changing shape of the family has meant that family lives have become less predictable than they were in the mid-twentieth century. The course of family living results in large part from the decisions and choices two adults make, moving in their own ways and at their own paces through their lives. Assuming that partners' respective beliefs, values, and behaviors mesh fairly well at first, any change in either can adversely affect the fit.

One consequence of ongoing adult developmental change in two individuals is that the union may be put at risk. If one or both change considerably over time, they may grow apart instead of together. A challenge

© Michael Heron/CORBIS

In a world of demographic, cultural, and political changes, there is no typical family structure. Today the postmodern family includes cohabiting families, single-parent families, lesbian and gay partners and parents, and remarried families. Whatever their form, families are entrusted with filling three basic functions for society—responsible child rearing, practical and economic support, and emotional support.

for contemporary relationships is to integrate divergent personal change into the relationship while nurturing any children involved.

How can partners make it through such changes and still stay together? Two guidelines may be helpful. The first is for people to take responsibility for their own past choices and decisions rather than blaming previous "mistakes" on their mates. In addition, it helps to recognize that a changing partner may be difficult to live with for a while. A relationship needs to be flexible enough to allow for each partner's individual changes—to allow family members some degree of freedom. At the same time, it's good to remember the benefits of family living and the commitment necessary to sustain it. Individual happiness and family commitment are not inevitably in conflict; research shows that a supportive marriage has a significant positive impact on individual well-being (Waite and Gallagher 2000).

> On the one hand, people value the freedom to leave unhappy unions, correct earlier mistakes, and find greater happiness with new partners. On the other hand, people are concerned about social stability, tradition, and the overall impact of high levels of marital instability on the wellbeing of children. The clash between these two concerns reflects a fundamental contradiction within marriage itself; that is, marriage is designed to promote both institutional and personal goals.... To make marriages with children work effectively, it is necessary for spouses to find the right balance between institutional and individual elements, between obligations to others and obligations to the self. (Amato 2004, p. 962)

Throughout this text we will continue to explore the tension between individualistic and familistic values and discuss creative ways that partners can alter a committed, ongoing relationship in order to meet their changing needs.

Marriages and Families: Four Themes

In this chapter we have defined the term *family* and discussed diversity and decision making in the context of family living. We can now state explicitly the four themes of this text.

1. Personal decisions must be made throughout the life course. Decision making is a trade-off; once we choose an option, we discard alternatives. No one can have everything. Thus, the best way to make choices is knowledgeably.
2. People are influenced by the society around them. Cultural beliefs and values influence our attitudes and decisions. Societal or structural conditions can limit or expand our options.
3. We live in a society characterized by considerable change, including increased ethnic, economic, and family diversity; by tension between familistic and individualistic values; by decreased marital and family permanence; and by increased political and policy concern about the needs of children and families. This dynamic situation can make personal decision making more challenging than in the past—and more important.
4. Personal decision making feeds into society and changes it. We affect our social environment every time we make a choice. Making family decisions can also mean choosing to become politically involved in order to effect family-related social change. Making family choices consciously, according to our values, gives our family lives greater integrity.

We continue our examination of the family in Chapter 2, "Exploring the Family," and in Chapter 3, which discusses the social context in which families make choices.

George and Gaynel Couran were married in 1916. "That was the girl for me. I got the woman I wanted," said George at the couple's eightieth wedding anniversary. Judging by her expression, Gaynel undoubtedly got the man she wanted. The Courans learned to balance individualism and familism over the course of their marriage.

Summary

- This chapter introduced the subject matter for this course and presented the four themes that this text develops. The chapter began by addressing the challenge of defining the term *family*.
- We, your authors, define *family* as any sexually expressive, parent–child, or other kin relationship in which people—usually related by ancestry, marriage, or adoption—(1) form an economic and/or otherwise practical unit and care for any children or other dependents, (2) consider their identity to be significantly attached to the group, and (3) commit to maintaining that group over time.
- Social scientists usually list three major functions filled by today's families: raising children responsibly, providing members with economic and other practical support, and offering emotional security.
- With relaxed institutional control, family diversity has progressed to the point that there is no typical family form today.
- Whether we are in an era of "family decline" or "family change" is a matter of debate.
- In addition to the trend of relaxed institutional control over family formation and family life generally, we examined three other contemporary societal trends that affect families: advancing communication and reproductive technologies, the changing racial and ethnic composition of American families, and economic recession and uncertainty.
- Marriages and families are composed of separate, unique individuals. Our culture values both families and individuals.
- Families provide members a place to belong and help ground identity development. Finding personal freedom within families is an ongoing, negotiated process.
- People make choices, either actively and knowledgeably or by default, that determine the courses of their lives. People must make choices and decisions throughout their life course. Those choices and decisions are limited by social structure and at the same time are causes for change in that structure.
- Change and development continue throughout adult life. Because adults change, relationships, marriages, and families are far from static. Every time one individual in a relationship changes, the relationship itself changes, however subtly.

Questions for Review and Reflection

1. Without looking at ours, write your definition of *family*. Then compare yours to ours. How are the two similar? How are they different? Does your definition have some advantages over ours?
2. Why is the family a major social institution? Does your family fulfill each of the family functions identified in the text? How?
3. What important changes in family patterns do you see today? Do you see positive changes, negative changes, or both? What do they mean for families, in your opinion?
4. What are some examples of a personal or family problem that is at least partly a result of problems in the society?
5. **Policy Question.** What are some changes in law and social policy that you would like to see put in place to enhance family life?

Key Terms

binational family 15
choosing by default 19
choosing knowledgeably 20
extended family 6
familistic (communal, or collective) values 21
family 4
family change perspective 10
family decline perspective 10
family identity 21
family policy 17
family structure 6
household 6
individualistic (self-fulfillment) values 22
nuclear family 6
postmodern family 7
self-concept 21
social institution 10
structural constraints 17
transnational family 15

Online Resources

Sociology CourseMate

www.CengageBrain.com

Access an integrated eBook, chapter-specific interactive learning tools, including flashcards, quizzes, videos, and more in your Sociology CourseMate, accessed through **CengageBrain.com.**

www.CengageBrain.com

Want to maximize your online study time? Take this easy-to-use study system's diagnostic pre-test, and it will create a personalized study plan for you. By helping you identify the topics that you need to understand better and then directing you to valuable online resources, it can speed up your chapter review. CengageNOW even provides a post-test so you can confirm that you are ready for an exam.

4

Our Gendered Identities

Jon Riley/Getty Images

As we think about family life, we need to consider gender issues. Cultural expectations about how boys and girls, men and women should behave and relate to each other are important influences on personal identities, family roles, and life choices. But to what extent have traditional expectations changed?

A statement from earlier editions of this textbook, "gender influences virtually every aspect of people's lives and relationships," is now being challenged. Some scholars assert that the significance of gender is declining. Others, however, see gender identity and gender inequality as continuing to be enormously important, but point to how our *thinking* about gender has changed.

From an earlier 1970s perspective, in which all women were seen to be disadvantaged compared to all men, we now look at gender in relation to its structural linkages to race, class, and sexual orientation, as well as to global interconnections (Andersen and Collins 2007b; Baca Zinn, Hondagneu-Sotelo, and Messner 2007; Theidon 2009). For example, a black woman immigrant from Haiti who is a single mother working as a domestic has a very different life from that of her employer, a white woman lawyer who is an Ivy League graduate with a professional husband. The husband's life is much different from that of a white male high school dropout who remains single into his forties because he finds himself financially unable to marry (Porter and O'Donnell 2006). Additionally, a women in another country whose soldier-husband has laid down his weapons may have domestic violence issues similar to those of a military wife in the United States (Meneses 2008; Sontag 2008). As noted in our analysis of race/ethnicity in Chapter 3, *within-group* differences have become an important theme in the study of gender.

Gendered Identities

We are using the term *gender* rather than *sex* for an important reason. The word **sex** is used in reference to male or female anatomy and physiology. We use the term **gender** (or **gender role**) far more broadly—to describe societal attitudes and behaviors expected of and associated with the two sexes (Duck and Wood 2006, p. 170).[1] Another concept, **gender identity**, refers to the degree to which an individual sees herself or himself as feminine or masculine.

A further complication occurs because a small number of people are born with ambiguous sexual characteristics or do not feel at ease with their sex as recorded at birth. "Issues for Thought: Challenges to Gender Boundaries" addresses variations in biology that affect sex and gender identification.

In this chapter, we will examine various aspects of gender. In doing so, we'll consider personality traits and cultural scripts typically associated with masculinity and femininity. For example, note the differences between women's and men's perceptions of fairness and equity as they divide the tasks associated with preparing for their weddings in "Issues for Thought: 'Wife' Socialization and the Heterosexual Wedding." Also in this chapter, we'll analyze gender inequality in social institutions. We'll discuss the possible influence of biology and examine the socialization process as we explore whether people are taught to behave as either females or males, are born that way, or simply adapt to the social structures and opportunities they find as they become adults. We'll discuss the lives of adults as they select from options available to them. And we'll examine the social movements that have arisen around gender issues. We'll speculate about what the future may hold in terms of gender equality.

Gender Expectations and Cultural Messages

We live in an ambiguous time regarding gendered attitudes and behavior. On the one hand, it is now taken for granted that women have careers and that most will work regardless of motherhood. Examples of women in nontraditional roles abound: women as astronauts, CEOs, and officers and enlisted personnel in the military. On the other hand, the media and research explore the continuing disadvantages faced by women and the uncertainty that many women have about their choices and the ability to realize them.

Men have begun to consider where they stand as well—in relationships, in the family, and at work. Some men have begun to move into traditionally female occupations, and married fathers are doing more at home than they used to (Bianchi, Robinson, and Milkie 2006). Women and men are asserting their individuality and joining as equals many areas of society that were, at one time, considered "off-limits" to the other gender. Frequently, however, we receive mixed messages from institutions such as the mass media.

Our actions, thoughts, and feelings come not from instinct, but from social messages, and often those messages tell us the wrong story about each other, leading, in the case of this discussion, to difficulties trying to sort out the roles we are expected to play and the roles we would like to play as men and women. Social theorist Erving Goffman (1967) notes that the messages we see on television, in magazines, online via our social networking sites, and so on, often present an idealized, one-dimensional stereotype of what women and men

[1] The distinction between *sex* and *gender*, first made by sociologist Ann Oakley (1972), is a dominant perspective in social science (Laner 2003). But not all social theorists agree with this conceptualization. Judith Butler (1990) argues that the two are essentially one—gender—and others agree that the biological as well as behavioral aspects of sex are socially constructed (Cresswell 2003).

Issues for Thought

"Wife" Socialization and the Heterosexual Wedding

Planning a wedding is more than picking a wedding gown, ordering flowers, and choosing a caterer. Research reveals that heterosexual wedding planning serves as a tool to prepare brides for their future roles as wives. The work involved in planning a wedding highly resembles the domestic and family work that married women have long performed. Weddings, thus, give brides a taste of, and practice for, their future roles as family and relationship managers.

Brides and grooms have a tendency to view themselves as equal participants in wedding planning work. However, when a closer look is taken, it becomes clear that wedding planning work is grossly unequal. For example, in a recent study, every single bride-to-be completed disproportionate amounts of the behind-the-scenes work, such as information gathering. It was found, for example, that brides had a greater familiarity with informational resources such as popular wedding guides and magazines. Yet not one groom had purchased, read, or mentioned wedding media when interviewed for this study. Additionally, every bride kept track of planning resources and information such as telephone numbers, business cards, and appointments in an organizer. No grooms, however, created or maintained any such organizer. The grooms, though, were not left out of the loop. The typical pattern of action included brides gathering information about a wedding location or caterer, and narrowing that information down to a set of choices which were then presented to the groom.

Brides also complete a disproportionate amount of kin work. This work includes anticipating family needs and facilitating ongoing family ties. In wedding planning, kin work ranges from anticipating special meal requirements of family and guests to making sure all appropriate family are invited, included, and acknowledged. Brides, for example, are much more likely to assist family members and guests with rides to and from the airport, hotel accommodations, and entertainment during their stay. Wedding planning kin work is the same sort of kin work married women have long been performing.

Parallel to the managerial role women play in performing household labor, brides take responsibility for wedding planning—becoming wedding managers. Brides take it upon themselves to oversee, follow up on, and supervise wedding activities. Brides, for example, are the ones who send letters, e-mails, or make telephone calls to the bridal party informing them of the schedule for the photographs, rehearsals, and so forth that the wedding party is expected to attend.

Wedding planning is a microcosm of the family work that takes place within heterosexual marriages. Brides are introduced to the world of kin work and the behind-the-scenes work it takes to construct and maintain family through planning a wedding. This is probably not the first time brides have experienced this work. Growing up, many girls are given kin work as chores, and they have probably seen their mothers, sisters, grandmothers, and aunts perform it. The wedding, however, often becomes her first major project in family work and the time when she transitions to being a major player in the game—the wife.

Critical Thinking

Think about the ways you have been socialized into a particular gender role. Discuss the household chores you did as a young person—were they different from those of your siblings or friends of the opposite sex? Did those chores have the effect of preparing you for any particular adult roles?

Source: Tamara Sniezek. You can read more of Professor Sniezek's research into weddings in her 2005 journal article: "Is It Our Day or the Bride's Day? The Division of Wedding Labor and Its Meaning for Couples," *Qualitative Sociology* 28(3):215–234.

"are." When our lives, lifestyles, and behaviors do not match up with these media-driven stereotypes, we sometimes feel *stigmatized.* To be stigmatized is to have others act disapprovingly toward us in such a way that we feel badly about ourselves.

American attitudes have grown more liberal regarding men's and women's roles. Few agree, for example, that "sons in a family should be given more encouragement to go to college than daughters," an expression of **traditional sexism** (Sherman and Spence 1997). Traditional sexism is the belief that women's roles should be confined to the family and that women are not as fit as men for certain tasks or for leadership positions. Such beliefs have declined since the 1970s (Twenge 1997a, 1997b). Some social theorists believe, however, that traditional sexism has not gone completely away. Research into transgendered identity (see "Issues for Thought: Challenges to Gender Boundaries") finds that discriminatory attitudes toward transgendered people are rooted in traditional sexism (Serano 2007).

A more subtle **modern sexism** has replaced traditional sexism. It takes the form of agreement with statements such as the following: "Discrimination in the labor force is no longer a problem" and "in order not to appear sexist, many men are inclined to overcompensate women" (Campbell, Schellenberg, and Senn 1997; Tougas et al. 1995). Yet, data for 2008 shows us that being a secretary was the top job for women, and the median wage for women was $36,000 (Douglas 2009, p. 289). Modern sexism denies that gender discrimination

Issues for Thought

Challenges to Gender Boundaries

We take for granted that sex is a dichotomy: You are either male or female. Yet somewhere between 1 and 4 percent of live births are **intersexual**—that is, the children have some anatomical, chromosomal, or hormonal variation from the male or female biology that is considered "typical." "Chromosomes, hormones, the internal sex structures, the gonads and the external genitalia all vary more than most people realize" (Fausto-Sterling 2000, p. 20; Gough et al. 2008).

In the 1950s intersex babies (then termed *hermaphrodites*) were assigned a gender identity by doctors, and parents were advised to treat them accordingly. The children typically underwent surgery to give them genitals more closely approximating the assigned gender.

Intersexuality emerged as an area of political activism with the formation of the Intersex Society of North America (ISNA) in 1993 (Gough et al. 2008). Members have demonstrated against arbitrary gender assignment and the surgical "correction" of intersexed infants, demanding the acceptance of gender ambiguity (Preves 2002). Some medical ethicists take the position that "the various forms of intersexuality should be defined as normal" (Lawrence McCullough, quoted in Fausto-Sterling 2000, p. 21; see also Ghosh 2009), and that surgical "corrections" are not only unethical, but serve to "reinforce the stigma through degradation and shame" (Gough et al. 2008, p. 494; Warne and Bhatia 2006).

Although some **transsexuals** (who have been raised as one sex while emotionally identifying with the other) still wish surgery to conform their bodies to their gender identity, others may simply adopt the dress and demeanor of the sex with which they identify, vary their appearance and self-presentation, or adopt a style that is not gender identified.

The term **transgendered** describes an identity adopted by those who are uncomfortable in the gender of their birth. They may be in transition to a new gender or simply wish to continue to occupy a middle ground. Some universities have established gender-neutral housing at the request of transgendered students (F. Bernstein 2004; Raymond and Gordon 2008). Some bureaucratic forms now include a "transgender" box as well as those for "male" and "female," suggesting the beginning of societal accommodation of a more complex sex/gender system.

Chaz Bono (formerly Chastity Bono) was raised as the daughter of entertainers Sonny Bono and Cher. At age forty, she decided to have gender reassignment. *Gender* (or sex) *reassignment* is a surgical procedure in which a person's primary and secondary sex organs are changed to that of the other sex. Although the public transformation from Chastity to Chaz has provided a positive treatment of the issue, such transformations prove difficult for the people undergoing reassignment, not because of the physical and psychological transformations, but because of the responses to the changes by friends and family—and even the public.

In 1998, classical pianist David Buechner became Sara Buechner. Buechner was, prior to 1998, a famous musician. After her gender reassignment, the public, friends, and family did not support the changes, and her career stalled. Like Chaz Bono's mother, Sara Buechner's mother had a great deal of difficulty accepting her child's desires and subsequent change to a woman. In both cases, like many others, eventually family, friends, and even the public become accustomed to the new person. Not every transgender story is as positive, but as more people choose to redefine themselves in this way, the rest of society will follow with relative levels of acceptance (Marikar 2009; Winerip 2009).

The biological, psychological, and social realities presented by intersexed or transgendered individuals are challenges to the notion that there are clearly demarcated masculine and feminine genders and gender roles. In turn, parents, physicians, mental health professionals, and educators are coping with ethical decisions regarding surgery and socialization for those born with ambiguous sex characteristics or who appear in childhood to have uncertain sexual identities (P. L. Brown 2006; Lerner 2003; Weil 2006).

Critical Thinking

Have transgendered individuals been politically visible in your campus or community? What are your own thoughts as to whether gender is a dichotomy or a continuum along which individuals may vary?

persists and includes the belief that women are asking for too much (Swim et al. 1995). Moreover, though work, family, and civic roles have changed and modernized, there is still a sense on the part of the average person that men and women are different in personality and aptitudes (Begley 2009).

Modern sexism is endemic in the mass media. The mass news and entertainment media present images and stories that suggest "full equality for women is real—that now . . . [women] can be or do anything they want—but then simultaneously suggest that most women prefer domesticity over the workplace. This reinforces the notion that women and men together no longer need to pursue greater gender equality at work and at home" (Douglas 2009, pp. 283–284). The repetition of such distorted messages leads to unhelpful and sometimes harmful outcomes. For example, males are made to worry that they should resemble *hypermasculine* (i.e.,

Image courtesy of The Advertising Archives

Mass media present us with an idealized, one-dimensional stereotype of ourselves. This has important connotations for our relationships, how we see ourselves, and how we see each other.

characterized by distorted or exaggerated masculine traits) media images, causing some to act aggressively towards other males in an effort to "prove" themselves (Cooper 2008; Kane 2009; C. Lee 2008).

You can probably think of some characteristics typically associated with being feminine or masculine. Stereotypically masculine people are often thought to have **agentic** (from the root word *agent*) or **instrumental character traits**—confidence, assertiveness, and ambition—that enable them to accomplish difficult tasks or goals. A relative absence of agency characterizes our expectations of women, who are thought to embody **communal** or **expressive character traits**: warmth, sensitivity, the ability to express tender feelings, and placing concern about others' welfare above self-interest.

The ways in which men are expected to show agency and women expressiveness are embedded in the culture around us. Let's examine some of our cultural messages about masculinity and femininity.

Masculinities We need to state the obvious: Men are not all alike. Recognizing this, scholars have begun to analyze **masculinities** in the plural, rather than the singular—a recent and subtle change meant to promote our appreciation for the differences among men.

An important cultural expectation is that a man should be occupationally or financially successful, or at least should be working to support his family—which should include children sired in marriage. A man is also expected to be confident and self-reliant, even aggressive. An alternative cultural message emphasizes adventure, sometimes coupled with violence and/or the need to outwit, humiliate, and defeat other men in barroom brawls, contact sports, and war (Katz 2006; Sullivan and McHugh 2009).

Scholars have expanded on this last idea. If a male finds that legitimate avenues to occupational success are blocked to him because of, for example, lack of education or racial/ethnic status, he might "make it" through an alternative route, through physical aggression or striking a "cool pose." The latter involves dress and postures manifesting fearlessness and detachment, adapted by some racial/ethnic minority males for emotional survival in a discriminatory and hostile society (Crook, Thomas, and Cobia 2009; Martin and Harris 2006; Smith and Beal 2007; Wester et al. 2006). White supremacy movements can be seen as a similar response to status disadvantage for less advantaged white males (Swain 2002, pp. 1–2 and Chapter 3).

During the 1980s, a new cultural message emerged. According to this message, the "liberated" male or "new man" is emotionally sensitive and expressive, valuing tenderness and equal relationships with women (Messner 1997, pp. 36–38, 41). Since then, another transformation of the ideal male image has occurred in response to the terrorist attacks of 9/11. Now, an image of unafraid "can-do" men who tackle fear and traumatic events head-on, providing "unambiguous and uncomplicated performances of masculinity," while at the same time publicly shedding tears after they deal with traumatic issues, is becoming a more prevalent image of masculinity in American society (Adelman 2009, p. 279).

Femininities There are a variety of ways of being a woman, according to cultural messages of **femininities**. The pivotal expectation for a woman requires her to offer emotional support. Traditionally, the ideal woman was physically attractive, not too competitive, a good listener, and adaptable. She served as a man's helpmate, aiding and cheering his accomplishments. She was further expected to be a "good" mother, putting her family's and children's needs before her own. This cultural message continues to be promoted in our mass media.

Communications theorist Sut Jhally (2007), using Goffman's analysis of *gender display* (gender display are the behaviors we exhibit because of our socialization as men or women), examined a variety of mass media products, such as television, film, and magazines. One element he examined was people's hands. He noted that female "hands are shown not as assertive or controlling

Davis Factor/CORBIS

More and more women are entering nontraditional occupations, such as the military.

of their environment but as letting the environment control them" (Jhally 2009, p. 6).

An expectation that emerged as more women entered the workforce and the feminist movement arrived is that of the "professional woman:" independent, ambitious, self-confident. This cultural model may combine with the traditional one to form the "superwoman" message, according to which a good wife and/or mother also efficiently attains career success and/or supports her children by herself. An emerging female expectation is the "satisfied single:" a woman (either heterosexual or lesbian, usually employed, and perhaps a parent) who is quite happy not to be in a serious relationship with a male.

Gender Expectations and Diversity The view of men as instrumental and women as expressive was based primarily on images of white, middle-class heterosexuals. The use of European American, middle-class heterosexual people and families as "normal" in social science research often causes social scientists and policy makers to interpret differences as deficiencies, leading to the stereotyping of different groups (Leidy et al. 2009; Parke and Buriel 2006).

The "strong black woman" cultural messages for black women range from "bitches and bad (black) mothers to modern mammies . . . black women are [stereotyped as] either extremely educated or a high school dropout, ambitious or listless, sexy or ugly" (Boylorn 2008, pp. 417–418; Collins 2004; see also Andersen and Collins 2007a; Squires 2007). Latinas and Asian women are stereotyped as being more submissive than non-Hispanic white women (Andersen and Collins 2007a; Covert and Dixon 2008; Gewertz 2009). Latino men are stereotyped as patriarchal, following a *machismo* cultural ideal of extreme masculinity and male dominance (Hondagneu-Sotelo 1996; McLoyd et al. 2000; Ramos-Sánchez and Atkinson 2009). Some Latinos engaging in this stereotypical machismo behavior may do so because of the history of Latinos in the United States. According to William Carrigan and Clive Webb (2009), racial prejudice by whites against Mexicans in the late 1800s through early 1900s emphasized Mexican men as having more feminine attributes such as cowardice and a preference for wearing "fancy" clothing. This demeaning legacy is an important part of the psychological and cultural history of Latinos that has contemporary ramifications.

Other research indicates that racial/ethnic differences in role expectations and behaviors, particularly for males, are actually not as strong as either stereotypes or sociohistorical perspectives have suggested. The preeminence of the ideology of the male provider role is a powerful theme in *all* racial/ethnic groups (e.g., Taylor, Tucker, and Mitchell-Kernan 1999). Yet this view has changed significantly over the course of contemporary American labor history, especially with the necessity of dual incomes (Cunningham 2008).

African American families have "flexible family roles," but the male's involvement in child care and other expressive roles does not have the same priority as the provider role, despite the difficulty encountered by African American males in fulfilling this role. Black men and women express preferences for egalitarian relationships (Cowdery et al. 2009; Furdyna, Tucker, and James 2008). African American men are more supportive of employed wives than white men are. Yet, gender ideology among African Americans does differentiate the sexes by the importance of the male provider role.

Women are likely to perform more of the household labor than men (though African American men do more than white men) (Cowdery et al. 2009). African American men show up as more conservative than white men in other ways—for example, in a stronger conviction that men and women are essentially different: Men are "manly," and women are "womanly," or soft and feminine (Haynes 2000, p. 834). Interestingly, this may be related to the pursuit of the traditional family structure that has long eluded most African Americans. In many African American families, the ability to have traditional gender relationships is evidence of economic success (Cowdery et al. 2009; Furdyna, Tucker, and James 2008).

Similarly complex gender patterns are observed in Latino families. For example, some Mexican American women engage in stereotyped *marianismo* where they carry the primary responsibility for housework and child care (Pinto and Coltrane 2008). But roles have been modified in the migration process and with women's entry into the labor force. Mexican American women do more housework and child care than men, but less than their counterparts who still live in Mexico or who are immigrants (Pinto and Coltrane 2008).

(Asian) Indo American women, studies show, typically find themselves on similar trajectories. Like Mexican American women, as they obtain greater levels of education and develop their own careers, these wives are making greater demands on their husbands to help out with the burden of domestic chores and child care (Bhalla 2008; Kallivayalil 2004). These are but a few examples of the complexity of role expectations and behavior in real-life families.

"It's her first bench-clearing brawl."

Traditional stereotypes of children define males as aggressive and competitive and girls as sensitive and concerned for others. Real behavior is far more varied than these stereotypes and depends very much on the situation.

To What Extent Do Women and Men Follow Cultural Expectations?

It is one thing to recognize cultural images but another to follow them. Consequently, we continue to ask: To what extent do individual men and women, boys and girls, exhibit gender-differentiated behaviors?

In adult life, women seem to have greater connectedness in interpersonal relations and, perhaps due to gender stereotypes, find themselves pushed into the caregiving professions in greater numbers than men, whereas men tend to be in more socially dominant, competitive, and achievement-oriented occupations (Beutel and Marini 1995; Webster and Rashotte 2009). But there is great individual variation, and the situational context accounts for much of the apparent difference between men and women (Gormley and Lopez 2010; Meier, Hull, and Ortyl 2010; Rosenfeld 2007; Webster and Rashotte 2009).

Moreover, behavior vis-à-vis the gendered expectations we've discussed generally fits an overlapping pattern (Basow 1992). We can visualize this as two overlapping distribution curves (see Figure 4.1). For example, although the majority of men are taller than the majority of women, the area of overlap in men's and women's heights is considerable, and some men are shorter than some women. It is also true that differences among women or among men (*within-group variation*) are usually greater than the average difference between men and women (*between-group variation*).

Although males and females differ little on basic traits and abilities, the opportunities available in the social structure affect the options of men and women and, ultimately, their behaviors as they adapt to those options. The "deceptive differences" (Epstein 1988) we observe or think we observe typically involve men and women assigned to different social roles. A woman secretary, for example, is expected to be compliant and supportive of her male boss's decisions. To observers, she seems to have a gentle and submissive personality, while he is seen to have leadership qualities (Eagly, Wood, and Diekman 2000; Meier, Hull, and Ortyl 2010; Ridgeway and Smith-Lovin 1999; Webster and Rashotte 2009).

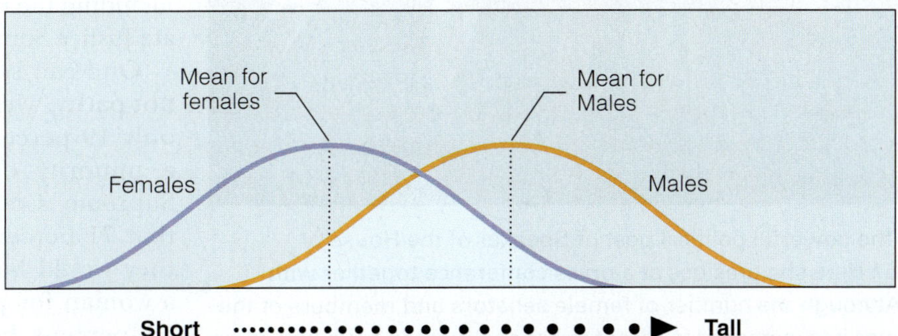

Figure 4.1 How females and males differ on one trait, height, conceptualized as overlapping normal distribution curves. Means (averages) may differ by sex, but trait distributions of men and women occupy much common ground.

The Gender Similarities Hypothesis

The preponderance of research on gender differences suggests that in fact they are few. Psychologist Janet Hyde (2005) offers a **gender similarities hypothesis** to replace the usual assumption of gender differences. The gender similarities hypothesis "holds that males and females are similar on most, but not all, psychological variables. . . . That is, men and women, as well as boys and girls, are more alike than they are different" (p. 581).

Hyde finds virtually no difference on most traits, a few moderate differences, and very few large differences. These conclusions apply even to math and verbal ability, self-esteem, and tendency toward aggression, areas where gender differences were thought to be pronounced. She did find evidence of gender differences (1) in motor performance, especially in throwing distance and speed; (2) in sexuality, especially male's greater incidence of masturbation and acceptance of casual sex; and (3) in physical aggressiveness. She did not find clear differences in relational aggression. Other research that fails to find confirmation of most stereotypical gender differences in emotions and emotional expression supports the gender similarities hypothesis (Else-Quest, Hyde, and Linn 2010; Hyde 2007).

Hyde goes on to argue that mistaken assumptions about gender differences have serious costs, hurting women's opportunities in the workplace, men's confidence in nontraditional family roles, and both sexes' confidence in their ability to communicate with each other. Despite the validity of Hyde's gender similarities hypothesis, virtually all societies, including our own, are structured around some degree of gender inequality.

Gender Inequality

Male dominance describes a situation in which the male(s) in a dyad or group assume authority over the female(s). On the societal level, male dominance is the assignment to men of greater control and influence over society's institutions and, usually, greater benefits. In this section we address gender difference and gender inequality in certain major social institutions: politics and government, religion, health, education, and the economy.

Male Dominance in Politics

As of 2009, in the U.S. Congress there were seventeen women in the Senate and seventy-six in the House of Representatives (U.S. House of Representatives 2009). In 2007, Democratic congresswoman Nancy Pelosi became Speaker of the House, the highest position in the House of Representatives and second after the vice president in the line of succession. A recent *New York Times* article quotes political strategists as saying that "[v]oters have grown more accustomed to women in powerful positions" (Toner 2007).

AP Photo/Paul Sakuma

Nancy Pelosi attained the powerful political post of Speaker of the House of Representatives in 2007. Here she presides at a press conference together with other House leaders. Although the number of female senators and members of the House of Representatives has increased in recent years and women have had some senior appointments in the executive branch in addition to Pelosi's congressional position, women remain a minority in positions of political power.

Beginning with the Clinton administration and continuing under President Barack Obama, women have been more visible in the executive branch of government as well. Hillary Clinton, the former first lady and a presidential contender herself, serves as secretary of state. Women justices have served on the Supreme Court, including the newest justice, Associate Justice Sonia Sotomayor.

One can see progress, though not parity, when women comprise only 19 percent of Congress and a minority of the cabinet and Supreme Court. Surveys report that 71 percent of the public say they would be willing to vote for a woman for president—but only 56 percent believe their family, friends, and coworkers are willing to do so (Rasmussen Reports 2008).

Male Dominance in Religion

Religion as an institution evidences male dominance as well. Although most U.S. congregations have more female than male participants, men more often hold positions of authority, while women perform secretarial, housekeeping, and low-level administrative chores (Chaves, Anderson, and Byassee 2009). As with politics, there are some striking exceptions that suggest future change. Women have been elected as bishops and denomination leaders in the African Methodist Episcopal, Anglican, United Methodist, and Presbyterian churches, but recent surveys suggest that women lead only 8 percent of congregations in the United States (Banerjee 2006a, 2006b; Butt 2009; Chaves, Anderson, and Byassee 2009; Gott 2010; "Professor Says" 2007).

The effects of personal religious involvement on women's daily lives are complex. The growth of evangelical Protestantism, Islamic fundamentalism, and the Latter-day Saints religion, along with the charismatic renewal in the Catholic Church, has fostered a traditional family ideal of male headship and a corresponding rejection of feminist-inspired redefinitions of family roles. We note that strict gender divisions in the home lead to family tension and decreased marital satisfaction, particularly for the wife. Such dissatisfaction increases the risk of divorce even in the most traditional of couples (Duba and Watts 2009; Vaaler, Ellison, and Powers 2009; Zink 2008).

On the other hand, actual practice among evangelicals seems more egalitarian than formal doctrine (Bartkowski 2001, Chapter 7). There is also a growing feminist movement among American Muslim women who seek to combine their religio-cultural heritage with equal rights for females. This feminism "signifies a commitment to faith that challenges secular feminist notions" about Islam and women (Karim 2009, p. 93).

Gender and Health

When it comes to health, we can no longer speak of male advantage. From birth onward, indeed prior to birth (fetal loss), males have higher death rates. Male infants have higher rates of infant mortality and adverse conditions (Heron et al. 2009, Table D). Nature recognizes this disparity, and in the United States, around 105 boys are born for every 100 girls, with boys outnumbering girls under age eighteen (U.S. Census Bureau 2009j).

Life expectancy for the total population dropped slightly to 77.7 years in 2006—80.2 years for females and 75.1 years for males, a difference of 5.1 years (Heron et al. 2009). The life expectancy gap between males and females peaked in 1979 at almost eight years and has been decreasing since (see Figure 4.2).

Gender difference in longevity has been attributed to greater risk factors for boys and men, including smoking and drinking, accidents, suicide, and murder victimization, as well as some not-well-understood vulnerability to infection and stress (Heron et al. 2009). Men also have far fewer doctor visits (i.e., checkups) than women, and men who are middle-aged and more traditional visit the doctor even less (Dotinga 2009; Painter 2006; Rabin 2006).

For years, medical researchers paid women little attention. But partly due to the feminist movement, "women's health has been a national priority" (Rabin 2006). Now men's advocacy groups are calling for increased attention to men's health and greater investment in research on their unique health conditions—funding for breast cancer research, for example, exceeds that for prostate cancer by 40 percent. In any case, we can applaud the increasing attention to gender equality in medical research.

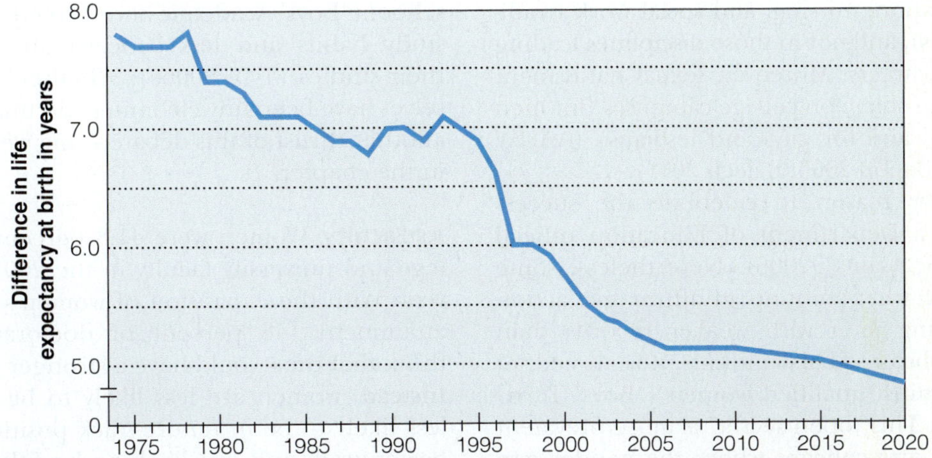

Figure 4.2 The difference in life expectancy between males and females, United States, 1975–2020. From a difference of almost eight years in 1979, this gap has been steadily decreasing. The years post-2006 are projections by the U.S. Census Bureau.

Gender and Education

Whether women or men are relatively disadvantaged in higher education is in dispute. (The relative circumstances of boys and girls in K–12 schooling will be discussed in the Gender and Socialization section later in this chapter.)

As Students Women have been the majority of college students since 1979 and now surpass men in the proportion of the total population that are college graduates (Lewin 2006c; "Women Catching Up" 2008). In 2007, women earned 57 percent of bachelor's and 60.5 percent of master's degrees, 50 percent of first professional degrees, and 50 percent of doctorates (U.S. Census Bureau 2010b, Table 288).

The changing gender balance in higher education—indeed, in high school completion, with 72 percent of girls but only 65 percent of boys graduating high school (Lewin 2006b)—has led to cries of alarm (e.g., "leaving men in the dust," Lewin 2006a, p. A1; "stagnation for men," "Study: Academic Gains" 2006). Advocates of attention to boys argue that with the advances made by women (attributable to feminism), it is now the "boys' turn." Otherwise, "many will needlessly miss out on success in life" ("Big [Lack of] Men" 2005).

In response to the assumption that women "have it made" and men are the disadvantaged category, counterarguments and data have been offered (see, e.g., Gandy 2005). First of all, men's college enrollments have *not* declined; they have simply not increased as rapidly as women's (Corbett, Hill, and St. Rose 2008; U.S. National Center for Education Statistics 2006). Second, any disadvantage to males depends on age and class. Among upper-income students of traditional age, *males*—white, black, Hispanic, and Asian—remain a majority of college enrollees (Cataldi, Laird, and KewalRamani 2009; Lewin 2006c), though barely so. Women's master's degrees are primarily in education, nursing, and social work (traditional female areas), and not in those disciplines leading to the most elite careers. Moreover, sexual harassment continues to be a problem on college campuses (for men as well as women, and for gays and lesbians) (AAUW Educational Foundation 2006; Dziech 2003).

"There is every reason to celebrate the success of women," says a Department of Education official ("Study: Academic Gains" 2006). Nevertheless, some colleges now have what amounts to affirmative action for men, admitting men with weaker records than some women applicants. This amounts, it is argued, to discrimination against qualified women ("Boys' Turn" 2006; Britz 2006). This "open secret" is more prevalent at smaller liberal arts colleges where the gender gap is more obvious (Jaschik 2009; Meyer 2009). The U.S. Commission on Civil Rights has begun to research the issue because, it says, ". . . some college administrators argue that they must discriminate against women or the gender balance at their institutions will become . . . off-kilter" (Heriot 2009).

Some education scholars believe that "the new emphasis on young men's problems . . . is misguided in a world where men still dominate the math–science axis, earn more money, and wield more power than women" (Lewin 2006a, p. 18). Such concerns may be misguided given the recent data released by the U.S. Department of Education. A new report suggests that reading scores for males at ages nine, thirteen, and seventeen have improved since 2004, and the gaps between boys and girls is decreasing (Rampey, Dion, and Donahue 2009). Additionally, recent research also points out the continued disparity in earnings between the sexes, with women, on average, earning just 77.1 cents for every dollar a man earns, which is down from 77.8 cents in 2007 (Institute for Women's Policy Research 2009).

The data have made visible two patterns. First, it becomes clear that the college achievement gap is greater among racial/ethnic groups *within* gender categories and especially points to black and Hispanic male disadvantage (Aronson 2003; Corbett, Hill, and St. Rose 2008). This has set off a debate over whether these trends show a worrisome achievement gap between men and women or whether the concern should be directed toward the educational difficulties of poor boys, whether they are black, white, or Hispanic (Cataldi, Laird, and KewalRamani 2009; Corbett, Hill, and St. Rose 2008; Lewin 2006a, p. 18).

A second and alarming pattern is the apparent difference between males and females in goals and attitudes toward schooling. Such attitudes have long-run implications for males' educational attainment, placement in the workforce, and ability to maintain a marriage that has a stable financial underpinning. A *USA Today* study found that 84 percent of girls but only 67 percent of boys think it is important to continue beyond high school ("Boys' Academic Slide" 2003). Boys have poorer study habits and less concern about doing well in their studies (Tyre 2006c). Whether the schools themselves have been unwelcoming and unadapted to boys is another thrust of this debate—one we will take up later in the chapter.

As Faculty Women were 41.8 percent of full-time college and university faculty in the 2007–2008 academic year. With the expansion of women's graduate degree attainment (48 percent of doctorates), one would think that they would have a stronger presence by now. Instead, women are less likely to be full-time faculty; less likely to be in tenure-track positions; less likely to be tenured; and less likely to be full professors (U.S. Department of Education 2009, Table 245; West and Curtis 2006). Disadvantage to women is especially strong at the more elite schools. Sixty-two percent of

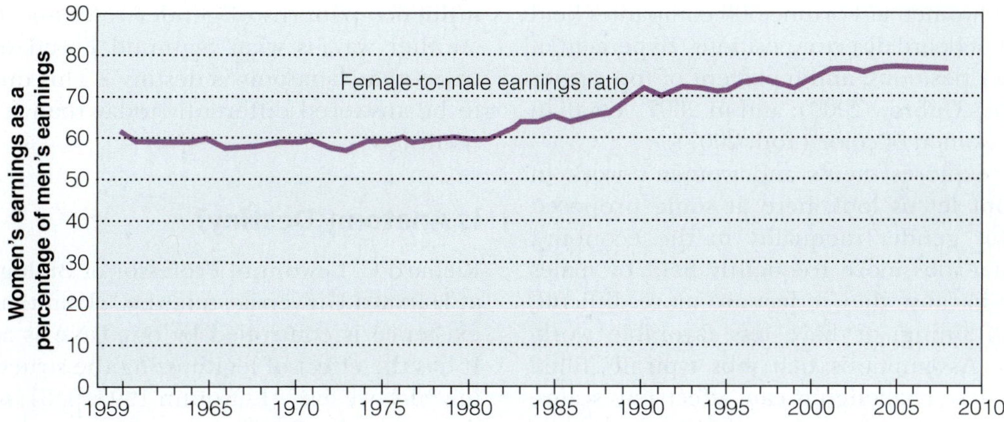

Figure 4.3 Female-to-male earnings ratio of full-time, year-round workers by sex: 1955–2008.

those hired by Ivy League universities in 2005 were men (Arenson 2005).

Little gain is seen in faculty racial/ethnic diversity. In 2007, 44.6 percent of college faculty were white males; 32 percent, white females; 2.8 percent, black females; 2.7 percent, black males; 2.5 percent Asian/Pacific Islander females; 4.8 percent, Asian/Pacific Islander males; 1.6 percent, Hispanic females; 1.9 percent Hispanic males; and less than 1 percent each, Native American males and females (Snyder, Dillow, and Hoffman 2009).

Male Dominance in the Economy

It is on gender inequality in the economy that most attention has been focused. Although the situation is changing, as you can see from Figure 4.3, men have been and continue to be dominant economically. Before examining the gendered pay differences, we would first like to discuss what appears to be economic role reversals for some married couples. According to a recent poll by the Pew Research Center (see Figure 4.6 later in the chapter), "only 4% of husbands had wives who brought home more income than they did in 1970, a share that rose to 22% in 2007" (Fry and Cohn 2010, p. 2). The reasons for this are many, but it is important to note that there are fewer married couples than in 1970, more women than men obtain college degrees, and in 2008 men were unemployed at three times the rate of women. Males accounted for about 75 percent of the 2008 unemployment rate (Borbely 2009; Fry and Cohn 2010, p. 2).

In 2008, women who were employed full time earned 80 percent of what men employed full time did (U.S. Bureau of Labor Statistics 2009a); this is down a full percentage point from 2006. Younger women between the ages of sixteen and twenty-four and between the ages of twenty-five and thirty-four earn a larger proportion (91 percent and 89 percent, respectively) of what men do (U.S. Bureau of Labor Statistics 2009a). Non-Hispanic white and Asian women both earned just under 80 percent of what males earned. Black and Hispanic female/male comparisons are more favorable to women, at 90 percent, but this is primarily because black and Hispanic men have much lower earnings than do white men (U.S. Bureau of Labor Statistics 2009a).

Even in the same occupational categories, women earn less than men. For instance, in 2008, in the highest-paying occupation, that of chief executive, women made $83,356, whereas men earned $103,948 on average (U.S. Bureau of Labor Statistics 2009a). The lowest paid occupational category, food preparation worker, also had a difference in pay, with women earning $17,576 and men earning $19,136 on average. Some analysts suggest the difference is related to choice of occupational specialty and practice setting; however, as evidenced by the differences in pay for the same profession at both ends of occupational earnings, such a simplistic explanation provides little clarity to a problem that has haunted women since the Industrial Revolution and that has devastating impacts on poverty, hunger, health, and quality of life.

Overall, the earnings gap between men and women narrowed in recent decades, but, as Figure 4.3 indicates, that gap is widening slightly. Some proportion of the convergence is due to falling wages for men or their increased time out of the labor force, but by and large the narrowing gap is due to rising wages for women as they have increased their human capital (education and skills) and labor force participation (England 2006). Yet, as discussed above, the pay gap between male and female college graduates has widened a bit since the 1990s.

Men also continue to dominate corporate America. "A decade ago it was possible to imagine that men and women with similar qualifications might one day soon be making identical salaries. Today that is harder to imagine" (Leonhardt 2006b, p. A1; see also "Women Still Lag"

2004). In 2008, "women at Fortune 500 companies held only 15 percent of board director positions, 16 percent of corporate officer positions, and 6 percent of top earner positions" (Tuhus-Dubrow 2009); and in 2007, less than 2 percent were women of color (Toth 2007).

Chapter 11 explores men's and women's work in more detail. But let us look here at some proposed explanations for gender inequality in the economy. Some argue that jobs more frequently held by males may pay better because they in fact are more difficult, require more training, or have less favorable working conditions. Assumptions that jobs typically filled by women are less challenging can affect pay scales. Women may themselves buy into gender stereotypes and believe they are less competent to achieve certain jobs or occupational levels. And as women enter the job pool for certain professional jobs (e.g., journalism), the field becomes more crowded and wages and salaries are less competitive (Blau, Brinton, and Grusky 2006).

Women also contend with employers' *assumptions* that women will opt out, which may affect their careers. This is where the costs of gender stereotyping come in. Employers may be less likely to select women for advanced training and positions with upward mobility potential even though the women affected may be highly ambitious, with a commitment to continuous employment (Laff 2007; Pinto 2009). This form of discrimination ultimately leads to less advancement and earnings for women. For this reason, it is more likely a woman's income will be seen as less essential to the family than a man's, and the family may favor his career over hers in terms of residential mobility, the taking of time-pressured jobs and promotions, and the like.

But not all of the wage gap is explainable by objective characteristics of men's and women's employment histories, skills, or women's own choices. It is likely that discrimination against women as employees continues to some degree. After various factors associated with earnings are taken into account, research finds a varying (by perhaps as much as a 22.9 percent) differential in earnings that is usually attributed to discrimination, albeit of a nonobvious sort (Blau and Kahn 2006; Institute for Women's Policy Research 2009; National Women's Law Center 2007).

We have been discussing gender inequality. The state of affairs can be nicely summed up by Figure 4.3, which illustrates the gains women have made economically *and* the gap that still hasn't closed. Male dominance in the United States today is, of course, more moderate than in our past or compared to contemporary societies that are more traditional or overtly oppressive of women. Still, cross-culturally and historically, it appears that virtually all societies have been characterized by some degree of male dominance.

This leads us to ask whether male dominance might be anchored in biology. To what extent does biology influence patterns of gender roles and behaviors? Put another way, is what Sigmund Freud once proposed true—that "anatomy is destiny"? This question is likely to be answered differently today than it was just a few years ago.

Is Anatomy Destiny?

Richard C. Lewontin, Professor of Biology and Zoology at Harvard University, said the "claim that all of human existence is controlled by our DNA is a popular one. It has the effect of legitimizing the structures of society in which we live" (Lewontin 1993, p. 61; see also Lewontin and Levins 2007). Lewontin is suggesting that some researchers attribute socially constructed human behavior to inherited genetics. In particular, these researchers look to race and gender differences, trying to find a genetic explanation for what most social scientists recognize as structurally created forms of inequality, often relying heavily on functionalist explanations of social organization—hence the term sociobiology (MacCallum and Hill 2006; Nielsen 2009). In other words, these researchers have privileged simplistic explanations for sociohistorical complexity.

Biological theories of gender difference were initially offered by ethologists, who study humans as an evolved animal species (e.g., Tiger 1969). Tiger, who primarily studied baboons, found males to be dominant and argued that *Homo sapiens* inherited this condition through natural selection. Newer data on nonhuman primates have challenged these conclusions as socially constructed myths. Primate species vary in their behavior, and within species there is some environmentally shaped variation (Bartlett 2009; Haraway 1989; Vogel et al. 2009; Wood and Eagly 2002, p. 721). The facts suggest that male and female behavior is not differentiated in a consistent way in the animal species most closely related to humans.

A subsequent sociobiology theory of gendered behavior focused on genes. This theoretical model is most often found in the realm of *evolutionary psychology*, where human behavior is thought to be associated with biological adaptation. In this view, in order to continue their genes, individuals act to maximize their reproduction or that of close kin. Different strategies characterize males (who seek to impregnate many females) and females (who seek the best conditions in which to nurture their small number of children) (Buss 2009; Buss and Shackelford 2008; Dawkins 1976). Other researchers reverse the order, suggesting that rather than viewing biology as impacting human behavior and society, we should instead examine the ways in which society and social interactions impact our biology (McIntyre and Edwards 2009).

Other evolutionary perspectives focus on the hunting–gathering era of early human evolution. Men, because of their greater physical strength and their freedom from reproductive responsibility, were able to hunt. But women, who might be pregnant or breastfeeding, gathered food that was naturally available close to home while they also cared for children. According to these evolutionary theories, circumstances elicited different adaptive strategies and skills from men and women that then became encoded in the genes—greater aggression and spatial skills for men, nurturance and domesticity for women. According to this perspective, these traits remain part of our genetic heritage and are today the foundation of gender differences in personality traits, abilities, and behavior (Maccoby 1998, Chapter 5). Newer research suggests that such traits merely reflect cultural differences (i.e., such traits vary from culture to culture).

The notions that current behaviors stem from our adaptation during the hunting–gathering era, discussed above, have been called into question, along with the conflation of evolution with adaptation. For example, physical size must be taken into account when analyzing the difference between males and females in such activities as throwing and spatial reasoning (Hooven et al. 2004; Yang et al. 2007). Another set of traits brought into question are empathy (female) and aggression (male). Recent research shows that basal testosterone levels (found in both males and females) has significant impact on the level of empathy or aggression in either sex. In other words, aggressive or empathetic behavior (or the lack thereof) has less to do with one's gender and more to do with levels of basal testosterone in the body at any given time (Carré and McCormick 2008; Mehta, Jones, and Josephs 2008; van Honk et al. 2004).

The genetic heritage is expressed through **hormonal processes** (as noted above).[2] However, the relationship between hormones and behavior goes in both directions: What's happening in one's environment may influence hormone secretion levels. Several studies have found, for example, that the hormonal levels of males in romantic relationships and those of new fathers undergo changes parallel to those associated with maternal behavior (e.g., lower testosterone and cortisol and detectable levels of estradiol) (Gray 2003; Gray, Ellison, and Campbell 2007; McIntyre et al. 2006; van Anders and Watson 2006, 2007). Testosterone rises in men in response to an athletic or other competition or in response to insults (Carré and McCormick 2008; Mehta, Jones, and Josephs 2008).

Biologists have relinquished deterministic models in their thinking about gender and family.[3] They present an evolutionary theory that acknowledges strong environmental effects on animal behavior. Much current biological theorizing leaves plenty of room for culture (e.g., Emlen 1995; Geary and Flinn 2001; Lewontin and Levins 2007; McIntyre and Edwards 2009; Nielsen 2009). In fact, cognitive psychologists continue to debate the existence and significance of gender differences; however, a growing body of important research shows that *stereotype threat* may have a greater impact on gendered differences in cognitive testing results. A stereotype threat is "the sense of threat that can arise when one knows that he or she can possibly be judged or treated negatively on the basis of a negative stereotype about one's group" (Goff, Steele, and Davies 2008, p. 92; see also Campbell and Collaer 2009; Harvard University 2005; Pinker 2005; Spelke 2005).

Sociologists who work from a biosocial perspective (e.g., Alan Booth and colleagues) are finding complex interactions among gender, social roles, and biological indicators rather than categorical gender differences (see Figure 4.4 for differing ideas of gender role development). It is safe to say that there is convergence on the opinion that in gender, as well as other behavior, biology interacts with culture in complex and constantly changing ways that cannot be reduced to biological determinism.

Although adult men and women seem to be converging in social roles and personal qualities, gender differences and separation still seem rather powerful in the younger years. We look now at the various theories and practices related to the socialization of boys and girls.

[2] **Hormones** are chemical substances secreted into the bloodstream by the endocrine glands; they influence the activities of cells, tissues, and body organs. The primary male sex hormones are androgens. Testosterone, produced in the male testes, is an androgen. Testosterone levels in males peak in adolescence and early adulthood, then slowly decline throughout the rest of a man's life. Females also secrete testosterone and other androgens, but in smaller amounts. The primary female hormones are estrogen and progesterone, secreted by the female ovaries.

Sex hormones influence *sexual dimorphism*—that is, differences between the sexes in body structure and size, muscle development, fat distribution, hair growth, voice quality, and the like. The degree to which hormones produce gender-differentiated behavior is disputed.

[3] Another area of biological research and theorizing on gender differences has to do with brain organization and functioning. *Brain lateralization* refers to the relative dominance and the synchronization of the two hemispheres of the brain. The argument was that male and female brains differ due to greater amounts of testosterone secreted by a male fetus. As a result, researchers believed different sides of the brain may be dominant in males and females, or males and females may differ in the degree to which the two brain halves work together (Blum 1997; Liu et al 2009; Springer and Deutsch 1994).

Overall, brain lateralization studies have produced unconvincing evidence concerning sex differences in brain organization or a connection to verbal, spatial, or mathematical abilities. Recent research finds no significant difference between the genders in either mathematical or language skills, instead noting that the brain functioning is asymmetrical in both sexes. Furthermore, gender differences in measured math ability and achievement have declined dramatically, arguing against a biological explanation (Hyde, Fenema, and Lamon 1990; Kimmel 2000, pp. 30–33; Liu et al. 2009; Pinel and Dehaene 2009; Rogers 2001; Sun and Walsh 2006; Wood and Eagly 2002, p. 720).

Gender as a Functional Role	Gender as a Situational Role
1. Gender role behaviors developed to meet functional system needs of the family; functional needs of nuclear family system create differentiation into an instrumental leader (father) and an expressive leader (mother); the two roles describe division of labor and other aspects of interaction within families.	1. Gender role differences depend up on cultural definitions; interaction requires both influential, agentic, proactive behaviors and acquiescent, expressive, reactive behaviors depending on the nature of the risk, characteristics of other individuals, and other situational facts.
2. Instrumental and expressive roles are equally valuable because they have equal functional importance; individuals recognize that, so the two roles are equally valued and rewarded; also, each role has its own ranking of assumed competence.	2. Instrumental and expressive roles are seen as unequal in importance, social esteem, and perceived value; instrumental and agentic attitudes and behaviors are favored; social-emotional and responsive attitudes and behaviors are less favored; also the instrumental role is associated with high general competence, whereas the expressive role is associated with low general competence; thus the two kinds of roles are associated with power and prestige structures in face-to-face interaction.
3. Childhood gender socialization entails learning either the instrumental (male) or expressive (female) role; by late adolescence, gender-appropriate attitudes and behaviors usually have been thoroughly internalized.	3. Socialization includes learning both superordinate and subordinate behaviors and attitudes; it also includes learning social cues to tell a person's place within situational social hierarchies.
4. Because of the functional importance of filling the two gender roles, socialization is repetitive and is so intense that the roles tend to be overlearned and individuals become encased in them; a fully socialized individual typically is only able to display one role set; fully socialized adults have difficulty understanding or displaying the complementary role to their own.	4. Because of the importance of situation-appropriate behavior, individuals learn considerable flexibility in displaying both instrumental and social-emotional attitudes and behaviors; an individual can display different role sets in different circumstances.
5. Changing gender role behaviors and attitudes (presumably in the direction of greater quality) would require changing the gender role socialization experiences of children from earliest childhood through late adolescence; such changes would need to be made in all or most families to change society; however, that would endanger the functioning of future families.	5. Changing gender role behaviors and attitudes (presumably in the direction of greater equality) would require devising situation-specific interventions to change structural characteristics of particular situations.

Figure 4.4 The functional role vision compared to the situational vision of gender.

Gender and Socialization

Psychologist Eleanor Maccoby, earlier associated with a review of research on sex differences that found them few and mostly unimportant (Maccoby and Jacklin 1974), has now come to see biology as grounding some *childhood* differences between the sexes, as well as children's tendency to prefer sex-segregated play.

Maccoby sees boys' rough play, earlier separation from adults, poor impulse control, and competition-seeking behavior, and girls' interest in young infants, earlier verbal fluency, and earlier self-regulation as biologically based. She attributes these differences to *prenatal* hormonal priming (see also Hines et al. 2002), noting that hormonal levels *during childhood* do *not* match these observed patterns. Nor do hormonal levels vary much by sex until adolescence. It is worth noting that she sees the biological influence as very specifically *not* marking the existence of generalized sex differences. However, an important question arises in regard to biological bases for sex differences concerning the relationship and interactions each child has with its same-gendered parent and the development of gender roles (Caldera, Huston, and O'Brien 1989; Feldman 2003). For example, if a female who conducts herself according to the expected gender roles has more interaction with a female child, would we not see a more pronounced development of those roles in that child?

Such questions bring us to look at biology and childhood in a different way. In contrast to other species, much of the behavior of humans involves behavior that is learned, not programmed as instinct. There is a lengthy period of dependency on parents or other adults during which this learning takes place (Geary and Flinn 2001). This process, termed **socialization**, is "[a] process by which people develop their human capacities and acquire a unique personality and identity and by which culture is passed from generation to generation" (Ferrante 2000, p. 521).

In this section we look specifically at *gender* socialization, but the socialization processes discussed here are applicable to other aspects of cultural values and behavioral expectations as well. First, we examine some theories of socialization, then we look at specific settings for gender socialization, and finally we address some current issues regarding boys and girls.

Children learn much about gender roles from their parents, whether they are taught consciously or unconsciously. Parents may model roles and reinforce expectations of appropriate behavior. Children also internalize messages from available cultural influences and materials surrounding them.

Theories of Socialization

There are a number of competing theories of gender socialization, each with some supporting evidence.

Social Learning Theory According to **social learning theory** (Bandura and Walters 1963), children learn gender roles as they are taught by parents, schools, and the media. Children observe and imitate *models* of gender behavior, such as parents, and/or they are *rewarded (or punished)* by parents and others for gender-appropriate or -inappropriate behavior. Fathers seem to have stronger expectations for gender-appropriate behavior than do mothers. Although this theory makes intuitive sense, researchers have found little association between children's personalities and parents' characteristics (Andersen 1988; Losh-Hesselbart 1987). Other research, especially on the realm of familial violence, suggests there is some association between children's aggressive behaviors and observed parental behavior (Button and Gealt 2010; Dunn 2005; Hoffman, Kiecolt, and Edwards 2005).

Self-Identification Theory Some psychologists think that what comes first is not rules about what boys and girls should do but rather the child's awareness of being a boy or a girl. In this **self-identification theory** (also termed *cognitive-developmental theory*), children categorize themselves as male or female, typically by age three. They then identify behaviors in their families, in the media, or elsewhere appropriate to their sex and adopt those behaviors. In effect, children socialize themselves from available cultural materials (Kohlberg 1966; Signorella and Frieze 2008).

Gender Schema Theory Similar to self-identification theory, gender schema theory posits that children develop a framework of knowledge (a **gender schema**) about what girls and boys typically do (Bem 1981). Children then use this framework to organize how they interpret new information and think about gender. Once a child has developed a gender schema, the schema influences how she or he processes new information, with gender-consistent information remembered better than gender-inconsistent information. For example, a child with a traditional gender schema might generalize that physicians are men even though the child has sometimes had appointments with female physicians. Overall, gender schema theorists see gender schema as maintaining traditional stereotypes. This theoretical framework continues to be tested and continues to show that younger children maintain more rigid gender stereotypes than do adolescents (Crouter et al. 2007; Signorella and Frieze 2008).

Symbolic Interaction Theory In **symbolic interaction theory** (Cooley 1902, 1909; Mead 1934), children develop self-concepts based on social feedback—the *looking-glass self* (see Chapter 2). Also important is their *role taking*, as they play out roles in interaction with significant others such as parents and peers. As children grow, they take on roles representing wider social networks, and eventually *internalize* norms of the community (termed by Mead *the generalized other*). Although this is a general theory of socialization, you can see how it can be applied to gender. Little girls play "mommy" with their dolls and kitchen sets, whereas little boys play with cars or hypermasculine action figures. But things are changing, and it is now likely that little girls as well as little boys play "going to work."

All the socialization theories presented here seem plausible, but none has conclusive research support. Self-identification theory and gender schema theory, as well as biologically deterministic theories, are especially lacking. It is also the case that gender socialization is a moving target in a rapidly changing social world. When noting the difficulties of these theories in trying to fully explain gendered behavior, keep in mind that human behavior is based on many factors. Our genes, our socialization, our interactions, our environment, and our cultural and social encounters are just a few of the things that impact who each individual "is."

The complexity and informational intake capabilities of our brains may never be fully known. But each encounter we have with another person, another object, with visual stimuli, with auditory stimuli, and so forth all work together to impact each of us in different ways. Thus, the social sciences have the most difficult of tasks—which is to try and make sense of who we are and how we got to where we are now. Sometimes, along the way, researchers bring their own biases into the mix, and we thus find ourselves combating deterministic theoretical models.

Regardless of the long-term value of each theoretical construct, all are ultimately valuable because they serve to move the scientific disciplines forward, allowing researchers to develop more sophisticated explanations of who we are.

Settings for Socialization

FOCUS ON CHILDREN

We'll turn now to some empirical findings regarding gender socialization in concrete and specific settings: the family, play and games among peers, media influences, and the schools. We saw in Chapter 3 that religious groups often specify appropriate gender roles, and they are also a setting for gender socialization.

Boys and Girls in the Family From the 1970s on, parents have reported treating their sons and daughters similarly.[4] "[T]he specialization of men for dominance and women for subordination that emerged [as a socialization pattern] in patriarchal societies has eroded with the weakening of gender hierarchies in postindustrial societies" (Wood and Eagly 2002, p. 717). Differential socialization still exists, but it is typically not conscious. Instead, it "reflects the fact that the parents themselves accept the general societal roles for men and women," though this is no longer universal (Kimmel 2000, p. 123). New analysis also reinforces parental roles as important in the socialization process, suggesting that low levels of parental involvement as well as negative and coercive parental behaviors are likely to contribute to negative behaviors in children—particularly in female adolescents (Kroneman et al. 2009; Svensson 2003).

Still, encouragement of gender-typed interests and activities continues. A study of 120 babies' and toddlers' rooms found that girls had more dolls, fictional characters, children's furniture, and the color pink; boys had more sports equipment, tools, toy vehicles, and the colors blue, red, and white. Fathers, more than mothers, enforce gender stereotypes, especially for sons; it is more acceptable, for example, for girls to be tomboys (Adams and Coltrane 2004; Bussey and Bandura 1999; Feldman 2003, p. 207; Kimmel 2000, Chapter 6; Marks, Lam, and McHale 2009; Pomerleau et al. 1990).

Exploratory behavior is encouraged more in boys than in girls (Feldman 2003, p. 207). Toys considered appropriate for boys encourage physical activity and independent play, whereas "girl toys" elicit closer physical proximity and more talk between child and caregiver (Athenstaedt, Mikula, and Bredt 2009; Caldera, Huston, and O'Brien 1989; Zahn-Waxler and Polanichka 2004). Even parents who support nonsexist child rearing for their daughters are often concerned if their sons are not aggressive or competitive "enough"—or are "too" sensitive (Blakemore and Hill 2008; Pleck 1992). Girls are increasingly allowed or encouraged to develop instrumental attitudes and skills. Meanwhile, boys are still discouraged from, or encounter parental ambivalence about, developing attitudes and skills of tenderness or nurturance (Blakemore and Hill 2008; Chaplin, Cole, and Zahn-Waxler 2005; Kindlon and Thompson 1999; Martin and Ross 2005; Pollack 1998).

Beginning when children are about five and increasing through adolescence, parents allocate household chores—both the number and kinds—to their children differentially, according to the child's sex. With African American children often an exception, Patricia will more likely be assigned cooking and laundry tasks; Paul will find himself painting and mowing (Burns and

Courtesy Deb Glover and Celeste Wheeler

Toys send messages about gender roles. What does this toy say?

[4] Because most of the classic research presented in this section has focused on middle-class whites, findings may or may not apply to other racial/ethnic or class groups. Racial/ethnic and class variation in child rearing is discussed in Chapter 10.

Homel 1989; McHale et al. 1990). Because girls' chores typically must be done daily, whereas boys' are sporadic, girls spend more time doing chores—a fact that "may convey a message about male privilege" (Basow 1992, p. 131). African American girls, however, are raised to be more independent and less passive. Research also indicates that African American boys as well as girls are socialized for roles that include employment and child care (Brown et al. 2009; Hale-Benson 1986; Staples and Boulin Johnson 1993; Theran 2009).

Although relations in the family provide early feedback and help shape a child's developing identity, play and peer groups become important as children try out identities and adult behaviors. In fact, the author of one review of psychological research argues that peers have much more influence on child and adolescent development in general than do parents (J. Harris 1998; Rose and Rudolph 2006).

Play and Games The role of **play** is an important concept in the interactionist perspective. In G. H. Mead's theory (1934), play is not idle time, but a significant vehicle through which children develop appropriate concepts of adult roles as well as images of themselves.

Boys and girls tend to play separately and differently (Aydt and Corsaro 2003; Maccoby 1998, 2002; McIntyre and Edwards 2009). Girls play in one-to-one relationships or in small groups of two and three; their play is relatively cooperative, emphasizes turn taking, requires little competition, and has relatively few rules. In "feminine" games such as jump rope or hopscotch, the goal is skill rather than winning (Basow 1992; Munroe and Romney 2006). Boys more often play in fairly large groups, characterized by more fighting and attempts to effect a hierarchical pecking order. Boys also seem to exhibit high spirits and having fun (Maccoby 1998; Munroe and Romney 2006). From preschool through adolescence, children who play according to traditional gender roles are more popular with their peers; this is more true for boys (Martin 1989).

Especially in elementary schools, many cross-sexual interaction rituals such as playground games are based on and reaffirm boundaries and differences between girls and boys. Sociologist Barrie Thorne (1992), who spent eleven months doing naturalistic observation at two elementary schools, calls these rituals **borderwork** (Aydt and Corsaro 2003).

Sports play a role, both the informal and organized sports of childhood and the images presented in the media (Hardin and Greer 2009; Messner 2002). Now girls have more organized sports available to them, as well as more media models of women athletes. Girls who take part in sports have greater self-esteem and self-confidence (Andersen and Taylor 2002; Dworkin and Messner 1999).

The Power of Cultural Images Media images often convey gender expectations. These images are called *media frames.* A media frame is the way a story has been created for the consumer (this includes television shows, commercials, magazine articles, photographs, radio shows, music, video games, etc.). A media frame is the way that the writers of a story make sense of the stories and events we are viewing, hearing, interacting with, and/or reading about. In other words, the media frame guides us through what the subject is and its meaningful qualities. Such framing has important implications for our gender expectations.

Children's programming more often depicts boys than girls in dominant, agentic roles (B. Carter 1991). On music videos, females are likely to be shown trying to get a man's attention. Some videos broadcast shockingly violent misogynistic (i.e., hatred of women) messages (Jhally 2007). In TV commercials, men predominate by about nine to one as the authoritative narrators or voiceovers, even when the products are aimed at women (Craig 1992; Kilbourne 1994). Cultural images in the media indicate to the audience what is "normal." In studying media frames, researchers "focus on *how* issues and other objects of interest are reported by news media as well as *what* is emphasized in such reporting" (Weaver, McCombs, and Shaw 2004, p. 257, emphasis in original).

The media coverage of the 2008 presidential election is an excellent recent example of the continuation of gender stereotypes that has haunted women politicians since the Suffragette movement (Baird 2008). Women who are government officials or running for political office are more likely to have reporters, television shows, and even opponents emphasize their physical appearance (how their hair looks, what kind of clothing they wear) and to discuss their children and marital status. Communication scholars have noted that "Palin's attractiveness resulted in frequent and varied references to her 'sexiness,' whereas Clinton was viewed as not feminine enough in pantsuits that covered her 'cankles'" (thick ankles) (Carlin and Winfrey 2009, p. 330; see also Bystrom 2006; Heldman, Carroll, and Olson 2005).

Socialization in Schools There is considerable evidence that the way girls and boys are treated differently in school is detrimental to both genders (Corbett, Hill, and St. Rose 2008; Sullivan, Riccio, and Reynolds 2009). School organization, classroom teachers, and textbooks all convey the message that boys are more important than girls. At the same time, some critics posit that school expectations are unreasonably difficult for the typical boy to meet.

Teachers' Practices Research shows that teachers pay more attention to males than to females, and males tend to dominate learning environments from nursery school

© Michael Newman / Photo Edit

Are boys behaving differently than girls in this photo? How does this fit with the discussion of gender and socialization in school? What does that discussion say about girls in school? Boys in school?

through college (Lips 2004; Zaman 2008). Researchers who observed more than 100 fourth-, sixth-, and eighth-grade classes over a three-year period found that boys consistently and clearly dominated classrooms. Teachers called on and encouraged boys more often than girls. If a girl gave an incorrect answer, the teacher was likely to call on another student, but if a boy was incorrect, the teacher was more likely to encourage him to learn by helping him discover his error and correct it (Sadker and Sadker 1994). Compared to girls, boys are more likely to receive a teacher's attention, to call out in class, to demand help or attention from the teacher, to be seen as model students, or to be praised by teachers. Boys are also more likely to be disciplined harshly by teachers (Epstein 2007; Kindlon and Thompson 1999).

In subtle ways, teachers may reinforce the idea that males and females are more different than similar. There are times when boys and girls interact together relatively comfortably—in the school band, for example. But in classrooms, teachers often pit girls and boys against each other in spelling bees or math contests (Thorne 1992).

African American Girls, Latinas, and Asian American Girls in Middle and High School Journalist Peggy Orenstein (1994) spent one year observing pupils and teachers in two California middle schools, one mostly white and middle class and the other predominantly African American and Hispanic and of lower socioeconomic status. Orenstein found that in both schools, girls were subtly encouraged to be quiet and nonassertive whereas boys were rewarded for boisterous and even aggressive behaviors.

However, African American girls were louder and less unassuming than non-Hispanic white girls were when they began school—and some continued along this path (Theran 2009). In fact, they called out in the classroom as often as boys did. But Orenstein noted that teachers' reactions differed. The participation, and even antics, of white boys in the classroom was considered inevitable and rewarded with extra attention and instruction, whereas the assertiveness of African American girls was defined as "menacing, something that, for the sake of order in the classroom, must be squelched" (p. 181). Orenstein further found that Latinas, along with Asian American girls, had special difficulty being heard or even noticed. Probably socialized into quiet demeanor at home and often having language difficulties, these girls' scholastic or leadership abilities largely went unseen. In some cases, their classroom teachers did not even know who the girls were when Orenstein mentioned their names.

In high school, Latina girls experience cross-pressures when the desire to succeed in school and move on to a career is in tension with the traditional assumption of wife and mother roles at a young age. Eighteen percent of sixteen- to seventeen-year-olds do not finish high school, compared to 8.4 percent of black and 4.5 percent of white girls (Cataldi, Laird, and KewalRamani 2009, Table 3). Factors such as poverty and language barriers, as well as the pressure to contribute to the family, affect the educational attainment of both boys and girls. But young Latinas, especially recent immigrants, seem torn between newer models for women as mothers *and* career women and the traditional model of marriage and homemaking (Canedy 2001). Nevertheless, the majority of Latinas and Latinos finish high school.

School Organization In 2007–2008 school year, 75.6 percent of all school employees were women (Coopersmith 2009, Table 3), although only a little over half (51 percent) of the principals were women (Battle 2009, Table 3). Eighty-five percent of elementary teachers and 59 percent of secondary teachers were women (Coopersmith 2009, Table 3). These numbers represent a change toward greater balance since 1982, when only 21 percent of principals, 24 percent of officials and administrators, and 49 percent of secondary teachers were women (U.S. Census Bureau 2003a, Table 252).

Programs and Outcomes One concern related to schooling has been whether girls are channeled into or themselves avoid the traditionally masculine areas in high school study. We don't really know the answer to this question. A recent review of 1,000 research studies (AAUW Educational Foundation 1999) reports that high school boys and girls now take similar numbers of science courses, but boys are more likely to take all three core courses: biology, chemistry, and physics. Girls enroll in advanced placement (AP) courses in greater numbers than boys, including AP biology. But fewer girls than boys get high enough scores on AP tests to get college credit. Girls take fewer computer courses, and they cluster in traditional female occupations in career-oriented programs (Halpern et al. 2007).

Girls versus Boys?

Girls have long been the primary focus of attention in examining the possible bias of educational institutions. The previous sections make a good case for such concern, and the 1994 Women's Equal Education Act declares girls an "under-served population." Despite the litany of difficulties girls and women may face in educational settings, the intention is to identify problems that need continued attention. In fact, girls are doing well on the whole. Women and girls "are on a tear through the educational system. . . . In the past 30 years, nearly every inch of progress . . . has gone to them" (Thor Mortenson of the Dell Institute for the Study of Opportunity in Higher Education, in Conlin 2003, p. 76).

In recent years, attention has turned to boys. Some writers attack the "myth of girls in crisis" (Sommers 2000a, p. 61). A resident scholar at the conservative think-tank American Enterprise Institute, Sommers in her critique goes beyond a concern for balance to argue that there is a "war on boys" (2000b). In Sommers's view, boys are actively discriminated against by the educational establishment (2000b, p. 60; see also 2000a, p. 23). "[B]oys are resented, both as the unfairly privileged sex and as obstacles on the path to gender justice" (2000b, p. 60; see also 2000a, p. 23).

Sommers and others point to the declining male share of college enrollments and note that on a number of indicators, girls do better in school: better grades, higher educational aspirations, and greater enrollment in AP and other demanding academic programs.

Currently, girls are even more likely to outnumber boys in higher-level math and science courses; however, in 2007 boys outscored girls in math in all grades tested (Snyder, Dillow, and Hoffman 2009). Girls also outnumber boys in student government, honor society, and student newspaper staffs. More boys fall behind grade level and more are suspended, and they are far more likely to be shunted into special education classes or to have their inattentive and restless behavior defined as deviant, and medicated. Indicators of deviant behavior—crime, alcohol, and drugs—show more involvement by boys. Other research also shows that boys have a greater incidence of diagnosis of emotional disorders, learning disorders, attention-deficit disorders, and teen deaths (Conlin 2003; Goldberg 1998; Sommers 2000a, 2000b).

To the argument that boys do better on SAT and other standardized tests, Sommers responds that the pool of girls taking the test is more apt to include disadvantaged and/or marginal students, whereas their male counterparts do not take these exams. Sommers's concerns may be misplaced, however. Other scholars note that when examining sex differences, socioeconomic and racial differences should be taken into account as well. When these are taken into account, the sex differences are no longer significant, but there is a correlation between race and class and a higher SAT score (Zwick 2001). In fact, in an examination of the most recent SAT data (see Table 4.1), we can see that the higher the test taker's family income, the better the scores (Total Group Report 2009, p. 4; see also Rampell 2009).

Other analysts do not necessarily share Sommers's allegations of active discrimination against boys. But they argue that attention to girls' educational needs and the success of men in the work world tended to obscure boys' problems in school. They see a mismatch between typical boy behavior—high levels of physical activity and more challenges to teachers and school rules—and school expectations about sitting still, following rules, and concentrating (Poe 2004). Moreover, a survey by the Public Education Network (Metropolitan Life Insurance Company 1997) found that 31 percent of boys in grades 7–12 felt that teachers do not listen to them, as compared with 19 percent of girls.

A recent research study (Meadows, Land, and Lamb 2005) sought to examine and compare the situations of boys and girls. The researchers took note of Sommers's critique regarding boys, as well as the research cited earlier on the disadvantaged situation of girls in schools. They noted Carol Gilligan's influential books (1982; Gilligan, Lyons, and Hanmer 1990), which argue that girls' strengths in relationships and emotional expressions are devalued in an individualistic and competitive American society and that girls become discouraged as they arrive on the threshold of adolescence (see also Pipher 1995).[5]

[5] Meadows et al. (2005) note that Gilligan's conclusions about gender differences are based on small numbers of interviews with girls (no boys) and on anecdotes and that she has never been willing to make her data available for review by other scholars.

Table 4.1 SAT Score by Family Income, 2009

SAT	Test Takers Percent	Critical Reading Mean	Mathematics Mean	Writing Mean
All Test Takers (N = 1,530,128)	**100**	**501**	**515**	**493**
		Family Income		
$0-$20,000	10	434	457	430
$20,000-$40,000	15	462	475	453
$40,000-$60,000	15	488	497	476
$60,000-$80,000	15	503	512	491
$80,000-$100,000	13	517	528	505
$100,000-$120,000	11	525	538	516
$120,000-$140,000	5	529	542	520
$140,000-$160,000	4	536	550	527
$160,000-$200,000	5	542	554	535
More than $200,000	7	563	579	560

Source: Adapted from The College Board (http://professionals.collegeboard.com, Table 11).

Essentially, Meadows and her colleagues asked: How goes it with boys and girls? For answers they turned to the status of boys and girls on twenty-eight social indicators of well-being, which are also combined into an index. These indicators measure seven life domains: material well-being, health, safety, productive activity, intimacy, place in the community, and emotional well-being (Meadows, Land, and Lamb 2005, p. 5). Meadows and her colleagues concluded that "gender differences in well-being, when they do exist, are very slight and that overall both boys and girls in the United States currently enjoy a higher quality of life than they did in 1985" (p. 1).

Other approaches to concerns about boys are exactly opposite to the approach of Sommers. Psychiatrist William Pollack's perspective is that "what we call . . . normal boy development . . . not only isn't normal, but it's traumatic and that trauma has major consequences" (quoted in Goldberg 1998, p. A-12; see also Kimmel 2001). To express vulnerability is to run the risk of victimization. Boys, particularly racial/ethnic minority youth, face a dilemma in that acting tough to protect themselves is threatening to adults (psychologist Dan Kindlon, cited in Goldberg 1998). One effort suggested by this line of thought is to take measures to decrease bullying (Kimmel 2001; Totura et al. 2009). Another is to encourage boys to express their emotions and to redefine the male role to include emotional expression (Espelage and Swearer, 2004; Zaman 2008).

Other proposals include the following: (1) accepting a certain level of boys' rowdy play as not deviant, (2) implementing more active learning-by-doing to permit physical movement in classroom settings, and (3) encouraging activities shared by boys and girls and boy–girl dialogues about gender (Kindlon and Thompson 1999). The bottom line may be the observation by Marie C. Wilson, president of the Ms. Foundation for Women: "We'd be so naive to think we could change the lives of girls without boys' lives changing" (quoted in Goldberg 1998, p. A-12). It may be that "girls and boys are on the same side in this issue."

In this section on socialization, we have examined how socialization shapes gender identities and gendered behavior. Socialization continues throughout adulthood as we negotiate and learn new roles—or as those already learned are renegotiated or reinforced. The varied opportunities we encounter as adults influence the adult roles we choose and play out, and the qualities and skills we develop. And those have changed in recent decades, in response to the Women's Movement and the men's movements that followed.

"We don't believe in pressuring the children. When the time is right, they'll choose the appropriate gender."

Social Change and Gender

The increasing convergence of men's and women's social roles, though incomplete, reflects a dramatic change from the more gender-differentiated world of the mid-twentieth century. Such changes are due not only to structural forces (especially economic) that led to women's increased entry into the labor force but also to active change efforts by women and their allies in the Women's Movement. Men's movements followed.

The Women's Movement

The nineteenth century saw a feminist movement develop, but from around 1920 until the mid-1960s there was virtually no activism regarding women's rights and women's roles.[6] Women did make some gains in the 1920s and 1930s in education and occupational level, but these were eroded during the more familistic post–World War II era.

Media glorification of housewife and breadwinner roles made them seem natural despite the reality of increased women's employment. But contradictions between what women were actually doing and the roles prescribed for them became increasingly apparent. Higher levels of education for women left college-educated women with a significant gap between their abilities and the housewife role assigned to them. Employed women chafed at the unequal pay and working conditions in which they labored and began to think that their interest lay in increasing equal opportunity. Betty Friedan's book *The Feminine Mystique* (1963) captured this dissatisfaction and made it a topic of public discussion. Further, the Civil Rights Movement of the 1960s provided a model of activism. In a climate in which social change seemed possible, dissatisfaction with traditional roles precipitated a social movement—the Second Wave of the Women's Movement. This movement challenged theretofore accepted traditional roles and strove to increase gender equality.

In 1961 President Kennedy set up a Presidential Commission on the Status of Women, and some state commissions were established subsequently. The National Organization for Women (NOW) was founded in 1966. Meanwhile, in Congress, the Civil Rights Act of 1964 had been amended by opponents (as a political tactic) to include sex—and it passed! Title VII of the Civil Rights Act gradually began to be enforced. Grassroots feminist groups with a variety of agendas and political postures developed across the country.

NOW had multiple goals—opening educational and occupational opportunities to women, along with establishing support services such as child care. As well, NOW recognized the commitment of a majority of women to marriage and motherhood and spoke to the possibility of "real choice" (National Organization for Women 1966). Although supporting traditional heterosexual marriage for those who chose it, the organization came to support the more controversial choice (in those times) of a lesbian lifestyle, as well as reproductive rights, including abortion.

Women vary in their attitudes toward the Women's Movement and in what issues are important to them. Figure 4.5 indicates "top priority" issues that were evident in a survey of women conducted in 2003.

Some women of color and white working-class women may find the Women's Movement irrelevant to the extent that it focuses on psychological oppression or on professional women's opportunities rather than on "the daily struggle to make ends meet that is faced by working class women" (Aronson 2003, p. 907; Langston 2007). Black women have always labored in the productive economy under duress or out of financial necessity and did not experience the enforced delicacy of women in the Victorian period. Nor were they ever housewives in large numbers, so the feminist critique of that role may seem irrelevant (Lessane 2007).

Chicano/Chicana (Mexican American) activism gave *la familia* a central place as a distinctive cultural value. Latinos of both sexes placed a high value on family solidarity, with individual family members' needs and desires subsumed to the collective good, so that Chicana feminists' critiques of unequal gender relations in *la familia* often met with hostility (Manago, Brown, and Leaper 2009).

Muslim women and Arabic women also view feminism through the lens of culture, religion, and community. Strict adherence to religious and cultural traditions are often at odds with western feminist views, yet many women are challenging sharia law and using the Qur'an to question patriarchy and demand women's rights (Karim 2009; Sayeed 2007).

African American and Latino women consider racial/ethnic as well as gender discrimination in setting their priorities (Arnott and Matthaei 2007). In fact, it is more precise to say their feminist views are characterized by *intersectionality*—structural connections among race, class, and gender (Baca Zinn, Hondagneu-Sotelo, and Messner 2007; Labaton and Martin 2004; Roth 2004; Yuval-Davis 2006).

In some ways, such as their experience with racial/ethnic discrimination and their relatively low wages, Chicanas are more like Mexican American men, who are also subordinated, than they are like non-Hispanic

[6] The "First Wave" of feminism began with a convention on women's rights that produced the Seneca Falls Declaration in 1848. Nineteenth-century women were also active in abolitionist and temperance movements. The First Wave of feminism came to an end when a major goal, voting rights for women, was achieved in 1920 (Rossi 1973).

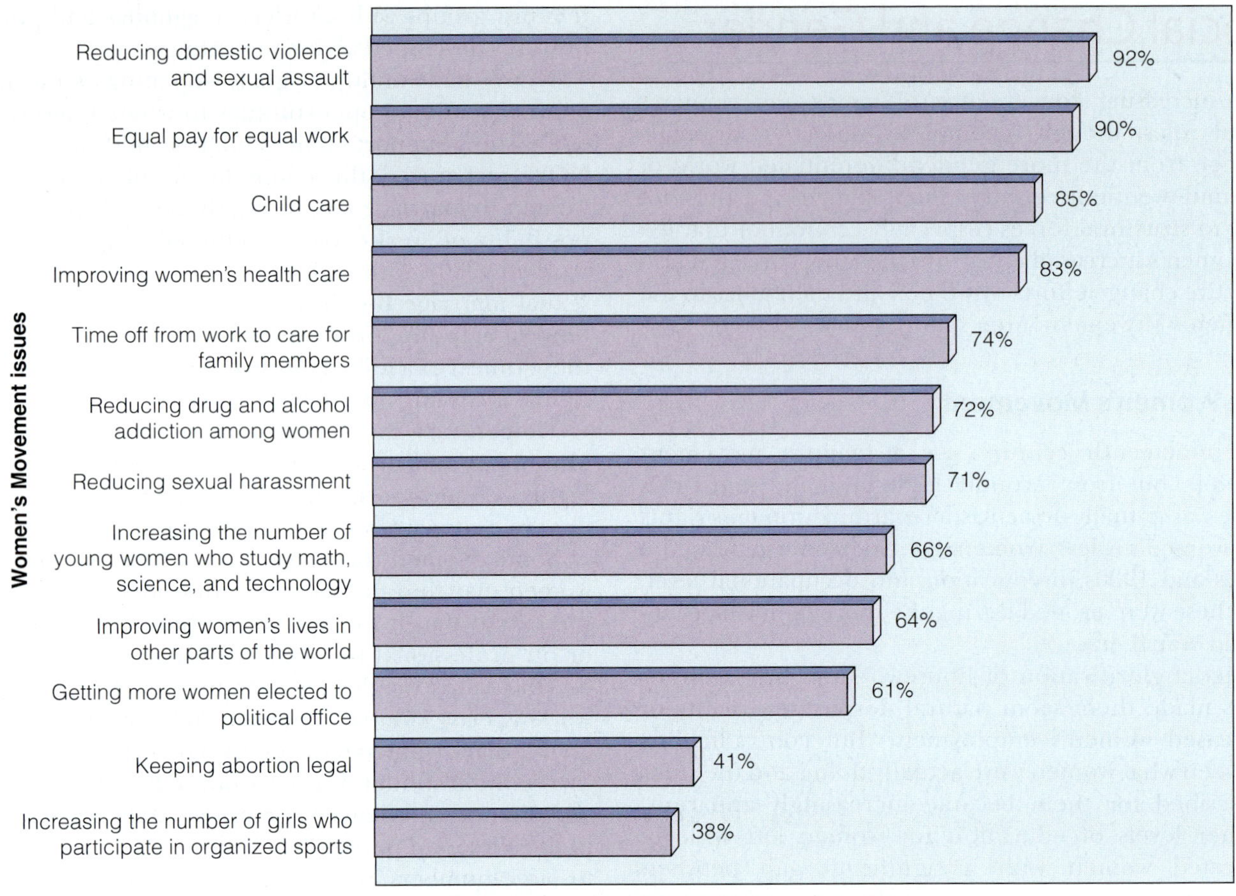

Figure 4.5 "Top priority" issues for the Women's Movement. More than 3,300 women were asked to indicate which issues they felt the Women's Movement should focus on. The 2003 survey was conducted for the Center for the Advancement of Women by Princeton Survey Research Associates.

Source: Center for the Advancement of Women 2003, p. 11 (www.advancewomen.org).

white women. Nevertheless, a Chicana feminism emerged during the 1960s and 1970s. Generally, Chicanas support women's economic issues, such as equal employment and day care, while showing less support for abortion rights than do Anglo women. Latinas formed some grassroots community organizations of their own to offer social services such as job training, community-based alternatives to juvenile incarceration, and bilingual child development centers. The Mexican American Women's National Association (now MANA) was established in 1974 (Segura and Pesquera 1995).

African American women are more critical of gender inequality than are white women (Kane 2000). A National Urban League report states that "a feminist perspective has much to offer Black America" (West 2003). African American women and men are more likely than whites to endorse political organizing for women's issues (Hunter and Sellers 1998). Sixty-eight percent of Latina women ($n = 354$) and 63 percent of African American women ($n = 352$) surveyed in 2001 as part of a national sample of 2,329 "strongly agree" that there is a need for a women's movement today (Center for the Advancement of Women 2003). Post Colonial, Third World, and Transnational Feminisms are led by women of color and Third World women. These movements developed out of western feminism's lack of attention to issues of racism, imperialism, colonial oppression, power, sexuality, and resistance to hegemony. These feminisms seek to create justice and equality across national borders (Gurel 2009).

There are other variations in attitudes toward the Women's Movement. Some women deplore the rise of feminism and encourage traditional marriage and motherhood as the best path to women's self-fulfillment (Enda 1998; Passno 2000). Many feminists would define the movement as one that advances the interests and status of women as mothers and caregivers, as well as workers (Showden 2009). Surveys in the 1980s indicate that large majorities reject the notion that the Women's Movement is antifamily (Hall and Rodriguez 2003).

Dan Koeck/The New York Times/Redux

Native Americans, members of what were once hunting and gathering and hoe cultures, have a complex heritage that varies by tribe but may include a matrilineal tradition in which women have owned (and may still own) houses, tools, and land. Native American women's political power declined with the spread of Europeans into their territories and the subsequent reorganization of Indian life by federal legislation in the 1920s. Recently, Native American women have begun to regain their power. Erma J. Vizenor is chairwoman of the White Earth Nation, the largest tribe in Minnesota. Dr. Vizenor, who holds a doctorate from Harvard, is one of 133 women tribal leaders.

The media often assert that a younger "post-feminist" generation does not support a women's movement. The assumption is that they may have a negative image of feminism or be latently feminist, but believe that women's rights' goals have already been achieved. Sometimes such articles assert that younger women are simply too busy with work and family to have the time to be active (Showden 2009).

Differences of opinion among women on issues related to sexuality and reproduction are undoubtedly divisive. Most recent research finds a complex array of definitions of feminism (Aronson 2003; Center for the Advancement of Women 2003), and cultural meanings of *feminism* do seem to vary by age cohort (Peltola, Milkie, and Presser 2004; Showden 2009).

Nevertheless, research suggests that "post-feminism" is a myth. Hall and Rodriguez, who did an extensive review of survey data, found an increase in support for the Women's Movement from the 1970s and 1980s to the middle or late 1990s (see also Bolzendahl and Myers 2004). Young adults age eighteen to twenty-nine reported more favorable attitudes than older cohorts (Hall and Rodriguez 2003, p. 895; see also Aronson 2003). "One might note that many of the ideologies associated with feminism have become relatively common place and speak to the success of feminism in attaining much broader acceptance of gender equality" (Schnittker, Freese, and Powell 2003, pp. 619–20). Although not all supporters of the Women's Movement self-identify as feminists, a majority (54 percent) "say that being a feminist is an important part of who they are" (Center for the Advancement of Women 2003).

Men's Movements

As the Women's Movement encouraged changes in gender expectations and social roles, some men responded by initiating a men's movement. The first National Conference on Men and Masculinity was held in 1975 and has been held almost annually since. The focus of this men's movement is on changes that men want in their lives and how best to get them. One goal has been to give men a forum—in consciousness-raising groups, in men's studies college courses, and, increasingly, on the Internet—in which to air their feelings about gender and think about their life goals and their relationships with others.

Kimmel (1995) divides today's men's movement into three fairly distinct camps: antifeminists, profeminists, and masculinists. *Antifeminists* believe that the Women's Movement has caused the collapse of the natural order, one that guaranteed male dominance, and they work to reverse this trend. The National Organization for Men (NOM) opposes feminism, which it claims is "designed to denigrate men, exempt women from the draft and to encourage the disintegration of the family" (Siller 1984, quoted in Kimmel 1995, p. 564).

According to Mark Kann, men's self-interest may lead to an antifeminist response even among men who wish women well in an abstract sense:

> I would suggest . . . that men's immediate self-interest rarely coincides with feminist opposition to patriarchy. Consider that men need money and leisure to carry out their experiments in self-fulfillment. Is it not their immediate interest to monopolize the few jobs that promise affluence and autonomy by continuing to deny women equal access to them? . . . Why should they commit themselves to those aspects of feminism that reduce men's social space? It is one thing to try out the joys of parenting, for example, but quite another to assume sacrificial responsibility for the pains of parenting. (Kann 1986, p. 32)

Profeminists support feminists in their opposition to patriarchy. They analyze men's problems as stemming from a patriarchal system that privileges white heterosexual men while forcing all males into restrictive gender roles (Ashe 2004). In 1983, profeminist men formed the National Organization for Changing Men (changed in 1990 to the National Organization for Men Against Sexism, or NOMAS), whose purposes are to transcend gender stereotypes while supporting

The Rise of Wives, 1970 to 2007

Share of husbands whose wives' income tops theirs

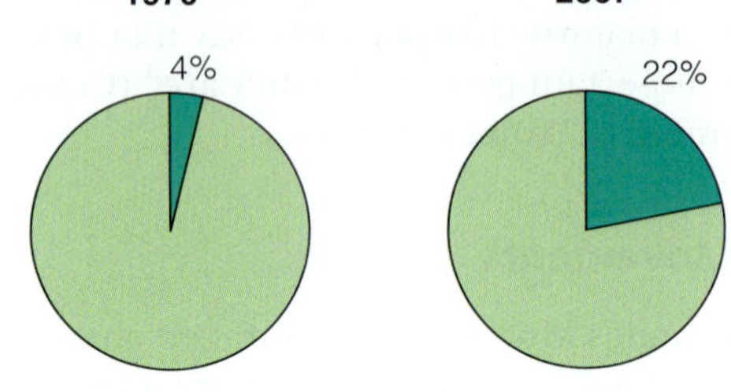

Among married women, which spouse has more education?

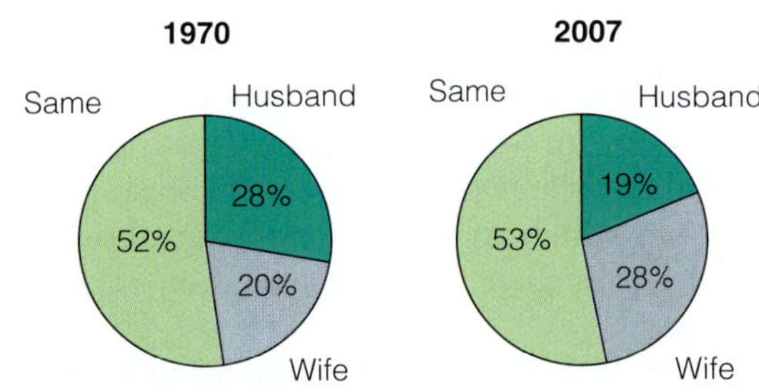

Figure 4.6 The Rise of Wives.

women's and gays' struggles for respect and equality ("Who We Are" 2009).

The newer *masculinists,* who emerged in the early 1990s, tend not to focus on patriarchy as problematic (although they might agree that it is). Instead, masculinists work to develop a positive image of masculinity, one combining strength with tenderness. Their path to this is through therapy, consciousness-raising groups, and rituals. Through rituals, men are to get in touch with their feelings and heal the buried rage and grief caused by the oppressive nature of corporate culture, the psychological and/or physical absence of their fathers, and men's general isolation due to a socialized reluctance to share their feelings (Kimmel 1995). Robert Bly's *Iron John* (1990) is a prominent example of these ideas.

In examining men's movements and their goals, it is important to appreciate that men's social situations vis-à-vis traditional roles are as diverse as women's. The idea of a universal patriarchy and male dominance is challenged by the obvious point that all men are not privileged in the larger society (Connell 2005; Hebert 2007), whether or not they are in gender relations. "When race, social class, sexual orientation, physical abilities, and immigrant or national status are taken into account, we can see that in some circumstances 'male privilege' is partly—sometimes substantially—muted" (Baca Zinn, Hondagneu-Sotelo, and Messner 2004, p. 170, citing Kimmel and Messner 1998).

Personal and Family Change

Sometimes, in response to available options, adults reconsider earlier choices regarding gender roles. For example, a small proportion of men choose to be full-time fathers and/or househusbands. Others may effect more subtle changes, such as breaking through previously learned isolating habits to form more intimate friendships and deeper family relationships.

Ironically, that very expansion in the range of people's opportunities may lead to mixed feelings and conflicts, both within oneself and between men and women as we confront the "lived messiness" of gender in contemporary life (Heywood and Drake 1997, p. 8). Stay-at-home moms may worry about the family budget and about their options if their marriages fail or if they desire to work when children are older. They may feel others consider them uninteresting or incompetent. Women who are employed may wish they could stay home full time with their families or at least have less hectic days and more family time. Moreover, a wife's career success and work demands may lead her into renegotiating gender boundaries at home, and that may produce domestic tension.

Modern men may be torn between egalitarian principles and the advantages of male privilege. For one thing, husbands are still expected to succeed as principal family breadwinners (see Figure 4.6 to see how some wives are now earning more than their husbands). The "new man" is expected to succeed economically *and* to value relationships and emotional openness. Although women want men to be sensitive and emotionally expressive, they also want them to be self-assured and confident.

Men often face prejudice when they take jobs traditionally considered women's (Simpson 2005; Snyder and Green 2008). They may also encounter more resistance than women when they try to exercise "family friendly" options in the workplace (Neal and Hammer 2007; Peterson 2004). This resistance men encounter, however, may also be a self-imposed perception in which they believe they will be viewed as "less committed to their company" should they access such options (Neal and Hammer 2007, p. 159). Such difficulties, coupled with technological advancements, have allowed some fathers to take the "daddy track" option. This is where more men work from home or opt for flexible work hours (Jarrell 2007; Shellenbarger 2007).

These conflicts are more than psychological. They are in part a consequence of our society's failure to provide support for employed parents in the form of adequate maternity and paternity leave or day care, for example. American families continue to deal individually with problems of pregnancy, recovery from childbirth, and early child care as best they can. Adequate job performance, let alone career achievement, is difficult for women under such conditions regardless of ability. Declining economic opportunities for non–college-educated men, coupled with criticisms of male privilege sparked by the Women's Movement, lead some men to feel unfairly picked on (Hebert 2007).

Today's men, like today's women, find it difficult to have it all (Jarrell 2007). If women find it difficult to combine a sustained work career with motherhood, men face a conflict between maintaining their privileges and enjoying supportive relationships. But many "will find that equality and sharing offer compensations to offset their attendant loss of power and privilege" (Gerson 1993, p. 274).

Chapter 11 discusses work and family in more detail, and Chapter 13 addresses family power.

The Future of Gender

"Gender is a ruling idea in people's lives—even where egalitarian ideology is common, as among young, affluent, educated Americans. . . . Despite the extraordinary improvements in women's status over the past two centuries, some aspects of gender have seemed exceptionally resistant to erosion in recent decades"—notably child raising and occupational achievement and pay. "[P]eople still think about women and men differently and . . . men still occupy most of the highest positions of political and economic power" (Jackson 2006, pp. 215, 229).

If men and women are seen through a lens of differential competence, if men and women continue to interact in situations in which they (men) have greater power and status, then assumptions about inherent status differences are supported. Moreover, gender differences may be maintained because of the power of gendered self-concepts. Men and women may have a psychological stake in the maintenance of these differences as important aspects of personal identity (Ridgeway 2006).

Yet sociologist Robert Max Jackson is convinced that the forces of history will sweep gender inequality aside. Two hundred years of change suggest that, indeed, gender is not embedded so deeply in society that it cannot change. "It is fated to end because essential organizational characteristics and consequences of a modern, industrial, market-oriented, electorally governed society are inherently inconsistent with the conditions needed to sustain gender inequality" (Jackson 2006, p. 241).

Looking at marriage and the family, sociologist Steven Nock expects marriages of "equally dependent spouses" to represent the future toward which American marriage is evolving. By this he means a model in which both spouses are earners as well as family caretakers, and they are dependent on their common earnings as the basis of their family life. In the short run, women's increased earnings have enabled them to leave a marriage of poor emotional quality. Yet the falling divorce rate suggests that in the long run this will not be the case because, as Nock says,

> . . . we are returning to a more traditional form of marriage than we have had in the last century. Marriage was historically based on extensive dependency by both partners. . . . I believe that the recent increases in marital stability reflect the gradual working out of the gender issues first confronted in the 1960s. If so, this implies that young men and women are forming new types of marriages that are based on a new understanding of gender ideals. And if so, the growth of equal dependency that we are likely to see in the next decade bodes well. (Nock 2001, pp. 773–74)

Gendered expectations and behaviors—both as they have and have not changed—underpin many of the topics explored throughout this text. For example, gender is important to discussions of family power, communication, and parental roles, as well as to work and family roles. In future chapters we will explore these topics, keeping in mind gendered expectations and social change.

Summary

- Roles of men and women have changed over time, but living in our society remains a somewhat different experience for women and for men. Gendered cultural messages and social structure influence people's behavior, attitudes, and options. But in many respects, men and women are more alike than different.
- Generally, traditional masculine expectations require that men be confident, self-reliant, and occupationally successful—and engage in "no sissy stuff." During the 1980s, the "liberated male" cultural message emerged, according to which men are expected to value tenderness and equal relationships with women. We have seen the return of respect to the physically tough and protective "manly man."
- Traditional feminine expectations involve a woman's being a man's helpmate and a "good mother." An emergent feminine role is the successful "professional woman." When coupled with the more traditional roles, this results in the "superwoman."
- Individuals vary in the degree to which they follow cultural models for gendered behavior. The extent to which men and women differ from each other and follow these cultural messages can be visualized as two overlapping normal distribution curves.
- Although there are significant changes, male dominance remains evident in politics, in religion, and in the economy.
- There are racial/ethnic and class differences in stereotypes, as well as some differences in actual gender and family patterns. This and other diversity has come to be expressed in responses to the women's and men's movements.
- Biology interacts with culture to produce human behavior, and the two influences are not really separable. Sociologists give considerable attention to the socialization process, for which there are several theoretical explanations. Advocates have expressed concern about barriers to the opportunities and achievements of both boys and girls.
- Underlying both socialization and adult behavior are the social structural pressures and constraints that shape men's and women's choices and behaviors. These have changed in recent decades, in part as a consequence of the Women's Movement and subsequent men's movements.
- Turning our attention to the actual lives of adults in contemporary society, we find women and men negotiating gendered expectations and making choices in a context of change at work and in the family. New cultural ideals are far from realization, and efforts to create lives balancing love and work involve conflict and struggle, but promise fulfillment as well.
- Whether gender will continue to be a moderator of economic opportunities and life choices in the future is uncertain, as men's and women's roles and activities converge, but men remain more advantaged. It is likely that gender identity will continue to be important to both men and women.
- Some social scientists predict that the shared economic and family roles emerging in younger marriages will produce more stable marriages.

Questions for Review and Reflection

1. What are some characteristics generally associated with males in our society? What traits are associated with females? How might these affect our expectations about the ways that men and women should behave? Are these images still influential?
2. Do you think men are dominant in major social institutions such as politics, religion, education, and the economy? Or are they no longer dominant? Give evidence to support your opinion.
3. Which theory of gender socialization presented in this chapter seems most applicable to what you see in the real world? Can you give some examples from your own experience of gender socialization?
4. Women and men may renegotiate and change their gendered attitudes and behaviors as they progress through life. What evidence do you see of this in your own life or in others' lives?
5. **Policy Question.** What family law and policy changes of recent years do you think are related to the women's and men's movements? What policies do you think would be needed to promote greater gender equality and/or more satisfying lives for men and women?

Key Terms

agentic (instrumental) character traits 83
borderwork 95
communal (expressive) character traits 83
femininities 84
gender 80
gender identity 80
gender role 80
gender schema theory of gender socialization 93
gender similarities hypothesis 86
hormonal processes 91
hormones 91
intersexual 82
male dominance 86
masculinities 83
modern sexism 81
play 95
self-identification theory of gender socialization 93
sex 80
social learning theory of gender socialization 93
socialization 92
symbolic interaction theory of gender socialization 93
traditional sexism 81
transgendered 82
transsexual 82

Online Resources

Sociology CourseMate

www.CengageBrain.com

Access an integrated eBook, chapter-specific interactive learning tools, including flashcards, quizzes, videos, and more in your Sociology CourseMate, accessed through CengageBrain.com.

www.CengageBrain.com

Want to maximize your online study time? Take this easy-to-use study system's diagnostic pre-test, and it will create a personalized study plan for you. By helping you identify the topics that you need to understand better and then directing you to valuable online resources, it can speed up your chapter review. CengageNOW even provides a post-test so you can confirm that you are ready for an exam.

5

Our Sexual Selves

From childhood to old age, people are sexual beings.[1] Sexuality has a lot to do with the way we think about ourselves and how we relate to others. It goes without saying that sex plays a vital role in marriages and other intimate partner relationships.

Despite the pleasure it may give, sexuality may be one of the most baffling aspects of our selves. Finding mutually satisfying ways of expressing sexual feelings can be a challenge.

In this chapter, we will look briefly at children's sexual development. We define sexual orientation and examine the situation of gay men, lesbians, and bisexual individuals in today's society. We will review the changing cultural meanings of sexuality through our history, as well as the varied sexual standards present in contemporary culture. We will discuss sex as a pleasure bond that requires open, honest, and supportive communication, and then look at the role sex plays throughout marriage.

We will look at some challenges that are associated with sexual expression. What happens when one or both partners has an affair? How has the emergence of HIV/AIDS as a pandemic disease affected sexual relationships and families? Finally, we will examine ways that sexuality, research on sex, and sex education have become political issues in our society.

Before we discuss sexuality in detail, we want to point out our society's tendency to reinforce the differences between women and men and to ignore the common feelings, problems, and joys that make us all human. The truth is, men and women aren't really so different. Many physiological parts of the male and female genital systems are either alike or analogous, and sexual response patterns are similar in men and women (Masters and Johnson 1966).

Space limits our ability to present much detail on the various possibilities of sexual expression, which include kissing, fondling, cuddling, and even holding hands, as well as more overtly sexual activities. We consider that you might have concerns about sexuality that are difficult to address in the limited space of this textbook.

Sexual Development and Orientation

Knowledge about children's sexual development and the emergence of sexual orientation is not as extensive as we would like, but we do know some things.

[1] Five online appendices give information on sexual and reproductive topics: Appendix A: Human Sexual Anatomy, Appendix B: Human Sexual Response, Appendix C: Sexually Transmitted Diseases, Appendix D: Sexual Dysfunctions and Therapy, and Appendix E: Conception, Pregnancy, and Childbirth. These appendices can be accessed at the book website.

Children's Sexual Development

"Human beings are sexual beings throughout their entire lives" (DeLamater and Friedrich 2002, p. 10). As early as twenty-four hours after birth, male newborns get erections, and infants may touch their genitals. In a study of almost one thousand children in Minneapolis and Los Angeles, pediatric researchers sought to establish a baseline of "normative" sexual behavior—that is, to indicate the normality of children's sexual interest to parents, social workers, and others. These researchers found that young children often exhibit overtly sexual behaviors.

Reports by "primary female caregivers," using the Child Behavior Checklist and Child Sexual Behavior Inventory, indicate that between the ages of two and five, a substantial number of children engage in "rhythmic manipulation" of their genitals, which the researchers term a "natural form of sexual expression" (DeLamater and Friedrich 2002, p. 10; see also Kellogg 2009; "Sexual Development" 2009). Children may also try to look at others who are nude or undressing or try to touch their mother's breasts or genitals. Sixty percent of boys and 44 percent of girls in this age group touched their own sex organs (Friedrich et al. 1998, Tables 3 and 4). Children also "play doctor," examining one another's genitals. There were few sex differences overall.

Researchers are interested in these physical manifestations of childhood sexual development. However, they place this in context, noting that overall sensual experiences from infancy onward shape later sexual expression, while attachment to parents in infancy and childhood provides the emotional security essential to later sexual relationships (DeLamater and Friedrich 2002; Kellogg 2009; "Sexual Development" 2009).

Early sexual behavior peaks at age five, declining thereafter until sexual attraction first manifests itself around age eleven or twelve. Children are maturing about two years earlier than they were one hundred years ago and much earlier than in 1500, when the average age of puberty was nineteen in England (Brink 2008; Sanghavi 2006; Steingraber 2007). As the age of puberty has declined, the age at marriage has risen, leaving a more extended period during which sexual activity may occur among adolescents and unmarried adults.

Sexual Orientation

As we develop into sexually expressive individuals, we manifest a sexual orientation. **Sexual orientation** refers to whether an individual is drawn to a partner of the same sex or the opposite sex. **Heterosexuals** are attracted to opposite-sex partners and **homosexuals** to same-sex partners.[2] **Bisexuals** are attracted to people of both sexes. A person's sexual orientation does not necessarily predict his or her sexual behavior; abstinence is a behavioral choice, as is sexual expression with partners of the nonpreferred sex. All these terms designate one's choice of sex partner only, not general masculinity or femininity or other aspects of personality.

We tend to think of sexual orientation as a dichotomy: One is either "gay" or "straight." Actually, sexual orientation may be a continuum. Freud, Kinsey, and many present-day psychologists and biologists maintain that humans are inherently bisexual; that is, we all have the latent physiological and emotional structures necessary for responding sexually to either sex.

From the interactionist point of view (see Chapter 2), the very concepts "bisexual," "heterosexual," and "homosexual" are social inventions. They emerged in scientific and medical literature in the late nineteenth century (Katz 2007, pp. 10–12; Seidman 2003, pp. 46–49, 56–58). Although same-sex sexual relations existed all along, the conceptual categories and the notion of sexual orientation itself were cultural creations. Developing a sexual orientation today may be influenced by the resultant tendency to think in dichotomous terms: Individuals may sort themselves into the available categories and behave accordingly. In time, social pressures to view oneself as either straight or gay may inhibit latent bisexuality or inconsistencies (Gagnon and Simon 2005; Katz 2007, pp. 25–27; Rosario et al. 2006; Schwartz 2007). In this light, the recent assertion of **asexuality** as a sexual orientation represents a challenge to the traditional dichotomy. *Asexuality* is described in "A Closer Look at Diversity: Is It Okay to Be Asexual?"

The reason some individuals develop a gay sexual orientation has not been definitively established—nor do we yet understand the development of heterosexuality. The American Psychological Association (APA) takes the position that a variety of factors impact a person's sexuality. The most recent literature from the APA says that "sexual orientation is most likely the result of a complex interaction of environmental, cognitive and biological factors . . . is shaped at an early age . . . [and evidence suggests] biology, including genetic or inborn hormonal factors, play a significant role in a person's sexuality," and that sexual orientation is not a choice and cannot be changed at will (American Psychological Association 2010).

Among gays and lesbians, sexual identity through a sense of being different might have been felt in childhood. Sexual attraction to same-sex people occurs as early as ten for boys and fourteen for girls. Same-sex sexual activity typically begins around age fourteen for males, whereas women's initial experiences tend to occur around age sixteen. "Coming out"—identifying oneself as gay to others—occurs on average just before or after high school graduation (Drasin et al. 2008; Savin-Williams 2006). Recent empirical research reaffirms these findings. Of 2,560 California high school students surveyed over a three-year period, 11 percent reported a gay or lesbian identification, approximately 12 percent identified as bisexual, and nearly 5 percent noted that they were questioning their sexuality (Russell, Clarke, and Clarey 2009).

Individuals vary in this process. A study of 156 lesbian, gay, and bisexual youths recruited from gay organizations and public colleges in New York City found that 57 percent consistently identified as gay or lesbian and were more certain and accepting of their same-sex sexuality, involved in gay social activities, and more comfortable with others knowing. Fifteen percent consistently identified as bisexual. Another 18 percent experienced a gradual transition to the establishment of a gay self-identity. Contrary to stereotype, female youth were more likely to have a consistent gay sexual orientation earlier than male youth (Rosario et al. 2006; see also Rosario, Scrimshaw, and Hunter 2008).

Deciding who is to be categorized as **gay**, **lesbian**, or bisexual for research purposes is not easy—How much experience? How exclusively homosexual? With survey respondents possibly concealing sexual orientation, this precludes any certain calculation of how many gay and lesbian individuals are in our society. Until fairly recently, it was stated that about 10 percent of adult individuals are gay or lesbian. However, the National Health and Social Life Survey (NHSLS; Laumann et al. 1994) suggested that the proportion of homosexual individuals in the population is probably lower. An analysis of combined NHSLS data and University of Chicago National Opinion Research Center (NORC) survey data found that 4.7 percent of men have had some same-sex experiences since age eighteen, whereas 2.5 percent had exclusively same-sex experiences over the last year. Of women, 3.5 percent report some adult same-sex experiences, whereas 1.4 percent had exclusively same-sex experiences over the last year (Black et al. 2000).

In terms of self-identification, the National Survey of Family Growth, conducted in 2002 and 2003 by the U.S. Centers for Disease Control and Prevention, found that approximately 4.1 percent of each sex in the eighteen to forty-four age range reported a gay, lesbian, or bisexual self-identification, whereas 90 percent identified as heterosexual (Mosher, Chandra, and Jones 2005, pp. 1–3, Table B; Gates 2006).

[2] Everyday terms are *straight* (heterosexual), *gay*, and *lesbian*. The term *gay* is synonymous with *homosexual* and refers to males or females. Often *gay* or *gay male* is used in reference to men, while *lesbian* is used to refer to gay women. The Committee on Lesbian, Gay, Bisexual, and Transgender Concerns of the American Psychological Association (1991) prefers the terms *gay male* or *gay man* and *lesbian* to *homosexual* because the committee thinks that the latter term may be associated with negative stereotypes.

A Closer Look at Diversity

Is It Okay to Be Asexual?

A majority of Americans are heterosexual—that is, attracted to potential partners of the opposite sex. Some Americans are **GLBT**: gay male, lesbian, bisexual, or transgendered, attracted to same-sex partners or those of either sex, as the case may be. A newly identified sexual orientation is asexuality. An unknown but probably small number of Americans simply do not experience sexual attraction to others. This is different from *celibacy* or *abstinence*, which is a *decision* not to have sexual relations, at least for a time, but not from a lack of desire.

Asexual individuals have emotional feelings and may desire intimate relationships with others, just not sexual ones. Some asexuals experience physical arousal or even masturbate, "but feel no desire for partnered sexuality" (Jay 2005).

Little research on asexuals exists; asexuals have been virtually invisible. In fact, by age forty-four, 97 percent of men and 98 percent of women have had sexual intercourse (Mosher, Chandra, and Jones 2005, p. 1). Such sexual activity, however, does not always mean that feelings of sexual desire exist.

In an exploratory study of asexuality conducted in 1994 and based on a national probability sample of British residents age eighteen through fifty-nine (Bogaert 2004), 1.05 percent reported themselves to be asexual even though 44 percent were or had been married or cohabitating. Women were more likely to report an asexual orientation than men, but age was not related to asexuality. An interesting finding of this study was that there were large differences between sexual and asexual people in education and social class, with asexuals more likely to have less education and lower social origins. Bogaert speculates that asexuality may be related to a less-advantaged social environment. Needless to say, this and other findings of the study need to be tested against further research conducted in other societies with diverse class structures.

The Asexual Visibility and Education Network (AVEN) was founded in 2001, as a networking and information resource (www.asexuality.org). This group would like to see *asexuality* become a recognized sexual orientation so that absence of sexual desire is not treated as dysfunctional but, rather, as a "normal" alternative. Clinicians vary in whether they agree, but as one example, Dr. Irwin Goldstein, director of the Boston University Center for Sexual Medicine, considers that "[l]ack of interest in sex is not necessarily a disorder or even a problem . . . unless it causes distress" (Duenwald 2005, p. 2).

Critical Thinking

Had you been aware of the concept of asexuality before reading about it here?

In your opinion, does our society define asexuality as dysfunctional? Can you think of examples that support your viewpoint? Might asexuality become recognized as a legitimate sexual orientation?

The existence of a fairly constant proportion of gays and lesbians in virtually every society—in societies that treat homosexuality harshly as well as those that treat it permissively—suggests a biological imperative (Bell, Weinberg, and Hammersmith 1981), as does the fact that 450 mammal and bird species engage in same-sex sexual activity (Roughgarden 2009a, 2009b; Mackay 2000, p. 22). No specific genetic differences between heterosexuals and gays have been conclusively established (Greenberg, Bruess, and Haffner 2002, p. 367; Roughgarden 2009a). Meanwhile, a biological imperative does not equal predetermined sexuality and means instead that a variety of factors influences sexual orientation. Research on biological influences on sexual orientation continues (Abrams 2007; Roughgarden 2009a).

Whether a same-sex sexual orientation finds expression is clearly affected by environment, apart from or in conjunction with any genetic dispositions. A study using data from the General Social Survey and the National Health and Social Life Survey found increases in same-sex partnering between 1998 and 2002, especially for women (Butler 2005). Butler points to changes in social norms and in the legal climate, as well as increasing economic opportunities for women, as likely factors shaping this change. Butler (along with other researchers) notes that the social climate impacts not only the public's perspectives on sexuality but also the kinds of research questions that are being explored regarding sexual orientation. Anne Fausto-Sterling, a noted professor of biology, put it best when she said, "we should debate what it is we want to understand about human sexuality, argue about the forms of knowledge we seek, and consider what the best ways of pursuing such knowledge might be" (2007, p. 55).

Theoretical Perspectives on Human Sexuality

There are various theoretical perspectives concerning marriage and families, as we saw in Chapter 2. Many of these have been applied to human sexuality. We can, for example, look at sexuality using a structure–functional perspective. In this case, we see sex as a focus of norms designed to regulate sexuality so that it serves the societal function of responsible reproduction.

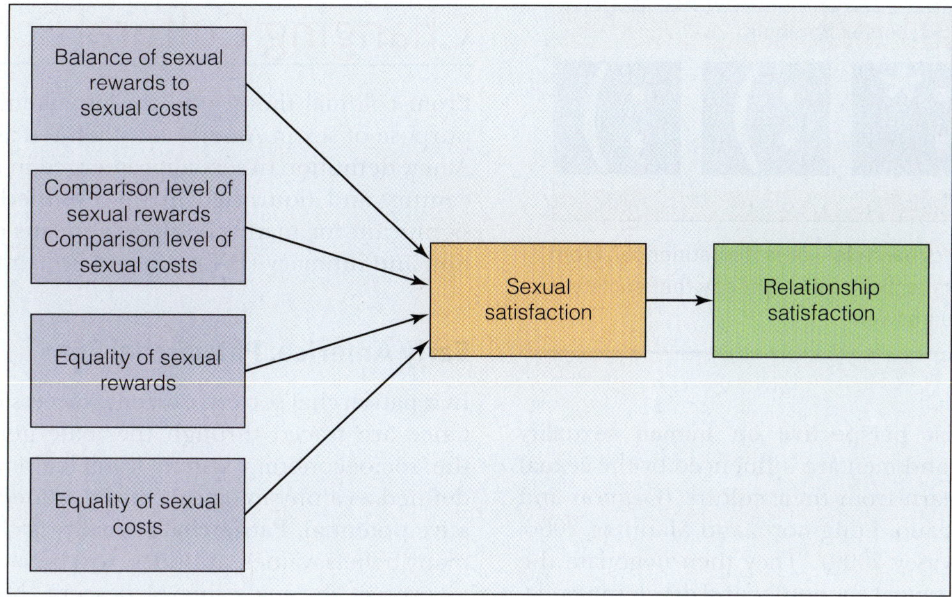

Figure 5.1 Model of factors associated with sexual and relationship satisfaction.

Those looking at sexuality from a biosocial perspective consider that humans—like the species from which they evolved—are designed so as to enable them to efficiently transmit their genes to the next generation. According to this biosocial perspective, men are naturally promiscuous, seeking multiple partners so as to distribute their genes widely, whereas women, who can generally have only one offspring a year, are inclined to be selective and monogamous (Dawkins 1976).

Both these perspectives have their limits. The structure–functional perspective tells us little about the emotions and pleasures of sexual relationships, whereas the biosocial perspective argues a genetic determinism that is contradicted by historical and cross-cultural variation in sexual behavior and relationships. Two more useful ways of looking at sexual relationships in a sociological perspective are exchange theory and interaction theory, both introduced in Chapter 2.

The Exchange Perspective: Rewards, Costs, and Equality in Sexual Relationships

From a general *exchange theory* perspective, women's sexuality and associated fertility are resources that can be exchanged for economic support, protection, and status in society. However, an exchange theory perspective that brings sex closer to our human experience is the **interpersonal exchange model of sexual satisfaction** (Lawrance and Byers 1995; Kisler and Christopher 2008).

Figure 5.1 shows us that in the interpersonal exchange model of sexual satisfaction, satisfaction depends on the *costs* and *rewards* of a sexual relationship, as well as the participant's *comparison level*—what the person expects out of the relationship. Also important is the *comparison level for alternatives*—what other options are available, and how good are they compared to the present relationship? Finally, in this day and age, expectations are likely to include some degree of *equality*. Research to test this model found that these elements of the relationship did indeed predict sexual satisfaction in married and cohabiting couples (Byers 2005; Lawrance and Byers 1995; Kisler and Christopher 2008); however, social class remained a necessary variable to take into consideration within this exchange model of sexual satisfaction (Neff and Harter 2003).

The Interactionist Perspective: Negotiating Cultural Messages

The *interactionist* perspective emphasizes the interpersonal negotiation of relationships in the context of sexual scripts: "*That* we are sexual is determined by a biological imperative toward reproduction, but *how* we are sexual—where, when, how often, with whom, and why—has to do with cultural learning, with meaning transmitted in a cultural setting" (Fracher and Kimmel 1992). Cultural messages give us legitimate reasons for having sex, as well as who should take the sexual initiative, how long a sexual encounter should last, how important experiencing orgasm is, what positions are acceptable, and whether masturbating is appropriate, among other things. Recently, cultural messages have concerned what sexual interaction or relationships are appropriately conducted over the Internet, as well as with the newer phenomenon of "sexting" via cell phones with video capabilities.

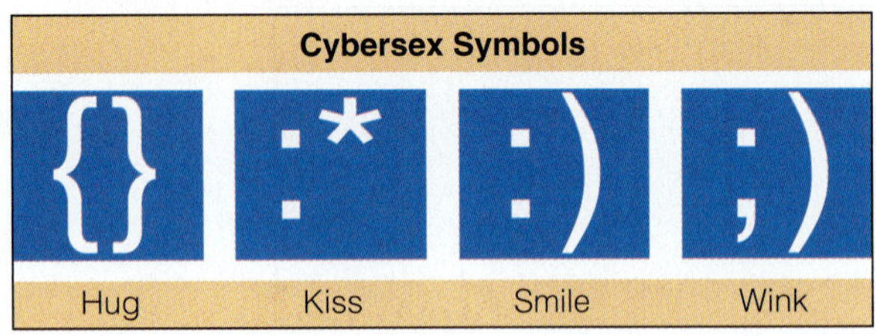

Cybersex. Is it sex—cyberstyle—or is it abstinence? From an interactionist perspective, we might say that society is still constructing the answer.

An **interactionist perspective on human sexuality** holds that women and men are influenced by the **sexual scripts** that they learn from their culture (Gagnon and Simon 2005; Giordano, Longmore, and Manning 2006; VanderLaan and Vasey 2009). They then negotiate the particulars of their sexual encounter and developing relationship (A. Stein 1989, p. 7; MacNeil and Byers 2009).

Sex partners assign meaning to their sexual activity—that is, sex is symbolic of something, which might be affection, communication, recreation, or play, for example. Whether each gives their sexual relationship the same meaning has a lot to do with satisfaction and outcomes. For example, if one is only playing while the other is expressing deep affection, trouble is likely. A relationship goal for couples becoming committed is to establish a joint meaning for their sexual relationship.

Sex has different cultural meanings in different social settings. In the United States (and elsewhere), messages about sex have changed over time.

© Paul Fusco/ Magnum Photos

Self-disclosure and physical pleasure are key qualities in building sexually intimate relationships. Tenderness is a form of sexual expression valued not just as a prelude to sex but also as an end in itself.

Changing Cultural Scripts

From colonial times until the nineteenth century, the purpose of sex in America was defined as reproductive. A new definition of sexuality emerged in the nineteenth century and flourished in the twentieth. Sex became significant for many people as a means of communication and intimacy (D'Emilio and Freedman 1988).

Early America: Patriarchal Sex

In a patriarchal society, descent, succession, and inheritance are traced through the male genetic line, and the socioeconomic system is male-dominated. Sex is defined as a physiological activity, valued for its procreative potential. **Patriarchal sexuality** is characterized by many beliefs, values, attitudes, and behaviors developed to protect the male line of descent. Men are to control women's sexuality. Exclusive sexual possession of a woman by a man in monogamous marriage ensures that her children will be legitimately his. Men are thought to be born with an urgent sex drive, whereas women are seen as naturally sexually passive; orgasm is expected for men but not for women. Unmarried men and husbands whose wives do not meet their sexual needs may gratify those needs outside marriage. Sex outside marriage is considered wrong for women, however.

Although the patriarchal sexual script has been significantly challenged, it persists to some extent and corresponds to traditional gender expectations. If masculinity is a quality that must be achieved or proven, one arena for doing so is sexual accomplishment or conquest. A 1992 national survey by the NORC (National Opinion Research Center) at the University of Chicago, based on a representative sample of 3,432 Americans age eighteen to fifty-nine, found that men were considerably more likely than women to perform, or "do," sex. For example, more than three times as many men as women reported masturbating at least once a week. Three-quarters of the men reported always reaching orgasm in intercourse, whereas the fraction for women was nearer to one-quarter. Men are also much more likely to think about sex (54 percent of men and 19 percent of women said they think about it at least once a day) and to have multiple partners. Men are also more excited by the prospect of group sex (Laumann et al. 1994). One might return to a biosocial perspective to explain these differences except that they are less pronounced among the youngest cohorts.

The Twentieth Century: The Emergence of Expressive Sexuality

A different sexual message has emerged as the result of societal changes that include the decreasing economic dependence of women and the availability of new methods of birth control. Because of the increasing emphasis on couple intimacy, women's sexual expression is more encouraged than it had been earlier (D'Emilio and Freedman 1988). With **expressive sexuality,** sexuality is seen as basic to the humanness of both women and men; there is no one-sided sense of ownership. Orgasm is important for women as well as for men. Sex is not only, or even primarily, for reproduction, but is an important means of enhancing human intimacy. Hence, all forms of sexual activity between consenting adults are acceptable.

The 1960s Sexual Revolution: Sex for Pleasure

Although the view of sex as intimacy continues to predominate, in the 1920s, an alternative message began to emerge wherein sex was seen as a legitimate means to individual pleasure, whether or not it was embedded in a serious couple relationship. Probably as a result, the generation of women born in the first decade of the twentieth century showed twice the incidence of nonmarital intercourse[3] as those born earlier (D'Emilio and Freedman 1988). This probably occurred mostly in relationships that anticipated marriage (Zeitz 2003). Further liberalization of attitudes and behaviors characterized the sexual revolution of the 1960s.

What was so revolutionary about the sixties? For one thing, the birth control pill became widely available; as a result, people were freer to have intercourse with more certainty of avoiding pregnancy.[4] At least for heterosexuals, laws regarding sexuality became more liberal. Until the U.S. Supreme Court decision in *Griswold v. Connecticut* (1965) recognized a right of "marital privacy," the sale or provision of contraception was illegal in some states. The idea that sexual and reproductive decision making belonged to the couple, not the state, was extended to single individuals and minors by subsequent decisions (*Eisenstadt v. Baird* 1972; *Carey v. Population Services International* 1977).

Americans' attitudes and behavior regarding sex changed during this period. In 1959, about four-fifths of Americans surveyed said they disapproved of sex outside marriage. In 2006, only 25 percent said it was "always wrong" (Smith 1999; Schott 2007). Not only did attitudes become more liberal, but behaviors (particularly women's behaviors) changed as well. The rate of nonmarital sex and the number of partners rose, while age at first intercourse dropped (Wells and Twenge 2005)—7.6 percent of young people were having sexual intercourse before the age of 13 (Eaton et al. 2008). The trend toward higher rates of nonmarital sex has continued. Now "almost all Americans have sex before marrying" (Finer 2007, p. 73).

Today, sexual activity often begins in the teen years. Table 5.1 shows the percentages of sexually experienced teens in each of the major racial/ethnic groups according to the Youth Risk Behavior Surveillance System, a national high school–based survey conducted by the U.S. Centers for Disease Control and Prevention (Eaton et al. 2008). Not surprisingly, sexual experience increases with age. In 2007, almost half (47.8 percent) of high school students had had sexual experience (49.8 percent of males and 45.9 percent of females), and 35 percent are currently sexually active. For the vast majority (85 percent) of teens who had experienced sex, their first experience was with a romantic partner, although some 7.8 percent of students were forced to have sex (Eaton et al. 2008; Ryan, Manlove, and Franzetta 2003).

Perhaps the most significant change the sexual revolution ushered in, among heterosexuals at least, has been in marital sex. "Today's married couples have sexual intercourse more often, experience more sexual pleasure, and engage in a greater variety of sexual activities and techniques than people surveyed in the 1950s" (Greenberg, Bruess, and Haffner 2002, p. 437). In the NORC study, 88 percent of married partners said they enjoy great sexual pleasure (Laumann et al. 1994).

Table 5.1 Sexual Experience of High School Students by Race/Ethnicity and Gender, 2005

	Percentage who . . . "Ever had Sexual Intercourse"		"Are Currently Sexually Active"	
Ethnicity	Males	Females	Males	Females
White	42%	44%	31%	34%
Black	75%	61%	51%	44%
Hispanic	58%	44%	36%	34%

Source: Eaton et al. 2006, Tables 44, 46.

[3] *Nonmarital sex* refers to sexual activity by people who are not married to each other, whether they have never married or are divorced, widowed, or currently married (although we usually use the term *extramarital sex* for this last situation). *Nonmarital sex* replaces the previously common term *premarital sex. Premarital* connotes the anticipation of marriage, reflecting the fact that before the sexual revolution, a substantial portion of nonmarital sexual activity took place between people who were formally engaged or informally pledged to marry or who would subsequently marry.

[4] It is important to note that both sexual liberation and the use of birth control were already in progress. "The pill did not create America's sexual revolution so much as it accelerated it" (Zeitz 2003).

The 1980s and 1990s: Challenges to Heterosexism

If the sexual revolution of the 1960s focused on freer attitudes and behaviors among heterosexuals, recent decades have expanded that liberalism to encompass lesbian and gay male sexuality. Until several decades ago, most people thought about sexuality almost exclusively as between men and women. In other words, our thinking was characterized by **heterosexism**—the taken-for-granted system of beliefs, values, and customs that places superior value on heterosexual behavior and that denies or stigmatizes nonheterosexual relations. However, since "Stonewall" (a 1969 police raid on a U.S. gay bar) galvanized the gay community into advocacy, gay males and lesbians have not only become increasingly visible but have also challenged the notion that heterosexuality is the one proper form of sexual expression.

Gay men and lesbians have won legal victories, new tolerance by some religious denominations, greater understanding on the part of some heterosexuals, and sometimes positive action by government. Some states and communities have passed sexual orientation antidiscrimination laws. Corporations also are increasingly likely to enact antidiscrimination policies.

The public's attitudes toward homosexuality, though never as favorable as toward nonmarital sex generally, became more favorable in the 1990s, after earlier high rates of disapproval. In the early 1970s, about 70 percent thought homosexual relations were "always wrong." In 1986, the Supreme Court decision in *Bowers v. Hardwick* declined to extend privacy protection to gay male or lesbian relationships, and homosexual conduct remained criminalized in some states. Then in a 2003 case (*Lawrence et al. v. Texas*), the Supreme Court reversed its earlier decision, striking down a Texas law criminalizing homosexual acts, thus legalizing same-sex sexual relations. Figure 5.2 shows that 56 percent of those surveyed in a Gallup poll agreed that "homosexual relations should be legal" ("Gay and Lesbian Rights" 2009).

Americans are divided over whether gay men and lesbians choose their sexual orientation, a split that shapes attitudes. People who see being gay as a choice are less sympathetic to lesbians or gay men regarding jobs and other rights (Loftus 2001). Americans are more likely to approve of civil rights protections for gays and lesbians than of a gay or lesbian lifestyle, and that approval has continued to strengthen since the 1970s. In 2006, 89 percent of Americans surveyed in a Gallup poll agreed that gays "should have equal job opportunities" (Saad 2006a). The workplace is "becoming friendlier" to gay, lesbian, and bisexual employees, and the vast majority of Forbes 500 companies include sexual orientation in their antidiscrimination policies (Fidas and Luther 2010). Gay employees are increasingly open about their sexual orientation ("The Office Closet Empties Out" 2006).

Homophobia—viewing homosexuals with fear, dread, aversion, or hatred—is still present in American society. A recent poll found that "most Americans oppose legalizing marriage between same-sex couples by 57 percent to 40 percent." What is interesting about these numbers, however, is that when those polled knew someone who is gay, lesbian, or bisexual, their support for gay and lesbian rights increased. In other words, the polls reflect what studies show: The more familiar we are with sexual minorities, the more likely we are to support sexual equality ("Gay and Lesbian Rights" 2009; Herek 2009a, 2009b).

As discussed in the previous paragraph, knowing a gay or lesbian person tends to make us more supportive of sexual rights. It seems, however, that semantics are also important when Americans are contemplating gay rights. For example, CBS and *The New York Times* polled Americans in 2009, and found that a majority (59 percent) favored allowing homosexuals to serve in the U.S. military, while the same poll showed that an

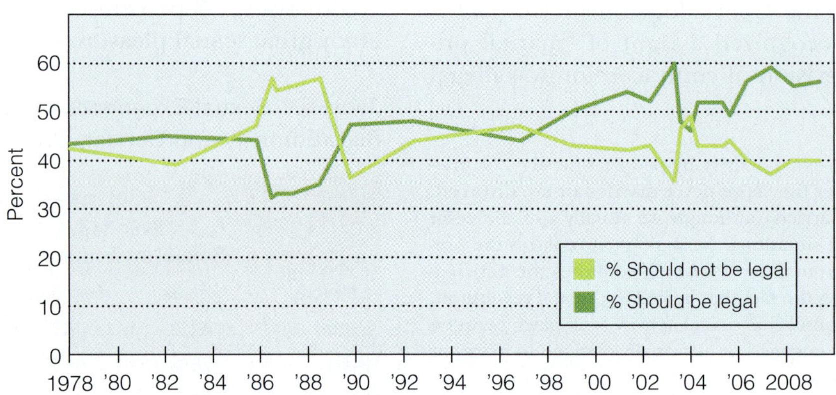

Figure 5.2 Do you think gay or lesbian relations between consenting adults should or should not be legal?

Joseph Sohm/Visions of America/Corbis

Lesbian and gay male unions and families have become increasingly visible over the past decade. Meanwhile, discrimination and controversy persist.

even stronger majority (71 percent) favored allowing gay men and lesbians to serve in the U.S. military. As readers can see, the pollsters used two different types of wording to ask the same question. In one question, they used the term "homosexuals," whereas in another question, they used the term "gay men and lesbians."

Comparing Gay Male and Lesbian Sexual Behaviors Sexual conduct, experience, and satisfaction have much to do with cultural trends. Leonore Tiefer notes that how we develop our desires and our expectations have very much to do with our "socially produced expectations [which] affect meaning and satisfaction" (Tiefer 2007, p. 246).

Philip Blumstein and Pepper Schwartz (1983), who studied a large national sample of 12,000 volunteers from the Seattle, San Francisco, and Washington, DC areas prior to the HIV/AIDS epidemic,[5] described lesbian relationships as the "least sexualized" of four kinds of couples: heterosexual cohabiting and married couples, lesbians, and gay men. Lesbians have sex less frequently than gay men, although it may be difficult to make comparisons because lesbians' physical relationship can take the form of hugging, cuddling, and kissing, not only genital contact (Peplau, Fingerhut, and Beals 2004; Frye 1992; Tracy and Junginger 2007). Nevertheless, lesbians report greater sexual satisfaction than do heterosexual women: "Their greater tenderness, patience, and knowledge of the female body are said to be the reasons" (Konner 1990, p. 26; see also Holmberg, Blair, and Phillips 2010). Gay male sexuality is more often "body-centered" (Ruefli, Yu, and Barton 1992), whereas lesbian sexuality is more person-centered. The conventional wisdom is that gay men may be more accepting of nonmonagamous relationships than are lesbians—or heterosexuals (Adam 2007; Christopher and Sprecher 2000). Some studies, especially those done prior to the HIV/AIDS epidemic, show that gay men have more transitory sex than lesbians. Other studies point out that even though gay men may say they are in open relationships, "they did not act on this option." At the same time, significant percentages of men in both homo- and heterosexual monogamous relationships had slept with someone other than their own partner since "their primary relationships began" (Adam 2007, pp. 123, 125). Casual sex among lesbians appears to be relatively rare.

We have discussed differences, but patterns of sexual frequency and satisfaction in gay and lesbian relationships resemble those of heterosexual marriage and cohabitation in some ways. In all couple types studied by Kurdek (1991)—gay, lesbian, heterosexual cohabitants, and married couples—sexual satisfaction within

[5] Although the Blumstein and Schwartz study was published in 1983, and is not a random sample, it "continues to be the most extensive study on the sexuality of gay and lesbian couples to date" (Christopher and Sprecher 2000, p. 1,007). These data are still being used by well-respected researchers (e.g., Kurdek 2006). Still, one must keep in mind that these data predate the AIDS epidemic and other societal changes that have an impact on sexuality and sexual expression.

As We Make Choices

Sexting—Five Things To Think About Before Pressing "Send"

1. Don't assume anything you send or post is going to remain private.
2. There is no changing your mind in cyberspace—anything you send or post will never truly go away.
3. Don't give into the pressure to do something that makes you uncomfortable, even in cyberspace.
4. Just because a message is meant to be fun doesn't mean the person who gets it will see it that way . . . many teen boys (29 percent) agree that girls who send such content "are expected to date or hook up in real life."
5. Nothing is truly anonymous.

Source: Adapted from *Sex and Tech: Results from a Survey of Teens and Young Adults*, by the National Campaign to Prevent Teen and Unplanned Pregnancy and CosmoGirl.com (2009), p. 2.

each group was associated with general relationship satisfaction and with sexual frequency. "Despite variability in structure, close dyadic relationships work in similar ways" (Kurdek 2006, p. 509; see also Holmberg and Blair 2009).

The Twenty-First Century: Risk, Caution—and Intimacy

Although pleasure seeking was the icon of sixties sexuality, warnings to be cautious in the face of risk characterizes contemporary times. Some heterosexual young adults see AIDS as a threat only for other people. Others do acknowledge the risk, but decide to take their chances. "Most emerging adults . . . say that fear of AIDS has become the framework for their sexual consciousness, deeply affecting their attitudes toward sex and the way they approach sex with potential partners," perhaps asking for a test result or insisting on condom use (Arnett 2004, p. 91). (HIV/AIDS is discussed in more detail later in this chapter.) Meanwhile, a number of singles have multiple partners over time; males tend to report higher rates of multiple partners, with 29 percent reporting "fifteen or more female sexual partners" compared to 9 percent of females stating they have had "fifteen or more male sexual partners in a lifetime" (Fryar et al. 2007, p. 3).

Sexting may be a new word to many older generations, but is a well-known and growing phenomenon among young people of all genders, sexualities, classes, and belief systems in our modern, technological era. According to a new survey, many teens and young adults have sent sexually provocative photographs and text messages over their cell phones to people they don't know, or that they want to date or hook up with. In addition, 71 percent of teen girls, 67 percent of teen boys, 83 percent of young adult women, and 75 percent of young adult men admit to sending sexually suggestive photos and text messages of themselves to people with whom they are in a romantic relationship. Many believe that their sexual images or text will remain with their romantic interest, yet 48 percent of young adult women and 46 percent of young adult men say "it is common for nude or seminude photos to get shared with people other than the intended recipient" (Sex and Tech 2009, pp. 2–3).

Today, there is risk in a sexual encounter. Critics of sexual liberation argue that this is especially disadvantageous for women (Shalit 1999). At the same time, a more liberal sexual environment offers the potential for expressive sexuality and true sexual intimacy. People now have more knowledge of the principles of building good relationships (whether or not they always succeed

"Should I come out to everyone all at once or one cubicle at a time?"

in putting them into practice). Now that the possibility of satisfying sexual relationships seems more attainable, how do men and women negotiate those sexual relationships inside and outside of marriage?

Negotiating (Hetero)sexual Expression[6]

Although relationships between the sexes are more equal today than in the past, many—though assuredly not all—women and men today may have internalized divergent sexual scripts, or messages. Today's heterosexuals negotiate sexual relationships in a context in which new expectations of equality and similarity coexist within a heritage of gender-related difference. Men may be somewhat more accepting of recreational sex than women are, and studies continue to show that women are more interested than men in romantic preliminaries (Purnine and Carey 1998).

The "pressure on men to be more sensitive, less predatory, and less macho has been mounting for several decades" (Schwartz and Rutter 1998, p. 48; see also Seal and Ehrhardt 2003). After the sexual revolution of the 1960s, men became more interested in communicating intimately through sex, whereas women showed more interest than before in physical pleasure (Pietropinto and Simenauer 1977; Seal, O'Sullivan, and Ehrhardt 2007). Masters and Johnson (1976) had argued that more equal gender expectations lead to better sex.

This discussion points again to the fact that cultural messages vary and that sexual relationships are negotiated in a social context. "Since early in the twentieth century the bonds between marriage and sexual activity have been unraveling" (Smith 2006, p. 26). In the next sections, we discuss nonmarital—outside of marriage/committed relationships—sexual activity. After that, we will examine sexuality within marriage/committed relationships—where most sexual activity takes place—and then look at what is known about racial/ethnic diversity in sexual expression. Keep in mind that sexual expression may include more than intercourse—activities ranging from genital intercourse, to oral and anal sex, to kissing and cuddling.

Four Standards for Sex Outside Committed Relationships

In the 1970s, sociologist Ira Reiss (1976) developed a fourfold classification of societal standards that illustrates the varied cultural messages about nonmarital sex.

[6] The idea that sexual expression is negotiated was developed in regard to heterosexual relationships; this principle may be applied to gay and lesbian relationships.

Today we can apply his typology to sex outside of all committed relationships. Reiss's four standards—abstinence, permissiveness with affection, permissiveness without affection, and the double standard—were originally developed to apply to premarital sex among heterosexual couples. However, they have since been applied to the sexual activities of unmarried people generally. (Later we'll discuss extramarital sex—that is, sexual relations of married people or cohabitants outside of their committed relationship.)

Abstinence The standard of **abstinence** maintains that, regardless of the circumstances, nonmarital intercourse is wrong for both women and men. Many contemporary religious groups, especially the conservative Christian and Islamic communities, encourage abstinence as a moral imperative.

The several years before 2008 saw an increase in rates of teen pregnancy (3 percent), births (4 percent), and abortions (1 percent) (Kost, Henshaw, and Carlin 2010, p. 2). That reversed a downward trend, as teen birth rates had declined 34 percent from 1991 to 2005 (Hamilton, Martin, and Ventura 2010), with accompanying declines in teen pregnancy rates (Dyess 2009; Gavin et al. 2009; Schlesinger 2010). The trend has reversed again: In 2008, the teen birth rate dropped, along with birth rates in most other age groups, a decline attributed in part to the recession (Hamilton, Martin, and Ventura 2010).

Generally, teens who do not engage in sexual activity give conservative values or fear of pregnancy, disease, or parents as their reasons (Blinn-Pike 1999; Rasberry and Goodson 2009, pp. 79, 81). A study of college students suggests that women who refrain from sexual activity do so because of an absence of love, a fear of pregnancy or sexually transmitted diseases (STDs), a belief that use of contraception will cause infections or cancer, or a belief system that endorses nonmarital virginity (Kaye, Sullentrop, and Sloup 2009). Men's hesitancy to pursue sexual involvement comes more often from feeling "inadequate or insecure" (Christopher and Sprecher 2000, p. 1,009).

Individuals adopt the abstinence standard for other reasons as well. Some women and men have withdrawn from nonmarital sexual relationships entirely to avoid bad experiences. Some withdraw from sexual risk, at least for a time, rather than feeling vulnerable in the open sexual climate of the sexual revolution (Rasberry and Goodson 2009). The feminist movement is cited as empowering women to be abstinent if they wish (Ali and Scelfo 2002).

Advocates of abstinence claim that it is "a new sexual revolution" (Laub 2005, p. 103; see also Herzog 2008) in a "campus life [that] has become so drenched in sexuality, from the flavored condoms handed out by a resident adviser to the social pressure of the hook-up scene."

Issues for Thought

"Hooking Up" and "Friends with Benefits"

Two similar new patterns of sexual behavior—"hooking up" and "friends with benefits"—made their appearance at the turn of the twenty-first century. Researchers believe that "hooking up" and "friends with benefits" have been around for a while, but are just now becoming visible to researchers and others not immersed in youth culture.

The "demise of the date and the rise of the hookup is a national trend," with dating coming about only after the hookup has turned into a lasting emotional attachment (England and Thomas 2007, p. 152; Bogle 2008, pp. 44, 48). Indeed, a growing body of research suggests that, at least among a majority of U.S. students, *dating*—preplanned couple outings—has virtually disappeared (Epstein et al. 2009; B. Wilson 2009). Now that same improvised sociability has been extended to "hooking up" or finding a "friend with benefits"—that is, pairing off from the group for a sexual encounter (Bogle 2008). In fact, the idea of the hookup has moved beyond the college to people who have diseases, disfigurements, and even psychological issues, and who have difficulty finding others who can understand their needs. Take, for example, cancer survivors. Many cancer survivors, once they divulge that history to someone they've been dating, often find themselves quickly abandoned by the love interest. As a result, new organizations and websites have emerged, creating a social space where people can "hook up" with others dealing with similar issues (Alexander 2010; Durham 2010).

The basic idea in hooking up and friends with benefits is that a sexual encounter means nothing more than just that—sexual activity. Hooking up can occur with no prior acquaintance between the parties and no further contact afterward. *Friends with benefits* is described as sex that takes place with friends, but without expectations for romantic love or commitment. At least that is the initial premise.

These sexual scripts may have emerged because many of today's young adults—who are delaying marriage, going to college, and developing careers—still want to have sex. They want some intimate connection without risking romantic disappointment and emotional loss. When hooking up or finding friends with benefits occurs among high school students, similar reasons may be in place. As one or both sex partners anticipate leaving for college, they may want to keep their options open (Edwards 2006; B. Wilson 2009).

What does this development mean for young lives and future marriage prospects? Reactions of social scientists range from alarm at the disappearance of a courtship path to marriage (Glenn and Marquardt 2001; Stepp 2007), to the thought that hooking up is simply the new way to begin a relationship that may become serious despite its initial intent (England and Thomas 2007; Epstein et al. 2009). By carefully outlining the positives and negatives of both dating and hooking up, one observer reminds us that dating also has drawbacks as a relationship development process (Bogle 2004/2008).

Meanwhile, some observers note that men continue to have greater relationship power in hookup settings, as indeed they did in the dating era (Bogle 2008). Now that there are more women than men on most college campuses, it is suggested that male power is reinforced inasmuch as competition among heterosexual women for the fewer available men is heightened. However, this is not necessarily the case, as men must negotiate the sexual scripts just as much as women (Manning, Giordano, and Longmore 2006; Pollack 2006; Smiler 2008).

There is considerable research on hooking up for such a newly recognized phenomenon. Maybe academics, shut up in their offices analyzing data, find vicarious enjoyment in the topic. More seriously, though, due to researchers' interest, we should in time learn more about how the gap between "hooking up" and "married with children" is to be bridged.

Critical Thinking

What do you think about the advisability of hooking up or having friends with benefits? How might a researcher from the interactionist perspective investigate the way that couples bridge the gap between "hooking up" and "married with children"?

At Princeton, a pro-abstinence organization, the Anscombe Society, was formed to support abstinence outside of traditional marriage and to provide a setting for exploration and discussion of the abstinence alternative (Peterson 2005b, p. B3). Other organizations and books (e.g., Doan and Williams 2008; Moffett 2007; Winner 2006) offer intellectually sophisticated and sexually frank discussions of this alternative.

Permissiveness with Affection The standard of **permissiveness with affection** permits nonmarital intercourse for both men and women equally, provided they have a fairly stable, affectionate relationship. This standard may be the most widespread sexual norm among unmarried individuals. A Gallup poll taken in 2008 found that 57 percent of Americans find sex between an unmarried man and woman "morally acceptable" ("Marriage" 2009).

In a 1997 national poll by *U.S. News & World Report* magazine, a majority of respondents under the age of forty-five said that adult nonmarital sex "generally benefits people" in addition to offering sexual pleasure.

A majority also felt that having had a few sexual partners makes it easier for a person to choose a sexually compatible spouse (Whitman 1997). The previously mentioned NORC survey concluded that we have sex mainly with people we know and care about. Seventy-one percent of Americans have only one sexual partner in the course of a year (Laumann et al. 1994).

Permissiveness without Affection Sometimes called recreational sex, **permissiveness without affection** allows intercourse for women and men regardless of how much stability or affection is in their relationship. Casual sex—intercourse between partners only briefly acquainted—is permitted.

About fifteen years ago, a *New York Times* article surprised many by describing a pattern among adolescents termed "**friends with benefits**" (Denizet-Lewis 2004). This article focused on teens "**hooking up**" casually for sexual encounters with friends and acquaintances, completely outside a romantic relationship context. Today, sociologists see this as a growing trend among adolescents and young adults. The point of the "hookup" seems to be that teens or young adults, who feel themselves to be unready for romance and commitment, are able to explore their sexuality in what is intended to be an emotionally neutral context. According to Dr. Kathleen Bogle, a sociologist who studies this phenomenon, dating used to be something that led up to sex, but in "the hookup era, something sexual happens, even though it may be less than sexual intercourse, that may or may not ever lead to dating" or romantic involvement (B. Wilson 2009; see also Bogle 2008, pp. 24–49). Of course, it doesn't always work out that way.

Sexual activity does not necessarily mean intercourse; oral sex is quite common (Bogle 2008, p. 25). "Issues for Thought: 'Hooking Up' and 'Friends with Benefits'" discusses this new sexual script.

The Double Standard According to the **double standard**, women's sexual behavior must be more conservative than men's. In its original form, the double standard meant that women should not have sex before or outside marriage, whereas men could. Within the context of marriage and committed relationships, femininity "is typically framed in terms of being sexually desirable rather than sexually desiring whereas masculinity connotes sexual aggression and prowess" (Elliott and Umberson 2008, p. 392). More recently, the double standard has required that women be in love to have sex, or at least have fewer partners than men have. Now it appears that there are even different expectations for males and females in "hooking up."

An exploratory study of this phenomenon among undergraduates at two Eastern colleges found some informal rules: Women should be less aggressive, should not hang around fraternity houses, and should have fewer partners than men. It was quite difficult for these college women to maintain reputation and self-esteem while engaging in hooking up—"the only game in town" (Bogle 2004, p. 99; see also Stepp 2007, p. 117).

At first glance, it would seem that men have greater sexual freedom and greater power in these relationships. Bogle, in fact, concludes: "[T]here is one crucial commonality . . . [of *hooking up* and dating, its predecessor sexual script]. . . . [*Men*] *have a greater share of power in both eras*" (p. 229; see also Bogle 2008, pp. 23, 173). Other research notes, however, that this is not necessarily the case; in fact, many men find these ever-transforming sexual scripts difficult to negotiate. Furthermore, young men seem to be as emotionally vulnerable as women and are, frequently, using the "hookup" as a means to find lasting and meaningful relationships (Epstein et al. 2009; Manning, Giordano, and Longmore 2006; Pollack 2006; Smiler 2008).

In our society generally, men and women may have different expectations, with men exposed to cultural conditioning that encourages them to separate sex from intimacy, whereas among women, sexual expression more often symbolizes connection with a partner and communicates intimacy. One observer also argues that gender differences in permissiveness may reflect differences in social power and vulnerability, prompting a woman's strategy of self-protection through adherence to conventional cultural expectations (Howard 1988).

Sexual Infidelity

Up to this point, we've been examining scripts for sex among noncommitted relationships. Now we will look at a different form of sex outside marriage and committed relationships—sexual infidelity, or "affairs."

As we will see in Chapter 7, marriage typically involves promises of sexual exclusivity—that spouses and committed partners will have sexual relations only with each other. Cohabiting and other committed relationships also involve expectations of fidelity, although to a somewhat lesser degree (Treas and Giesen 2000). In this era of expressive sexuality, "people still feel that the self-disclosure involved in sexuality symbolizes the love relationship and therefore sexuality should not be shared with extramarital partners" (Reiss 1986, pp. 56–57). Americans believe in fidelity and sexual exclusivity regardless of a legally binding commitment to one another (see Chapter 7), but it seems that beliefs and actions to not always quite match up, and some find themselves unable to completely adhere to their own expectations.

Although infidelity is found in virtually any society and throughout our known history, the proscription against extramarital sex is stronger in the United States than in many other parts of the world. Ninety-two percent of Americans consider extramarital affairs "morally wrong" (Newport 2009). Cohabiting couples also generally expect each other to be sexually faithful (94 percent, compared to 99 percent of married couples). However, the rate of sexual infidelity is higher among cohabiting couples than among married couples (Treas and Giesen 2000).

As you will see in Chapters 7 and 8 of this text, long-term relationships (including marriages and cohabitations) are generally founded on the agreements, by both parties, of fidelity. Some researchers distinguish among emotional infidelity, sexual infidelity, and combined emotional and sexual infidelity. The latter is most disapproved. Emotional (without sexual) infidelity is least disapproved (Blow and Hartnett 2005). The impacts of any form of infidelity, however, are lasting. Sexual infidelity is engaging in sexual relations with someone who is not one's own marriage or committed partner. Some researchers define emotional infidelity as an "intense, primarily emotional, nonsexual relationship" with someone who is not one's own marriage or committed partner (Potter-Efron and Potter-Efron 2008, p. 2). Both of these forms of infidelity have long-term, sustained negative impacts on the marriage or committed relationship (Meier, Hull, and Ortyl 2009).

Statistics on sexual infidelity are based on what people report: Some spouses or committed partners hesitate to admit an affair; others boast about affairs that didn't really happen. Social researcher Pepper Schwartz (2009) says that "over a lifetime approximately 25 to 50 percent of married men and women are going to cheat on their partner. Make that 50 percent plus of cohabiters" (see also Chapters 7 and 8 of this text). Although these rates are lower than those found in earlier research, "these percentages translate into a significant number of Americans who have experienced sex with someone other than their spouse at least once" (Christopher and Sprecher 2000, p. 1,006). A survey conducted in 2002 by the Centers for Disease Control and Prevention found that 92 percent of married men and 93 percent of married women had sexual contact with only one opposite-sex partner (the spouse) during the past year. This compares to 80 percent of male and female cohabitants whose sexual relations were limited to their cohabiting partner. New research out of the University of Washington finds that "the lifetime rate of infidelity for men over 60 increased to 28 percent in 2006, up from 20 percent in 1991. For women over 60, the increase is more striking: to 15 percent, up from 5 percent in 1991" (Parker-Pope 2008, p. D1), which suggests that women's infidelity is on the rise.

Of married men, 3.4 percent reported a lifetime experience of affairs with other men; 5.3 percent of cohabiting men reported such experiences. Of married women, 7.2 percent reported some sexual experience with other women, and 10.8 percent of cohabiting women did so. (The higher rates for women are probably due to the much looser definition of "sexual experience" for women (Mosher, Chandra, and Jones 2005, Tables 1, 2, 8.)

"Hey look, before this goes any further, I should probably tell you we're married."

Risk Factors Sociologists Judith Treas and Deirdre Giesen (2000) developed a conceptual model of risk factors for extramarital sex. They tested this model with data from the 1992 National Health and Social Life Survey, a national probability sample, which included 2,870 married or cohabiting individuals ages eighteen through fifty-nine.[7]

Treas and Giesen found that entering an extramarital affair is a rational decision. That is, affairs are generally *not* spontaneous (the result of too much alcohol, for example), nor are they the consequence of overwhelming romantic passion. Rather, "[p]eople contemplating sexual infidelity described considered decisions" (Treas and Giesen 2000, p. 49). In a recent study, researchers also found that loneliness is an important factor in one's decision to be unfaithful. This study found that the conditions of many undocumented workers in the United States is such that loneliness, as well as fear of deportation, led to unsafe sexual practices and an increased risk of sexually transmitted disease (Hirsch et al. 2009).

Although the book you are reading focuses on the United States, there is some important research examining sexual infidelity in other countries. This research provides evidence of cross-cultural similarities when it comes to love and sexual infidelity. For example, in all parts of the world, the decision to engage in sexual

[7] This study draws on the National Health and Social Life Survey data set (Laumann et al. 1994), but analyzes only data from married and cohabiting respondents.

infidelity appears to be unrelated to feelings of love the adulterer has for his or her partner, but instead comes from a complex interplay of sexuality, identity, ideology, ego, access, and even peer pressure (Hirsch et al. 2009/2010).

Not surprisingly, individuals who have a stronger sex interest and who have more permissive sexual values and more past sex partners are more likely than others to engage in sexual infidelity (Treas and Giesen 2000). Lower satisfaction with a marital or cohabiting relationship is another unsurprising risk factor. Relationship dissatisfaction is a motive more important to women. Sexual dissatisfaction and declines in frequency are also associated with affairs, especially for men (Blow and Hartnett 2005). In fact, research shows that the risk of extramarital affairs for both genders is "significantly higher among marriages characterized by spousal violence, divorce proneness, a past experience of marital separation, or the practice of spending relatively little time together," but marital and sexual satisfaction seemed to be less important to someone's decision to have an extramarital affair (DeMaris 2009, p. 605).

Opportunity plays a role. Couples who lead separate lives and who have jobs requiring travel are more likely to have extramarital affairs (Treas and Giesen 2000). Workplace opportunity per se was not a significant factor for lifetime rates of extramarital affairs, but it was associated with having an affair in the last twelve months. The researchers speculate that if an opportunity came along at a low point in the marriage, it might be taken advantage of. Additionally, women's economic independence may have something to do with their increasing rates of extramarital sex. Women are working longer hours, traveling more, and have the same access to cell phones, text messaging, and so on that men have to create and nurture intimate connections outside of marriage or committed relationship (Parker-Pope 2008).

The 1990s saw the emergence of a new brand of marital infidelity—adultery on the net, or **cyberadultery**. The Internet has created new opportunities for individuals to develop secret relationships (Jayson 2008a; Potter-Efron and Potter-Efron 2008; Whitty and Quigley 2008). The emotional connection may lead to a meeting—and then perhaps to a sexual relationship. At the same time, the Internet makes it more likely that a partner or employer will be able to find out about an affair (Cooper 2004; Crooks and Baur 2005). Such a discovery often triggers a couple's move into therapy.

Historically, societies have depended on community pressures to control disapproved sexual activity of any sort. Shared social networks of family and friends, as well as church attendance, seemed to operate as social controls discouraging infidelity (Hutson 2009).

Union duration of marriage or cohabitation, which can be a measure of both *investment* in the relationship and *habituation,* showed a positive relationship with likelihood of extramarital sex during the union. This provides some support for the **habituation hypothesis**—that is, that familiarity reduces the reward power of a sexual encounter with a spouse or partner compared to a new relationship (Liu 2000). At the same time, union duration is also a simple measure of exposure to the risk of an extramarital affair (Treas and Giesen 2000).

Previous researchers have found gender differences evident in the analysis of patterns of extramarital sex (Harris 2003a), with more husbands than wives having had an affair sometime during their marriage (Laumann et al. 1994; Schwartz 2009). If a wife has an affair, she is more likely to do so because she feels emotionally distanced by her husband. Men who have affairs are far more likely to do so for the sexual excitement and variety they hope to find. Moreover, "men feel more betrayed by their wives having sex with someone else; women feel more betrayed by their husbands being emotionally involved with someone else" (Glass 1998, p. 35; Begley 2009; Blow and Hartnett 2005). However, when other risk factors are controlled, gender differences may be reduced or even eliminated (Treas and Giesen 2000).

Effects of Sexual Infidelity The secrecy required by an affair erodes the connection between partners. When discovered, the betrayal may spark jealousy—or it may create a crisis that motivates a search for the resolution of more general relationship problems (Crooks and Baur 2005; Snyder, Baucom, and Gordon 2008).

An affair *can* have positive effects such as encouraging closer relationships, paying greater attention to couple communication, and placing a higher value on the family (Olson et al. 2002). But only a small percentage of couples see an improved relationship (Blow and Hartnett 2005). Not only has trust been eroded and feelings been hurt, but the uninvolved spouse may also have been exposed to various sexually transmitted diseases—not a rare occurrence (Crooks and Baur 2005). For many partners, concern about HIV/AIDS heightens anger and turmoil over affairs. The uninvolved partner may feel exploited financially as well, because money has been unilaterally spent on an intimate outside the relationship (T. Smith 2006).

Research among married individuals is mixed as to whether infidelity "causes" divorce. That seems to depend on the previous level of marital satisfaction, the motives attributed to the unfaithful spouse, attitudes toward infidelity in general, and the efforts of both spouses to work things out (Blow and Hartnett 2005).

Recovering from an Affair Given that affairs do occur, people will have much to think about if they discover that their spouse has had (or is having) one. The uninvolved mate will need to consider how important the affair is relative to the marital relationship as a whole.

Can she or he regain trust? In some cases, the answer is no; trust never gets reestablished, and the heightened suspicion gets incorporated into other problems the couple might have (Baucom, Snyder, and Gordon 2009, p. 325).

Whether trust can be reestablished depends on several factors. One is how much trust there is in the first place. For this reason, new relationships may be especially vulnerable to breaking up after an affair. Many couples do recover from an affair; however, "it's hard to do without a therapist" (S. Glass 1998, p. 44; see also Baucom et al. 2006). Therapists suggest that doing so requires that the offending partner:

- apologize sincerely and without defending her or his behavior.
- allow and hear the verbally vented anger and rage of the offended partner (but not permit physical abuse).
- allow for trust to rebuild gradually and to realize that this may take a long time—up to two years or more.
- do things to help the offended partner to regain trust—keep agreements, for example, and call if he or she is running late.

Meanwhile, the offended partner needs to decide whether she or he is committed to the relationship and, if so, needs to be willing to let go of resentments as much as is possible (Snyder, Baucom, and Gordon 2008). Finally, the couple should consider relationship counseling (described in Chapter 12). According to Shirley Glass, "The affair creates a loss of innocence and some scar tissue. I tell couples things will never be the same. But the relationship may be stronger" (1998, p. 44; 2003).

Sexuality throughout Marriage and Committed Relationships

It might surprise you that various aspects of nonmarital sex are more likely to be studied than are those within marriage and that sexual activities of teens receive more research attention than those of adults (L. Davis 2006). "More is known about sexuality in marriage at this time than has ever been true in the past. But we still have only a limited view of how sexuality is integrated into the normal flow of married life" (Christopher and Sprecher 2000, p. 1,013).

Research in recent years has been much better methodologically, but has tended to focus on sexual frequency: How often do married couples have sex, and what factors affect this frequency? Before we get to the answers, we need to say something about how the information is gathered. "Facts About Families: How Do We Know What We Do? A Look at Sex Surveys" discusses the history and progress of research on sexuality.

How Often?

Social scientists are interested in sexual frequency because they like to examine trends over time and to relate these to other aspects of intimate relationships. For the rest of us, "How often?" is typically a question motivated by curiosity about our own sexual behavior compared to that of others. Either way, what do we know?

Married couples have sex more often than single individuals, though less often than cohabiting couples (Christopher and Sprecher 2000; T. Smith 2006; Yabiku and Gager 2009). In the NORC survey, described earlier in this chapter, the average frequency of sex for sexually active, married respondents under age sixty was seven times a month. About 40 percent of married individuals said they had intercourse at least twice a week (Laumann et al. 1994). Of course, these figures are averages: "People don't have sex every week; they have good weeks and bad weeks" (Pepper Schwartz, quoted in Adler 1993).

So does the ratio of good to bad weeks change over the course of a marriage? Yes: You have fewer good weeks (sorry).

Fewer Good Weeks To examine sexual frequency throughout marriage, Call, Sprecher, and Schwartz (1995) looked at the responses of 6,785 marrieds with a spouse in the household (and 678 respondents who were cohabiting) in the NSFH data set described earlier. Like researchers before them and since (T. Smith 2006), they found that sexual activity is highest among young marrieds. About 96 percent of spouses under age twenty-five reported having had sex at least once during the previous month. The proportion of sexually active spouses gradually diminished until about age fifty, when sharp declines were evident. Among those fifty to fifty-four years old, 83 percent said they had sex within the previous month; for those between sixty-five and sixty-nine, the figure was 57 percent; 27 percent of respondents over age seventy-four reported having had sex within the previous month.

The average number of times that married people under age twenty-five had sex is about twelve a month. That number drops to about eight times a month at ages thirty through thirty-four, then to about six times monthly at about age fifty. After that, frequency of intercourse drops more sharply; spouses over age seventy-four average having sex less than once each month.

It used to be that describing sexuality over the course of a marriage would be nearly the same as discussing sex as people grow older. Today, this is not the case. Many

Facts about Families

How Do We Know What We Do? A Look at Sex Surveys

How do we know what Americans do sexually? In serious social science, researchers strive for *representative samples* that reflect, or represent, all the people about whom they want to know something.

Pioneering Research

The pioneer surveys on sex in the United States were the Kinsey reports on male and female sexuality (Kinsey, Pomeroy, and Martin 1948; 1953). Kinsey used volunteers; he believed that a statistically representative survey of sexual behavior would be impossible because many of the randomly selected respondents would refuse to answer or would lie.

Recent Surveys

More recent scientific studies on sexual behavior have used random samples. In 1992, the National Opinion Research Center (NORC) at the University of Chicago conducted interviews with a representative sample of 3,432 Americans, age eighteen to fifty-nine—the National Health and Social Life Survey (Laumann et al. 1994). Eighty percent agreed to be interviewed—an impressively high response rate.

Respondents were questioned in ninety-minute face-to-face interviews. To provide some anonymity for the more sensitive part of the interview—questions about oral and anal sex, for example—specific sexual behavior questions were asked by means of a questionnaire. The respondent wrote answers and sealed them in an unlabeled envelope.

Findings of the National Health and Social Life Survey may be generalized to the U.S. population under age sixty with a high degree of confidence. Indeed, the results have been welcomed as the first-ever truly scientific nationwide survey of sex in the United States. Because the NORC sample included only people under sixty, however, it cannot tell us anything about the sexual activities of older Americans.

Another study of sex among married individuals (Call, Sprecher, and Schwartz 1995) sought to compensate for the NORC study's deficiencies by using another national data set, the National Survey of Families and Households (NSFH). Between 1987 and 1988, the NSFH staff, affiliated with the University of Wisconsin, did in-person interviews with a representative national sample of 13,000 respondents age eighteen and over (Sweet, Bumpass, and Call 1988), and the survey was repeated between 1992 and 1994. Considered very reliable, the NSFH data are used as a basis for analysis regarding many topics discussed in this text. Some analyses have combined the National Survey of Families and Households and NORC data (Black et al. 2000).

A more recent survey, the National Survey of Family Growth, was conducted in 2002 and early 2003, by the U.S. Centers for Disease Control and Prevention. This survey also had an almost 80 percent response rate. It consists of in-person, in-home interviews with 12,571 people—4,928 men and 7,642 women. Measures of sexual behavior were collected by means of computer-assisted self-interviewing. This survey was limited to those fifteen through forty-four years of age, with different analyses involving various age combinations within this range (Mosher, Chandra, and Jones 2005). A new edition of this survey is currently taking place, with data collection ongoing. To see for yourself the process that takes place in this kind of research, explore the *Planning and Development of the Continuous National Survey of Family Growth* that is available online.[a]

NORC continues to conduct a biennial General Social Survey that includes questions about sexual behavior. It publishes extensive reports on sexual behavior (e.g., Smith 2006), as well as providing current data on attitudes of the general public toward sexual activity. Additionally, in a study titled, National Children's Study, NORC is conducting a longitudinal study of American children from prior to birth to the age of twenty-one in an effort to study environmental influences on children's health and development.

Conclusions based on survey research on sensitive matters such as sexuality must always be qualified by an awareness of their limitations—the possibility that respondents have minimized or exaggerated their sexual activity or that people willing to answer a survey on sex are not representative of the public. Nevertheless, with data from these national sample surveys, we have far more reliable information than ever before.

a. http://www.cdc.gov/nchs/data/series/sr_01/sr01_048.pdf

couples are remarried, so that at age forty-five, or even seventy, a person may be newly married. Nonetheless, we may logically assume that young spouses are in the early years of marriage.

Young Spouses

Young spouses have sexual intercourse more frequently than do older mates. Young married partners, as a rule, have fewer distractions and worries. The high frequency of intercourse in this age group may also reflect a self-fulfilling prophecy: These couples may have sex more often partly because society expects them to.

After the first few years, sexual frequency declines (T. Smith 2006). Why so? The sexual intensity of the honeymoon period subsides, and "from then on almost everything—children, jobs, commuting, housework, financial worries—that happens to a couple conspires to reduce the degree of sexual interaction while almost nothing leads to increasing it" (Greenblatt 1983, p. 294).

Indeed, later research does indicate that pregnancy, the presence of small children, and a less than certain birth control method are factors that reduce sexual activity in young marriages.

Researchers have begun to wonder how sexual relations in early marriage might differ between couples who have established a sexual relationship before marriage and those who did not (Sprecher 2002), but there has been little examination of the transition from premarital to marital sex.

Spouses in Middle Age

On average, as people get older, they have sex less often. Physical aging is not the only explanation for the decline of sexual activity over time, although it appears to be the most important one. Marital satisfaction was the second largest predictor of sexual frequency.

Sexual satisfaction, marital satisfaction, and sexual frequency are interrelated throughout marriage (Byers 2005; Crooks and Baur 2005; Sprecher and Schwartz 1994; T. Smith 2006; Elliott and Umberson 2008). However, "even among couples who rate their marriages as very happy and among those who say they are still 'in love,' frequency of intercourse declines with age," and some of the decline is gendered with more women reporting lower levels of desire then men as they age (T. Smith 2006, p. 13; Elliott and Umberson 2008).

Despite the declining frequency of sexual intercourse, respondents in a variety of small studies emphasized the continuing importance of sexuality (Greenblatt 1983; Elliott and Umberson 2008). They pointed to the total marital relationship rather than just to intercourse—to such aspects as "closeness, tenderness, love, companionship and affection" (Greenblatt 1983, p. 298)—as well as other forms of physical closeness such as cuddling or lying in bed together. In other words, with time, sex may become more broadly based in the couple's relationship. During this period, sexual relating may also become more sophisticated, as the partners become more experienced and secure (Purnine and Carey 1998).

Older Partners

In our society, images of sex tend to be associated with youth, beauty, and romance; to many young people, sex seems out of place in the lives of older adults. Not too many years ago, public opinion was virtually uniform in seeing sex as unlikely—even inappropriate—for older people. With Masters and Johnson's work in the 1970s, indicating that many older people are sexually active, public opinion began to swing the other way. Then, in the 1980s, researchers began to caution against the romanticized notion that biological aging could be abolished (Cole 1983, pp. 35, 39). Of course, physical changes associated with aging do affect sexuality (Christopher and Sprecher 2000, p. 1,002).

In a nationally representative sample surveyed by the American Association of Retired Persons, a majority (56 percent) of those individuals forty-five and older agreed that a satisfying sexual relationship is important to one's quality of life. But they rated family and friends, health, being in good spirits, financial security, spiritual well-being, and a good relationship with a partner as more important than a fulfilling sexual connection (Jacoby 2005). Thus, "it stands to reason that individuals and couples... who have developed the capacity over the years to experience optimal sexuality have much to teach the rest of us" (Kleinplatz et al. 2009, p. 15). For example, when asked what they would tell younger generations about sexual enjoyment, elderly respondents who had been in a committed relationship twenty-five years or longer told researchers that good sex over the long term includes patience and practice. To illustrate this metaphorically, one respondent told the researchers, "instead of rushing by the windows in a train, one watches the scenery." Reminiscing during lovemaking also enhanced both the sexual desire and the sexual experience in elderly lovemaking (Melby 2010, p. 4; Kleinplatz et al. 2009).

Men and women in their late forties both placed an equal and high priority on sex. Additionally, 73 percent of people aged fifty-seven to sixty-four and 53 percent of people aged sixty-five to seventy-four remain sexually active, but by age sixty, a gender gap becomes evident. Sixty-two percent of men but only 27 percent of women gave sex a high priority (DeLamater and Sill 2005; Lindau et al. 2007; Melby 2010, p. 4).

Some older partners shift from intercourse to petting as a preferred sexual activity. On the other hand, sexual intercourse does not necessarily cease with age. Among the sexually active, 90 percent said they found their mates "very attractive physically" (Greeley 1991). Sexually active spouses over age seventy-four have sex about four times a month. Indeed, retirement "creates the possibility for more erotic spontaneity, because leisure time increases" (Allgeier 1983, p. 146). New research warns, however, that although maintaining a healthy sex drive into the "golden years" is normal, care needs to be taken to ensure that people who choose to accept a decreasing sex drive as they age are not treated as "victims of a pathology" (Marshall 2009, p. 219).

When health problems do not interfere, both women's and men's emotional and psychological outlooks are as important as age in determining sexual functioning. Factors such as monotony, lack of an understanding partner, mental or physical fatigue, and overindulgence in food or alcohol may all have a profound negative effect on a person's capacity for sexual expression. Another important factor is regular sexual activity—as in "use it or lose it" (Marshall 2009, p. 218).

What about Boredom?

Jokes about sex in marriage are often about boredom. Among social scientists, one explanation often offered for the decline in marital sexual frequency is **habituation**—the decreased interest in sex that results from the increased accessibility of a sexual partner and the predictability in sexual behavior with that partner over time. Decreases due to habituation seem to occur early in the marriage; sexual frequency declines sharply after about the first year of marriage no matter how old (or young) the partners are. The reason for "this rather quick loss of intensity of interest and performance" appears to have two components: "a reduction in the novelty of the physical pleasure provided by sex with a particular partner and a reduction in the perceived need to maintain high levels of sexual behavior" (Call, Sprecher, and Schwartz 1995, p. 649; see also Liu 2000).

However, research by Erickson (2005) and by Elliott and Umberson (2008) suggests that the decline in sexual frequency may be more complex than the previous explanation. They use social theorist Arlie Hochschild's (1983) concept, **emotion labor**, in which women, through their gendered work at home, display certain emotions that they believe are expected of them—in other words, it's a gendered management of emotions. This emotion labor includes all of the pressures of work, running the household, dealing with children's needs, and so on—the burdens of women's daily lives. Such work is exhausting, oftentimes leading to, the authors suggest, reduced sex drive on the part of women. The authors suggest that the complexities found in reduced sex drive among women may have quite a bit to do with the fact that women are exhausted from their emotion work that is endemic to running a household, as well as the exhaustion that comes from displaying emotions that are expected but that they don't feel in the course of their daily and family lives.

"Owen, look—the good sex fairy."

Given that the decline in marital frequency occurs most sharply early in marriage and only gradually after that, these researchers reasoned that "it is difficult to determine ... whether habituation to sex actually occurs" throughout the marriage (Call, Sprecher, and Schwartz 1995, p. 647). Comparisons of first-married and remarried couples can shed some light on this. Remarried respondents reported somewhat higher rates of sex frequency compared to people in first marriages who were the same age, and this was particularly true for those under age forty. Because people who remarry do renew the novelty of marital sex with a new partner, this finding is evidence for the habituation hypothesis (Call, Sprecher, and Schwartz 1995).

Sexual Satisfaction in Marriage and Other Partnerships

All this discussion of the frequency of intercourse may tempt us to forget that committed partners' sexuality is essentially about intimacy and self-disclosure. In other words, sex between partners—heterosexual partners and gay and lesbian partners as well—both gives pleasure and reinforces the relationship. A relatively recent study found that those who "reported both the greatest emotional satisfaction and the greatest physical pleasure in their intimate relationships were those who were partnered in a monogamous relationship" (Hendrick 2000, p. 4). Another study comparing cohabiting, married, and single individuals found that cohabiting and married individuals had the highest—and equal—levels of physical pleasure, with emotional satisfaction with sex greatest among married people (Waite and Joyner 2001).

Despite declining sexual frequency, sexual satisfaction remains high in marriages over the life course (of course, the less satisfied may have opted for divorce); 88 percent report that they are "extremely" or "very physically pleased" (Laumann et al. 1994; see also Christopher and Sprecher 2000, p. 1,003). General satisfaction with sexual relationships was also characteristic of gay and lesbian couples.

Race/Ethnicity and Sexual Activity

Table 5.1 reports differences in the sexual experience of high school students. As discussed previously in this chapter, there is variation between racial and gender groups when it comes to sexual activities. Additionally, a study in the *American Journal of Public Health* noted that, in 2006 (the most recent year that data was collected), the vast majority of men from all racial groups had only one sex partner. The prevalence, however, "of multiple sexual partnerships varied substantially by race/ethnicity. Non-Hispanic black and Hispanic men (28 percent and 18 percent, respectively) were more likely to have had multiple sexual partners than were non-Hispanic white men (13 percent) and men of other racial/ethnic groups (9 percent)" (Adimora, Schoenbach, and Doherty 2007, p. 2,232). Comparisons between white males and females and their black and Hispanic counterparts about experience with oral and anal sex vary with the particular item. Overall, whites are more likely to have had "unconventional sex" (Mosher, Chandra, and Jones 2005, Tables 1, 2, p. 12).

African Americans and non-Hispanic whites are more similar than dissimilar in at least some aspects of their sexual behavior, and any dissimilarities are related to socioeconomic status, not race (Knox and Zusman 2009). Asians report fewer sexual partners over a lifetime and tend to have their first sexual experiences later than whites and Hispanics. For Hispanic men, the more acculturated into the mainstream American culture they are, the more casual sexual encounters they have (Meston and Ahrold 2010). Research on *married couples* suggested that sexual frequency does not vary significantly with race, social class, or religion (Christopher and Sprecher 2000).

Gay/lesbian sexuality, like heterosexual behavior, has been explored among African Americans mostly in the context of problems (e.g., AIDS) and at the lower end of the social scale. An exception is found in the analysis of the 2000 census data on black same-sex households, which make up 14 percent of all such households. Black same-sex households tend to be less well off economically than other same-sex households. They are more likely to be raising children (Dang and Frazer 2004).

Social scientists writing about gay black male sexuality believe it is not as visible as among whites because blacks may find white gay subcultures alien, and they may tend to be integrated into heterosexual communities and extended families that strongly disapprove of homosexuality (Bowleg et al. 2003; Mays, Cochran, and Zamudio 2004). Similar issues are found in the more traditional Latino and Asian cultures where heterosexuality is emphasized. For example, the "machismo" image is a strong component of Latino culture, and assertions of virility are an important part of traditional Asian cultures as well (Calzo and Ward 2010, p. 1,104). As part of that social integration, as well as the racism that men of color perceive in the gay community (Han 2008), black and Latino gay men may be more likely to be bisexual than exclusively homosexual and less likely to assert a gay identity even when engaged primarily in same-sex relations (Sandfort and Dodge 2008). This pattern of engaging in sex with other men while maintaining a straight masculine identity has been labeled "the down low" (Denizet-Lewis 2003; Malebranche 2007).

Black lesbians are relatively invisible due to their smaller numbers and integration into extended family relationships. The issues faced by black gay and bisexual men tend to be relatively invisible as well. The black lesbians in a qualitative study of 530 lesbians and 66 bisexual women were well-educated, middle-class women in their thirties, who first became conscious of their attraction to women at around age fourteen, with first same-sex sexual experiences at age nineteen. Their adult relationships have been generally satisfying and close (Mays and Cochran 1999).

Now let us turn to a more general discussion of sexual expression as conceptualized by sex researchers William Masters and Virginia Johnson, who initiated contemporary sex therapy.

Sex as a Pleasure Bond: Making the Time for Intimacy

The convergence of sexual satisfaction with general satisfaction serves to support Masters and Johnson's (1976) view of sex as a **pleasure bond**, by which partners commit themselves to expressing their sexual feelings with each other.

In sharing sexual pleasure, partners realize that sex is something partners do with each other, not to or for each other. Each partner participates actively, as an equal in the sexual union. Further, each partner assumes **sexual responsibility**—that is, responsibility for his or her own sexual response. When this happens, the stage is set for conscious, mutual cooperation. Partners feel freer to express themselves sexually.

Just as it is important for families to arrange their schedules so that they may spend time together, it's also important for couples to plan time to be alone and intimate (Marano 2010; Masters, Johnson, and Kolodny 1994). Planning time for intimacy involves making conscious choices. Boredom with sex after many years in a marriage may be at least partly the consequence of a decision by default.

Therapists suggest that couples might create romantic settings at home or—if they can afford it—take a weekend retreat. Partners may choose to set aside at least one night a week for themselves alone where they can cuddle and watch movies, for example. Another idea is leisurely going out together for a cup of coffee together. Partners do not have to have intercourse during these times: They should do only what they feel like doing. But scheduling time alone together does mean mutually agreeing to exclude other preoccupations and devote full attention to each other. The point is to have "us time," so this time together should not be spent discussing finances, family, or work.

© The Newark Museum / Art Resource, NY

This suggestion may be easier for parents with young children who are put to bed fairly early. A common complaint from parents of older children is that the children stay up later and, by the time they are teenagers, the parents no longer have any private evening time together. One woman's solution to this problem:

> Our house shuts down at 9:30 now. That doesn't mean we say "It's your bedtime, kids. You're tired and you need your sleep." It means we say, "Your dad (or your mom) and I need some time alone." The children go to their rooms at 9:30. Help with homework, lunch money, decisions about what they'll wear tomorrow—all those things get taken care of by 9:30 or they don't get taken care of. (Monestero 1990)

The important thing, these therapists stress, is that partners don't lose touch with either their sexuality or their ability to share it with each other. In other words, as Patti Newbold, who lost her husband, sadly notes, "marriage isn't about my needs or his needs or about how well we communicate about our needs. It's about loving and being loved" (Marano 2010, p. 71).

We have been talking about human sexual expression as a pleasure bond. It is terribly unfortunate that sexuality can also be associated with disease and death. Indeed, the fact that it is so difficult to make a transition to the next topic points to the multifaceted, even contradictory, nature of contemporary human sexual expression.

Sexual Expression, Family Relations, and HIV/AIDS

HIV/AIDS has now been known for about thirty years. The HIV, or "human immunodeficiency virus," which produces AIDS, has existed longer than that, but it was only in 1981 that AIDS was recognized as the cause of a rapidly increasing number of deaths.

An HIV infection eventually progresses to full-blown AIDS. AIDS stands for "acquired immunodeficiency syndrome"; it is a viral disease that destroys the immune system. With a lowered resistance to disease, a person with AIDS becomes vulnerable to infections and other diseases that other people easily fight off. "Facts About Families: Who Has HIV/AIDS?" presents some details on the demographics and transmission modes of HIV/AIDS.

The rates of new HIV diagnoses increased 15 percent between 2004 and 2007 (U.S. Centers for Disease Control and Prevention 2009, p. 6), with about 56,000 people becoming infected each year (Kates et al. 2009, p. 8). The rise of new HIV cases comes at the same time as county and state, and federal budgets for HIV/AIDS/STD prevention funding were cut or remained flat (Kates et al. 2009, pp. 6–7, 15). Because of its lethal character—over 583,298 deaths in the United States through 2007 (U.S. Centers for Disease Control and Prevention 2009)—we focus here on HIV/AIDS. Appendix C describes various STDs and presents information on transmission modes, prevention, and treatment.

A theme of this text is that social, political, economic, and cultural conditions affect people's choices. We examine here the impact of HIV/AIDS as a societal phenomenon that has changed the consequences of decisions about sexual activity and one that intersects with other social characteristics.[8]

HIV/AIDS and Heterosexuals

Some heterosexual adults have responded to the threat of AIDS with changed behavior, but many others have not. As you can see from Figure 5.3, the incidence of AIDS transmission is growing among heterosexuals, making up 31 percent of all new cases by 2007. Heterosexuals report increased use of condoms and fewer partners than in the past (T. Smith 2006).

[8] We discussed, in Chapter 3, that poor people (including a substantial portion of people of color) have lower rates of education, and when they do have access to education, it is often of poorer quality. What this combination of factors suggests to many contemporary researchers examining this issue is that poverty denies access to education about diseases such as HIV/AIDS (as well as knowledge of prevention). Furthermore, poverty denies access to medical care and resources, which also may be of help at preventing this and other transmittable (but preventable) diseases.

Facts about Families

Who Has HIV/AIDS?[a]

Over one million people are living with HIV or full-blown AIDS: 40 percent black, 38 percent white, 16 percent Hispanic, and less than one percent each Asian/Pacific Islander and Native American/Alaska Native. The cumulative total of AIDS cases reported through 2007 is over a million, with around 56,000 new cases diagnosed each year. There have been over 580,000 deaths since AIDS was first identified in 1981 (Altman 2005; U.S. Centers for Disease Control and Prevention 2009, Tables 4, 8; "HIV/AIDS Epidemic in the United States" 2009, p. 1).

On the positive side, infections are being caught in the early stages, and new treatments have enabled longer lives for those with the virus (Antiretroviral Therapy Cohort Collaboration 2008).[b] On the other hand, the increase in infections suggests a growing sense of complacency among groups at risk of contracting the disease (Cooter and Stein 2009). Estimates are that 21 percent of those with HIV have not been tested and are unaware of their condition ("HIV/AIDS Epidemic in the United States" 2009, p. 1).

Age and HIV/AIDS

HIV/AIDS has most affected young and middle-aged adults. As of 2007, around 70 percent of AIDS cases were diagnosed in people in the twenty-five through forty-four age range, with the greatest increase in diagnoses going to those age forty to forty-four, who accounted for 15 percent of all new cases. The proportion of HIV/AIDS cases among teenagers is small, under one percent (U.S. Centers for Disease Control and Prevention 2009, p. 6, Tables 1, 3), but keep in mind that individuals who are older at diagnosis may have been infected as adolescents. Expanded testing and treatment of HIV-infected pregnant women have lowered the rate of new cases of prenatal transmission to fewer than 2 percent of births to infected women ("Pregnancy and Childbirth" 2007, n.p.). There were only twenty-eight new cases of AIDS in children in 2007 (U.S. Centers for Disease Control and Prevention 2009, Table 5).

We seldom think of AIDS as affecting older individuals, but around 10 percent of cases are found among those age fifty and up. Only 1.5 percent of AIDS cases are reported for individuals age sixty-five and older, but that is over 15,853 cases among senior citizens (U.S. Centers for Disease Control and Prevention 2009, Table 3). Currently, there are efforts to create programs to educate older Americans about risks and precautions concerning HIV/AIDS (Villarosa 2003).

Gender and HIV/AIDS

Men accounted for 74 percent of AIDS cases diagnosed in 2007, among adolescents and adults. The dominant source of AIDS among males is having sex with other men (53 percent), with intravenous drug use and heterosexual contacts also significant causes of infection. Cumulatively, 80 percent of AIDS cases among women arose from heterosexual contact, and 20 percent from intravenous drug use (U.S. Centers for Disease Control and Prevention 2007, p. 7, Table 3).[c]

Critical Thinking

Pick one of the previously mentioned demographic categories—for example, teen women. What ideas can you think of for an HIV/AIDS prevention program for this group? You may want to

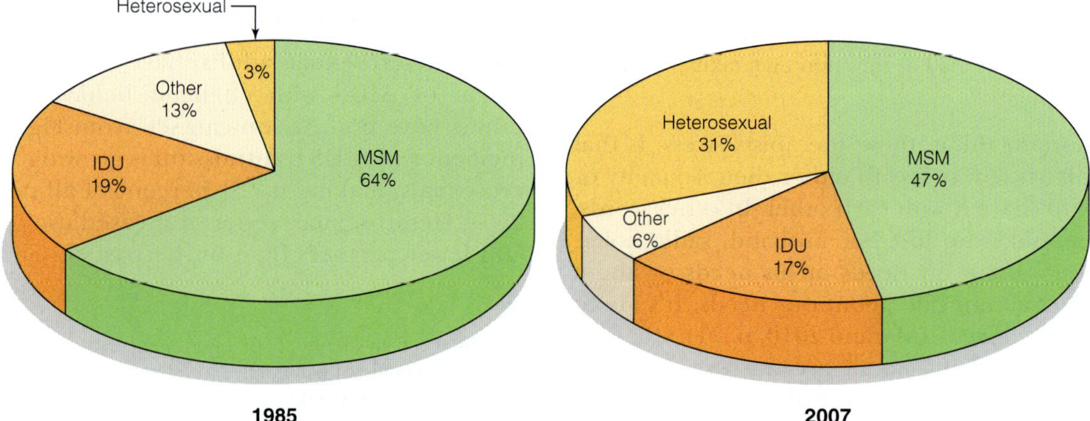

Figure 5.3 The transformation of AIDS diagnoses. What was once considered a "gay disease" has become more prevalent in the heterosexual population.

consult Appendix C, "Sexually Transmitted Diseases," on the website.

a. The term HIV/AIDS is used in general references to this sexually transmitted disease. When speaking about numbers of cases, HIV (the virus that causes AIDS) and AIDS (the active disease) are often distinguished. Most of those who become infected with the HIV virus will progress to full-blown AIDS. The incidence (number of new cases) and prevalence (current cases) of HIV infection are only estimates, as there is no population-wide screening program. Many people who may be HIV-positive are not tested, and test results are not always reported consistently. Consequently, most of the data in these sections on the social distribution of HIV/AIDS are based on AIDS cases, as those are more definite in diagnosis and are reported more accurately.

b. Initially, many cases of AIDS arose through infection from blood transfusions, but this mode of transmission declined after 1985, when donated blood began to be rigorously screened for HIV. Blood transfusion accounted for less than one percent of cases in 2007 (U.S. Centers for Disease Control and Prevention 2009, Table 4).

c. Infection from woman-to-woman sexual contact is rare (U.S. Centers for Disease Control and Prevention 2007).

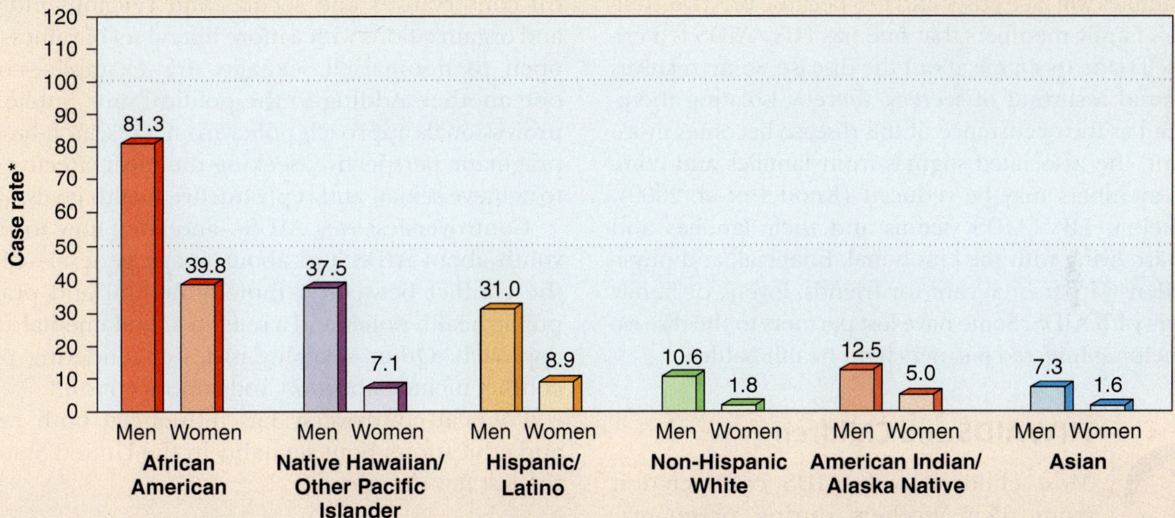

Figure 5.4 Estimated rates of AIDS cases reported among adults and adolescents by race/ethnicity, 2005.*

*Number of cases per 100,000 in respective racial/ethnic and gender group.

Number of cases per 100,000 in respective racial/ethnic and gender group. Source: U.S. Centers for Disease Control and Prevention 2009, Table 6b.

They may insist on a recent blood test verification of HIV status or, more often, condom use. "Even for many [young adults]... who have been on the conservative side in their behavior, AIDS is part of their consciousness. ...They realize that even if they have been careful in their sexual behavior, their partners may not have been, and that puts them at risk" (Arnett 2004, p. 91).

In an effort to reduce potential contact with the disease, some heterosexuals opt for periods of celibacy. Given the increasing heterosexual transmission of HIV/AIDS (see Figure 5.3), "women should embrace a philosophy of always protecting themselves from HIV" ("Third of New HIV Cases" 2004). Perhaps 20 percent of gay men marry at least once (K. Butler 2006b; J. Gross 2006d), and upwards of 70 percent of "straight-identified men having sex with men are married" (DeNoon 2006). Consequently, some heterosexual women may be regularly exposed to the virus if their husbands are sexually active with men.

HIV/AIDS and Gay Men

Many gay men modified their sexual behavior in the 1980s. Multiple, frequent, and anonymous sexual contacts had been common elements of lifestyle and sexual ideology for many gay men (Blumstein and Schwartz 1983). However, attitudes and behavior changed enough, at least among men in their thirties and over, to have dramatically reduced the incidence of new cases among gay males for a time, but we saw a 25 percent increase in new cases of male-to-male transmission of HIV/AIDS from 2004 to 2007 (U.S. Centers for Disease Control and Prevention 2009, Table 1).

Meanwhile, life expectancy (average number of years remaining to those treated between age twenty and thirty-five) is now between thirty and forty years with antiretroviral therapy (Antiretroviral Therapy Cohort Collaboration 2008, Table 2). As the mood in the gay community lightened since the early days of HIV/AIDS in the 1980s, some gay men have returned to unprotected sex (barebacking) with many and anonymous partners, and we have seen a surge of HIV infections among younger gay men ("HIV/AIDS Epidemic in the United States" 2009). Gay activists and public health professionals have expressed concern that drug ads with pictures of relatively hearty gay men convey a misleading message about the difficulties of living with AIDS, a message that may reduce caution and prevention (Cooter and Stein 2010, pp. 14–15; M. Gross 2006).

HIV/AIDS and Family Crises

Some families will face crises and loss because of AIDS. Telling one's family members that one has HIV/AIDS is a crisis in itself. Due to shame about the disease, some relatives grieve amid a shroud of secrecy, thereby isolating themselves. But as the occurrence of this disease becomes more prevalent, the associated stigmas from families and community members may be reduced (Knodel et al. 2009). Nevertheless, HIV/AIDS victims and their families and friends are living with the emotional, financial, and physical burdens of personal care for friends, lovers, or family members with AIDS. Some have lost partners to the disease or are helping infected partners fight health battles.

HIV/AIDS and Children

Most children with AIDS contracted it from their mothers during pregnancy, at birth, or through breast milk. This form of AIDS transmission has declined dramatically due to voluntary prenatal HIV testing of pregnant women and the subsequent administration of prenatal drug therapies.

Women who have tested positive for HIV/AIDS are not always willing to give up the prospect of motherhood; some are deciding to have children after diagnosis now that the risk of transmission may be drastically reduced by medication. In fact, if "women take these drugs before and during birth, and their babies are given drugs after birth, HIV transmission is reduced from 25 percent to less than 2 percent (fewer than 2 in 100)" ("Pregnancy and Childbirth" 2007, n.p.). Men with HIV are beginning to hope for parenthood also, with a procedure called "sperm washing" designed to minimize transmission to a female partner (Cichocki 2009; Kolata 2002a).

Children with AIDS have a unique array of treatment requirements and are often in the hospital. Some are abandoned by their parents to hospital care. Others are raised by grandparents or foster parents. A new set of problems has arisen as babies with AIDS enter their teens. Clinical professionals report behavioral, emotional, and cognitive problems among some of these babies who have survived to adolescence. Public health workers have begun to take note of the teens' needs for services (Dee 2005; Hazra, Siberry, and Mofenson 2010).

HIV/AIDS and other sexually transmitted diseases are more than a medical or a family problem—they are conditions imbued with social meanings and consequences. Politics enters into decisions about policy related to HIV/AIDS—and policy regarding sexuality in general.

The Politics of Sex

One of the most striking changes over the past several decades has been the emergence of sexual and reproductive issues as political controversies. Religious and political conservatives and secular and religious individuals and organizations with a more liberal set of values—more open to nonmarital sexuality, for example—confront one another. Adding to the political mix, public health professionals approach policy from a research-based and pragmatic perspective, seeking the most effective means to achieve sexual and reproductive health goals.

Controversies over AIDS—and over how to educate youth about AIDS and about sex in general—illustrate the conflict between a morally neutral and pragmatic public health policy and a religious fundamentalist moral approach. Other sexuality issues engendering political conflict include abortion and contraception.

Political controversy has influenced both research and education about sexuality in the United States over the last few decades.

Politics and Research

At first, the emergence of AIDS seemed to legitimate sex research and lead to the funding of research on sexual behavior because of the implications for controlling the AIDS epidemic (Christopher and Sprecher 2000). The need for more comprehensive and current data on sexual behavior twice led to efforts to mount federally funded national sample surveys to be conducted by teams of well-respected social scientists. The studies were initially funded, but then Congress canceled a pilot study on the grounds that a sex survey would be too controversial. NORC conducted a much smaller, though national, sample survey without federal funds through the support of grants from private agencies.

A planned survey of 24,000 teens in grades seven to eleven was also canceled ("U.S. Scraps" 1991). Ironically, comparisons with other countries suggest that our society's tendency to deny sexuality at the same time we encourage it sends mixed messages that, among other negative consequences, probably help account for the unusually high rates of teen pregnancy and abortion in the United States (Dyess 2009; Risman and Schwartz 2002). The climate for the scientific study of sexuality has been hostile enough that "only the brave study sex" (Carey 2004). Whether this trend holds in the near future remains to be seen, although there have been some signs of change via the actions on the part of the Obama administration.

The politicization of research has taken other forms. Some reports of research that do not support the government position on an issue have been removed from government websites or changed after initial posting (Lewontin 2004; Rest and Halpern 2007; Simoncelli 2005). For example, a review of many studies which concluded that abortion does *not* cause breast cancer (contradicting the position of the National Right to Life movement) was removed from the National Cancer Institute website (Shulman 2008). On January 12, 2010, a new page was uploaded onto the National Cancer Institute website that noted scientists "concluded that having an abortion or miscarriage does not increase a woman's subsequent risk of developing breast cancer" (U.S. National Cancer Institute 2010). Research on sex education which found that providing information about contraception to teens does *not* increase their sexual activity was removed from the U.S. Centers for Disease Control and Prevention (CDC) website. The CDC fact sheet on condoms was changed to de-emphasize the protective value of condoms vis-à-vis HIV infection (Shulman 2008). On February 8, 2010, the U.S. Center for Disease Control and Prevention website uploaded a new page that said, "Consistent and correct use of male latex condoms can reduce (though not eliminate) the risk of STD transmission" ("Condoms and STDs: Fact Sheet for Public Health Personnel" 2010).

Adolescent Sexuality and Sex Education

Indeed, adolescents are sexually active; 47.8 percent of high school students responding to the 2007 Youth Risk Behavior Surveillance (Eaton et al. 2008) have had sexual intercourse. What may surprise you is that teen sexual intercourse has declined since 1991; in that year, 54 percent of high school youth had had intercourse. Studies suggest that males have changed more than females; a slim majority of high school males (50.2 percent) were virgins in 2007 (Eaton et al. 2008; Risman and Schwartz 2002). The downward trend in adolescent sexual intercourse (and births) predates the emphasis on "abstinence-only" sex education programs (Dailard 2003; "Improvements" 2006).

Experts attribute the decline in sexual intercourse to comprehensive sex education and to fear of sexual disease. Some have argued that sociosexual values have simply become more conservative generally, but that possibility has not been adequately researched (N. Bernstein 2004a; Risman and Schwartz 2002; Santelli et al. 2007). Data from the National Survey of Family Growth (1995 and 2002 waves) indicate that 86 percent of the decline in pregnancy risk is due to improved contraception (regular use, better methods), whereas only 14 percent is due to delayed sex (Santelli et al. 2007). These declines in pregnancy risk reversed in 2005, but the downward trend in teen births resumed in 2008 (Hamilton, Martin, and Ventura 2010).

Sociologist Frank Furstenberg, who has long researched teen sex, reproduction, and parenthood, as well as the transition to adulthood, believes that young people have observed how difficult it is in today's economy to establish a satisfying life if parenthood comes too early. He thinks that teenagers "getting the picture" might be a key element, as they strive to delay sex and prevent pregnancy to avoid the difficult lives they have seen around them (in N. Bernstein 2004a).

The decline in teen sexual activity has slowed in the twenty-first century, virtually "flat-lining" since 2001, except for declines in current sexual activity of black youth (Brenner et al. 2006; Feijoo 2004; "Improvements" 2006). Moreover, in assessing the decline of teen sexual activity, it is important to note that a lot depends on one's definition of sexual activity. Yes, sexual intercourse is less frequent among adolescents than in the past. It is also true that teens exhibit surprisingly high rates of oral sex: 55 percent of males ages fifteen through nineteen and 54 percent of females engage in oral sex (Mosher, Chandra, and Jones 2005, Tables 3 and 4). Many adolescents do not consider oral sex to be "sex" so they can still consider themselves virgins. They also seem to be attracted to oral sex because it does not present a risk of pregnancy (true) or of sexually transmitted disease (not true).

Sex Education Current controversy centers on whether sex education should be "abstinence only" or "abstinence plus" (also termed "comprehensive"). Since 1996, the federal government has taken the official position that abstention from sexual relations unless in a monogamous marriage is the only protection against sexually transmitted disease and pregnancy—and that abstinence is the only morally and rationally appropriate principle of sexual conduct. "Abstinence-only" programs may mention contraception, if at all, only to cite allegedly high failure rates. Programs are urged to convey to students that nonmarital sex for people *of any age* is likely to have harmful physical and psychological effects (J. Brody 2004; Dailard 2002).

Surveys of parents indicate that they prefer that an "abstinence-plus" sex education program be presented in the schools, one that would include contraception and AIDS prevention as well as promotion of abstinence. As Figure 5.5 indicates, more than 74 percent of adults "approve of health education classes that teach about sex and abstinence," and 49 percent believe abstinence-only classes have some impact on preventing teen pregnancy (Rasmussen Reports 2009). Yet, a substantial and growing number of school sex education programs are "abstinence only," as government funding is limited to such programs (Lindberg, Santelli, and Singh 2006).

Research indicates that comprehensive sex education programs (those that include contraception) do not lead to any earlier commencement of sexual activity; in fact,

Percentage of adults who say that sex education is primarily the responsibility of parents (not schools) **	80%
Percentage of married adults who say that sex education is primarily the responsibility of parents (not schools) **	83
Percentage of unmarried adults who say that sex education is primarily the responsibility of parents (not schools) **	74
Percentage of adults who also approve of school health classes that include sex education **	74
Percentage of parents of high school students who say sex education should cover . . .	
HIV/AIDS	99
How to talk with parents about sex and relationship issues*	98
The basics of how babies are made, pregnancy, and birth	97
Waiting to have sexual intercourse until older	96
How to get tested for HIV and other STDs	96
How to deal with the emotional issues and consequences of being sexually active*	96
Waiting to have sexual intercourse until married*	94
How to talk with a girlfriend or boyfriend about "how far to go sexually"*	94
Birth control and methods of preventing pregnancy	93
How to use and where to get contraceptives	85
Abortion*	83
How to put on a condom*	79
That teens can obtain birth control pills . . . without permission from a parent*	73
Homosexuality and sexual orientation*	73

Figure 5.5 Who should teach children about sex, and what parents want sex education to teach their children.

* Questions marked with an asterisk were asked of only half the sample.

**Questions marked with a double asterisk were asked in a 2009 telephone survey by Rasmussen Reports.

Source: Survey of 1,001 parents of children in seventh to twelfth grade sponsored by National Public Radio (NPR)/Kaiser Family Foundation/Kennedy School of Government (2004). The survey was conducted in September/October 2003. *The high school parent subsample = 450.

** Rasmussen Reports National Survey of 1,000 Adults, conducted January 12-13, 2009.

Reports National Survey of 1,000 Adults, conducted January 12–13, 2009.

research indicates that comprehensive sex education delays the start of sexual activity. "Encouraging abstinence and urging better use of contraception are compatible goals" (Kirby 2001, p. 18). There is as yet no evidence that "abstinence-only" programs are effective in delaying sex or preventing pregnancy, nor are they scientifically accurate. The federal government's own study of the effectiveness and accuracy of its federally funded abstinence-only education programs found them wanting ("The Abstinence-Only Delusion" 2007; Begley 2007; J. Brody 2004; "Conclusions Are Reported" 2007; Kirby, Laris, and Rolleri 2006; Crosse 2008, p. 5). In fact, the only abstinence-based education program that was effective (although only slightly) at delaying sex would not have qualified to be taught in middle schools because it did not meet the federal mandated guidelines. This recent study examined abstinence-focused education and found a link between such education and a reduction in sexual activity in twelve-year-old African American children. This study of 662 children found that, two years after the abstinence-focused course, the children who took it had slightly reduced sexual activity, compared with those who had taken a traditional sex education course (Guttmacher Advisory 2010; Jemmott, Jemmott, and Fong 2010; Schlesinger 2010).

While abstinence-only education is ineffective in delaying sex, early research found that virginity pledges taken in certain circumstances seemed to delay adolescent sexual activity (Bearman and Brückner 2001), but later research has found no difference in delay of sexual activity between those who take the pledge and those who do not (Rosenbaum 2009; Tanne 2009; Thomas 2009). Recent research also found that once these teens become sexually active, they do so without precautions and have higher rates of pregnancy and STDs than other teens (Altman 2004; Rosenbaum 2009, p. e114).

Those results compare adolescents who are still minors. A study based on the National Longitudinal Study of Adolescent Health, which compared young adults (nineteen through twenty-five) who had made a virginity pledge and those who had not, found that contraceptive use did not differ at this later point. Both groups had high rates of intercourse (89.7 percent and 75 percent, respectively) and other sexual activity. In other words, "by the time they become young adults, some 81 percent of pledgers have engaged in some type of sexual activity" (Rector and Johnson 2005, p. 13).

Sex education needs to take into account the teen propensity to engage in oral sex and to consider it risk-free despite high rates of STDs among youth (Halpern-Felsher et al. 2005). Moreover, the first experience for a small proportion of teens—7.8 percent—is forced sex (Eaton et al. 2008). Some others' experiences are ambiguous as to wantedness (Houts 2005).

Sex education programs may emphasize peer pressure, troubled families and neighborhoods, or hormonal processes and rarely consider the broad array of teen motivations for sexual activity. It seems that both adolescent males and females seek sex because they expect it to meet needs for intimacy, sexual pleasure, and social status (Ott et al. 2006). These issues need to be taken into account in sex education programs. Long-time sex education researcher Douglas Kirby and his colleagues have identified some programs that seem effective in discouraging early sexual activity and sexual risks (Kirby, Laris, and Rolleri 2006).

Sexual Responsibility

People today are making decisions about sex in a climate characterized by political conflict over sexual issues. Premarital and other nonmarital sex, homosexuality, abortion, and contraception represent political issues as well as personal choices. Public and private communication must rise to new levels. The AIDS epidemic has brought the importance of sexual responsibility to our attention in a dramatic way.

Making knowledgeable choices is a must. Because there are various standards today concerning sex, all individuals must determine what sexual standard they value, which is not always easy. Today's adults may be exposed to several different standards throughout the course of their lives. Even when individuals feel that they have clear values, applications to particular situations may be difficult. A person who believes in the standard of sexual permissiveness with affection, for example, must determine when a particular relationship is affectionate enough.

Making these choices and feeling comfortable with them requires recognizing and respecting your own values, instead of just being influenced by others when in a sexual situation. Anxiety may accompany the choice to develop a sexual relationship, and there is considerable potential for misunderstanding between partners. This

Eric K. K. Yu/CORBIS

Intimacy and sexuality require communication—physical as well as verbal—from both partners. Sexuality has become more expressive and less patriarchal in the United States, and each generation finds itself reevaluating sexual assumptions, behaviors, and standards.

section addresses some principles of sexual responsibility that may serve as guidelines for sexual decision making.

One obvious responsibility concerns the possibility of pregnancy. Partners should plan responsibly whether, when, and how they will conceive children and then use effective birth control methods accordingly.

A second responsibility concerns the possibility of contracting STDs or transmitting them to someone else. Individuals should be aware of the facts concerning HIV/AIDS and other STDs. They need to assume responsibility for protecting themselves and their partners. They need to know how to recognize the symptoms of an STD and what to do if they get one (see Appendix C).

A third responsibility concerns communicating with partners or potential sexual partners. As we've seen in this chapter, sex may mean many different things to different people. A sexual encounter may mean love and intimacy to one partner and be a source of achievement or relaxation to the other. Honesty lessens the potential for misunderstanding and hurt between partners.

A fourth responsibility is to oneself. In expressing sexuality today, each of us must make decisions according to our own values. A person may choose to follow values held on the basis of religious commitment or put forth by ethicists or by psychologists or counselors. People's values change over the course of their lives, and what's right at one time may not appear so later. Despite the confusion caused both by internal changes as our personalities develop and by the social changes going on around us, it is important for individuals to make thoughtful decisions about sexual relationships.

Summary

- Social attitudes and values play an important role in the forms of sexual expression that people find appropriate and enjoyable.
- Despite decades of conjecture and research, it is still unclear just how sexual orientation develops and whether it is genetic or socially shaped. Recent decades have witnessed increased acceptance of gay, lesbian, bisexual, and transgender (GLBT) individuals, though some disapproval, discrimination, and hostility remain.
- Whatever one's sexual orientation, sexual expression is negotiated amid cultural messages about what is sexually permissible or desirable. In the United States, these cultural messages have moved from patriarchal sex, based on male dominance and on reproduction as its principal purpose, to a message that encourages sexual expressiveness in myriad ways for both genders equally.
- Four standards of nonmarital sex are abstinence, permissiveness with affection, permissiveness without affection, and the double standard—the latter diminished since the 1960s, but is still alive. Extramarital sex is not approved, but it does occur and represents a challenge to marital trust.
- Marital sex changes throughout the life course. Young spouses have sex more often than do older mates. Although the frequency of sexual intercourse declines over time and through the length of a marriage, some 27 percent of married people over age seventy-four are sexually active.
- Making sex a pleasure bond, whether a couple is married or not, involves cooperation in a nurturing, caring relationship. To fully cooperate sexually, partners need to develop high self-esteem, to break free from restrictive gendered stereotypes, and to communicate openly.
- HIV/AIDS has had an impact on relationships, marriages, and families.
- Sexuality, sexual expression, and sex education are public issues at present, and different segments of American society have divergent views.
- Whatever the philosophical or religious grounding of one's perspective on sexuality, there are certain guidelines for personal sexual responsibility that we should all heed.

Questions for Review and Reflection

1. Give some examples to illustrate changes in sexual behavior and social attitudes about sex. What might change in the future?
2. Do you think that sex is changing from "his and hers" to "theirs"? What do you see as some difficulties in making this transition?
3. Discuss what you've learned about the nature of sexual relationships. What did you find useful and relevant to everyday life? What seems remote from real-world experience?
4. How do you think HIV/AIDS affects sex and sex relationships—or does it?
5. **Policy Question.** What role, if any, has government policy played in sex education, research and information on sex, and sexual regulation?

Key Terms

abstinence 117
asexual 110
asexuality 109
bisexual 109
cyberadultery 121
double standard 119
emotion labor 125
expressive sexuality 113
friends with benefits 119
gay 109
GLBT 110
habituation 125
habituation hypothesis 121
heterosexism 114
heterosexuals 108
HIV/AIDS 127
homophobia 114
homosexuals 108
hooking up 119
interactionist perspective on human sexuality 112
interpersonal exchange model of sexual satisfaction 111
lesbian 109
patriarchal sexuality 112
permissiveness with affection 118
permissiveness without affection 119
pleasure bond 126
sexting 116
sexual orientation 108
sexual responsibility 126
sexual scripts 112

Online Resources

Sociology CourseMate

www.CengageBrain.com

Access an integrated eBook, chapter-specific interactive learning tools, including flash cards, quizzes, videos, and more in your Sociology CourseMate, accessed through CengageBrain.com.

www.CengageBrain.com

Want to maximize your online study time? Take this easy-to-use study system's diagnostic pre-test, and it will create a personalized study plan for you. By helping you identify the topics that you need to understand better and then directing you to valuable online resources, it can speed up your chapter review. CengageNOW even provides a post-test so you can confirm that you are ready for an exam.

6

Love and Choosing a Life Partner

Almost three-quarters of young adults believe in "one true love," and more than 90 percent would like a "soul mate" (Robison 2003; Whitehead and Popenoe 2001). We all want to be loved, and most of us expect to be in a committed relationship—if not now, then in the future. Being in a committed relationship involves selecting someone with whom to become emotionally and sexually intimate and, often, with whom to raise children. Accordingly, the choice of a partner is a major life course decision. In Chapter 1, Figure 1.2, "The Cycle of Knowledgeable Decision Making," illustrates that making knowledgeable decisions requires an awareness of one's personal beliefs and values, as well as conscious consideration of alternatives and serious thought about the probable consequences. You may want to refer to Figure 1.2 as you study this chapter.

Research suggests that the best way to choose a life partner is to look for someone to love who is socially responsible, respectful, and emotionally supportive. It is also important that the person is committed both to the relationship and to the value of staying together. Lastly, it helps if that person also demonstrates good communication and problem-solving skills (Bradbury and Karney 2004; Hetherington 2003).

Equally important, research findings suggest looking for a mate with values that resemble one's own, because similar values and attitudes are strong predictors of ongoing happiness and relationship stability. Although romantic love is usually a very important ingredient (Amato 2007), successful life partnerships are also based on partners' maturity, common goals, qualities of friendship, and the soundness of their reasons for getting together (Gaunt 2006; Lacey et al. 2004).

In this chapter, we'll look at some things that influence the choice of a life partner and subsequent relationship satisfaction. We will examine how a relationship develops and proceeds from first meeting to commitment. We will also discuss interreligious and interracial unions. We'll examine research on how cohabiting before marriage affects marital stability. To begin, we explore some things that we know about love.

Nearly three-quarters of women and almost two-thirds of men marry by age thirty; by age forty, more than 80 percent of Americans have married (Goodwin, McGill, and Chandra 2009). By age twenty-four, more Americans are married than cohabiting (Saad 2008b). Therefore, the topic of choosing a marriage partner is critically important. Meanwhile, we need to note here that research and published counseling advice on choosing a committed life partner have focused almost solely on heterosexual, *marital* mate selection. One reason for this situation is that choosing a marriage partner is more easily identifiable for researchers—one is either married or not—whereas the existence and nature of committed, lifelong relationships outside marriage are harder to identify and research.

Furthermore, although more than three-quarters of Americans who have divorced remarry within ten years (Bramlett and Mosher 2001), research tends to focus on choosing a spouse for a first marriage. However, much of what is said in this chapter can probably be applied to choosing a partner for a committed nonmarital relationship and for remarriages as well. Research specifically related to choosing a spouse for remarriage is discussed in Chapter 16.

Love and Commitment

"With respect to love, the gap between everyday people and family scholars is surprisingly wide.... [M]ost researchers have avoided the topic.... Yet attitude surveys reveal that the great majority of Americans view love as the primary reason for getting and staying married" (Amato 2007, p. 306).

> Romantic love can be defined in multiple ways. For example, one definition might be that romantic love is a strong emotional bond with another person that involves sexual desire, a longing to be with the person, a preference to put the other person's interests ahead of one's own, and a willingness to forgive the other person's transgressions. (Amato 2007, p. 206)

With the obvious exceptions of physical and emotional abuse, loving involves the acceptance of partners for themselves and "not for their ability to change themselves or to meet another's requirements to play a role" (Dahms 1976, p. 100). People are free to be themselves in a loving relationship, and to expose their feelings, frailties, and strengths (Armstrong 2003). Related to this acceptance is caring, or empathy—the concern a person has for the partner's growth and the willingness to "affirm [the partner's] potentialities" (May 1975, p. 116; Jaksch 2002).

Psychologist Erich Fromm (1956) chastises Americans for their emphasis on wanting to *be loved* rather than on learning to *love*. Many of the ways we make ourselves lovable, Fromm writes, "are the same as those used to make oneself successful, 'to win friends and influence people.' As a matter of fact, what most people in our culture mean by being lovable is essentially a mixture between being popular and having sex appeal" (p. 2). Showing empathy, of course, is something very different and is essential in loving relationships (Ciaramigoli and Ketcham 2000). Rollo May defines empathy, or caring, as a state "composed of the recognition of another; a fellow human being like one's self; of identification of one's self with the pain or joy of the other" (1969, p. 289). In addition to empathy, loving someone requires commitment.

Maintaining a loving relationship requires commitment of both partners (Dixon 2007). Committing oneself to another person involves working to develop a relationship "where experiences cover many areas

Jack Hollingsworth/Photolibrary

Marriages between individuals with a relatively secure attachment style that take place after about age twenty-five and are between partners who grew up in intact (nondivorced) families are the most likely to be satisfying and stable. But having grown up as a child of divorce does *not* mean that an individual will *necessarily* have an unhappy or unstable marriage.

of personality; where problems are worked through; where conflict is expected and seen as a normal part of the growth process; and where there is an expectation that the relationship is basically viable and worthwhile" (Altman and Taylor 1973, pp. 184–87; Amato 2007).

Committed lovers have fun together; they also share more tedious times. They express themselves freely and authentically (Smalley 2000). Committed partners view their relationship as worth keeping, and they work to maintain it despite difficulties or disagreements (Amato 2007; Love 2001). **Commitment** is characterized by this willingness to work through problems and conflicts as opposed to calling it quits when problems arise. In this view, commitment involves consciously investing in the relationship (Etcheverry and Le 2005). Then too, committed partners "regularly, routinely, and predictably attend to each other and their relationship no matter how they feel" (Peck 1978, p. 118). Psychological research expands upon these ideas; the following section is an example.

Sternberg's Triangular Theory of Love

In research on relationships varying in length from one month to thirty-six years, psychologist Robert Sternberg (1988a, 1988b, 2006) found three components necessary to authentic love: intimacy, passion, and commitment (see also Overbeek et al. 2007). According to **Sternberg's triangular theory of love**, *intimacy* "refers to close, connected, and bonded feelings in a loving relationship. It includes feelings that create the experience of warmth in a loving relationship... [such as] experiencing happiness with the loved one;...sharing one's self and one's possessions with the loved one; receiving...and giving emotional support to the loved one; [and] having intimate communication with the loved one" (Sternberg 1988a, pp. 120–21).

Passion "refers to the drives that lead to romance, physical attraction, sexual consummation, and the like in a loving relationship" (Sternberg 1988a, pp. 120–21). *Commitment*—the "decision/commitment component of love"—consists of not only deciding to love someone, but also deciding to maintain that love. **Consummate love** (see Figure 6.1), composed of all three components, is "complete love,... a kind of love toward which many of us strive, especially in romantic relationships" (Sternberg 1988a, pp. 120–21).

The three components of consummate love develop at different times, as love grows and changes: "Passion is the quickest to develop, and the quickest to fade.... Intimacy develops more slowly, and commitment more gradually still" (Sternberg, quoted in Goleman 1985). Passion, or "chemistry," peaks early in the relationship but generally continues at a stable, although fluctuating, level and remains important both to our good health

Facts about Families

Six Love Styles

Relationships evidence different characteristics or personalities. John Alan Lee (1973) classified six love styles, initially based on interviews with 120 white, heterosexual respondents of both genders. Lee subsequently applied his typology to same-sex relationships (Lee 1981). Researchers then developed a Love Attitudes Scale (LAS): eighteen to twenty-four questions that measure Lee's typology (Hendrick, Hendrick, and Dicke 1998). Although not all subsequent research has found all six dimensions, this typology of love styles has withstood the test of time, has proven to be more than hypothetical, and may even have cross-cultural relevance (Lacey et al. 2004; Le 2005; Masanori, Daibo, and Kanemasa 2004).

Love styles are sets of distinctive characteristics that loving or lovelike relationships take. The word *lovelike* is included in this definition because not all love styles amount to genuine loving as this chapter defines it. People may incorporate different aspects of several styles into their relationships. What are Lee's six love styles?

1. **Eros** (AIR-ohs) is a Greek word meaning "love"; it forms the root of our word *erotic*. This love style is characterized by intense emotional attachment and powerful sexual feelings or desires. When erotic couples establish sustained relationships, these are characterized by continued emotionally intense sexual interest. A sample question on the Love Attitudes Scale (LAS) designed to measure eros asks respondents to agree or disagree with the following: "My partner and I have the right chemistry between us" (Hendrick, Hendrick, and Dicke 1998).
2. **Storge** (STOR-gay) is an affectionate, companionate style of loving. This love style focuses on deepening mutual commitment, respect, friendship over time, and common goals. Storgic lovers' basic attitudes to their partners are one of familiarity: "I've known you a long time, seen you in many moods" (Lee 1973, p. 87). Storgic lovers are likely to agree that "I always expect to be friends with the one I love" (Hendrick, Hendrick, and Dicke 1998).
3. **Pragma** (PRAG-mah) is the root word for *pragmatic*. Pragmatic love emphasizes the practical element in human relationships and rational assessment of a potential partner's assets and liabilities. Arranged marriages are often examples of pragma. So is a person who decides very rationally to get married to a suitable partner. The following is one LAS statement that measures pragma: "A main consideration in choosing a partner is/was how he/she would reflect on my family" (Hendrick, Hendrick, and Dicke 1998).
4. **Agape** (ah-GAH-pay) is a Greek word meaning "love feast." Agape

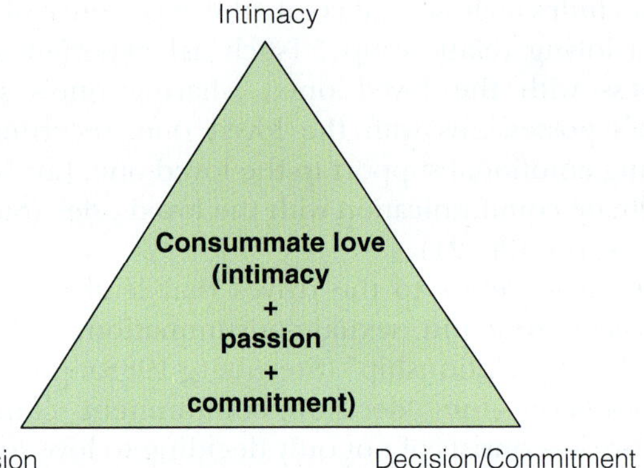

Figure 6.1 The three components of love: triangular theory.

Source: Adapted from "Triangular Love," by Robert J. Sternberg (1988a), Figure 6.1, p. 121. In Robert J. Steinberg and Michael L. Barnes (eds.), *The Psychology of Love*. Copyright © 1988 Yale University Press. Adapted by permission.

(Kluger 2004) and to the long-term maintenance of the relationship (Love 2001). Intimacy, which includes conveying and understanding each other's needs, listening to and supporting each other, and sharing common values, becomes increasingly important as time goes on. In fact, psychologist and marriage counselor Gary Smalley (2000) argues that a couple is typically together for about six years before the two feel safe enough to share their deepest relational needs with one another.

Commitment is essential; however, commitment without intimacy and some level of passion is hollow. In other words, all these elements of love are important. Because these components not only develop at different rates but also exist in various combinations of intensity, a relationship is always changing, if only subtly (Sternberg 1988b). In addition to Sternberg's model, attachment-theory scholars (see Chapter 2) offer insight into loving relationships.

Attachment Theory and Loving Relationships

Applying attachment theory to loving relationships, we can presume that people with more secure attachment styles would have less ambivalence about emotional closeness and commitment. "Secure attachment, in part, depends on regarding the relationship partner as being available in times of need and as trustworthy" (Kurdek 2006, p. 510). In Figure 6.2, attachment style is incorporated in *beliefs and attitudes about the partner or the relationship*.

We might therefore conclude that those with a *secure* attachment style are better prospects for a committed relationship (Rauer and Volling 2007). An *insecure/anxious* emphasizes unselfish concern for a beloved's needs even when that requires personal sacrifice. Often called *altruistic love*, agape emphasizes nurturing others with little conscious desire for a return other than the intrinsic satisfaction of having loved and cared for someone else. Agapic lovers would likely agree that, "I try to always help my partner through difficult times" (Hendrick, Hendrick, and Dicke 1998).

5. **Ludus** (LEWD-us) focuses on love as play or fun. Ludus emphasizes the recreational aspects of sexuality and enjoying many sexual partners rather than searching for one serious relationship. Of course, ludic flirtation and playful sexuality may be part of a more committed relationship based on one of the other love styles. LAS questions designed to measure ludus include the following: "I enjoy playing the game of love with a number of different partners" (Hendrick, Hendrick, and Dicke 1998).
6. **Mania**, a Greek word, designates a wild or violent mental disorder, an obsession, or a craze. Mania involves strong sexual attraction and emotional intensity, as does eros. However, mania differs from eros in that manic partners are extremely jealous and moody, and their need for attention and affection is insatiable. Manic lovers alternate between euphoria and depression. The slightest lack of response from a love partner causes anxiety and resentment. Manic lovers would be likely to say, "When my partner doesn't pay attention to me, I feel sick all over" or "I cannot relax if I feel my partner is with someone else" (Hendrick, Hendrick, and Dicke 1998). Because one of its principal characteristics is extreme jealousy, we may learn of manic love in the news when a relationship ends violently. Of Lee's six love styles, mania least fits our definition of love, described earlier.

How do these love styles influence relationship satisfaction and continuity? Psychologists Marilyn Montgomery and Gwendolyn Sorell (1997) administered the LAS to 250 single college students and married adults of all ages. They found that eros can last throughout marriage and is related to high satisfaction. Agape is also positively associated with relationship satisfaction (Neimark 2003). Interestingly, Montgomery and Sorell found storge to be important only in marriages with children. Ludus did not necessarily diminish relationship satisfaction among those who are mutually uncommitted. However, ludic attitudes have been empirically associated with diminished long-term relationship and marital satisfaction (Le 2005; Montgomery and Sorell 1997).

attachment style entails "fear of abandonment" with consequent possible negative behaviors such as unwarranted jealousy or attempts to control one's partner. An *avoidant* attachment style leads one to pass up or shun closeness and intimacy either by evading relationships altogether or demonstrating ambivalence, seeming preoccupied, or otherwise distancing oneself (Benoit and Parker 1994; Fletcher 2002; Hazen and Shaver 1994).

The attachment style of one's partner can either magnify or lessen the effects of one's own attachment style. For example, if both individuals are insecure and anxious, the relationship will be characterized that way as well. On the other hand, a person with an insecure attachment style who is in a committed relationship with someone having a secure attachment style may gradually learn to feel more secure (Banse 2004). Individual or relationship therapy may help people change their attachment style.

Attachment theory and Sternberg's triangular theory of love are not the only ways of looking at love, of course. "Facts about Families: Six Love Styles" analyzes love in yet a third way. Still another way to better understand love is to think about what love is *not*. We turn now to an examination of three things love isn't: martyring, manipulating, and limerence.

Three Things Love Isn't

Love is not inordinate self-sacrifice. And, loving is not the continual attempt to get others to feel or do what we want them to—although each of these ideas is frequently mistaken for love. Nor is love all those crazy feelings you get when you can't get someone out of your mind. We'll examine these misconceptions in some detail.

Martyring **Martyring** involves maintaining relationships by consistently minimizing one's own needs while trying to satisfy those of one's partner. Periods of self-sacrifice are necessary through difficult times. However, as a premise of a relationship, excessive self-sacrifice or martyring is unworkable. Martyrs may have good intentions, believing that love involves doing unselfishly for others without voicing their own needs in return. Consequently, however, martyrs seldom feel that they receive genuine affection. A martyr's reluctance to express his or her needs is damaging to a relationship, for it prevents openness and intimacy.

Manipulating Manipulators follow this maxim: If I can get her [or him] to do what I want done, then I'll be sure she [or he] loves me. **Manipulating** means seeking to control the feelings, attitudes, and behavior of your partner or partners in underhanded ways rather than by directly (not abusively!) stating your case. When not getting their way, manipulators are likely to find fault with a partner, sometimes with verbal abuse. "You don't really love me," they may accuse. Manipulating, like martyring, can destroy a relationship.

Limerence Have you ever been so taken with someone that you couldn't get him or her out of your mind? Although the object of your attention may be unaware of your feelings, you review every detail of the last time you saw him or her and fantasize about how you might actually develop a relationship. Psychologist Dorothy Tennov (1999 [1979]) named this situation limerence (LIM-er-ence). She makes the following points: First, limerence is not just "lust" or sexual attraction. People in limerence fantasize about being with the limerent object in all kinds of situations—not just sexual ones. Second, many of us have experienced limerence. Third, limerence can possibly turn into genuine love, but more often than not, it doesn't.

People discover love; they don't simply find it. The term *discovering* implies a process—developing and maintaining a loving relationship require seeing the relationship as valuable, committing to mutual needs, satisfaction, and self-disclosure, engaging in supportive communication, and spending time together. We now turn to factors that affect how that love pla ys into the selection of a life partner.

Mate Selection and Relationship Stability

Designed to apply to same-sex unions as well as to heterosexual marriages, Figure 6.2 depicts a model of factors that affect relationship stability—whether partners remain together over time (Kurdek 2006). Relationship stability, happiness, and satisfaction depend upon how the partners interact with each other as well as on the perceived social support the couple receives from family members, friends, and the community in general. How partners interact with each other, in turn, depends upon a person's ideas about the partner and the relationship. These beliefs and attitudes depend, in turn at least partly, upon the personality traits that each partner brings to the union (Kurdek 2006, p. 510).

As an example, let's say that Fran and Maria are considering marriage. Each wonders about the odds of

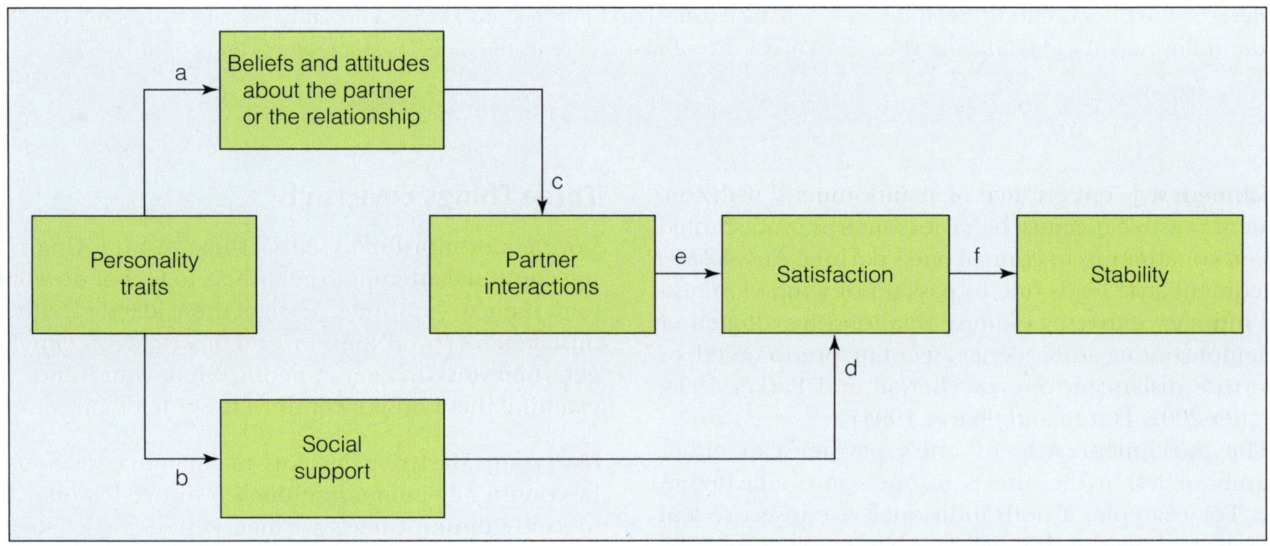

Figure 6.2 A time-ordered sequential model of relationship outcomes.

"The model has six components that form a time-ordered sequence of six linkages (letters a through f). The [personality traits] component refers to personality traits partners bring to their relationships that affect both the manner in which the relationship events are appraised (...[beliefs and attitudes about the relationship]; Link a) and the quality of perceived social support that is received (Link b)....The [beliefs and attitudes about the partner or the relationship] component refers to beliefs and attitudes about the partner or the relationship that affect how partners interact with each other (Link c).... The component social support underscores the view that intimate relationships coexist with other personal relationships, particularly those involving friends and family members....The partner interactions component represents how partners behave toward one another and [along with social support, Link d] forms another basis for overall satisfaction with the relationship (Link e)....Relationship satisfaction refers to the overall level of positive affect experienced in the relationship and the extent to which important personal needs are being met in the relationship and is one determinant of relationship stability (Link f)" (adapted from Kurdek 2006, pp.510–11).

staying married (**marital stability**). First, Maria and Fran need to take their personality traits into account. Is Fran thoughtful, dependable, reliable, and honest? Is Maria? Is one or both prepared to support a family? What beliefs and attitudes do they have about each other and about their relationship? Does Fran believe that marriage to Maria is likely to result in marital satisfaction? Or is Fran marrying Maria despite misgivings about her or the relationship? Does Maria believe that marital stability is likely for her? Or does she see this marriage as likely to end in divorce but "worth a try" anyway? Positive attitudes about the relationship, coupled with realistically positive assessments of a prospective spouse's personality traits, are important to marital stability.

According to this model, Maria and Fran's respective personality traits influence the degree of social support that they will receive—and believe that they receive—from family members and friends. More perceived social support will result in greater marital satisfaction. Then too, Fran and Maria's beliefs and attitudes about each other and about their relationship will affect how they interact with each other. Will they—do they now—interact primarily in supportive ways? Do they handle conflict well? Supportive interaction results in greater marital satisfaction. Greater marital satisfaction, in turn, results in the greater likelihood of marital stability.

Other chapters in this text focus on various aspects of partner interactions and social support. Here we focus on choosing a partner who is best predisposed psychologically to maintain a stable and committed relationship.

Psychologists and counselors advise choosing a partner who is integrated into society by means of school, employment, a network of friends, and who fairly consistently demonstrates supportive communication and problem-solving skills (Cotton, Burton, and Rushing 2003). We're reminded that, "Heavy or risky drinking is associated with a host of marital difficulties including infidelity, divorce, violence and conflict" (L. Roberts 2005, p. F13). The same can be said for other forms of substance abuse (Kaye 2005, F15). Furthermore, research shows that relationships are more likely to be stable when partners' parents have not been divorced.

The Intergenerational Transmission of Divorce Risk

Either because they know the statistics, have divorced friends, or have experienced their parents' divorce, many young adults are cautious about getting married and possibly going through the pain and economic upheaval of divorce, especially if they plan to have children (Arnett 2004; Wallerstein 2008). It is important to remember that assuredly not all children of divorced parents will themselves divorce. No one is suggesting that a child of divorced parents be automatically rejected as a future spouse, and not all researchers agree that there is an intergenerational transmission of divorce risk (Li and Wu 2008). However, "[s]tudies based on large national samples consistently show that parental divorce increases the risk of marital instability in offspring" (Hetherington 2003, p. 325; Teachman 2004). Cross-national research has also found this to be true in industrialized countries besides the United States (Dronkers and Harkonen 2008). When both spouses come from divorced families, the probability of their own divorce is still higher (Amato and DeBoer 2001; Wolfinger 2005).

Family scholars refer to this phenomenon as the **intergenerational transmission of divorce risk**: A divorced parental family transmits to its children a heightened risk of getting divorced. Noting that "apparently, there is something in the divorce experience beyond that of parental conflict that exacerbates problems in stability in intimate relations in offspring" (Hetherington 2003, p. 326), researchers have suggested the following four hypotheses to explain the intergenerational transmission of divorce risk. Children of divorce are themselves more likely to get divorced because they have:

1. more—and more serious—personality problems
2. neither been exposed to nor learned supportive communication or problem-solving skills
3. less commitment to the relationship
4. more accepting attitudes toward divorce (Dunne, Hudgins, and Babcock 2000; Hetherington 2003; Hetherington and Kelly 2002; Wolfinger 2005)

We might also hypothesize that children of divorce, as a category, are less likely to have developed a secure attachment style, discussed previously.

After what we've said here, it is important to emphasize that children of divorce will themselves not *necessarily* divorce (Zimmerman and Thayer 2003). Research shows that a supportive, well-adjusted partner "can play a protective role" in minimizing the intergenerational transmission of divorce risk. Prominent researcher on children of divorce, E. Mavis Hetherington (2003) has described her findings on this point:

> Under conditions of low stress with a supportive partner, there was no difference in couple instability between the offspring of divorced and nondivorced parents. For these well-married youths in a benign environment, no intergenerational transmission of marital instability was found. Under conditions of high stress, there was a marginally significant trend for the offspring of divorced parents, even with a supportive partner, to show somewhat more marital instability than those from nondivorced families. (p. 328)

Minimizing Mate Selection Risk

Mate selection plays a part in the intergenerational transmission of divorce risk because individuals from divorced families are themselves more inclined to have the characteristics described earlier and to choose partners who have them. Hetherington (2003) reports her findings concerning **mate selection risk** as follows:

> Youths from divorced families were more likely to select high-risk partners who were also from divorced families and who were impulsive, socially irresponsible, and had a history of antisocial behaviors such as alcohol and drug abuse, minor misdemeanors, troubles with the law, problems in school and at work, fighting, and an unstable job history. (p. 328)

Other research has found that *mate selection risk* may apply to adult children of alcoholics as well as to those of divorce (Olmsted, Crowell, and Waters 2003). What can one do to minimize mate selection risk?

A first step in minimizing mate selection risk is to let go of misconceptions we might have about love and choosing a partner. Selecting a partner wisely involves balancing any insistence on perfection against the need to be mindful of one's real needs and desires. In the absence of adequate role models for maintaining a supportive relationship, many of us may embrace misconceptions about finding a partner. For instance, we might believe that "I can be happy with anyone I choose, if I work hard enough," or that "Falling in love with someone is sufficient" (Cobb, Larson, and Watson 2003, p. 223). However, working things out requires both partners' willingness and ability to do so; just one's own willingness to work hard at a marriage is not enough. Furthermore, if having fallen in love is assumed to be enough to make a union last, then other, potentially detrimental partner characteristics may be minimized. Generally, long-term relationships built on "respect, mutual support and affirmation of each other's worth are more likely to survive" (Hetherington 2003, p. 322).

Later in this chapter, the section "Some Things to Talk About" gives other ideas on assessing your own and a prospective partner's values and attitudes. Of course, it's important to be truthful when relating with a potential partner, as well as to ascertain how truthful a partner is being (S. Campbell 2004). Some couples go to counseling to assess their future compatibility and commitment (Marech 2004). Others may access marital compatibility tests on the Internet. Although we, your authors, are unable to attest to the efficacy of these, they do stimulate couple discussions about important topics. At this point, we turn to the social science analogy of choosing a mate in a marketplace.

The Marriage Market

Imagine a large marketplace in which people come with goods to exchange for other items. In nonindustrialized societies, a person may go to market with a few chickens to trade for some vegetables. In more industrialized societies, people attend hockey equipment swaps, for example, trading outgrown skates for larger ones. People choose partners in much the same way: They enter the *market* (traditionally called the **marriage market**) armed with resources—personal and social characteristics—and then they bargain for the best "buy" that they can get.

Arranged and Free-Choice Marriages

In much of the world, particularly in parts of Asia and Africa that are less Westernized, parents have traditionally arranged their children's marriages. In **arranged marriage**, future spouses can be brought together in various ways. For example, in India, parents typically check prospective partners' astrological charts to assure future compatibility. Traditionally, the parents of both prospective partners (often with other relatives' or a paid matchmaker's help) worked out the details and then announced the upcoming marriage to their children. The children may have had little or no say in the matter, and they may not have met their future spouse until the wedding. However, today it is more common for the children to marry only when they themselves accept their parents' choice. Unions like these, sometimes called "assisted marriages," can be found among some Muslim groups and other recent immigrants to the United States (Ingoldsby 2006b; MacFarquhar 2006). Research shows that—at least at first—couples who have had more input report greater marital satisfaction (Madathil and Benshoff 2008).

Arranged marriage is still practiced, but the custom is waning (Zang 2008). Arranged marriage was observed throughout most of the world into the twentieth century—and well into the eighteenth century in Western Europe. As pointed out in "My Family: An Asian Indian American Student's Essay on Arranged Marriages," we can still find arranged marriages in many parts of the less industrialized world today. The majority of young couples in cultures that have traditionally practiced arranged marriage continue to heed extended family members' opinions about a prospective mate (Zhang and Kline 2009).

The fact that marriages are arranged doesn't mean that love is ignored by parents. Indeed, marital love may be highly valued. However, couples in arranged marriages are expected to develop a loving relationship *after* the marriage, not before (Tepperman and Wilson 1993). A study that compared marital satisfaction among arranged marriages in India to those more

My Family

An Asian Indian American Student's Essay on Arranged Marriages

The college student who wrote the following essay is the daughter of Asian Indian immigrants to California. Her essay points out that some people in the United States experience arranged marriages today and that arranged marriage is changing.

My parents had an arranged marriage twenty-three years ago and are still married to this day. Their wedding day was the first time they saw each other, and even then it was just a quick glance. A mutual friend of both families mentioned… that their kids would be a good match. So my mom's parents… interviewed my dad. My grandparents took into consideration various things like my dad's height, weight, education, family background, age, income, house, and health….

My dad's parents did the same thing to my mom. They went to see… whether they liked her. One of their main concerns was what their grandchildren would look like. So they wanted a tall, pretty, healthy wife for their son. Both sets of parents agreed to the other's child, and the deal was made. Both sets of my grandparents went home to tell their son and daughter that they were getting married. There were no questions asked by my parents. Out of respect for their parents, they agreed to be married. Actually, this is incorrect, because they didn't really agree; they couldn't have agreed [because] they were never asked. Basically they weren't given an option. However, neither of my parents argued; they just went along with their parents' wishes.

When I asked my parents if they were disappointed when they first saw each other on their wedding day, they said no. They did not fall in love at first sight either, but they thought their parents did a good job in finding them a spouse…. Neither of my parents regret[s] marrying each other even though they really didn't have much of a choice. They are happy with their lives, their children, and each other.

Arranged marriages in the East Indian culture are a lot different today than they were [twenty-three years ago]. I have friends my own age who have had arranged marriages. Now they get the opportunity to actually meet the person whom their parents have in mind for them. Better yet, they get to decide whether or not they want to marry that person.

A friend of mine just went to India with her parents to get married. Once she got there she discovered that her family members had already picked out about fifteen different men from whom she could choose. She interviewed all of them with her parents. She crossed off the names of the ones she wasn't interested in and had a second interview with the remaining men on her list. With three men left on her list after the second interview, her parents decided that she could meet these men alone without any parent chaperons….

She ended up liking one of them. She said she was very attracted to him. He was a dentist, tall, had a nice body, very polite, and treated her like a princess. She married this guy and brought him over to California. She couldn't be happier. She told me that she doesn't think that she would have ever been able to find such a wonderful husband without the help of her family. She is very grateful to them.

As for my two brothers and me, my parents have not necessarily expected us to have an arranged marriage. But before we do get married they want us to possess the best qualities, mainly a high education, good manners, respect for others, and high self-esteem, which will enable us to choose a partner of equal qualities….I did not have an arranged marriage. I married my husband because I truly loved him. However, before I made the decision to get married, I did try to make sure that we would be compatible and have similar goals.

I sometimes wonder what it would be like to have an arranged marriage. What would the wedding night be like? How could two people who don't really know each other or love each other make love? I did not feel comfortable enough to ask my parents or my friend about this. But it is something that I wonder about.

Critical Thinking

What are some advantages of arranged marriage? Some disadvantages? In what ways might personal choice be involved in arranged marriages today?

freely chosen in the United States found no differences in marital satisfaction between the two groups. According to the authors, "Although this is not a case in favor of arranged marriages, it provides no support for a position opposing this tradition" (Myers, Madathil, and Tingle 2005, p. 189). Meanwhile, with global Westernization, arranged marriages are less and less common, especially among those with higher education (D. Jones 2006; Hoelter, Axinn, and Ghimire 2004).

The United States is an example of what cross-cultural researchers call a **free-choice culture**: People choose their own mates, although often they seek parents' and other family members' support for their decision. Immigrants who come to the United States from more collectivist cultures, in which arranged marriages have been the tradition, face the situation of living with a divergent set of expectations for selecting a mate. Some immigrant parents from India, Pakistan, and other countries arrange for spouses from their home country to marry their offspring. Either the future spouse comes to the United States to marry the young person, or the young person travels to the home country for a wedding ceremony, after which the newlyweds usually live in the United States (Dugger 1998). In this case, the marriage is typically characterized

Although the arranged marriage of this couple in Northern India (right) may seem to be a world apart from the more freely chosen marriage of this couple in the United States (left), bargaining has occurred in both of these unions. In arranged marriages, families and community do the bargaining, based on assets such as status, possessions, and dowry. In freely chosen marriages, the individuals perform a more subtle form of bargaining, weighing the costs and benefits of personal characteristics, economic status, and education.

by the greater Westernization of one partner (the young person who has lived in the United States) and the spouse's simultaneous need to adjust not only to marriage but also to an entirely new culture.

The incidence of **cross-national marriages** like these may decline as the required visa for an immigrating spouse is far harder to come by now than prior to September 11, 2001. Furthermore, American-born children of immigrants may see themselves as too Americanized for this approach to finding a partner (MacFarquhar 2006). Whether unions are arranged or not, we can think of choosing a marital partner as taking place in a market.

Regarding arranged marriages, parents go through a bargaining process not unlike what takes place at a traditional village market. They make rationally calculated choices after determining the social status or position, health, temperament, and, sometimes, physical attractiveness of their prospective son- or daughter-in-law. Professional matchmakers often serve as investigators and go-betweens, just as we might engage an attorney or a stockbroker in an important business deal.[1]

With arranged marriage, the bargaining is obvious. The difference between arranged marriages and marriages in free-choice cultures may seem so great that we are inclined to overlook an important similarity: *Both*

[1] Sometimes, as in the Hmong culture, the exchange involves a *bride price,* money or property that the future groom pays the future bride's family so that he can marry her. More often, the exchange is accompanied by a *dowry,* a sum of money or property the female brings to the marriage. As one example, Asian Indians have traditionally practiced the dowry system, now illegal there but still widespread (Self and Grabowski 2009; Srinivasan and Lee 2004). A woman with a large dowry can expect to marry into a higher-ranking family than can a woman with a small dowry, and dowries are often increased to make up for qualities considered undesirable (M. Kaplan 1985, pp. 1–13). For instance, parents in eighteenth-century England increased the dowries of daughters who were pockmarked.

© Edward Keating/The New York Times

The man on the decorated horse is an investment banker from New York who has traveled to Jaipur, India, to marry a native Asian Indian woman. The marriage had been arranged in India by the groom's mother. The couple will return to New York to live. "I always knew I'd probably end up getting married to someone who wasn't very American, because I'm not myself in some ways," he said.

involve bargaining. What has changed in free-choice societies is that individuals, not family members, do the bargaining.

Social Exchange

The ideas of bargaining, market, and resources used to describe relationships come to us from exchange theory, discussed in Chapter 2. A basic idea of exchange theory is that whether relationships form or continue depends on the rewards and costs they provide to the partners. Individuals, it is presumed, want to maximize their rewards and avoid costs, so when they have choices, they will pick the relationship that is most rewarding or least costly.

This analogy is to economics, but in relationships, individuals are thought to have other sorts of resources to bargain besides money: physical attractiveness, intelligence, educational attainment, earning potential, personality characteristics, family status, the ability to be emotionally supportive, and so on. Individuals may also have costly attributes, such as belonging to the "wrong" social class, religion, or racial/ethnic group, being irritable or demanding, and being geographically inaccessible (a major consideration in modern society). The increasing number of single people with children in today's market may find parenthood to be a costly attribute (Goldscheider, Kaufman, and Sassler 2009).

The Traditional Exchange Historically, women have traded their ability to bear and raise children, coupled with domestic duties, sexual accessibility, and physical attractiveness, for a man's protection, status, and economic support. This traditional exchange characterizes marriages in many immigrant groups that have recently arrived in the United States (Hill, Ramirez, and Dumka 2003). Evidence from classified personal ads shows that the traditional exchange still influences heterosexual relationships in general. Men are more likely to advertise for a physically attractive woman; women, for an economically stable man. Although women increasingly have their own employment and income, women continue to expect greater financial success as a category from prospective husbands than vice versa (Buss et al. 2001; Fitzpatrick, Sharp, and Reifman 2009). National data that looked at black, Hispanic, and white males found that the probability of a man's getting married largely depends on his earning power (Edin and Reed 2005; Lichter, Qian, and Mellott 2006; Schoen and Cheng 2006).

Bargaining in a Changing Society "As gender differences in work and family roles blur, individuals' criteria for an acceptable mate are likely to change" (Raley and Bratter 2004, p. 179). For instance, research that looked at heterosexual mate preferences in the United States over the past sixty years showed that men and women—but especially men—have increased the importance that they put on potential financial success in a mate, while a woman's domestic skills have declined in importance (Siegel 2004; Sweeney and Cancian 2004). One study indicates that, for today's young man, a woman's high socioeconomic status increases her sexiness (Martin 2005).

As gender roles become more alike, exchange between partners may increasingly include "expressive, affective, sexual, and companionship resources" for both partners. In fact, a high-earning woman might bargain for a nurturing, housework-sharing husband, even if his earning potential appears to be lower than hers (Press 2004; Sprecher and Toro-Morn 2002). As college-educated young women approach occupational and economic equality with potential mates, the exchange becomes more symmetrical than in the past, with both genders increasingly looking for physical attractiveness, emotional sensitivity, and earning potential in one another (Buss et al. 2001; Montoya 2008). Marriages based on both partners' contributing roughly equal economic and status resources are more egalitarian. Changes in men's roles toward greater emotional expressiveness may improve relationship communication and satisfaction.

Desiring wives who can make good money, college-educated men are now much more likely to marry college-educated women than a few decades ago. In fact, today *both* men and women are likely to want a spouse with more education or who earns more than they do (King and Allen 2009; Raley and Bratter 2004).[2] The fact that college-educated women and men tend to marry one another points to another concept associated with mate selection—assortative mating.

Assortative Mating—A Filtering Process Individuals gradually filter, or sort out, those who they think would not make the best life partner or spouse. Research has consistently shown that people are willing to date a wider range of individuals than they would live with or become engaged to, and they are willing to live with a wider range of people than they would marry (Jepsen and Jepsen 2002). For instance, one study has found that women are less likely to consider the economic prospects of their male partners when deciding whether to cohabit than when deciding about marriage (Manning and Smock 2002). Social psychologists call this process **assortative mating** (or, sometimes, *assortive mating*). Assortative mating raises another factor shaping partner choice—the tendency of people to form committed, and especially marital, relationships with others with whom they share certain social characteristics. Social scientists term this phenomenon **homogamy**.

Homogamy: Narrowing the Pool of Eligibles

Individuals tend to make relationship choices in socially patterned ways, viewing only certain others as potentially suitable. The market analogy would be to choose only certain stores or websites at which to shop. Each shopper has a socially defined **pool of eligibles**: a group of individuals who, by virtue of background or birth, are considered most likely to make compatible mates.

Americans tend to choose partners who are like themselves in many ways. People tend to form committed relationships with people of similar race, age, education, religious background, and social class (Kossinets and Watts 2009). As an example, the Protestant, Catholic, and Jewish religions, as well as the Muslim and Hindu religions, have all traditionally encouraged **endogamy**: marrying within one's own social group.

The opposite of endogamy is **exogamy**, marrying outside one's group, or **heterogamy**—that is, choosing someone dissimilar in race, age, education, religion, or social class. For example, age and educational heterogamy have been more pronounced among black individuals than among whites, partly because an "undersupply" of educated black men prompts black women to partner with considerably older or younger men with less education (Surra 1990). Overall, however, with "the loosening of relationship conventions," more older women are dating or marrying men at least five years younger—the media-hyped "cougar" phenomenon (Kershaw 2009b). This "loosening of relationship conventions" evidences itself in other types of heterogamy as well.

As young adults experience increased independence from family influence, we can expect a rise in interracial and interethnic unions (Rosenfeld 2008). In spite of a trend toward less religious homogamy and a lessened tendency of Asian, Hispanic, and European Americans—such as Irish, Italians, or Poles—to marry within their own ethnic groups, homogamy is still a strong force (Fu and Heaton 2008).[3] About 7.5 percent of U.S. marriages involve spouses of different races or a Hispanic married to a non-Hispanic (U.S. Census Bureau 2010b, Table 60). The growth in race/ethnic intermarriage *rates* for Asians and Hispanics has declined some since the 1990s (although their numbers continued to rise). More than 90 percent of non-Hispanic and of black couples are racially homogeneous. About 60 percent of Asian Americans and 75 percent of Hispanics marry within their group (Lee and Edmonston 2005). However, nearly 54 percent of Native Americans marry outside their race, and more than 80 percent of Arab Americans marry outside their ethnicity (Kulczycki and Lobo 2002). Interracial and interethnic marriage and cohabitation rates involving African Americans have continued to increase significantly (Qian and Lichter 2007).

With regard to socioeconomic class and education, although people today are marrying across small class distinctions, they still are not doing so across large ones. For instance, individuals of established wealth or high

[2] As a result of this situation, finding an acceptable spouse could prove problematic for both women and men. "If both sexes are looking to marry ['up,' or] hypergamously, there is a mismatch between the preferences of men and women" (Raley and Bratter 2004, p. 168).

[3] "It often comes as a surprise to whites born after 1980 that crossing the ethnic boundaries to date or marry had social consequences in recent American ethnic history. The dating and marriage of, for example, an Italian American and an Irish American [in the first half of the twentieth century] not only raised eyebrows in each community but often brought disappointment and even estrangement from family members" (C. Gallagher 2006, p. 143).

© Joel McLeister/Star Tribune, Minneapolis-St. Paul

These Hmong immigrants in St. Paul, Minnesota, are celebrating the Hmong New Year, which also serves as a courting ritual. As in Laos, teenagers line up—boys on one side, girls on the other—and play catch with desirable potential mates. Catching the ball begins conversation. Tossing the ball gives girls a chance to meet boys under conditions approved by their parents. In Minnesota, however, the traditional Laotian black cloth ball is often replaced with a fluorescent tennis ball (Hopfensperger 1990, p. 1B). Because virtually all participants are Hmong, the ritual helps to ensure racial/ethnic homogamy.

education levels seldom marry those who are poor or who have low educational achievement (Fu and Heaton 2008). We know relatively little about religious, racial, or socioeconomic homogamy in cohabiting relationships, but we would presume—given the filtering process of assortative mating—that cohabiting couples exhibit less homogamy than married couples. All in all, at least with regard to marriage, an individual is likely to choose someone who is similar in basic social characteristics. We'll look at a hypothetical case to see why this is so.

Reasons for Homogamy

Andrea is attracted to Alex (and vice versa), who is a college student like herself. Andrea's parents are upper-middle class. They live in the expensive section of her hometown, have a housekeeper, and frequently have parties by their pool. Catholic, they go to Mass every Sunday. Alex's parents are working class. They are separated. His mother lives in an apartment and works as a checker in a supermarket. The family believes in "being good people," but do not belong to any organized religion.

How likely is it that Andrea and Alex will marry? If they do marry, what sources of conflict might occur? We can begin to answer these questions by exploring four related elements that influence both initial attraction and long-term happiness. For one thing, people often find it easier to communicate and feel more at home with others from similar education, social class, and racial or ethnic backgrounds (Lewin 2005). Alex is likely to have attitudes, mannerisms, and vocabulary different from those of Andrea. Each may feel out of place in surroundings that the other considers natural. Two other factors—geographic availability and social pressure—are important reasons that many relationships are generally homogamous.

Geographic Availability **Geographic availability** (traditionally known in the marriage and family literature as *propinquity* or *proximity*) has historically been a reason that people meet others who are like themselves (Harmanci 2006; Travis 2006). For instance, as the size of various immigrant communities in the United States grows, the geographic availability of eligibles in the same ethnicity increases, resulting in ethnic homogamy (Gowan 2009; Qian and Lichter 2007). Geographic segregation, which can result from either discrimination or strong community ties, contributes to homogamous marriages (C. Gallagher 2006; Iceland and Nelson 2008; Lichter et al. 2007). Intermarriage patterns within the American Jewish community are an example. Only about 6 percent of Jews married non-Jews in the late 1950s. Now that the barriers that used to exclude Jews from certain residential areas and colleges are gone, about half marry gentiles (Sussman 2006).

Geographic availability also helps to account for educational and social class homogamy. Middle-class people tend to socialize together and send their children to the same schools; upper- and lower-class people do the same. Unless they had met in a large, public university or online, it is unlikely that Alex and Andrea would have become acquainted at all.

Today, first encounters may occur in cyberspace, and people meet others as far away as other continents. Websites such as InterRacialMatcher.com facilitate heterogamy. However, the Internet may actually encourage endogamy among religious or racial/ethnic groups, who can advertise online for homogamous dating partners (e.g., allhispanicdating.com; asianromance.com; blacksingles.com; christian.com; jewishconnect.com; meetmuslimsingles.com; see also Desmond-Harris 2010). Illustrating these points, Russel K. Robinson, a black gay man writing in the *Fordham Law Review*, describes his experience as follows:

> Although I lived on the wealthy, predominantly white west side of [Los Angeles], the Internet created opportunities for me to interact with men in [less wealthy areas of the city]—men I almost certainly would not meet randomly while going through my daily routine.....Even as the Internet increases romantic opportunity, it also channels interactions....Like many dating websites, Match.com

> prompts the user to indicate which races he will and will not date....[I]f a white user is interested only in white romantic partners, he can easily structure his screen so that he never even has to view nonwhite profiles. (Robinson 2008, 2791–92)

The Internet also allows us to meet people with similar values and attitudes if not similar in socioeconomic characteristics, such as vegetarians or humanitarian social activists (K. Baker 2008). Then too, online daters' mutual ability to access the Internet and then to travel, if necessary, to meet each other face-to-face assures some degree of educational and/or financial homogamy. We know of no research on the actual effect of the Internet on marital homogamy, and we'd like to suggest that this question would be a good one for future research—perhaps yours.

Social Pressure A second reason for homogamy is social pressure. Interethnic relationships are more likely to develop when young adults are relatively independent of parental influence and/or when one's parents have an ethnically diverse network of friends (Rosenfeld and Byung-Soo 2005). Meanwhile, for the majority of us, cultural values encourage marrying someone who is socially similar to ourselves. Andrea's parents, friends, and siblings may not approve of Alex because he doesn't exhibit the social skills and behavior of their social class. Meanwhile, Alex's mother and friends may say to him, "Andrea thinks she is too good for us. Find a girl more like our kind."

Sometimes, social pressure results from a group's concern for preserving its ethnic or cultural identity. Arab, Asian, or Hispanic immigrants may pressure their children to marry within their own ethnic group to preserve the culture (Kitano and Daniels 1995; S. M. Lee 1998). Whether blatant or subtle, social pressure toward homogamy can be forceful. Making knowledgeable choices involves recognizing the strength of social pressure and deciding whether to act in accordance with others' expectations.

We've discussed some reasons for homogamy, but not all marriages are homogamous, of course. Heterogamy refers to marriage between those who are different in race, age, education, religious background, or social class.

Examples of Heterogamy

How does marrying someone from a different religion, social class, or race/ethnicity affect a person's chances for a happy union? In general, marriages that are homogamous are more likely to be stable because partners are more likely to share the same values and attitudes when they come from similar backgrounds (Furstenberg 2005; Gaunt 2006). As an example, Islamic marriage counselor Aneesah Nadir suggests that, in a homogamous Muslim marriage, both spouses—not just one—are likely to find value in referring to the Quran for answers to disagreements (Nadir 2009).

In this section, however, we examine the relationship between heterogamy and marital success. We will discuss interfaith marriages, and then look at interracial and interethnic unions. First, however, it is worth noting that partners can experience cultural differences even when they share a religious, racial, or ethnic category. For instance, Muslims (as well as those of other religions) may not only practice their religion to varying degrees but also be of different ethnicities (Nadir 2009). As a second example, with regard to race, the U.S. black population is itself culturally diverse because it includes black individuals whose ancestors have been in this country for generations as well as recent immigrants from Africa or the Caribbean (Kent 2007). Similarly, the category "Asian" includes individuals from a variety of nations and cultures.

Interfaith Marriages It is estimated that between 30 percent and 40 percent of Jewish, Catholic, Mormon, Muslim, and a higher percentage of Protestant adults and children in the United States live in interfaith or interdenominational households (D'Antonio et al. 1999). Being highly educated seems to lessen individuals' commitment to religious homogamy (Petersen 1994). Religions that see themselves as the one true faith and people who adhere to a religion as an integral component of their ethnic/cultural identity (for example, some Catholics, Jews, and Muslims) are more likely to encourage homogamy, sometimes by pressing a prospective spouse to convert (Bukhari 2004). Often, religious bodies are concerned that children born into the marriage will not be raised in their religion (Sussman 2006).

Some switching, no doubt, also takes place because partners agree with the widely held belief that interreligious marriages tend to be more stressful and less stable than homogamous ones—a belief supported by research (Mahoney 2005). One probable reason that religious homogamy improves chances for marital success involves value consensus. Religion-based values and attitudes may come into play when negotiating leisure activities, child-raising methods, investments and expenditures of money, and appropriate spousal roles (Curtis and Ellison 2002). Meanwhile, analysis of data from a national random telephone survey of Protestant and Catholic households concluded that although marital satisfaction was less for interdenominational couples, the difference disappeared when the interdenominational couple had generally similar religious orientations, good communication skills, and similar beliefs about child raising (Hughes and Dickson 2005; Williams and Lawler 2003).

One study conducted with homogamously married Christian, Jewish, and Islamic couples found strong religious beliefs to be associated with less couple conflict. Shared religiosity gave them a shared sense of purpose and commitment to permanence, coupled with a willingness to forgive the spouse when conflicts emerged (Lambert and Dollahite 2006). One research team has attributed the higher rate of marital happiness associated with religious homogeneity almost entirely to the positive effect of church attendance: Homogamously married partners go to church more often and at similar rates and, as a result, show higher marital satisfaction and stability (Heaton and Pratt 1990).

Some recent research shows a declining effect of religious differences on marital satisfaction over the past several decades due to the greater effect of couples' gender, work, and co-parenting concerns (Myers 2006; Williams and Lawler 2003).

Interracial/Interethnic Marriages **Interracial marriages** include unions between partners of the white, black, Asian, or Native American races with a spouse outside their own race. As defined by the U.S. Census Bureau, Hispanics are not a separate race but, rather, an ethnic group. Unions between Hispanics and others, as well as between different Asian/Pacific Islander, Hispanic, or black ethnic groups (such as Thai–Chinese, Puerto Rican–Cuban, or African American—black Caribbean) are considered **interethnic marriages**.

Interracial unions have existed in the United States throughout our history (Maillard 2008). However, not until June 1967 (*Loving v. Virginia*) did the U.S. Supreme Court declare that interracial marriages must be considered legally valid in all states. At about the same time, it became impossible to gather accurate statistics on interracial marriages. Many states no longer require race information on marriage registration forms, so these data are incomplete at best.

Available statistics show that the proportion of interracial and interethnic marriages is fairly small (between 7 and 8 percent of the adult U.S. population, or 4.5 million couples) (U.S. Census Bureau 2010b, Table 60). Although this proportion has steadily increased since 1970, when the proportion was just one percent, growth in interracial and interethnic marriage may recede somewhat in the future as immigrant groups become large enough to provide an ample pool of eligibles within their own ethnic categories (Lee and Edmonston 2005; Qian and Lichter 2007). If we count cohabiting couples, the percentage today of racially or ethnically heterogeneous couples would be somewhat higher than the statistics for married couples because (due to the assortative mating process) cohabiting couples are less homogamous than married couples (Batson, Qian, and Lichter 2006; Joyner and Kao 2005).

As shown in Figure 6.3, of all interracial marriages in 2008 (this does not count Hispanic–non-Hispanic unions), about 20.5 percent (481,000 couples) were black–white (U.S. Census Bureau 2010b, Table 60).[4] The vast majority of the remainder were combinations of whites with Asians, Native Americans, and others. Two-thirds of black-white marriages involved black men married to white women. Among Hispanic marrieds, about one-third have a spouse of non-Hispanic origin (U.S. Census Bureau 2010b, Table 60).

[4] Native-born African Americans are significantly more likely to intermarry racially than are black recent immigrants from the West Indies or Africa (Batson, Qian, and Lichter 2006).

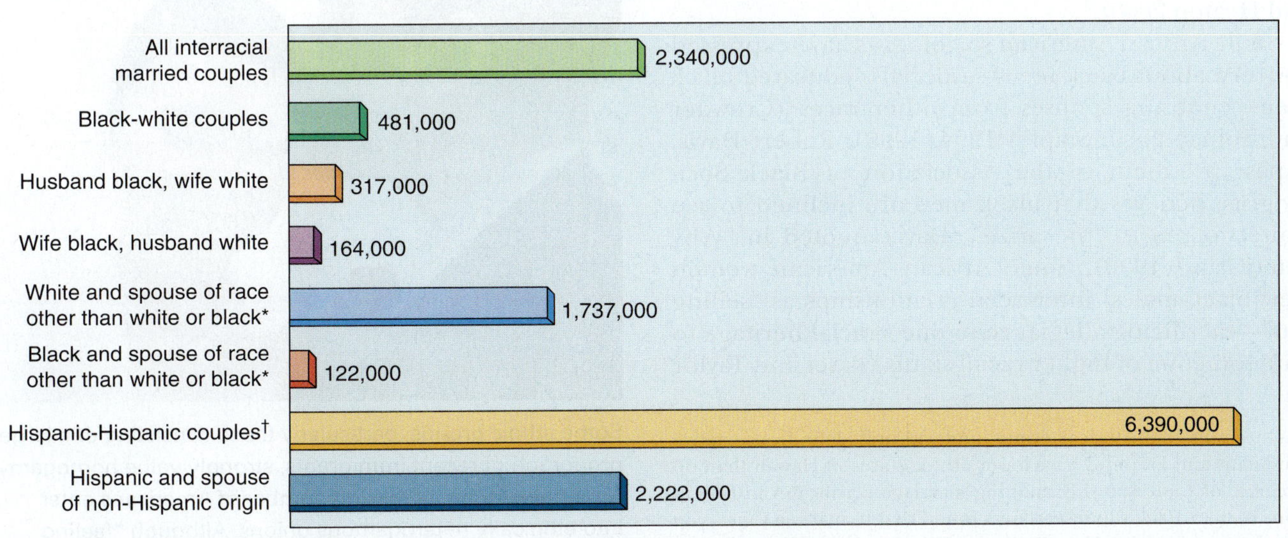

Figure 6.3 Number of interracial and Hispanic–non-Hispanic married couples, 2008.

Source: U.S. Census Bureau 2010b, Table 60.

Reasons for Interracial and Interethnic Unions Much attention has been devoted to why people marry or form other romantic unions interracially. One apparent reason among racial/ethnic groups that are relatively small in number is simply that they have a smaller pool of eligibles in their own race/ethnicity and are also more likely than larger racial/ethnic groups to interact with others of different races (Qian and Lichter 2007; Robinson 2008).

Another explanation is the **status exchange hypothesis**—the argument that an individual might trade his or her socially defined superior racial/ethnic status for the economically or educationally superior status of a partner in a less-privileged racial/ethnic group (Kalmijn 1998). In this regard, racial stereotypes may play a part:

> [A] society dominated by Euro-Americans will unsurprisingly privilege a standard of beauty and cultural styles that is a mirror image of itself, even if that image is a media distortion.... [I]nterviews with Asian men and women [found] that a sizable minority of respondents preferred whites as potential or current mates because of their preference for "European" traits including tallness, round eyes, buffness for men and more ample breasts for women. (C. Gallagher 2006, p. 150)

Applying the status exchange hypothesis to black–white intermarriage would suggest marrying "up" socioeconomically on the part of a white person who, in effect, trades socially defined superior racial status for the economically superior status of a middle- or upper-middle-class black partner. Little research has been done to test this hypothesis, but a recent study of intermarriage among native Hawaiians, Japanese, Filipinos, and Caucasians in Hawaii supports the hypothesis (Fu and Heaton 2000).[5]

Some African American sociologists have expressed concern about black men—especially educated black men—choosing spouses from other races (Crowder and Tolnay 2000; Staples 1994, 1999). Robert Davis, a past president of the Association of Black Sociologists, believes that black men are inclined to see white women as "the prize" (Davis, quoted in "Why Interracial" 1996). Some African American women view black males' interracial relationships as "selling out"—sacrificing allegiance to one's racial heritage to date someone of higher racial status (Paset and Taylor 1991). In a paper on this topic, a Latina student wrote the following:

> It is not just in the African American community that this is happening....I have noticed when a Mexican American man gets educated, he usually ends up dating and marrying an Anglo female. Being with an Anglo female is more of a trophy to the Mexican man....I would like to meet an educated Mexican male and date him but there are not that many around. I am not totally set on just dating a Mexican male, but you hardly see white males dating other races. Sometimes it seems there is little hope for Hispanic and African American females to ever find a good partner. (Torres 1997)

Having said this, we note that research on interracially married couples has generally found that "with few exceptions, this group's motives for marriage do not appear to be any different from those of individuals marrying...within their own race" (Porterfield 1982, p. 23). As with homogamous couples, those in heterogamous relationships find their partners by means of social exchange in a marriage market (Fryer 2007). When asked about their motives for marrying heterogamously, the most common answers they give are love and compatibility (Porterfield 1982).

Interracial/Interethnic Heterogamy and Marital Stability

Marital success can be measured in terms of two related, but different factors: (1) stability—whether or how long the union lasts, and (2) the happiness of the partners.

Some ethnic groups, particularly those consisting of a large proportion of recent immigrants, strongly value homogamy. Nevertheless, an increasing number of Americans enter into ethnically heterogamous unions. Although "feeling at home"—a factor that encourages homogamy—may be difficult at first, some individuals thrive on the cultural variety characteristic of interracial or interethnic relationships.

[5] As a result of historical events and cultural definitions, native Hawaiians and Filipinos have lower ethnic status in Hawaii than do Japanese or Caucasians. Examining marriage certificates in Hawaii from 1983 to 1994, the researchers found that to marry a Caucasian or a Japanese, native Hawaiians and Filipinos had to have higher economic or educational status than those who married within their own ethnic group. At the same time, Japanese and Caucasians who married native Hawaiians or Filipinos were "of lower status in their own group" (Fu and Heaton 2000, p. 53).

Marital *stability* is not synonymous with marital *happiness* because, in some instances, unhappy spouses remain married, whereas less unhappy partners may choose to separate. Just as information on interracial/interethnic marriages is incomplete, so is information on their divorces. Only about half the states and the District of Columbia report race/ethnicity on divorce records. What evidence we have on whether interracial/interethnic marriages are more or less stable than intraracial/intraethnic unions comes from national survey data.

One study that analyzed data from the National Survey of Families and Households (NSFH) showed that partners in interethnic unions—both married and cohabiting—reported lower relationship quality than did those in same-ethnic unions (Hohmann-Marriott and Amato 2008). In general, research suggests that marriages that are homogamous in age, education, religion, and race are the most stable (Bratter and King 2008; Larson and Hickman 2004).

However, a recent study based on analysis of data from 23,139 married couples "failed to provide evidence that interracial marriage *per se* is associated with an elevated risk of marital dissolution." Instead, the risk of divorce or separation among the interracial couples sampled was similar to that of the race of the spouse from the more divorce-prone race. Accordingly, "Mixed marriages involving Blacks were the least stable followed by Hispanics, whereas mixed marriages involving Asians were even more stable than endogamous White marriages" (Zhang and Van Hook 2009, p. 104).

Additionally, these researchers found black husband–white wife pairings to be the least stable of all the marriage types they looked at:

> One plausible interpretation of these results is that they reflect persistent racism and distrust directed toward Blacks, particularly Black men in the United States. The qualitative findings from Yancey (2007) indicated that Whites who married Blacks experienced more firsthand racism as compared to Whites who married other non-Black minorities. Specifically, White women reported encountering more racial incidents with their Black husbands (e.g., inferior service, racial profiling, and racism against their children) and more hostilities from families and cohorts as compared to other interracial pairings. Research in communication and cultural studies echoed Yancey's findings and found that the above-mentioned social pressures tend to increase social isolation of Black-White unions, especially from the White community, and consequently negatively impact the survival of these marriages. (Zhang and Van Hook 2009, p. 105)

We can offer at least three explanations for any differences in the marital stability that may exist among interracial or interethnic couples. First, significant differences in values and interests between partners can create a lack of mutual understanding, resulting in emotional gaps and increased couple conflict (Durodoye and Coker 2008; Lincoln, Taylor, and Jackson 2008). Second, such marriages may create conflict between the partners and other groups, such as parents, relatives, and friends. Continual discriminatory pressure from the broader society may create undue psychological and marital distress (Bratter and Eschbach 2006; Childs 2008). If they lack a supporting social network, partners may find maintaining their union in times of crisis more difficult. Also, a higher divorce rate among heterogamous marriages may reflect the fact that these partners are likely to be less conventional in their values and behavior, and unconventional people may divorce more readily than others (see Hohmann-Marriott and Amato 2008).

Interracial/Interethnic Heterogamy and Human Values

One recent study of unmarried interracial couples in college found *higher* relationship satisfaction compared to same-race couples (Troy, Lewis-Smith, and Laurenceau 2006). A comparison of Mexican American–non-Hispanic white marriages with those of homogamous white and homogamous Mexican American couples found little difference in marital satisfaction among the three groups (Negy and Snyder 2000). Whether these findings would apply to all interethnic or interracially married couples is unknown.

In any case, it is important to note the significance of human values. Many people do not want to limit their social contacts—including their life partners—to socially similar people. Although many people may retain a warm attachment to their racial or ethnic community, and some ethnic groups strongly value homogamy, social and political change has been in the direction of breaking down racial and ethnic barriers. People committed to an open society find intermarriage to be an important symbol, whether or not it is a personal choice, and do not wish to discourage this option (Dunleavy 2004; Moran 2001).

The data on homogamy may be interpreted to mean that, regardless of differences in race or ethnicity, common values and lifestyles contribute to relationship stability. A heterogamous pair may have common values that transcend their differences in background. Some problems of interracial (or other heterogamous) marriages have to do with social disapproval and lack of social support from either race (Felmlee 2001; Gullickson 2006). However, individuals can choose to work to change the society into one in which heterogamous marriage will be more accepted and hence will pose fewer problems.

Moreover, opinion polls and other research show that Americans are becoming less disapproving of interracial dating and marriage (Carroll 2007a; J. Jones

2005). Also, Americans are now more likely to have a close confidant of another race, suggesting that interracial bridges among people are increasing (Hulbert 2006). Still, among both blacks and whites, a minority of individuals strongly disapprove of interracial marriage (Jacobson and Johnson 2006). To the degree that racially, religiously, or economically heterogamous marriages increase in number, they are less likely to be troubled by the reactions of society.

Again, we see that private troubles—or choices—are intertwined with public issues. Some ethnic groups strongly value homogamy. Meanwhile, it is also true that if people are able to cross racial, class, or religious boundaries and at the same time share important values, they may open doors to a varied and exciting relationship. Chapter 10 explores raising children in interracial families. In our society, choice of life partners, whether homogamous or heterogamous, typically involves developing an intimate relationship and establishing mutual commitment. The next section examines these processes.

Developing the Relationship and Moving Toward Commitment

Social scientists have been interested in the process through which a couple develops their relationship and mutual commitment. What first brings people together? What keeps them together?

Meandering Toward Marriage and First Meetings

Young people today "meander toward marriage," feeling that they'll be ready to marry when they reach their late twenties or so (Arnett 2004, p. 197). Experiencing unprecedented freedom, today's young adults often express the need to explore as many options as possible before "settling down." As one young woman explained:

> I think everyone should experience everything they want to experience before they get tied down, because if you wanted to date a black person, a white person, an Asian person, a tall person, short, fat, whatever, as long as you know you've accomplished all that, and you are happy with who you are with, then I think everything would be OK. I want to experience life and know that when that right person comes, I won't have any regrets. (Quoted in Arnett 2004, p. 113)

Some young couples "hook up" for nonrelationship or "recreational" sex (see Chapter 5). They may find sexual pleasure in "friends with benefits" as they experiment with many relationships before they think about looking for a spouse (Kan and Cares 2006; Manning, Giordano, and Longmore 2006). According to sociologist Kathleen Bogle (2008), the emergence of the "hookup" is "a major shift in the culture over the past few decades"—a shift from dating with a focus on developing a long-term, possibly marital relationship to getting together only for a sexual encounter. "Bogle says the hookup is what happens when high school seniors and college freshmen suddenly begin to realize they won't be marrying for five, ten, or fifteen years" (Wilson 2009; see also Meier and Allen 2009; Wallace 2007).

Despite its growing appeal among college students, hooking up has unfortunately been empirically linked to known risky behaviors such as alcohol abuse and engaging in sexual intercourse without using a condom (Gute and Eshbaugh 2008). As discussed in Chapter 5, hooking up can also evidence the sexual double standard as men more often see the hookup primarily as providing sexual gratification whereas women are more likely to hope that a hookup could be the beginning of a relationship (Bogle 2008). Then too, casual dating such as this can be associated with date or acquaintance rape, as discussed in "Issues for Thought: Date or Acquaintance Rape."

First Meetings Americans tend to believe that they find more socially desirable personality traits in those who are physically attractive. An examination of research studies on mate preferences since 1939 shows that physical attractiveness increased as a value over the past century and is especially important upon first meeting and in the early stages of a relationship (Malakh-Pines 2005; Tender 2008).

The majority of couples meet for the first time in face-to-face encounters, such as at school, work, a game, or a party. However, more couples today, especially those who are older, meet through singles' ads or online (Ellin 2009). Development of a face-to-face romantic relationship moves from initial encounter to discovery of similarities and self-disclosure (Knobloch, Solomon, and Theiss 2006). However, meeting for the first time online is a bit different.

Internet relationships—sometimes coupled with Internet background checks—progress through "an inverted developmental sequence." That is, without first seeing one another, two people who find each other intriguing gradually get to know one another through keyboard discussions. Then, too, as noted earlier, emerging niche websites introduce people who share specific characteristics, such as not wanting children, or being dog owners or vegetarians (Kirby 2005). This development makes it possible to establish the groundwork for rapport from the beginning, rather than having rapport develop as people gradually discover more about each other. Over time, emails become more intimate, and a powerful connection may be established (Merkle and

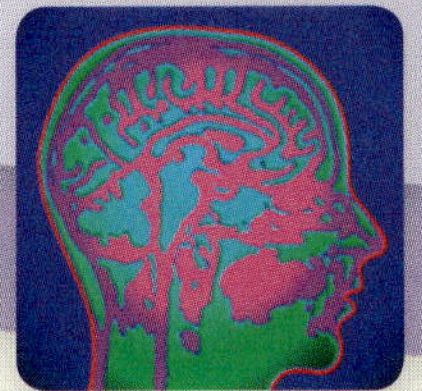

Issues for Thought

Date or Acquaintance Rape

Contrary to the impression that we are likely to get from the media, most rape victims know their rapists (G. Cowan 2000). **Date** or **acquaintance rape**—being involved in a coercive sexual encounter with a date or other acquaintance—emerged as an issue on college campuses over the past two decades, but date rape no doubt plagued the dating scene for a long time before that (Friedman, Boumil, and Taylor 1992).

Often, excessive use of alcohol is involved (Foran and O'Leary 2008; Peralta and Cruz 2006). Findings from various research studies over the past decade show that sexually coercive men tend to dismiss women's rejection messages regarding unwanted sex and differ from noncoercive men in their approach to relationships and sexuality: They date more frequently; have higher numbers of sexual partners, especially uncommitted dating relationships; prefer casual encounters; and may "take a predatory approach to their sexual interactions with women."

Closely related to the concept of date rape is *sexual coercion* (Ryan and Mohr 2005). Some researchers have noted the existence of female-initiated sexual coercion—although significantly fewer women than men are sexually coercive, and when they are coercive, they use less forceful techniques. Men's experiences with being coerced most often do not advance beyond kissing or fondling, whereas women's experiences most often result in unwanted, sometimes violent intercourse (Christopher and Sprecher 2000).

Many female victims blamed themselves, at least partially—a situation that can result in still greater psychological distress (Breitenbecher 2006). One reason victims blame themselves has to do with **rape myths**: beliefs about rape that function to blame the victim and exonerate the rapist (G. Cowan 2000). Rape myths include the ideas that (1) the rape was somehow provoked by the victim (for example, she "led him on" or wore provocative clothes); (2) men cannot control their sexual urges, a belief that consequently holds women responsible for preventing rape; and (3) rapists are mentally ill, a belief that encourages potential victims to feel safe with someone they know, no matter what (G. Cowan 2000). Increasingly, college men report that they recognize the male's responsibility for rape; this finding may be evidence that campus rape-prevention information and workshops make a difference (Domitrz 2003).

Critical Thinking

What can you do to help prevent date rape? What should you do if you or a friend is raped by an acquaintance? What would or should you do if a friend or acquaintance of yours was known to be the perpetrator of a date or acquaintance rape?

At its 1985 national convention, members of Pi Kappa Phi fraternity unanimously adopted a resolution not to tolerate any form of sexually abusive behavior on the part of their members. The fraternity also produced this poster and distributed it to all its chapters. The illustration is a detail from the painting *The Rape of the Sabine Women*. Beneath the large message, a smaller one reads, "Just a reminder from Pi Kappa Phi. Against her will is against the law."

Richardson 2000; Tender 2008). However individuals meet, what is it that draws and keeps them together? One way to explore this process involves the idea of a developing relationship as moving around a wheel.

The Wheel of Love

According to this theory, the development of love has four stages, which is a circular process—a **wheel of love**—capable of continuing indefinitely. The four stages—rapport, self-revelation, mutual dependency, and personality need fulfillment—are shown in Figure 6.4, and they describe the span from attraction to love.

Rapport Feelings of rapport rest on mutual trust and respect. A principal factor that makes people more likely to establish rapport is similarity of values, interests, and background (Gottlieb 2006)—social class, religion, and so forth. The outside circle in Figure 6.4 is meant to convey this point. However, rapport can also be established between people of different backgrounds, who may perceive one another as an interesting contrast to themselves or see qualities in one another that they admire.

Self-Revelation **Self-revelation**, or *self-disclosure*, involves gradually sharing intimate information about oneself. People have internalized different views about how

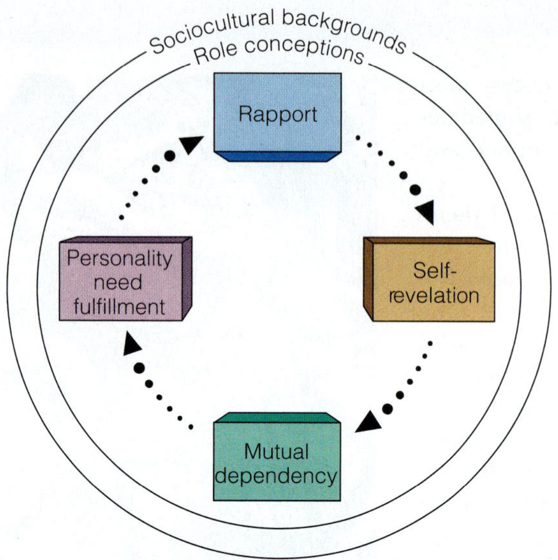

Figure 6.4 Reiss's wheel theory of the development of love.
Source: From *Family Systems in America,* 3rd ed., by I. Reiss © 1980 Wadsworth, a division of Cengage Learning.

much self-revelation is proper. The middle circle of Figure 6.4, "Role conceptions," signifies that ideas about social class-, ethnic-, or gender-appropriate behaviors influence how partners self-disclose and respond to each other's self-revelations and other activities.

For most of us, love's early stages produce anxiety. We may fear that our love won't be returned. Maybe we worry about being exploited or are afraid of becoming too dependent. One way of dealing with these anxieties is, ironically, to let others see us as we really are and to share our motives, beliefs, and feelings (Peck and Peck 2006). As reciprocal self-revelation continues, an intimate relationship may develop while a couple progresses to the third stage in the wheel of love: developing interdependence, or mutual dependency.

Mutual Dependency In this stage of a relationship, the two people desire to spend more time together and thereby develop interdependence or, in Reiss's terminology, *mutual dependency*. Partners develop habits that require the presence of both partners. Consequently, they begin to depend on or need each other. For example, watching a good DVD may now seem lonely without the other person because enjoyment has come to depend not only on the movie but on sharing it with the other. Interdependency leads to the fourth stage: a degree of mutual personality need fulfillment.

Need Fulfillment As their relationship develops, two people find that they satisfy a majority of each other's emotional needs. As a result, rapport increases, leading to deeper self-revelation, more mutually dependent habits, and still greater need satisfaction. The relationship is one of ongoing emotional exchange and mutual support. Along this line, social scientist Robert Winch (1958) once proposed a theory of complementary needs, whereby we are attracted to partners whose needs complement our own (Malakh-Pines 2005). Sometimes people take this idea to mean that "opposites attract." This may make intuitive sense to some of us, but needs theorists more often argue that we are attracted to others whose strengths are *harmonious* with our own (Klohnen and Mendelsohn 1998; Schwartz 2006). Couples also tend to be matched on sex drive and attitudes about sex (Lally and Maddock 1994; Murstein 1980). "As We Make Choices: Harmonious Needs in Mate Selection" further explores these ideas. As partners develop mutual need satisfaction and interdependence, they gradually define their relationship. Part of defining a relationship should involve, according to counselors, talking about serious questions (Pendley 2006). What are some things that deserve discussing?

Some Things to Talk About

Talking about the relationship that you and your partner want may bring up differences, many of which can be worked out. If value differences are uncovered and cannot be worked out—for example, about whether or not to have children—it might be better to end the relationship before committing to a union that cannot satisfy either partner. Openly and honestly discussing matters like the ones that follow is important to successful mate selection (Pendley 2006):

1. When should a relationship be dissolved and under what circumstances? How long and in what ways would you work on an unsatisfactory relationship before dissolving it?
2. What are your expectations, attitudes, and preferences regarding sex?
3. Do you want children? If so, how many? Whose responsibility is birth control?
4. If you have children, how will you allocate child-rearing responsibilities? Do the two of you agree on child-raising practices, such as whether to spank a child?
5. What is the financial situation of each partner as he or she comes into the union? How will the couple manage any prior debt, credit problems, and their existing financial situations in general?
6. Will partners equally share breadwinning and homemaking responsibilities, or not? How will money be allocated? Who will be the owner of family property, such as family businesses, farms, or other partnerships?
7. Do you expect your partner to share your religion? Will you attend religious services together? If you are of a religion different from that of your mate, where will you worship? What about the children's religion?

As We Make Choices

Harmonious Needs in Mate Selection

Finding a spouse with needs that are in harmony with one's own means matching different (but complementary) needs in some cases. In other cases, finding the "right" partner involves matching similar needs. The following three areas in which couples' needs should be similar are suggested by prominent sociologist Pepper Schwartz (2006) as important for a happy, long-term match:

1. **Personal Energy.** Your marriage may have more chance for success when your general energy level matches your partner's. "Whenever a couple spends time together their energy levels come into play.... While lovers may be willing to accommodate a leisurely stroll along the beach or a speed walk up the nearest mountain, at the end of the day, constant accommodation can be taxing and frustrating" (Schwartz 2006, p. 17).
2. **Outlook.** "People's attitudes and mood ranges from cheerful and upbeat to serious and earnest.... There is nothing wrong with either of these two emotional approaches to the world, but [it can be frustrating] if one person always feels the other is 'raining on her parade.'... Meanwhile, the partner's take on this may be to see that kind of optimism as simplistic or even scary... [and to] stop trusting their partners' instinctive impulse to see the brightest side of everything" (Schwartz 2006, p. 18).
3. **Predictability.** "If you draw comfort from surrounding yourself with familiar patterns and places, you are not going to be happy with someone for whom the very thought of predictable days, weeks, and places fills them with an urge to run.... The opposite of this need for predictability is the passion for variety.... [I]f the person who craves variety and the person who craves predictability find themselves together, they are going to feel betrayed and angry and worst of all, trapped" (Schwartz 2006, p. 21; see also Smithson and Baker 2008).

Critical Thinking

Do you agree with Pepper Schwartz that couples' needs should be similar in these three areas? Can you think of examples that would support Schwartz's points? Can you think of exceptions? Can you think of other situations in which the best match would be between partners with similar needs? Can you think of areas in which partners' different needs might complement one another?

8. What are your educational goals? How about your prospective partner's?
9. How will each of you relate to your own and to your partner's relatives?
10. What is your attitude toward friendships with people of the opposite sex? How about cyberfriends? Would you ever consider having sex with someone other than your mate? How would you react if your partner were to have sex with another person?
11. How much time alone do you need? How much are you willing to allow your partner?
12. Will you purposely set aside time for each other? If communication becomes difficult, will you go to a marriage counselor?
13. What are your own and your partner's personal definitions of *intimacy, commitment,* and *responsibility*?

Discussing topics such as these is an important part of defining a couple's relationships.

Defining the Relationship

From an interaction-constructionist perspective (see Chapter 2), qualitative research with serious dating couples shows that they pass through a series of fairly predictable stages (Sniezek 2002, 2007) by means of which they further define their relationship. Hinting, testing, negotiating, joking, and scrutinizing the partner's words and behavior characterize this process. As one example, a thirty-two-year-old emergency room worker described reading her partner's joking about marriage—and his use of the word *yet*—as a possible sign that he had considered marrying her:

> It was right here in our kitchen I put it (the food) down on his plate and I'm like "prison food." And he said "Um gee and we're not even married yet." And that was like the first joke. It stuck in my mind. (Sniezek 2007)

As the relationship progresses toward an eventual wedding, the "marriage conversation" is introduced. In the research being described here, women were more likely to initiate marriage talk—cautiously and indirectly: "Yeah it's like so what are you thinking? Where is this relationship heading?" In other cases, the marriage conversation began more directly. One woman raised the question of marriage when her partner suggested that they live together:

> When he asked me to move in with him, I told him I felt uncomfortable living with someone and not being married—a moral issue for me. So we talked about [the probability of getting married] at that time. (Sniezek 2007)

Once marriage talk is initiated, the couple faces negotiating a joint definition of the relationship as premarital. If one partner rejects the idea that the relationship should lead to marriage, several responses can occur. In some cases, one partner's marriage hopes may be relinquished, although the relationship continues. In other cases, a partner may deliver an ultimatum. Sometimes an ultimatum results in marriage; in other cases, stating an ultimatum causes an irreparable rift in the relationship.

Finally, most couples do not define themselves as "really" engaged until one or more ritualized practices take place—buying rings, setting a wedding date, public announcements to family and friends, holding engagement parties, and so on. These practices make the redefinition of the relationship increasingly public and "hardened" (Sniezek 2007).

In another qualitative study on this subject, two social scientists conducted lengthy interviews with 116 individuals in premarital relationships. They examined the process by which these partners gradually committed to marriage (Surra and Hughes 1997). From the interviews, the researchers classified the respondents' relationships in two categories: *relationship-driven* and *event-driven.*

Relationship-driven couples followed the evolving, wheel-like pattern described earlier. However, in event-driven relationships, partners vacillated between commitment and ambivalence. Often they disagreed on how committed they were as well as why they had become committed in the first place. The researchers called this relationship type *event-driven* because events—fighting, discussing the relationship with one's own friends, and making up—punctuated each partner's account.

It's probably no surprise that event-driven couples' satisfaction with the relationship fluctuated over time. Although often recognizing their relationships as rocky, they do not necessarily break up, because positive events (for example, a discussion about getting married or an expression of approval of the relationship from others) typically follow negative ones. At least some event-driven couples would probably be better off not getting married. We turn now to an even more serious issue—that of dating violence.

Dating Violence—A Serious Sign of Trouble

Sometimes we need to make decisions about continuing or ending a relationship that is characterized by physical violence and/or verbal abuse. Physical violence occurs in 20 percent to 40 percent of dating relationships (Luthra and Gidycz 2006)—a high, "most surprising incidence" (Johnson and Ferraro 2000, p. 951). Most incidents of aggression involve pushing, grabbing, or slapping. Between 1 percent and 3 percent of college students have reported experiencing severe violence, such as beatings or assault with an object. Researchers are concerned that dating violence among teens is widespread and that many teens—as well as others—apparently minimize violence or view it as to be expected in certain situations (Hoffman 2009; Prospero 2006; Sears et al. 2006).

Both genders engage in physical aggression (Ryan, Weikel, and Sprechini 2008). However, by far, the more serious injuries result from male-to-female violence (Johnson and Ferraro 2000). Furthermore, women are more inclined to "hit back" once a partner has precipitated the violence, rather than to physically strike out first (Luthra and Gidycz 2006).

Dating violence typically begins with and is accompanied by verbal or psychological abuse (Lento 2006) and tends to occur over jealousy, with a refusal of sex, after illegal drug use or excessive drinking of alcohol, or upon disagreement about drinking behavior (Cogan and Ballinger 2006; Ryan, Weikel, and Sprechini 2008).

Researchers have found it discouraging that about half of abusive dating relationships continue rather than being broken off (Few and Rosen 2005). Given that the economic and social constraints of marriage are not usually applicable to dating, researchers have wondered why violent dating relationships persist. Evidence suggests that having experienced domestic violence in one's family of origin—even chronic verbal abuse in the absence of physical violence—is significantly related to both being abusive and to accepting abuse as normal (Cyr, McDuff, and Wright 2006; Tshann et al. 2009). A recent qualitative study of twenty-eight female undergraduates in abusive dating relationships found that some of these women felt "stuck" with their partner (Few and Rosen 2005). A majority had assumed a "caretaker identity," similar to martyring. As one explained:

> I always was a rescuer in my family. I felt that I was rescuing him [boyfriend] and taking care of him. He never knew what it was like to have a good, positive home environment, so I was working hard to create that for him. (p. 272)

Others felt stuck because they wanted to be married, and their dating partner appeared to be their only prospect: "I think near the end, one of the reasons I was scared to let go was: 'Oh, my God, I'm twenty-seven.' I was worried that I was going to be like some lonely old maid" (p. 274).

What are some early indicators that a dating partner is likely to become violent eventually? A date who is likely to someday become physically violent often exhibits one or more of the following characteristics:

1. Handles ordinary disagreements or disappointments with inappropriate anger or rage
2. Has to struggle to retain self-control when some little thing triggers anger

3. Goes into tirades
4. Is quick to criticize or to be verbally mean
5. Appears unduly jealous, restricting, and controlling
6. Has been violent in previous relationships (Island and Letellier 1991, pp. 158–66)

Dating violence is never acceptable. Making conscious decisions about whether to marry a certain person raises the possibility of not marrying him or her. Letting go of a relationship can be painful. Next, we'll look at the possibility of breaking up.

The Possibility of Breaking Up

Returning to Reiss's wheel theory of love, we note that once people fall in love, they may not necessarily stay in love. Relationships may "keep turning," or they may slow down or reverse themselves. Sometimes love's reversal, and eventual breakup, is a good thing: "Perhaps the hardest part of a relationship is knowing when to salvage things and when not to" (Sternberg 1988a, p. 242). Being committed is not always noble, as in cases of relationships characterized by violence or consistent verbal abuse, for example (partner abuse is discussed in Chapter 13). Committed love will require some sacrifices over the course of time. However, as one therapist put it, "Love should not hurt" (Doble 2006).

According to the exchange perspective, dating couples choose either to stay committed or to break up by weighing the rewards of their relationship against its costs. As partners go through this process, they also consider how well their relationship matches an imagined, ideal one. Partners also contemplate alternatives to the relationship, the investments they've made in it, and barriers to breaking up. (This perspective is also used when examining people's decisions about divorce, as discussed in Chapter 15.)

When a partner's rewards are higher than the costs, when there are few desirable alternatives to the relationship, when the relationship comes close to one's ideal, when one has invested a great deal in the relationship, and when the barriers to breaking up are perceived as high, an individual is likely to remain committed. However, when costs outweigh rewards, when there are desirable alternatives to the relationship, when one's relationship does not match one's ideal, when little has been invested in the relationship in comparison to rewards, and when there are fewer barriers to breaking up, couples are more likely to do so.

Even when a couple does not break up, recent research on dating couples has found support for the *principle of least interest* whereby the less involved partner wields more power in and control over the continuation or ending of the relationship (Waller 1951). Relatedly, some research has found that the lesser valued partner in a relationship is more inclined toward jealousy and yet also more willing to forgive the more highly valued partner for relationship indiscretions (Sidelinger and Booth-Butterfield 2007). However, high relationship satisfaction and stability are associated with equal emotional involvement (Crawford, Feng, and Fischer 2003; Sprecher, Schmeeckle, and Felmlee 2006). Having examined the processes through which individuals and couples move as they select a spouse, we turn to a discussion of cohabitation as a step in choosing a marriage partner.

"Put me on your do-not-call list."

Cohabitation and Marital Quality and Stability

Cohabitation serves different purposes for different couples: Living together "may be a precursor to marriage, a trial marriage, a substitute for marriage, or simply a serious boyfriend–girlfriend relationship" (Bianchi and Casper 2000, p. 17). Since the 1970s, the proportion of marriages preceded by cohabitation has grown steadily, and by 1995, a majority of marriages followed this pattern (Bumpass and Lu 2000). Cohabitation as a "substitute for marriage" is discussed at length in Chapter 8. Here we address cohabitation as a stage in choosing a spouse. Specifically, we will explore this question: How does cohabiting affect subsequent marital quality and stability?

Since about 1990, the proportion of cohabitors who eventually married their partners has declined (Seltzer 2000, p. 1,252). This situation is largely due to the fact that cohabiting has become more socially acceptable, a cultural change that "contributes to a decline in cohabiting partners' expectations about whether marriage is the 'next step' in their own relationship" (Seltzer 2000, p. 1,249). Another reason that fewer cohabitors are marrying has to do with economics: Poor cohabiting couples are less likely to marry (Gibson-Davis 2009; Lichter, Qian, and Mellott 2006).

Nevertheless, at least half of today's married couples between ages eighteen and forty-nine report having lived together before their wedding (Saad 2008b). Many of them began cohabiting with definite plans to marry their partner. "Thus, first-time cohabitors often believe their union is part of the marriage process" (Guzzo 2009a, p. 198). On the other hand, cohabitors may gradually come to believe that they'll marry eventually. One study found that cohabitors who had talked about future marriage had "generally been living with their partners for about two years, indicating that the issue of greater permanence in their relationships surfaces over time" (Sassler 2004, p. 501). All else being equal, cohabiting couples who identify as conservative Protestants are more likely than other cohabitors to marry (Eggebeen and Dew 2009).

Many young people today follow the intuitive belief that "cohabitation is a worthwhile experiment for evaluating the compatibility of a potential spouse, [and therefore] one would expect those who cohabit first to have even more stable marriages than those who marry without cohabiting" (Seltzer 2000, p. 1,252; see also Manning 2009; "Marriage" 2008). Among high school seniors, about two-thirds agreed that "[i] t is usually a good idea for a couple to live together before getting married in order to find out whether they really get along" (The National Marriage Project 2009, Figure 18).

At this point, research in inconclusive on whether doing so is really a good idea. Interestingly, however, a study of 120 heterosexuals cohabiting for about one year found that those who lived together to test their compatibility had more negative couple communication and generally poorer quality relationships than those who reported cohabiting for other reasons (Rhoades, Stanley, and Markman 2009).

So far, there has not been much research on whether cohabitation that is limited only to one's future spouse increases or decreases the odds of marital success. We can report that findings from a national representative sample show the divorce rate for serial cohabitors to be twice that for women who cohabited only with their eventual husbands (Lichter and Qian 2008). A second study that also used a national representative sample (of 6,577 women) found that premarital cohabitation that was limited to the woman's future husband did not increase the couple's likelihood of divorce (Teachman 2003). This situation also appears to be true for remarriages: Cohabiting with only one's future second spouse has been found not to increase divorce likelihood (Teachman 2008a).

Meanwhile, research over the past twenty years has consistently shown that marriages which are preceded by more than one instance of cohabitation are *more* likely to end in separation or divorce than are marriages in which the spouses had not previously cohabited at all (Xu, Hudspeth, and Bartkowski 2006). However, one study shows that these findings apply to non-Hispanic whites but not to African Americans or Mexican Americans, for whom cohabiting may be a more normative life course event, as discussed in Chapter 8 (Phillips and Sweeney 2005). Why might serial cohabitation before marriage be related to lower marital stability? Hypotheses to answer this question can be divided into two categories—*experience* and *selection*—both of which are supported to some degree by research.

First, the **experience hypothesis** posits that cohabiting experiences themselves affect individuals so that, once married, they are more likely to divorce (Seltzer 2000). For example, serial cohabitation may adversely affect subsequent marital quality and stability inasmuch as the experiences actually weaken commitment because "'successful' cohabitation demonstrates that reasonable alternatives to marriage exist" (Thomson and Colella 1992, p. 377). There is also evidence that "young adults become more tolerant of divorce as a result of cohabiting, whatever their initial views were," possibly because "cohabiting exposes people to a wider range of attitudes about family arrangements than those who marry without first living together" (Seltzer 2000, p. 1,253; see also Dush, Cohan, and Amato 2003; Popenoe and Whitehead 2000).

A related hypothesis suggests that some cohabiting couples, who would not have married if they had been simply dating but not living together, do end up marrying just because getting married seems to be the expected next thing to do. We can assume that it is less difficult to end an unsatisfactory dating relationship than a cohabiting one. Furthermore, research has found that cohabitors who marry after having a nonmarital birth experience lower marital relationship quality than do nonparent cohabitors who eventually marry (Tach and Halpern-Meekin 2009). This finding may result from the fact that cohabiting parents are more likely to marry mainly because they feel that they should. Choosing by default, couples may "slide" from cohabiting into marrying, rather than making more deliberative decisions (Stanley, Rhoades, and Markman 2006; Stanley 2009).

Second, the **selection hypothesis** assumes that individuals who choose serial cohabitation (or who "select" themselves into cohabitating situations) are different from those who do not; these differences translate into higher divorce rates. Serial cohabitors are more likely to have low relative education and income as well as less effective problem-solving and communication skills—factors related to divorce (Amato et al. 2008; Lichter and Qian 2008; Thornton, Axinn, and Xie 2007). Furthermore, those who choose serial cohabitation may have more negative attitudes about marriage in general and more accepting attitudes toward divorce.

An important international study lends considerable support to the selection hypothesis (Liefbroer and Dourleijn 2006). This study looked at the effects of cohabitation on marital stability in several countries and found that cohabiting had no negative effect on marital stability in countries such as Norway, where cohabiting is more common than in the United States. The researchers reasoned that in societies where cohabitation is about as common as marriage, those who live together before marrying would not be significantly different from those who do not. Therefore, no selection effect would be operating. The fact that this research found no negative effect of cohabitation on marital stability in societies where there would be little selection effect supports the selection hypothesis. Other support for the selection hypothesis is the finding that negative effects of cohabitation apply more strongly for non-Hispanic whites than for blacks or Mexican Americans, the latter two racial/ethnic groups having a higher percentage of cohabitors (Phillips and Sweeney 2005).

© Digital Vision/Getty Images

Love is a process of discovery that involves continual exploration and sharing. Choosing a supportive partner is an important factor in developing a satisfying long-term relationship. Creating and maintaining that union involves recognizing that challenges will arise and committing to face and overcome them.

Maintaining a satisfying long-term relationship is challenging, if only because two people, two imaginations, and two sets of needs are involved. Differences *will* arise because no two individuals have exactly the same points of view. Relationships can more often be permanently satisfying, counselors advise, when spouses learn to care for the "unvarnished" other, not a "splendid image" (Van den Haag 1974, p. 142). In this regard, sociologist Judith Wallerstein, reflecting on her own marriage of fifty years, writes:

> I certainly have not been happy all through each year of my marriage. There have been good times and bad, angry and joyful moments, times of ecstasy and times of quiet contentment. But I would never trade my husband, Robert, for another man. I would not swap my marriage for any other. This does not mean that I find other men unattractive, but there is all the difference in the world between a passing fancy and a life plan. For me, there has always been only one life plan, the one I have lived with my husband. (Wallerstein and Blakeslee 1995, p. 8)

Choosing a supportive partner is an important factor in developing this kind of long-term love and relationship satisfaction.

Summary

- Loving is a caring, responsible, and sharing relationship involving deep feelings, and it is a commitment to intimacy. Genuine loving in our competitive society is possible and can be learned.
- Love should not be confused with martyring, manipulating, or limerence.
- People discover love; they don't simply find it. The term *discovering* implies a process—developing and maintaining a loving relationship require seeing the relationship as valuable, committing to mutual needs satisfaction and self-disclosure, engaging in supportive communication, and spending time together.
- Historically in Western cultures, marriages were often arranged in the marriage market, as business deals. In some of the world that is less Westernized, some marriages are still arranged. Some immigrant groups in the United States (and other Westernized societies) today practice arranged or "assisted" marriage.

- Whether marriage partners are arranged, "assisted," or more freely chosen, social scientists typically view people as choosing marriage partners in a marriage market; armed with resources (personal and social characteristics), they bargain for the best deal they can get.
- Although gender roles and expectations are certainly changing, some aspects of the traditional marriage exchange (a man's providing financial support in exchange for the woman's childbearing and child-raising capabilities, domestic services, and sexual availability) remain. Nevertheless, couples today are increasingly likely to value both partners' potential for financial contribution to the union.
- An important factor shaping partner choice is homogamy, the tendency of people to select others with whom they share certain social characteristics. Despite the trend toward declining homogamy, it is still a strong force, encouraged by geographical availability, social pressure, and feeling at home with people like ourselves.
- Committed relationships develop through building rapport and gradually negotiating the relationship as premarital, leading to marriage.
- Serial cohabiting (although not necessarily cohabiting before marriage only with one's future spouse) has been shown to increase the likelihood of divorce. The suggested reasons for this involve the *selection hypothesis* and the *experience hypothesis.*

Questions for Review and Reflection

1. Sternberg offers the triangular theory of love (Figure 6.1). What are its components? Are they useful concepts in analyzing any love experience(s) you have had?
2. Explain reasons why marriages are likely to be homogamous. Why do you think homogamous unions are more stable than heterogamous ones? How might the stability of interracial or interethnic relationships change as society becomes more tolerant of these?
3. If possible, talk to a few married couples you know who lived together before marrying, and ask them how their cohabiting experience influenced their transition to marriage. How do their answers compare with the research findings presented in this chapter?
4. This chapter lists topics that are important to discuss before and throughout one's marriage. Which do you think are the most important? Which do you think are the least important? Why?
5. **Policy Question.** What social policies, if any, presently exist to discourage couples who are experiencing dating violence from getting married? What new policies might be enacted to further discourage dating violence?

Key Terms

arranged marriage 144
assortative mating 148
commitment 139
commitment (Sternberg's triangular theory of love) 139
consummate love 139
cross-national marriages 146
date rape (acquaintance rape) 155
endogamy 148
exogamy 148
experience hypothesis 160
free-choice culture 145
geographic availability 149
heterogamy 148
homogamy 148
interethnic marriages 151
intergenerational transmission of divorce risk 143
interracial marriages 151
intimacy (Sternberg's triangular theory of love) 139
manipulating 142
marital stability 143
marriage market 144
martyring 141
mate selection risk 144
passion (Sternberg's triangular theory of love) 139
pool of eligibles 148
rape myths 155
selection hypothesis 160
self-revelation 155
status exchange hypothesis 152
Sternberg's triangular theory of love 139
wheel of love 155

Online Resources

Sociology CourseMate

www.CengageBrain.com

Access an integrated eBook, chapter-specific interactive learning tools, including flash cards, quizzes, videos, and more in your Sociology CourseMate, accessed through CengageBrain.com.

www.CengageBrain.com

Want to maximize your online study time? Take this easy-to-use study system's diagnostic pre-test, and it will create a personalized study plan for you. By helping you identify the topics that you need to understand better and then directing you to valuable online resources, it can speed up your chapter review. CengageNOW even provides a post-test so you can confirm that you are ready for an exam.

Marriage: From Social Institution to Private Relationship

Marital Status: The Changing Picture

The Time-Honored Marriage Premise: Permanence and Sexual Exclusivity

Facts about Families: Marital Status—The Increasing Proportion of Unmarrieds

The Expectation of Permanence

Expectations of Sexual Exclusivity

Issues for Thought: Three Very Different Subcultures with Norms Contrary to Sexual Exclusivity

From "Yoke Mates" to "Soul Mates"— A Changing Marriage Premise

Weakened Kinship Authority

Finding One's Own Marriage Partner

Marriage and Love

Deinstitutionalized Marriage

Institutional Marriage

Companionate Marriage

Individualized Marriage

Individualized Marriage and the Postmodern Family—*Decline* or Inevitable *Change*?

Deinstitutionalized Marriage—Examining the Consequences

Focus on Children: Child Outcomes and Marital Status: Does Marriage Matter?

Facts about Families: Marriage and Children in Poverty

A Closer Look at Diversity: African Americans and "Jumping the Broom"

Valuing Marriage—The Policy Debate

Policies from the Family Decline Perspective

Policies from the Family Change Perspective

Happiness and Life Satisfaction: How Does Marriage Matter?

Marital Satisfaction and Choices Throughout Life

Preparation for Marriage

Age at Marriage, Marital Stability and Satisfaction

The First Years of Marriage

Creating Couple Connection

Between 80 and 90 percent of American adults today are, have been, or will be married for at least part of their lives (Stevenson and Wolfers 2007). Seventy-five percent of those in their twenties plan to marry someday (Bergman 2006a). Consistently, surveys show married people to be happier and healthier than unmarrieds. In research reported by sociologist Cherlin (2005), "One question asked of adults was whether they agreed with the statement, 'Marriage is an outdated institution.' Only 10 percent of Americans agreed—a lower share than any developed nation except Iceland" (Cherlin 2005, p. 44).

Nevertheless, according to a national Gallup poll, fewer than two-thirds of American adults under age fifty think that it's very important for a committed couple to marry—even when they plan to spend the rest of their lives together (Saad 2006b). That's a major change from sixty years ago, when marriage seemed the only option for the vast majority of committed (heterosexual) couples. Nevertheless, although the situation is much less clear-cut than now, marriage in the United States continues to be the most socially acceptable—and stable—gateway to family life.

In this chapter and the one that follows, we explore marriage as a changing institution, along with other ways to fashion family life. This chapter describes what distinguishes marriage from other couple relationships, then examines the changing nature of marriage, and ends with an exploration of recently married couples' relationships. We will see that getting married announces a personal life course decision to one's relatives, to the community, and, yes, to the state. Despite wide variations, marriages today have an important element in common: the commitment that partners make publicly—to each other and to the institution of marriage itself (Cherlin 2004; Goode 2007 [1982]). Put another way, getting married—as opposed to cohabiting, for instance—is not only a private relationship but also a publicly proclaimed commitment. We'll further explore research on the benefits of marriage for adults and children, and examine government initiatives to strengthen marriage. We begin by looking at marital status in the United States today.

Marital Status: The Changing Picture

Do you have friends who are "living together"? Maybe they are raising children. Maybe you know someone who says that she or he is "happily divorced." Do you know married couples who don't have children, either because they're putting it off or they don't want children at all? If you're in your twenties or thirties, you may have trouble believing that these situations were far from ordinary not long ago. However, marriage is different now than it was in the days of our parents and grandparents. Figure 7.1 shows the marriage, divorce, and birth rates in the United States from 1950 to between 2007 and 2008. As you can see from that figure:

1. The marriage rate has generally declined—from 11.1 marriages (that is, weddings) per 1,000 population in 1950, to 7.1 in 2008 (Tejada-Vera and Sutton 2009, Table A). In 1960, nearly 90 percent of women and men between ages thirty-five and forty-four were

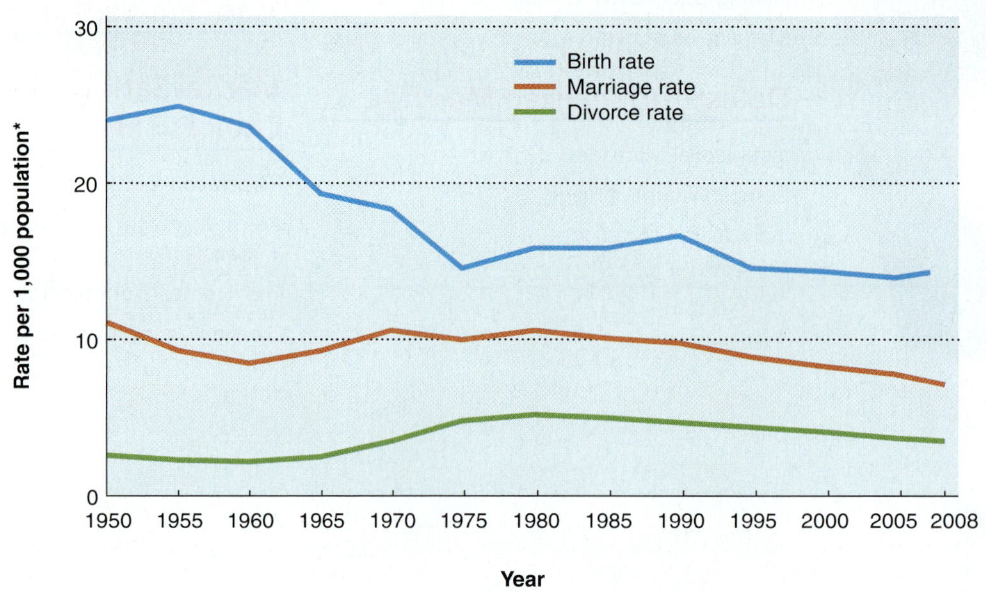

Figure 7.1 U.S. marriage, divorce, and birth rates, 1950 to 2007–08

Sources: Hamilton, Martin, and Ventura 2009, p. 2; Tejada-Vera and Sutton 2009, Table A; U.S. Census Bureau 2007a, Table 72.

married, compared with about 70 percent today (The National Marriage Project 2009, Figure 3).

2. The divorce rate is higher today than in 1960, when there were 2.2 divorces per 1,000 population. In 2008, that figure was 3.5 (Tejada-Vera and Sutton 2009, Table A). With ups and downs, the U.S. divorce rate has climbed since the nineteenth century. In the 1920s, the divorce rate accelerated somewhat. Then between about 1965 and 1975, the divorce rate doubled—a phenomenon that some policy makers call the *divorce revolution* (Popenoe 2007). By the mid-1970s, divorces reached an all-time high. Although the rate has slowly but steadily declined since then, it remains significantly higher than it was fifty years ago.
3. The birth rate has steadily declined since 1950—from 24.1 births per 1,000 population in 1950, to 14.3 in 2007 (Hamilton, Martin, and Ventura 2009, p. 2).[1]

Zigy Kaluzny-Charles Thatcher/Getty Images

Marking a couple's commitment, weddings are public events because the community has a stake in marriage as a social institution. Publicly proclaiming commitment to the marriage premise can help to enforce a couple's mutual trust in the permanence of their union. More and more, however, marriage seems to be reserved for the middle and upper classes—those who feel that they can afford this component of the American dream.

These three indicators—marriage, divorce, and birth rates—present a changing picture of marriage over the past sixty years. Today, 57 percent of U.S. adults are currently married (U.S. Census Bureau 2009a, Table A1; 2010b, Table 56)—a proportion that has been slowly declining over the past several decades. Although this situation results partly from a continuing trend of generally rising divorce rates since the early twentieth century, it also marks a fairly dramatic change from a few decades ago (Coontz 1992, 2005b). Throughout the first half of the twentieth century, the trend was for more people to marry and at increasingly younger ages.[2] Moreover, about 80 percent of those unions lasted until the children left home (Scanzoni 1972). In the 1960s, that trend reversed, and since then, the tendency has been for smaller and smaller proportions of Americans to be married. "Facts About Families: Marital Status—The Increasing Proportion of Unmarrieds" further explores marital status in the United States today.

One reason for these changes—perhaps seeming ironic at first glance—is that we increasingly expect to find love in marriage. How would expecting to find love in marriage be associated with fewer of us being married? The following sections answer this question. To begin, we examine the time-honored marriage premise, with its expectations for permanence and sexual exclusivity.

The Time-Honored Marriage Premise: Permanence and Sexual Exclusivity

Why does a marriage today require a wedding, witnesses, and a license from the state? Around four hundred years ago in Western Europe, the government, representing the community, officially became involved in marriage (House 2002; Thornton 2009). For about one century before that, Roman Catholic Canon Law included rules, or canons, that regulated European marriage—although the canons, difficult to enforce in widely separated rural villages, were often ignored (Halsall 2001; House 2002; Therborn

[1] Rates per 1,000 population are not the ideal way to present these data, because population characteristics, such as the fact that the U.S. population has aged, are not taken into account. However, rates per 1,000 population are the only data available for presenting this long-term, historical comparison. The fertility rate for women of childbearing age (15 to 44) evidences the same trend as in Figure 7.1 (Hamilton, Martin, and Ventura 2009, Figure 1).

[2] For men, median age at first marriage in 1890—the year when the government first began to calculate and report this statistic—was 26.1. For both women and men, median ages at first marriage fell from 1890 until 1960, when they began to rise again. Around 1950, family sociologists described a standard pattern of marriage at about age twenty for women and twenty-two for men (Aldous 1978).

Facts about Families

Marital Status—The Increasing Proportion of Unmarrieds

The proportion of unmarrieds age eighteen and over climbed from 28 percent of the total population in 1970, to 43 percent in 2008 (U.S. Census Bureau 2010b, Table 56). Figure 7.2 compares marital status proportions for non-Hispanic white, Hispanic, African American, and Asian women and men. As you can see in Figure 7.2, for instance, Asian Americans are most likely to be married and least likely to be divorced. African Americans are likely to be never married, followed by Hispanics. Cohabitors, more fully explored in Chapter 8, may be never married, divorced, or widowed.

The Never-Married

There is a growing tendency for young adults to postpone marriage until they are older. By 2009, the median age at first marriage for both men and women had risen to 25.9 for women and 28.1 for men (U.S. Census Bureau 2010a, Table MS-2).

As a consequence of postponing marriage, the proportion of singles in their twenties has risen dramatically. In 1970, 36 percent of women age twenty through twenty-four were never-married; by 2008, that figure had risen to 79 percent. The ranks of never-married men age twenty through twenty-four have increased from 55 percent in 1970 to 87 percent in 2008 (Saluter and Lugaila 1998; U.S. Census Bureau 2010b, Table 57).

This proportion of unmarrieds is striking when compared with the 1970s—and all the more striking when compared with the 1950s. However, this situation is not so unusual in a broader time frame. That is, the percentage of never-married men and women age twenty through twenty-four today is comparable to the proportion of young adults never married at the turn of the twentieth century (Arnett 2004).

The Divorced

The growing divorce rate has contributed to the increased number of singles. In 2008, 9 percent of men and 12 percent of women age eighteen and over were divorced. These proportions show a sharp increase from 1980, when 4 percent of men and 6 percent of women were divorced (U.S. Census Bureau 2000, Table 53; U.S. Census Bureau 2010b, Table 56). Although the divorce rate is no longer rising, it is stable at a high level, and the divorced will continue to be a substantial component of the unmarried population. Chapter 15 addresses divorce.

The Widowed

Unlike the other unmarried categories, the proportion of widowed women and men has remained about the same over the past several decades—between 2 and 3 percent for men, and between 9 and 12 percent for women (U.S. Census Bureau 2010b, Table 56). Death rates declined throughout the twentieth century, reducing the chances of widowhood for the young and middle-aged—although the wars in Afghanistan and Iraq unfortunately remind us that the widowed can be young as well. Meanwhile, the proportion of older people in the population has increased, and an older person has a greater risk of losing a spouse. Furthermore, widows (though not widowers) find it difficult to remarry, due to the significantly higher number of older women than older men, a situation discussed in Chapter 17.

Critical Thinking

How do you think the decreasing proportion of marrieds has affected American society in general and child raising in particular? What changes in cultural attitudes have helped to cause the high proportion of unmarrieds today? What structural factors have helped to cause the high proportion of unmarrieds?

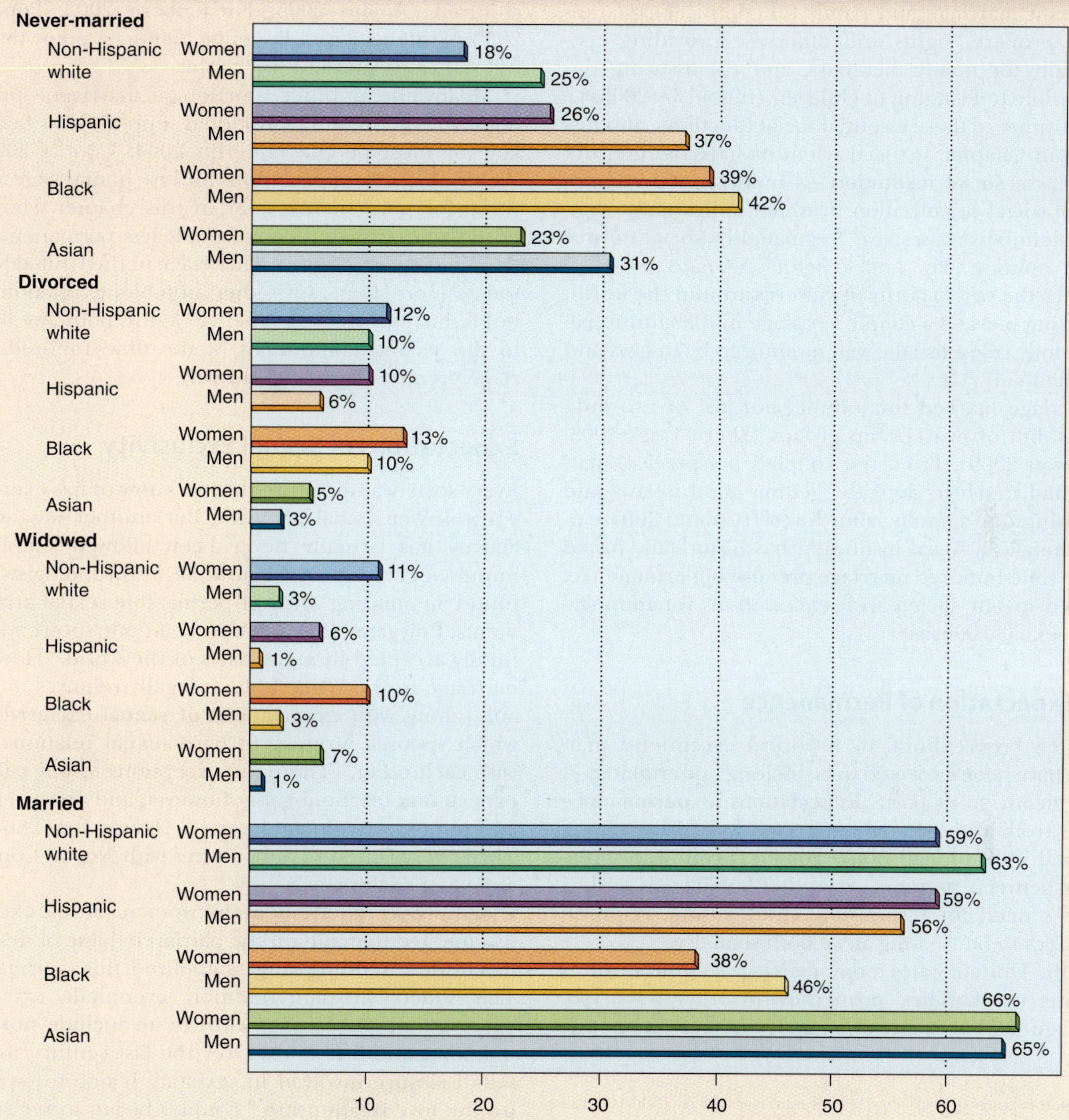

Figure 7.2 Marital status of the U.S. population, age 18 and over, 2008, by race/ethnicity and age

Source: U.S. Census Bureau 2010b, Table 57.

2004).[3] Even in the absence of Canon Law, communities throughout the world, represented by kinship groups or extended families, had always claimed a stake in two important marriage and family functions: (1) guaranteeing property rights and otherwise providing economically for family members, and (2) assuring the responsible upbringing of children (Ingoldsby 2006a).

Partly due to these essential social functions, also discussed in Chapter 1, social scientists have defined the family as a **social institution**—a fundamental component of social organization in which individuals, occupying defined statuses, are "regulated by social norms, public opinion, law and religion" (Amato 2004, p. 961).[4] In the vast majority of cultures around the world, a wedding marked a couple's passage into institutionalized family roles, usually well monitored by in-laws and extended kin.

Marriage marked the joining, not just of two individuals, but of two kinship groups (Sherif-Trask 2003; Thornton 2009). From the couple's perspective, marriage had much to do with "getting good in-laws and increasing one's family labor force" (Coontz 2005b, p. 6). Family as a social institution has historically rested on the time-honored **marriage premise** of permanence, coupled in our society with expectations for monogamous sexual exclusivity.

The Expectation of Permanence

With few cross-cultural or historical exceptions, marriages have been expected to be lifelong undertakings—"until death do us part." **Expectations of permanence** derive from the fact that marriage was historically a practical institution (Coontz 2005b). Economic agreements between partners' extended families, as well as society's need for responsible child raising, required marriages to be "so long as we both shall live."

In the United States today, marriage seldom involves merging two families' properties. In other ways, too, marriage is less critically important for economic security. Furthermore, marriage today is less decisively associated with raising children, although marriage remains significantly related to better outcomes for children (Amato 2005; Furstenberg 2003; Popenoe 2008; Whitehead and Popenoe 2006)—a point that we will return to later in this chapter.

Meanwhile, another function of marriage—providing love and ongoing emotional support—has become key for most people (Cherlin 2004; Coontz 2005b). We explore how expectations for love in marriage affect those for permanence later in this chapter. Here we note that marriage is considerably less permanent now than in the past. However, marriage in the United States today, more than any other non-blood relationship, holds the hope for permanence. At this point, we'll turn to the second component of the time-honored marriage premise—sexual exclusivity.

Expectations of Sexual Exclusivity

Every society and culture that we know of has exercised control over sexual behavior. Put another way, sexual activity has virtually never been allowed simply on impulse or at random. Meanwhile, anthropologists have found an amazing array of permissible sexual arrangements. **Polygamy** (having more than one spouse) is culturally accepted in many parts of the world.[5] However, marriage in the United States legally requires monogamy, along with **expectations of sexual exclusivity**, in which spouses promise to have sexual relations only with each other. (There are exceptions to our cultural expectation for monogamy, however, and three of these exceptions are touched on in "Issues for Thought: Three Very Different Subcultures with Norms Contrary to Sexual Exclusivity.")

In Europe, requirements for women's sexual exclusivity emerged to maintain the patriarchal line of descent; the bride's wedding ring symbolized this expectation. The Judeo-Christian tradition eventually extended expectations of sexual exclusivity to include not only wives but also husbands. Over the last century, as "the self-disclosure involved in sexuality [came to] symbolize the love relationship," couples began to see sexual exclusivity as a mark of romantic commitment (Reiss 1986, p. 56).

Today, expectations of sexual exclusivity have broadened from the purely physical to include expectations of emotional centrality, or putting one's partner first. Indeed, some marriage counselors now speak of "emotional affairs" (Herring 2005; Meier, Hull, and Ortyl

[3] The Netherlands first enacted a civil marriage law in 1590 (Gomes 2004). England passed its first Marriage Act in 1653 but did not require a legal marriage license until 1754 (House 2002). Shortly after Europeans established colonies in the United States, they enacted rules for marriage similar to those that they had known in Europe (Cott 2000). In the four hundred years since then, our federal and state governments have generated a massive number of marriage-related laws and court decisions. For instance, polygamy has been illegal in the United States since 1878, and due to laws enacted at the turn of the twentieth century, unmarried cohabitation is still illegal in some states, although the laws are seldom enforced (Hartsoe 2005). Also, before issuing a marriage license, some states require blood tests for various communicable diseases. Many states have waiting periods, ranging from seventy-two hours to six days, between the license application date and the wedding ("Chart: State Marriage License" 2006).

[4] Social scientists typically point to five major social institutions: family, religion, government or politics, the economy, and education.

[5] Polygamy can be divided into two types. *Polygyny*, a form of polygamy whereby a man can have multiple wives, "is a marriage form found in more places and at more times than any other" (Coontz 2005b, p. 10). However, polygyny is not always that frequent, because many men cannot afford multiple wives. Polyandry is rare (Stephens 1963). *Polyandry*—a woman's having many husbands—is still less frequent.

Issues for Thought

Three Very Different Subcultures with Norms Contrary to Sexual Exclusivity

Although a very substantial majority of Americans value monogamy as a cultural standard, there are subcultural exceptions. This box looks at three of these subcultural exceptions, each one very different from the others—polygamy, polyamory, and swinging.

Polygamy

Polygamy has been illegal in the United States since 1878, when the U.S. Supreme Court ruled that freedom to practice the Mormon religion did not extend to having multiple wives (*Reynolds v. United States* 1878). Today, some activists are pursuing U.S. legalization of polygamy (Stacey and Meadow 2009).

Although a 2006 Gallup poll found that one-quarter of Americans think that most Mormons endorse polygamy (Carroll 2006), this is not the case. The Church of Jesus Christ of Latter-day Saints (LDS) no longer permits polygamy. Nevertheless, there are dissident Mormons (not recognized as LDS by the mainstream church) who follow the traditional teachings and take multiple wives (Woodward 2001, p. 50). Some multiple wives have argued that polygyny is a feminist arrangement because the sharing of domestic responsibilities benefits working women (D. Johnson 1991; Joseph 1991).

Federal law prohibits prospective immigrants who practice polygamy from entering the United States. However, polygamy has been found in New York among some immigrants from countries in which it is practiced (Bernstein 2007). Civil libertarians argue that the Supreme Court should rescind its *Reynolds* decision on the grounds that the right to privacy permits this choice of domestic lifestyle as much as any other (Slark 2004).

Polyamory

Polyamory means "many loves" and refers to marriages in which one or both spouses retain the option to sexually love others in addition to their spouse (Polyamory Society n.d.).

Deriving their philosophy from the sexually open marriage movement, which received considerable publicity in the late 1960s and 1970s, polyamorous spouses agree that each may have openly acknowledged sexual relationships with others while keeping the marriage relationship primary. Unlike in swinging, outside relationships can be emotional as well as sexual. Couples usually establish limits on the degree of sexual and/or emotional involvement of the outside relationship, along with ground rules concerning honesty and what details to tell each other (Macklin 1987, p. 335; Rubin 2001). "Polyamorists are more committed to emotional fulfillment and family building than recreational swingers" (Rubin 2001, p. 721).

Some polyamorous couples are raising children. The Polyamory Society's Children Educational Branch offers advice for polyamorous parents and maintains a PolyFamily scholarship fund, as well as the Internet-based "PolyKids Zine," and "PolyTeens Zine," both designed to present "uplifting PolyFamily stories and lessons about PolyFamily ethical living" (Polyamory Society n.d.). Like polygamy, polyamory has received some media attention in the last several years, and polyamorists are working toward greater social acceptance. Some polyamorists want to establish legally sanctioned group marriages and have begun to organize in that direction (Anderlini-D'Onofrio 2004). Conservative groups, such as the Institute for American Values, see such moves as evidence of an emergent "radical sensibility" that threatens American values and harms children (Marquardt n.d., p. 30; Kurtz 2006).

Swinging

Swinging is a marriage arrangement in which couples exchange partners to engage in purely recreational sex. Swinging gained media and research attention as one of several "alternative lifestyles" in the late 1960s and early 1970s (Rubin 2001). At that time, it was estimated that about 2 percent of adults in the United States had participated in swinging at least once (Gilmartin 1977).

Although little research has been done on swinging in the past few decades, "lifestyle practitioners," as some swingers now prefer to be called, still exist as a minority subculture. It has been estimated that there are now about 3 million married swingers in the United States, an increase of about one million since 1990. Some of this growth is probably due to the Internet, which helps to link potential swingers (Rubin 2001).

Interestingly, as a category, swingers tend to be middle-aged, middle-class, and more socially and politically conservative than one might expect (Jenks 1998; Rubin 2001). Although they often face the challenge of managing jealousy, swingers emphasize the lifestyle's positive effects—variety, for example (deVisser and McDonald 2007). Former swingers who have given up the lifestyle point to problems with jealousy, guilt, competing emotional attachments, and fear of being discovered by other family members, friends, or neighbors (Macklin 1987).

A couple considering a sexually nonexclusive marriage must take into account not only personal values and relationship management challenges but also the increased risk of being infected with HIV/AIDS. However, condoms are typically available at swing clubs, and "the fear of disease has apparently not inhibited the recent growth of swinging" (Rubin 2001, p. 723).

Critical Thinking

What do you think about these exceptions to monogamy? Do you see them as threatening to American values? If so, why? If not, why not? Does one or more of them seem reasonable to you while others do not? If so, why? If not, why not?

2009). With over 90 percent of us believing an affair is morally wrong ("Marriage" 2008), Americans are less accepting of extramarital sex than are people in many monogamous societies. (Although the vast majority of Americans say that they disapprove of extramarital sex, the picture is somewhat different in practice. Sexual infidelity is explored in Chapter 5.)

To summarize, the marriage premise has changed somewhat over the past century. Expectations for permanence have diminished while those for sexual exclusivity have been extended to include not just physical sex but also emotional centrality. The following section explores how these changes came about.

From "Yoke Mates" to "Soul Mates"—A Changing Marriage Premise

Chapter 1 points to an individualist orientation in our society. In eighteenth-century Europe, **individualism** emerged as a way to think about ourselves. No longer were we necessarily governed by rules of community. Societies changed from **communal**, or **collectivist**, to **individualistic**. In individualistic societies, one's own self-actualization and interests are a valid concern. In collectivist societies, people identify with and conform to the expectations of their extended kin. Western societies are characterized as individualistic, and individualism is positively associated with valuing romantic love (Dion and Dion 1991; Goode 2007 [1982]). (By *Western,* we mean the culture that developed in Western Europe and now characterizes that region and Canada, the United States, Australia, New Zealand, and some other societies.)

The Industrial Revolution and its opportunities for paid work outside the home, particularly in the growing cities and independent of one's kinship group, gave people opportunities for jobs and lives separate from the family. In Europe and the North American colonies, people increasingly entertained thoughts of equality, independence, and even the radically new idea that individuals had a birthright to "the pursuit of happiness" (Coontz 2005b). These ideas were manifested in dramatically unprecedented political events of the late 1700s, such as the U.S. Declaration of Independence and the French Revolution.

The emergent individualistic orientation meant a generally diminished obedience to group authority, because people increasingly saw themselves as separate individuals, rather than as intrinsic members of a group or collective. Individuals began to expect self-fulfillment and satisfaction, personal achievement, and happiness. With regard to marriage, an emergent individualist orientation resulted in three interrelated developments:

1. The authority of kin and extended family weakened.
2. Individuals began to find their own marriage partners.
3. Romantic love came to be associated with marriage.

Weakened Kinship Authority

Kin, or extended family, include parents and other relatives, such as in-laws, grandparents, aunts and uncles, and cousins. Some groups, such as Italian Americans, African Americans, Hispanics, and gay male and lesbian families, also have "fictive" or "virtual" kin—friends who are so close that they are hardly distinguished from actual relatives (Furstenberg 2005; Sarkisian, Gerena, and Gerstel 2006). In collectivist, or communal, cultures, kin have exercised considerable authority over a married couple. For instance, in traditional African societies, a mother-in-law may have more to say about how many children her daughter-in-law should bear than does the daughter-in-law herself (Caldwell 1982).

In Westernized societies, however, kinship authority is weaker. By the 1940s in the United States, at least among white, middle-class Americans, the husband–wife dyad was expected to take precedence over other family relationships. Sociologist Talcott Parsons noted that the American kinship system was not based on extended family ties (1943). Instead, he saw U.S. kinship as comprised of "interlocking conjugal families" in which married people are members of both their **family of orientation** (the family they grew up in) and their **family of procreation** (the one formed by marrying and having children). Parsons viewed the husband–wife bond and the resulting family of procreation as the most meaningful "inner circle" of Americans' kin relations, surrounded by decreasingly important outer circles. However, Parsons pointed out that his model mainly characterized the American middle class. Recent immigrants and lower socioeconomic classes, as well as upper-class families, still relied on meaningful ties to their extended kin.

Although the situation is changing, the extended family (as opposed to the married couple or nuclear family) has been the basic family unit in the majority of non-European countries (Ingoldsby and Smith 2006). In the United States, extended families continue to be important for various European ethnic families, such as Italians, and for Native Americans, blacks, Hispanics, and Asian Americans, as well as other immigrant families (Gowan 2009; Kent 2007; Mather 2009; Richardson 2009).

Norms about extended-family ties derive both from cultural influences and from economic or other practical circumstances (Hamon and Ingoldsby 2003; Wong, Yoo, and Stewart 2006). Immigrants from many

"The Dinner Quilt," *Faith Ringgold, 1986*

less-developed nations work in the United States and send money to extended kin in their home countries (Ha 2006). Among Hispanics, *la familia* ("the family") means the extended as well as the nuclear family.

More and more Hispanics today value the primacy of the conjugal bond (Hirsch 2003). Meanwhile, like the Italians that Gans (1982 [1962]) studied in the 1960s, many Hispanics live in comparatively large, reciprocally supportive kinship networks (Sarkisian, Gerena, and Gerstel 2006; Lugo Steidel and Contreras 2003). For example, many Puerto Rican families have lived in "ethnically specific enclaves" and may rely as much on extended kin as on conjugal ties (Wilkinson 1993). Asian immigrants are also likely to emphasize extended kin ties over the marital relationship (Glick, Bean, and Van Hook 1997).

We can sometimes get a glimpse of mainstream American individualism through the eyes of fairly recent immigrants from more collectivist societies. For example, a Vietnamese refugee describes his reaction to U.S. housing patterns, which reflect nuclear, rather than extended-family, norms:

> Before I left Vietnam, three generations lived together in the same group. My mom, my family including wife and seven children, my elder brother, his wife and three children, my little brother and two sisters—we live in a big house. So when we came here we are thinking of being united in one place. But there is no way. However, we try to live as close as possible. (quoted in Gold 1993, p. 303)

American housing architecture similarly discourages many Muslim families—from India, Pakistan, or Bangladesh, for example—who would prefer to live in extended-family households (Nanji 1993).

All this is not to say that extended-family members are irrelevant to non-Hispanic white families in the United States. Nuclear families maintain significant emotional and practical ties with extended kin and parents-in-law (Lee, Spitze, and Logan 2003). A qualitative study with a sample that was 95 percent white showed that uncles often mentor nephews or nieces (Milardo 2005). Extensive data from the Longitudinal Study of Generations show that young adults today highly value their parents and extended families (Bengston, Biblarz, and Roberts 2007). However, as individuals and couples increasingly become more urban—and more geographically mobile—the power of kin to exercise social control over family members declines. If an individualist orientation has weakened kinship authority, it has also led to the desire to find one's own spouse.

Finding One's Own Marriage Partner

Arranged marriage has characterized collectivist societies (Hamon and Ingoldsby 2003; Ingoldsby 2006b; MacFarquhar 2006; Sherif-Trask 2003). Because a marriage joined extended families, selecting a suitable mate was a "huge responsibility" not to be left to the young people themselves (Tepperman and Wilson 1993, p. 73).

Analyzing arranged marriage in contemporary Bangladesh, sociologist Ashraf Uddin Ahmed notes that an individual's finding his or her own spouse "is thought to be disruptive to family ties, and is viewed as a child's transference of the loyalty from a family orientation to a single person, ignoring obligations to the family and kin group for personal goals" (Ahmed, quoted in Tepperman and Wilson 1993, p. 76). Moreover, there is concern that an infatuated young person might choose a partner who would make a poor spouse.

Ahmed argues that the arranged marriage system has functioned not only to consolidate family property but also to keep the family's traditions and values intact. But as urban economies developed in eighteenth-century Europe and more young people worked away from home, arranged marriages gave way to those in which individuals selected their own mates. Love rather than property became the basis for unions (Coontz 2005b).

Marriage and Love

Throughout the first five thousand years of human history in all the world's cultures that we know of, people probably fell in love, but they weren't *expected* to do so with their spouses. Marriage was thought to be "too vital an economic and political institution to be entered into solely on the basis of something as irrational as love" (Coontz 2005b, p. 7). Love—an intense, often unpredictable, and possibly transitory emotion—was viewed as threatening to the practical institution of marriage. Valuing romance could lead individuals to ignore or challenge their social responsibilities.[6]

However, with time, the ideology of romantic love came to be expected of marriage (Meier, Hull, and Ortyl 2009). In family historian Stephanie Coontz's words, basing marriage on love and companionship

> represented a break with thousands of years of tradition. . . . Critics of the love match argued . . . that the values of free choice and egalitarianism could easily spin out of control. If the choice of a marriage partner was a personal decision, . . . what would prevent young people . . . from choosing unwisely? If people were encouraged to expect marriage to be the best and happiest experience of their lives, what would hold a marriage together if things were "for worse" rather than "for better"? (2005b, pp. 149–50)

To use Coontz's metaphor, couples were no longer yoked together (like field oxen). "Where once marriage had been seen as the fundamental unit of work and politics, it was now viewed as a place of refuge from work, politics, and community obligations—a haven in a heartless world" (Coontz 2005b, p. 146; Lasch 1977). A successful marriage came to be measured by how well the union met its members' emotional needs.

To summarize this section, emergent individualism in eighteenth-century Europe meant that people, increasingly valuing personal satisfaction and happiness, began to associate romantic love with marriage and, hence, to want to find their own marriage partners, a practice that both resulted from and further caused weakened kinship authority. Couples were no longer bound by the yoke of kin control. As you might guess, the nature of marriage changed. We'll explore that change next.

[6] An interesting way that Europe's twelfth- and thirteenth-century noblemen and women managed love's threat to marriage as a social institution was the practice of *courtly love*. As we have seen, most marriages in the upper levels of society during this period were based on pragmatic considerations, not love. But, as the saying went then, "marriage is no real excuse for not loving" (quoted in Coontz 2005b, p. 6). Among Europe's noblemen and women, romantic love was expressed in relationships outside marriage in which a knight worshipped his lady, and ladies had their favorites. These relationships involved a great deal of idealization and could be adulterous but were not necessarily sexually consummated (Stone 1980). The distinction between romance and marriage was also evident in the lower classes (Coontz 2005b, p. 7).

Deinstitutionalized Marriage

Coontz asserts that love and expectations for intimacy have "conquered marriage" (2005b). What does she mean? Coontz is talking about what family sociologist Andrew Cherlin (2004) has called the **deinstitutionalization of marriage**—a situation in which time-honored family definitions and social norms "count for far less" than in the past (p. 853). For instance, childbearing outside of marriage, once severely stigmatized, now "carries little stigma" (Cherlin et al. 2009a, p. 919; but also see Usdansky 2009a, 2009b).

The following sections present and expand upon Cherlin's analysis of the shift from *institutional* to *companionate* to *individualized* marriage. As we discuss these three kinds of marriage, we need to remember that they are abstractions, or *ideal types*.[7] In reality, marriages approximate these types to varying degrees.

Institutional Marriage

We have witnessed a gradual historical change in Western and Westernized societies away from **institutional marriage**—that is, marriage as a social institution based on dutiful adherence to the time-honored marriage premise, particularly the norm of permanence (Cherlin 2004, 2009a; Coontz 2005b; Thornton 2009).

> Once ensconced in societal mandates for permanence and monogamous sexual exclusivity, the institutionalized marriage in the United States represented the age-old tradition of a family organized around economic production, kinship network, community connections, the father's authority, and marriage as a functional partnership rather than a romantic relationship. . . . Family tradition, loyalty, and solidarity were more important than individual goals and romantic interest. (Doherty 1992, p. 33)

Institutional marriage generally offered practical and economic security, along with the rewards that we often associate with custom and tradition (knowing what to expect in almost any situation, for example). With few exceptions over the past five thousand years, institutional marriage was organized according to patriarchal authority, requiring a wife's obedience to her husband and the kinship group. It is also true that, legally, institutional marriage could involve what today we define as wife and child abuse or neglect. Child and wife abuse were not recognized as social problems in this country until the 1960s and 1970s respectively.

Across cultures, the strength and scope of patriarchal authority varied, however. As an extreme example, in ancient Rome, the *paterfamilias* (family father), having

[7] In this context, the word *ideal* indicates that a type exists as an idea, not that it is necessarily good or preferable.

absolute authority over his wife and children, could legally kill them or sell them into slavery.[8] No matter how old they were, sons were subject to the authority of the *paterfamilias* until he died. A daughter lived under her father's rule until she married, when her father's authority over her was legally transferred to her husband (Long 1875; S. Thompson 2006). In the United States, of course, patriarchal authority never approached anything near that of the ancient Roman *paterfamilias.*

New York Public Library Digital Image Collection

The married couple embedded in this family of Eastern European immigrants who arrived in New York City in 1832 may be in love, but they were not *expected* to find love in marriage. Instead, their union is held together by strong expectations of permanence, bolstered by the social control of the kinship group.

Companionate Marriage

By the 1920s in the United States, family sociologists had begun to note a shift away from institutional marriage, and, in 1945, the first sociology textbook on the American family (by Ernest Burgess and Harvey Locke) was titled *The Family: From Institution to Companionship.* By **companionate marriage**,

> Burgess was referring to the single-earner, breadwinner-homemaker marriage that flourished in the 1950s. Although husbands and wives in the companionate marriage usually adhered to a sharp division of labor, they were supposed to be each other's companions—friends, lovers—to an extent not imagined by the spouses in the institutional marriages of the previous era. . . . Much more so than in the 19th century, the emotional satisfaction of the spouses became an important criterion for marital success. However, through the 1950s, wives and husbands tended to derive satisfaction from their participation in a marriage-based nuclear family. . . . That is to say, they based their gratification on playing marital roles well; being good providers, good homemakers, and responsible parents. (Cherlin 2004, p. 851)

With companionate marriage, middle-class Americans often dreamed of attaining "the white picket fence." That is, they saw marriage as an opportunity for idealized domesticity within the "haven" of their own single-family home.[9] (This is why we have drawn a picket fence to symbolize the companionate marriage bond in Figure 7.3.) Meanwhile, women's increasing educational and work options, coupled with their expectations for marital love, sowed the seeds for the demise of companionate marriage (Cherlin 2004; Coontz 2005c).

An individualistic orientation views each person (both husband *and* wife) as having talents that deserve to be actualized. In this climate, women in companionate marriages began to pursue opportunities for self-actualization, as well as to expect a husband's expressive support for their doing so (Jackson 2007). Furthermore, women challenged centuries of previously ignored domestic violence. Given the tension between gender inequality and expectations for emotionally supported self-actualization, the companionate marriage "lost ground" (Cherlin 2004, p. 852).

By the 1970s, observers noted a movement away from people's finding of personal satisfaction primarily in acceptable role performance—for example, in the role of husband/breadwinner or wife/homemaker. Research on college students showed a shift in self-orientation away from defining themselves according to the roles they played. More and more, they identified themselves in terms of their individual personality traits. But individuals' appreciation for the esteem they get from playing their roles well "buttresses the institutional structure" (Turner 1976, p. 1,011; Babbitt and Burbach 1990). As one result, critics began to warn that American culture was becoming "narcissistic": Individuals appeared less focused on commitment or concern for future generations (Bellah et al. 1985; Lasch 1980).

[8] The occasions on which the *paterfamilias* actually exercised his authority to kill family members were uncommon, however (S. Thompson 2006).

[9] Companionate marriages of the 1950s "were exceptional in many ways. Until that decade, relying on a single breadwinner had been rare. For thousands of years, most women and children had shared the tasks of breadwinning with men. . . . Also new in the 1950s was the cultural consensus that everyone should marry, and that people should do so at a young age. The baby boom of the 1950s was likewise a departure from the past, because birthrates in Western Europe and North America had fallen steadily during the previous 100 years" (Coontz 2005c).

Feminists defined this situation somewhat differently: Attention to domestic abuse, unequal couple decision making, and unfair division of household labor—as well as a wife's ability to more easily leave an intolerable situation through divorce—could be good things (Hackstaff 2007). Some celebrated the fact that American culture would finally begin to make room for "thinking beyond the heteronormative family" (Roseneil and Budgeon 2004, p. 136; Stacey 1996). Coontz summarizes the situation more neutrally: "For better or worse," over the past thirty years, "all the precedents established by the love-based male breadwinner family were . . . thrown into question" (2005b, p. 11; 2005c). However one saw it, by the late 1980s, companionate marriage—which had lasted for but a minute in the long hours of human history—had largely given way to its successor, individualized marriage.

As an ideal type, the *companionate marriage* that characterized most of the twentieth century emphasized love and compatibility, as well as separate gender roles. However, in reality, couples represent this ideal type to varying degrees. Although this Russian immigrant couple, who own and operate a small Los Angeles grocery store, illustrate companionate marriage in *some* ways, they do not fit the definition of companionate marriage in at least one important way: They share the family provider role.

Individualized Marriage

Four interrelated characteristics distinguish **individualized marriage**:

1. It is optional.
2. Spouses' roles are flexible—negotiable and renegotiable.
3. Its expected rewards involve love, communication, and emotional intimacy.
4. It exists in conjunction with a vast diversity of family forms.

Partly because marriage is optional today, brides, grooms, and long-married couples have come to expect different rewards from marriage than people did in the past. They continue to value being good partners and, perhaps, parents. However, today's spouses are less likely to find their only, or definitive, rewards in performing these roles well (Byrd 2009). More than in companionate marriages, partners now expect love and emotional intimacy, open communication, role flexibility, gender equality, and personal growth (Cherlin 2004, 2009a; Meier, Hull, and Ortyl 2009). Over the course of about three centuries, couples have moved "from yoke mates to soul mates" (Coontz 2005b, p. 124).

Intense romantic feelings have been associated with greater marital happiness and may serve to get a married couple through bad times (Udry 1974; Wallerstein and Blakeslee 1995). There can be a downside to all this though. The idealization and unrealistic expectations implicit in individualized marriage can cause problems. Social theorist Anthony Giddens argues that expectations for a relationship based on intimate communication to the extent that "the rewards derived from such communication are the main basis for the relationship to continue" often lead to disappointment: "[M]ost ordinary relationships don't come even close" (Giddens 2007, p. 30). Giddens may be overstating the case. Probably many marriages do come close. However, the fact remains that such high expectations may be associated with the following results:

1. A person's deciding not to marry, because she or he can't find a "soul mate" who can promise this level of togetherness;
2. A high divorce rate (although assuredly there are other reasons for divorce, too, as described in Chapter 15);
3. A lower birth rate as individuals focus on options in addition to raising children, a topic addressed in Chapter 9.

One theme of this text is that society influences people's options and thereby impacts their decisions. To the extent that they are legally, financially, and otherwise able, people today organize their personal, romantic, and family lives as they see fit (Byrd 2009). Some

Figure 7.3a The institutional marriage bond. Couples are "yoked" together by high expectations for permanence, bolstered by the strong social control of extended kin and community.

Figure 7.3b The companionate marriage bond. Couples are bound together by companionship, coupled with a gendered division of labor, pride in performing spousal and parenting roles, and hopes for "the American dream"—a home of their own and a comfortable domestic life together.

Figure 7.3c The individualized marriage bond. Spouses in individualized marriages remain together because they find self-actualization, intimacy, and expressively communicated emotional support in their unions.

engage in "dyadic innovation" (Green 2006, p. 182)—that is, they fashion their relationships with little regard to traditional norms. As a twenty-eight-year-old woman told an interviewer:

> Marriage, just because it's a piece of paper, doesn't necessarily mean it's a relationship or a long-standing relationship. A long-standing relationship can be a boyfriend. If you're with somebody and you love them, I don't really care about the piece of paper. So marriage really never enters my mind. (in Byrd 2009, p. 324)

To summarize, "How good is your relationship?" is often a question equal in importance to "Are you married?" (Giddens 2007).

In this climate, a wide variety of family forms emerge. What today we call the *postmodern* family (see Chapter 1), characterized by "tolerance and diversity, rather than a single-family ideal," takes many forms (Doherty 1992, p. 35). As noted in Chapter 1, some observers view the deinstitutionalization of marriage as a loss for society, a "decline" that hopefully can be turned around (e.g., Whitehead and Popenoe 2006). Others see the deinstitutionalization of marriage simply as an inevitable historical change (e.g., Coontz 2005b, 2005c).

Individualized Marriage and the Postmodern Family—*Decline* or Inevitable *Change*?

Those who view individualized marriage as a *decline* assert that our culture's unchecked individualism has caused widespread moral weakening and self-indulgence. They say that Americans, more self-centered today, are less likely than in the past to choose marriage, are more likely to divorce, and are less child-centered (Blankenhorn 1995; Popenoe 2007, 2008; Stanton 2004a, 2004b; Whitehead and Popenoe 2008). From this point of view, the American family has broken down.

Others, in contrast, see the deinstitutionalization of marriage as resulting from inevitable social *change*. These thinkers point out that, for one thing, people who look back with nostalgia to the good old days may be imagining incorrectly the situation that characterized marriage throughout most of the nineteenth and twentieth centuries. For instance, large families with many children and higher death rates for parents with young children meant that many children were not raised in two-parent households (Coontz 1992). Moreover, we cannot go back:

> [J]ust as we cannot organize modern political alliances through kinship ties or put the farmers' and skilled craftsmen's households back as the centerpiece of the modern economy, we can never reinstate marriage as the primary source of commitment and caregiving in the

modern world. For better or worse, we must adjust our personal expectations and social support systems to this new reality. (Coontz 2005c)

In a climate characterized by debate between spokespersons from these opposing perspectives, researchers and policy makers examine the social consequences of deinstitutionalized marriage.

Deinstitutionalized Marriage: Examining the Consequences

In her seminal 1995 presidential address to the Population Association of America, family demographer Linda Waite (1995) asked rhetorically, "Does Marriage Matter?" She concluded that indeed it does, for both adults and children. After thoroughly reviewing prior research that compared the well-being of family members in married unions with that of those in unmarried households, Waite reported that, as a category, spouses:

- had greater wealth and assets.
- earned higher wages.
- had more frequent and better sex.
- had overall better health.
- were less likely to engage in dangerous risk taking.
- had lower rates of substance abuse.
- were more likely to engage in generally healthy behaviors.

Comparing children's well-being in married families with that of those in one-parent families, Waite found that, as a category, children in married families:

- were about half as likely to drop out of high school.
- reported more frequent contact and better-quality relationships with their parents.
- were significantly less likely to live in poverty.

Since her address, many sociologists and policy makers have further researched and debated Waite's findings. In the section following this one, we will examine the responses of policy makers. Here we review a sampling of demographic data and research findings on the question, "Does marriage matter?"

National income and poverty data apparently support Waite's argument that marrieds are financially better off. The median income for married-couple families in 2007 was $72,589, compared with just $44,358 and $30,296 for unmarried, male- and female-headed households, respectively (U.S. Census Bureau 2010b, Table 683). As Table 7.1 indicates, even when a wife is not in the labor force, married-couple households earn from $2,000 to $4,000 more annually than do unmarried male householders. This income gap is dramatically higher when marrieds are compared with unmarried female householders (U.S. Census Bureau 2010b, Table 683). Clearly, these data support the argument that higher income is positively associated with marriage. Furthermore, since Waite's address, studies have continued to find that, compared to unmarrieds, spouses in enduring marriages generally have better physical and mental health (Dush, Taylor, and Kroeger 2008; Liu 2009; Popenoe 2008; Williams, Sassler, and Nicholson 2008).

However, research also suggests that the association between marriage and positive outcomes is more complex than Waite indicated. For example, marrieds, on average, are less often depressed than the widowed and the divorced. But those in first marriages are not necessarily less depressed than either the remarried or the never married (Bierman, Fazio, and Milkie 2006; LaPierre 2009). Then, too, in addition to being married, education, a comfortable income, and (among blacks) not having to suffer from society-wide racism improve mental health (Bierman, Fazio, and Milkie 2006; Mandara et al. 2008). Finally, marrieds have more frequent sex than unmarrieds when all unmarrieds are categorized together, but they do not have more frequent sex than cohabiting couples (Waite 1995).

An early criticism of Waite's claims was that much—although not all—of the association between marriage and positive outcomes was due to *selection effects.* In researchers' language, people may "select" themselves into a category being investigated—in this case, marriage—and this self-selection can yield the results for which the researcher was testing. Increasingly,

Table 7.1 Median Income of Families by Types of Family in Constant (2007) Dollars: 1990 to 2007

	All Married-Couple Families	Married-Couple Families, Wife in Paid Labor Force	Married-Couple Families, Wife Not in Paid Labor Force	Unmarried Male Family Householder	Unmarried Female Family Householder
1990	$61,354	$71,937	$46,544	$44,669	$26,039
2000	$71,157	$83,361	$48,140	$45,425	$30,963
2007	$72,589	$86,435	$47,329	$44,358	$30,296

Source: U.S. Census Bureau 2010b, Table 683.

individuals with superior education, incomes, and physical and mental health are more likely to marry (Bierman, Fazio, and Milkie 2006; England and Edin 2007; Goodwin, McGill, and Chandra 2009, Figure 6; Schoen and Cheng 2006; Teitler and Reichman 2008). The **selection hypothesis** posits that many of the benefits associated with marriage—for example, higher income and wealth, along with better health—are therefore actually due to the personal characteristics of those who choose to marry (Cherlin 2003). For example, married women are more likely than those who are cohabiting or heading single-family households to inherit wealth (Ozawa and Lee 2006). Being positioned to inherit wealth from one's family of origin is a personal characteristic that *precedes* getting married.

Nevertheless, not all the benefits associated with marriage are accounted for by selection effects. In contrast to the selection hypothesis, the **experience hypothesis** holds that something about the *experience* of being married itself causes these benefits—a point that we will return to at the end of this chapter. Figure 7.4 illustrates the selection and the experience hypotheses. Meanwhile, considerable research has focused on examining the relationships between marriage and the consequences for children.

Child Outcomes and Marital Status: Does Marriage Matter?

The proportion of children under age eighteen living with two married parents declined steadily over the past forty years—from 85 percent in 1970, to 77 percent in 1980, to 67 percent in 2008 (U.S. Federal Interagency Forum on Child and Family Statistics 2006, 2009). About 20 million children under age eighteen (27 percent of all U.S. children) live in single-parent households (U.S. Federal Interagency Forum on Child and Family Statistics 2009). Twenty-three percent of all U.S. children reside in single-mother households, with another 4 percent living with single fathers. Nearly half (49 percent) of all single-parent families are non-Hispanic white. Blacks comprise 29 percent of single-parent families; Hispanics, 19 percent; and Asians, 2 percent (U.S. Census Bureau 2010b, Tables 66, 69).

Some "single" parents have cohabiting partners. Of all U.S. children, about 4.6 million (6 percent) live with a parents or parents who are cohabiting. Of children who live with cohabiting couples, about half (2.3 million) live with both of their unmarried biological or adoptive parents (U.S. Census Bureau 2009a, Table S0901; U.S. Census Bureau 2009d, Table C3; U.S. Federal Interagency Forum on Child and Family Statistics 2009).

Considerable research supports Waite's overall conclusion that growing up with married parents is better for children (Kreider and Elliott 2009a, 2009b; Magnuson and Berger 2009; Popenoe 2008). For instance, when compared with teens in homes with two married biological parents, those in single-parent and cohabiting families are more likely to experience earlier premarital intercourse, lower academic achievement, and lower expectations for college, together with higher rates of school suspension and delinquency (Carlson 2006; Manning and Lamb 2003; VanDorn, Bowen, and Blau 2006). In addition, studies that compared economically disadvantaged six- and seven-year-olds from families of various types found fewer problem behaviors among children in married families (Ackerman et al. 2001). Other research has found that, among couples with comparable incomes, married parents spend more on their children's education (and less on alcohol and tobacco) than do cohabiting parents (DeLeire and Kalil 2005). Furthermore, a recent analysis of national data found that, when compared to those in other family forms, married mothers exhibited the healthiest prenatal behaviors (Kimbro 2008).

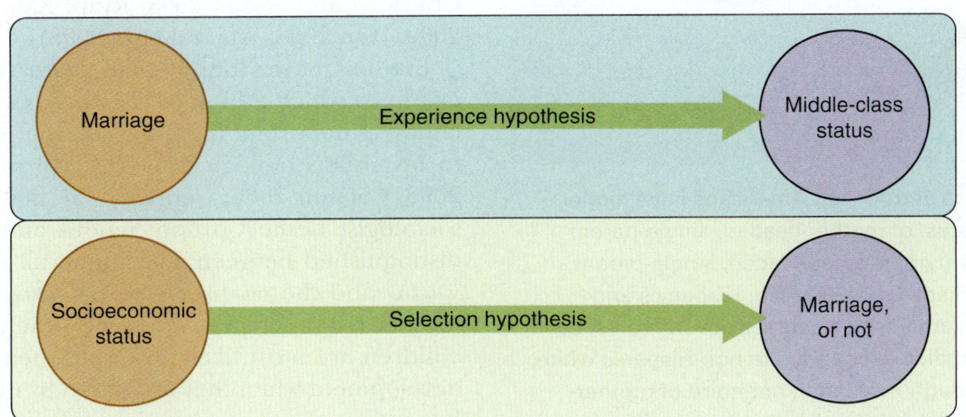

Figure 7.4 Causal order: Experience hypothesis, selection hypothesis

Source: Adapted from Marsh et al. 2007, p. 739.

As the experience hypothesis would suggest, one reason that, as a category, children with married parents evidence better outcomes may be the *experience* of growing up in a married-couple household. With its presumption of permanent commitment to the family as a whole, marriage "allows caregivers to make relationship-specific investments in the couple's children—investments of time and effort that, unlike strengthening one's job skills, would not be easily portable to another relationship" (Cherlin 2004, p. 855; Popenoe 2008).

However, as with the benefits of marriage for adults, researchers, working to unravel the statistical correlation between marriage and positive child outcomes, have uncovered complexities. For instance, findings differ according to how the variable *marriage* is defined.

Rhoberazzi/Getty Images

Although Hispanics and African Americans have higher percentages, or rates, of mother-headed, single-parent families, the majority of mother-headed, single-parent families are non-Hispanic white. Also, Hispanics and African American families have higher poverty rates, but the majority of families in poverty are non-Hispanic white. Furthermore, although more than one-third of mother-headed, single-parent families live below the official poverty level, nearly two-thirds do not.

Results differ when the variable *marriage* allows an investigator to compare the effects of having two biological, continuously married parents with those having a remarried stepparent. Using data from the National Longitudinal Survey of Youth, one study (Carlson 2006) compared outcomes for adolescents in several family structures. Similar to prior research, this study found fewer behavior problems among teens who lived with their continuously married biological parents. However, adolescents born outside of marriage but whose biological parents later married or were cohabiting, or whose mother married a stepfather, had more behavior problems than teens whose biological parents were continuously married (Carlson 2006). Furthermore, transitions to and from various family structures have been found to result in poorer outcomes for children (Bures 2009; Magnuson and Berger 2009).

In addition to refining the marriage variable, researchers have proposed supplementary or alternative causes for children's marriage-associated benefits. For one thing, children raised by married families are less likely to live in poverty—a situation that has serious negative effects on child outcomes (Moore et al. 2009). ("Facts about Families: Marriage and Children in Poverty" describes various effects of growing up in poverty.) We know that married parents are less likely to live below poverty level, but factors in addition to marital status are related to poverty as well. For example, in a study focused on Hispanic children, researchers showed that, for Mexican American children, poverty is related to a combination of marital status and the number of children in the household, the latter "an important predictor of poverty regardless of marital status" (Crowley, Lichter, and Qian 2006).

Beside marital status and poverty, still other factors correlate with children's outcomes—the child's neighborhood and peers, family conflict, parental nurturance and involvement in the child's school activities, parents' participation in religious services, and parents' available social support (Broman, Li, and Reckase 2008; Crawford and Novak 2008; Ryan, Kalil, and Leininger 2009; Wen 2008; Wu and Hou 2008).

Studies have found that *father involvement*—the extent to which a biological father is engaged with his child—is important regardless of whether he is married to his child's biological mother (Bronte-Tinkew et al. 2008; Carlson 2006; Cooper et al. 2009). Accordingly, sociologist Leslie Gordon Simons and her colleagues distinguished between what they call the *marriage perspective* and the *two-caregivers perspective*: "What we label the marriage perspective rests on the assumption that children are most likely to display healthy growth and development when they are raised by married parents." In contrast, the two-caregivers perspective contends that children do best when raised by two caregivers rather than by a single caregiver (Simons et al. 2006, p. 805).

Facts about Families

Marriage and Children in Poverty

More than 13.3 million U.S. children under age eighteen live at or below poverty; children comprise 36 percent of this nation's poor (U.S. Census Bureau 2010b, Table 697). More than 17 million children live in "near poor" conditions—that is, at less than 125 percent of poverty level (U.S. Census Bureau 2009a, Table S1703). In recent years, poverty rates have declined for African Americans and Hispanics. Nevertheless, 14 percent of white, 12 percent of Asian, 34 percent of African American, and 28 percent of Hispanic children live in poverty (U.S. Census Bureau 2010b, Table 696; see also Moore et al. 2009). Figures such as these may lead us to think of poverty in terms of black or Hispanic families, but the majority of poor children are non-Hispanic white. Despite lower *rates* of poverty, non-Hispanic whites predominate in sheer numbers, comprising nearly two-thirds of all poor children in the United States (U.S. Census Bureau 2010b, Table 696).

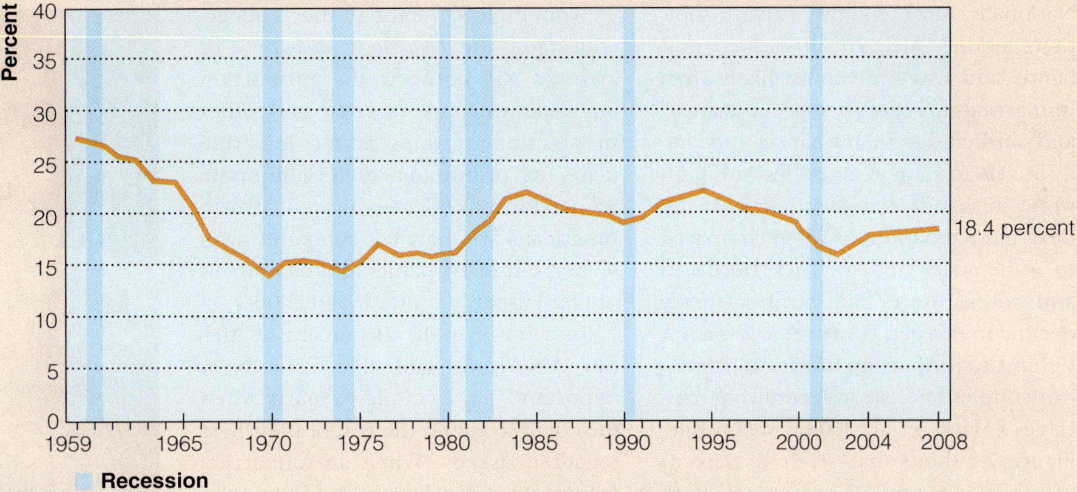

Figure 7.5 U.S. poverty rate for children under age 18, 1959 to 2008
Sources: Proctor and Dalaker 2003; U.S. Census Bureau 2009f, Table 690.

Regardless of their parents' marital status, children growing up in poverty often do not have enough nutritious food; are more likely to live in environmentally unhealthy neighborhoods; have more physical health, socioemotional, and behavioral problems; must travel farther to attain health care; attend poorly financed schools; do less well academically; and are more likely to drop out (Goosby 2007; Moore et al. 2009; Teachman 2008b). Furthermore, the rate of severe violence toward children is about 105 per 1,000 in families below the poverty line, compared to about 30 per 1,000 children in other families (Gelles and Cavanaugh 2005).

Economic hardship in childhood, even in a two-parent married family, particularly when it lasts for a long time or occurs in adolescence, is related to lowered emotional well-being in early adulthood (Sobolewski and Amato 2005; Vandewater and Lansford 2005). Not having enough money causes stress, which often leads to mothers' depression, parental conflict, and general household turbulence. Household turbulence and mothers' depression, in turn, are associated with lower parent–child (especially teen) relationship quality, a situation that results in a child's lower psychological well-being (Goosby 2007; Jackson, Choi, and Bentler 2009; Sobolewski and Amato 2005; Teachman 2008b).

As Figure 7.5 illustrates, the child poverty rate for all races calculated together was about 27 percent in 1959, but beginning with President Lyndon Johnson's War on Poverty[a] in the 1960s, it dropped consistently during the 1970s, to a low of about 14 percent. A decade later, a series of economic recessions occurred along with the phasing out of many War on Poverty measures. As a result, the child poverty rate began to rise in the late 1970s, then fell again after about 1993. However, the rate began to rise again in 2000. In 2008, the child poverty rate was 18.4 percent—up from 15.6 percent at the turn of the twenty-first century (Proctor and Dalaker 2003; U.S. Census Bureau 2010b, Table 697).

The War on Poverty offered *structural* strategies to decrease poverty, such as community meal programs and health centers, legal services, summer youth programs, senior centers, neighborhood development, adult education, job training, and family planning (Garson n.d.). Commitment to the War on Poverty diminished after the 1970s, with national rhetoric shifting to debates focused on individual responsibility. Today, however, scholars and some policy makers are again insisting that the United States must pay attention to ecological and structural supports for children and families regardless of—or in addition to—concerns about changing family structure (Cherlin 2009a; Moore et al. 2009; Popenoe 2009).

a. War on Poverty measures, first proposed in 1964 by President Lyndon Johnson and enacted by Congress in the subsequent Economic Opportunity Act, allocated federal funds to reduce poverty. You may have heard of War on Poverty programs, such as the Job Corps or the Neighborhood Youth Corps, Head Start, or Adult Basic Education. Although the majority of War on Poverty measures have ended, Head Start and the Job Corps continue to exist.

A Closer Look at Diversity

African Americans and "Jumping the Broom"

Nationally representative surveys show that, among African Americans, husbands and wives are more likely than unmarrieds to report being "very happy" and satisfied with their finances and family life (Blackman et al. 2006). Although white husbands consistently report the most marital happiness when compared to white wives and to black husbands and wives, there had been a steady decline in this gap (Corra et al. 2009). A significant proportion of African American couples have strong, enduring marriages (Marks et al. 2008). Meanwhile, Figure 7.2 shows that—with 46 percent of black men and 38 percent of black women currently married—African Americans are considerably less likely to be wed than are other U.S. racial/ethnic groups. A large body of literature, written by both blacks and whites, is accumulating on the structural–cultural reasons for this situation (McAdoo 2007; Saad 2006c; Wilson 2002). Chapter 3 explores this literature.

Nonetheless, among the college-educated, the *marriage disparity*, or *marriage gap* between the proportion of blacks who are married and other racial/ethnic groups is far less dramatic. According to a 2006 Gallup poll, 55 percent of college-educated African Americans are married, compared with 57 percent of Hispanics and 65 percent of non-Hispanic whites (Saad 2006c).

In a recent poll, 69 percent of African Americans said that it is "very important" for a couple to marry when they plan to spend the rest of their lives together. Asked, "When an unmarried man and woman have a child together, how important is it to you that they legally marry?" college-educated African Americans were *more* inclined than either Hispanics or non-Hispanic whites to say that marrying in this situation is "very important." The figures were 55 percent of blacks, 46 percent of Hispanics, and 37 percent of non-Hispanic whites (Saad 2006c). Furthermore,

Although somewhat controversial because it can be a reminder of slavery, jumping the broom at African American weddings is going through some revival as black couples plan wedding celebration rituals designed to incorporate their cultural heritage.

Analyzing data on 867 African American children from the Family and Community Health Study, Simons and her colleagues found that "child behavior problems were no greater in either mother-grandmother or mother-relative families than in those in intact nuclear families." At least among blacks, these researchers found mother-grandmother families to be "functionally equivalent" (Simons et al. 2006, p. 818). Then too, other extended kin in black families—uncles, for example—may be involved in child care (Richardson 2009).

Interestingly, research based on a national representative sample of more than 10,000 U.S. teens found that the negative effects of time lived with a single mother were less serious for black and Hispanic adolescents than they were for whites. Why might this be? First, although nonmarried parenthood remains somewhat stigmatized in the United States (Usdansky 2009a, 2009b), it is noteworthy that this stigma may be minimal within the black community where single-parent families are more normative (Heard 2007). Accordingly, "The common history among blacks allows for the emergence and primacy of social supports, such as women-centered kinship networks, coresidence with extended family, and strong ties to the church, which can buffer the negative effects of stress caused by family instability" (Heard 2007, p. 336). (For more on blacks and marriage, see "A Closer Look at Diversity: African Americans and 'Jumping the Broom.'")

As with the benefits of marriage for adults, researchers hypothesize that selection effects explain much—although not all—of marriage's advantage for children. We've seen that, on average, individuals who marry are better educated and have higher incomes. As parents, they live in neighborhoods more conducive to successful child raising. Less likely to be stressed due to financial problems, they are more likely to practice effective parenting skills (Manning and Brown 2006; also see Teachman 2008b). In her address to the Population Association of America, Waite acknowledged the contribution of selection effects to child outcomes. She added, however, that "we have been too quick to assign *all* the responsibility to selectivity here, and not quick enough to consider the possibility that marriage *causes* some of the better outcomes we see . . . " (1995, p. 497, italics in original).

To summarize, a large body of research shows that marriage is associated with benefits for adults and children. However, this relationship is complex, and much of it may be due to variables other than marital status as well as to selection effects (Teachman 2008b).

attitude surveys consistently show that African Americans value marriage, perhaps more than non-Hispanic whites do (Bramlett and Mosher 2001; Johnson and Staples 2005; Saad 2006c).

The news media have focused so frequently on poverty-level African Americans and on the relatively low proportion of married blacks that we may forget about the 10.6 million (40 percent of) African Americans who *are* married (U.S. Census Bureau 2010b, Table 56). Google "African American marriage" and you'll find several websites marketing wedding products and services to middle-class blacks. One book, *Jumping the Broom* (Cole 1993) is a wedding planner for American blacks. If you're not African American, there's a fairly good chance that you have not heard of jumping the broom. What is it?

For African Americans, the significance of the broom originated among the Asante in what is now the West African country of Ghana. Used to sweep courtyards, the handmade Asante broom was also symbolic of sweeping away past wrongs or warding off evil. Brooms played a part in Asante weddings as well. To culminate their wedding ceremony, a couple might jump over a broom lying on the ground or leaning across a doorway. Jumping the broom symbolized the wife's commitment to her new household, and it was sometimes said that whoever jumped higher over the broom would be the family decision maker (DiStefano 2001; Prahlad 2006).

Among slaves brought to the Americas, jumping the broom continued. Not allowed to marry legally, slaves sometimes jumped a broom as an alternative ceremony to mark their marital commitment. The association of jumping the broom with slavery has stigmatized the tradition for some African Americans. However, the ritual is coming back as more middle-class blacks seek culturally relevant wedding celebrations (African Wedding Guide n.d.; Anyiam 2002; DiStefano 2001).

Critical Thinking

How do you think that jumping the broom might be used to symbolize the time-honored marriage premise? Why would it be important to incorporate traditions that are relevant to one's own culture into a wedding ceremony? Why do you think we hear relatively little about African Americans' weddings or marriages?

A theme of this text is that research findings expand our knowledge so that we can better make decisions knowledgeably. One thing that the research implies is that, although generally marriage is advantaged, additional factors affect individual outcomes, and the disadvantages for some ethnic groups may not be as severe as for the population as a whole.

Just as researchers have responded in various ways to Waite's address, policy makers have had conflicting reactions. More conservative policy leaders, associated with the *decline* and "family breakdown" perspective, once hoped to effect a "family turnaround" (Whitehead and Popenoe 2003). They noted "a greater emphasis on short-term gratification and on adults' desires rather than on what is good for children" that they attributed to government welfare programs and to decreased attention to religious principles (Giele 2007, p. 76).

Today, these policy makers appear to have given up on a broad "family turnaround." In the words of sociologist David Popenoe (2008):

> [Realistically] there is probably not much that government policies or social action can do to change the situation. If major change is to come about it will have to occur through a broad cultural shift, reflected in the hearts and minds of the citizenry, in the direction of stronger interpersonal commitments and families. . . . Still, there surely are actions that societies can take to try to improve the situation and not make it worse; actions that discourage cohabitation and encourage marriage, at least when children are involved. (pp. 15–16)

On the other hand, policy makers who see marriage simply as *changing* recognize that many families are struggling but criticize the solutions offered by conservatives and propose their own. The following section explores this policy debate.

Valuing Marriage—The Policy Debate

Policy advocates from a marital *change* perspective are mainly concerned about the high number and proportions of parents and children living in poverty. They view poverty as causing difficult child-raising environments with resulting negative outcomes for some—though not all—of America's children. From this viewpoint, family struggle results from structural conditions, such as recession. Accordingly, these spokespersons argue for structural, or ecological (such as neighborhood-level), solutions.

From the *decline* perspective, on the other hand, concerns about "family breakdown" include the high number of federal dollars spent on "welfare" for poverty-level single mothers, coupled with the irresponsible socialization of children (Giele 2007). They define the causes for these concerns as primarily cultural, such as changes in individuals' values and attitudes regarding marriage. Therefore, they offer motivational and educational programs to effect a family "turnaround."

Policies from the Family Decline Perspective

An important goal from the *decline* perspective is to return to a society more in line with the values and norms of companionate marriage. As means to that end, advocates have established programs to encourage marital permanence. Many religions insist on premarital counseling as a way to dissuade couples in inappropriate matches from marrying and to encourage those who do marry to stay together (Nock 2005; Nadir 2009; Ooms 2005).

Covenant Marriage Some conservative Christian organizations and legislators advocate **covenant marriage**. In covenant marriage, partners agree to be bound by a marriage "covenant" (stronger than an ordinary contract) that will not let them get divorced easily ("Covenant Marriages Ministry" 1998). Between ten and twenty years ago, three states—Louisiana, Arizona, and Arkansas—enacted covenant marriage laws. Twenty other states have considered, but failed to pass, covenant marriage laws (Leon 2009).

How does covenant marriage work? Before their wedding, couples choose between two marital contracts, conventional or covenant. If legally bound by a marriage covenant, couples are required to get premarital counseling and may divorce only after being separated for at least two years or if imprisonment, desertion for one year, adultery, or domestic abuse is proved in court. In addition, a covenant couple must submit to counseling before a divorce (Brown and Waugh 2004).

Typically, fundamentalist Christian religions are enthusiastic about covenant marriage, whereas feminists and other critics are not ("Couple Support" 2006; Leon 2009; Sanchez et al. 2002). For instance, critics point out that proving adultery or domestic abuse in court may be difficult and expensive, while living in a violent household can be deadly (Gelles 1996).

Despite promoters' early enthusiasm, covenant marriage has failed to become a serious social movement, never having spread beyond the original three enacting states. Relatively few couples in the states where it is available have opted for covenant marriage ("More Binding Marriage" 2004). In addition to covenant marriage, the federal Healthy Marriage Initiative encourages marital stability (Chaney 2009; Graefe and Lichter 2007).

Government Initiatives States have promoted marriage education, some offering money incentives for couples to participate. Other state initiatives include home visitation programs for families that might be targeted for government assistance because of a variety of reasons, such as a birth to a teenager or an unstable marriage; mentoring, marriage counseling, communication skills, and anger management workshops; state-funded resource centers that provide information on marriage; and state websites that include marriage enrichment information and links to service-related sites (Dion 2005; Ooms 2005).

As part of the federal Healthy Marriage Initiative (HMI), these programs largely began after 2004, when Congress reauthorized the Temporary Assistance for Needy Families (TANF), or "welfare reform" program.[10] Although this program has been less emphasized after the presidency of George W. Bush, HMI's family-related goals continue to include, among other things, ending the dependence of single parents on government benefits by promoting not only job preparation but also marriage (Carlton et al. 2009; Healthy Marriage Initiative 2009). Proponents argued that giving single mothers "accurate information on the value of marriage in the lives of men, women, and children," along with marriage skills education, encourage marriage and reduce divorce (Ooms 2005; Rector and Pardue 2004).

The disparity in marriage rates between the poor and those who are not poor has become significant enough that social scientists have coined a term for this situation—the *marriage gap*. Meanwhile, critics of programs specifically designed to motivate people to marry argue that low-income Americans value marriage and would like to marry, but marriage is difficult to achieve for many of them. Low-income single mothers want trustworthy, steadily employed husbands who will help with both finances and child care (Burton et al. 2009; Joshi, Quane, and Cherlin 2009). As a young, college-educated woman in a qualitative study of African American single mothers explained, "I realized that when I do decide to enter marriage, my partner must have the same ambitions as me or similar to [mine].... Not too many men my age or older have the ambition that I have" (in Holland 2009, p. 173). For rich and

[10] The 1996 Personal Responsibility and Work Opportunity Reconciliation Act, or "welfare reform bill," effectively ended the federal government's sixty-year guarantee of assisting low-income mothers and children. The federal Aid to Families with Dependent Children (AFDC) program ended in 1997, and a different federal program, Temporary Assistance for Needy Families (TANF), ensued. TANF limits assistance to five years for most families, with most adult recipients required to find work within two years.

Evelyn Hockstein/MCT/Landov

The disparity in marriage rates between the poor and those who are not poor has become significant enough that social scientists have coined a term for this situation—the *marriage gap*. Low-income Americans value marriage and would like to marry, but marriage appears difficult to achieve for many, although certainly not all, of them.

poor alike, a wedding symbolizes personal achievement (Cherlin 2004; Mandara et al. 2008). After interviewing women in low-income neighborhoods, two researchers concluded that, for poor women, marriage

> has become an elusive goal—one they feel ought to be reserved for those who can support . . . a mortgage on a modest row home, a car and some furniture, some savings in the bank, and enough money left over to pay for a "decent" wedding. (Edin and Kefalas 2007, p. 508; also see Gibson-Davis 2009; King and Allen 2009)

Due to declining work opportunities for the less well educated and consequent high unemployment rates for men in poor neighborhoods, many potential husbands in these communities cannot promise a steady income (Burton and Tucker 2009; Harris and Parisi 2008; Huston and Melz 2004).

Relieving poverty will require solutions other than—or at least in addition to—promoting marriage.

The Relationship between Marriage and Poverty Data that relate child poverty rates to children's living arrangements show that residing with married parents does significantly lessen the likelihood of growing up in poverty (Kreider and Fields 2005, Table 2). As you can see from Table 7.2, when all races are taken together, 4.6 percent of married-couple families live below the official poverty line. This figure compares with 13.3 percent of single male-householder families and 28.3 percent of single female-householder families. We might conclude that encouraging people to get married would work *somewhat* to lessen poverty (Amato 2005; Thomas and Sawhill 2005).

However, the association between marriage and poverty is hardly the whole story. Table 7.2 shows that—despite the fact that they are married—4.5 percent of white, nearly 8 percent of Black, about 13 percent of Hispanic, 6.5 percent of Asian, and about 10 percent of American Indians or Alaska Natives live in poverty. Obviously, marriage alone is not sufficient to alleviate poverty. For one thing, as shown in Table 7.2, female householders with no spouse present are more than twice as likely as their male counterparts to live in poverty (28.3 percent, compared with 13.2 percent). In addition to marital status, low wages for women contribute to poverty (Ozawa and Lee 2006).

Moreover, a majority of unmarried families is not living in poverty. We must conclude that marriage contributes to a family's economic well-being, but a child's

Table 7.2 U.S. Families Below Poverty Level*

Family Type	Married couple	Male householder, no spouse present	Female householder, no spouse present
All races, number	2,910,000	671,000	4,087,000
White, number	2,278,000	440,000	2,400,000
Black, number	346,000	177,000	1,484,000
Hispanic, number	903,000	139,000	881,000
Asian, number	178,000	26,000	57,000
American Indian/Alaska Native, number	32,785	**	62,062
All races, %	4.6	13.2	28.3
White, %	4.5	11.5	25.1
Black, %	7.9	20.4	36.6
Hispanic, %	13.3	14.7	36.0
Asian, %	6.5	11.6	15.4
American Indian/ Alaska Native, %	10.2	**	37.6

*Data are for 2006, except American Indian/Alaska Native data, which are 2008. Percentages in poverty for all races for married couples with children and for female householders with children in 2008 were 6.5 and 36.3, respectively.
**Data unavailable.

Sources: U.S. Census Bureau 2009a, Table S1702; U.S. Census Bureau 2009f, Table 694.

having married parents is not absolutely necessary to grow up above the poverty line.

Policies from the Family Change Perspective

Many policy makers maintain that Americans are struggling with economic and time pressures that get in the way of their ability to realize family values (Ozawa and Lee 2006; Teitler et al. 2009). As remedies for poverty, policy leaders in this camp propose structural solutions such as support for education, job training, drug rehabilitation, improved job opportunities, neighborhood improvements, small business development, and parenting skills education (Amato 2005; S. Brown 2004; Ozawa and Lee 2006). Indeed, "[l]ow-income communities have been neglected for so long that the resources needed to rebuild them will require a major shift in public priorities over an extended period of time, possibly generations" (Huston and Melz 2004, p. 956).

Andrew Cherlin (2009a) argues that in a climate of "contradiction" between the American values of commitment to marital stability and individual freedom and happiness, it is a bit naïve today to think that encouraging people to get or stay married will work to better facilitate raising children responsibly. He finds marital stability virtually impossible to enhance in our American values climate, and therefore argues that it is not pragmatic to continue to insist on legal marriage as a public policy goal. Instead, he argues for *family stability*—supporting children and therefore their parents in whatever family form they find themselves (Cherlin 2009a).

Unfortunately, finding resources for ecological and structural support for families is even more difficult today than prior to the recession that began in 2008. Not only are resources more scarce, but also politicians and others debate whether (a) "welfare" encourages single parenthood while lessening the motivation to work, or (b) some form of family "safety net" is necessary and should not be stigmatized (DeParle 2009).

Having looked at research and policy on the question of whether marriage matters, we can conclude that marriage does matter, at least for those who can afford to get married. We end this chapter with a discussion of how marriage contributes to spouses' happiness and life satisfaction.

Happiness and Life Satisfaction: How Does Marriage Matter?

No longer a "marker of conformity," a wedding today marks a couple's public announcement that they have chosen marriage, among other available options, as a way to define and live their lives (Cherlin 2004, p. 856). Marriage, more than any other relationship, promises to shore up that love, helping partners to keep it, once discovered.

Academic research (e.g., Wienke and Hill 2009) and opinion polls show that both husbands and wives are far more likely than others to say that they are "very happy." Nearly two-thirds (62 percent) of marrieds say they are "very happy," compared to less than half (45 percent) of unmarrieds (Carroll 2005; Taylor, Funk, and Craighill 2006). What is it about the experience of being married that works to create this difference?

For one thing, there are some pragmatic reasons that spouses (and cohabitors, but to a lesser degree) benefit from an *economy of scale*. Think of the saying, "Two can live as cheaply as one." Although this principle is not entirely true, some expenses, such as rent, do not necessarily increase when a second adult joins the household (Thomas and Sawhill 2005; Goode 2007 [1982]; Waite 1995). Then, too, the promise of permanence associated with the marriage premise accords spouses the security to develop some skills and to neglect others because they can count on working in complementary ways with their partners (Goode 2007 [1982]; Nock 2005). Furthermore, "[s]pouses act as a sort of small insurance pool against life's uncertainties, reducing their need to protect themselves *by themselves* from unexpected events" (Waite 1995, p. 498).

In addition, marriage offers enhanced social support (Manning and Brown 2006). Marriage can connect people to in-laws and a widened extended family, who may be able to help when needed—for instance, with child care, transportation, a down payment on a house, or just an emotionally supportive phone call. The enhanced social support that often accompanies marriage works to encourage the union's permanence (Giddens 2007). For example, family and friends send anniversary cards, celebrations of the years the couple has spent together and reminders of the couple's vow of commitment. Beginning with a public ceremony, marriage makes for what sociologist Andrew Cherlin (2004) calls *enforced trust*:

> Marriage still requires a public commitment to a long-term, possibly lifelong relationship. This commitment is usually expressed in front of relatives, friends, and religious congregants. . . . Therefore, marriage . . . lowers the risk that one's partner will renege on agreements that have been made. . . . It allows individuals to invest in the partnership with less fear of abandonment. (p. 854)

Furthermore, marriage offers *continuity*, the experience of building a relationship over time and resulting in a uniquely shared history. And, finally, marriage provides individuals with a sense of obligation to others, not only to their families but also to the broader community (Goode 2007 [1982]; Wolfinger and Wolfinger 2008). This, in and of itself, gives life meaning (Waite 1995, p. 498).

Marital Satisfaction and Choices Throughout Life

Our theme of making choices throughout life surely applies both to couples anticipating marriage as well as to decisions made during the early years of marriage. We'll examine these topics now.

Preparation for Marriage

Given today's high divorce rate, clergy, teachers, parents, policy makers, and others have grown increasingly concerned that individuals be better prepared for marriage. High school and college family life education courses are designed to prepare individuals of various racial/ethnic groups for marriage (Coalition for Marriage, Family and Couples Education 2009; DeMaria 2005; Fincham, Hall, and Beach 2006). Premarital counseling, which often takes place at churches or with private counselors, is specifically oriented to couples who plan to marry. For example, many Catholic dioceses require premarital counseling before a couple may be married by a priest. Christians of other denominations, and Islam, Jewish, and other religions offer premarital

AP Images/Erik S. Lesser

As an effort to improve family life, this neighborhood restoration project involves the community in effecting structural, as opposed to cultural or attitudinal, change.

counseling as well. Illustrating the connection between private lives and public interest, a few states now require premarital counseling for engaged couples under age eighteen (Holloway 2008; Murray 2006).

Premarital counseling goals involve helping the couple to evaluate whether their relationship should lead to marriage; develop a realistic, yet hopeful and positive vision of their future marriage; recognize potential problems; and learn positive problem-solving and other communication skills (Dinkmeyer 2007; Holloway 2008). Some programs have been developed especially for those contemplating post-divorce cohabitation or remarriage, particularly when children are involved (Gonzales 2009).

Research designed to assess how effective these programs are shows that they do improve a couple's communication skills and relationship quality, at least in the short term (Blanchard et al. 2009). Unfortunately, however, we have little data on the relationship between premarital counseling and relationship stability. Furthermore, "a lack of racial/ethnic and economic diversity in the samples prevented reliable conclusions about the effectiveness of [premarital counseling] for disadvantaged couples, a crucial deficit in the body of research" (Hawkins et al. 2008, p. 723).

Among other factors, success depends upon the personality characteristics of each partner, as well as on couple characteristics, such as the interactional styles with which they begin the program, influences from their families of origin, and their motivation to learn from the program (Murray 2004). One study found that those who become actively involved in premarital counseling are more likely to value marriage and to be kind and considerate to begin with (Duncan, Holman, and Yang 2007). Overall, however, family experts see these programs as important, especially for those under age eighteen and for adult children of troubled or divorced families (Dinkmeyer 2007; Holloway 2008). Psychologist Scott Stanley identifies four benefits of premarital education:

> (a) it can slow couples down to foster deliberation, (b) it sends a message that marriage matters, (c) it can help couples learn of options if they need help later, and (d) there is evidence that providing some couples with some types of premarital training . . . can lower their risks for subsequent marital distress or termination. (Markman, Stanley, and Blumberg 2001, p. 272)

The idea of "slowing couples down" prompts questions about the relationship between age at marriage and the union's stability.

Age at Marriage, Marital Stability and Satisfaction

In the 1950s, men tended to marry at about age twenty-four and women at about age twenty-two (Aldous 1978). We've seen that the median age at first marriage today is about twenty-six for women and twenty-eight for men—considerably older than at mid-twentieth century. Nevertheless, "Although much attention has been paid to the increasing age at first marriage in the United States, many Americans continue to marry at young ages. More than one-quarter of young women and more than 15 percent of young men marry before their twenty-third birthday" (Uecker and Stokes 2008, p. 844). Is there a "right" age to marry?

Over the past several decades, researchers have given considerable attention to the relationship between age at first marriage and marital stability. Findings consistently show that the odds of marital stability increase with age at marriage (Amato et al. 2007). Those who marry young are, on average, more emotionally immature and impulsive and less apt to be educationally, financially, or psychologically prepared to responsibly choose a partner or perform marital roles (Clements, Stanley, and Markman 2004; Martino, Collins, and Ellickson 2004). Low socioeconomic origins, poor communication and problem-solving skills, premarital pregnancy, lack of interest in school, and financial struggles are associated with marrying early (Larson and Hickman 2004; Uecker and Stokes 2008). Teen marriages (the majority between eighteen- and nineteen-year-olds) are the least stable (Bramlett and Mosher 2001; McGinn 2006b).

Typically, policy makers have developed programs encouraging teens to postpone marriage. Meanwhile, when they do occur, early marriages would benefit by recognition and support:

> Given early marriage's known association with marital dissolution, it is important to pay adequate attention to . . . individuals who marry in early adulthood. . . . Early marriage comes with its own set of difficulties, however, and if understanding and supporting all marriages—be they early, normative, or late—is a goal of scholarship and policy, this population should garner more attention from both researchers and policy makers. (Uecker and Stokes 2008, p. 844, 845)

Until recently, research on age at first marriage focused solely on marital stability. However, a 2009 analysis of findings from several major national surveys examined the relationship between age at first marriage and marital happiness and satisfaction (Glenn, Uecker, and Love 2009). Findings show that marriages occurring today, when spouses are between ages twenty-two and twenty-five, are most likely to be not only stable but also happy. Spouses who first married after age thirty reported lower marital satisfaction even as they were likely to stay married.

Based on a thorough review of prior research, Glenn, Uecker, and Love (2009) offer possible explanations. For one thing, more "set-in-their-ways" older spouses may find it more difficult to fashion a compatible life together. Also, marrying after about age thirty may mean selecting a spouse from a market in which "lots of the good ones are gone." Or it may suggest that an individual has been searching for the perfect partner—a situation that can only lead to later disappointment. Despite lower satisfaction levels, however, age at first marriage does act as a deterrent to divorce. If they are older, mildly unhappy partners may feel hesitant to reenter singlehood, the dating game, or the marriage market. Some advice from the study:

> The findings of this study *do* indicate that for most persons, little or nothing in the way of marital success is likely to be gained by deliberately delaying marriage beyond the mid twenties. For instance, a 25 year old person who meets an excellent marriage prospect would be ill-advised to pass up that opportunity only because he/she feels not yet at the ideal age for marriage. Furthermore, delaying marriage beyond the mid twenties will lead to the loss during a portion of young adulthood of any emotional and health benefits that a good marriage would bring. . . . On the other hand, it is extremely important to stress that the findings of this study should not lead anyone of any age to panic and thus make a bad choice of a spouse. (Glenn, Uecker, and Love 2009, pp. 42–43)

The First Years of Marriage

The first years of marriage tend to be the happiest, with gradual declines in marital satisfaction afterward (Dush, Taylor, and Kroeger 2008; Tach and Halpern-Meekin 2009). Why this is true is not clear. One explanation points to life cycle stresses as children arrive and economic pressures intensify; others argue that falling in love and new marriage are periods of emotional intensity from which there is an inevitable decline (Glenn 1998; Whyte 1990). We do know something about the structural advantages of the early years of marriage, and it is likely that these contribute to high levels of satisfaction. For one thing, partners' roles are relatively similar or unsegregated in early marriage. Spouses tend to share household tasks and, because of similar experiences, are better able to empathize with each other.

In the 1950s, marriage and family texts characteristically referred to the first months and years of marriage as a period of adjustment, after which, presumably, spouses had learned to play traditional marital roles. Today we view the first months and years of marriage more as a time of role-*making* than of role-*taking*.

From the interaction-constructionist theoretical perspective (see Chapter 2), **role-making** refers to modifying or adjusting the expectations and obligations traditionally associated with a role. Role-making involves issues explored more fully in other chapters of this text. Newlyweds negotiate expectations for sex and intimacy (Chapter 5), establish communication (Chapter 12) and decision-making patterns (Chapter 13), balance expectations about marital and job or school responsibilities (Chapter 11), and come to some agreement about becoming parents (Chapter 9) and how they will handle and budget their money. When children are present, role-making involves negotiation about parenting roles (Chapter 10). Role-making issues peculiar to remarriages are addressed in Chapter 16. Generally, role-making in new marriages involves creating, by means of communication and negotiation, identities as married people (Rotenberg, Schaut, and O'Connor 1993). The time of role-making is not a clearly demarcated period but continues throughout marriage.

Couples must also accomplish certain tasks during this period. In general, "the solidarity of the new couple relation must be established and competing interpersonal ties modified" (Aldous 1978, p. 141; Rotenberg, Schaut, and O'Connor 1993). Getting through this stage requires making requests for change and negotiating resolutions, along with renewed acceptance of each other. Indeed, research by psychoanalyst John Gottman shows that communication as newlyweds tends to influence the later happiness—and even the permanence—of the marriage (Gottman et al. 1998; Gottman and Levenson 2000, 2002). The couple constructs relationships and interprets events in a way that reinforces their sense of themselves as a couple (Wallerstein and Blakeslee 1995). Relationships with parents change (Sarkisian and Gerstel 2008). Perhaps expectedly, a recent study in Switzerland found that newlyweds were happier when relatives were supportive but not interfering (Widmer et al. 2009).

A national study undertaken by family researchers at Creighton University in Omaha identified three main, potentially problematic topics for couples in first marriages: (1) money—balancing job and family, dealing with financial debt brought into the marriage by one or both spouses, and what to do with money income; (2) sexual frequency; and (3) agreeing on how much time to spend together—and finding it! Challenges associated with learning to balance work and/or college courses and a marital relationship are real (Christopherson 2006). Feeling supported by parents and extended kin helps (Kurdek 2005). Other issues the couples in the Creighton study mentioned above involved expectations about who would do household tasks (and how well), communication challenges, and problems with in-laws (Brennan 2003; Risch, Riley, and Lawler 2004). A more general, necessary goal for couples in early marriage is to create couple connection.

Creating Couple Connection

Partners who desire enduring emotional relationships must keep their relationship as a high priority. Some research suggests that, on average, today's marriages are happier when both spouses are employed (Schoen, Rogers, and Amato 2006). Also, husbands and wives who engage in supportive communication and who together pursue leisure activities that they both enjoy are more

Because, more than others, a married couple can count on continuity, bolstered by enforced trust, spouses are freer to plan for a future together.

compatible and satisfied with their marriage (Crawford et al. 2002; Johnson et al. 2005; Kurdek 2005).

Research on marital satisfaction also suggests that couples who make time for shared new experiences are more happily married (Burpee and Langer 2005). Assuredly for wives, time spent together is important to marital happiness (Gager and Sanchez 2003). An important psychologist and expert on marital communication, John Gottman, offers this advice:

> Happy, solid couples nourish their marriages with plenty of positive moments together. . . . Too often, families lead complex—even grueling—lives in which they sacrifice the happy times for more materialistic, fleeting goals. . . . Sundays at the office take the place of Sundays at the park. But if you want to keep your marriage alive, it's essential to rediscover—or perhaps simply make time for—those experiences that make you feel good about your spouse and your marriage. (1994, p. 223)

Comparative analysis of data collected from national samples in 1980 and 2000 revealed that spouses spend less time interacting with each other now than they did twenty-five years ago. (However, their reported marital satisfaction had not declined significantly, partly because they were more satisfied with the decision-making equality in their marriage [Amato et al. 2003].) Nevertheless, increased emphasis on other matters, such as managing debt, job pressures and long work hours, or children's needs, can result in exhaustion, increased conflict, and slow emotional erosion (Dew 2008; Roberts and Levenson 2001). Noting that "[l]ove is not an express lane concept," observers suggest creating daily "connecting moments" when you can be alone together and pay attention to your relationship (Brennan 2003; Brotherson 2003).

Keeping one's marriage vital requires that partners consciously and continuously strive to maintain intimacy. An emotionally meaningful relationship does not develop long term "by drift or default" (Cuber and Harroff 1965, p. 145). Satisfaction with the marital relationship has a great deal to do with the choices that partners make. One important set of decisions involves practicing positive communication skills. Research that followed 135 Denver couples over thirteen years, from the time they were engaged and into their marriages, concluded that "the seeds of marital distress and divorce are sown for many couples before they say 'I do.' . . . [N]egative premarital and early marital interactions . . . prime a marriage for the erosion of positivity over time" (Clements, Stanley, and Markman 2004, p. 621). Building better communication skills is addressed in Chapter 12.

Summary

- The marriage premise involves permanence and—for Western societies—monogamous sexual exclusivity.
- New norms for love-based marriage gradually became prevalent in Europe throughout the 1700s and 1800s. Expectations for personal happiness and love in marriage have changed the marriage premise over the past three hundred years.
- Marriages and families have become deinstitutionalized. Marriage has changed from institutionalized, to companionate, to individualistic.
- Overall, researchers consistently find a significant correlation between marriage and many positive outcomes for both adults and children, but the relationship is more complicated than it first appears because some of the benefits associated with marriage are due to selection effects.
- Scholars and policy makers who view individualized marriage and the postmodern family as indications that the institution of marriage and family is in "decline" and "breakdown" have proposed ways to effect a turnaround—such as covenant marriage and the Healthy Marriage Initiative.
- Scholars and policy makers who view individualized marriage and the postmodern family as results of inevitable historical change, resulting in struggle for some families more than for others, have proposed structural solutions to poverty and family struggle—such as higher wages for women, neighborhood development, an adequate minimum wage, and more employment opportunities.

- Optional and less permanent than in the past, marriage continues to offer benefits; married adults are more likely than others to say that they are happy with their lives. Being married continues to help bolster the marriage premise, due largely to family and community social support that results in enforced trust.
- There is society-wide concern about preparation for marriage. Premarital counseling and family life education are two approaches that have been developed, but we need more research data on their effectiveness.
- Partners change over the course of a marriage, so a relationship needs to be adaptable if it is to continue to be emotionally satisfying.
- Spouses in the first years of marriage engage in role-making, a process that includes—among other things—negotiating issues surrounding money, sexual frequency, and time together.

Questions for Review and Reflection

1. Discuss the marriage premise, with its expectations of permanence and sexual exclusivity. Describe how love has changed the marriage premise over the past three centuries. What does family demographer Stephanie Coontz mean when she says that "love conquered marriage"?
2. Pointing out the pros and cons of each, compare and contrast companionate marriage and individualized marriage.
3. Explain the connection between federal "welfare reform" and the National Marriage Initiative.
4. Recognizing the possibility of selection effects, what are some ways that the experience of being married can enhance happiness and life satisfaction?
5. **Policy Question.** Are you more inclined to agree with policy leaders from the family decline or from the family change perspective? Using research evidence from this chapter, explain the reasons for your answer.

Key Terms

collectivist society 172
communal society 172
companionate marriage 175
covenant marriage 184
deinstitutionalization of marriage 174
expectations of permanence 170
expectations of sexual exclusivity 170
experience hypothesis 179
family of orientation 172
family of procreation 172
individualism 172
individualistic society 172
individualized marriage 176
institutional marriage 174
kin 172
marriage premise 170
polyamory 171
polygamy 170
role-making 189
selection hypothesis 179
social institution 170
swinging 171

Online Resources

Sociology CourseMate

www.CengageBrain.com

Access an integrated eBook, chapter-specific interactive learning tools, including flash cards, quizzes, videos and more in your Sociology CourseMate, accessed through CengageBrain.com.

www.CengageBrain.com

Want to maximize your online study time? Take this easy-to-use study system's diagnostic pre-test, and it will create a personalized study plan for you. By helping you identify the topics that you need to understand better and then directing you to valuable online resources, it can speed up your chapter review. CengageNOW even provides a post-test so you can confirm that you are ready for an exam.

8

Living Alone, Cohabiting, Same-Sex Unions, and Other Intimate Relationships

Jon Riley/Getty Images

When answering national polls, nearly all Americans say that our families are very important to us. Our families are essential to us, yet they are likely to be different from the "traditional" family of the mid-twentieth century—as we saw in Chapters 1 and 7. Today's "postmodern" family is characterized by a diversity of family forms. As we look at various living arrangements in this chapter, we will examine some of these family forms. In the process, we will find that the distinction between being single and being married is not that sharp today. Many people who are legally single are embedded in families of one form or another.

Many college students today think of "being single" as not being in a romantic relationship. By this way of thinking, a person in a dating relationship or cohabiting would not be single. To the U.S. Census Bureau, however, *single* means *unmarried*, and many researchers tend to use these terms interchangeably. In this chapter, we will examine what social scientists know about the large and growing number of singles: the never-married, the divorced, and the widowed.

Marriage as a social institution is explored in Chapter 7. In this chapter, we'll discuss a variety of living arrangements other than marriage. We will explore cohabitation, as well as same-sex families. We'll also look at living alone, residing with one's parents, and living communally, or in groups. To begin, we'll examine some reasons for the increasing proportion of unmarrieds in our society today.

Reasons for the Increasing Proportion of Unmarrieds

Figure 7.2, in Chapter 7, shows the proportions of never-married, divorced, and widowed individuals by various racial/ethnic categories. These percentages are considerably higher than in past decades. In 1970, less than 28 percent of U.S. adults were single. Today that number is about 44 percent (Saluter and Lugaila 1998, Figure 1; U.S. Census Bureau 2010b, Table 56). Much of this change is due to a growing proportion of widowed elderly. However, the high proportion of singles also results from a high divorce rate and young adults' postponing marriage, together with a dramatically escalating cohabitation rate. Several social factors—demographic, economic, technological, and cultural—encourage Americans to postpone marriage, not to marry at all, or to choose to divorce rather than stay married.

Demographic, Economic, and Technological Changes

One reason for the growing proportion of singles is *demographic*, or related to population numbers. A high rate of heterosexual marriage presumes that there are matching numbers of marriage-age males and females in the population. Therefore, the **sex ratio**—the number of men to women in a given society or subgroup—influences marital options and singlehood.[1] Throughout the nineteenth and early twentieth centuries, the United States had more men than women, mainly because more men than women migrated to this country and, to a lesser extent, because a considerable number of young women died in childbirth. Today this situation is reversed due to changes in immigration patterns and greater improvement in women's health. In 1910, there were nearly 106 men for every 100 women. The sex ratio was 100, or "even," a few years after the end of World War II, in about 1948. In 2008, there were about 97 men for every 100 women (U.S. Census Bureau 2010b, Table 7).

Beginning with middle age, there are increasingly fewer men than women in every racial/ethnic category. Sex ratios differ somewhat for various racial/ethnic categories, however. For instance, at younger ages, the sex ratio is lower for blacks and Native Americans than for Hispanics or non-Hispanic whites. Incarceration rates as well as employment prospects also affect individuals' odds of marrying (Dixon 2009; King and Allen 2009).

In addition to demographics, *economic* factors have increased the proportion of nonmarrieds. For one thing, expanded educational and career options for college-educated women over the past several decades have encouraged many of them to postpone marriage:

> With so many options open to them, and with so little pressure on them to marry by their early twenties, the lives of young American women today have changed almost beyond recognition from what they were 50 years ago. And most of them take on their new freedoms with alacrity, making the most of their emerging adult years before they enter marriage and parenthood. (Arnett 2004, p. 7)

In addition, many middle-aged and older career and/or divorced women tend to look on marriage skeptically, viewing it as a bad bargain once they have gained financial and sexual independence (Levaro 2009; Swartz 2004; Zernike 2006).

Moreover, research shows that people today view marriage as a status that needs to be financially affordable. The fact that many men's earning potential has declined, relative to women's, may make marriage less attractive to both genders (Raley and Bratter 2004). Growing economic disadvantage and uncertainty

[1] The sex ratio is expressed in one number: the number of males for every 100 females. Thus, a sex ratio of 105 means that there are 105 men for every 100 women in a given population. More specialized sex ratios may be calculated—for example, the sex ratio for specific racial/ethnic categories at various ages or the sex ratio for unmarried people only.

appear to have made marriage less available to many who might want to marry but feel that they can't financially afford it (Gibson-Davis 2009; King and Allen 2009; Roberts 2009).

In addition to economics, *technological* changes over the past sixty years have affected the proportion of singles. Beginning with the introduction of the birth control pill in the 1960s, improved contraception has contributed to the decision to delay or forego marriage. With effective contraception, sexual relationships outside marriage and without great risk of unwanted pregnancy became possible (Gaughan 2002; Coontz 2005b). Moreover, as discussed in Chapter 1, reproductive technologies such as artificial insemination, offer the possibility for planned pregnancy to unpartnered heterosexual women as well as to same-sex couples. In addition to these structural reasons for the increasing proportion of nonmarrieds, cultural changes have played a part.

The increase in the number and proportion of unmarrieds in our society is a result of many factors, including unfavorable sex ratios, especially in older age categories; economic constrictions; improved contraception; and changing attitudes toward marriage and singlehood, which have resulted in more young adults postponing marriage.

Cultural Changes

As discussed in Chapter 2, social scientists note a fairly new life cycle stage called *emerging adulthood:* Young people today spend more time in higher education and/or exploring options regarding work, career, and family making than in the past (Arnett 2000; Furstenberg 2008). Although Americans of all ages have helped to increase the proportion of singles, emerging adulthood accounts for much of the greater proportion of unmarrieds today.

Several other cultural changes over the past few decades also account for the growing proportion of nonmarrieds. First, attitudes toward nonmarital sex have changed dramatically over past decades. With about two-thirds of adults of all ages approving, sexual intercourse outside marriage has become widely accepted ("Marriage" 2008). Currently, "hooking up"—discussed in Chapter 6 and called "recreational sex" in the 1960s—has gained attention (Wilson 2009).

Second, as American culture gives greater weight to personal autonomy, many find that—at least "for now"—singlehood is more desirable than marriage (Furstenberg 2008; Meier and Allen 2009). As one young man explained:

> It would kind of bum me out to be married. One day I was at work and my friend called me up from Florida and said, "What are you doing?" I'm like, "Just working," and he said, "Can you come down?" I'm like, "When?" and he's like, "Tomorrow," and I'm like, "Well, let me see what I can do." So I took a week off all of a sudden and went down to Florida. And I know I'd never be able to do that if I was married. (in Arnett 2004, p. 101)

A young woman evidences a similar attitude:

> I hope to be married by the time I'm 30. I mean, I don't see it being any time before that. I just think I have a lot of life left in me, and I want to enjoy it. There's so much out there, not that you couldn't see it with your husband, but why have to worry "Is he going to get mad at this?" Just go out and enjoy life and then settle down, and you'll know you've done everything possible that you wanted to do, and you won't regret getting married. (in Arnett 2004, p. 103)

Being single has become an acceptable option, rather than the deviant lifestyle that it was once thought to be. During the 1950s, people (including social scientists) tended to characterize the never-married as selfish, neurotic, or unattractive. The divorced were also stigmatized. These views have changed so much that the popular press today enthusiastically runs stories about those who are "embracing the solo life" (Hurwitt 2004; Sanders 2004).

Then too, getting married is no longer virtually the only way to gain adult status. Before about 1940, the most legitimate reason for leaving home, at least for women, was to get married. Today, 45 percent of young men and 39 percent of young women say that they first left home for other reasons, often to attend college and/or "to gain independence." The nationwide General Social Survey (GSS), conducted by the National Opinion Research Center (NORC), found that people now see becoming self-supporting as the first transition to adulthood, followed by no longer living with one's parents, having a full-time job, completing school, being able to support a family financially, and—sixth on the list—getting married (T. Smith 2003). As more young adults choose to claim independence simply by moving, marriage has lost its monopoly as the way to claim adulthood (Arnett 2004; Furstenberg et al. 2004).

Moreover, cohabitation is emerging as a socially accepted alternative to marriage (Cherlin 2009a). Among teens, about 70 percent say it's okay for couples to live together before they get married, and fewer than half (45 percent) of adults today think that it is "morally wrong" to have a baby outside of marriage (Lyons 2004; "Marriage" 2008). Forty-two percent of U.S. adults believe that an unmarried couple that has lived together for one year is just as committed as a couple that has been married for one year ("Marriage" 2008). Although beliefs such as these are considerably less likely among many recent immigrants and members of some religions, young adults in general experience greater independence and less parental pressure to marry than in the past (Arnett 2004; Rosenfeld 2008).

Finally, the changing nature of marriage itself may render marriage less desirable now than in the past (Cherlin 2009a). Marriage has become less strongly defined as permanent, and high divorce rates have led at least some singles to fear a potential divorce of their own. This fear reduces the likelihood that they will marry (Waller and Peters 2008). Historically, the expectation of permanence offered a significant benefit to getting married (Amato et al. 2007). If marriage is losing its permanent status, then

> [i]ndividuals, as a result, have less faith that a successful marriage is possible, and they transfer support for marriage into support for other coupling arrangements, such as cohabitation—arrangements that are easier to dissolve if (and when) problems arise. (Willetts 2006, p. 125)

To summarize, it appears that much of the increase in singlehood results from (1) low sex ratios, particularly in certain regions and among specific age and racial/ethnic groups; (2) increasing educational and economic options for some, coupled with growing financial disadvantage for others; (3) technological changes regarding pregnancy; and (4) changing cultural attitudes toward marriage and singlehood: greater acceptance of premarital sex and emphasis on personal autonomy, development of singlehood and cohabitation as acceptable lifestyles, marriage having lost its monopoly as a way to claim adulthood, and the diminished permanence of marriage. We can apply the exchange theoretical perspective (see Chapter 2) to this issue of less compelling reasons to get married. Overall, as people weigh the costs against the benefits of being married, marriage offers fewer benefits now, relative to being single, than in the past. If fewer Americans are married today, what are singles' various living arrangements?

Singles—Their Various Living Arrangements

As a category, singles make a variety of choices about how to live. Some live alone; others, with parents; still others, in groups or communally. Some unmarrieds cohabit with partners of the same or opposite sex. This section explores these living arrangements.

Living Alone

The number of one-person households has increased dramatically over past decades. Individuals living alone now make up over 28 percent of U.S. households—up from just 8 percent in 1940 (U.S. Census Bureau 1989, Table 61; U.S. Census Bureau 2008a). Figure 8.1 gives the percentage of U.S. adults living alone, by age. As you can see from the figure, the likelihood of living alone increases with age. This is true for all racial/ethnic groups and is markedly higher for older women than for older men (U.S. Census Bureau 2010b, Table 58).

Asians and Hispanics of all ages are less likely to live alone than are blacks or non-Hispanic whites. Although the social science literature tends to focus on middle-class blacks as married, researchers have pointed to a growing number of middle-class, never-married black singles who live alone (Marsh et al. 2007). Significantly less likely to be married than other racial/ethnic groups (see Figure 7.2), blacks are more likely than others to be living by themselves, particularly in older age groups. More collectivist Asian and Hispanic cultures help to discourage living alone in these ethnic groups. Of course, some who live alone are actually involved in long-term committed relationships.

Living Alone Together

An emerging lifestyle choice is *living alone together (LAT)*. Here a couple is engaged in a long-term relationship, but each partner also maintains a separate dwelling (A. Roberts 2005). The number of these relationships is difficult to ascertain, because the U.S. Census Bureau does not measure them. However, European social scientists have noted this family form. According to David Popenoe, codirector of the National Marriage Project at

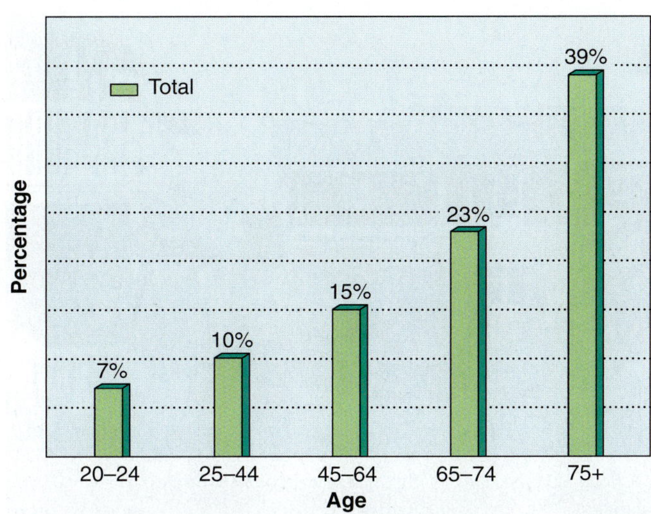

Figure 8.1 Percentage of people over 19 years old living alone, by age, 2008

Source: Calculated from U.S. Census Bureau 2010b, Table 58.

Rutgers University, LAT is clearly an emerging trend in the United States. We know this partly from anecdotal evidence and "partly [from] the fact that every other significant European trend in family life has turned out to be happening in America" (Popenoe, quoted in Brooke 2006). Although we know relatively little about LAT, it is apparently at least partly motivated by a desire to retain autonomy. As one woman said, "I like my own life, my own identity and want to keep it. I like having the things I love around me." As one man put it, "I am as devoted as any husband to her, . . . but I like my alone time and being around my stuff, not [hers]" (in Brooke 2006).

For an older adult, living alone together "allows for unencumbered contact with adult children from previous relationships while protecting their inheritance and offering freedom from caregiving as a prescribed duty. . . Separate homes also allow a tangible line of demarcation in terms of gender equity and the distribution of household labor" (Levaro 2009, p. F10). Some young adults in LAT relationships reside with their parents (S. Smith 2006).

Living with Parents

A large proportion of young adults today are living with one or both parents. In Table 8.1, we see that the percentage of young adults living at home has increased moderately since 1960. In 2008, 56 percent of men and 48 percent of women age eighteen through twenty-four lived with their parents. For men and women age twenty-five to thirty-four, the proportions are 15 percent and 10 percent, respectively (U.S. Census Bureau 2009e, Table AD-1). Overall, about 11 percent of all adults over age eighteen live with their parents. Some adults who live with their parents have never moved out, but others—called boomerangers—have left home and then returned (Arnett 2004; Wang and Morin 2009).

Table 8.1 Percentage Living with their Parents, Sex and Year

	Age 18–24	Age 25–34
Men		
1960	52	11
1995	58	15
2002	55	14
2008	56	15
Women		
1960	35	7
1995	47	8
2002	46	8
2008	48	10

Source: U.S. Census Bureau 2009e, Table AD-1.

Back in 1940, the proportion of adults under age thirty living with their parents was quite high. Sociologists Paul Glick and Sung-Ling Lin suggest why:

> The economic depression of the 1930s had made it difficult for young men and women to obtain employment on a regular basis, and this must have discouraged many of them from establishing new homes. Also, the birth rate had been low for several years; this means that fewer homes were crowded with numerous young children, and that left more space for young adult sons and daughters to occupy. (Glick and Lin 1986, p. 108)

These same reasons apply to many young people today.

Looking at Table 8.1, you will note that the proportion of young adults living with parents declined slightly between 1995 and 2002. As Figure 3.1 illustrates, median household income rose between 1995 and 2002. We can argue that a better economy during that period helped to reduce the percentage of adults living with their parents.

Not surprisingly, the economic recession that began in 2008 led to an increase in boomerangers (Palmer 2008). In one national poll, 10 percent of adults between ages eighteen and thirty-four said they had recently moved back home due to the poor economy (Wang and Morin 2009). A high unemployment rate adds to singles' job-finding difficulties. Then too, "in recent decades, young adults [have been] taking longer to find secure, well-compensated employment" (Danziger and Rouse 2008, F8). Moreover, even before the recent recession, housing in urban areas was too expensive for many singles to maintain their own apartments.

Although many observers focus on economic reasons as primary causes for living with parents, some others see this trend as resulting from "an indulgent parenting style" that demands little of young adult offspring (Pisano 2005). However, it is also true that parents may appreciate the companionship and help of their live-in adult children (Arnett 2004; Straus 2009). Researchers and journalists who have interviewed parents and adult children note that the "generation gap," which in past decades might have made financial dependency and close living annoying to one or both generations, seems to have vanished. According to sociologist Barbara Risman, parents and adolescents or emerging adults today have more in common in lifestyle and values than did baby boomers and their depression/World War II–era parents (in Jayson 2006a). On the other hand, conflict with parents can precipitate the decision to move out and take up residence with a romantic partner (Sassler 2004).

We need to note here that living with parents can occur in a variety of circumstances. Some ethnic groups, such as the Hmong, expect single women to reside with their parents until marriage. Unmarried women who have babies, especially those who became mothers in their teens, may be living with parents. Formerly married young men and women may return to their parental home after divorce. Just as economic considerations, desire for emotional support, or need for help with child raising may lead young singles to live with parents, similar pressures may encourage singles to fashion group or communal living arrangements.

Group or Communal Living

Groups of single adults and perhaps children may live together. Often these are simple roommate arrangements. But some group houses purposefully share aspects of life in common. **Communes**—that is, situations or places characterized by group living—have existed in American society throughout its history and have widely varied in their structure and family arrangements.[2]

Living communally has declined in the United States since its highly visible status in the 1960s, when many communes were established as ideological retreats from what their founders saw as the misguided American life characteristic of the 1950s. However, some communes that were established then still exist. Furthermore, small-scale and nonideological versions of group living have more recently surfaced (Jacobs 2006). For example, the recession that began in 2008 prompted 12 percent of single adults between ages eighteen and thirty-four to acquire a roommate, and another 2 percent took in a boarder (Wang and Morin 2009).

Courtesy of Matt Kramer

Cohousing started in Denmark and spread to the United States in the early 1980s. Residents own their own homes, with residences clustered closely to leave open space, which is community-owned. Cohousing complexes, which typically combine private areas with communal kitchens—and, often with community gardens—offer alternative living arrangements and can be a way to cope with some of the problems of aging, unattached singlehood, or single parenthood.

Communal living, either in single houses or in cohousing complexes that combine private areas with communal kitchens and "family rooms," may be one way to cope with some of the problems of aging, unattached singlehood, or single parenthood ("Cohousing" 2006). In a small but growing number of cohousing complexes, people of diverse races, ethnicities, and ages choose to reside together, sharing some meals and recreational activities. Communal living is designed to provide enhanced opportunities for social support and companionship. More commonly, financial considerations and the desire for companionship encourage romantically involved singles to share households. We turn now to a discussion of "living together," or cohabitation.

[2] In some communes, such as the traditional Israeli kibbutzim (Spiro 1956) and nineteenth-century American groups such as the Shakers and the Oneida colony (Kephart 1971; Kern 1981), all economic resources are shared. Work is organized by the commune, and commune members are fed, housed, and clothed by the community. Other communes may have some private property. Sexual arrangements also vary among communes, ranging from celibacy to monogamous couples (the kibbutzim and some communes in the United States) to the open sexual sharing found in both the Oneida colony and some modern American groups. Children may be under the control and supervision of a parent, or they may be raised more communally, with a de-emphasis on biological relationships and responsibility for discipline and care vested in the entire community.

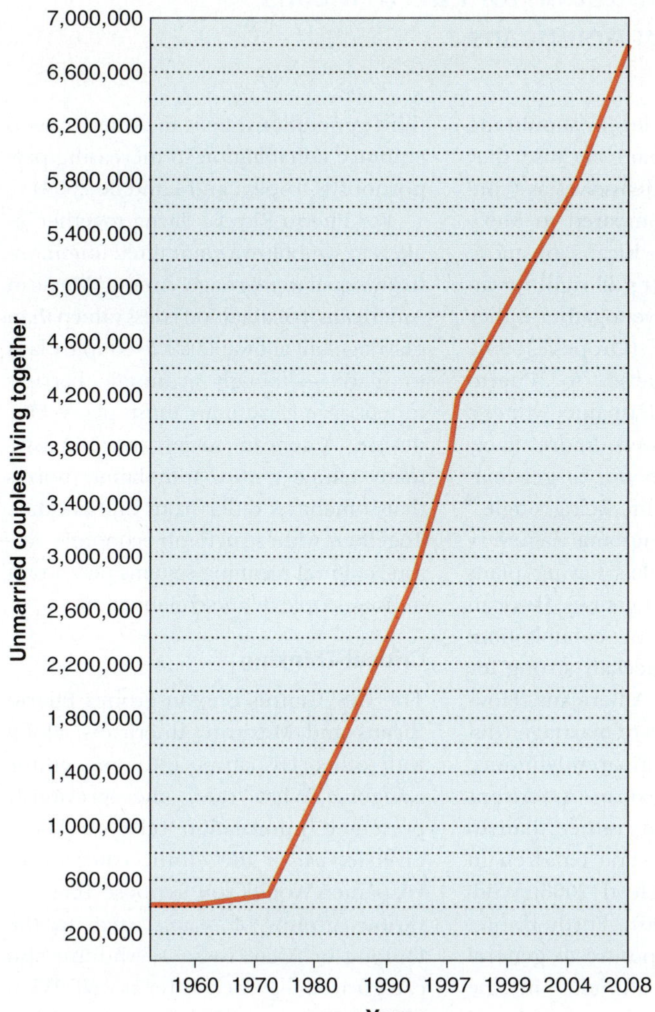

Figure 8.2 Unmarried heterosexual couples living together in the United States, 1960–2008

Sources: Edwards 2009; Glick and Norton 1979; Schneider 2003; Simmons and O'Connell 2003; U.S. Census Bureau 2007a, Table 61.

Cohabitation and Family Life

Cohabitation, or nonmarrieds living together, gained widespread acceptance over the past several decades and is "widely viewed as one of the most important changes in family life in the past 40 years, dramatically altering the marital life course by offering a prelude to or a replacement for marriage" (S. Smith 2006, p. 7). Not only in the United States but in other industrialized nations as well, "living together" has dramatically increased. In this country, the cohabitation trend spread widely in the 1960s, took off sharply in the 1970s, and has risen steadily ever since, as Figure 8.2 illustrates. Today, about 6.8 million U.S. heterosexual couples cohabit (Edwards 2009). This number may be an undercount, because cohabitors do not necessarily move into separate housing. Instead, they may live together in a parental home or reside with roommates and therefore would not be included in a census count (Manning and Smock 2005).

By 2005, an estimated one-half of U.S. women age fifteen through forty-five had cohabited with a male partner at some time in their lives—an increase of nearly 10 percent since 1995 (Chandra et al. 2005, Table 47). The proportion of teenage cohabitors is fairly small; nevertheless, the likelihood of a fifteen- to nineteen-year-old's currently cohabiting nearly tripled in the twenty-five years between 1980 and 2005 (Houseknecht and Lewis 2005).

By 2008, opposite-sex, unmarried-couple households were 5 percent of all households (U.S. Census Bureau 2009b, Table S1101). Six percent of all households with children are headed by cohabiting partners (Kreider and Elliott 2009b, pp. 6 and 8). About 10 percent of infants under age one—but just 1 percent of children age twelve to seventeen—live with cohabiting parents. "This [age] difference may indicate both the fact that the prevalence of cohabitation has risen over the last 10 to 15 years and the fact that cohabiting couples have high rates of dissolution, so they may not remain together for 12 to 17 years after the child's birth" (Kreider and Elliott 2009b, p. 16). The incidence of cohabitation is expected to escalate further as future generations become still more accepting of this family form (Lyons 2004). Furthermore, new generations are growing up in cohabiting families and thereby may be socialized to take cohabiting for granted (Seltzer 2004).

Approximately three-quarters of cohabitants are under age forty-five (U.S. Census Bureau 2008b, Table UC4). Nevertheless, the proportion of middle-aged cohabitors has increased over the past two decades. Middle-aged and older cohabitors are generally in relationships of longer duration, and—as you might expect—they are more likely to be divorced (King and Scott 2005). Approximately 5 percent of cohabitants are age sixty-five and over—a 50 percent increase since 1990 (U.S. Census Bureau 2000, Table 57; 2008b Table UC4). Older singles express less desire to marry (or remarry) than do younger singles (Mahay and Lewin 2007). Older couples have found that living together absent legal marriage may be economically advantageous, because they can retain some financial benefits that are contingent on not being married (King and Scott 2005). With regard to older couples,

> Financial considerations are often at the forefront of decisions to forgo marriage. New couples are aware of their children's fear for their inheritance and for that reason may. . . refrain from marriage. . . . When it comes to marriage and money, widows often say straight out that they are unwilling to risk the financial security of a departed husband's pension. (Levaro 2009, p. F10)

Comparing marrieds to cohabitors, analyses of data from several sources find cohabitors to be younger, less

A Closer Look at Diversity

The Meaning of Cohabitation for Puerto Ricans, Compared to Mexican Americans

You probably have an idea of what cohabitation means to you, and you may assume that living together signifies the same thing to all of us. But researchers who have analyzed national survey data to study cohabitation among various racial/ethnic groups have uncovered interesting differences (Castro Martin 2002; Manning 2004). Cohabiting means different things to different people—and to different categories of people (Landale, Schoen, and Daniels 2009).

For instance, Puerto Rican women have a long history of **consensual marriages** (heterosexual, conjugal unions that have not gone through a legal marriage ceremony). The tradition of consensual marriages probably began among Puerto Ricans due to lack of economic resources necessary for marriage licenses and weddings: "Although nonmarital unions were never considered the cultural ideal, they were recognized as a form of marriage and they typically produced children" (Manning and Landale 1996, p. 65). Therefore, for Puerto Ricans in the continental United States, cohabitation symbolizes a committed union much like marriage, and they don't necessarily feel the need to marry legally should the woman become pregnant because they have already defined themselves as (consensually) married. Compared to Mexican Americans, Puerto Ricans are more likely to agree that "[i]t's all right for an unmarried couple to live together if they have no plans to marry" (Oropesa 1996).

Meanwhile, compared to Puerto Ricans (and to non-Hispanic whites), Mexican Americans were more likely to agree that "[i]t is better to get married than go through life being single." Mexican Americans weigh marriage very positively, and a couple's having plans to marry significantly increases Mexican Americans' approval of cohabitation. These findings are especially strong for foreign-born Mexican Americans. However, economic barriers to marriage (discussed in Chapter 7) apparently induce many low-income Mexican Americans to continue to cohabit, rather than to marry, and to raise several children in cohabiting families (Lloyd 2006; Wildsmith and Raley 2006). Furthermore, as a result of their exposure to general cultural values and attitudes in the United States, we can expect second- and third-generation Mexican Americans to embrace cohabitation in increasing proportions (Oropesa and Landale 2004).

For Puerto Ricans, "living together" is likely to symbolize a committed union, virtually equal to marriage. Among Mexican Americans, cohabitation is less valued than marriage but allowable if the couple plans to marry—although economic barriers to marriage can thwart those plans. Our diverse American society encompasses many ethnic groups with family norms that sometimes differ from one another. Together with structural/economic factors, cultural meaning systems play a part in how people define cohabitation.

Critical Thinking

The U.S. Census Bureau groups Puerto Ricans and Mexican Americans, along with other Hispanics, into one ethnic category. What does the previously presented information tell you about diversity *within* the ethnic category of Hispanic? Would you suppose that the various groups of Asians, such as the Hmong or Asian Indians, who are also categorized together, differ as well? What about African Americans, or whites?

educated, earning less income, less likely to own their own homes, more likely to be nonwhite, and likely to have experienced more transitions in living arrangements as children (S. Ryan et al. 2009; Schoen et al. 2009; Thornton, Axinn, and Xie 2007; U.S. Census Bureau 2008b, Table UC4). Research shows that some of these trends begin in adolescence: Cohabiting women were found to have had lower academic achievement and fewer parental resources in adolescence (Amato et al. 2008). Relatively conservative religious affiliation, attendance, and fervor are negatively related to cohabitation (Eggebeen and Dew 2009). Nevertheless, people from all social classes, educational categories, and religious persuasions have cohabited.

Cohabitation as an Acceptable Living Arrangement

As "A Closer Look at Diversity: The Meaning of Cohabitation" suggests, cohabiting means different things to different people. Generally, however, "[c]ohabitation is very much a family status, but one in which the levels of certainty about commitment are less than in marriage" (Bumpass, Sweet, and Cherlin 1991, p. 913; see also Thornton, Axinn, and Xie 2007). British demographer Kathleen Kiernan (2002) has described a society-wide, four-stage process through which cohabitation becomes a socially acceptable living arrangement, equal in status to marriage.

In the first stage, the vast majority of heterosexuals marry without living together first. We saw this stage in the United States until the late 1970s. In the second stage, more people live together but mainly as a form of courtship before marriage, and almost all of them marry with pregnancy. Today, some cohabitants consider their lifestyle a means of courtship, or *premarital cohabitation.* As one young woman explained, "We wanted to try it out and see how we got along, because I've had so many long-term relationships. I just wanted to make sure we were compatible. And he's been married before, and he felt the same way" (in Arnett 2004, p. 108). Living together as a means of selecting a committed life partner is explored in Chapter 6.

In the third stage, cohabiting becomes a socially acceptable alternative to marriage. A couple no longer feels it necessary to marry with pregnancy or childbirth, and people routinely take an unmarried partner to work or family get-togethers. Nevertheless, in stage three, legal and social differences remain between marriage and "just" living together. In the fourth stage, cohabitation and marriage become virtually indistinguishable, both socially and legally. In this stage, the numbers of married and cohabiting couples are about equal, and a cohabiting couple may have several children (Kiernan 2002).

Social historian Stephanie Coontz (2005b) characterized the United States as "transitioning from stage two to stage three at the end of the twentieth century" (p. 272).[3] Perhaps in some large metropolitan areas of this country—where "cohabitation has replaced marriage as a first union experience for a growing majority of young adults" (Lichter and Carmalt 2009, p. F12)—cohabitation has fully reached stage three. According to Coontz, Sweden is an example of a society in stage four. Norway is a second example. Interestingly, in Norway where cohabitation is common and virtually institutionalized, cohabitors' relationships are more like those of marrieds than in the United States (Hansen, Moum, and Shapiro 2007).

Will the United States ever get to stage four? Coontz is skeptical, because "people [in the United States] still place much more importance on getting married than Swedes do" (2005b, p. 272). "As We Make Choices: Some Things to Know about the Legal Side of Living Together" discusses the legal implications of cohabiting in the United States today.

Cohabitation as an Alternative to Unattached Singlehood and to Marriage

In a qualitative study of 120 heterosexual cohabitors, nearly two-thirds ranked, "I wanted to spend more time with my partner" as their first reason for moving in together (Rhoades, Stanley, and Markman 2009). Some couples begin to live together shortly after their first date; others wait for months or longer (Sassler 2004). Accounts of how cohabitation begins suggest that cohabiting does not always result from a well-considered decision. As one twenty-three-year-old woman who had been living with her parents explained,

> I was looking for my own apartment at this time. . . . He was like, "Why don't you just move in with me?" I was like, "Let's give it some time," or whatever. So I dated him for like a month and then finally all my stuff ended up in his house. (in Sassler 2004, p. 496)

Some cohabitants view living together as an alternative to dating or unattached singlehood (Manning and Smock 2005). As one respondent told her interviewer:

> Um, he had came over, and we had talked and. . . he had spent the night and then from then on he had stayed the night, so basically . . . he just honestly never went home. I guess he had just got out of a relationship, the person he was living with before, he was staying with an uncle and then once we met, it was like love at first sight or whatever and um, he never went home, he stayed with me. (in Manning and Smock 2005, p. 995)

Psychologist Jeffrey Arnett (2004) has dubbed those who live together as an alternative to being single *uncommitted cohabitors.*

Other cohabitors view living together as an alternative to marriage (Cherlin 2009a; Willetts 2006). As they construct their own definitions of commitment, we can think of these couples as *committed cohabitors* (Arnett 2004; Byrd 2009). As one cohabitor explained:

> We've been together 10 years. We met at college. . . . We graduated and started living together. . . . We never say never, but we certainly don't have any plans to [marry]. We're very happy being unmarried to each other. (in Sachs, Solot, and Miller 2003)

And as a thirty-two-year old woman who has been in a monogamous relationship for ten years explained:

> I have friends who have been married and divorced already in the time that we have been together. . . . And I think I like the luxury of the fact that every day that we are together I know we are together because we both choose to be and not because we feel some artificial obligation to be together. (in Byrd 2009)

People's reasons for living together as an alternative to marrying often include the belief that marriage signifies loss of identity or stifles partners' equality and communication (Moore, McCabe, and Brink 2001; Willetts 2003). In the United States today, this view is unusual among young adults, and committed cohabitors are generally older (Arnett 2004).

The Cohabiting Relationship

As a category, cohabiting couples differ from married couples in several ways. First, cohabitors are less homogamous, or alike in social characteristics, than are marrieds. At 12 percent, cohabiting couples are about twice

[3] In the early twentieth century, living together outside marriage was illegal in every state. Due to laws enacted at the turn of the twentieth century, unmarried cohabitation has remained illegal in a handful of states, although the laws are seldom enforced. The American Civil Liberties Union has sued to overturn anticohabitation laws in states where they still exist (Jonsson 2006).

As We Make Choices

Some Things to Know about the Legal Side of Living Together

When unmarried partners move in together, they may encounter regulations, customs, and laws that cause them problems, especially if they're not prepared. Consulting a lawyer is strongly advised. Some potential trouble spots:

Domestic Partners

- In many areas and employment sites, opposite- and same-sex unmarried couples may register their partnership and then enjoy some rights, benefits, and entitlements that have traditionally been reserved for marrieds, such as access to joint health insurance.
- Registering as **domestic partners** usually requires joint residence and finances, plus a statement of loyalty and commitment.

Residence

When two unmarried people are renting, landlords may ask each to sign the lease—a legally binding contract—so that each is held responsible for all rent and associated costs.

Bank Accounts

Any couple can open a joint bank account, but one partner can then withdraw money without the other's approval.

Power of Attorney for Finances

Important when one partner becomes incapacitated, a document establishing power of attorney for finances allows the authorized partner to pay bills, run the partner's business, file taxes, and so on.

Credit Cards

If an unmarried couple shares a credit card, both partners are legally responsible for all charges made by either of them, even after the relationship ends. Creditors generally will not remove one person's name from an account until it is paid in full.

Property

Have a written agreement about what happens to property that was purchased together should the relationship end.

Insurance

- The routine extension of auto and home insurance policies to "residents of the household" cannot be presumed to include nonrelatives.
- Anyone may name anyone else as the beneficiary on a life insurance policy. However, insurance companies sometimes require an "insurable interest," generally interpreted to mean a conventional family tie.

as likely as marrieds to be interracial (Gates 2009b, p. ii). Compared with married women, cohabiting women are more likely to earn more and be several years older than their partners (Fields 2004). Cohabitors have been more likely than marrieds to be nontraditional in many ways, including attitudes about gender roles, and to have parents with nontraditional attitudes and/or who have divorced (Baxter 2005; Cunningham 2005; Davis, Greenstein, and Gertelsen Marks 2007; Teachman 2004).

On average, cohabiting relationships are relatively short-term. Half last less than one year, because the couple either break up or marry (Bumpass and Lu 2000). However, one national survey found that 39 percent of unmarried couples were still together after five to seven years (Bianchi and Casper 2000, p. 17). Still, "[c]ompared with married couples, cohabitors are much more likely to break up" (Seltzer 2000, p. 1,252). Reasons include the fact that, for the most part, cohabiting partners are not committed to their relationship in the same way that married partners are. Then, too, cohabitation may not include widely held norms to guide behavior to the degree that marriage does. As a result, the relationship may suffer as partners struggle to define their situation. Finally, lack of social support may negatively impact the stability of cohabitation "as members of the [cohabiter's acquaintance] network . . . provide the partners possibilities for other intimate relationships" (Willetts 2006, p. 114).

Uncertainty about commitment, together with less well-defined norms for the relationship, may be reasons that, compared to marrieds, cohabitants pool their finances to a lesser extent (Kenney 2004; King and Scott 2005); are less likely to say that they are happy with their relationships and find them less fair (Skinner et al. 2002); report a higher incidence of depression than marrieds (Kim and McKenry 2002; Lamb, Lee, and DeMaris 2003); place greater importance on sexual frequency (Yabiku and Gager 2009); and have more sex outside the relationship than marrieds do (Treas and Giesen 2000).

However, research that analyzed data from the National Survey of Families and Households (NSFH) has found that the relationship quality of "*long-term*" cohabiting couples (who were together for at least four years) differed little from marrieds in conflict

Wills and Living Trusts

If you have no will or living trust when you die, your property will pass to individuals designated by state law—usually legal spouses and blood relatives. A surviving partner could inherit nothing, not even property that he or she paid for.

Health Care Decision Making

Anyone too ill to be legally competent should have an agent to act for him or her in medical decision making. Many cohabitants want their partners to play this role. To be sure that medical personnel honor this desire, designate your partner as decision maker through a "durable power of attorney for health care" document.

Children

With the 1972 case of *Stanley v. Illinois* (405 U.S. 645), an unmarried mother is no longer entitled to sole disposition of the child in many states. Although courts have placement discretion, unmarried couples should stipulate in writing that custody is to go to the partner if the other parent dies. Note also that financial obligations for child support do not depend on marital status.

Some—but not all—courts grant visitation rights to a nonbiological, same-sex co-parent should the relationship end. Unmarried parents to a partner's child should consider three documents:

- Co-parenting Agreement spelling out the rights and responsibilities of each partner
- Nomination of Guardianship that adds language to a will or living trust
- Consent to Medical Treatment allowing the co-parent to authorize the child's medical procedures

Breaking Up

Ending a cohabiting relationship is not to be taken lightly:

- Couples who do not stipulate in writing—and preferably with an attorney's assistance—paternity, property, and other agreements can expect legal hassles. See an attorney about the laws in your state.
- Ending a registered domestic partner agreement in California and some other states requires a formal property settlement agreement and a dissolution proceeding in court (Clifford, Hertz, and Doskow 2007).

Critical Thinking

Does having to worry about the legal aspects of cohabitation lessen what appear to be some of the advantages of living together? Why, or why not?

levels, amount of interaction together, or relationship satisfaction. One thing did differ, however: For both marrieds and long-term cohabitors, relationship satisfaction declined with the addition of children to the household, but this decline was more pronounced for cohabitors (Willetts 2006). Other research has found that, compared with younger cohabitors, older cohabiting couples generally report higher relationship quality. Among younger cohabitors, lack of plans for marriage is associated with lower relationship satisfaction (King and Scott 2005). One study found that cohabiting men with intentions to marry their partner do more housework than do other cohabiting males (Ciabattari 2004).

Cohabitation and Intimate Partner Violence Evidence also exists of considerable domestic, or intimate partner violence (IVP), in cohabiting relationships (Brownridge and Halli 2002; DeMaris 2001)—more than among marrieds or dating partners. This situation may also be due to a combination of relatively low commitment (Johnson and Ferraro 2000) and conflict over "rights, duties, and obligations" (Magdol et al. 1998, p. 52). In addition, selection effects—the situation (discussed more thoroughly in Chapter 7) in which individuals "select" themselves into a category being investigated—in this case, cohabitation—probably help to account for these findings. As we have seen, individuals who live together without marrying tend to be less well educated and poorer than marrieds, and—although domestic violence occurs at all economic and education levels—low income and education are statistically associated with higher levels of domestic violence (Schumacher et al. 2001).

Although not as often as one might expect, IVP can result in the dissolution of the relationship (DeMaris 2001). Research on the economic consequences of cohabitors' breaking up finds similarities to getting divorced. On average, men experience moderate financial decline, whereas women's economic decline is more pronounced (Avellar and Smock 2005). Counselors stress the importance of being fairly independent before deciding to cohabit, understanding one's motives, having clear goals and expectations, and being honest with and sensitive to the needs of both oneself and one's partner. This is especially necessary when children are involved.

© Royalty-Free/CORBIS

According to Pamela J. Smock, associate director at the Institute for Research at the University of Michigan, Ann Arbor, cohabiting "has become the typical and, increasingly, the majority experience of persons before marriage and after marriage" (quoted in "What Happened? . . ." 2003). On average, cohabiting relationships are relatively short-term. Half last less than one year, because the couple either break up or marry. Cohabiting men with intentions to marry their partner are likely to do more housework than other cohabiting males.

Cohabiting Parents and Outcomes for Children

FOCUS ON CHILDREN

Today, between 10 and 20 percent of all births occur to a cohabiting mother (Chandra et al. 2005, Table 16; Lichter and Carmalt 2009). About half of all nonmarital births occur to cohabiting couples (Dye 2005; Hamilton et al. 2006). Perhaps half or more of births to cohabitors are planned (Lichter and Carmalt 2009; Manning 2001). As shown in Figure 8.3, 38 percent of cohabiting heterosexual households contain children under age eighteen—a proportion only five percentage points lower than that of married-couple households with children (U.S. Census Bureau 2009c, Table UC3; U.S. Census Bureau 2010b, Table 65). Six percent of children under age eighteen (about 4.6 million) live with a parent or parents who are cohabiting. Of children who live with cohabiting couples, half live with both of their unmarried biological or adoptive parents (U.S. Census Bureau 2009a, Table S0901; U.S. Census Bureau 2009d, Table C3; U.S. Federal Interagency Forum on Child and Family Statistics 2009).

These statistics describe a situation at one point in time. However, "it is important to keep in mind that as children age, they may spend time in several [living] arrangements" (Kreider and Elliott 2009a, p. 16). More than ten years ago, demographers estimated that about one in four U.S. children would live in a family headed by a cohabiting couple "at some point during childhood" (Graefe and Lichter 1999, p. 215). Today—due to the increasing incidence of cohabiting and of childbearing among unmarried couples—we estimate this proportion to be higher (Lichter and Carmalt 2009).

Although a large majority of cohabiting couples with children have one child, a significant number (about 1.5 million cohabiting couples) are raising two or more children (Chandra et al. 2005, Table 9). Research from at least three national samples has found this situation to be more characteristic of black and Hispanic cohabitors than of non-Hispanic whites, who are more likely to marry upon becoming pregnant (Chandra et al. 2005, Table 18; Manning 2004).

A qualitative study with thirty cohabiting working-class childfree couples found that most intended to defer having children—many until after they marry, if they do (Sassler, Miller, and Favinger 2009). In another qualitative study, in-depth interviews with twenty-four childless cohabitors who had had some college found that they associated their desire to be in the middle class with marrying in the event that they had children. For these couples, cohabitation "appears to serve as a staging area, a time when couples can be together, complete schooling, and get fiscally established prior to marrying and beginning families" (Sassler and Cunningham 2008, p. 22).

Having a child while cohabiting does not necessarily increase a couple's odds of staying together, but conceiving a child during cohabitation and then marrying before the baby is born apparently does increase union stability. Why would this be? "Although birth in cohabitation indicates a decision to remain together during pregnancy, it also represents a decision not to commit to marriage" (Manning 2004, p. 677). Cohabiting parents who see a father's involvement in parenting as very important are more likely to stay together (Hohmann-Marriott 2009). Perhaps ironically, the fear of divorce among unmarried parents

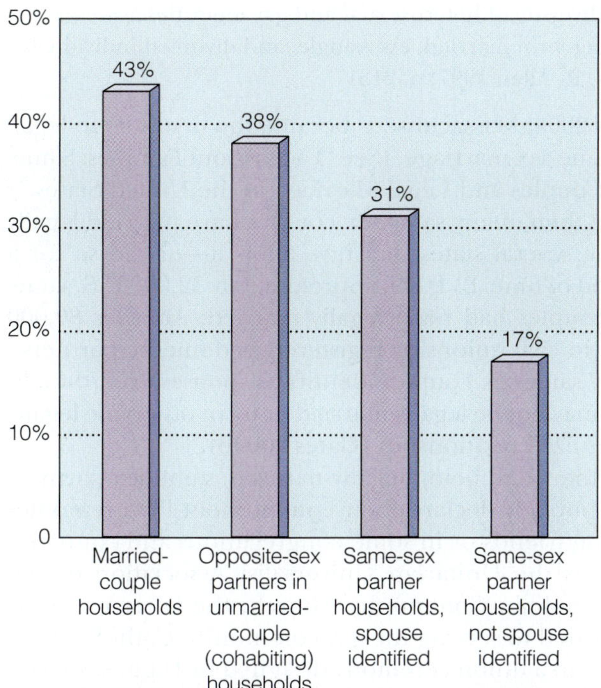

Figure 8.3 Percentage of children under age 18 in four U.S. household types, 2008

Note: Unmarried partners' children refers to at least one biological child under age 18 of either parent. Percentages for opposite-sex cohabiting households are for 2007.

Sources: Gates 2009b, Figure 13; U.S. Census Bureau 2009c, Table UC3; U.S. Census Bureau 2010b, Table 69.

may reduce their likelihood of marrying (Waller and Peters 2008).

Children's Outcomes For many families, "[c]ohabitation may not be an ideal childrearing context precisely because of the stress associated with the uncertainty of the future of the union" (S. Brown 2004, p. 353). Because cohabiting couples are significantly less likely to stay together than marrieds, it has been noted that many children in cohabiting-couple families will experience a series of changes, or transitions in their family's living arrangements (Lichter and Carmalt 2009; Raley and Wildsmith 2004). This cumulative instability is related to problematic outcomes for children (Cavanagh 2008). "Residential and other household changes associated with the formation of new partnerships may disrupt well-established patterns of [parental] supervision" (Thomson et al. 2001, p. 378; see also Heard 2007; Magnuson and Berger 2009). Other research has found a relationship between a mother's overall stress (which negatively affects parenting) and her forming a coresidential relationship with a nonbiological father to her child (Cooper et al. 2009).

Accordingly, many family scholars have expressed concern regarding outcomes for adolescents and younger children living in opposite-sex, cohabiting families (Booth and Crouter 2002; S. Brown 2004). For example, research that compared economically disadvantaged children from families of various forms found more problem behaviors among children in various types of unmarried families, including cohabiting unions (Ackerman et al. 2001; M. J. Carlson 2006). Other research has found that, among couples with comparable incomes, cohabiting parents spend less on their children's education than do marrieds (DeLeire and Kalil 2005).

When compared to those living with two married biological parents, adolescents who have lived with a cohabiting parent are more likely to experience earlier premarital intercourse, higher rates of school suspension, and antisocial and delinquent behaviors, coupled with lower academic achievement and expectations for college (Albrecht and Teachman 2003; S. Brown 2004; M. J. Carlson 2006). Having a cohabiting male in the household who is not the biological father appears not to enhance adolescents' outcomes when compared with living in a single-mother household (Manning and Lamb 2003). Nevertheless, research also shows that, compared to growing up in a single-parent home, children do benefit economically from living with a cohabiting partner, provided that the partner's financial resources are shared with family members (Manning and Brown 2006).

A relatively new area for court determination of child custody concerns children of cohabiting parents who separate. Some courts treat nonmarital relationships as "sufficiently marriage-like" for marital law to apply (Judge Heather Van Nuys in "Court Treats" 2002). Some proponents of the idea that only legally married couples should be treated as married oppose court involvement in custody issues of unmarried parents. However, "Courts aren't trying to contribute to the demise of traditional families. But they recognize the reality of families today and functional parents" (Duke University Law School Dean, Katherine Bartlett, quoted in Biskupic 2003, p. 2A).

As cohabitation becomes increasingly common, we become more aware that today's pluralistic family is comprised of many forms. We turn now to another relationship type that exemplifies the pluralistic family—same-sex couples.[4]

[4] Not only cohabiting and same-sex couples add diversity to the postmodern family. Transgendered identity—physically changing surgically and/or with the use of hormones from male to female or vice versa—further complicates a traditional view of family life. As an example, a man who married a woman in 1988 thereafter gradually changed gender. The couple stayed together. Is their marriage "gay"? On another note, some states do not recognize sex changes. If the former male, now a female, were to remarry now in those states, she would be allowed only to marry a female (Boylan 2009).

Same-Sex Couples and Family Life

Google GLBT (gay, lesbian, bisexual, and transgendered) organizations, and you'll find websites for blacks, Latinos/as, Jews, and Muslims, among others. Lesbian and gay singles make up a diverse category of all ages and racial/ethnic groups. In 2008, there were approximately 565,000 same-sex couple households in the United States, about evenly divided between gay male and lesbian couples (Gates 2009b).[5, 6]

Families of same-sex couples include lesbian co-parents, as well as an array of combinations of lesbian mothers and biological fathers, surrogate mothers, and gay biological fathers (less frequent) (Goldberg 2010; C. Patterson 2000). A family studies professor describes the diversity apparent in her own lesbian family as follows:

> My partner and I live with our two sons. Our older son was conceived in my former heterosexual marriage. At first, our blended family consisted of a lesbian couple and a child from one partner's previous marriage. After several years, our circumstances changed. My brother's life partner became the donor and father to our second son, who is my partner's biological child. My partner and I draw a boundary around our lesbian-headed family in which we share a household consisting of two moms and two sons, but our extended family consists of additional kin groups. For example, my former husband and his wife have an infant son, who is my biological son's second brother. All four sets of grandparents and extended kin related to our sons' biological parents are involved in all our lives to varying degrees. These kin comprise a diversity of heterosexual and gay identities as well as long-term married, ever-single, and divorced individuals. (K. R. Allen 1997, p. 213)

In 2004, Massachusetts became the first state to legalize same-sex marriage. (See "Facts About Families: Same-Sex Couples and Legal Marriage in the United States.") Since then, many same-sex couples have married legally in the several states that now allow it—or did so for a period of time. By 2009, approximately 32,000 U.S. same-sex couples had been legally married. Another 80,000 were in civil unions or registered as domestic partners.[7] Many same-sex couples identify as spouses even though they may not be legally married or in an otherwise legally recognized relationship (Gates 2009b).[8]

Other than being legally married, same-sex partners may publicly declare their commitment in ceremonies among friends or in some congregations and churches, such as the Unitarian Universalist Association or the Metropolitan Community Church, the latter expressly dedicated to serving the gay community. Catholics have access to a union ceremony designed by Dignity, a Catholic support association, although the Catholic Church does not recognize these unions ("Registration of Holy Union . . ." 2008).

Secular commitment ceremonies for gay men and lesbians are common enough to have sparked a number of wedding-planning businesses for same-sex couples (e.g., twobrides.com, twogrooms.com). Same-sex couples also use other commitment markers, such as joint estate planning, buying a house together, wearing rings, or hyphenating their last names (Porche and Purvin 2008; Reczek, Elliott, and Umberson 2009; Suter, Daas, and Bergen 2008). Registering as domestic partners (described in "As We Make Choices: Some Things to Know about the

[5] The Census Bureau conducts an annual American Community Survey (ACS) between decennial censuses. The number of same-sex couples reported by the 2008 ACS was considerably lower than the 780,000 reported in 2006. "This is likely a result of changes in the format and processing of the 2008 ACS that reduced the probability of respondents making errors" (Gates 2009b, p. 2). For a detailed account of how this error originally occurred—and how it was corrected in the 2008 ACS—see Gates 2009a.

[6] Until the 2000 census, calculations of unmarried couples did not include same-sex partners. Therefore, comparing estimates from before 2000 with census data thereafter is inappropriate.

Beginning with the 2000 census, unmarried same-sex couples were counted as such. Because Massachusetts legalized same-sex marriage in 2004, there was hope that the 2010 census would calculate same-sex married, as well as unmarried, couples. However, the 2010 census does not count married same-sex couples as married; instead it counts them as unmarried. This situation is largely due to the Census Bureau's interpretation of the federal Defense of Marriage Act (which defines marriage as necessarily "between one man and one woman") as not permitting an enumeration of same-sex couples as married. However, the Census Bureau has announced a large-scale project to improve future data collection on same-sex couples, and it is anticipated that questions on their marital status will appear in the future (O'Connell and Lofquist 2009; Quinn 2009; "Same-Sex Couples . . ." 2009).

[7] The terms *domestic partnership* and *civil union* both refer to officially recognized unions according to which unmarried couples enjoy some (although not all) rights and benefits ordinarily reserved for marrieds. However, the term *civil union* is used to refer to various states' granting same-sex couples a legal status virtually equivalent to marriage. The term domestic partnership is typically used to refer to same- or opposite-sex unmarried partner benefits offered by some employers, cities, counties, and states. Generally, domestic partnerships grant couples lesser status and fewer benefits than do civil unions. However, California, Oregon, and Washington use the term *domestic partnership* for legislation similar or equivalent to civil union laws in other states ("Marriage, Domestic Partnerships, and Civil Unions . . ." 2009).

[8] Same-sex couples living together in long-term, committed relationships are not a recent development. According to social historian Samuel Kader (1999), same-sex committed couples date back to the Old Testament, and commitment ceremonies between same-sex partners were not unknown in early Christianity. More recently, scholars "have uncovered a long and complicated history of gay relationships in nineteenth-century America. Sometimes women passed as men to form straight-seeming relationships; sometimes men or women lived together as housemates but were really lovers; sometimes individuals would marry but still carry on romantic, sometimes lifelong same-sex intimate relationships" (Seidman 2003, p. 124).

Legal Side of Living Together") can have emotional significance for same-sex couples who may do so partly as a way of publicly expressing their commitment.

Demographically, same-sex couples who identify as spouses (even if not legally married) are much like heterosexual marrieds in several respects. Same-sex couples who identify as spouses have an average age of fifty-two, average household incomes of $91,558, and 31 percent are raising children. "That compares with an average age of fifty, household income of $95,075, and 43 percent raising children for married heterosexual couples" ("Report: Gay Couples Similar . . ." 2009). Additionally, in both couple types, a little over 20 percent have a college degree, about 80 percent own their own homes, and 6 to 7 percent are interracial (Gates 2009b).[9]

Same-sex couples live in virtually every county of every state (Gates 2009b). Often they find community in urban areas that have high concentrations of gays and lesbians, along with strong activist organizations. But lesbians and gays also live in the suburbs and smaller towns. The Internet has changed life for many gay men and lesbians, especially those living in rural areas. Accessing websites such as PlanetOut.com, homosexuals from all over the world can meet and interact online regardless of geographical boundaries (Gudelunas 2006).

Although discrimination assuredly persists, attitudes toward GLBT rights generally have become more accepting over the past twenty-five years. Gallup polls have shown a gradual increase—from 34 percent in 1983 to 57 percent in 2008—in agreement with the idea that being gay or lesbian is an "acceptable alternative lifestyle" (Saad 2008a; see also Newman 2007). Then too, more employers, cities, and states are extending various benefits to same-sex couples—health insurance for an employee's partner, for example (Surdin 2009).

The Same-Sex Couple's Relationship

In many respects, same-sex relationships are similar to heterosexual ones. Like heterosexuals, same-sex partners highly value love, faithfulness, and commitment (Meier, Hull, and Ortyl 2009). Research indicates that the need to resolve issues of sexual exclusivity, and power and decision making is not much different in same-sex pairings than among heterosexual partners (Kurdek 2006). However, research shows that same-sex partners of both genders are likely to evidence more equality and role sharing than couples in heterosexual marriages (Kurdek 2007; Parker-Pope 2008).

Nevertheless, a recent study of thirty-two New York City black lesbians in stepfamilies (that is, one partner brought her child or children into a same-sex cohabiting relationship) found that for these women constructing "family" meant following traditional heterosexual gender roles to some degree. Specifically, biological mothers in these stepfamilies were more involved not only in child care but also in housework. The author argues that following heterosexually "appropriate" marital roles may be especially important for lesbian mothers who previously bore their children in heterosexual contexts, because "they willingly moved from validated relationships with men to . . . often stigmatized, same-sex unions. Given this status change, these mothers may find 'appropriate' gender construction that much more important" (Moore 2008, p. 353).

Same-sex couples must daily negotiate their private relationship within a heterosexual—often, heterosexist—world (Oswald and Masciadrelli 2008; Suter et al. 2006). A comparison of same-sex couples with married heterosexual couples found that the former spent more time discussing the state of their relationship. The researchers suggest that this difference may reflect the absence of a legal bond: "It appears that to some degree heterosexual married couples may take for granted that they are bound together through legal marriage, whereas gays and lesbians must frequently 'take the pulse' of the relationship to assess its status" (Haas and Stafford 2005, p. 56).

A traumatic example of living out a private relationship amid heterosexism occurred in 2009, when a Florida hospital prevented a distraught lesbian from being at her dying partner's bedside ("Federal Court Dismisses Lawsuit . . ." 2009). "This is an anti-gay city and state," the hospital receptionist reportedly explained (Parker-Pope 2009). One year later, President Obama ordered that any hospital that received federal funds through Medicare or Medicaid must grant hospital visiting rights to same-sex partners (Stolberg 2010). Nevertheless, discrimination against same-sex couples persists in many areas of their lives.

Discrimination adds stress for same-sex couples and may result in lowered mental health and relationship quality (Otis et al. 2006). In addition, the potential for discrimination gives partners unique avenues for dealing negatively with couple conflict. "For example, 'outing' one's partner is not an issue for heterosexuals but is a surprisingly common weapon for gay people in an abusive relationship" (Burke and Owen 2006, p. 6; Sorenson and Thomas 2009).

Same-Sex Intimate Partner Violence Stress resulting from discrimination was once thought to be one reason that statistics indicated higher rates of intimate partner violence (IVP) among same-sex couples versus among heterosexual couples. However, recent analysis has uncovered methodological deficiencies in earlier reports of higher IPV among same-sex couples, and current research suggests that the rates are

[9] Interestingly, same-sex unmarried partners and different-sex cohabiting partners have similar rates of being interracial—13 percent of same-sex unmarried partners and 12 percent of different-sex cohabiting partners (Gates 2009b, p. 11).

Facts about Families

Same-Sex Couples and Legal Marriage in the United States

The 1974 U.S. Supreme Court decision in *Singer v. Hara* defined marriage as a union between one man and one woman (*Singer v. Hara* 1974). Nevertheless, the federal government has traditionally recognized the right of individual states to create, interpret, and enforce laws regarding marriage and families. Consequently, the battle over legal marriage for same-sex couples has largely been fought within individual state courts and legislatures.

Lawsuits Claiming Discrimination and Varied State Responses

Beginning in the late 1990s, same-sex couples in several states filed lawsuits claiming that barring lesbians and gays from legal marriage is unconstitutional because it discriminates against same-sex couples. Some (although not all) courts have agreed and ordered their state legislatures to address this problem by passing new, nondiscriminatory laws. Results have been varied. In 2004, Massachusetts became the first state to allow gay and lesbian couples to marry legally. About 10 percent of all states now allow same-sex marriage. However, marriage in these states remains "an incomplete legal status, because same-sex marriages are denied federal recognition of their relationship by virtue of the 1996 federal [Defense of Marriage Act, or] DOMA" (Oswald and Kuvalanka 2008, p. 1060). (DOMA is described later in this boxed material.) Other states have passed *civil union* laws.

Civil unions allow same-sex partners access to virtually all marriage rights and benefits on the state level, but none on the federal level. For instance, a couple would have state-regulated rights to joint property and tenancy, inheritance without a will, and hospital visitation and health care decisions for their partners. However, they cannot collect federal Social Security benefits upon a partner's death, nor can a non-U.S. partner become a U.S. citizen upon joining a civil union (Oswald and Kuvalanka 2008).

Meanwhile, some states have amended their state constitutions to stipulate that marriage in that state is to be defined only as heterosexual. As an example, in 2008, California voters (by a margin of 52 percent to 48 percent) passed the California Marriage Protection Act (Proposition 8), a state constitutional amendment declaring that "only marriage between a man and a woman is valid or recognized in California." Proposition 8 overturned a prior California court ruling which said that same-sex couples have a constitutional right to marry.

However, a state constitution does not outrank a federal court ruling, and in August 2010, a federal court ruled that California's Proposition 8 violated the U.S. constitution because it discriminated against a category of U.S. citizens without a rational basis for such discrimination. Proponents of Proposition 8 had argued that to allow same-sex marriage would erode traditional marriage, but the federal judge who struck down Proposition 8 ruled that, "Tradition alone…cannot form the rational basis for law" (McKinley and Schwartz 2010).

This decision, however, does not definitively determine the legality of same-sex marriage because it applies only to one jurisdiction and because the case is expected to advance to the U.S. Ninth Circuit Court of Appeals and from there to the United States Supreme Court (Schwartz 2010). How a U.S. Supreme Court ruling might affect the existing Federal Defense of Marriage Act and the various state laws permitting or prohibiting same-sex marriage (and domestic partnership) remains to be seen.

The Federal Defense of Marriage Act (DOMA)

States usually recognize one another's legal decisions. This *principle of reciprocity* would require a state to recognize a legal marriage performed in another state. However, to allow states *not* to follow the principle of reciprocity regarding same-sex marriages, the United States passed the 1996 **Defense of Marriage Act (DOMA)**. The Defense of Marriage Act is a federal statute declaring marriage to be a "legal union of one man and one

---

about the same for both couple types (Sorenson and Thomas 2009). Meanwhile, society-wide responses to same-sex violence "can be described as neglectful at best" (Sorenson and Thomas 2009, p. 349; Kulkin et al. 2007):

> Restraining orders, a legal remedy that is widely used when a victim is trying to end the relationship that requires the abuser to have either no or only peaceful contact with the victim . . . are not available to gay men and lesbians in [some] states. In addition, social services are not always welcoming; lesbian victims of IPV report not feeling comfortable seeking domestic violence services that generally are geared to heterosexual females. And most shelters do not accept male clients, making such services off limits to gay male IPV victims. (Sorenson and Thomas 2009, p. 349)

Gay activists argue that domestic violence laws need to specifically include lesbian and gay partners, and police must be trained to more effectively address intimate partner violence among same-sex couples (Kulkin et al. 2007). In sum, the problem of same-sex IVP "is exacerbated" by a political climate that often "treats gays and lesbians as a marginalized population" (Burke and Owen 2006, p. 7).

"There's nothing wrong with our marriage, but the spectre of gay marriage has hopelessly eroded the institution."

Robert Mankoff/Bios/Cartoonbank

woman," withholding federal recognition of legal same-sex marriages in any state, and relieving states of the obligation to grant reciprocity to marriages performed in another state. As a result of DOMA, a large majority of states have passed laws or state constitutional amendments that refuse to allow legal marriage in that state and/or recognize a marriage obtained by same-sex couples in another state (Oswald and Kuvalanka 2008).

In 2009 a bill, named the Respect for Marriage Act, was introduced into Congress. If passed, the act will repeal DOMA ("Legislation Introduced . . ." 2009).

A Proposed Federal Amendment to the U.S. Constitution

A proposed federal amendment to the U.S. Constitution would define marriage as between one man and one woman and ban same-sex marriage in the United States while allowing states to create civil unions or domestic partnerships (Allen and Cooperman 2004; Page and Benedetto 2004). Because the originators of the U.S. Constitution intended for amendments not to be undertaken lightly, they made them very difficult to pass. Passing a U.S. constitutional amendment requires a two-thirds majority in both the U.S. House of Representatives and Senate. Then the amendment must be approved by three-fourths of the states. A constitutional amendment that would define marriage as between one man and one woman has not passed in Congress.

This range—from legal same-sex marriage in several states to a possible federal constitutional amendment that would ban same-sex marriages across the country—points up the serious public divide in the United States regarding same-sex marriage. For further details on legal marriage for same-sex couples in the United States and throughout the world, visit the following websites: American Civil Liberties Union (aclu.org); Partners Task Force for Gay and Lesbian Couples (buddybuddy.com); and DOMA Watch (domawatch.org).

Critical Thinking

Today it would be difficult to escape the public debate over whether, on the one hand, the family as institution is inappropriately threatened or, on the other hand, tolerance for diversity is fitting when the issue is legal marriage for same-sex couples. What do you think? Is the institution of marriage and family threatened by same-sex marriage? Why, or why not? Can you back up your opinion with facts?

Same-Sex Parents and Outcomes for Children

Enough same-sex couples are establishing families with children that, by the early 2000s, observers noted a "gay baby boom" (Johnson and O'Connor 2002). A 2008 census bureau survey found that 31 percent of same-sex couples who identified themselves as married, and 17 percent of other same-sex households now include children under age eighteen (Gates 2009b, Figure 13). (See also Figure 8.3.) These children were born to the union, were adopted, or were born in prior heterosexual relationships.

Same-sex couples become parents through adoption, foster care, planned sexual intercourse, or artificial insemination (Bell 2003; Gomes 2003; Mundy 2007). Some—but certainly not all—courts permit a lesbian partner to adopt the biological child of the other partner or will grant joint adoption to same-sex couples, ensuring legal parenthood to both members of the couple raising a child (Human Rights Campaign 2007).

Religions vary in their policies regarding such families. For example, the Catholic Church officially opposes both legal marriage and adoption by same-sex couples (Buchanan 2006; Egelko 2008; LeBlanc 2006a). Courts also vary in their receptiveness to same-sex families.

© San Francisco Examiner/Lacy Atkins

Lesbian couples may take advantage of AID (artificial insemination by donor) technology so that one partner gives birth to a baby they both want. Research indicates that children of lesbian or gay male parents are generally well adjusted and have no noticeable differences from children of heterosexual parents.

Some courts have permitted a lesbian co-parent to adopt a biological child born to her partner, ensuring legal parenthood to both members of the couple raising a child (Human Rights Campaign 2007). Many courts grant joint adoption to gay male couples. However, some states prohibit same-sex couples from adopting children. Florida, for example, prohibits same-sex couple adoption, although it does allow them to serve as foster parents (Waddell 2005).[10]

Among lesbian couples, one partner may give birth to a child that both partners parent. When a couple decides to follow this course, the women face a series of decisions: Who will be the biological mother? How will a sperm donor be chosen? What will they call themselves as parents? How will they negotiate parenthood within a heterosexual society? Where and from whom will they find support? (Chabot and Ames 2004; Goldberg and Smith 2008).

[10] The Williams Institute on Sexual Orientation, Law and Public Policy, affiliated with the UCLA School of Law, estimates that Florida's prohibiting adoption by GLB individuals and same-sex couples costs the state $2.5 million annually in unnecessary foster care expenses (Goldberg, Badgett, and Cooper 2009).

Compared to that regarding heterosexuals, the amount of research on same-sex parents is small but growing. One study has found that lesbian partners who become parents are more likely than heterosexual wives to remain committed to full-time work as well as to motherhood (Peplau and Fingerhut 2004). Another study focused on the relationship quality of twenty-nine lesbian couples who gave birth to their first child by means of artificial insemination. These researchers found that, similar to heterosexual couples, lesbian partners' relationship satisfaction declined with the transition to parenthood. This situation was largely due to having less time to be alone as a couple after the baby was born (Goldberg and Sayer 2006).

"Living in a society fixated on labels and family terminology," lesbian couples are often asked, "Who is the real mom?" (Chabot and Ames 2004, p. 354). One nonbiological mother illustrates this point:

> I think a lot of people have issue with that . . . you're not *really* the mother if you're not the biological mother. You're just sort of playing this role, or something. Maybe you're just the one who's also responsible, but you're not "*the mom.*" We don't care what anybody else thinks. We both are the moms. (in Chabot and Ames 2004, p. 354)

Then, too, issues of support from the couple's extended families may cause tension:

> Biological mothers' families may undermine the nonbiological mother's relationship to the child, seeing her as "less of a mother." . . . Another possibility is that biological mothers' families . . . meet or even surpass nonbiological mothers' expectations for support, but their frequent presence or greater involvement ultimately causes conflict between the partners. (Goldberg and Sayer 2006, p. 97)

Meanwhile, same-sex parents emphasize their similarity to heterosexual parents: "We go to story time at the library and worry about all the same food groups" (in M. Bell 2003). "Contrary to stereotypes of these families as isolated from families of origin, most report that children had regular (i.e., at least monthly) contact with one or more grandparents, as well as with other adult friends and relatives of both genders" (Patterson 2000, p. 1,062). A wide network of adult friends and relatives may even include ex-husbands. A lesbian mother who, like her partner, brought a daughter into the relationship from a heterosexual previous marriage, explains:

> [B]oth of [the girls'] fathers live very close. We stayed right within the same school district that I was in with the little one. Little Monica's father being just in the next school district over. So, the fathers were always there visiting and taking care of [the girls], especially my ex-husband when . . . I was back in school, so . . . he always had the responsibility of being there when they got home [from school]. (in Hequembourg 2007, p. 169)

Children's Outcomes Research from an accumulation of more than one hundred studies finds children of gay male and lesbian parents to be generally well adjusted, with no noticeable differences from children of heterosexual parents in cognitive abilities, behavior, or emotional development. There is no evidence that children of same-sex parents are confused about their gender identity, either in childhood or adulthood, or that they are more likely to be homosexual (Goldberg 2010; Meezan and Rauch 2005).

Although not necessarily refuting these findings, sociologists note that the research methodologies of many of these studies are not rigorous, largely because it is very difficult to locate representative samples of gay male and/or lesbian parents. Sociologist Tim Biblarz argues that insufficient long-term, large-scale research exists to determine whether being raised by same-sex parents affects sexual identity (Jayson 2009). The research that we do have—which is largely on lesbian, white, and middle- or upper-middle class parents—concludes that same-sex parents, especially those who identify as spouses, are much like married heterosexuals in their parenting practices (Goldberg 2010). Its members having themselves reviewed the literature, the American Academy of Pediatrics officially supports gay male and lesbian couples' adopting, bearing, and raising children (Perrin 2002).

Meanwhile, like children of other minority groups, those in same-sex families may experience prejudice from friends, classmates, or teachers. Regarding relationships with schools, the Family Pride Coalition urges same-sex parents to

> [t]ell the teachers who is in your family and names your children use to identify them, and provide a glossary of correct terms for lesbian and gay families. Give the library a list of books, videos and other resource materials . . . , and encourage school administrators and librarians to purchase these materials for the school. (Brickley et al. 1999)

In a heterosexist society, adult children of same-sex parents face questions about coming out about their parents (Goldberg 2007, 2010). Children of same-sex parents have formed a support group called COLAGE (Children of Lesbians and Gays Everywhere) and maintain a website (www.colage.org). Their purpose is to "engage, connect, and empower people to make the world a better place for children of lesbian, gay, bisexual, and/or transgender parents and families." Being allowed to marry legally might be a benefit to children being raised in same-sex households, because marriage is associated with increased "durability and stability of the parental relationship" as well as enhanced in-law, grandparent, and other extended-family investment (Meezan and Rauch 2005, p. 108; Goldberg 2010; Wildman 2010). We turn now to the debate over legal marriage for same-sex couples.

The Debate over Legal Marriage for Same-Sex Couples

In 2000, the Netherlands became the first country to allow same-sex partners to marry.[11] At the time of this writing, several other European countries including Portugal, as well as Argentina, Canada, Iceland, and South Africa, now allow same-sex marriage (Barrioneuvo 2010; Partners Task Force for Gay and Lesbian Couples 2009).[12] Meanwhile, the United Nations Commission on Human Rights has been unable to pass a resolution to add sexual preference as a reason that people's human rights must not be violated. The motion was dropped "in the midst of intense pressure" from the Vatican and the Conference of Islamic States ("United Nations Drops" 2004). We can conclude that the **culture war**—deep conflict over matters concerning human sexuality and gender—is global.

The conservative Family Research Council website (www.frc.org), one of several that speak out against same-sex marriage, urges people to "Take a Stand for Marriage!" Other websites, such as Gay and Lesbian Advocates and Defenders (GLAD), the Partners Task Force for Gay and Lesbian Couples, or the National Black Justice Coalition advocate for the other side (www.glad.org; www.buddybuddy.com; www.nbjc.org). Having first emerged as a remote possibility in the 1970s, legal marriage for gay and lesbian couples "became a front-line issue" after 1991, when gay activists formed the Equal Rights Marriage Fund (Seidman 2003; Taylor et al. 2009). "Facts about Families: Same-Sex Couples and Legal Marriage in the United States" outlines political developments regarding legal marriage for same-sex couples.

As shown in Figure 8.4, 57 percent of Americans favor allowing same-sex couples to enter into legal agreements, such as civil unions and domestic partnerships, that would give them many of the same rights as married couples. Our country is about evenly split between those who favor (46 percent) and who oppose (48 percent) allowing gays and lesbians to adopt children. Just as attitudes have become more accepting about GLBT rights generally, public opposition to legal same-sex

[11] For a detailed account of developments regarding same-sex legal marriage around the world, see the following: Human Rights Campaign (www.hrc.org); Lambda Legal (www.lambdalegal.org); American Civil Liberties Union (www.aclu.org); and "Legal Marriage Report: Global Status of Legal Marriage," Partners Task Force for Gay and Lesbian Couples 2009, at buddybuddy.com.

[12] U.S. citizens are allowed to marry in Canada. However, at this writing, their unions are not recognized by either the United States government or the vast majority of state governments. "Another complication arises if a couple wishes to divorce. They would not be able to do so in their resident state if their state did not recognize the marriage in the first place. To get a divorce, one of the partners would need to reside in Canada for a year" (Partners Task Force for Gay and Lesbian Couples 2006c).

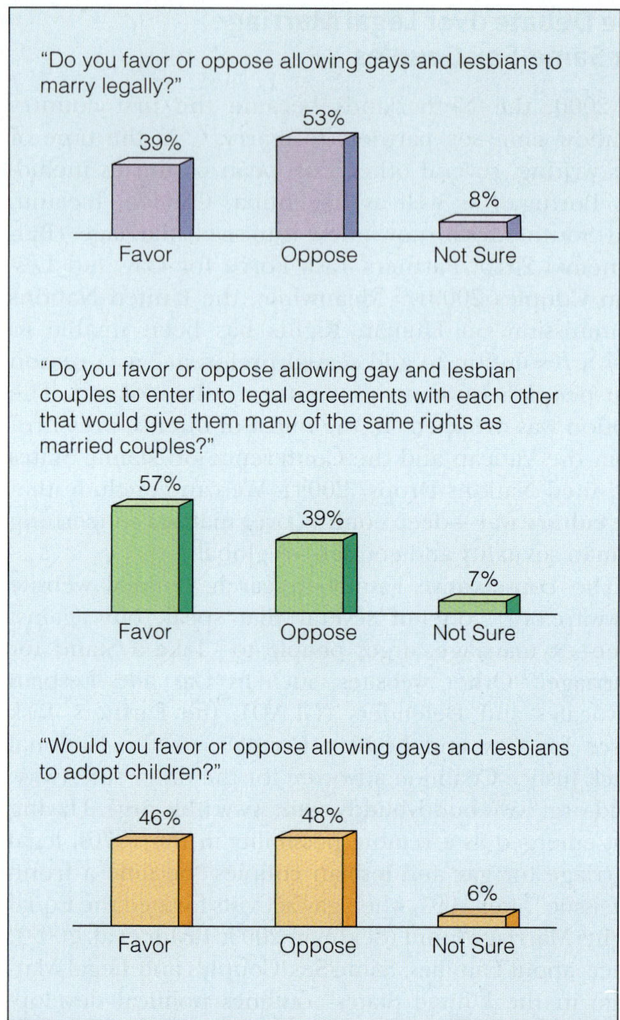

Figure 8.4 American public opinion regarding legal marriage, domestic partnerships/civil unions, and adoption for same-sex couples, 2008–2009.
Source: Pew Research Center 2008, 2009c.

marriage has softened somewhat since the mid-1990s, when about only 25 percent of Americans believed that same-sex marriage should be legal (Vestal 2009). Thirty-nine percent of Americans say that they favor legal marriage for same-sex couples, while 53 percent oppose (Pew Research Center 2009c). Scholars see the national divide over legal same-sex marriage as a mark of cultural ambivalence resulting from conflicting core values: the sanctity of marriage versus personal freedom and civil rights (Brumbaugh et al. 2008). What are the arguments against and for legal marriage for same-sex partners?

Arguments for Legal Marriage as Heterosexual Only Not all religions oppose legal same-sex marriage. The Mormon and Catholic churches, the National Association of Evangelicals, and Islam and Orthodox Jewish congregations oppose legal same-sex marriage. "On the other side are the Unitarians, the United Church of Christ, the Union for Reform Judaism, the Soka Gakkai branch of Buddhism, and dissident groups of Mormons, Catholics, and Muslims" (Egelko 2008, p. A10). Christian social psychologist David Myers, making a "Christian Case for Gay Marriage," argues that if marriage is good for people and society, as discussed in Chapter 7, then marriage should be an option for everyone, including lesbians and gays (Myers and Scanzoni 2006). However, for religious fundamentalists and other conservative groups, the move to legalize marriage is an "attempt to deconstruct traditional morality" (Smolowe 1996a; J. Wilson 2001).

Those who favor defining legal marriage as only heterosexual are more likely to value traditional gender roles (as well as traditional family structure) and to live in communities in which those values are reinforced through daily communication with like-minded neighbors (McVeigh and Diaz 2009). Proponents of legal marriage as only heterosexual argue that heterosexual marriage alone has deep roots in history, as well as in the Judeo-Christian and other religious traditions (Hartocollis 2006; McKinley and Schwartz 2010).They further claim that only heterosexual married parents can provide the optimum family environment for raising children and that legalizing same-sex marriage would weaken an institution already threatened by single-parent families, cohabitation, and divorce (Blankenhorn 2007). Some contend that "[e]ven more ominously, permitting gays to marry would open the door for all sorts of people to demand the right to marry—polygamists, children, friends, kin—even more than two partners" (Seidman 2003, p. 128).[13] Finally, they argue that legal marriage for same-sex couples is unnecessary, given legislation, such as civil unions in some states, which give virtually all the rights of marriage to same-sex couples without the title "married" or "spouse" (Seidman 2003).

Arguments for Legal Same-Sex Marriage In her book, *Beyond (Straight and Gay) Marriage* (2008), American University law professor Nancy Polikoff argues that all family forms need to be valued under the law. Same-sex families comprise a family form that is not going to disappear; if marriage is thought to be good for spouses and children emotionally, financially, and healthwise, then to deny these benefits to a significant number of individuals is unethical and socially costly (Rauch 2004).

[13] This fear is not entirely unfounded. In 2003, the U.S. Supreme Court struck down laws criminalizing sodomy (interpersonal sexual acts that do not allow for procreation, such as oral sex or anal intercourse). At that time, the Supreme Court ruled that individuals have "the full right to engage in private conduct without government intervention." Today some advocates seek the same considerations for proponents of bigamy (Kurtz 2006; Soukup 2006). Moreover, changing the legal definition of marriage as necessarily "between one man and one woman" could affect not only the gender stipulation but also the requirement that marriage take place between only two individuals (Kurtz 2003; Stacey and Meadow 2009).

Those who favor legalized same-sex marriage further argue that denying lesbians and gays the right to marry legally violates the U.S. Constitution because it discriminates against a category of citizens (Schwartz 2010). Legal marriage yields economic and other advantages. For instance, hospital visitation rights would be guaranteed to a same-sex spouse. As another example,

> The right to divorce is a benefit associated with marriage that often goes unmentioned. Relationships end, and marriage provides the opportunity for a legal chaperon when partners are unable or unwilling to manage their separation, dissolution, and post-divorce parenting in a productive manner. Legal marriage for LGBT partners would protect the interest of all members of the family upon dissolution, just as it does for heterosexual partners. (Allen 2007, p. 181)[14]

Allowing same-sex legal marriage would facilitate child custody cases in the event of dissolution (Polikoff 2008; Hare and Skinner 2008). Chapter 15 further explores dissolution of same-sex unions and of unmarried heterosexual relationships.

However, due to the federal Defense of Marriage Act (DOMA), which defines marriage as only between "one man and one woman," even same-sex couples that are legally married in states that allow it cannot receive federal benefits designated for married couples (Clifford, Hertz, and Doskow 2007; Oswald and Kuvalanka 2008). There are more than one thousand federal laws in which marital status is a factor, including the rights to veterans' benefits, for example ("Federal Marriage Benefits Denied..." n.d.; U.S. General Accounting Office 1997). Other federal laws that apply only to legally married partners include those granting Social Security benefits to a widowed or disabled spouse, the right of legally married partners to inherit from one another without a will, or laws making it possible for the immigrant spouse of a U.S. citizen to also become a citizen.[15]

Proponents of gay and lesbian rights further argue that creating domestic partnerships or civil unions, instead of allowing marriage for same-sex partners, creates second-class citizens (Allen 2007; Leff 2006; Seidman 2003). As one lesbian spouse, legally married in Massachusetts, said:

> Same-sex marriage not only makes me take my relationship more seriously, it's making me take my country more seriously. I always felt oppressed and not a part of America, not really. But this seems like finally there is a light in the dark, like finally . . . the government is saying that my relationship counts and I count, too. (in Lannutti 2007, p. 141)

Many children of gay male or lesbian couples also view the legalization of same-sex marriage as giving them security and comfort (P. L. Brown 2004; Goldberg 2007). Relatedly, one mother described her daughter's school experience:

> She would be quite open about [our family] in school and answer, "I have two moms." And kids would say to her, "Well, they can't be married." And she would say we're married because that's how we always represented ourselves. So she had a boy in her class that would say, "They're not married, they can't be married!" So I figured it was such a thrill for her to be able to say, with confidence, "They're married, and yes it is legal," and "I'm just like you." (in Porche and Purvin 2008, p. 153)

Interestingly, however, although many lesbians and gays support the claim for same-sex marriage in principle, in Massachusetts where same-sex marriage has been legal since 2004, a minority of same-sex couples has chosen to marry. A recent qualitative study of Massachusetts same-sex couples who had been together for twenty years or more sheds light on this development. One reason that committed same-sex couples may not marry when given the option is that they have already "spent thousands of dollars instituting all the legal protections they felt they needed and did not see a need to complicate those arrangements by changing their status through a marriage recognized only by Massachusetts." Attitudes of other participants in this study resembled those of some heterosexual cohabitating couples. They said that "marriage is made 'not by some sort of legal sanctions' but by the commitment of the people in the relationship to each other" (Porche and Purvis 2008, p. 155). Gay men and lesbians themselves have been divided somewhat on the desirability of legalized same-sex marriage, at least for themselves ("Gays Want the Right" 2004).

Dissenting Arguments among Lesbians and Gay Men With the majority of states offering *no* legal recognition at all for same-sex unions, some GLBT spokespersons argue that too much emphasis is placed on advocating for same-sex marriage when activist resources would be better spent working for wider enactment of civil unions (Leff 2009). Furthermore, some gays and lesbians have opposed legal same-sex marriage in principle. Generally they have objected to mimicking a traditionally patriarchal institution based on property rights and institutionalized husband–wife

[14] Couples who marry in states where same-sex marriage is legal, then return to their own states where it is not legal, can expect to encounter difficulties in the unforeseen event of a later desire to divorce. Same-sex divorce is impossible in a state that does not recognize the marriage, and getting divorced in the state where a couple was married can be challenging. Most states have a residency requirement for divorce, some as long as one year (Clifford, Hertz, and Doskow 2007).

[15] Under federal law, legally married spouses can petition for immigration and citizenship status for their foreign-born husbands or wives. In 2009, a bill was introduced in the U.S. Congress that would similarly allow American citizens and legal immigrants to pursue U.S. residency for their same-sex partners (Preston 2009). At this writing, the outcome of this proposed legislation has not been determined.

roles and characterized by a high divorce rate.[16] Opponents have also objected to giving the state power to regulate primary adult relationships (Peele 2006).

Moreover, they have stressed that legalizing same-sex unions would further stigmatize any sex outside marriage, with unmarried lesbians and gay men facing heightened discrimination ("Monogamy: Is It for Us?" 1998; Seidman 2003). We can't say how representative the following statement is, but it does illustrate the viewpoint of at least one lesbian when contemplating the possibility of legalized same-sex marriage in her state:

> I don't want to get married so this marriage thing is going to make it harder for me to find a person to be in a relationship with. I know that because I don't want to get married, women will think I'm not a good potential partner, and move on. . . . It sucks, because . . . now I have to limit myself to the other non-marrying kinds out there—like finding a great girl wasn't hard enough already! (in Lannutti 2007, p. 145)

Whether and to what extent allowing same-sex couples to legally marry increases their personal life satisfaction is a matter for future research. In the following section, we turn to a discussion of life satisfaction among the unmarried.

Although there is undeniable evidence for the physical and psychological benefits of marriage, unattached singles do point to benefits of their lifestyle. Among these are less irritation with coresident family members and a greater sense of control over their lives. Moreover, when we think of singlehood as a continuum, we realize that not all singles—even those who live alone—are socially unattached, disconnected, or isolated. Maintaining close relationships with family and friends is associated with positive adjustment and satisfaction among singles.

Maintaining Supportive Social Networks and Life Satisfaction

Perhaps not surprisingly, life satisfaction is associated with income as well as marital status (Pelham 2008). As discussed in Chapter 7 and illustrated in Table 7.1, many singles and single parents, particularly women, just do not make enough money (U.S. Census Bureau 2010b, Table 700). Many work more than one low-paying job, and then take care of their homes and children (Huston and Melz 2004). For them, "career advancement" means hoping for a small raise or just hanging on to a job in the face of growing economic insecurity. Pursuing higher educational opportunities means rushing to class one evening a week after working all day. Moreover, research shows that poor women have less-effective private safety nets than do others, because their families and friends are also very likely to be poor and overburdened financially and emotionally (Harknett 2006). These women are dealing with work, parenting, and low-income issues, enjoying neither the stereotypical "swinging singles" lifestyle characterized by personal freedom and consumerism nor the commitment of marriage.

As pointed out in Chapter 7, research and polls consistently find that, as a group, marrieds are happier than singles (Carroll 2005; Taylor, Funk, and Craighill 2006; Wienke and Hill 2009). Research also shows that, regardless of whether they are legally married, people in secure interpersonal heterosexual or same-sex relationships—and those who socialize often with friends and family—are happier than are those who spend considerable time alone (Harter and Arora 2008; Pelham 2008; Wienke and Hill 2009).

If we think of the various living arrangements of unmarrieds as forming a *continuum of social attachment* (Ross 1995), we realize that not all singles are socially unattached, disconnected, or isolated. In sociologist Catherine Ross's (1995) research with a nationally representative sample of about two thousand adults who

[16] With irony, San Francisco columnist Mark Morford questions why same-sex couples would *want* to marry: "Show me a single scientific experiment where fully 50 percent of the results turn out negative and induce collapse and emotional breakdown and childhood therapy and Xanax and alcoholism and screaming, and I'll show you a scientist who will quickly scrap the whole thing and start over" (Morford 2006).

For singles, it's important to develop and maintain supportive social networks of friends and family. Single people place high value on friendships, and they are also major contributors to community services and volunteer work.

were interviewed in 1990, people in close relationships—whether or not married and whether or not living alone—were significantly less depressed than those with no intimate partner at all (see also Pelham 2008). Furthermore, the relationship between being involved and not being depressed held *only* for those in happy, or supportive, arrangements.

One young woman, single by choice, actually planned her own wedding ceremony—to herself. She wore white, carried a bouquet, and invited about twenty friends. She "chose to join herself in matrimony" a few days after her thirtieth birthday. Her friend, serving as officiator, asked, "Do you promise to love, honor, and respect yourself from this day forward for as long as you live?" "I do," answered the woman. She was subsequently declared "wedded to life" (Seligman 2006). Those who view themselves as "wedded to life"—by choice—are probably more satisfied with their lives than are those who are single against their wishes.

Meanwhile, for unattached singles, living alone can be lonesome. However, living alone does not necessarily imply a lack of social integration or meaningful connections with others (Trimberger 2005). Nevertheless, unattached singles have tended to report feeling lonely more often than have marrieds (Harter and Arora 2008; Pelham 2008). Poor and older singles are especially likely to be lonely, perhaps because the low incomes and ill health that tend to accompany old age make socializing very difficult. Besides age and income, being single as a result of divorce apparently affects loneliness (Kim and McKenry 2002).

Sociologist E. Kay Trimberger (2005) argues that the "heaviest thing" for unattached, middle-aged women is the "idea of the couple, and that's so internalized." Trimberger identifies the following "pillars of support" for unattached single women: a nurturing home, satisfying work, satisfaction with their sexuality, connections to the next generation, a network of friends and possibly family members, and a feeling of community.

Some research has found cohabitants to be midway between unattached singles and marrieds in mental and physical well-being (Kurdek 1991), while other studies have shown no difference between cohabitants and other singles, "suggesting that the protection effects of marriage are not as applicable to cohabitation" (Kim and McKenry 2002, p. 905). However, marriage also involves a set of obligations and the responsibility of coping with both the burdens of other family members and the disappointments that come with family life. Valuing personal autonomy, Americans may find these obligations emotionally stressful (Gove, Style, and Hughes 1990). There are some areas in which nonmarrieds may feel better off than the married. Less irritation and a greater sense of control over one's life can be among the advantages of being single (Hughes and Gove 1989).

All of us need support from people whom we are close to and who care about us. Isolation increases feelings of unhappiness, depression, and anxiety (Umberson et al. 1996), whereas being socially connected "seems to keep stress responses . . . from running amok," according to UCLA psychologist Shelley Taylor (quoted in "Save the Date" 2004). Maintaining close relationships with parents, siblings, and friends is associated with positive adjustment and life satisfaction (Kurdek 2006; Soons and Liefbroer 2009; Spitze and Trent 2006). A social network that can function as "a parent safety net" is important to positive parenting practices among unmarried mothers (Ryan, Kalil, and Leininger 2009).

Vicky Kasala

Besides a variety of living arrangements, factors such as age, sex, residence, religion, and economic status contribute to the diversity and complexity of single life. An elderly man or woman existing on Social Security payments and meager savings has a vastly different lifestyle from two unmarried professionals living together in an urban area. Also, the experience of being unmarried differs according to whether one is single by choice or involuntarily.

A crucial part of one's support network involves valued friendships. Despite changing gender roles, men remain less likely than women to cultivate psychologically intimate relationships with siblings or same-sex friends (Levy 2005; Weaver, Coleman, and Ganong 2003). Indeed, a man may be more open and disclosing with a woman friend (Wagner-Raphael, Seal, and Ehrhardt 2001). One study of men in the construction industry found that many of them, rather than building truly supportive friendships, talked instead about horseplay, alcohol consumption, risk taking, and physical prowess, and generally engaged in one-upmanship (Iacuone 2005). Men (as well as women) who do not establish friendships based on emotional honesty run the risk of feeling socially isolated. In addition to friendships, other sources of support for singles include group living situations, religious fellowships, and volunteer work (Lyons 2003; Mustillo, Wilson, and Lynch 2004). Singles also reach out to their families of origin (Arnett 2004; Bengston, Biblarz, and Roberts 2002). However a person chooses to live the single life, establishing a sense of belonging by maintaining supportive social networks is important.

Summary

- Since the 1960s, the number of unmarrieds has risen dramatically. Much of this increase is due to young adults' postponing of marriage, coupled with the rise in the incidence of cohabitation.
- One reason people are postponing marriage today is that increased job and lifestyle opportunities may make marriage less attractive.
- The low sex ratio—fewer men for women of marriageable age—has also caused some women to postpone marriage or put it off entirely.
- Attitudes toward marriage and singlehood have changed, so that being unmarried is more often viewed as preferable, at least "for now."
- More and more young unmarrieds are living in their parents' homes, usually at least partly as a result of economic constraints.
- Some unmarrieds have chosen to live in communal or group homes.
- A substantial number and growing percentage of heterosexual unmarrieds are cohabiting.
- As heterosexual cohabitation becomes more acceptable, more and more cohabiting households include children either born to the union or from a previous relationship.

- The relative instability of heterosexual cohabiting unions has led to some, apparently warranted, concern for the outcomes of children living in cohabiting families.
- Some couples live together in gay male or lesbian unions; a little more than one-third of lesbian and nearly one-quarter of gay male households include children either from the same-sex union or from a previous (often heterosexual) relationship.
- Same-sex couples must daily negotiate their private relationship within a heterosexual—and often, heterosexist—world.
- Research finds that children raised by same-sex couples are not significantly different from those raised by heterosexual parents.
- Congruent with the emergence of the pluralistic family, we are witnessing a national and global debate over whether legal marriage should be extended to include lesbians and gay men.
- However one chooses to live the single life, it is important to maintain supportive social networks.

Questions for Review and Reflection

1. Individual choices take place within a broader social spectrum—that is, within society. How do social factors influence an unmarried individual's decision regarding his or her living arrangements?
2. What do you see as the advantages and disadvantages of cohabitation compared to marriage?
3. What does current research tell us about the outcomes generally of children raised in homes with two married biological parents, compared to those raised in cohabiting families?
4. On average, do the outcomes of children raised by heterosexual parents differ from the outcomes of those raised by same-sex couples?
5. **Policy Question.** Do you think that legalizing same-sex marriage is a good idea? Give arguments based on facts to support your opinion.

Key Terms

cohabitation 199
communes 198
consensual marriages 200
culture war 211
Defense of Mrriage Act (DOMA) 208
domestic partners 202
sex ratio 194

Online Resources

Sociology CourseMate

www.CengageBrain.com

Access an integrated eBook, chapter-specific interactive learning tools, including flash cards, quizzes, videos, and more in your Sociology CourseMate, accessed through CengageBrain.com.

www.CengageBrain.com

Want to maximize your online study time? Take this easy-to-use study system's diagnostic pre-test, and it will create a personalized study plan for you. By helping you identify the topics that you need to understand better and then directing you to valuable online resources, it can speed up your chapter review. CengageNOW even provides a post-test so you can confirm that you are ready for an exam.

10

Raising Children in a Diverse Society

"Whoever came up with the Peace Corps motto, 'The toughest job you'll ever love,' probably wasn't a parent" (Picker 2005, p. 46). Although raising children may be a joyful and fulfilling enterprise, parenting today takes place in a social context that makes child rearing an enormously difficult task. For most of human history, adults raised children simply by living with them and thereby providing examples and socialization into adult roles. From an early age, children shared the everyday world of adults, working beside them, dressing like them, sleeping near them.

At least in Europe, the concept of childhood as different from adulthood did not emerge until about the seventeenth century, according to historian Phillipe Ariès (1962). As education became available to all children, not just those of the wealthy, and as they spent more of their time in school, children gradually spent less time participating in the everyday lives of adults. One result is that today we regard children as people who need special training, guidance, and care (Apple 2006). Nevertheless, compared to sixty years ago, U.S. society can seem indifferent to the needs of parents and their children. For instance, the rate of child poverty in the United States exceeds that of the nation as a whole and is considerably higher than in other wealthy industrialized nations (Moore et al. 2009; U.S. Census Bureau 2010b, Table 697).

In this chapter, we will discuss the parenting process in the United States, a society that is diverse economically, by race/ethnicity, and in terms of family structure. As you study this chapter, we encourage you to note the *intersection* of these circumstances: how the parenting process is influenced by ways that gender, race/ethnicity, and social class interconnect, or overlap within a family structure, or form. As just one example, within the single-parent family form, parenting is a different experience for a low-income father of color than for a middle-class, non Hispanic white mother.

We'll begin by looking at some general characteristics of the parenting process today. Next we'll examine how gender affects parenting. We will then describe parenting styles, noting that the authoritative parenting style is advised by child development experts. We'll address ways that parenting differs according to race/ethnicity. We'll describe grandparents who serve as parents.

Other issues related to children appear throughout this text. Child outcomes related to cohabitation and same-sex couples are addressed in Chapter 8. Combining work and parenting roles is explored in Chapter 11. Suggestions about how best to communicate with children appear in Chapter 12. Violence against children is discussed in Chapter 13. The economic concerns of divorced parents, as well as their children's outcomes, are addressed in Chapter 15. Issues unique to stepparents are considered in Chapter 16. Here we address the parenting *process* in a diversity of social circumstances.

Parents in Twenty-First Century America

As shown in Figure 10.1, married couples comprise just under two-thirds (64 percent) of families with a joint child under age eighteen. Single-mother families represent almost one-quarter (24.6 percent) of parenting family groups. The remaining parental family groups

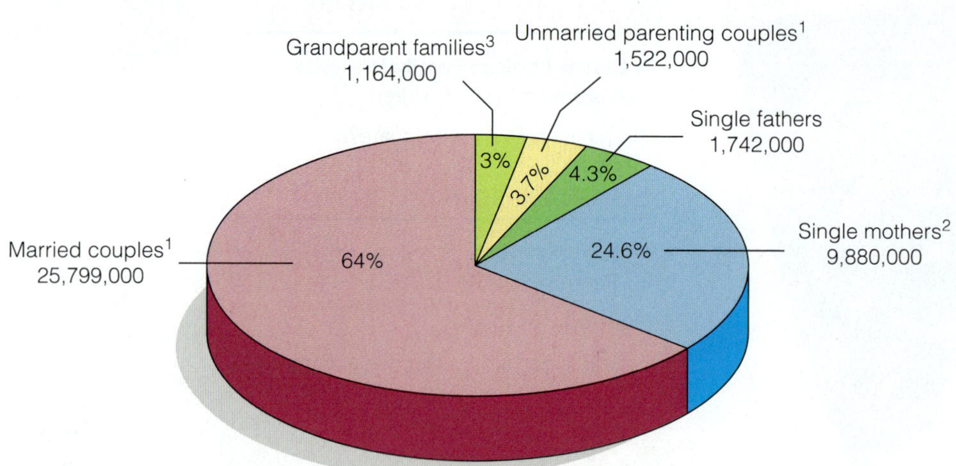

[1]Have at least one joint never-married child under age eighteen in the home.
[2]Parent may have a partner, but none of the children is also the child of the cohabiting partner.
[3]Grandparent householder with grandchildren for whom the grandparent is responsible.

Figure 10.1 Family Groups with Children under Age 18, 2009

Source: Calculated from U.S. Census Bureau 2010a, Table FG10. Percentages do not total exactly 100 percent due to rounding errors.

include single fathers, unmarried cohabiting couples with at least one joint child under age eighteen, and grandparent families (U.S. Census Bureau 2010a, Table FG10). According to Census Bureau definitions, a single parent can be either cohabiting or not.

In addition to variations in family form, many parents display a marked fluidity in living arrangements, resulting in a degree of complexity not remarked upon by researchers until fairly recently. For example, a single mother may move from her own apartment to live with her mother, then move once more to reside with other relatives or a romantic partner. Then too, **multipartnered fertility** (a person's having children with more than one partner) can mean that a father resides, perhaps temporarily, with one or more of his children but not with others (Harknett and Knab 2007). As a result, the parenting situations discussed in this chapter should be understood as changeable.

Regardless of their living arrangements or family structure, parents today face a myriad of questions that would not have been imagined just a few decades ago: How much fast food is too much? Should I let my child walk to school without a chaperone? Should I believe the teacher who says my child needs medication? Does my teenager spend too much time on Facebook? What should I tell my child about terrorism?

© Kim Gunkel/iStockphoto

Raising a child with disabilities reminds us that parents and children can evidence resilience, which is enhanced by strong familial bonds.

Parenting Challenges and Resilience

We would not want to point out the difficulties facing today's parents without first noting some positives. In general, parents now have higher levels of education and are likely to have had some exposure to formal knowledge about child development and child-raising techniques. Many fathers are more emotionally involved than several decades ago (Bianchi, Robinson, and Milkie 2006). In many respects, technology has improved our quality of life. The Internet offers countless sources of information for parents dealing with just about any situation. New communication technologies allow parents and children to keep in virtually continual contact and make being in touch with other family members far easier and more likely than a generation ago (Devitt and Roker 2009).

Nevertheless, parents face difficulties and make mistakes. It helps to know that children can be remarkably **resilient**: Children (and adults) can demonstrate the capacity to recover from or rise above adverse situations and events (Coyle et al. 2009; Goldman 2006; Werner and Smith 2001). Furthermore, research indicates that "[a]dults who acknowledge and seem to have worked through difficulties of their childhood are apparently protected against inflicting them on their children" (Belsky 1991, p. 124). There is also evidence that one caring, conscientious adult can generate a resilient child (Johnson 2000; Soukhanov 1996). Meanwhile, the family ecology perspective (see Chapter 2) leads us to look at ways that the larger environment challenges parents today.

Some Ways That the Social Environment Makes Parenting Difficult Here we list six societal features that make parenting difficult:

1. In our society, the parenting role conflicts with the working role, and employers typically place work demands first (Barnett et al. 2009; Bass et al. 2009; Marshall and Tracy 2009). A majority of American parents say they worry about juggling the demands of work and family and wish they could spend more time with their children (Erickson and Aird 2005; Snyder 2007).
2. Today's parents raise their children in a pluralistic society characterized by diverse and conflicting values. Parents are but one of several influences on children. Among others are schools, television, movies, music, and the Internet. Concerns about outside influences

may be greater for immigrant parents whose cultural values differ from some that they encounter in the United States (Driscoll, Russell, and Crockett 2008). But high percentages of all American parents worry about negative messages in the media, protecting their children from drugs and alcohol, or about the possibly problematic influences of other kids on their child (Farkas, Johnson, and Duffett 2002).

3. Various experts have publicized the fact that parents influence their children's health, weight, eating habits, math and language abilities, behaviors, and self-esteem. Although much parenting advice is useful, the emphasis on how parents influence their children can lead us to feel anxious about our performance as parents.[1]
4. Today's parents often find themselves sandwiched between simultaneously caring for children and elderly parents. Although caregiving can increase life satisfaction, stress can build as family members juggle employment, housework, child care, and parent care (Cullen et al. 2009).
5. In many areas of the United States, community appreciation for and assistance to parents has diminished over the past fifty years. The proportion of children under eighteen in our population—about one-quarter—represents a substantial drop from the 1960s, when more than one-third of Americans were children (U.S. Census Bureau 2010b, Table 8). Accordingly, the proportion of households with children has dropped from almost half in 1960 to fewer than one-third. Therefore, the parenting role is less predominant today. As parenting has become one lifestyle choice among many, society-wide support has diminished for the child-rearing role, once taken for granted as central (Whitehead and Popenoe 2008).
6. Today's parents are given full responsibility for successfully raising "good" children, but their authority is often questioned. For example, the state may intervene in parental decisions about schooling, discipline and punishment, medical care, and children's safety as automobile passengers ("Home School Laws" 2010; "HPV Policy" 2007; Jervey 2004).

As a result of these factors, being a parent today can be far more challenging than many nonparents realize. It's no wonder that parents, especially when employed, are considerably more stressed than nonparents (Carroll 2007c). Then too, a parent's physical illness, as well as raising a child with special needs, can add stresses peculiar to these situations, and recent government budget cuts have meant diminished resources for children with special needs (Firmin and Phillips 2009; Ontai 2008).

A Stress Model of Parental Effectiveness

As we saw in Chapters 7 and 8, considerable research shows that growing up with married parents is statistically related to better child outcomes (Kreider and Elliott 2009a; Magnuson and Berger 2009). Researchers attribute much of this finding to differential stress levels. Rather than family structure itself, stresses that are peculiar to family forms other than marriage account for divergent child outcomes. Being raised in a supportive family atmosphere is statistically related to more desirable outcomes for children, regardless of family structure (Doohan et al. 2009; Schoppe-Sullivan, Schermerhorn, and Cummings 2007).

According to a **stress model of parental effectiveness** (see Figure 10.2), stress that parents experience—from sources such as job demands, financial worries, concerns about neighborhood safety, feeling stigmatized due to negative stereotypes associated with living in a nonmarital family form, or racial/ethnic discrimination—cause parental frustration, anger, and depression, increasing the likelihood of household conflict. Parental depression and household conflict, in turn, lead to poorer parenting practices—inconsistent discipline, limited parental warmth or involvement, and lower levels of parent-child trust and communication. Poorer child outcomes result (Benner and Kim 2010; Burrell and Roosa 2009; Jackson, Choi, and Bentler 2009; Teachman 2009; White et al. 2009). Having social support mediates, or diminishes, this adverse relationship (Lee et al. 2009).

The Transition to Parenthood

More than forty years ago, in what has become a classic analysis, social scientist Alice Rossi asserted that the **transition to parenthood** is difficult for several reasons. Many first-time parents approach child rearing with little experience. Moreover, new parents abruptly assume

[1] Today you can read about how to raise "respectful" (Cartmell 2006; Rigby 2006), "happy" (Adkins 2007; Biddulph and Biddulph 2007), optimistic and "depression-proofed" (Murray and Fortinberry 2006), "successful" (Brodkin 2006; Burt and Perlis 2006), "well-adjusted" (Gangstad 2006), "confident" (Apter 2007), "socially skilled" (Markway and Markway 2006), "charitable" (Weisman 2006), "kind" (Siegel 2006), "resourceful" (Nelsen, Erwin, and Duffy 2007), "generous" (Gallo and Gallo 2005), and "balanced" kids (Campbell and Suggs 2006). You can read about how to raise kids to "lead change" (Gustafson 2009), or "make a change" (Tim Smith 2006), kids destined for "true greatness" (Kimmel 2006)—even "athletic stars" (Dance and Place 2006). Advice may be specifically directed to parents who are raising boys (Cox 2006; M. Jones 2006; Lewis 2007), girls (Preuschoff 2006; Trevathan and Goff 2007), twins (Gottesman 2006; Heim 2007), children who are deaf (Marschark 2007), children with special needs (Winter 2006), and "gifted" children (Klein 2007), as well as those who are "strong-willed" (Pickhardt 2005), shy (Markway and Markway 2006), or "spirited" (Kurcinka 2006). You can learn to raise great children properly by using "6 keys" (Leman 2006), "8 steps" (Gallo and Gallo 2005), "12 secrets" (Wright 2006a), "13 dynamics" (Inman and Koenig 2006), "52 brilliant ideas" (Dosani and Cross 2007), "101 truths" (Scott 2006), or "135 tools" (Arnall and Elicksen 2007).

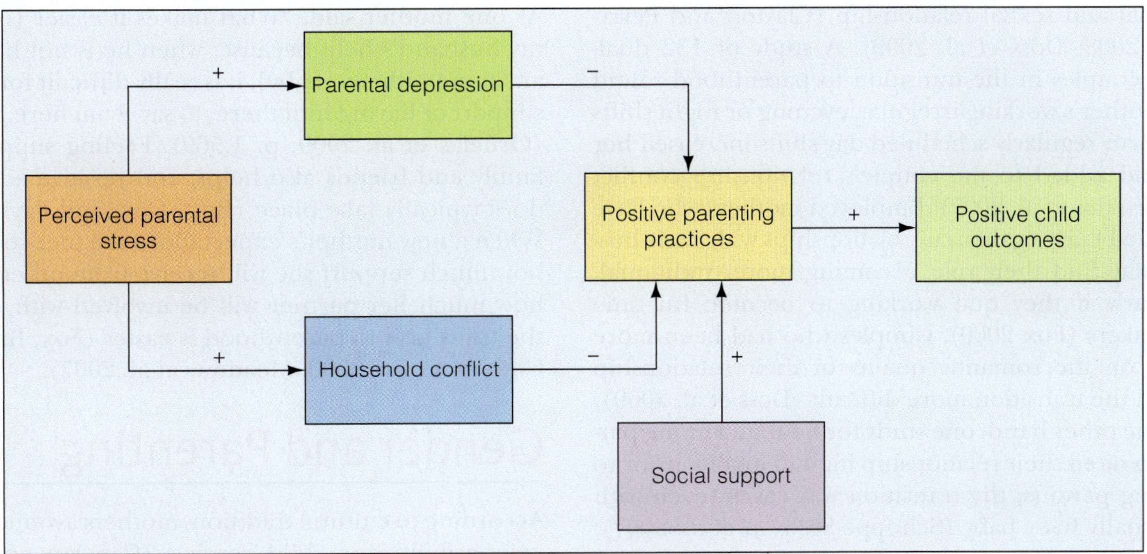

Figure 10.2 Stress Model of Effective Parenting. In this figure, plus signs (+) depict positive relationships between variables, and minus signs (-) depict negative ones. Greater use of positive parenting practices results in more positive outcomes for children. However, higher stress levels result in more (+) parental depression and more (+) household conflict. Parents might feel stressed due to job or educational demands; financial difficulties; concerns about neighborhood safety; or feeling stigmatized as a result of racial/ethnic discrimination or negative stereotyping associated with nonmarital family forms. Increased parental depression and household conflict result in diminished (-) use of positive parenting practices. Meanwhile, higher levels of perceived social support—due to high levels of family cohesion, private safety nets, or policies and programs that support parents—are positively related (+) to effective parenting practices, hence to positive child outcomes.

Sources: This figure was designed by Agnes Riedmann and derived from research findings from the following: Baxter 1989; Benner and Kim 2010; Broman, Li, and Reckase 2008; Bronte-Tinkew, Horowitz, and Scott 2009; Brush 2008; Burrell and Roosa 2009; Goosby 2007; Jackson, Choi, and Bentler 2009; Joshi and Bogen 2007; Lee et al.

twenty-four-hour duty, caring for a dependent and fragile infant (Rossi 1968). Often surprised at how disruptive an infant can be, new parents report being bothered by the baby's interrupting their sleep, work, and leisure time. In the words of one new mother, "[Y]ou have to run to bathe yourself because the child is going to wake up" (in Ornelas et al. 2009, p. 1,564).

Moreover, parents are more likely than in the past to be geographically distant from their own parents and other relatives who might give advice and help. For example, a Mexican immigrant mother told an interviewer:

> In Mexico, when you have a baby, well your mother is always there, or your family is there. . . . They help you like to pick him up, to hold him, to change him. All of that. So, you come here, and you find yourself alone and with a little baby that you don't even know how to pick up. (in Ornelas et al. 2009, p. 1,568)

More disconnected from friends and others than before the baby's arrival, nonimmigrant new mothers also report feeling isolated (Paris and Dubus 2005). Employed mothers of infants, especially those who have jobs with inflexible hours and little opportunity for advancement, are more likely to feel stressed (Marshall and Tracy 2009). Along with other factors, the difficulties associated with a new baby result in postpartum depression in about 10 percent of new mothers (Formichelli 2001).[2]

Meanwhile, a study of low-income black families found that mothers who were more pleased about their pregnancy were less likely later to view parenting as burdensome (Ispa et al. 2007). Becoming a parent typically involves what one researcher has called the *paradox of parenting:* New parents feel overwhelmed, but the motivation to overcome their stress and do their best proceeds from the stressor itself—the child as a source of love, joy, and satisfaction (Coles 2009).

For couples, the transition to parenthood means less time spent relaxing together and declines in their

[2] It helps to know that babies differ even at birth; the fact that a baby cries a lot does not necessarily mean that she or he is receiving the wrong kind of care (Rankin 2005). Infants may have different "readabilities"—that is, varying clarity in the messages or cues they give to tell caregivers how they feel or what they want (R. Bell 1974). Although new parents' attitudes, overall mood, and self-esteem influence how they view their babies, it also appears that babies have varied temperaments at birth. Some are "easy," responding positively to new foods, people, and situations, and transmitting consistent cues (such as tired cry or hungry cry). Other infants are more "difficult." They have irregular habits of sleeping or eating that sometimes extend into childhood; they may adapt slowly to new situations and stimuli; and they may cry endlessly, for no apparent reason (Komsi et al. 2006; Roisman and Fraley 2006; Thomas, Chess, and Birch 1968).

emotional and sexual relationship (Clayton and Perry-Jenkins 2008; Doss et al. 2009). A study of 132 dual-income couples in the transition to parenthood found that a mother's working irregular, evening or night shifts rather than regularly scheduled day shifts increased her stress and added to the couple's relationship conflict (Perry-Jenkins et al. 2007). Employed mothers who have established fairly egalitarian relationships with their husbands may find their role becoming more traditional, particularly if they quit working to become full-time homemakers (Fox 2009). Couples who had been more focused on the romantic quality of their relationship may find the transition more difficult (Doss et al. 2009).

On the other hand, one study found that, among parents who rated their relationship high in quality prior to becoming parents, the transition was easier, even with an unusually fussy baby (Schoppe-Sullivan et al. 2007).

Tetra Images / Getty Images

Transition to parenthood can be difficult for a number of reasons, including upset schedules and lack of sleep. It's a paradox that (1) new parents feel overwhelmed, while (2) inspiration to overcome their stress and do their best is provided by the stressor itself—the child as a source of profound delight.

As one mother said, "What makes it easier [is] having my husband's help because, when he is not here and I am alone with my [baby], it is really difficult for me. The support of having him there, to say 'I am here,' [helps]" (Ornelas et al. 2009, p. 1,569). Feeling supported by family and friends also helps, and positive adjustment does typically take place (Bost, Cox, and Payne 2002). When a new mother's expectations are met concerning how much support she will receive from others and/or how much her partner will be involved with the baby, the transition to parenthood is easier (Fox, Bruce, and Coombs-Orme 2000; Meadows et al. 2007).

Gender and Parenting

According to cultural tradition, mothers assume primary responsibility for child rearing (Cancian and Oliker 2000). Whether employed or not, a mother is generally expected to be the child's primary **psychological parent**, assuming—with self-sacrifice when necessary—major emotional responsibility for the safety and upbringing of her children (Springer, Parker, and Leviten-Reid 2009). Historically, fathers have been expected to be breadwinners and not necessarily competent in or desirous of nurturing children on a day-to-day basis (Gerson 1997). Today, however, our culture prescribes that "good" fathers not only assume considerable (usually primary) financial responsibility but also actively participate in the child's care (Troilo and Coleman 2008).

The theoretical perspective that emphasizes social reality as constructed (Chapter 2) reminds us that family members adapt culturally understood roles to their own situations.[3] Put another way, individuals "do" family, especially in a postmodern society characterized by fluidity in family forms (Hertz 2006b). How do cultural expectations regarding mother- and fatherhood correspond with the daily experiences of mothers and fathers? Put another way, how does each gender "do" parenthood?

Doing Motherhood

Whether single, cohabiting, or married, mothers typically engage in more hands-on parenting than do fathers, and they take primary responsibility for their children's upbringing (Hook and Chalasani 2008; Newport 2008).[4] Perhaps not surprisingly, adolescents of

[3] As discussed in Chapter 7, from the social constructionist perspective, individuals engage in role making: We adjust, or "make," rather than simply "take" our roles.

[4] An obvious exception involves gay men who choose to parent. "Gay men who choose to parent, either as a couple or alone, must cope with the fact that they will be challenging societal notions regarding the absence of a woman as the primary caregiver. Under this assumption, many men, both gay and nongay, will struggle with questions concerning their ability to parent based solely on their exposure to traditional gender scripts" (Berkowitz and Marsiglio 2007, p. 367).

both genders are likely to name their mother as their closest family confidant (Nomaguchi 2008). A study of employed, coupled heterosexual parents found that mothers often define "quality time" differently from fathers. Fathers are more likely to see quality time with their children as being home and available if needed. Mothers more often see quality time as having heart-to-heart talks with their children or engaging in child-centered activities (Snyder 2007).

Moreover, heterosexual fathers see themselves as more involved with their children than their partners do (Mikelson 2008). A mother may try to manage her child(ren)'s relationship with their father by encouraging father–child activities and constructing for them a positive image of him (Seery and Crowley 2000). "Despite much attention in recent years to the . . . 'new, nurturing father,' . . . women still do most child raising and homemaking" (Arendell 2000, p. 1,198; Dermott 2008). This intense daily contact with children is viewed ambivalently by many mothers—as a source of great life satisfaction but causing frustration and stress (Warner 2006).

Some women quit successful careers to accommodate their mothering role (Stone 2007; Tyre 2006b). As mothers have entered the labor force in greater numbers, many men have been encouraged by their family's need and the redefinition of male roles to want to play a larger part in the day-to-day care of their families (Bass et al. 2009; Bianchi, Robinson, and Milkie 2006). When mothers see fathers as competent parents—and when fathers believe that their child's mother has confidence in them—fathers are more likely to be highly involved (Fagan and Barnett 2003). Stressful for virtually all parents, mothering as a single parent is generally even more so.

Single Mothers

About 38 percent of all births occur to unmarried women (U.S. Census Bureau 2010b, Tables 80, 85). As discussed in Chapter 8, some of these births are to women in same-sex couples. In addition, between one-quarter and one-half of all nonmarital births occur to cohabiting heterosexual couples (Carter 2009; Dye 2005; Hamilton et al. 2006). We can therefore conclude that between 15 and 20 percent of all births occur to uncoupled, single mothers. The intersection of gender with family form is evident in the fact that single women, dramatically more often than single men, assume responsibility for child rearing (Brush 2008).

The category *single mother* is diverse by race/ethnicity, immigration experience, education, and socioeconomic class. Many single mothers never intended to raise their children without a partner. On the other hand, some women have purposefully decided to raise a child as a single parent.

Single Mothers by Choice Some single women adopt or, using donor sperm and artificial insemination, purposefully conceive and intend to raise their child without a partner. Called **single mothers by choice**, these women tend to be in their thirties or early forties, middle- or upper-middle class, European American, and relatively highly educated (Bock 2000).

Sociologist Rosanna Hertz (2006a) describes several stages in the decision to become a single mother by choice. First, a woman begins to realize that finding a partner first, then becoming a parent is unlikely to pan out for her. Next, she begins to investigate options regarding adoption or nonstandard insemination procedures. She also mobilizes support from family and friends. After the baby has entered her life, she continues to construct her roles around providing financial support and caring for her child. Researchers have given relatively little attention to the parenting practices of single mothers by choice. More numerous today—and receiving far more research attention—are single mothers by circumstance.

Single Mothers by Circumstance For the majority of women, the decision to be a single mother is less than deliberate (Hertz 2006a). **Single mothers by circumstance** arrive at this status in a variety of ways. Some women, becoming mothers while married or cohabiting, believed that their relationship would last but have since divorced or separated. Others realized that their relationship was not permanent, and the pregnancy may have been unplanned, but they chose to bear the child rather than have an abortion (Carter 2009). As one never-married college student and single mother told an interviewer, "My heart felt ready for the baby. I knew it was something I could do with or without a spouse" (in Holland 2009, p. 173).

As a category, single mothers' median family incomes are considerably lower than either married mothers' or single fathers, and single mothers are more likely to live in poverty, as shown in Tables 7.1 and 7.2. Some single mothers fantasize about marrying a responsible partner: "Wouldn't that Prince Charming dream be nice just once in awhile?" (in Gemelli 2008, p. 112). Others may have wanted to wed but did not find a man whom they considered acceptable (Holland 2009). Some single mothers keep the fathers of their children at a distance due to poor relationships with them, safety concerns for their children, apprehension about the father's illegal activities, or their seeing him as generally unreliable (England and Edin 2007).

Nevertheless, single mothers are well aware that to be married is the cultural ideal. One told an interviewer, with reference to her never-married status:

> Even though I have come so far, I have a car, I have a house, not just an apartment, and I'm a CNA [certified nursing assistant] and I will never have to work a minimum wage job again ever. My kids aren't in want for anything really important, but . . . I'm nowhere. I'm at the bottom, you know. (in Gemelli 2008, p. 112)

In a society that strongly advocates a two-parent child-rearing model,[5] single mothers report feeling stigmatized (LaRossa 2009; Thornton 2009; Usdansky 2009a, 2009b). A low-income single mother told her interviewer, "I've had to do motherhood in a hostile environment" (in Gemelli 2008, p. 106). As pointed out in Chapter 9, disgrace attached to unwed motherhood has diminished since the mid-twentieth century. Nevertheless, popular culture continues to shame or dishonor single mothers, particularly those whose children were born out of wedlock (e.g., Coulter 2009). Negative attitudes about unmarried parenthood encourage society-wide reluctance to provide resources for single mothers and their children (Mollborn 2009).

Meanwhile, single mothers evidence creativity and resilience as they construct support networks to help with finances, housing, child care, and other needs (Chu-Yuan Lee et al. 2009; King, Mitchell, and Hawkins 2010; Levine 2009). For instance, an association called CoAbode facilitates house sharing for single mothers (coabode.com). As another example, single mothers maintain the Internet-based M.O.M.S. support group that offers practical assistance, such as providing business clothes for those in need (www.singlemoms.org). In addition, single mothers may rely on brothers, brothers-in-law, grandfathers, uncles, or male cousins to serve as father figures for their children (Juffer 2006; Richardson 2009).

A **private safety net**, or social support from family and friends, is associated with children's better adjustment (Ryan, Kalil, and Leininger 2009). But social support from extended family is not always without cost. For example, a single mother told of her father's offering to pay for her family's medical insurance but only on the unspoken condition that she listen while he regularly criticized her. Single mothers, especially when low-income, undertake an "ungainly balancing act . . . as they walk a tightrope of reciprocity, social isolation, and material support frequently coupled with humiliating condemnation" (Brush 2008, p. 128).

To improve life for themselves and their children, many single mothers choose further education. This decision is not without added stress, however (Duquaine-Watson 2007). Given their work and parenting obligations, finding time to attend assigned off-campus activities or meetings to plan group projects poses problems. Moreover, some instructors make unappreciated, stereotypic assumptions. As one student explained, "We were going to be starting to talk about welfare laws and programs the following week and [my instructor] wanted to know if I would be comfortable sharing my experiences with the rest of the class. I never even got welfare" (in Duquaine-Watson 2007, p. 234).

For single mothers who do receive welfare, legislative changes have meant added stress (Gemelli 2008). As noted in Chapter 7, the 1996 "welfare reform bill" dismantled the federal Aid to Families with Dependent Children (AFDC) program. A new federal program, Temporary Assistance for Needy Families (TANF), replaced AFDC. Intended to encourage both marriage and the work ethic, TANF limits to five years what had previously been open-ended assistance and requires that most recipients be employed.[6] For many single mothers, TANF has meant unsatisfying work at poverty-level wages, new day care struggles, and less time with their children (Cook et al. 2009; Neblett 2007).

In accordance with the stress model of parental effectiveness, single mothers' time constraints, generally poorer economic resources, and resultant higher depression levels—not family structure per se—result, on average, in less effective parenting behaviors (Guzzo and Lee 2008; Teachman 2009). Instead of between-group comparisons of children raised by single mothers with those raised in two-parent homes, researchers sometimes make within-group comparisons of children raised in various single-mother families. In these latter

Given work and other demands, more than 50 percent of mothers tell pollsters that they wish they had more time with their children. One way that these middle-class mothers cope with time pressures is by taking their toddlers to their yoga class. One thing that may be sacrificed, however, is mom's time for personal relaxation.

[5] The two-parent model is culturally potent enough that, in one instance, a Vermont judge threatened to rescind custody from a lesbian biological mother because she refused to allow her former partner access to their daughter (Ring 2009).

[6] As one woman said in response to welfare changes meant to encourage the work ethic, "It's funny that low-income women or women living in poverty can stay at home and be a bad role model, but a middle class mother or wealthy mother is not a bad role model when they stay home. It's like America has two standards and it's based on class" (in Gemelli 2008, p. 101).

cases, variations in income, education, stress, and depression levels largely explain child-outcome differences (Brush 2008; Crawford and Novak 2008). Not surprisingly, stress is less pronounced among single mothers with relatively higher education, fewer children, better jobs, and more personal resources (Lleras 2008).

Doing Fatherhood

Over the past decade, research on fathers has increased dramatically as policy makers and social scientists have concerned themselves with the importance of fathers to mothers' and children's lives. In general, these studies show that a father's involvement in his child's upbringing is related to positive cognitive, emotional, and behavioral outcomes from infancy into adolescence.[7] On the flip side of the coin, father absence has generally been associated with adverse effects on children's cognitive, moral, and social development (Bronte-Tinkew et al. 2008; Dermott 2008; J. Jones 2008; Mitchell, Booth, and King 2009).[8]

However, this situation is more complicated than suggested by these generalizations (Pan and Farrell 2006). Incidences of a father's substance abuse and of father-perpetrated partner violence and child abuse remind us that encouraging father contact is not always best for children (Blazei, Iacono, and McGue 2008; Lee, Bellamy, and Guterman 2009; Osborne and Berger 2009; Salisbury, Henning, and Holdford 2009). Furthermore, **social fathers** (nonbiological fathers in the role of father, such as stepfathers) do not seem to improve *adolescents'* outcomes when compared with living in a single-mother household (Bzostek 2008). Indeed, a mother's male relatives—for example, the child's uncle or grandfather—may be better and more reliable parent figures than a romantic partner (Jayakody and Kalil 2002). Nevertheless, research does show that, compared to growing up in a single-mother home, younger children benefit economically from living with a social father, provided that he shares his financial resources with the family (Manning and Brown 2006).

Married fathers are increasingly invested in their children's daily lives as they engage in breadwinning, planning, sharing activities, and teaching their children (Gaertner et al. 2007; Whitehead and Popenoe 2008). Children's interaction with fathers often differs from that with their mothers as fathers more typically play with or engage in leisure activities with their children than do mothers (Cancian and Oliker 2000). Although we tend to stereotype low-income fathers of color as unmarried and absent, interviews with young African American and Latino fathers in New York City uncovered married fathers who were actively involved in their children's upbringing. Better educated fathers with more satisfying jobs showed higher levels of parental engagement (Wilkinson et al. 2009). Experiencing high levels of workplace stressors, including low levels of employee self-direction, adds to fathers' stress, resulting in less effective parenting (Goodman et al. 2008).

Married-Couple Families with a Stay-at-Home Father In 2008, about 140,000 married-couple families had a stay-at-home father (U.S. Census Bureau 2010b, Table 68)—a situation that has since increased with men's job losses during the recession that began in 2008 (Bar 2009; O'Reilly 2009). Some of these men have been laid off or closed family-owned businesses and remain out of the workforce (Aasen 2009; Kershaw 2009a). Others have wives who earn more than they could and question sending their children to day care when the father could stay home (St. George 2010; J. A. Smith 2009).

Fathers' responses to these situations tell us something about the joys of daily experiencing the little things that growing children say and do (Swager 2009). Their responses also point out the relative lack of status associated with parenting, at least in some circles. For example, one stay-at-home father, recently laid off from a Fortune 500 company, told a *New York Times* reporter, "To go from the 24-7, high-end, deal-making prestige of working for places that are written about in newspapers to this, it took a long time to get comfortable. . . . It's humbling " (Kershaw 2009a).

Single Fathers

Compared to mothers, the proportion of fathers who serve as the principal parent is dramatically small. Among families with children under age eighteen, about 4 percent are single-father families—5 percent for blacks and non-Hispanic whites, 3 percent for Hispanics and Asians. About half of these nearly 2 million fathers are never married. A significant proportion are divorced, and a much smaller fraction, widowed (U.S. Census Bureau 2010b, Tables 66 and 67). The majority of single fathers care for just one child, but some are parenting three or more (U.S. Census Bureau 2010b, Table 64).

[7] Not only is father involvement often good for children, but it can also benefit the broader community. There is evidence that fatherhood changes a man toward greater altruism for the rest of his life. Based on data from the National Survey of Families and Households (NSFH), researchers found that, compared with men who have never been fathers, middle-aged men of all social classes who at some point in their lives had become fathers and were highly engaged with children were significantly more likely to have altruistically oriented social relationships and to be involved in service organizations (Eggebeen, Dew, and Knoester 2009).

[8] We note here that "father absence" can be other than simply residential absence and can, even among married fathers, include psychological absence, or indifference with minimal positive father-child interaction. Of course, residential fathers have more opportunity to develop psychological presence than do nonresident fathers (Krampe 2009).

Single fathers typically assumed their role because they "stepped up" in difficult and unforeseen circumstances: "You gotta do what you gotta do" (in Coles 2009). In some cases, single fathers have considered their relationship with their own fathers, learned from their past, and want to do things differently. As one single, black father said, "A lot of people take their father not being there when they were young as a bad thing. But I just took the good out of it and took what he did do and took what I'm not going to do like him" (in Coles 2009, p. 1,328). Single fathers often know that extended family support is available, but may not rely on it: "I call my sister occasionally for advice, but I have a strong autonomous streak in me. I'd rather do it myself" (in Coles 2009, p. 1,329).

Whether single or married, poor or financially better off, fathers as primary parents report fighting stereotypes as odd, unmasculine, or weak (Troilo and Coleman 2008). Watched and evaluated as parents, they feel that they have to prove themselves capable (Coles 2009). In response, single fathers have organized various support groups (e.g., www.athomedad.org).

Nonresident Fathers

Nonresident fathers are biological or, much less often, adoptive fathers who do not live with one or more of their children. Less true for divorced fathers, never-married nonresidential fathers move in and out of their children's lives (Amato, Meyers, and Emery 2009; Roy, Buckmiller, and McDowell 2008). Due to multipartnered fatherhood, a father may be living with one or more of his biological children but "nonresident" with regard to others. Then too, a nonresident father may be serving as a social father to one or more children whom he did not conceive, usually because he lives with a woman who had at least one child from a previous relationship (McMahon et al. 2007).

Although often stereotyped as "absent" and disinterested (Troilo and Coleman 2008), many nonresident fathers express love and genuine concern for their children: "These two guys . . . are the reason I live, you know" (in Coles 2009, p. 1,334; also see Wilkinson et al. 2009). A study of fifty nonresident fathers who had previously been arrested for drug problems found that many saw their children daily, several times a week, or weekly (McMahon et al. 2007). Indeed, the majority of nonresident fathers maintain some presence in their children's lives and provide them with various kinds of practical support, at least while the children are young. Some economically disadvantaged fathers take on significant child care responsibility as a vehicle for expressing their contribution to the family's well-being (Amato, Meyers, and Every 2009; England and Edin 2007). Researchers have found that a nonresident father's being involved depends on his employment status, age, education, religious participation, and substance abuse history as well as on his family background (Goldscheider et al. 2009; Knoester, Petts, and Eggebeen 2007; McMahon et al. 2007). One recent study shows that nonresident fathers are more involved when their child is male (Bronte-Tinkew and Horowitz 2010).

In addition, a nonresident father's involvement largely depends upon his relationship with his child's mother and, to a lesser extent, her extended family (Guzzo 2009b; Marsiglio 2008; Ryan, Kalil, and Ziol-Guest 2008). He tends to be more highly involved when his relationship with his child's mother is generally without conflict (Jackson, Choi, and Franke 2009). Involvement is enhanced when the father has been involved prenatally, possibly because he assumes an identity as father during the prenatal period (Cabrera, Fagan, and Farrie 2008a; Doherty 2008; Marsiglio 2008). The next section explores what children need, regardless of the family form in which they reside.

What Do Children Need?

Children of all ages need encouragement, adequate nutrition and shelter, parental interest in their schooling, and consistency in rules and expectations. Parental guidance should be congruent with the child's age or development level (Barnes 2006; Mental Health America 2009).

Children's Needs Differ According to Age

Children's needs differ according to age. Infants need to bond with a consistent and dependable caregiver. To develop emotionally and intellectually, they need affectionate, intimate relationships as well as conversation and variety in their environment. Discipline is never appropriate for babies because they cannot understand its purpose and are unable to change their behavior in response (Brazelton and Greenspan 2000; Hall 2008).

Preschool children need opportunities to practice motor development as well as wide exposure to language, especially when people talk directly to them (Cowley 2000). They also need consistent, clear definitions of what behavior is unacceptable (Del Vecchio and O'Leary 2006; Dorman 2006). School-age children need to practice accomplishing goals appropriate to their abilities and to learn how to get along with others. To better accept criticism as they get older, they need realistic feedback regarding task performance—neither exaggerated praise nor aggressive criticism. They also need to feel that they are contributing family members by being assigned tasks and taught how to do them (Dinkmeyer, McKay, and Dinkmeyer 1997; Hall 2008; Jayson 2005b).

Although the majority of teenagers do not cause familial "storm and stress" (Kantrowitz and Springen 2005), the teen years do have the special potential for reducing marital quality and sparking parent-child conflict (Cui and Donnellan 2009; Whiteman, McHale, and Crouter 2007). As they search for identity and begin to define who they are and will be as adults, adolescents need firm guidance, coupled with parental accessibility and emotional support (Guilamo-Ramos et al. 2006; D. Walsh 2007). Teens also need to learn effective methods for resolving conflict (Tucker, McHale, and Crouter 2003).

Despite stereotypical ideas to the contrary, influences from teens' peers are not necessarily negative and can, in fact, be positive (Hall 2008). Furthermore, parents can and do influence their teenagers' behavior (Dillon et al. 2008; Bersamin et al. 2008; Longmore et al. 2009). It's important for parents to remember "the obvious fact that most adolescents make it to adulthood relatively unscathed and prepared to accept and assume adult roles" (Furstenberg 2000, p. 903). Regardless of age, children have been shown to benefit from an authoritative parenting style (Junn and Boyatzis 2005).

Experts Advise Authoritative Parenting

Parents gradually establish a *parenting style*—a general manner of relating to and disciplining their children. As shown in Table 10.1, we can distinguish among authoritarian, permissive, and authoritative parenting styles (Baumrind 1978; Maccoby and Martin 1983). The **authoritarian parenting style** is low on emotional warmth and nurturing but high on parental direction and control. The authoritarian parent's attitude is, "I am in charge and set/enforce the rules, no matter what" (Gaertner et al. 2007). Parents who employ this style are more likely to spank their children or use otherwise harsh punishment (Grogan-Kaylor and Otis 2007). Unnecessarily high parental direction or control has been associated with a child's decreased sense of personal effectiveness or mastery over a situation, even among children as young as four (Moorman and Pomerantz 2008).

Karan Kapoor / Getty Images

The children in this family have different needs that correspond with their varied ages. Meanwhile, all children need encouragement along with consistent parental expectations and rules. Authoritative parents are emotionally involved with their children, setting limits while encouraging them to develop and practice their talents.

Table 10.1 Parenting styles

		Parental Warmth	
		Low	**High**
Parental Monitoring	**High**	Authoritarian	Authoritative/Positive
	Low	Permissive-Emotional Neglect	Permissive-Indulgent

Parenting styles combine two dimensions: (1) parental warmth, and (2) parental expectations, coupled with monitoring of their children. When both warmth and monitoring are high, parents are said to exhibit an authoritative parenting style. At least for white, middle-class children, research consistently shows that an authoritative parenting style is the most effective of the four possible styles.

The **permissive parenting style** gives children little parental guidance. Although low on parental direction or control, permissive parenting may be high on emotional nurturing—a situation, characterized as *indulgent,* that leads to the classic "spoiled child." A second variant of the permissive style is low on *both* parental direction *and* emotional support—a situation of *emotional neglect.* Authoritarian and permissive parenting styles are associated with children's and adolescents' depression and otherwise poor mental health, low school performance, behavior problems, high rates of teen sexuality and pregnancy, and juvenile delinquency (Hall 2008; Waldfogel 2006).

Child psychologists prefer the **authoritative parenting style**, sometimes called *positive parenting.* This style, characterized as warm, firm, and fair, combines emotional nurturing and support with conscientious parental direction (although not excessive control). Authoritative parents would agree with the statements, "I consider my child's wishes and opinions along with my own when making decisions," "I value my child's school achievement and support my child's efforts," and "I expect my child to act independently at an age-appropriate level" (Manisses Communications Group 2000, p. S1). Authoritative parenting involves encouraging the child's individuality, talents, and emerging independence, while also consciously setting limits and clearly communicating and enforcing rules (Brooks and Goldstein 2001; Ginott, Ginott, and Goddard 2003).[9] Authoritative parents monitor their children's activities and whereabouts while giving appropriate consequences for misbehavior when warranted (Waldfogel 2006).

Regardless of family structure, authoritative parents are more likely than others to have children who do better in school and are socially competent, with relatively high self-esteem and cooperative, yet independent, personalities (Crawford and Novak 2008; Fivush et al. 2009; Jackson-Newsom, Buchanan, and McDonald 2008). Positive effects of authoritative parenting last into adulthood (Schwartz et al. 2009). "A Closer Look at Family Diversity: Parenting LGBT Children" asks you to consider how an authoritative parenting style would apply to this situation.

When two parents are involved, their collaboration or working together renders them more effective, especially when both parents use the authoritative parenting style (Feinberg, Kan, and Hetherington 2007; Kjobli and Hagen 2009; Simons and Conger 2009). An interesting study of two-parent Mexican American families found that children and their parents were happier when parents agreed with and supported one another (Formoso et al. 2007). Collaborative parenting reduces stress and enhances parents' feelings of competence (Jackson, Choi, and Franke 2009), as well as partners' relationship satisfaction (Ehrenberg et al. 2001; Kluwer, Heesink, and Van de Vliert 2002). A sample of married and cohabitating working-class parents of first graders found that families in which both parents practiced an authoritative parenting style were most effective in raising well-adjusted children. Families in which only one parent used an authoritative parenting style were more effective than those in which neither parent did (Martin, Ryan, and Brooks-Gunn 2007; Meteyer and Perry-Jenkins 2009).

Psychological Control versus Authoritative Parenting As opposed to direct forms of parental control, such as asking direct questions, explicitly stating expectations, and giving time-outs or denying privileges, **psychological control** involves using manipulative strategies such as inducing guilt or withdrawing signs of affection. Rather than conveying unconditional love for the child while correcting misbehavior, psychological control relies on negative cues, such as refusing to acknowledge the child.

The underlying message is that the child's behavior has hurt the parent's feelings. To reduce tension, the child is expected to comply with the parent's wishes. At least among Latino and European American adolescents, and among African American girls, psychological control has been found to hinder children's emergent sense of agency or mastery over their behavior and future goal attainment. Depression can result (Bean and Northrup 2009; Mandara and Pikes 2008; Soenens, Vansteenkiste, and Sierens 2009).

[9] Limits are best set as house rules and stated objectively in third-person terms. A parent may say, for example, "The time to be home is 10 o'clock." With preschoolers, limits need to be set and stated very clearly: A parent who says, "Don't go too far from home" leaves "too far" to the child's interpretation. "Don't go out of the yard at all" is a wiser rule.

A Closer Look at Family Diversity

Parenting LGBT Children

Parenting a child who is lesbian, gay, bisexual, or transsexual (LGBT) can be not only pleasurable and broadening but also emotionally challenging ("For Parents . . ." 2004). When a lesbian, gay male, or bisexual child "comes out," or discloses his or her identity to family members, the parent may feel confused, ambivalent, alone, embarrassed, and/or angry (Martin et al. 2009). Even parents who view themselves as progressive, readily accepting GLBT friends and acquaintances, may be surprised at their feelings of disappointment and grief upon finding out that their child is lesbian, gay, or bisexual. If homosexuality is against the parent's religion, a child's coming out can be even more disconcerting. It helps to recognize the following facts:

- All cultures and historical periods include individuals who have identified themselves as gay, lesbian, bisexual, or transgender.
- The American Psychological Association and the American Pediatric Association do not consider being GLBT as a psychological disorder.
- GLBT adolescents and young adults may feel guilty about their sexual orientation, worried about responses from their families and friends, and fearful of discrimination in clubs, sports, college, or the workplace ("Gay and Lesbian Adolescents" 2006).
- Hiding one's sexual orientation can be extremely stressful and isolating. Adolescents and adult children come out because they want to live their lives openly and honestly without deception ("Questions and Answers" n.d.; Wright and Perry 2006).
- The physical and mental health of GLBT youth is better when they feel social support (Wright and Perry 2006).
- Parents' acceptance of their child's sexual identity allows for open discussions about the child's dating relationships and related issues, such as ways to deal with prejudice and discrimination or how to reduce risks associated with HIV/AIDS ("For Parents . . ." 2004).

Experts advise that, whatever a parent's feelings when a child comes out, the child needs assurance that she or he is loved just as much as before:

> Can you imagine the feelings of a youngster who bravely tells his or her parents that they are gay only to be confronted by an anger which may be so severe that they are put out of the house, or told that he or she has brought shame to the family? Yet this happens and it is a fact that gay people occasionally commit suicide because they have been so badly ostracized and made to feel alienated. ("If Your Child . . ." 2008).

As parents work through their feelings, they may want to talk their situation over with others. Professionals urge parents not share the information without their child's consent. An exception involves talking with a counselor. Other resources are available as well. PFLAG (Parents, Families, and Friends of Lesbians and Gays) is a national organization comprised of local educational and support groups, as well as Internet resources.

Critical Thinking

How might the stress model of effective parenting be applied to this situation of a GLBT child's coming out to her or his parents? How might an authoritarian parent's reaction to their child's coming out differ from the response of an authoritative parent?

Before leaving this discussion, we need to note that some scholars view the authoritarian/permissive/authoritative model as biased. For instance, one study shows that authoritative parenting is a more important prediction of behavior for children of European descent than for the Hmong (Supple and Small 2006). Some scholars argue that the model is ethnocentric, or Eurocentric—that is, it uses European, white, middle-class beliefs about parenting as the standard to which all others are compared—often unfavorably (Farver et al. 2007). This point is developed throughout the section "Racial/Ethnic Diversity and Parenting," later in this chapter. The next section focuses on the question of whether spanking is ever appropriate.

Is Spanking Ever Appropriate?

Spanking refers to hitting a child with an open hand without causing physical injury. In 2007, a California state legislator proposed legislation that would have outlawed spanking children under three years old. Had the proposal become law, California would have joined the approximately fifteen European nations in which spanking children is illegal (Straus 2007). However, the California-based suggestion met enough negative media response that the idea was dropped, and the proposed bill was revised to involve only more serious forms of corporal punishment, such as kicking or hitting a child with an implement (Steinhauer 2007). Whether spanking children is ever a good idea is controversial (Coombs-Orme and Cain 2008; Larzelere 2008).

Analysis of data from the 13,000 respondents in the National Survey of Families and Households found that about one-third of fathers and 44 percent of mothers had spanked their children during the week prior to being interviewed. Boys, especially those under age two, are spanked the most often. Children over age six are spanked less often, but some parents spank their children during early adolescence (Guzzo and Lee 2008).

Mothers spank more often than fathers. Younger, less-educated parents in households with more children and less social support, parents who argue a lot with their children, sociopolitical conservatives, those with a fundamentalist religious orientation, and parents who live in relatively violent neighborhoods are more likely to spank (Button 2008; Ellison and Bradshaw 2009). The stress of first-time parenthood is associated with spanking (Guzzo and Lee 2008). One study found that single mothers who become more seriously involved in a romantic relationship, whether with the biological father of their child or not, are more likely to spank their children. The authors speculated that the mothers experienced increased strains as they incorporated the child into their developing relationship (Guzzo and Lee 2008).

A leading domestic violence researcher, sociologist Murray Straus (2007) advises parents never to hit children of any age under any circumstances. At least among European American children, being frequently spanked in childhood is linked to later behavior problems, as well as to depression, suicide, alcohol or drug abuse, physical aggression against one's parents in adolescence, and later to abusing one's own children and to intimate partner violence (Berlin et al. 2009; Lansford and Dodge 2008). Straus has argued that spanking teaches children a "hidden agenda"—that it is all right to hit someone and that those who love you hit you. This confusion of love with violence sets the stage for domestic violence. Then, too, especially when a parent spanks in anger—which is never advised—"spanking can escalate and apparently does mix in with more severe hitting" (Kazdin and Benjet 2003, p. 102; Roberto, Carlyle, and Goodall 2007). Infants and babies under two years old should never be spanked (Coombs-Orme and Cain 2008). Spanking or vigorously shaking an infant can lead to permanent damage, even death.

Meanwhile, some researchers contend that Straus and his colleagues may be overstating the case (Saadeh, Rizzo, and Roberts 2002). For instance, psychologist Marjorie Gunnoe (cited in S. Gilbert 1997) theorizes that spanking is most likely to have negative results for children only when they perceive being spanked as an aggressive act. She hypothesizes that children under age eight tend to think it is their parent's right to spank them. However, recent research does show that corporal punishment has generally negative effects (Christie-Mizell, Pryor, and Grossman 2008; Mulvaney and Mebert 2007).

The American Academy of Pediatrics advises that children under two years old and adolescents should *never* be spanked and recommends that parents learn disciplinary methods other than spanking (American Academy of Pediatrics 1998). Straus has argued that spanking usually accompanies other, more effective discipline methods such as explaining or denying privileges. These nonspanking discipline methods are effective by themselves, and parents should be encouraged to follow the principle, "just leave out the spanking part" (Straus 1999a, p. 8; Straus 2007). In general, middle- and upper-middle-class parents are less likely than low-income parents to spank. Low-income parents "may be unaware of current American Academy of Pediatrics policy recommendations about spanking. Or they may consciously disagree with them" (Guzzo and Lee 2008).

Social Class and Parenting

There are effective and ineffective parents in all social classes (Jackson, Choi, and Bentler 2009). Meanwhile, this section examines some ways that social class impacts parental alternatives and choices. You'll recall a theme of this text: Decisions are influenced by social conditions that expand or limit one's options. Virtually all opportunities and experiences, or *life chances*, are influenced by **socioeconomic status (SES)**—one's position in society, measured by educational achievement, occupation, and/or income. Parenting is no exception (Furstenberg 2006; Lareau 2006).

Research shows that family education and income have more influence on parenting behaviors and children's outcomes than do race/ethnicity or family structure in and of itself (Gibson-Davis 2008). We have seen that parents who are less stressed and relatively content practice more positive child-rearing behaviors (Burrell and Roosa 2009; Gibson-Davis 2008). Reduced stress and emotional well-being, in turn, are statistically correlated with higher socioeconomic status.

Middle- and Upper-Middle-Class Parents

In this climate of economic uncertainty, even middle- and upper-middle-class parents with relatively high education have suffered layoffs, salary reductions, and reduced health and retirement benefits (Coy, Conlin, and Herbst 2010). Having already tightened their belts, some have trouble paying their bills (Pew Research Center 2009b). Nevertheless, compared with lower-SES parents, those with higher income can better afford to provide for their children's needs and wants. For instance, more than 90 percent of households with annual incomes of $100,000 have Internet access, compared with 50 percent of those making between

Parents' and children's life experiences are significantly related to their socioeconomic status. Middle- and upper-middle-class parents tend to emphasize concerted cultivation of their children's development and talents.

$25,000 and $35,000 (U.S. Census Bureau 2010b, Table 1118). Then too, higher-SES parents have the resources to hire household help or purchase devices such as baby-monitoring equipment that might help with parenting (Knoester, Haynie, and Stephens 2006; Nelson 2008).[10] Furthermore, they reside in neighborhoods conducive to successfully raising and educating their children.

More highly educated parents have fewer children on average (U.S. Census Bureau 2010b, Table 92) and are likely to emphasize **concerted cultivation** of their child's talents and overall development. According to this parenting model, they more often praise their children; play with or talk to them "just for fun"; read to them; create and enforce rules about watching television; engage their children in extracurricular lessons, clubs, and sports; take them on outings; enroll them in private or charter schools; and say that there are people in the neighborhood whom they can count on (U.S. Census Bureau 2009h, Tables D5-D30).

More so than in low-income neighborhoods, middle- and upper-class children are likely to have neighborhood and school friends who share their parents' values and can therefore serve as parallel socialization agents (Hall 2008). Then too, volunteering at their children's schools, and monitoring other students' and even teachers' behavior, highly educated parents secure educational advantages for their children. Should problems arise at school, higher-SES parents are likely to have network contacts with community professionals who can help and may even challenge school officials' decisions (Hassrick and Schneider 2009).

Higher-SES parents are likely to get parenting information from professional sources such as books or the Internet (Radey and Randolph 2009). Often using the authoritative parenting style, they negotiate with their children in ways meant to foster language and critical thinking skills, self-direction, initiative, and self-advocacy (Lareau 2006; Shinn and O'Brien 2008). This parenting model well prepares children for success in the broader society because schools and professions value the self-direction, critical thinking, and self-advocacy that these children learn at home. But can parents take concerted cultivation too far?

Hyperparenting—The "Hurried Child" and "Helicopter Parents" According to some observers, many higher-SES parents engage in **hyperparenting**. Dubbed "helicopter parents," they hover above, meddling excessively in their children's lives.[11] Typically, they scramble to be "perfect," providing their children with more than is either necessary or beneficial (Warner 2006). Some parents have become vulnerable to marketing that prods "good" parents to spend unnecessarily large amounts of money on baby gear and toys, among other things (Deveny 2007; Purcell 2007). For many, excessive spending on their children cuts into their ability to save for emergencies, retirement, or college (Paul 2008).

Critics warn that many higher-income parents not only give their children too much but also engage

[10] Ironically, although possibly enhancing parental freedom, baby-monitoring devices can also increase anxiety levels because they encourage defining the infant as extremely fragile (Nelson 2008). Can you think of other parental aids that might have similar effects?

[11] For example, some nutritionists are concerned that many parents have become overzealous, even obsessive, in efforts to engender good eating habits in their children—not allowing a child to eat cake at a birthday party, for instance ("What's Eating Our Kids?" 2009). And camp counselors report being contacted by anxious parents because their child looked sleepy or unhappy in a group photo ("Helicopter Parents" 2007). College personnel report being emailed by irate parents because there was too much salt in the cafeteria chicken or their undergraduate's roommate ate their ramen noodles ("Mom Needs an A" 2007).

them in too many scheduled activities—private lessons, extracurricular activities associated with school or church, and organized recreational programs. "If the hearth was the center of the home in the 19th century, the calendar is really the center of many middle class homes" (Lareau, in "Class in America" 2003). Expecting achievement in these endeavors, parents may place too many demands on their children, even encouraging them to compete for places in the most preferred preschools, for example (Saulny 2006). Filling their own needs while believing that they are acting in the best interest of their children, these parents may be determined to raise "trophy kids" (Perrow 2009).

Although there is some evidence that tightly scheduling a child may not be harmful (Cloud 2007), developmental psychologist David Elkind (1988) warned a generation ago that "scheduled hyperactivity" (Kantrowitz 2000) can produce the "hurried child," not to mention frazzled parents (Elkind 2007a, 2010; Warner 2006). The over-scheduled, or "hurried child" is denied free playtime while encouraged to assume too many challenges and responsibilities too soon (Elkind 2007a, 2007b).[12] Hurried children suffer the stress induced by the pressure to accomplish (Anderson and Doherty 2005). Or they may abandon goal-directed academic and/or extracurricular activities (Su 2007).

As the hurried child enters young adulthood, some helicopter parents meddle inappropriately in their college student's educational experiences or attempt to negotiate job offers, salary, and benefits for their offspring (Armour 2007; Blanck 2007; "Mom Needs an A" 2007). Some individuals who see themselves in negative descriptions of helicopter parents find the criticism unfair, especially in this unsettling economy and because they pay considerably for their children's education.

Nevertheless, psychologists warn that helicopter parents risk turning their children against them. Furthermore, excessive hovering denies youth opportunities to develop self-confidence or problem-solving skills (Su 2007). Some parents have created an organization called "Putting Family First" (www.puttingfamilyfirst.org) that supports parents who want to reduce their children's involvement in organized activities and have more unscheduled family time (Kantrowitz 2000).

Compared with life in higher-SES families, "childhood looks different" in families of lower socioeconomic status where children grow up with less supervised play, fewer scheduled activities, and more unplanned interaction with extended family members and friends (Lareau 2003a). Sociologists Elliot Weininger and Annette Lareau (2009) have noted an inconsistency. Higher-SES parents determine to promote self-direction in their children but exercise subtle forms of control that can undermine their intent. Conversely, lower-SES parents tend to espouse obedience but often grant children considerable autonomy (as they play outside unsupervised, for example), thereby limiting emphasis on conformity.

"So many toys—so little unstructured time."

Working-Class Parents

Working-class parents work at construction, manufacturing, repair, installation, and service jobs such as health care assistants, that require at least a high school education and pay higher than minimum wage. More so than with higher-SES parents, working-class parents have suffered the negative effects of declining factory work and union power; decreased wages and benefits; insecurities associated with temporary work; and escalating housing, utilities, and transportation costs.

Working-class parents do not necessarily view the concerted development parenting model as good parenting. In fact, they may view this model as negative, creating demanding children (Guzzo and Lee 2008). Instead, they tend to follow the **facilitation of natural growth parenting model**, according to which children's abilities are allowed to develop naturally (Lareau 2006). Some working-class parents employ the authoritative parenting style. Nevertheless, much parent-child communication tends to be authoritarian, emphasizing obedience and conformity and less often eliciting children's feelings or opinions (Lareau 2003a, 2006). Working-class parents are more likely to tell their children what to do rather than trying to persuade them with reasoning. When dealing with professionals (e.g., doctors, religious clergy, teachers, public officials), working-class

[12] A related issue involves schools' "hurrying" of children with the increased use of standardized testing and decreased emphasis on music, art, or time for spontaneity and play (Cloud 2007; Trudeau 2006; Tyre 2006a).

parents are likely to encourage their children to keep their thoughts and questions to themselves (Shinn and O'Brien 2008).

Many working-class parents are involved in their children's schools and do promote academic success in their children (Cooper, Crosnoe, et al. 2009; Woolley and Grogan-Kaylor 2006). However, the natural growth parenting model, coupled with the authoritarian parenting style, does not correspond well with the middle-class culture and expectations of schools and professions. Although higher-SES children appear to gain a sense of entitlement, working-class children are likely to grow up with feelings of discomfort, constraint, and distrust regarding their school and work experiences (Lareau 2003a; Lucas 2007). For children from working-class families who embark upon professional careers, this sense of not fitting in can persist (Lubrano 2003).

Low-Income and Poverty-Level Parents

The majority of low-income and poverty-level parents work at minimum- or less-than-minimum-wage jobs with irregular and unpredictable hours and no employer-subsidized medical insurance or other benefits. Because more and more low-income jobs are part-time and also because working even full-time at minimum wage does not pay enough to live above poverty level, many low-income parents have two or three jobs (Ames, Brosi, and Damiano-Teixeira 2006). Analysis of data from the National Longitudinal Survey of Youth (NLSY) shows that single mothers who work part-time in low-wage jobs with nonstandard hours generally raise their children in poorer-quality home environments (Lleras 2008).[13] Irregular work schedules in low-wage jobs with little autonomy and high supervisor surveillance, coupled with housing or neighborhood troubles as well as financial worries, cause stress.

Living in rented homes, apartments, or motel rooms, they struggle with rent burdens, utility payments, and housing instability (Berger, Heintze, et al. 2008; Ehrenreich 2001). Moreover, many poor families move from city to city to live with relatives or to search for jobs. This situation makes it difficult for a parent to establish support systems and hinders children's chances for school continuity and success (Molyneux 1995). In sharp contrast to higher-SES parents, many low-income parents struggle to give their children a few "extras," such as a "respectable" birthday party, school field trips, or a high school class ring (Lee, Katras, and Bauer 2009; Mistry et al. 2008).

With fewer resources, lower-income parents are less likely to live in neighborhoods that value education or encourage high achievement (Coles 2009; England and Edin 2007; Henry et al. 2008). In fact, items that middle-class Americans take for granted, such as relatively safe, gang-free neighborhoods, are often unavailable (Loukas et al. 2008), and parental control is more difficult to achieve in neighborhoods characterized by antisocial behavior (Gayles et al. 2009; Moore et al. 2009).

Furthermore, poverty-level families are more likely than others to live with air pollution, and to have poorer nutrition, more illnesses such as asthma, schools that are less safe, and limited access to quality medical care (Downey and Hawkins 2008; Seccombe 2007). Children living in poverty—more often disabled or chronically ill than other children—have expensive health care needs that welfare or other social services do not always or completely cover (Cohen and Bloom 2005; Levine 2009).

About 8 percent of children who are raised in poverty (compared with about 5 percent of children raised in families that are not poor) have emotional or behavioral difficulties (Simons et al. 2006, p. 3; Teachman 2008b). "Facts about Families: Marriage and Children in Poverty," in Chapter 7, further describes children's outcomes that result from growing up in poverty.

Homeless Families Over the past three decades, extreme poverty, a shortage of affordable housing, job erosion, home foreclosures, declining public assistance, lack of affordable health care, domestic violence, substance addiction, and mental illness have helped to create a significant number of homeless families—a phenomenon that would have been unthinkable forty years ago (National Coalition for the Homeless 2009c).

Families with children are among the fastest-growing segments of the homeless population, a situation that has become more pronounced since the beginning of the recession that began in 2008. Partly as a result of changes to welfare laws, described earlier in this chapter, approximately 40 percent of the homeless are mothers

[13] Specifically, what does it mean to say that a low-income single mother's home environment is less than desirable? In the National Longitudinal Survey of Youth (NLSY), *home environment* is operationally defined (see Chapter 2) using measures of cognitive stimulation, maternal responsiveness, and safety of the physical environment. For three- to six-year-olds, cognitive stimulation involves eight measures that are whether the parent helps the child learn (1) numbers, (2) shapes, (3) colors, and (4) the alphabet; (5) whether the mother reads to the child at least three times a week; (6) whether the child has ten or more books; (7) whether the family gets at least one magazine regularly; and (8) whether there is a record or tape player in the home. Maternal responsiveness involves four measures that are whether the mother (1) talks to the child, (2) kisses or hugs the child, (3) answers the child's questions verbally, and (4) voices positive feelings about the child. Physical environment has four items that are whether (1) the play environment appears safe, and whether the rooms are reasonably (2) clean, (3) lighted, and (4) uncluttered (Lleras 2008).

and children, with children under age eighteen making up about one-quarter of the homeless (Seccombe 2007). Fathers, some of whom are single parents, are also found among the homeless (National Coalition for the Homeless 2009a, 2009c).

Homeless parents, especially those who have been without housing for a longer time, move often and have little in the way of a helpful social network ("Homeless Families with Children" 2001). Getting children to school and supervising their homework—not to mention being actively involved in a child's classroom—become extremely difficult for homeless parents. Although families benefit from entering shelters, life in a homeless shelter is itself stressful. Some shelters require that the family leave during the day, regardless of the weather: "How can this mother go out and look for a job or even look for a place to live when she's got three kids, and it's raining, or it's cold?" Problematic rules involve bedtimes, mealtimes, keeping children quiet, and the requirement that children be with their parents at all times. Other stressors occur as well. For example, one mother told of a single male resident's "getting fresh with my older girl" (Lindsey 1998, p. 248).

Social class may be more important than race/ethnicity in terms of parental values and interactions with children (Lareau 2003b, 2006). Middle-class parents of all racial/ethnic groups are more alike than different, and so are poverty-level parents. Upper-middle-class black parents perform their role differently than do working-class black parents or those living below poverty level (Peters 2007). At the same time, social scientists do look at how various ethnic groups evidence culturally specific parenting behaviors (Cohen, Tran, and Rhee 2007). The major focus of the following section is on parenting behaviors and challenges that are specific to various racial, ethnic, and religious minorities.

John Moore/Getty Images

Families benefit from homeless shelters, but living there can be stressful in itself. Stress-inducing regulations involve bedtimes and mealtimes, along with the expectation that children be quiet or with their parents at all times.

Racial/Ethnic Diversity and Parenting

As a beginning, we need to note two factors. First, there is considerable overlap among class and racial/ethnic categories. For instance, although the upper middle class now includes substantial numbers of people of color, particularly Asians, it is still largely non-Hispanic white. Many African American and Hispanic families are now solidly middle class, but these race/ethnic groups remain overrepresented in low-income and poverty categories. A second factor to note is that there is considerable ethnic diversity *within* the following groups. For instance, Asian Americans include a broad range of ethnicities, including Chinese, Japanese, Korean, Vietnamese, and Asian Indians, among others.

African American Parents

Evidence suggests that African American parents' attitudes, behaviors, and hopes for their children are similar to those of other parents in their social class (Peters 2007). Nevertheless, the impact of race remains important. For instance, even when social class is taken into account, it appears that African American mothers (but not fathers) are more likely than European Americans to spank their children. However, spanking may not have the same negative effects on black children as it does on European American children. Among blacks, physical punishment is more acceptable and hence more likely to be viewed by both the parent and the child as an appropriate display of maternal warmth and positive parenting (Jackson-Newsom, Buchanan, and McDonald 2008). It follows that comparing African American parents to other ethnic groups can be seen as Eurocentric (Dodson 2007).

As with other race/ethnic minorities, African Americans' parental attitudes and behaviors are similar to other parents in their socioeconomic status (SES). Nevertheless, the intersection of gender and race with SES means that this father, culturally expected to be an effective breadwinner, also risks race discrimination as he navigates a job search in this recession economy. He is pictured here at a New York State employment services office in Brooklyn.

Besides putting up with research findings that are possibly biased against them, even higher-SES African Americans remain vulnerable to discrimination (Lacy 2007; Welborn 2006). So simple a matter as buying toys becomes problematic. Black dolls only? Should the child choose? What if the choice is a white Barbie doll? For middle-class African American parents, forging a unique *black middle-class* identity and then instilling this identity into their children is a major undertaking (Lacy 2007).

Native American Parents

Native American parents have been described as exercising a permissive parenting style that some critics have viewed as bordering on neglectful. However, describing Native American parenting in this way smacks of Eurocentrism (Seideman et al. 1994). Traditionally, Native American culture has emphasized personal autonomy and individual choice for children as well as for adults. Before the arrival of Europeans and for some time thereafter, Native Americans successfully raised their children by using nonverbal teaching examples and "light discipline," possibly coupled with "persuasion, ridicule, or shaming in opposition to corporal punishment or coercion." Native Americans continue to respond with warmth to their children's needs and also to "respect children enough to allow them to work things out in their own manner" (R. John 1998, p. 400; Seideman et al. 1994).

Given the problems of substance abuse and high teenage suicide rates documented among Native American youth, we might conclude that the traditional method of raising Native American children is no longer effective, due to changes in the broader society. However, valuing their cultural heritage, many Native Americans have been reluctant to assimilate into the broader society—and this reluctance may mean a rejection of the authoritative parenting style advised by European American psychologists. Meanwhile, the use of tribal elders "to help mitigate the loss of parental involvement and early nurturant figures in the lives of Native American adolescents" is important to many tribes (R. John 1998, p. 404).

Meanwhile, researchers have noted that Native American parents and children demonstrate resilience. For example, a longitudinal study of twenty-nine Navajo Native American mothers who as teenagers bore infants found that, twelve to fifteen years later, many had completed or gone beyond high school (Dalla et al. 2009). Moreover, although single-parent households do occur in Native American communities, the extended family serves as an instrument of group solidarity by reinforcing cultural standards and expectations, and lending practical assistance. With symbolic and actual leadership status in family communities, Native American grandparents often monitor grandchildren and may fully adopt the parenting role when necessary (Letiecq, Bailey, and Kurtz 2008).[14]

[14] However, despite the idea that the extended family may be strongly institutionalized among Native Americans and the resultant possibility that raising grandchildren might be less stressful for Native American grandparents, one study has found that Native American grandmothers raising their grandchildren were *more* depressed than were their European American counterparts (Letiecq, Bailey, and Kurtz 2008).

Hispanic Parents

Hispanic parents have been described as more authoritarian than their non-Hispanic counterparts. However, as with other racial/ethnic minorities, it may be that this description is Eurocentric and therefore inaccurate. The concept of **hierarchical parenting**, which combines warm emotional support for children with a demand for significant respect for parents, older extended-family members, and other authority figures, may more aptly apply to Hispanic parents. Hierarchical parenting is designed to instill in children a more collective value system rather than the relatively high individualism that European Americans favor (McLoyd et al. 2000).

This collectivism has been found to be functional. For instance, a recent study that compared Mexican American with European American parents in Southern California found that family cohesion (*familismo*) lessened the relationship between economic stress and negative parenting (Behnke et al. 2008; see also Martyn et al. 2009). Research shows similar positive effects of family cohesion for Vietnamese American as well as for families of other ethnicities, including European Americans (Lam 2005; Vandeleur et al. 2009).

Hispanic parents teach their children the traditions and values of their cultures of origin while often coping with a generation gap that includes differential fluency and different attitudes toward speaking Spanish (Gonzales et al. 2006; Pew Research Center 2009a; Smokowski, Rose, and Bacallao 2008). As in other bicultural families, intergenerational conflicts may extend into many matters of everyday life as the younger generation becomes more assimilated into U.S. culture. For example, "My mother would give me these silly dresses to wear to school, not jeans," complained a fifteen-year-old Mexican American female (Suro 1992, p. A-11). As Hispanic immigrant parents adjust to U.S. culture, they are likely to place less emphasis on *familismo* and to become increasingly permissive, the consequences of which can be detrimental to adolescents' behavior (Baer and Schmitz 2007; Driscoll, Russell, and Crockett 2008).

Asian American Parents

Despite often being portrayed as affluent, Asian Americans are found in lower socioeconomic strata and may experience economic hardship (Ishii-Kuntz et al. 2009). Nevertheless, compared to the average of 29.4 percent for all Americans over twenty-four years old, 52.6 percent of Asian Americans have completed four years or more of college (U.S. Census Bureau 2010b, Table 224). Ironically, meanwhile, the Asian American parenting style is often characterized as authoritarian (Greenfield and Suzuki 2001) and even hostile (McBride-Chang and Chang 1998). Research findings are mixed regarding the success of the expert-preferred authoritative parenting style among Asian Americans, again suggesting that the model may be Eurocentric (Pong, Johnston, and Chen 2010).

Social scientists have offered an alternative parenting concept, the **Confucian training doctrine**. This parenting model is named after the sixth-century Chinese social philosopher Confucius, who stressed (among other things) honesty, sacrifice, familial loyalty, and respect for parents and all elders. The Confucian training doctrine blends parental love, concern, involvement, and physical closeness with strict and firm control, or "training" (Chao 1994; McBride-Chang and Chang 1998). "Training" may involve parents' use of guilt, shame, and moral obligation to control their children's behavior (Farver et al. 2007). However, the extremely strong ties between Asian American parents and their children have been found to lessen parent-child conflict, along with potential negative effects of shaming (Benner and Kim 2009; Park, Vo, and Tsong 2008).

Like other ethnic minorities, Asian Americans have suffered from discrimination (Lau, Takeuchi, and Alegria 2006; Tong 2004). Moreover, Asian immigrant parents may face conflicts with their children when expecting traditional behavior characteristic of the homeland while their children assimilate into the American culture and no longer adhere to traditional expectations regarding dating, for example, or marital monogamy (Ahn, Kim, and Park 2008; Farver et al. 2007). Then too, Asian American youth must contend with high expectations created by the stereotyping of Asians as a "model," or "super" minority (Abboud 2006).

Parents of Multiracial Children

According to the 2000 census, which was the first to offer citizens the option of identifying themselves as more than one race, nearly 7 million Americans are of mixed race ("Mixed Race Americans" 2009; Roth 2005). Of those, more than 40 percent are children under age eighteen. As multiracial children reach childbearing ages and as racial heterogamy loses its taboo, the number of multiracial births is expected to climb (Qian and Lichter 2007).

Raising biracial or multiracial children has unique challenges, although it is not without rewards as well (Rockquemore and Laszloffy 2005). One challenge may be tension between parents and children—and between the parents themselves—over cultural values and attitudes. For instance, Euro-American parents, particularly white single mothers who are living in mostly white communities, may find that "[y]ou have to seek, to go out of your way to give them that African

© Bob Daemmrich / The Image Works

At this festival marking Eid, the end of Ramadan, this Muslim community in central Texas gathers for afternoon prayers. Muslim parents hope that their children will remain true to their religious tradition. Meanwhile, like parents of other minority religions in the United States, they must help their children face fear of ridicule and actual discrimination.

American side" (respondent, quoted in O'Donoghue 2005, p. 148).

A small, qualitative study of eleven East Coast white women who were raising biracial black-white teens unexpectedly found that—because their physical characteristics made it possible—some adolescents (three females) chose to embrace a Latina identity as a way to deal with racial ambiguity (O'Donoghue 2005). One psychologist surveyed multiracial adults and asked whether they thought that their parents had been prepared to raise children of mixed race. The majority did not believe so (Dunnewind 2003). Today, however, many schools are more sensitive to the needs of multiracial children (Wardle 2000), and more resources are available for parents raising multiracial children. According to one recent study, multiracial and multi-ethnic families that foster an explicit family identity as multicultural, multiracial, or multiethnic have happier, better-adjusted children (Soliz, Thorson, and Rittenour 2009). Chapter 9 also addresses these issues.

Religious Minority Parents

Ethnicity is often associated with religious belief. For example, Chinese Americans are likely to be Buddhists; Asian Indian Americans are likely to be Hindu or Sikh. In a Christian dominant culture, diverse ethnoreligious affiliations affect parenting for many Americans. For instance, Muslims have their own holy days, such as Ramadan, which may not be taken into account in public schools' scheduling. Wearing flowing robes and, more often, head scarves or veils (called *hijab*), Muslims report that they fear ridicule and face discrimination from employers and others (American Moslem Society 2010; "Muslim Parents Seek" 2005).

American parents of religious minorities generally hope that their children will remain true to their religious heritage amid a majority culture that seldom understands and is sometimes threatening ("Muslim Parents Seek" 2005; F. R. Lee 2001).[15] One solution has been the emergence of religion-based summer camps for children of Bahia, Buddhist, Catholic, Hindu, Jewish, Mormon, Mennonite, Muslim, and Sikh parents, among others (www.mysummercamps.com).

Raising Children of Racial/Ethnic Identity in a Racist and Discriminatory Society

A parent's feeling victimized by racism adds stress to an already stressful parenting process (Benner and Kim 2009; Brody et al. 2008). Families of color (or religious minorities) attempt to serve as an insulating environment, shielding children from and/or confronting injustices (Brody et al. 2008; Brown et al. 2007; Cohen, Tran, and Rhee 2007). Most engage in **race socialization**—developing children's pride in their cultural heritage while warning and preparing them about the possibility of encountering discrimination (Scottham and Smalls 2009; Umana-Taylor et al. 2009). Higher levels of race socialization are associated with parents' having been discriminated against, their higher sense of personal efficacy, and greater concern that their children will actually encounter racism (Benner and Kim 2009; Brody et al. 2008; Crouter et al. 2008).

Valuing one's cultural heritage while simultaneously being required to deny or "rise above" it to advance poses problems for individuals and between parents and their children. For instance, Native Americans must often choose between the reservation and an urban life that is perhaps alienating but may present greater economic opportunity (Seccombe 2007). Latinos may see a threat to deeply cherished values of family and community in the competitive individualism of the mainstream American achievement path (McLoyd

[15] This desire that their children maintain their ethno-religious heritage is a principal reason for some immigrant parents' preference that their children marry homogamously, sometimes in arranged marriages (see Chapter 6).

et al. 2000). Asian Americans may follow the "model minority" route to success but experience emotional estrangement from their culturally traditional parents (Kibria 2000). We turn now to a discussion of another variation in the parenting experience—grandparents as parents.

Grandparents as Parents

About 11 percent of U.S. grandparents are raising grandchildren (Lumpkin 2008). More than 3.6 million children under age eighteen are living in a grandparent's household, a few with only their grandfather, many with two grandparents, and many more with only their grandmother (King, Mitchell, and Hawkins 2010; U.S. Census Bureau 2010b, Table 70). Having risen dramatically over the past ten years, the number of grandparents raising children or residing with and helping to raise their grandchildren is expected to rise, especially in today's recession economy (Spratling 2009).

Taken together, unmarried parenthood, divorce or separation, poverty, substance abuse, HIV/AIDS, domestic violence, abandonment, and incarceration account for a very large majority of grandparent families, or **grandfamilies** (Henderson et al. 2009). Unsurprisingly, the family often views a grandparent's assuming the role of primary parent as a crisis. One study found that grandparents' coping strategies involved relying on their religious faith as well as imagining that the situation would somehow "just go away" (Lumpkin 2008). Handling family crises is addressed in Chapter 14.

Sylvie de Toledo is a social worker whose nephew was raised by her mother after her sister's suicide. As a result of this experience, Toledo founded a support group called Grandparents as Parents (GAP) "to meet the urgent and ongoing needs of grandparents and other relative caregivers raising at-risk children" (www.grandparentsasparents.org). As Toledo writes,

> Sometimes the call comes at night, sometimes on a bright morning. It may be your child, the police, or child protective services. "Mama, I've messed up. . . ." "We're sorry. There has been an accident. . . ." "Mrs. Smith, we have your grandchild. Can you take him?" Sometimes you make the call yourself—reporting your own child to the authorities in a desperate attempt to protect your grandchild from abuse or neglect. Often the change is gradual. At first your grandchild is with you for a day, then four days, a month, and then two months as the parents slowly lose control of their lives. You start out baby-sitting. You think the arrangement is temporary. You put off buying a crib or moving to a bigger apartment. Then you get a collect call from jail—or no call at all. (Toledo and Brown 1995, p. 9)

At other times, the change is more sudden, as when a grandchild's parents are killed in an auto accident (Landry-Meyer and Newman 2004).

Becoming a primary parent requires considerable adjustment for grandparents (Lumpkin 2008). Living with children in the house is a significant change after years of not doing so (Dolbin-MacNab 2006). A grandparent's circle of friends and work life may change. He or she may retire early, reduce work hours, or try to negotiate more flexible ones. On the other hand, a grandparent may return to work to finance raising the child(ren). In either case, a grandparent's finances may suffer while paying for items such as additional beds, food, and clothing. To help, under the **formal kinship care** system, some states offer financial compensation to grandparents (or other relatives, such as aunts) who raise their grandchildren as state-licensed foster parents.[16] "Facts about Families: Foster Parenting" further discusses foster parenting.

The Center for Law and Social Policy finds formal kinship care to be generally good for children. Compared with children in nonrelative foster care, those fostered by relatives are less likely to have tried to run away, and more likely to say that they feel loved, like those with whom they live, and want their current placement to be their permanent home (Conway and Hutson 2007). However, a few critics argue that, at least with regard to black children, formal kinship care is overused and detrimental to families in the long run because it fails to emphasize reunification with the children's parents (Harris and Skyles 2008).

Grandparents' raising grandchildren is typically characterized by family members' ambivalence (Letiecq, Bailey, and Kurtz 2008). Unsure whether or when their grandchildren will return to the parental home, grandparents may "learn a . . . stance of detachment to cope with the shifts they are sure to experience and probably even applaud" (Nelson 2006, p. 822). Furthermore, there are often questions about the possible legal termination of the parent's parental rights (McWey, Henderson, and Alexander 2008). When parental rights are not terminated, grandparents who are responsible for the children in their care lack legal rights over them (Letiecq, Bailey, and Porterfield 2008).

Some grandchildren being raised by a grandparent see one or both parents either regularly or sporadically; but generally these relationships are complex, often marked with difficulties. In a qualitative study with white, black, and mixed-race children being raised by grandparents, some children hoped for reunification

[16] However, some grandparents report having trouble navigating their state's kinship care system due to, among other reasons, fear and distrust of the child welfare system and daunting bureaucratic regulations (Letiecq, Bailey, and Porterfield 2008).

Facts about Families

Foster Parenting

Every state government has a department that monitors parents' treatment of their children. An example is California's Department of Child Protective Services. When government officials determine that an individual under age eighteen is being abused or neglected, they can take temporary or permanent custody of children and remove them from the parental home to be placed in **foster care**. As wards of the court, foster children are financially supported by the state.

About 460,000 children are in foster care in the United States. There would be more, but there are not enough foster parents or other facilities to fill current needs ("Foster Care" 2005; Wingett 2007). Seventy-one percent of foster care takes place in a licensed foster parent's home—47 percent with nonrelatives, and 24 percent with relatives. The remainder of children in foster care live in various arrangements, including group homes (6 percent) or institutional settings (10 percent), such as Nebraska's Boystown (which also accepts girls) (U.S. Department of Health and Human Services 2009a; www.boystown.org).

The mean age of children in foster care is 9.7 years. Children stay in foster care for an average of about two years, but 20 percent stay for only one to five months, and nearly 10 percent remain until age eighteen when they "age out." Although the rate of children in foster care is higher for African Americans than for other race/ethnic groups, the highest percentage of children in foster care are white (40 percent), followed by 31 percent for blacks, 20 percent of Hispanics, and 5 percent of mixed-race children (U.S. Department of Health and Human Services 2009a).

Very often without family support, those who "age out" of the system—for the most part, youths who were older upon becoming foster children and the developmentally neediest—face serious challenges as they work toward assuming adult roles (Osgood et al. 2005). They are more likely than other young adults to become imprisoned, homeless, unemployed, or pregnant outside marriage (Koch 2009). In 2009, Congress passed a bill encouraging states to extend foster care services until age twenty-one. According to this legislation, the federal monies pay for half of these services, with states and counties responsible for the remainder (Koch 2009). About half of the states extend Medicaid health insurance coverage beyond age eighteen for former foster children and/or offer them scholarships or free public college tuition.

Among others, motivations for becoming a foster parent include fulfilling religious principles, wanting to help fill the community's need for foster homes, enjoying children and hoping to help them, providing a companion for one's only child or for oneself, and earning money. Technically not salaried, foster parents are "reimbursed" in regular monthly stipends by the government.

Although the ultimate goal in half of the cases is reunification of foster children with their parents or principal caretakers, about one-quarter of foster children are available for adoption (U.S. Department of Health and Human Services 2009a). Some foster parents see fostering as a step toward adopting (Baum, Crase, and Crase 2001). We end with the words of Jo Ann Wentzel, senior editor of the magazine *Parenting Today's Teen* and foster mother to more than seventy-five children over the course of her career:

> I don't regret anything I've ever done for any of my [foster] kids. . . . Every once in a while, a kid will track me down and leave a cryptic message on my answering machine, which says, I know I was a pain-in-the-butt when I lived with you but I really learned a lot from you. . . . Or maybe they will tell me about their successes and claim it was because of something we did or said. They tell me they called because they wanted us to know they turned out good [sic] or because they respected our opinion on something. (Wentzel 2001, p. 2)

Critical Thinking

From the structure-functional perspective, discussed in Chapter 2, foster parents are functional alternatives to biological or adoptive parents. What are some ways, do you think, that the foster parent system is functional? What are some instances in which it could be dysfunctional?

with their parents while the majority had accepted the situation (Dolbin-MacNab and Keiley 2009).

The extent to which children benefit from a grandparent's intervention has just begun to be studied, and results are mixed (Dunifon and Kowaleski-Jones 2007). On the one hand, a grandparent's living in the home of a poor single mother is advantageous inasmuch as it adds income, from Social Security benefits, for example (Barnett 2008; Mutchier and Baker 2009). In addition, researchers and social workers generally maintain that grandparents provide stability, family cohesiveness, and solidarity while often enhancing young children's cognitive development (Dunifon and Kowaleski-Jones 2007; Spratling 2009). On the other hand, not all grandparents who are raising their grandchildren employ effective parenting practices (Barnett 2008). Grandmothers have been found to be most sensitive and beneficial to infants (Dunifon and Kowaleski-Jones 2007).

Research is also just beginning on the responses and feelings of adults who were raised by their grandparents. One study found that some adult children were grateful and felt a strong bond with their grandmothers whereas others evidenced distance and distrust (Dolbin-MacNab and Keiley 2009). Social service agencies have initiated educational and coping programs for grandfamilies (Dolbin-MacNab 2006; Ross and Aday 2006). The National Center on Grandfamilies promotes awareness of grandfamilies and gives advice on how to help grandparents meet their various needs (www.grandfamilies.org).

Parenting Young Adult Children

Children benefit from parents' emotional support throughout their twenties and after (Kantrowitz and Tyre 2006). As adolescents make the transition to adult roles, parent-child relations often grow closer and less conflicted (Arnett 20004, Chapter 3; Straus 2009).[17] At the same time, young adults may be angry or depressed over lingering childhood issues or difficulties with assuming adult roles (Arnett 2004; Galambos and Krahn 2008). Meanwhile, concerns over the young adult's sometimes faltering transition to adulthood can cause parental ambivalence and parent-child conflict (Hay, Fingerman, and Lefkowitz 2007).

Polls show that a significant majority of higher-SES parents lend or give their children money to repay student loans, buy a car, help with rent or credit card debt, or to put a down payment on a house (Harris 2008). One interesting study found that parents tend to provide money not only to their neediest but also to their most successful children, the latter in anticipation of help from the child as the parent grows older (Fingerman et al. 2009).

Recession, unemployment, and underemployment, along with a decline in affordable housing, make launching oneself into independent adulthood especially difficult today (Danziger and Rouse 2008, F8; Wadler 2009; Wang and Morin 2009). As one result, more and more young adult children either do not leave the family home, or return to it as "boomerangers" after college, divorce, or upon finding first jobs unsatisfactory (Bodnar 2007; Trumbull 2009). As reported in Chapter 8, more than half of men and almost half of women age eighteen through twenty-four live with one or both parents, and a significant fraction of older adults do too (U.S. Census Bureau 2009e, Table AD-1).

Parents should feel comfortable in setting reasonable household expectations. One way to do this is to negotiate a parent-adult child residence-sharing agreement (Wadler 2009). Following are some issues to negotiate:

1. How much money will the adult child be expected to contribute to the household? When will it be paid?
2. What benefits will the child receive?
3. Who will have authority over utility usage?
4. What are the standards for neatness?
5. Who is responsible for cleaning what and when?
6. Who is responsible for cooking what and when?
7. How will laundry tasks be divided?
8. What about noise levels?
9. What about guests? When are they welcome, and in what rooms of the house? Will the home be used for parties?
10. What are the expectations about informing other family members of one's whereabouts?
11. What will be the rules about using the personal possessions of others?
12. If the adult child has returned home with children, who is responsible for their care?

More detailed residence-sharing agreements are available on the Internet, some for salc (e.g., "Boomerang Kids Contract" 2009). Although a residence-sharing agreement can help temporarily, the goal of the majority of parents is for their adult children to move on. Accomplishing this may be complicated by differing ideas on just what a parent owes an adult child. Our culture offers few guidelines about when parental responsibility ends or how to withdraw it.

Toward Better Parenting

What are some steps that we can take to improve parenting in the United States? Studies show that optimal parenting involves the following factors:

- Supportive family communication (Leidy et al. 2009; Lindsey et al. 2009)
- Involvement in a child's life and school (Cooper, Crosnoe, Suizzo, and Pituch 2009)
- Private safety nets—that is, support from family and/or friends (Lee et al. 2009; Ryan, Kalil, and Leininger 2009)

[17] A possible exception involves offspring from non- or nominally religious families who in young adulthood embrace Orthodox Judaism or Christian or Muslim fundamentalism. In these cases, the children may be concerned that their parents lack appropriate religious fervor and/or—at least in the case of fundamentalist Christianity—may not be saved. Meanwhile, some parents can find their child's new fundamentalism "appalling" ("Religion's Generation Gap" 2007).

White Packert/Getty Images

Good parenting involves having adequate economic resources, being involved with the child, using supportive communication and having support from family and/or friends, along with workplace and broader social policies that bolster all families.

- Adequate economic resources (Guzzo and Lee 2008)
- Workplace policies that facilitate a healthy work-family balance and support parenting in other ways as well (Aber 2007; Bass et al. 2009)
- Safe and healthy neighborhoods that encourage positive parenting and school achievement (Dudley 2007)
- Society-wide policies that bolster all parents (Marshall and Tracy 2009)

Chapter 12 explores the first factor listed, supportive family communication. Here we note some existing programs designed to improve child rearing, and then discuss further ways to promote better parenting.

Over the past several decades, many national organizations have emerged to help parents. Some programs serve parents in general. One of these is Thomas Gordon's Parent Effectiveness Training (PET) (Gordon 2000). Another is Systematic Training for Effective Parenting (STEP) (Center for the Improvement of Child Caring n.d.). Both STEP and PET combine instruction on effective communication techniques with emotional support for parents. Some other parent education classes incorporate anger management training (Fetsch, Yang, and Pettit 2008). However, arguing that there remains a "fundamental lack of knowledge about infant cognitive skills and alternative strategies for dealing with troublesome behavior," advocates increased promotion of basic knowledge about child development (Coombs-Orme and Cain 2008).

Meanwhile, programs have been designed to improve parenting in specific situations. For example, a variety of intervention programs aim to help teenage and/or substance-abusing parents (Tolan, Szapocznik, and Sambrano 2007). Other programs have been developed for low-income parents and for grandparents (Dolbin-MacNab 2006; Ross and Aday 2006). Some curricula are designed for particular racial/ethnic groups (Center for the Improvement of Child Caring n.d.; Kumpfer and Tait 2000).

Moreover, there are programs intended to increase fathers' involvement, some fairly successful (Cowan et al. 2009; Fagan 2008; Hawkins et al. 2008). Because still more children could benefit from fathers' economic support and additional contact, policy makers advise further interventions that facilitate father involvement (Amato, Meyers, and Emery 2009; Teachman 2009).

In line with the family decline perspective, discussed in Chapters 1 and 7, some policy makers promote marriage as the most effective way to enhance father involvement. According to this perspective,

> [I]t is the institution of marriage that helps men to "sign on" to fatherhood. By choosing to make a legal, social and public commitment to a spouse, a man voluntarily agrees—often well ahead of the actual arrival of a child—to take on the legal and social role of a father. (Whitehead and Popenoe 2008, p. 18; see also Doherty 2008 and Gillmore et al. 2008)

From the family change perspective, on the other hand, there is need for "shifting the paradigm in support of multiple family forms" (Jones 2008, p. 208).

What are some ways that social policy could better support all parents, regardless of family structure? The stress model of effective parenting suggests that reducing parents' stress would improve parenting. Accordingly, "Improving the socioeconomic conditions of parents, particularly among the most vulnerable, might improve parenting outcomes across all relationship types" (Guzzo and Lee 2008, p. 58).

Moreover, because free time to engage in leisurely social interaction and activities is crucial to psychological well-being (Harter and Arora 2008), work and society-wide policies aimed at freeing up time for mothers and fathers would improve parenting. More concerted attention on the part of employers to parental child-raising needs and responsibilities would help, along with their greater recognition that good parenting is essential to a civil society.

Then too, elementary school administrators might schedule children's performances and parent-teacher conferences so that they are less likely to conflict with parents' work schedules (Barnett et al. 2009). And single parents in particular would benefit from more—and more affordable—day care services (Ornelas et al. 2009). Also, college regulations might be widened to better accommodate student parents. An example would be an institution's explicitly stating that exams can be made up in the case of a child's illness (Duquaine-Watson 2007).

We've seen that informal social support has been found to mitigate stress and hence to be related to more positive parenting (Lee et al. 2009; Ryan, Kalil, and Leininger 2009). But policy makers also urge greater civic and community activism on the part of parents (Dudley 2007; Whitehead and Popenoe 2008). Some parent-education programs include instruction on how to become more civically involved or engage in community activism (Doherty, Jacob, and Cutting 2009). "Pediatrics is politics," the late pediatrician Benjamin Spock once said (quoted in Maier 1998). He meant that good parenting involves working for better neighborhoods, communities, and family-centered social policies—and these, in turn, result in better parenting.

Summary

- Family form, gender, socioeconomic class, and race/ethnicity intersect to result in parenting experiences for individuals.
- The family ecology theoretical perspective reminds us that society-wide conditions influence the parent-child relationship, and these factors can place emotional and financial strains on parents.
- We began by considering reasons why parenting can be difficult today. We noted that work and parent roles often conflict.
- The stress model of effective parenting posits that stressors of various sorts lead to parental depression and household conflict, which in turn result in less positive parenting practices and ultimately in poorer child outcomes.
- Although more fathers are involved in child care today, mothers are the primary parent in the vast majority of cases and continue to do the majority of day-to-day child care.
- Not only mothers' but fathers' roles can be difficult, especially in a society like ours, in which attitudes have changed so rapidly and in which there is no consensus about how to raise children and how mothers and fathers should parent.
- Child psychologists prefer the authoritative parenting style, although some scholars describe the authoritarian/permissive/authoritative parenting style typology as ethnocentric or Eurocentric.
- The need for supportive—and socially supported—parenting transcends social class and race or ethnicity. At the same time, we have seen that parenting differs in some important ways, according to economic resources, social class, and whether parent and child suffer discrimination due to religion, racial/ethnic status, or sexual orientation of the parents. Raising children in lower socioeconomic strata is a very different experience from parenting in wealthier social classes.
- Higher-SES parents tend to follow the *concerted cultivation parenting model*, whereas working-class parents are more likely to adhere to the *facilitation of natural growth model*.
- Besides concerns for basic necessities, such as food, clothing, shelter, and health care, poverty-level parents may live in depressingly blighted neighborhoods.
- A trend over the past several decades has been for an increasing number of grandparents to serve as primary parents, often as a result of some crisis in the child's immediate family.
- More than 460,000 children are in foster care today, many of them in formal *kinship care*.
- To have better relationships with their children, parents are encouraged to accept help from others (friends and the community at large as well as professional caregivers), to build and maintain supportive family relationships (the subject matter for Chapter 12), and to engage in community or civic activism.

Questions for Review and Reflection

1. Describe reasons why parenting can be difficult today. Can you think of others besides those presented in this chapter?
2. Compare these three parenting styles: authoritarian, authoritative, and permissive. What are some empirical outcomes of each? Which one is recommended by most experts? Why?
3. How does parenting differ according to social class? Use the family ecology theoretical perspective to explain some of these differences.
4. What unique challenges do African American, Native American, Hispanic, and/or Asian American parents face today, regardless of their social class? How would *you* prepare an immigrant child or a child of color to face possible discrimination?
5. **Policy Question.** Describe some social policies that could benefit all low-income parents, regardless of their gender, race/ethnicity, or family structure.

Key Terms

authoritarian parenting style 263
authoritative parenting style (also known as positive parenting) 264
concerted cultivation 267
Confucian training doctrine 272
facilitation of natural growth parenting model 268
formal kinship care 274
foster care 275
grandfamilies 274
hierarchical parenting 272
hyperparenting 267
multipartnered fertility 255
permissive parenting style 264
private safety net 260
psychological control 264
psychological parent 258
race socialization 273
resilient 255
single mothers by choice 259
single mothers by circumstance 259
social fathers 261
socioeconomic status (SES) 266
stress model of parental effectiveness 256
transition to parenthood 256

Online Resources

Sociology CourseMate

www.CengageBrain.com

Access an integrated eBook, chapter-specific interactive learning tools, including flash cards, quizzes, videos, and more in your Sociology CourseMate, accessed through CengageBrain.com.

www.CengageBrain.com

Want to maximize your online study time? Take this easy-to-use study system's diagnostic pre-test, and it will create a personalized study plan for you. By helping you identify the topics that you need to understand better and then directing you to valuable online resources, it can speed up your chapter review. CengageNOW even provides a post-test so you can confirm that you are ready for an exam.

11

Work and Family

© Ariel Skelley/GettyImages/Taxi

Providing and caring for all family household members, including dependents and the elderly, is integral to our definition of families. Until recently, historically speaking, cooperative labor for survival was the dominant purpose of marriage. Women as well as men engaged in economically productive labor not limited to the personal care of family members.

"Where do you work?" is a new question in human history. Only since the Industrial Revolution has working been considered separate from family living, and only since then have the concepts "employed" and "unemployed" emerged. With the Industrial Revolution, economic production moved outside the household to factories, shops, and offices. Although human beings have always worked, it was not until the industrialization of the workplace in the nineteenth century that people characteristically became wage earners, hiring out their labor to someone else and joining a **labor force.**[1]

First men and then women have become workers in the labor force. How has that affected family life? In this chapter, we'll look at the interrelationship of work and family roles for both women and men. We'll look at paid employment and unpaid household work. We'll consider how people use their time to meet work and family responsibilities and consider whether time spent with children has been cut short. And we'll look at the strategies and choices partners use to manage their work and their family relations.

Women in the Labor Force

As the Industrial Revolution got under way, women by and large remained in the home, depending on social class, of course. Women of lower social classes, immigrant women, women of color, and widowed women often supported themselves and their families by taking in laundry, marketing baked goods, working as domestic labor in other people's homes, and housing boarders; before they married, they may have worked in factories. Still, it was largely men who held "jobs" and were visible in economic production.

Women's Entry into the Labor Force

As family size declined and especially as the need for clerical workers and light factory workers expanded, women began to enter the labor force. Industrialization gave rise to bureaucratic corporations, which depended heavily on paperwork. Clerical workers were needed, and not enough men were available. Textile industries sought workers with a dexterity thought to be possessed by women. The expanding economy needed more workers, and women were drawn into the labor force in significant numbers beginning around 1890. As Figure 11.1 shows, women's participation in the labor force has increased greatly since the beginning of the nineteenth century.

This trend accelerated during World War I, the Great Depression, and World War II, and then slowed following the war. As soldiers came home, the government encouraged women to return to their kitchens. Despite these cultural pressures, the number of wage-earning women rose again. Material expectations increased for housing and consumer goods, and families became more likely to think of college education for the kids.

Beginning in about 1960, the number of employed women began to increase rapidly. Stagnant and declining earnings for men and economic uncertainty for previously successful industries led more families to require a second earner. The growth in the divorce rate left women uncertain about the wisdom of remaining out of the labor force and, hence, dependent on a husband's earnings. The women's movement emerged and was a strong force for anti–sex discrimination laws that opened formerly male occupations to women. The movement also altered attitudes about careers for women. By 1979, a majority of married women were employed outside the home.

At first, the largest group of wage-earning women consisted of young unmarried women; relatively few women worked during child-rearing years. Although many mothers remained at home while children were small, by 1970, half of wives with children between ages six and seventeen earned wages, and that figure increased to 76.2 percent in 2007 (U.S. Census Bureau 2010b, Table 585; U.S. Bureau of Labor Statistics 2009c, Bulletin 2307).

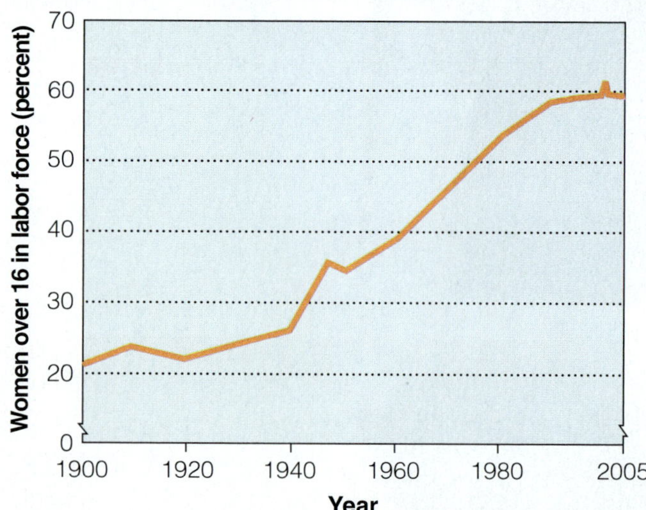

Figure 11.1 The participation of women over age sixteen in the labor force, 1900–2005

Source: Thornton and Freedman 1983; U.S. Census Bureau 1998, 2010b, Table 575.

[1] The term *labor force* refers to those people who are employed or who are looking for a paid job.

Keith Brofsky/Jupiterimages

Women have entered the labor force in greater and greater numbers since the 1960s.

Mothers of young children were the last women to move into employment outside the home. In 2007, 61.5 percent of wives with children under age six were paid employees. In fact, 57.8 percent of married mothers of children under age one had joined the labor force. Even larger proportions of single women were employed: 78 percent of those with children age six to seventeen, and 67.4 percent of those with children under six (U.S. Census Bureau 2010b, Tables 585, 586).

The *rate* of increase in employment has been greater for white women than black women, who historically had been more likely to work for wages (England, Garcia-Beaulieu, and Ross 2004). Now, white women—with a labor force participation rate of 59.2 percent—are catching up to black women at 61.3 percent. Fifty-nine percent of Asian women and 56.2 percent of Hispanic women are employed (U.S. Census Bureau 2010b, Table 575). Attitudes changed along with behavior. By the late 1990s, fewer than 20 percent of women and men disapproved of married women working (Sayer, Cohen, and Casper 2004, Table 1). Urban and rural women carry a particularly heavy burden, as both types of communities have been hit tremendously hard by the long-term changes in the American economy. Nearly "one in five rural married women contribute the majority of the couple's earnings, representing a 56 percent increase since 1970. The proportion of urban married women as primary and sole breadwinners increased by 65 percent over the same time period" (Smith 2008, p. 23).

Women's Occupations

When women are in the labor force and work for pay (sometimes termed "market work"), what kinds of jobs do they hold? Occupational distribution of women differs from that of men, as Figure 11.2 indicates.

The pronounced tendency for men and women to be employed in different types of jobs is termed **occupational segregation**. Figure 11.2 depicts the major occupational categories of employed women for 2008. As you can see, 24.5 percent of all employed women were office or sales workers. Only 15.2 percent of employed women were in management, business, or finance positions, whereas 21.1 percent were in professional work (U.S. Bureau of Labor Statistics 2009c, Table 10). Asian American (46 percent) and white women (40.6 percent) were the most likely to hold managerial or professional jobs, compared to black (31.3 percent) and

© James Marshall/The Image Works

Women in blue-collar jobs are still a minority, although more women are entering these jobs, which tend to pay better than traditional women's jobs in service or clerical work.

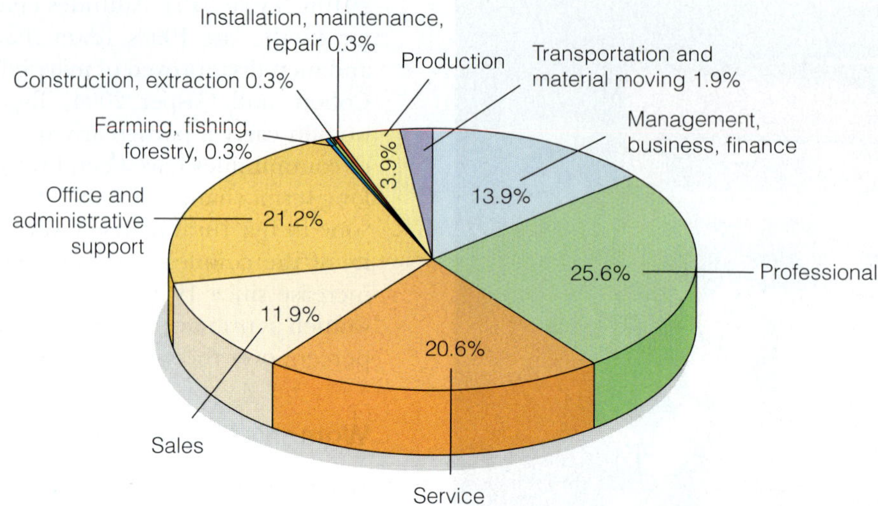

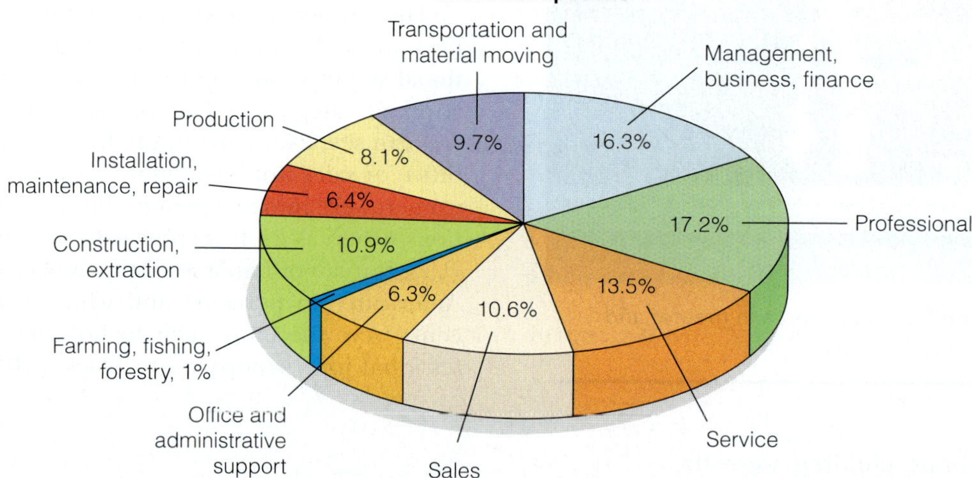

Figure 11.2 The jobs held by women and men, 2005. The percentages in each sector of the pie charts tell us what percentages of women and what percentages of men hold certain jobs. For example, 25 percent of women have professional employment whereas 20 percent are in service occupations. Seventeen percent of men are in professional jobs, whereas 13 percent are service workers.

[a] Percentages may not add to 100 percent due to rounding.

Source: U.S. Bureau of Labor Statistics 2009c. *Women in the Labor Force: A Databook,* Table 10.

Hispanic women (23.5 percent) (U.S. Bureau of Labor Statistics 2009c, Table 12).

Jobs typically held by men and women differ *within* major occupational categories, with men more likely to hold the upper-level jobs within each sector. Even though women are proportionately more likely to be professionals than men, they occupy the lower-paying ranks. For example, women are 27.2 percent of the country's dentists, but 96.3 percent of the dental assistants; 34.4 percent of lawyers, but 87.7 percent of paralegals and legal assistants; 30.5 percent of physicians, but 91.7 percent of registered nurses (U.S. Bureau of Labor Statistics 2009c, Table 11). This occupational segregation contributes to the difference between men's and women's average earnings.

The Wage Gap

Differences in earnings persist in comparisons of employed women and men. Women who worked full time in 2008 earned eighty-eight cents for every dollar men earned (U.S. Bureau of Labor Statistics 2009c, Table 16). The **wage gap** (the difference in earnings between men and women) varies considerably depending on occupation and tends to be greater in the more elite, higher-paying occupations (Weinberg 2004). For instance, the starkest difference in pay occurs in the highest-paying occupation, that of physician. In this occupation in 2008, women on average earned $95,766 or just 60.8 percent of men's earnings ($157,510) (Cheeseman and Rosenthal 2008, Table B). The difference was thought to be related to choice of occupational specialty and practice setting (for example, pediatrics, which pays less, is a popular choice of female physicians); however, U.S. Census researchers Cheeseman and Downs (2007) show that the problem is endemic throughout all occupations. For example, males who enter the nursing profession make higher wages than women who work in the same profession. To some extent, men's and women's employment remains segmented into dual labor markets, with women in a narrower range of jobs offering fewer benefits and advancement opportunities.

Men continue to dominate corporate America. In 2010, less than 3 percent of the highest-earning executives in Fortune 500 companies were women ("Women CEOs" 2010). Although racism blocks the path to management for nonwhite or Hispanic men, both racism and sexism block the path for nonwhite and Hispanic women, who hold only two executive positions and who make up 3.2 percent of the boards of directors positions in the top 500 American corporations (Angelo 2010; Soares, Carter, and Combopiano 2009). In 2010, only one (and the first) African American woman held a CEO position in the *Fortune 500* list of top companies (Angelo 2010).

Occupational segregation (that is, differentiation in jobs of men and women) declined from 1960 to 1990, at all levels of the occupational range. The decline was most pronounced for the college-educated. "But it is also clear that men and women continue to occupy separate spheres in the world of work. It is also clear that the pace of change has slowed" (Cotter, Hermsen, and Vanneman 2004, pp. 13–14). Another important point is the growing divide among women (and men) who have or do not have a college education. Increasingly, the earnings of less-educated men and women, especially men, are falling behind those of more highly educated individuals (Wessel 2010).

Whether the wage gap is due to discrimination or represents men's and women's differing job choices (some of which are impacted by family obligations) is disputed (Boraas and Rodgers 2003, p. 14). Do women's family responsibilities lower their career achievement, and, if so, is the pay gap a result of personal choice? We have discussed the wage gap more generally in Chapter 4. Here, we focus on the relationship between lesser earnings and women's motherhood role.

The concept of the **motherhood penalty** describes the fact that motherhood has a tremendous negative lifetime impact on earnings, a long-term gender-earnings gap. "Women still earn a small proportion of what men earn [over a lifetime] . . . and remain financially dependent on men for income during the child-rearing years and indeed throughout much of their adult lives" (Hartmann, Rose, and Lovell 2009, p. 125). Furthermore, the motherhood penalty has not declined over time despite women's increasing education, involvement in the labor force, somewhat less discrimination, and more opportunities to advance their careers (National Women's Law Center 2010; Goodman 2009; Hegewisch and Liepmann 2010).

A study conducted by the National Women's Law Center (NWLC) found that women were simply paid less than men for the same amount and kind of work. This accounted for much of the difference between the earnings of women and men. Married mothers work approximately one hour less per day in the labor market than married fathers; although this impacts the wages of married mothers, it is not enough to explain the differences between all women's and all men's pay (U.S. Bureau of Labor Statistics 2008). Citing the 2003 U.S. General Accounting Office research on the gender gap, the NWLC found that when factors such as "marital status, race, number and age of children, and income, as well as work patterns such as years of work, hours worked, and job tenure" are controlled for, women make 80 percent of what men do (National Women's Law Center 2010, p. 3). A recent class-action lawsuit against Wal-Mart exemplifies this pattern at the lower end of the pay scale. In 2010, Wal-Mart Corporation settled the largest sex-discrimination lawsuit in history when it agreed to pay damages in the amount of $86 million to over 200,000 female employees in California for paying them less than it paid its male employees (Stempel 2010). Things appear even worse for women at the higher end of the pay scale. Here, women are paid even less than their male counterparts, averaging seventy-five cents to every dollar earned by a man. For example, female CEOs make on average $1,500 per week whereas their male counterparts average $2,000 weekly (Censky 2010).

The Great Recession was impacting the global economy at the time of this writing. Regardless of whether or not the economic outlook has improved between then and now, both women and men will see long-term impacts on job and income prospects. Many commentators examining the Great Recession offer an additional, tongue-in-cheek term for the current economic woes: mancession (a merging of the words man and *recession*). The reason for this is because the hardest hit in this most recent economic downturn have been men—particularly the lesser educated, those who are poorer, and men of color (Elsby, Hobjin, and Şahin 2010; Hartmann, English, and Hayes 2010; Wessel 2010). At the same time, however, women's participation in the labor force continues to increase. Although 75 percent of those unemployed in 2008 were men, women compose an ever larger share of the employed, increasing from 46.4 percent at the end of 2007 to nearly half (47.4 percent) in December 2009 (Borbely 2009; Hartmann, English, and Hayes 2010; Taylor et al. 2010, p. 2). This has important ramifications for familial relationships—especially around the division of labor where women typically bear the majority of child care and domestic duties.

Opting Out, Stay-at-Home Moms, and Neotraditional Families

"The housewife" has vanished, more or less. That would be a woman who views her adult role as one devoted to the home, while she remains economically dependent on the earnings of her husband, the breadwinner. Today, though, 67.7 percent of women with children under eighteen are in the labor force, as are 69.4 percent of married mothers (U.S. Census Bureau 2010b, Table 586; U.S. Bureau of Labor Statistics 2009c, Table 6). Are there no traces left of the housewife?

The movement of women into the labor force has dropped a percentage point or so from its 2000 peak (see Figure 11.1), but some of this may be due to the changing demographics of the American population, rather than a retreat back into the house. The percentage of mothers who return to work within the year after a birth has dropped slightly from a 1998 peak of 59 percent to 57.3 in 2006 (Dye 2008, Figure 3), but has remained relatively steady over the years. These data suggest that workingwomen generally continue to do so, even after giving birth to a child. As has been discussed previously, and later in this chapter, economic trends in the United States are such that mothers will have increasing pressure to enter or remain in the labor force.

In 2009, 22 percent of married women with children under fifteen were "stay-at-home" mothers, while 7 percent of fathers were. These parents gave "to care for home and family" as their reason for not participating in the labor force. Each of these "stay-at-home" mothers and fathers had employed husbands or wives who worked fifty-two weeks in the last year (U.S. Census Bureau 2009e, Table SHP-1).

We don't know from these bare-bones data whether these mothers (and fathers) plan to remain out of the labor force, having made a commitment to being a full-time parent, or whether they plan to return to work. We also don't know what their occupations are, although highly educated mothers and those with higher-level occupations are more likely to be employed, and they return to the labor force more quickly after giving birth (Johnson and Downs 2005). The long view of the American economy is such that the trend of stay-at-home fathers may actually increase, whereas many mothers are likely to become the new family breadwinners (Belkin 2009). Research from the United States Federal Reserve shows that males in the United States bear the largest brunt of unemployment. Since 1980, following each recession, men have lost ground by an average of 1.2 percent, whereas women have lost an average of .73 percent. This kind of chronic job loss suggests that American males will increasingly have difficulty finding and keeping their jobs (Elsby, Hobijn, and Şahin 2010, Table 1).

Opting Out Opting out was conceived of in more limited terms than a complete withdrawal from the labor force, as the young women interviewed or informally surveyed spoke of part-time jobs or leaving the labor force for a few years. Little evidence exists that substantial "**opting out**" has in fact occurred (see Gerson 2010, p. 240, note 21 for additional sources). Economist Heather Boushey of the Center for Economic and Policy Research (2005a; 2006) suggests, based on her analysis, that a weak labor market since 2001 had led to a very slight downturn in labor force participation for both women and men, whereas labor force participation of single women and of high school dropouts continued to grow (Porter 2006). Since 2001, we have seen a trend in which women are becoming the majority of workers in the American labor market (Belkin 2009, p. O11).

A look at the choices of more affluent women, such as graduates of elite universities, found that these women also did not leave the workforce after having children, at least not for very long—58 percent were never out of the job market for more than six months, and on average, the women spent 1.6 years out of the labor force. Most were married and had children (Goldin 2006). For example, interviews with African American women lawyers, technology experts, corporate managers, and entrepreneurs indicate that they are concerned about the need to build financial security for their families and, often, the need to help extended-family members. "Among highly educated women aged 25 to 45, the effect of having children on women's labor force participation has been negligible since 1984, and remains so today" (Boushey 2006). In fact, the job losses felt by men during the current economic downturn has many highly educated and affluent mothers returning to the labor force, many of them sooner than they had intended (Greenhouse 2009; Belkin 2009). Moreover, some companies are beginning to develop reentry programs for women who have taken time out of the labor force (Joyce 2007b; McGinn 2006a).

Stay-at-Home Moms In 2009, 26 percent of mothers of children under fifteen in married-couple families were stay-at-home mothers, wives of steadily employed men who remained out of the labor force for the entire year, giving as their reason "taking care of home and family" (U.S. Census Bureau 2009e, Table SHP-1; Jayson 2009). These data give no indication of whether this arrangement is temporary or permanent. Given that most women leave the labor force for relatively short periods over a lifetime, "stay-at-home mom" is a status that is temporary for the majority of women. But what would women prefer? The Gallup Poll has been asking that question for many years. In 1978, a decisive majority favoring employment over the traditional homemaker role of women appeared in poll data for the first time. "Since then, no clear consensus in either direction has emerged, with small majorities of women sometimes opting for working outside the home and, . . . [at other times] small majorities favoring the traditional role of family caretaker" (Moore 2005). In 2007, the poll showed that a slight majority of American women preferred paid employment over the traditional role of family caretaker (Saad 2007).

Neotraditional Families There are families, termed **neotraditional families** (Wilcox 2004, pp. 209–11), for whom a traditional division of labor is the ideal:

> This [neotraditional] order is appealing to men and women who are discontented with . . . family modernization, the lack of clarity in gender roles . . . , and the pressures associated with combining two full-time careers. It is also appealing to women who continue to identify with the domestic sphere, who wish to see homemaking and nurturing accorded high value, and who wish to have husbands who share their commitment to family life. . . . Men who continue to seek status as domestic patriarchs who have the primary earning responsibility and at least titular authority over their families are also attracted to this order. (Wilcox 2004, p. 209)

Wilcox associates this family model with evangelical Christianity, as well as Orthodox Judaism, traditional Catholicism, and Mormonism; and suggests it is most likely to be found in the middle and working classes of the outer suburbs and in rural areas (Wilcox 2004, p. 210). Kathleen Gerson, interestingly, finds a heightened sense of egalitarianism coming from men and women who were raised in neotraditionalist families. She finds that although terms such as *equality* and *egalitarian* are elusive concepts to define, nonetheless these men and women are hoping "to find a lifelong partner, to balance work and family, and to share breadwinning and caretaking" (2010, p. 107).

Wilcox found active conservative Protestants more likely than mainline Protestants to agree that men should be breadwinners and women homemakers. Interestingly, all groups showed a decline in this viewpoint from the 1970s to the 1990s, though "active conservative Protestants" remain at almost 60 percent support for this model (Wilcox 2004, Figure 3.3). It stands to reason that economic pressures force many neotraditional women into the labor force, though they are likely to organize that work as much as possible around part-time or in-home work, or take substantial time out of the labor force when children are small (Eikhof, Warhurst, and Haunschild 2007; Cordes 2009).

Noah Berger/The New York Times/Redux

Some women have chosen to opt out of the labor force to raise their children at home. This former executive may return to the labor force eventually.

Men's Occupations

The work situations of men are many and varied as Figure 11.2 shows us. For example, many of the blue-collar jobs that paid good wages to earlier generations of men have vanished, and men without college degrees have experienced eroding incomes. "'In the past guys could drop out of school after finishing high school, or even without finishing, and go into a factory and get a steady job with benefits. ... But there has been a deterioration in young men's economic position'" (sociologist Valerie Oppenheimer, quoted in Porter and O'Donnell 2006). Between 1979 and 2003, there was no gain for those with some college but no degree, while high school grads' earnings declined 8 percent (Mincy 2006; Wessel 2010). Hartmann, English, and Hayes (2010) research suggests this trend continues. For example, men without a high school degree in 2009 have a 7.8 percent unemployment rate, whereas men with college degrees have a 2.6 percent unemployment rate (Hartmann, English, and Hayes 2010, p. 33). As discussed elsewhere in this book, the unemployment rates are even higher for men of color.

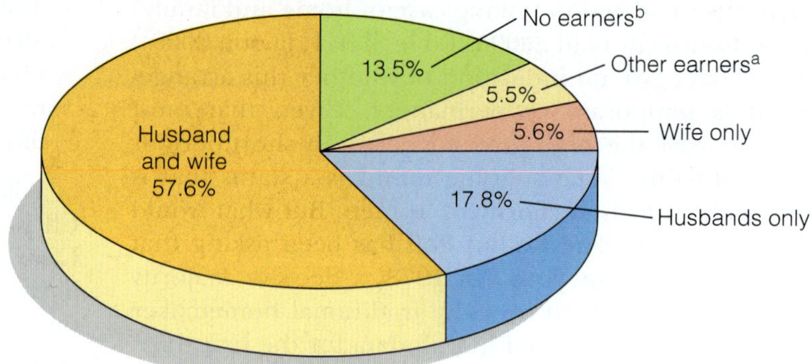

Figure 11.3 Married-couple families by number and relationship of earners, 2007

Source: U.S. Bureau of Labor Statistics 2006d, Table 23.

[a] Includes husband and other family member(s); wife and other family member(s); other earners, neither husband nor wife.

[b] The spouses may be unemployed, retired, disabled, institutionalized, or imprisoned. (The term *unemployed* refers to people who are in the labor force and are looking for work but who presently have no job.)

Yet, the provider role is an important one for men of all social classes. What is the present state of the provider?

The Provider Role

What sociologist Jessie Bernard terms the **good provider role** for men emerged in this country during the 1830s. Before then, a man was expected to be "a good steady worker," but "the idea that he was *the* provider would hardly ring true" (Bernard 1986, p. 126), because in a farm economy both husband and wife had roles in producing the family's income. The provider role (and its counterpart, the housewife role) lasted into the late 1970s. The proportion of married-couple families in which only the husband worked gradually declined from 42 percent in 1960 to 17.8 percent in 2007 (Wilkie 1991; U.S. Bureau of Labor Statistics 2009c, Table 23; and see Figure 11.3).

As Figure 11.3 indicates, in the vast majority (57.6 percent) of married couples, both husband and wife are now employed. In 5.6 percent of married couples, only the wife is employed. Although the role of family wage earner is no longer reserved for husbands, many Americans still believe that the man should be the principal provider for his family, and it works out that way in practice to some degree.

Overall, whether single or married, parent or not, men work more hours than women and are more likely (89.5 percent) to work full time than are women (75.4 percent). Employed wives contribute over a third (36 percent) of a family's income (U.S. Bureau of Labor Statistics 2009c, Tables 20, 24). Men continue to be primary breadwinners in the majority of couples, and most men (in all racial/ethnic groups) identify with this role (Coltrane 2000).

> [S]ocietal notions of the meaning of work for men and women are still quite distinctive. Both men and women may view working as a choice for women, even when the woman has no real alternative to being employed. In contrast, there is a strong societal imperative for men to be employed outside the home, and those who choose not to do so are viewed skeptically. (Taylor, Tucker, and Mitchell-Kernan 1999, p. 756)

In fact, men's success—as measured in terms of employment and higher earnings—still seems to be important in "facilitating marriage and enhancing marital stability" (Bianchi and Casper 2000, p. 31). Although social pressure may push men to view their lives through the lens of job status and earnings, Kathleen Gerson notes that, "when fathers found themselves doing all of the breadwinning despite a preference for sharing [domestic duties], their ambivalence spilled into daily domestic life" (2010, p. 78).

It is also difficult to live up to societal expectations that may not mesh with the reality of economic opportunities. This situation is especially applicable to blue-collar and racial/ethnic minority husbands in the twenty-first-century economy where "basic economic shifts ... leave men with shrinking opportunities for secure, well-paid, and unionized work" (Gerson 2010, p. 203). Moreover, husbands who want to share household work and child care will not find it easy to do so while continuing as the primary breadwinner (Cordes 2009). For this reason, partners who want to create new options for themselves need to work for changes in the public and corporate spheres, an option explored later in this chapter.

Some husbands today are rejecting the idea that dedication to one's job or occupational achievement is the ultimate indicator of success; in fact, 73 percent of men say they want a job or career that is fulfilling (*Time Opinion Poll on Gender* 2009). Some are choosing less-competitive careers and are spending more time with their families. Four-fifths of men age twenty through thirty-nine who were interviewed in 2000 rated a work schedule that would give them more family time as a more desirable job quality than challenging work or high income. Seventy percent of these younger men said they would exchange money for time with their families—compared to 26 percent of men over sixty-five. This suggests an important generational change, and one that might be happening because a substantial majority of the younger men (70 percent) had working mothers (Grimsley 2000). In a recent poll, nearly half of American men said that companies should provide more flexible work schedules to both men and women (Halpin and Teixeira 2009, p. 412 Table 3). Surprisingly, even during an economic recession, a Harris poll shows that 37 percent of fathers with children under the age of eighteen would leave their job if their significant other made enough to support the family, and 38 percent would accept less pay in exchange for more time to spend with their children (Careerbuilder.com 2007). Although this is down from the previously referenced 2000 poll, it shows a significant level of dissatisfaction with the *work–life*[2] balance for men, even in the face of economic insecurity.

Meanwhile, there is an effort on the part of some social scientists (e.g., Christiansen and Palkovitz 2001) to change the *meaning* of the standard male provider role so that it is seen to be as much a form of family work and fathering as "hands-on" parenting. Men with children work increased hours compared to childless men, on average.

Anthropologist Nicholas Townsend (2002) interviewed thirty-nine men who graduated from the same northern California high school in the 1970s; thirty were non-Hispanic white, six were Hispanic, and three were Asian American. Regardless of ethnicity, the men described their lives and goals in terms of "the package deal," which was composed of marriage, children, home ownership, and a steady job. Work was seen to be part of being a good father: "Everybody has a purpose in life. It's the same basic, mundane thing. You get up, you go to work, you come home. Your purpose is to provide for your family" (Skip, quoted in Townsend 2002, p. 117). Although these men desired to spend more time with their children and thought that important, in reality their time was devoted to paid work—many had two jobs or put in extensive overtime.

Still, it appears that there are two distinct models for the father-as-provider role. Some fathers (*good providers*) work *more* hours than childless men, whereas others (*involved fathers*) work *fewer* hours. A man's ideological commitment to one or the other role makes a difference.

[2] Work–life balance is the attempt men and women make to balance their work (the demands of job/career) and life (family, leisure, personal activities) in such a way as to find enjoyment and satisfaction in both.

© David Sacks/Jupiterimages

© Bill Aron/PhotoEdit

Many men today expect to work at home doing child care or domestic work, as well as to hold a job.

And "it seems clear that a shift away from the provider role and toward the involved father role [has occurred] in recent years" (Kaufman and Uhlenberg 2000, p. 934). Thus, some fathers try to decrease the demands of the workplace in order to participate more at home.

Why Do Men Leave the Labor Force?

Men may relinquish employment as a positive choice: the desire to spend more time with their children. But they may also not be employed because of poor health or disability, or their loss of a job may have developed into long-term unemployment.

Men may be dissatisfied with the competitive grind or the nature of their work, and find themselves in a situation—a working wife who earns enough to support the family or an early retirement package—that permits them to seek new options (J. Smith 2009; Tyre and McGinn 2003). Some couples may size up the situation and recognize that the woman is more desirous of pursuing a career, or has a higher-earning career, and/or is more successful than the man, and they can decide as a couple to reverse roles. In nearly 26 percent of couples, wives earn more than their husbands (U.S. Bureau of Labor Statistics 2009c, Table 25). For a variety of reasons, including the demise of secure employment at all economic levels, labor force participation rates have fallen for men (Krueger 2004).

Although they are a small minority, some men have relinquished breadwinning to become **househusbands**: men who stay home to care for the house and family while their wives work. About 158,000 fathers with children under fifteen remained out of the labor force for that purpose in 2009 (U.S. Census Bureau 2010c, Table FG8). The Census Bureau only considers those whose wives worked full time as **stay-at-home dads.** Although few men—0.4 percent—are stay-at-home dads by this definition (Fields 2004, Table 5), some 20 percent of fathers of preschool children whose mothers were employed were principle caregivers. This number, however, fluctuates between the regular school year and the summer months, as well as by income level (J. Johnson 2005, Table 2; Laughlin and Rukus 2009, slide 21).

In 26 percent of gay male couples with children, one parent often stays at home: "To some gay men, the idea of entrusting the care of a hard-won child to someone else seems to defeat the purpose of parenthood" (Bellafante 2004). These couples will, of course, have a male earner, which underscores the fact that the options for men who would like to give more time to their families are limited because men in our society typically earn more than women do. Consequently, whatever their preferences, many heterosexual couples find themselves needing to encourage the man's dedication to his job or career in the interests of the family's overall financial well-being (Lewin 2009; Smith 2009).

Although fathers who are primary parents express more sense of isolation than stay-at-home mothers and may experience the loss of a career-based identity, being a househusband is not the lonely choice it once was. Local groups, national organizations, and Internet chat rooms bring househusbands together, and mothers at home are more welcoming of their male counterparts than they used to be.

As with many aspects of family life, choice is the key to a man's satisfaction with the househusband role, as is mutual understanding by the couple about the specifics of their division of labor (Cordes 2009; Gerson 2010; Lewin 2009; Smith 2009; Tyre 2009).

Two-Earner Marriages—Work/Family Options

As recently as 1968, there were equal proportions of dual-earner and provider–housewife couples: 45 percent of each (Hayghe 1982). Today, **two-earner marriages**, in which both partners are in the labor force, are the statistical norm among married couples.

Even though we may tend to think of two-earner couples as ones in which both partners are employed nine to five, spouses display considerable flexibility in how they design their two-earner unions. (Households headed by single parents, of course, have more constraints on their choices.) These arrangements are ever-changing and flexible, varying with the arrival and ages of children and with both spouses' job opportunities and working conditions, and involving experimentation with different solutions for managing work and family commitments.

Although these work–family arrangements are fluid, we have observed certain patterns. In this section, we examine some ways in which couples choose to structure their work commitments and family life: the two-career marriage, part-time employment, shift work, working at home, and temporarily leaving the labor force.

Two-Career Marriages

Careers differ from *jobs* in that they hold the promise of advancement, are considered important in themselves—not just a source of money—and demand a high degree of commitment. Career men and women work in occupations that usually require education beyond the bachelor's degree, such as medicine, law, academia, financial services, and corporation management.[3]

[3] Higher-income men tend to be married to higher-income women, as the tendency to marry homogamously (see Chapter 6) would suggest. One effect of the trend toward dual-earner families is increasing inequality between families with two high-status, high-paying careers and those with two poorly paid jobs (Paul 2006; Schwartz and Mare 2005). Families depending on one woman's income fare even worse.

Some dual-earner couples choose to work together in a joint business.

The vast majority of two-earner marriages would not be classified as *dual career* because the wife's or the husband's employment does not have the features of a *career*. Nevertheless, the dual-career couple is a powerful image. Most of today's college students view the **two-career marriage** as an available and workable option.

For two-career couples with children, family life can be hectic, as partners juggle schedules, chores, and child care. Career wives, in particular, often find themselves in a paradoxical situation. The career world tends to view the person who splits time between work and family as less than professional, yet society encourages working women to do exactly that (Hochschild 1997). Two-career families often outsource domestic work and are likely to employ an in-home caregiver, a **nanny.**

Part-Time Employment

A little over 25 percent of women worked part-time in 2008 (compared to 10.5 percent of men; U.S. Bureau of Labor Statistics 2009c, Table 20). Mothers try to scale back their employment while children are preschoolers (children under six years old); however, only 6.3 percent of mothers with preschool-aged children were unemployed in 2008. By the time a child is nine months old, nearly 60 percent of all mothers are back at work—the majority working full-time, with only 22 percent of these mothers working only part-time (Han et al. 2008, p. 17).

Greater family and personal time is a clear benefit of part-time employment, but there are costs. As it exists now, part-time work seldom offers job security or benefits such as health insurance. And part-time pay is rarely proportionate to that of full-time jobs. For example, a part-time teacher or secretary usually earns well below the wage paid to regular staff. In higher-level professional/managerial jobs, a different problem appears. To work "part-time" as an attorney, accountant, or aspiring manager is to forgo the salary, status, and security of a full-time position and still to put in forty hours a week.

Shift Work

Sometimes one or both spouses engage in **shift work**, defined by the Bureau of Labor Statistics as any work schedule in which more than half an employee's hours

A San Francisco choreographer goes back to work, taking her new baby to a ballet rehearsal—another way to combine work and family.

A Closer Look at Family Diversity

Diversity and Child Care

Extreme Child-Care Maneuvers

By Sue Shellenbarger for *The Wall Street Journal* May 20, 2009

It was a hand-off reminiscent of a spy movie.

Rushing from a client meeting earlier this month, advertising consultant Ted Villa wheeled his Jetta into an office-building parking lot, whipped out his cellphone and reported his location to his business partner and wife, Nancy Snow Villa. Moments later, Ms. Villa piloted their SUV into a nearby spot, their three small children riding in back. After a brief bathroom break inside the building for the kids, Mr. Villa hopped into the SUV and drove away with the children. Leaving the Jetta where he parked it, Ms. Villa raced into the building for her own client meeting.

Ted Villa and Nancy Snow Villa swap work and child-care duties throughout the day in order to spend as much time with their three children as possible.

Time elapsed: less than 10 minutes. Money spent on child-care help: zero.

In a shift that is speeding a change in marital roles, the complex dance of the dual-earner couple is escalating to new extremes. Forced by the recession to cut costs while snapping up every opportunity to work, husbands and wives are swapping roles and bending work schedules at levels never seen before. Layoff victims are squeezing in freelance work amid family duties. Couples are coordinating their calendars down to the minute.

This new marital choreography in some ways "is a throwback to the kind of family that prevailed for most of the 20th century," when families tended to do everything for themselves without hiring child care or housekeeping help, says Stephanie Coontz, an author on the history of marriage and research director of the Council on Contemporary Families, Chicago. In other ways, the trend is historically unprecedented—accelerating a move toward more equitable sharing of responsibility and power between husbands and wives. "We're moving into uncharted territory here," Ms. Coontz says. "It would be a fascinating social experiment—if it weren't so painful."

Marriage expert Thomas Bradbury likens the pressures to the treadmill stress tests used to screen cardiac patients.

"Some couples will pass the test, a few will not," says Dr. Bradbury, a psychology professor and co-director of the Relationship Institute at the University of California, Los Angeles. Healthy marriages will grow stronger, but the hardships will bring others' weaknesses "into sharp relief," requiring mindful effort to survive.

Some scenes from the new dual-earner two-step:

Tag-team parents: The Villas started exUrban, a marketing and advertising concern, after he was laid off late last year. To hold down child-care costs and spend as much time as possible with Jane, age 5; Sam, 3; and Ben, 7 months, the Needham, Mass., couple swap roles throughout the day. They plan client meetings week-by-week to avoid conflicts, then fit writing, creative work and planning "in the gaps" between appointments, time with the children and housework, calling only occasionally on sitters or family members for help, Ms. Villa says.

On the day of the parking-lot hand-off, "Ted had meetings all morning. I had meetings all afternoon, and the kids needed to be picked up at noon" at the Montessori school, where they're all enrolled, she says. She picked them up, Mr. Villa met her at her client's office, and he took over family duties from there. "Some of our colleagues say, 'How sustainable is this?'" Ms. Villa says. But for now, she adds, it's what both she and her husband want.

With extensive planning, the Villas find time for family and work.

The tag-team act gets tougher for people who lack control over their work hours. Sabrina Holmes, mother of a 2-year-old son, can't afford to pay for his $700-a-month child-care center with the office jobs she is able to get.

The Green Valley, Ill., mother stopped using paid child care and found flexible work at home instead, as a call-center agent for LiveOps.com. Ms. Holmes has begun splicing her work in every waking hour her husband is home to help with their son.

The downside: Randy, her steelworker husband, works rotating shifts, moving from daytime to evening to graveyard hours every few weeks. That

are before 8 a.m. or after 4 p.m. It has been estimated that in one-quarter of all two-earner couples, at least one spouse does shift work; one in three if they have children (Presser 2000). Some spouses use shift work for higher wages or to ease child care arrangements. In 2004 (the most recent data available), 17.7 percent of all workers worked in shift work, with men making up the preponderance of shift workers (19.1 percent), while 16.1 percent of women worked in shift work. Fathers tend to work more weekend days than mothers (McMenamin 2007, pp. 9, 11).

"Tag team" and "split shift" are just a couple of colloquial terms used for dual-income earners who do shift work, as well as single parents who juggle multiple friend and family child care resources in a given day (Gornick, Presser, and Batzdorf 2009). The terms represent the clockwork timing necessary to exchange childcare duties from one working parent to the other one or more times a day. These kinds of handoffs are typically scheduled weeks in advance and are more often used by parents who have some control over their work schedules. For example, one parent drives to a means Ms. Holmes's workday moves too, interspersed with the naps and meals of her rambunctious son.

Not surprisingly, she sometimes finds it hard to "keep my eyes open," Ms. Holmes says. Also, "you kind of give up your free time with each other." On many days, "when my husband gets home from work, I go in my office, shut the door and that's it," she says. Meanwhile, her husband is doing more laundry, cleaning and yardwork. The result: Both of them are "getting spread pretty thin."

Dueling dockets: Melissa and Joel Selcher, both managers in high-pressure jobs, want to make sure at least one of them is available at all times in case one of their children, Lily, 9 months, or Jackson, 3, needs to be picked up at their child-care center. They also want to stay on top of their jobs amid layoffs and the recent acquisition of Mr. Selcher's company.

To coordinate their calendars, they've developed "a complex bartering system," Ms. Selcher says.

At the beginning of each month, the Burlingame, Calif., couple send each other meeting lists, then decide which commitments take precedence. One partner's meeting with an executive vice president beats out the other's meeting with a vice president.

If one spouse is making a presentation or running a meeting, "that person gets trump power," Ms. Selcher says. And each has the power of the veto; "we don't accept or agree" to a new meeting "unless we check with the other one," she says. They also have developed an emergency-alert code for getting in touch: If one partner rings the other's cellphone three times without leaving a message, that means "step out of your meeting and call me," she says. They used it recently when Jackson threw up at day care and had to be picked up midday.

Ms. Selcher acknowledges that the carefully orchestrated system "feels like a constant juggle." But for them, it works. "We're trying to make the right call for both of us," she says. "It's not just what's best for me or what's best for him, but what's best for the whole family unit."

Pooling assets: Eva Silva Travers, a Studio City, Calif., mother of two, and her husband, Joe Travers, were accustomed to separate checking accounts when they married, and kept them that way for a while. But now, coping with her layoff last October as a creative-department manager, and his reduced income as a touring musician, they've pooled their assets for the first time in a joint account.

"It's easier and less stressful to pay the bills out of joint money," she says. "Not having those little nickel-and-diming conversations is such a stress reliever."

She also has begun tracking Mr. Travers's schedule closely on tours, so they can plan Internet calls rather than relying on costly world cellphones for spontaneous calls, as they did in the past.

"Good things can come from hard times," says Ms. Travers, who is currently a freelancer on Elance.com. "This has taught us to be more of a couple, really. Just managing our work and money and schedules is a skill. . . . It takes a conscientious effort. The recession has forced our hand in making that change, which is ultimately really good."

To weather the strain, couples need consciously to acknowledge the stress and "make allowances for it," Dr. Bradbury says. Get help if needed, such as taking a class on relationships, committing to time alone together or seeing a therapist.

Second, cut your partner some slack. If you see him or her becoming overwhelmed, "do more: drive the kids, go to the grocery, cook dinner, pay the bills, whatever," he says. But "don't crow about how helpful you are," because that "can make your partner feel worse."

Third, "set up a firewall" against frustration, to prevent it from spilling over into your relationship and eroding the good feelings you have for each other, he says.

Instead of attacking or unloading on your partner, try to offer gestures of support or affection. And "even in those moments when he or she is driving you nuts," Dr. Bradbury says, remind yourself of why you fell in love—and focus on those qualities.

* Write to Sue Shellenbarger at sue.shellenbarger@wsj.com.

Critical Thinking

What family theory or theories could you use to analyze this situation?

Source: Shellenbarger, Sue. 2009. "Extreme Child-Care Maneuvers." *The Wall Street Journal* May 20, D1.

predetermined location with the children he's taken care of during the morning hours; he gets out and takes his wife's car to work, while she gets into his car and takes the children home where she will stay with them for the afternoon (Shellenbarger 2009).

Shift workers not only face physical stress with night work or frequently changing schedules, but shift work also reduces the overlap of family members' leisure time, and that can affect the marriage: "To the extent that social interaction among family members provides the 'glue' that binds them together, we would expect that the more time spouses have with one another, the more likely they are to develop a strong commitment to their marriage and feel happy with it" (Presser 2000, p. 94). Unsurprisingly, then, shift work is associated with a decrease in marital stability. For single parents the results of shift work can be devastating. Because of the increase in women's shift work (especially at night), an increasing number of single mothers find themselves forced to leave their children unattended, which has tragic consequences for their children (Gornick, Presser, and Batzdorf 2009).

Doing Paid Work at Home

Home-based work (working from home, either for oneself or for an employer) has increased dramatically over the past decades—a 55 percent increase between 1990 and 2000 (Bergman 2004). The number of self-employed has increased 25 percent from around 3.47 million in 1999 to 4.34 million in 2005, while the number of people working from home increased nearly 20 percent (from 9.48 to 11.33 million) between those same years (Tozzi 2010; U.S. Census Bureau 2005, Table 1).

Home-based work used to involve *piecework*, sewing or flower making, for example. This mode of home production is declining due to competition from low-wage workers overseas. It still exists, particularly in the assembly of medical kits, circuit boards, jewelry, and some textile work, but many home-based workers are educated and are engaged in professional services such as law, accounting, computer programming, consulting, marketing, finance, and so on (Tozzi 2010). Other home-based businesses include the direct selling of cosmetics, kitchenware, and other products, as well as working as an independent contractor to handle customer service calls (Armour 2006). In fact, in 2005 (the most recent data available), 42 percent of people working exclusively from home had family incomes of $75,000 or greater, and 46.5 percent held a bachelor's degree or higher (U.S. Census Bureau 2005, Table 1).

Home-based work now includes working from home for an employer, perhaps through telecommuting—connecting to the office, customers, clients, or others by the Internet, telephone, videoconferencing, or other means. In 2008, 21.1 percent of workers worked at home as part of their primary job, and 55 percent of them were self-employed. Two-thirds were managerial or professional employees. A little over half of home-based workers are women, and they make up 37.8 percent of all self-employed people (U.S. Bureau of Labor Statistics 2009c, Table 36/2009d, Tables 6 and 7; U.S. Census Bureau 2007a, Table 592/2005, Table 1).

The reason women give most often for working at home is to catch up with work, but 32 percent of women with children under the age of six say it is to "coordinate work with personal/family needs" (Wight and Raley 2009, Table 1). Remarking on the advantages of flexibility, mothers of young children were the most likely see telecommuting favorably: "I can take care of the sick child and get my work done. A win-win situation" (Hill, Hawkins, and Miller 1996, p. 297).

As the author of a study of women in a home-based direct-selling business noted, however, "many women soon discovered . . . that they had exchanged one set of challenges for another. Mothers employed at home report problems with interruptions . . . ; they are often asked to . . . run errands for relatives, to watch neighbors' children when bad weather closes the school, or to keep an eye out for the older kids" (Kutner 1988; see also Gudmunson et al. 2009).

A study comparing office-based employees to teleworkers found that teleworkers were no more likely than the office workers to feel they had enough time for family life. Some said that they tended to work more hours than they would otherwise (Hill, Hawkins, and Miller 1996, p. 297). Indeed, work–family flexibility may be a double-edged sword. The families of some teleworkers "struggled because workplace and schedule flexibility blurred the boundaries between work and family life" (p. 293). Home-based workers faced the same tension between career advancement—which required putting in long work hours—and family time as did employees working in a more conventional setting (Berke 2003; Gudmunson et al. 2009).

Unpaid Family Work

Unpaid family work involves the necessary tasks of attending both to the emotional needs of all family members and to the practical needs of dependent members (such as children or elderly parents), as well as maintaining the family domicile.

Caring for Dependent Family Members

Our cultural tradition and social institutions give women principal responsibility for raising children. Moreover, our culture designates women as "kinkeepers" (Salari and Zhang 2006), whose job it is to keep in touch with—and, if necessary, care for—parents, adult siblings, and other relatives. The vast majority of informal elderly care is provided by female relatives, usually daughters and (albeit less often) daughters-in-law (Piercy 2007).

Family responsibilities and resources in meeting the needs of elderly, ill, or disabled family members are topics included in Chapters 14 and 17, although many of the chapters deal with the emotional aspects of family life. In this chapter, we look more closely at housework and child care.

Housework

Utopians and social engineers alike once shared a hope that advancing technology and changed social arrangements would make obsolete the need for families to cook, clean, or mind children (D. Hayden 1981). But collective arrangements proposed by utopians and early feminists never caught on. Servants, who had done much of the work for earlier middle-class housewives, entered factory work or took other, better jobs, and middle-class women were left to do their own housework (Cowan 1983). Technology seems merely to have raised

Doris Lee (1905–1983), Thanksgiving, 1935. Oil on canvas.

the standards rather than making housework less time-consuming. For example, instead of changing clothes at infrequent intervals, we now do so daily, although it will most likely be a woman washing those dirty clothes (Cowan 1983; Newport 2008).

The Second Shift Housework—even with the decline—remains substantial. Including child care, many employed wives (and some husbands) put in what sociologist Arlie Hochschild calls a **second shift** of unpaid family work that amounts to an extra month of work each year (Hochschild 1989).

Increased immigration has provided a class of women who will do child care and cleaning for affluent, dual-career families. But despite changing attitudes among couples and media portrayals of two-earner couples who share housework, women in fact continue to do more of it. Although the gap has lessened (Artis and Pavalko 2003), data from about 8,500 participants in a University of Michigan study showed that women, on average, spend twenty-seven hours a week on housework (compared to forty hours in 1965), whereas men increased their housework time from twelve hours in 1965 to sixteen hours in 1999, but this dropped down to thirteen hours in 2005 (Institute for Social Research 2002; Swanbrow 2008).

Women's revolutionary entry into the labor force would seem to require a concurrent restructuring of household labor. Husbands *are* doing somewhat more around the house than they did twenty years ago. But "women continue to feel responsible for family members' well-being and are more likely than men to adjust their work and home schedules to accommodate others" (Coltrane 2000, p. 1212).

Who Does the Housework? A researcher commenting on the Michigan study said: "Women have shown a massive decline in the time spent in housework and a massive increase in paid work. Men have picked up a bit of the slack at home, but at some point have said, 'I've put the dishes in the dishwasher five nights this week. What else do you want from me?'" (K. Peterson 2002, p. D-06). Husbands are typically more willing to do child care—especially "fun" activities—than housework, although nearly as many women take care of the children on a daily basis as well as do the housework (S. Berk 1985; Hochschild 1989; Newport 2008). According to the U.S. Bureau of Labor Statistics *American Time Use Survey*, women spend 2.1 hours daily engaged in domestic chores, while men spend only 1.3 hours. Women spend 1.73 hours caring for children (such as bathing, feeding, reading to, playing with, and so on), whereas men spend 0.84 hours in these activities (2009d, Table 9; Hartmann, English, and Hayes 2010, p. 4). This imbalance exists regardless of employment status (Galinsky, Aumann, and Bond 2009).

Over the long history of the United States, men's participation in household labor has been consistently less than that of women, and it has long been thought to be generally related to the degree of equality of earnings between the spouses and the proportionate share of those earnings produced by the wife. Where the disagreements amongst social scientists occur is the impact that men's unemployment has on their level of participation in domestic chores and child care. For example, some researchers thought that when men are unemployed they may actually do less (Coltrane 2000)—that perhaps being a breadwinner is so symbolically important that unemployed family men are reluctant to do anything that might seem to undermine their manhood, such as labor traditionally considered women's work (Shelton and John 1993).

Recent research into this issue suggests a more complex picture. For example, in 2008, it was found that employed women spent an average of 2.52 hours in housework and caregiving per day, whereas an employed man spent 1.59 hours doing the same housework and caregiving. Unemployed women, in 2008, spent an average of 3.96 hours engaged in domestic duties and child care, whereas unemployed men spent an average of 2.87 hours per day (Hartmann, English, and Hayes 2010, Table 5; U.S. Bureau of Labor Statistics 2009d). These data appear to reinforce what authors and journalists are suggesting: that, after the initial trauma (or blow to the ego) of job loss, unemployed men do increase their participation in housework and child care duties (Cooke 2006; della Cava 2009, Eckel 2010). A longitudinal study of women's and men's participation in household duties from 1976 to 2005 shows that women are engaged in fewer hours of domestic chores while men are doing more. For example, the University of Michigan's Panel Study of Income Dynamics, conducted since 1968, shows that women spent twenty-six hours per week doing housework in 1976, whereas they spent approximately seventeen hours per week in

2005. During this same time frame, men's housework doubled from six hours per week to thirteen hours per week; men's child care duties have also tripled since the mid-1960s (Galinsky, Aumann, and Bond 2009; Kelleher 2007; Sullivan and Coltrane 2008; Swanbrow 2008).

This pattern of less housework time also was thought to characterize those men whose wives earn more than they do (Brines 1994; Hochschild 1989; Tichenor 1999; see also Kroska 1997), but other research suggests quite the opposite. According to social researcher Stephanie Coontz, married women who outearn their partners have husbands that contribute more to household duties and are more likely to have greater marital stability (Coontz 2007; see also Bianchi, Robinson, and Milkie 2006; Cooke 2006; Crary 2008; Sullivan and Coltrane 2008).

Ways in which individual families manage vary. Some two-earner couples hire household help, especially in upper-income white families, and purchase the services of immigrant, racial/ethnic minority, and working-class people for housekeeping and child care work or other chores (Coontz 2007; Ehrenreich and Hochschild 2002; Kelleher 2007). Researchers note that women more often coordinate paid services as well as do more housework themselves.

Another housework option might appear to be help from children. Some studies find that children, especially in single-parent families, help significantly with housework, while others find that children in married-couple families do more work. In any case, "while many children do some household labor . . . their contribution is typically occasional and their time investment small" (Shelton and John 1996, p. 311; see also Coltrane 2000, pp. 1225–26).

Another issue is that housework can have a meaning beyond simple household maintenance. Performing certain household tasks considered traditionally feminine (or masculine) may reinforce a masculine or feminine gender identity. "Housework is not just the performance of basic household tasks but it is also a symbolic expression of gender relations, particularly between wives and husbands" (Artis and Pavalko 2003, p. 748; see also Gilbert 2008). Recent polls show that even with the increased egalitarian division of household labor, there remains a tendency to split the tasks along gender lines. For example, men say their household tasks tend to include car upkeep, yard work, and investment decisions, whereas women tend to do more meal preparation and dish washing, grocery shopping, cleaning the house and laundry, and child care (Newport 2008). That said, however, this division of labor does not seem to incorporate the "moral quality" that it was once thought to have.

Researchers at the Families and Work Institute note that regardless of the "precise objective degree of responsibility men are assuming for various aspects of family work, it has clearly become more socially acceptable for men to be and to say they are involved in child care, cooking and cleaning over the past three decades than it was in the past" (Galinsky, Aumann, and Bond 2009, p. 18). American couples who divide the household duties more equitably have greater marital satisfaction and lower incidences of divorce than couples with more traditional divisions of household labor (Cooke 2006; Hall and MacDermid 2009; Sullivan and Coltrane 2008). Psychologist Joshua Coleman suggests that men's participation in domestic chores offers increased opportunities for intimacy amongst couples, noting "if a woman feels stressed out because the house is a mess and the guy's sitting on the couch while she's vacuuming, that's not going to put her in the mood" (Crary 2008).

Anderson Ross/Jupiterimages

Children do some household labor, but it is more often a socialization device or family group activity than a substantial sharing of parents' household tasks.

Race/Ethnicity and Other Factors In some ethnic groups, such as Vietnamese and Laotian, housework is significantly shared, if not by husbands, by household members other than the wife/mother (P. Johnson 1998). Among African Americans, adult children living at home, extended kin, and nonresident fathers are likely to share housework and child care (Gerson 2010). The latter may provide child care or help with repairs.

Research on racial/ethnic differences finds that the pattern of men's spending less time than women in housework occurs in white, black, Asian Indian, and Hispanic families. However, black men spend more time in unpaid family work than do white men (Bhalla 2008; Barajas and Ramirez 2007; Gerson 2010). One explanation offered for black men's greater participation in housework is that they have more egalitarian attitudes, at least in this domain, and that African American wives are more likely to be employed and to have earnings that are closer to equality compared to their husbands than is true for other groups (Forry, Leslie, and Letiecq 2007; Gerson 2010). However, when factors other than race/ethnicity that affect men's household labor were taken into account—such as age, number of children, sex-role attitudes, and wives' sex-role attitudes—race/ethnicity was no longer so significantly associated with household labor time. In other words, the differences among white, black, and Hispanic men's household labor time may reflect other differences among them, as well (Coontz 2007; Kelleher 2007; Sullivan and Coltrane 2008).

Is Housework Vanishing? One of the ways in which families have adjusted to women's entry into the labor force is to scale down what is thought necessary—assisted by microwaves, fast food, and so forth, and sometimes by paid services. The University of Michigan researchers use the term *vanishing housework* in noting that as men and women are both putting in more hours of employment, the total amount of time a couple spends on housework has declined. "This may mean that women who work, and especially those who work in high-paying jobs, cut back the amount of time they spend on cooking and cleaning by living with a little more dust and baking fewer homemade cookies, or simply that, because both spouses work, these families are more likely to be able to hire someone to do housework while both spouses maintain careers" (Achen and Stafford 2005, p. 12).

Another reason for the decline in housework may be a related change in culture. A study that looked at different cohorts of women found that younger women do less housework, suggesting that "socialization about family life, gender, and household labor may have been substantially different for newer cohorts" (Artis and Pavalko 2003, p. 758).

The Leisure Gap Women interviewed by sociologist Arlie Hochschild

> tended to talk more intently about being overtired, sick, and "emotionally drained." . . . They talked about how much [sleep] they could "get by on.". . . These women talked about sleep the way a hungry person talks about food. (Hochschild 1989, p. 9)

She and other researchers concluded that the second shift for women means a "**leisure gap**" between husbands and wives, as women sacrifice leisure—and sleep—to accomplish unpaid family work.

After a long day on the job, Cabral and Denys get some sleep on the seventeen-mile shuttle bus trip from the plant to Moline, Illinois, where they live. Longer hours of employment mean that time families spend on housework is "vanishing."

But according to recent research, the leisure gap seems to have vanished, at least so far as work demands are concerned. In their research based on time diaries, Bianchi, Robinson, and Milkie (2006) add employment hours and household work hours to get total time spent in work for men and women. Men, it is true, spend fewer hours in housework, but they spend more in paid employment. North American women spent an average of fifty-two to fifty-seven hours on employment plus domestic work (van der Lippe 2010, p. 51; Treas and Drobnič 2010).

Still, women have half an hour less than men of leisure time. Moreover, a lot depends on what is meant by "leisure." "Because women tend to be the coordinators of family life, it is often difficult for them to take time for themselves independent of household responsibilities" (Mattingly and Bianchi 2003, p. 1001). What counts as leisure time for women often involves their organizing of family activities for others. For example, while a mother is enjoying a child's birthday party, she is simultaneously managing the occasion. Mothers' ostensibly "leisure" time includes time spent with children and a great deal of multitasking, or "contaminated" leisure, as they do household tasks or supervise children while engaging in recreational activities. Free time away from the household is less available to women than men (Mattingly and Bianchi 2003).

Another component of leisure time is not related to a division between genders, but to a national division. The United States has the highest annual average of weeks worked than any other country. Americans worked an average of 46.7 weeks in 2005 (most recent data available), whereas the average for workers in the other industrialized nations was 42.6 weeks. Because the United States does not have federally mandated minimum vacation time nor federally mandated paid holidays (as opposed to all other members of the Organization for Economic Cooperation and Development—OECD), Americans work more during the year than all other workers in industrialized nations (Mishel, Bernstein, and Shierholz 2009, p. 367, Table 8.6). The implications of this for American families is important because the inability to escape work-life demands, even for a short time, are correlated with depression, anxiety, marital conflict, and so on.

Fairness and Marital Happiness A conclusion easily drawn from research is that employed women are carrying an unfair share of domestic tasks. But do couples themselves see it that way? That depends on the meaning of household work to the couple and what they consider "fair."

Although, overall, unequal shares of household labor are associated with marital dissatisfaction, this relationship is altered by perceptions of fairness. Citing a number of studies, Michelle Frisco and Kristi Williams (2003) found perceived fairness to be more strongly associated with marital happiness (and, in their own study, with the likelihood of divorce) than differences in actual hours spent in domestic work. To a wife or woman partner, a man's taking up *some,* if not an equal share of, household tasks may signify caring.

Interesting is that men and women perceive "fair share" differently. Of those men in dual-earner families who perceived that they were doing *more than their fair share,* 43 percent were actually doing *less than half* the housework. In other words, they did not think it would be fair for them to do as much as half the housework. Meanwhile, of women who perceived themselves to be doing a *fair* share, almost two-thirds were doing *all or more* of the housework. An uneven split seemed fair to them (Frisco and Williams 2003 [the Frisco and Williams study used the *Marital Instability Over the Life Course* data set]; White and Booth 1991; see also Greenstein 2009 for international comparisons). Probably both men and women have in mind as a standard of comparison the breadwinner–housewife model. Men, then, are doing more, whereas women are unloading some of their former responsibility. That seems "fair." And men may lump housework and employment together and add that up to feel the total burden of family responsibility is a fair one (Lavee and Katz 2002). The relatively comparable men's and women's total hours of paid and household work reported by Bianchi, Robinson, and Milkie (2006) would support this conclusion.

Gay Men, Lesbians, and Housework Given that gay couples are composed of people of the same gender, how does their household division of labor work out and what impact does it have on the relationship?

A small qualitative study of forty-three gay male and thirty-six lesbian couples explored these questions. Each partner was employed full-time, and there were no children residing with the couples (which is the majority pattern among gay/lesbian couples). The study looked at who performed some traditionally female tasks—it provides some interesting insights, though given the small sample, it cannot be conclusive.

Partners were asked how often they performed six tasks compared to how often their partner did. Generally, lesbian couples' division of labor was more egalitarian than that of gay male couples. The researcher was most interested in the impact on the relationship. Perceived equality was closely tied to relationship satisfaction and that, in turn, to relationship stability (Kurdek 2007). As with heterosexual couples, research shows that the amount of hours individual members of a

Sean Prior/Shutterstock

The second shift is probably more enjoyable when shared by both partners.

couple work in paid labor has the greatest influence on the division of household labor (Sutphin 2006).

In the next section, we will examine how partners juggle household labor demands, along with employment.

Juggling Employment and Family Work

The concept of juggling implies a hectic and stressful situation. A great deal of research and other writings on the subject suggest that today's typical dual-earner family or a family with a working single parent is a hectic one (e.g., Hochschild 1989, 1997). This is particularly true when children are in the home, and more so for single men and married and single women than for married men due to the greater "role overload" of the first three groups (Kiecolt 2003, p. 34).

Work, Family, and Leisure: Attitudes and Time Allocation

An influential study of changes in time at work concluded that working people are spending significantly more hours at work than in the recent past (Schor 1991). In their book based on data from the Current Population Survey, sociologists Jerry Jacobs and Kathleen Gerson affirmed this conclusion. They point to an "increasing mismatch between our economic system and the needs of American families" (Jacobs and Gerson 2004, back cover)

American workers lead the industrial world in the number of hours worked—with the average worker working 8.44 hours a day or 42.5 hours per week, and producing "$63,885 of wealth per year, more than their counterparts in all other countries" ("U.N.: U.S. Workers" 2007; U.S. Bureau of Labor Statistics 2009d, Table 4; U.S. Census Bureau 2010b, Table 589). A little over 26 percent of all employees now work more than forty hours per week, with 10 percent working between fifty and sixty hours a week. Just over 5 percent of the labor force held two or more paid jobs in 2008, with slightly higher proportions of women than men (U.S. Census Bureau 2010b, Tables 588, 589, 596).

Virtually every researcher studying work–family time hears expressions of time pressure, and of feeling rushed and stressed (e.g., Jacobs and Gerson 2004; Bianchi, Robinson, and Milkie 2006). Yet Bianchi and her colleagues argue that such stress is concentrated in the children's early years and especially for women with demanding careers, as well as for single mothers, whereas Jacobs and Gerson see more pervasive problems for working families. These different conclusions as to whether work hours have increased are difficult to resolve, but they seem to reflect methodological differences. Bianchi and her colleagues argue that their time diary methodology is more accurate because it is specific and timely—study participants are "walked" through activities of the preceding twenty-four hours. Jacobs and Gerson point to the small size of time diary samples and to other methodological issues and argue the merits of their Current Population Survey data.

Jacobs and Gerson do a careful analysis of theirs and the time diary studies and conclude that each is measuring different things. The hours worked per week by each employee have not changed much over recent decades. But the weeks devoted to work by family members have increased dramatically because of women's entry into the labor force. Total hours of work are expanded by the increasing tendency for women to work full-time and not leave the labor force for an extended period.

Some interesting research has been designed to assess the impact of women's entry into the labor force on health, marital quality, and marital stability. One such study has found women to have increasingly good (self-reported) health as labor force participation and working hours have increased. Both women's increased education and their employment have contributed to better health, contrary, perhaps, to expectation. Although there was a short-term diminishment of health attributed to the stress of coping with work and family in children's younger years, once children entered school, superior health rebounded. Overall, women have gained in health as employment has become the norm (Schnittker 2007).

A Gallup poll asked individuals whether they have enough time to do what they want. About 55 percent of those age eighteen through thirty-four and 58 percent of those aged thirty-five to fifty-four—the ages of employment and active parenting—say they do not have enough time (Carroll 2008). For a majority of Americans, rest and relaxation time, time for friends and hobbies, and even time for sleep is not what they would

"Hey, Baby, I just dropped the kids off at school, and now I'm going to the grocery store, and then I'm going home and unloading the car—am I making you hot?"

Facts about Families

Where Does the Time Go?

We've talked about employment and household labor. What do people do with the rest of their time?

An American Time Use Survey was conducted in 2008 by the U.S. Bureau of Labor Statistics (2009d). Some 21,000 people were asked to keep time diaries, recording what activities they engaged in and for how much time. The reports of these many individuals were averaged to come up with typical days for different groups. Let's look at employed parents of children under eighteen and see what happens in an average day.[a]

First there are the basics. Just over an hour (1.14 hours) was spent in *eating and drinking*. Around nine hours (9.15) were spent in such *personal care* activities as sleeping, bathing, dressing, and health care.

Work averaged just under six hours (5.77) for men, and just over three hours (3.3) for women (remember that some people work part-time and that all days are not workdays). On average, employed women spent almost two and a half hours (2.36) on *household activities*—the domestic labor—while these tasks occupied an hour and a quarter (1.25) of men's time.

These totals did not include child care, which fell into the category of *caring for and helping household children*. Women spent an hour and a half (1.51) on caring for household children, while men spent less than an hour (.85).

Shopping—*consumer goods purchases*, as the survey termed it—took almost an hour of an employed mother's daily time (.49), while fathers devoted a half an hour to shopping (.28). Men were able to devote more of their time to *leisure and sports* (4.42 hours) than were women (3.93 hours). The most common use of leisure time for all was watching television.

Men and women participated in *organizational, civic, and religious activities* at about the same rate, each spending about a half of an hour on an average day. Men spent an average of .12 and women spent an average of .16 hour in *caring for and helping nonhousehold* members; and in *educational activities* women spent nearly double the amount men did. *Telephone calls, mail, and email* communication rounded out the day (at .08 hour for men and .22 hour for women).

So what does it all mean? Despite amounts of time in some categories so small as to seem trivial, we can see some interesting things in these figures. The American Time Use Survey shows that women spend more than double the time than men do in the care of the household and its members, adding one more study to those that show a gender disparity. However, men spent a great deal more time in paid employment than did women.

In other areas, there is little difference in time use between men and women. The time men and women devote to organizational, civic, religious, and educational activities and to helping nonhousehold members is similar. Still, men have more leisure time, whereas women do more shopping (more likely to be grocery shopping than "fun" shopping). Women spend twice as much time as men in communication activities and more time on personal care, a large portion of which is sleeping.

Critical Thinking

How do you spend *your* time? Has the time you spend in various activities changed throughout your life? These data are for employed people who have children at home. If your situation is different, is your time use different as well?

Source: U.S. Bureau of Labor Statistics 2009d, Table 8.

a. This survey divides people by those with children under six years and those with children between the ages of six and seventeen. To simplify the table, we added the percentages from both and divided by two.

like it to be (Saad 2004). For more on these and similar issues, see the "Facts About Families: Where Does the Time Go?" box, which reports data from a major government survey on how employed parents spend their time on an average day.

Another study using a national data set found that "wives' full-time employment is associated with greater marital stability" while not affecting quality one way or the other (Schoen, Rogers, and Amato 2006). Still another study looked at gender changes and marital quality and found that most gender-related changes had no negative impact on marital quality, but there was increased marital conflict attributable to "work-family demands based on the combination of wives' employment and preschool-age children" (Rogers and Amato 2000, p. 747). This suggests, once again, that perhaps the negatives for families with employed women are focused on the preschool years of those with children.

There is some indication that younger workers have different attitudes toward work–family balance than did their predecessors. Social scientists see a "gender convergence" in attitudes and values regarding work and family roles. Both men and women want a balance of work and family in their lives (Cohen 2007b, p. A13; Monahan Lang, and Risman 2007).

A 2002 study sponsored by the American Business Collaboration (composed of such prominent corporations as IBM and Johnson and Johnson, with additional support from the Ford Foundation) and conducted by the Families and Work Institute surveyed some 2,800 adults from four generations of workers: (1) "matures" (born 1945 and earlier); (2) "baby boomers" (born between 1946 and 1964); (3) "Generation X" (born between 1965 and 79); and (4) "Generation Y" (born between 1980 and 1994). Respondents were asked if they put work before family ("work-centric"), put family before work ("family-centric"), or prioritized both equally ("dual-centric").

As Figure 11.4 indicates, a majority of the two youngest generations described themselves as family-centric, some as dual-centric, with few likely to style themselves as work-centric. Their predecessors, the baby boomers, were comparatively more work oriented and less family oriented, although a majority of boomers selected the dual-centric and family-centric orientations together. Matures (not included in Figure 11.4) were similar to Generations X and Y in being less work-centric, but were also less family-centric than all other generational groups. A majority were dual-centric (Families and Work Institute 2004).

We will look now at how children in two-earner marriages are doing, and then at parents.

How Are Children Faring?

Before women with children entered the work force in large numbers, working mothers were considered problematic by child development experts and the public. Now they are taken for granted. A 2001 survey of women (not all of them mothers) found more than 90 percent in agreement with the statement that a woman can be a good mother and have a successful career (Center for the Advancement of Women 2003). More recent studies conclude that maternal employment does not cause behavior problems in children (Vander Ven et al. 2001; see also Agee, Atkinson, and Crocker 2008), and another study of more than 6,000 children studied at age twelve found no difference between the children whose mothers were employed or not employed during the child's first three years (E. Harvey 1999). What is notable in much of the research, however, is the startling correlations between low family income and childhood problems (Jackson, Choi, and Bentler 2009).

"Quality time? Do I have to?"

Overall, this continues to be the prevailing view. Furthermore, the economic benefit to children of working mothers cannot be overlooked. Family income tends to be favorably associated with various child outcome measures. Important for parents, though, is keeping their child's needs in the forefront in the face of daily pressures. Recent studies have found that mothers who work part-time are better at this than those who work full-time—and may indeed spend more time helping their children with homework than even full-time homemakers. Before the era of working mothers, so-called full-time mothers did not spend all their time with children, but devoted more time than today's mothers to household work or volunteer work. And some of those mothers—of larger families, especially—made use of paid help in caring for children.

"The puzzling thing about the reallocation of mothers' time to market work [employment] is that it appears to have been accomplished with little effect on children's well-being," noted sociologist Suzanne Bianchi in her presidential address to the Population

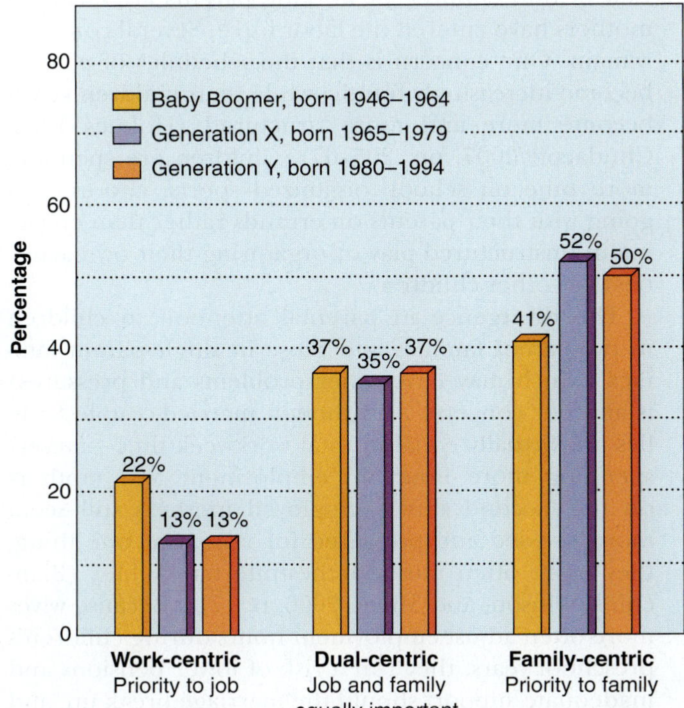

Figure 11.4 Priority given to work, family, or both by 2,800 workers surveyed in 2002: Generational differences

Source: Families and Work Institute 2004.

Association of America (Bianchi 2000). A variety of studies indicate that parents today spend as much or more time with children as in the past (Milkie et al. 2004; Bianchi, Robinson, and Milkie 2006; and see Figures 11.5 and 11.6). Figure 11.5 presents total weekly hours parents spent with children in 1975 and 2000. That time has increased for married fathers and married mothers. It has, however, decreased for single mothers, though it remains substantial.

The data on "total time" reflect the time a parent spends in the presence of children. Figure 11.6 presents the time parents spend in "primary child care," that is, active caretaking, whether that takes the form of routine care or enrichment activities. Mothers and fathers spent more time in child care in 2000 than did parents in previous measured years going back to 1965. (Time spent doing child care was measured in time diary studies done by various universities using samples ranging from 1,200 to over 5,000; Bianchi, Robinson, and Milkie 2006, Chapter 2).

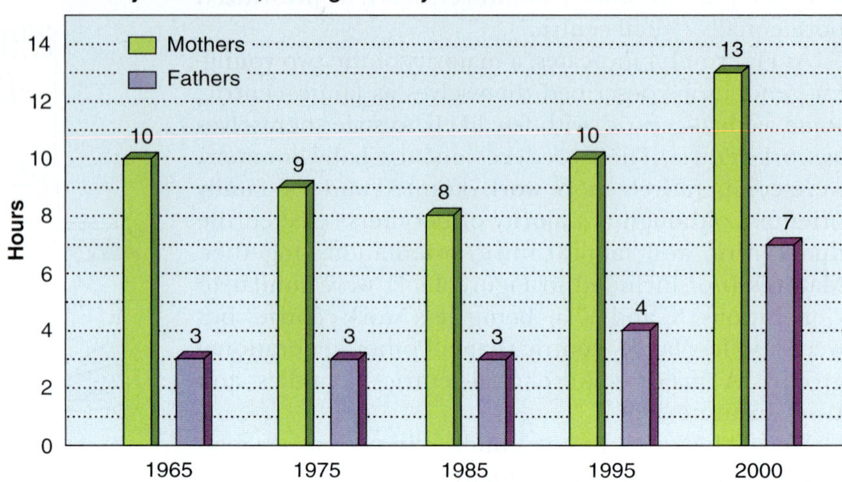

Figure 11.6 Primary child care, average weekly hours, mothers and fathers, 1965–2000

Source: From Bianchi, Robinson, and Milkie, *The Changing Rhythms of American Family Life*, 2006, Figure 4.3, p. 72. Reprinted by permission of the Russell Sage Foundation.

How did mothers, especially, accomplish an increase in time with children while at the same time dramatically increasing employment hours? (Incidentally, time spent in personal care [sleeping, grooming and eating] and free time remained relatively stable [Bianchi, Robinson, and Milkie 2006, Figure 5.1]). They cut back on housework and spent somewhat less time doing things just with spouses. In part, they multitasked; parents spent time with children (and often each other) in children's activities or those of the parents. Today's families are smaller, so that parental attention is less divided; moreover, the increase in father's time with children (for married parents) means increased total attention for children.

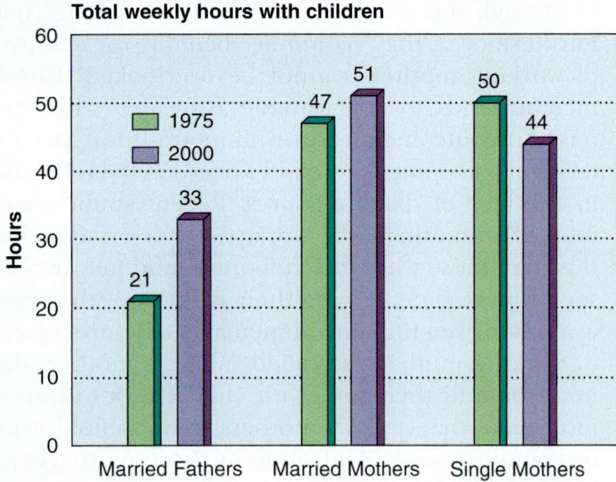

Figure 11.5 Total weekly hours spent with children for married fathers, married mothers, and single mothers, 1975 and 2000

Source: From Bianchi, Robinson, and Milkie, *The Changing Rhythms of American Family Life*, 2006, Figure 4.1, p. 63. Reprinted by permission of the Russell Sage Foundation.

These results present an optimistic and reassuring view of how children of working parents are faring as mothers have entered the labor force. Several concerns remain. One concern is that the schedules of parents become increasingly frantic, while their children's lives become more and more structured (Holmes 1998; Chudacoff 2007, pp. 205–07). Children are spending more time on school, organized sports, chores, and going with their parents on errands rather than engaging in unstructured play or organizing their own activities with other children.

The divergence in parental attention to children in two-parent families and those in single-parent families (which may have other problems and pressures) is another concern. And though married-couple families are virtually equal in total workweek time—fathers spending more hours in employment and mothers on the "second shift"—employed mothers still seem more stressed and pressured for time. For one thing, they more often must "orchestrate family life" (Bianchi, Robinson, and Milkie 2006, p. 171). Because wives more often adjust employment hours during children's preschool years, they run a risk of lower pensions and inadequate support should the marriage break up, and they may not have the careers they might have had otherwise. This leads us to the issue of how parents are faring as they juggle paid and unpaid work.

How Are Parents Faring?

This chapter focuses on work and family in marriages (rather than other family forms) for two reasons. First, the vast majority of research on the interface between paid employment and family labor concerns marrieds. Second, single parenting is addressed in some detail in Chapter 15.

> Although the rough edges of the work–family conflict may be particularly sharp for single parents, two-earner marriages assuredly have them also. Whether one is single or married, "career and family involvement have never been combined easily in the same person." (Hunt and Hunt 1986)

An ideal for modern family is to share wage-earning and family responsibilities on an equal basis and, for men, to be an involved father. Indeed, more fathers are taking off work following the birth of a child, and they are more visible in parenting classes, in pediatricians' offices, and dropping off and picking up children in day care centers.

A man, regardless of parental status, who gives family priority may have to deal with challenges to his masculinity or resentment from coworkers. Employers may not see unpaid family work as important or believe that employees, especially males, should allow family responsibilities to interfere with labor force involvement (Hochschild 1997). As a result, workers report that they are reluctant to take advantage of family benefits that are theoretically available (Jacobs and Gerson 2004, p. 6). Some husbands report having lied to bosses or taken other evasive steps at work to hide conflicts between job and family. One man told his boss that he has "another meeting" so that he can leave the office each day at 6 p.m.: "I never say it's a meeting with my family."

The previous discussion applies to working parents generally. In the next section, we will look at some stresses peculiar to *two-career* marriages—keeping in mind the distinction between *two-earner* couples and *two-career* couples made earlier in the chapter.

Two-Career Marriages Some decades ago, as the two-career marriage was emerging as an ideal lifestyle available to all young couples, Hunt and Hunt (1977) noted that dual-career families require a support system of child care providers and household help that depends heavily on ability to pay. That means it is inherently limited to a small number of families. Moreover, the success of today's two-career union is premised on the existence of a labor pool of low-paid, but highly dependable, household help. The vast majority of such help is provided by women, many of whom have their own families to worry about (Romero 1992). Even parents who can afford to pay for it find that locating such help may be difficult.

Two-career partners need the dexterity to balance not only career and family life but also her and his careers so that both spouses prosper professionally in what they see as a fair way. Two careers requiring travel may present added problems as parents "scramble to patch things together" for overnight child care (Shellenbarger 1991). The balance between partners may be upset by career fluctuations as well as family time allocations. The contrast between one career that is going well and one that is not may be hard on the partner on the down side. But the marriage may "operate as a buffer, cushioning the negative impacts of failures or reversals in one or the other career" (Hertz 1986, p. 59). When the marriage is rewarding, compromises, such as turning down opportunities that would require relocation, are acceptable because of the importance given to marriage as well as career.

Sociologist Rosanna Hertz (1986) found that the two-career couples she studied were realistic, though sometimes regretful, about some benefits of the traditional relationships they are giving up. Although men acknowledged that their wives provided less support, they appreciated the excitement, and the status, associated with an achieving wife. Some of them had considered or made career changes that would not have been possible if wives had not been successful wage earners. Both partners claimed fulfillment from and assigned emotional meaning to an egalitarian dual-career marriage: "She has a sense of a full partnership and she should" (in Hertz 1986, p. 75).

Commitment was perceived as truer: "Working . . . has decreased my dependence. . . . That makes it into much more of a voluntary relationship" (in Hertz 1986, p. 75). Very visible to Hertz was the way in which communication was enhanced by similar lives, making possible a higher level of mutual support than in conventional couples: "These couples . . . [had] a different level of understanding about each other's lives, a level that is intimate and empathic" (p. 77).

The couples Hertz studied did report conflict over balancing time, commitment, and career moves. Indeed, the geography of two careers presents a significant challenge to couples.

The Geography of Two Careers Because career advancement often requires geographic mobility—and even international transfers—juggling two careers may prove difficult for married or committed partners. A career move for one may make the other a **trailing spouse** who relocates to accommodate the partner's career. Increasingly, couples turn down transfers because of two-career issues. As a result, some large companies now offer career-opportunity assistance to a trailing spouse, such as hiring a job search firm, facilitating intercompany networking, attempting to locate a position for the spouse in the same institution, or providing career counseling (Jio 2008).

Although wives still move for their husband's career more often than the reverse, the number of trailing husbands has increased, and studies show that the benefits are much better for the trailing husband than for the trailing wife (Shauman and Noonan 2007). More two-career marriages today are based on a conscious mutuality to which partners have become accustomed by the time a career move presents itself. Such couples are less likely to have problems with a female-led relocation than are more traditional marrieds. For many spouses, trailing is preferable to commuting, another solution to the problem of career opportunities in two locations.

To Commute or Not to Commute? Social scientists have called marriages in which spouses live apart **commuter marriages**. The vast majority of commuting couples would rather not do so, but endure the separation for the sake of career or other goals. Since research began on commuter marriages in the early 1970s, social scientists have drawn different conclusions. Some studies suggest that the benefits of such marriages—greater economic and emotional equality between spouses—counter their drawbacks. Other research focuses on difficulties in managing the lifestyle. One conclusion to be drawn from the research is that commuters who are able to have frequent reunions are happier with the lifestyle than those who cannot.

In 2008, just under 3.5 percent of married Americans lived apart (U.S. Census 2010b, Table 66). One study of commuter couples compared life satisfaction for 90 commuting and 133 single-resident, two-career couples. Almost three-fourths of the commuters saw their partner weekly. The researchers were surprised to find that the commuters experienced less stress and overload than the single-residence couples: "Perhaps there is some restructuring in the commuting two-residence couple that simplifies life or perceptions of it. Perhaps short separations facilitate compartmentalization, allowing commuters to keep work life and family life in well-separated spheres, and to confront the demands of each role in alternation rather than simultaneously" (p. 405). Then, too, the commuter couples had significantly fewer babies and young children than did single-residence couples; commuter marriages probably work better in the absence of dependent children (G. Stern 1991).

Commuter marriages are not new or novel—American men have long worked in transient professions where they are gone for extended periods of time (that is, truck drivers, traveling sales, soldiers, and so on). What is different about modern commuter couples is that it is increasingly common for the wife to be the commuter in the couple, instead of the husband. The introduction of children increases the stress in commuter marriages—especially for a spouse who is the primary caregiver, because that spouse becomes a de facto single parent for the duration the commuting spouse is absent. It is suggested that approximately 800,000 children in the United States live in commuter families.

"Every Monday, Jaime Cangas, 40, kisses his wife Karen, 36, goodbye as she leaves their Plano, Texas, home and heads toward the airport. As a consultant for Accenture, she will be gone until late Thursday night, working with clients in faraway cities. Jaime, who sells and markets security software, will drop off their children, Caroline, 7, at school, and Mitchell, 3, at day care. He shops for groceries during his lunch break, then picks them both up at 6. When they get home, the kids blow kisses at Mommy through the webcam" (Cullen 2007). Although this arrangement has its stressors, research suggests more serious strains come about when the commuting ends and the couple or family reunites under the same household. Each member in the relationship has become used to the living arrangement, so an adjustment period becomes necessary after the commuting spouse moves back into the family home (Tessina 2008).

Couples who have been married for shorter periods seem to have more difficulties with commuter marriages. Perhaps because of their history of shared time, more established couples in commuter marriages have a greater "commitment to the unit" (H. Gross 1980; Rhodes 2002).

Social Policy, Work, and Family

Despite the benefits of employment to women and their families, and despite societal pressures and gender-role changes leading to high female employment, neither public policy nor families have fully adapted to this change. This section examines policy issues regarding work and family. Policy issues center on two questions: "What is needed?" and "Who will provide it?"

What Is Needed to Resolve Work–Family Issues?

Researchers and other work–family experts are in general agreement that single-parent and two-earner families are in need of more adequate provisions for child and elder care, family leave, and flexible employment scheduling.

Child Care Policy researchers define **child care** as the full-time care and education of children under age six, care before and after school and during school vacations for older children, and overnight care when employed parents must travel. Child care may be paid or unpaid and provided by relatives or others, including one of the parents.

In her study of dual-earner couples, sociologist Rosanna Hertz (1997) explored parents' approaches to child care and found they fell into three categories. One is the **mothering approach to child care**, whereby the couple prefer that the wife care for the children. An initial strategy of overtime or a second job for the husband often proves to be unworkable, so the wife does have to enter the labor force. But the couple maintains as traditional a division of labor as they can, with the mother working as much as possible during hours the children are sleeping or in school.

In the **parenting approach to child care**, parents share family care, and structure their work to this end. They accept part-time work, for example, and the lower incomes that go with it. But primarily, these are "labor force elites" (Hertz 1997, p. 370), who can be sure of commanding a full-time job when they want to, or whose part-time earnings produce substantial income. In blue-collar or lower-income families, shift care or the periodic unemployment of men produces a parenting approach. In 2005, 18 percent of fathers were principle sources of child care for preschoolers during mothers' day shift (U.S. Census Bureau 2008c).

In the **market approach to child care**, career-oriented couples hire other people to care for their children. We now look at child care in this sense. There are essentially three types of nonrelative child care. Paid care may be provided in the child's home by a nanny, an **in-home caregiver** who lives in or comes to the house daily. The term **family child care** refers to care provided in a caregiver's home, often by an older woman or a mother who has chosen to remain out of the labor force to care for her own children. Parents who prefer family day care seem to be seeking a family-like atmosphere, with a smaller-scale, less routinized setting. Perhaps they also desire social similarity of caregiver and parent to better ensure that their children are socialized according to their own values.

Center care provides group care for a larger number of children in child care centers. The use of child care centers has increased rapidly, partly because of the growing scarcity of in-home caregivers, as relatives or neighbors who formerly cared for children now join the labor force themselves. Increased use of center care is also due to the perception that it offers greater safety and a strong preschool curriculum.[4]

By the time they enter school, an estimated 44 percent of children have been in a nonrelative child care arrangement. This is more common for black and non-Hispanic white children, a little less so for Asian or Pacific Islander children, and least common among Hispanics (Dye and Johnson 2007, Table 2). Black mothers, who relied heavily on kin networks in the past, saw that option decline by the 1990s, as grandmothers and other relatives entered the labor force themselves (Brewster and Padavic 2002). Nonrelative care is also more common for children in families above the poverty level than for those in lower-income families (Dye and Johnson 2007, Table 3).

Of children of employed mothers in 2006, 28.8 percent were in organized care—day care centers, Head Start, or preschool. Slightly more than 4 percent had in-home care; 6.2 percent had family day care; and the remainder had other arrangements, no care, or multiple arrangements. Relative care was heavily used—25.6 percent of children were in the care of grandparents, with fathers caring for 24 percent; sibs or other relatives cared for 11 percent; and mothers themselves cared for 5.5 percent (by bringing children to the office or other work site, including self-employment work at home; U.S. Census Bureau 2008b, Table 1B).

Now there is extensive research on the developmental outcomes of various child care arrangements. See "As We Make Choices: Child Care and Children's Outcomes" for a discussion of this research.

About 20.8 percent of children age nine to eleven and 31.3 percent of those age twelve to fourteen whose mothers were employed full time were in **self-care**—that is, without adult supervision—for an average of seven hours a week (U.S. Census Bureau 2008b, Table 4). Self-care is more common in white upper-middle- and middle-class families than in black, Latino, or low-income settings, perhaps because of differences in neighborhood safety (U.S. Census Bureau 2008b, Table 4).

Low-income, single-parent, rural, and Hispanic parents are especially likely to have relatives take care of their children (Capizzano, Adams, and Ost 2006). Hispanic parents seem to prefer either relative or family day care rather than center care, a choice attributed to wanting a "warm and family-like atmosphere" rather than a "formal and cold" child care center. Family day care may also be seen as providing a personal relationship between the parent and the caregiver and, perhaps, a bilingual setting (Chira 1994).

African American parents prefer a center for its perceived educational benefits, whereas white parents' preference is more likely to be for the social interaction experiences a center provides for children. Some families may seek a provider of their own racial/ethnic group who will maintain the cultural context children have at home or, at a minimum, a white caregiver or center that will provide "racial safety"—that is, will not

[4] With regard to safety, it is important to note that despite a smattering of confirmed cases, concerns about abuse of children in day care have largely proved unfounded; studies indicate that children are at greater risk of abuse in their own homes (Finkelhor, Hotaling, and Sedlak 1991). "Overall, child care is quite safe" (Wrigley and Dreby 2005, p. 729), and center care is safer than care in private homes.

Facts about Families

Child Care and Children's Outcomes

Parents who have to make decisions about child care want to know two things: What are the characteristics of quality child care? And what effect does being in child care have on children? We address child care quality in "As We Make Choices: Selecting a Child Care Facility." Here we look at outcomes for children who have spent time in child care in their early years.

Psychologist Jay Belsky drew considerable attention when he reported an early finding that infants in their first year who are in nonparental care for twenty or more hours per week "are at elevated risk of being classified as insecure in their *attachments* to their mothers at 12 or 18 months of age" (Belsky 1990, p. 895; 2008, p. 9).[a] This set off the "day care wars" (Carey 2007), in which Belsky has continued to engage in dialogue with other child care researchers about whether time in child care is harmful to children and in what circumstances (2002).

A multiple-site longitudinal study, organized by the National Institute of the Child Health and Human Development (NICHD), began in 1991, and has now followed more than 1,300 children from shortly after birth through sixth grade (Belsky et al. 2007; Belsky 2008). The study looks at the impact of various types of child care compared to maternal care. (Commentators on the NICHD research find it noteworthy that the focus of the NICHD study is on *mothers.* A child is considered to be in care when not with the mother—that is, care by the father is considered "child care" [U.S. National Institute of Child Health and Human Development 2002].) Professor Belsky was one of the thirty researchers initially involved in the study, and has continued to participate. He is one of the authors of the latest reports on the NICHD study.

The conclusion first drawn from NICHD research was that children in nonrelative care and children cared for by their own parents differed little in development and emotional stability at fifteen months and three years (U.S. National Institute of Child Health and Human Development 1999). Yet, at the three-year point, child care did have a negative relationship to maternal sensitivity ("how attuned the mother is to the child's wants and needs") and child engagement ("how connected or involved a child appeared to be when relating to his or her mother"). But that finding did not hold for children in *quality care* (NICHD Early Child Care Research Network 1999a; U.S. National Institute of Child Health and Human Development 1999; Belsky 2008).

Moreover, favorable outcomes in terms of cognitive and linguistic skills were associated with *quality* of care, described as "when child care providers talk to children, encourage them to ask questions, respond to children's questions, read to them, challenge them to attend to others' feelings, and to different ways of thinking" (U.S. National Institute of Child Health and Human Development 1999; NICHD Early Child Care Research Network 1999b; Belsky 2008).

As the children approached age five and entered kindergarten, those who had spent longer hours in child care over time were found to have more behavior problems and conflicts with adults (as reported by parents, teachers, and the children themselves). That was true even when quality and type of care were taken into account (NICHD Early Child Care Research Network 2003a).

Although Professor Belsky made much of the results, his co-researchers argued that these were not serious problems—that, in fact, more serious behavior problems were evidenced by children who had not been in day care at all. They also pointed to the fact that problem behavior was confined to a minority of day care children—more than 80 percent of children long in care did *not* exhibit any behavior problems ("Day-Care Researchers" 2001). In this view, the findings had a "lack of clinical significance" (Dworkin 2002, p. 167), meaning that they did not signal a level of trouble that should cause concern. New research upholds these findings but does suggest a slight correlation between length of day care attendance and impulsiveness and risk taking in adolescence, particularly in children who were placed in low-quality day care where the caregivers were more authoritarian and children's free play was limited (Fox 2010; Stein 2010; Vandell et al. 2010).

Moreover, children in high-quality center care outperformed children not in care in measures of cognitive skills and language development (NICHD Early Child Care Research Network 2000b). Family background factors and maternal sensitivity were more important in their impact on children's adjustment than was time in child care (NICHD Early Child Care Research Network 2003a). The small size of the negative effects, the good adjustment of the preponderance of children, and the greater importance of parental influence in terms of the effects of extended child care were reassuring (Vandell et al. 2010).

Research continued through the first 4½ years of the children's lives, their day care years. The latest report

act in a racist way with their children (Uttal 2004). Black children are "more likely than the other groups to be in center-based care across most categories of children examined. The same can be said for the low use of center-based care and the high use of relative care among Hispanic children: these findings persist regardless of the child or family characteristic examined" (Capizzano, Adams, and Ost 2006, p. x).

Average monthly child care costs for infants exceed the costs a family would spend in food. "A family in the United States with one infant faced average prices in 2008 of $4,560 to $15,895 a year for center-based child on the NICHD study (Belsky et al. 2007; Vandell et al. 2010) assesses the situation of these children since entering school and draws the following conclusions:

1. Change over time has seen some earlier negative or positive effects vanish, while others take their place. The research, too, captures only one point in time in an ongoing process.
2. Children with more experience in child care center settings continued to evidence more behavior problems; however, these problems are more strongly correlated with low-quality child care and poverty. Also, length of time in nonfamilial child care is associated with impulsiveness and risk taking in adolescence. Why this is so remains a mystery, but the researchers speculate that it may be peer interaction and authoritarian child care providers in a center group setting that elicits disruptive behavior.
3. Nonrelative care, mostly center care, is associated with negative effects; however, high-quality care is a protective factor for children of fragile or at-risk families (Vandell et al. 2010, p. 739; see also Burchinal et al. 2010).
4. High-quality care of any kind is associated with better vocabulary.
5. "[P]arenting quality proved to be a far stronger and more consistent predictor of tested achievement and teacher-reported social functioning than was child-care experience" (Belsky et al. 2007, p. 696).
6. The developmental impact of child care on individual children may thus not be so significant, because child development outcomes of child care are "smaller in size and less pervasive than those associated with families and parenting" (Belsky et al. 2007, p. 698). But the "*collective* consequences" of a certain amount of problem behavior associated with children's child care experience can affect "classrooms, schools, communities, and society at large" (Belsky et al. 2007, p. 698).
7. "The current findings suggest that the quality of early child care experiences can have long-lasting (albeit small) effects on middle-class and affluent children as well as those who are economically disadvantaged" (Vandell et al. 2010, p. 750).

There continue to be criticisms of the study, most notably, the question of a "selection effect." The researchers were not, of course, able to assign families randomly to each type of child care; the choices of the parents may reflect something distinctive about the family that is the key factor affecting outcomes. A different and later study took advantage of developments in methodology to counter the effect of selection bias. The focus of this study was on only the first year of the child's life. Results indicated that the mother's working full-time in the first year was associated with negative cognitive and behavioral outcomes; these negative outcomes did not occur when mothers worked part-time in the first year, postponed work, or did not work for the first three years (J. Hill et al. 2005).

Child care researchers consider the policy implications of the research. Belsky (2002) argues for tax or other policies to support full-time parental care in the home, especially during the first year. NICHD research suggests that intervention programs might be effective in enhancing the parenting skills that their research suggests is more important for development than whether or not the child spends time in day care, especially for those children who did not have high-quality child care in their first years. "Experimental studies of high-quality early intervention programs have demonstrated that these programs can enhance social, cognitive, and academic development of economically disadvantaged children" (Belsky et al. 2007; Vandell et al. 2010, p. 738).

Other child care scholars agree with the NICHD researchers that subsidies should be available to permit parents to cut back work hours. At the same time, they urge attention to improving the quality of out-of-home care. They also believe child care can make a positive contribution to social development if done well (Maccoby and Lewis 2003).

Critical Thinking

If you were the mother of a new baby, would you find this research useful in making your decision about returning to work? Or would you be more inclined to rely on the advice of family members or other parents—or your child's reactions to child care? What would you like researchers to find out about children in child care?

a. "**Attachment** represents an active, affective, enduring, and reciprocal bond between two individuals that is believed to be established through repeated interaction over time" (Coleman and Watson 2000, p. 297, citing Ainsworth et al. 1978).

care" while parents of four-year-old children averaged "$4,055 to $11,680 a year in child care fees in 2008" ("Parents and the High Price" 2009, p. 1). Many parents using paid care change their arrangements each year because a caregiver quits, the cost is too high, the hours or location are inconvenient, the child is unhappy, or the parent dislikes the caregiver. As they struggle to find quality, affordable child care, many parents must make more than one arrangement for each child. As they patch together a series of child care arrangements, the system becomes increasingly unpredictable ("Parents and the High Price" 2009, p. 2).

As We Make Choices

Selecting a Child Care Facility

Universal, comprehensive, government-funded day care does not exist in the United States today. Although some parents have access to child care facilities through government programs or their employers, many parents are on their own in selecting a child care facility.

Some parents arrange their work schedules to care for their children, while others hire a nanny or recruit relatives into this role. Here we make some suggestions to parents who are choosing from commercially available child care.

State laws, which vary in both provisions and enforcement, establish minimal standards, and professional organizations like the American Academy of Pediatrics have developed guidelines for quality child care. We outline some of the things we think parents should consider when exploring and choosing child care for their children, drawing on the American Academy of Pediatrics guidelines as well as other sources.

Some criteria are very tangible and specific, like the ratio of children to adults. Some are more qualitative and can best be judged by the parent during visits, including post-placement visits to the child care facility. Some are only applicable to center care, whereas others are relevant to family day care as well.

© Bob Ebbesen/Alamy

Child care centers and preschools provide care for many children during the workday. Although children may not receive as much adult attention as they might with a single caregiver or with family day care, they benefit from greater interaction with other children and a preschool curriculum.

- *Low child-to-staff ratio.* Positive caregiving is associated with a low child-to-staff ratio, especially for very young children. State guidelines vary, but experts believe they tend to be too minimal. Best would be six to eight infants per two caregivers, six to twelve one- to two-year-olds per three teachers, and fourteen to twenty older preschoolers per two teachers.
- *Stable staff.* Some staff turnover is inevitable, but it should not exceed 25 percent a year. If children must constantly adjust to changes in personnel, they cannot build the warm and trusting relationships that they need with caregivers. It is also important to learn how much attention is given to preparing children for a caretaker's departure and to helping them adjust to new staff.
- *A well-trained staff.* Trained staff members are likely to be more responsive, more stimulating, and more creative in their activities with children. Because child care workers are poorly paid, it is difficult to find centers with staff members who are highly educated or trained in early childhood education. The ideal situation is for staff to be knowledgeable about child development and to participate in workshops or other ongoing training in best practices. Ask about staff education and plans for further training. In family day care settings, ask whether other family members or others who are not formally "staff" are nevertheless involved in caring for the children.
- *Cultural sensitivity.* Caregivers should be knowledgeable about the diverse racial/ethnic, religious, and social class cultures of this society and should be aware that children may come from various types of families, such as traditional nuclear, dual-earner, gay/lesbian, single-parent, divorced, or remarried.
- *Other staff qualities.* A warm personality and interpersonal sensitivity are essential. Caregivers who let children express their feelings and who will take their views into account are desirable. Because staff members will have an influence on the child's language acquisition, being verbally fluent and well-spoken is an asset. Some parents may have specific preferences, such as male or female caregivers or both, or minority or bilingual staff. Parents seeking family child care may have a specific type of home environment in mind and should consider how well their values and lifestyle match those of the caretaker.

- *Age-appropriate attention.* Babies need a responsive adult who coos and talks to them. One-year-olds need a staff member who will name things for them. Two-year olds need someone who reads to them. Older children can profit from social interaction and activities with other children as well as with adult caregivers.
- Adults should be responsive to children and interact with them, not limit themselves to a directive, organizing role. Do they greet the child warmly? Do they seem interested in what the child is doing or saying? They should make eye contact and perhaps bend to their level when speaking with children, not brush the children off or have a ho-hum attitude. How staff members interact with children can best be ascertained by observation in visits to the center.
- *Age-appropriate and stimulating activities and play spaces.* Experts differ on how academic a preschool program should be, and parents differ in how "educational" a program they are looking for. Look for a facility that also fosters play and community activities such as trips to the zoo or fire station—and one that prepares children for learning rather than offering a first-grade program in preschool. In any case, parents should pick a child care facility that is a good match for their values in this regard. You should find that staff members have a well-thought-out rationale for their program that they can easily describe.
- On the negative side, avoid child care centers or family day care environments that seem to provide only custodial care or allow lots of TV watching. What kinds of indoor and outdoor spaces are there for constructive and imaginative child play? What toys, books, and games are available? What are the ages of the other children who will be with your child in care?
- *Discipline.* Inquire about how staff handle the minor behavior problems that inevitably arise with children. Child experts typically recommend "time-outs," with physical discipline to be avoided. States vary in their laws regarding whether child caretakers are permitted to spank children. Where this is legally permissible, there may be centers or family caretakers who are indeed committed to the use of physical discipline—of course, parents may vary in terms of whether this is acceptable to them. You should both inquire and observe how "incidents" are handled, and ascertain whether the child care facility's policy and practice match what you want for your children. Use of physical discipline suggests that the caretakers are not well trained in handling problems and may create a somewhat fearful atmosphere for children as well.
- *A relationship with parents.* Parent–caregiver relationships will vary depending on whether the child is in family day care or a center. Any child care facility should welcome parental involvement, in the form of visits at a minimum; be wary of facilities that do not allow unannounced visits. You should feel supported in your parental role by the family caretaker or center staff (rather than distanced or unduly criticized). You should feel included in the child's daily life in child care. Especially important is how and how well family caretakers or center staff members communicate with you about problems.
- *Practical and financial considerations.* You will be told the basic hours and fees, but you also need to know what happens when the child is sick or the family leaves town and the child does not attend as usual. Can arrangements be made to have children arrive earlier or leave later than normal center hours on occasion? Regularly? Is transportation provided? If so, how costly is it, and how reliable?
- *Recommendations from other parents.* Talk to other parents about the facility. If you don't know any parents with children in the center, ask for names and phone numbers of parents who have children enrolled there, and talk to them about the facility. If a center declines to give you this information, try to determine whether the reason is that the facility's board adopted a privacy policy to protect parents or whether the management is being elusive and defensive.
- *Visits.* Visit the day care center as often as you can—and, if possible, unannounced—both before and after selecting a facility.
- *Accreditation.* The National Association for the Education of Young Children (NAEYC) is an accrediting agency for child care centers. If you plan to use center care, you might want to check the association's website (www.naeyc.org) for listings of accredited centers in your state. Although not all good child care centers have taken this step, accreditation by the NAEYC is a good sign.

Critical Thinking

What qualities do you think are most important in choosing a child care center? How would you compare in-home care, family day care, or center care on the qualities you think are important?

Sources: American Academy of Pediatrics 1992; Coordinated Access for Child Care 2001; Find Care 2002; Galinsky 2001; NICHD Early Child Care Research Network 2000a, 2003b; U.S. National Institute of Child Health and Human Development 2002; Watson 1984; Working Moms Refuge 2001.

Family day care and many child care centers are usually open weekdays only and close by 7 p.m. Some parents, such as single mothers on shift work or those who travel, need access to twenty-four-hour care centers. Child care is difficult to find for mildly ill youngsters too sick to go to their regular day care facility, although there are now centers beginning to fill this need (National Association for Sick Child Day Care 2010). Adding to the difficulty of finding day care is parents' need for *quality child care.* "As We Make Choices: Selecting a Child Care Facility" offers guidelines for evaluating the quality of a child care setting.

Elder Care There are some parallels between workers' responsibility for child care and for elder care. **Elder care** involves providing assistance with daily living activities to an elderly relative who is chronically frail, ill, disabled, or just in need of assistance. Many parents of the large baby boom generation are in their eighties and may live far away from their adult children. An estimated 34 million Americans are taking care of their aging parents. Some workers have retired early or just quit to care for parents, whereas others have turned down promotions, switched to part-time work, taken leaves of absence, or simply taken time off from work (Piercy 2007).

The need for companies to offer employees help with elderly dependents beyond unpaid family leave is becoming more recognized. Given that 90 percent of U.S. companies recently surveyed had a workforce of fifty-five years and older, many American companies are now offering elder care benefits as a recruiting tool (Woldt 2010). Supervisors may offer flexibility on an individual basis, but formal programs of assistance for elder care are in the beginning stages. Some 27 percent of companies now offer elder care benefits (Joyce 2007a). In addition to a graying population needing some assistance, a new phenomenon is taking root—older Americans finding new careers in taking care of the elderly. According to Paraprofessional Healthcare Institute, in 2008, some 28 percent of professional elder care workers were over the age of fifty-five (Leland 2010, p. 14; *Older Direct-Care Workers* 2010, p. 2). Care of the elderly is discussed in more detail in Chapter 17.

Family Leave **Family leave** involves an employee being able to take an extended period of time from work, either paid or unpaid, for the purpose of caring for a newborn, for a newly adopted or seriously ill child, for an elderly parent, or for their own health needs, with the guarantee of a job upon returning. The concept of family leave incorporates maternity, paternity, ill-child, and elder care leaves.

The 1993 Family and Medical Leave Act mandates up to twelve weeks of unpaid family leave for workers in companies with at least fifty employees. But unpaid leave will not solve the problem for a vast majority of employees, as most working parents need the income. More employers are now offering paid maternity leave. In 1981, only 37 percent of first-time mothers who had worked during pregnancy took paid leave (maternity leave, sick leave, or vacation). By 2003 (most recent data available), that number had increased to 49 percent. Women's unpaid leave reached an all-time high of 45 percent by 1996, where it remained until 2000, declining since that time to 39 percent. Another 8.5 percent took disability leave in 2003. Twenty-five percent of these first-time mothers quit their jobs, while 3.8 percent were let go. This last percentage—first-time mothers being fired from their jobs—has increased from a low of 2 percent in 1996 (Johnson 2007).

According to the Institute for Women's Policy Research, approximately 93 percent of the top 100 American companies offer one or more weeks of paid maternity leave, with the majority offering between five and eight weeks (Lovell, O'Neill, and Olsen 2007, p. 1). As for the remainder of the private sector, parental leave was far more dismal, with some 8 percent finding paid family leave available. Not surprisingly, the workers with the highest rates of paid family leave available were those in management, professional, and related fields (14 percent), whereas just 4 percent of those who worked in production, transportation, and material moving had paid family leave available ("National Compensation Survey" 2007, Table 19) "'Gen X and Gen Y men [men born later than 1964] are demanding to have the ability to play a larger role in family life than their fathers did," states Joan Williams, director of Work/Life Law at American University ("More New Dads" 2005, p. Bus. 1).

Flexible Scheduling About 27.5 percent of full-time workers have flexible schedules (U.S. Bureau of Labor Statistics 2009c, Table 30). **Flexible scheduling** includes such options as **job sharing** (two people share one position), working at home or telecommuting, compressed workweeks, flextime, and personal days (days off for the purpose of attending to a personal matter such as a doctor's appointment or a child's school program). Compressed workweeks allow an employee to concentrate the workweek into three or four or sometimes slightly longer days. **Flextime** involves flexible starting and ending times, with required core hours.

Flexible scheduling, although not a panacea, can help parents share child care or be at home before and after an older child's school hours. Some types of work do not lend themselves to flexible scheduling (see "A Closer Look at Family Diversity: Diversity and Child Care" earlier in this chapter), but the practice has been adopted by the federal government and by some companies because it offers employee-recruiting advantages, prevents turnover, and frees up office space when some employees work at home. Even when not formally offered, it may be possible.

Economist Edith Josten noted that employees who are allowed some flexibility in deciding when to begin and end work have reduced incidences of dissatisfaction, and those who choose to work longer hours in a day (allowing for a shorter workweek) complain less about job-related fatigue (2002, pp. 87-88). Employees who have flexible hours report enhanced job satisfaction and loyalty to the employer, but they find that flextime does not alleviate all or even most family–work conflicts. For one thing, women are slightly less likely to have this option than men are, though they are more in need of it given the typical division of labor in the home (U.S. Bureau of Labor Statistics 2009c, Table 30).

Who Will Provide What Is Needed to Resolve Work–Family Issues?

Policy experts, lawmakers, employers, parents, and citizens disagree over who has the responsibility to provide what is needed regarding various work–family solutions. A principal conflict concerns whether such solutions as child care or family leave should be government policy or constitute privileges for which a worker must negotiate.

The countries of northwestern Europe, which have a more pronatalist and social-welfare orientation than the United States, tend to view family benefits as a right (Lewis 2008). There is "the pervasive belief . . . that children are a precious national resource for which society has collective responsibility" (Clinton 1990, p. 25). Putting this belief into practice, most European countries are committed to *paid* maternity (or parental) leave for up to at least six months and usually much longer (Lewis 2008). Accustomed to a lack of family policy at the federal level, American parents sometimes turn their attention to local schools as a source of help for the care of older children in after-school programs and younger children in preschool programs and all-day kindergarten.

As you've read elsewhere in this chapter, some large corporations demonstrate interest in effecting **family-friendly workplace policies** that are supportive of employee efforts to combine family and work commitments. Such policies include on-site child care centers, sick-child care, subsidies for child care services or child care locator services, flexible schedules, parental or family leaves, workplace seminars and counseling programs, and support groups for employed parents. Such research as exists on outcomes for employers suggests that these policies help in recruitment, reduce employee stress and turnover, enhance morale, and thus increase productivity ("Balancing Work and Life" 2009).

But family-friendly policies are hardly available to all American workers (Heymann, Earle, and Hayes 2007). Professionals and managers are much more likely than technical and clerical workers to have access to leave policies, telecommuting, or flexible scheduling ("National Compensation Survey" 2007, Table 19). "At the high end, the big corporations are stepping up to provide benefits to help families, and at the lower end, as women leave welfare, there's now much more support for the idea that they deserve help with child care. But the blue-collar families, the K-Mart cashier, get nothing" (work–family policy expert Kathleen Sylvester, quoted in Lewin 2001b).

An estimated 40 percent of the workforce is made up of unmarried people. Single individuals or childless workers have begun to complain about what they see as the privileging of parents of young children when they themselves may have family caregiving needs: for elderly parents, siblings, or friends with whom they maintain caregiving relationships. They may find it onerous to cover for coworkers who are on leave or out of the office. They may feel that simple fairness should permit some flexibility in their schedules as well, for personal needs. Some companies have begun to accommodate these workers by instituting sabbaticals, "flexible culture," and "employee-friendly" policies, redefining policies previously characterized as "family-friendly" (Joyce 2006; 2007a).

We have devoted attention to work–family policies because these issues so strongly influence the options and choices of individual families. We would like to think that family-friendly companies represent the future of work. After all, "children . . . are 'public goods'; society profits greatly from future generations as stable, well-adjusted adults, as well as future employees and tax payers" (Avellar and Smock 2003, p. 605). Nevertheless, these voluntary programs and benefits do depend on cost constraints and corporate self-interest and are not likely to be so available during economic downturns or restructuring. Moreover, family-friendly programs need to be more comprehensive in terms of benefits and more widely available to all echelons of workers. However, keep in mind that most workers need extensive family support only during the period in which they are parenting young children. From that perspective, the challenge looks less daunting.

Entering the political arena to work toward the kinds of changes families want is one aspect of creating satisfying marriages and families. But employed couples also want to know what *they* can do themselves to maintain happy marriages. We now turn to that topic.

The Two-Earner Marriage and the Relationship

As you have been reading throughout this chapter, there are many challenges associated with two-earner marriages. But research shows that multiple roles (such as employee, spouse, parent) does not add to stress

© Stewart Cohen/Index Stock Imagery

This dual-earner couple have common job experiences—something traditional spouses do not have an opportunity to share.

(provided there is enough time to accomplish things), and in fact may enhance personal happiness. Research also points to the heightened satisfaction, excitement, and vitality that two-earner couples can have because these partners are more likely to have common experiences and shared worldviews than do traditional spouses, who often lead very different everyday lives. At the same time, conflict may arise in two-earner marriages as couples negotiate the division of household labor and more generally adjust to changing roles.

Gender Strategies

How a couple allocates paid and unpaid work and then justifies that allocation can be thought of as a *gender strategy*, a way of working through everyday situations that takes into account an individual's beliefs and deep feelings about gender roles, as well as her or his employment commitments (Hochschild 1989). In today's changing society, conscious beliefs and deeper feelings about gender may conflict. For example, a number of men in Hochschild's study of working couples articulated egalitarian sentiments, but had clearly retained gut-level traditional feelings about sex differences. Tensions exhibited by many of Hochschild's respondents were a consequence of "faster-changing women and slower-changing men" (p. 11).

Even when spouses share similar attitudes about gender, circumstances may not allow them to act accordingly. In one couple interviewed by Hochschild, both partners held the traditional belief that a wife should be a full-time homemaker. Yet because the couple needed the wife's income, she was employed, and they shared housework on a nearly equal basis. How couples manage their everyday lives in the face of contradictions reflects a consciously or unconsciously negotiated gender strategy.

One gender strategy used by wives who would like their husband to do more, but know he won't and are reluctant to insist, is to compare their husbands to other men "out there" who apparently are doing even less. A common gender strategy, according to Hochschild (1989), is to develop *family myths*—"versions of reality that obscure a core truth in order to manage a family tension." For example, when a husband shares housework in a way that contradicts his traditional beliefs and/or feelings, couples may develop a myth alleging the wife's poor health or incompetence to protect the man's image of himself. A common family myth defines the wife as an organized and energetic superwoman who has few needs of her own, requires little from her husband, and congratulates herself on how much she can accomplish.

Sociologist Bradford Wilcox (2004) uses the term *"enchanted" economies of gratitude* (p. 137, referencing Hochschild) in his study of evangelical families (to explain evangelical husbands' greater-than-average expressions of appreciation for their wives' household work). The commitment of the couple to a religiously based traditional division of labor is an anomaly in the context of today's ideal of egalitarian sharing. The evangelical wife's greater household labor is a "gift" that has symbolic significance for their religious and family world, and the husband reciprocates with "emotion work" (Wilcox 2004, Chapter 5).

Maintaining Intimacy While Negotiating Provider Roles and the Second Shift

Two kinds of changes are involved in moving toward more egalitarian family roles: Women come to share the provider role, while men take greater responsibility for household work. In considering the provider role, we turn to the notion of *meaning* again: Is women's sharing of the provider role a *threat,* so that men fear losing masculine identity, women's domestic services, and power?

Or is a woman's sharing the provider role a *benefit,* because men benefit materially from wives' employment and earnings and from a partner's enthusiasm for the wider world? Recent research suggests that men are more apt to see women's employment as a benefit. As a result, there is an ideological shift of men toward egalitarianism (Gerson 2010, pp. 107, 117).

Household work seems to be the greater arena for stress and conflict as roles change. Study after study shows that marital satisfaction is greater when wives feel that husbands share fairly in the household work. But a woman's employment does not necessarily lead to a husband's sharing of household work (Greenstein 2009).

Although husbands may now carry a greater share of the family work than in the past, getting comfortable with transitions in marital roles is not a quick and easy process. But when the transition proceeds from a mutual commitment to achieve an equitable relationship, the result may be greater intimacy. It follows from the general principle articulated in Chapter 1 that initial choices may need to be revisited over the life cycle. Gender issues may be revisited as partners adjust to changing work–family realities and as children enter the picture and then grow older. A first step is to address conflict.

Accept Conflict as a Reality The idea that marital partners may sometimes have competing interests departs from the more romanticized view that sees marriages and families as integrated units with shared desires and goals. As a first step toward maintaining intimacy during role changes, partners need to recognize their possibly competing interests and to expect conflict (Gerson 2010, p. 123).

Accept Ambivalence After accepting conflict as a reality, the next step in maintaining intimacy as spouses adjust to two-earner marriages is for both to recognize that each may have ambivalent feelings. The following excerpt from one young husband's essay for his English composition class is illustrative of a man's dilemma in assessing fairness in the division of labor: "I'm in school six days a week. My wife works between 40 to 50 hours a week. So I do the majority of the cooking, cleaning, and laundry. To me this is not right. But am I wrong to think so?" Women may also be ambivalent. They want their husbands to be happy, they want their husbands to help and support them, they feel angry about any past inequalities, and they feel guilty about their declining interest in housekeeping and their decreasing willingness to accommodate their husbands' preferences. Furthermore, men who participate have opinions about how child rearing or housework should be done. As a husband begins to pitch in, his wife may resent his intrusion into her traditional domain.

Empathize A next step is to empathize. This may be difficult, for it is tempting instead to point out where a partner falls short. But if couples are to maintain intimacy, they must make sure that *both* partners "win." Wives are often irritated by observing that husbands may underestimate the number of hours that household labor takes (Galinsky, Aumann, and Bond 2009; Kelleher 2007; Swanbrow 2008). It is never easy to adjust to new roles, and men especially may feel they have a lot to lose. Men can gain, too, of course: They develop domestic skills, their marriage is enhanced, there is more money, and they benefit from spending time with their children. In Hochschild's study (1989), some fathers who felt they had been emotionally deprived in relationships with their own fathers took great pleasure in creating more satisfying family relationships with and for their children.

As husbands empathize, they need to be aware that their willingness to participate in household tasks is vitally important to wives, especially to employed wives. A husband's sharing carries a symbolic meaning for a wife, indicating that her work is recognized and appreciated and that her husband cares (Crary 2008).

Strike an Equitable Rebalance Researchers who studied 153 Pennsylvania couples with children in school concluded the following: "Our data imply that the adjustment of individual family members, as well as harmonious family relationships, requires a *balance* among the very different and often conflicting needs and goals of different family members" (McHale and Crouter 1992, pp. 545–46, italics in original). Once equity is habitual, calculation and constant comparison are no longer necessary; some observers point out that the balance need not be an exactly calculated fifty-fifty split.

Show Mutual Appreciation Once partners have committed themselves to striking a balance, they need to create ways to let each know the other is loved. Traditional role expectations are relatively rigid and limiting, but they can be a way of expressing love and caring. When a wife cooks her husband's favorite meal or a husband can pay for family travel, each feels cared about. As spouses relinquish some traditional behaviors, they need to create new ways of letting each other know they care. Many people have noted the potential of shared work and of shared provider and caregiving roles for enriching a marriage (Galinsky, Aumann, and Bond 2009; van der Lippe 2010).

This discussion of the second shift has been framed in terms of marriage, the relationships of husbands and wives as they negotiate this marital challenge. Marriage *is* most likely to draw on cultural expectations of a traditional division of labor. But the second shift exists in other family forms. In heterosexual cohabiting couples, the woman does less household labor and the man more than in marriage, whereas the domestic division of labor is rather egalitarian in gay and lesbian couples. Single women and men also have work to do to maintain their households, especially if they are parents. Single men tend to do more than married men, whereas single women do less than married women. Interestingly, remarried couples are more likely to share housework than are men and women in a first marriage (Coltrane 2000; Patterson 2000), as are couples who cohabited before marriage (Rhoades et al. 2006). We should keep in mind that employees are embedded in diverse families and that partners may come up with a variety of ways of accomplishing providing and caregiving.

Despite the unresolved tensions of the second shift, research by sociologist K. Jill Kiecolt (2003) suggests that employed men and women are largely happy with their home lives. She set out to explore a thesis developed by Arlie Hochschild (1997) in her study of workers at one company. Hochschild concluded that family life for employed people is so hectic that work becomes a refuge, a place where individuals would prefer to be. Hochschild's was a case study, so no statistical conclusions could be drawn.

Testing this thesis with General Social Survey data from National Opinion Research Center (NORC) over the period between 1973 and 1994, Kiecolt found that only 13 percent of workers saw it that way. In the most recent year she studied, over 40 percent of respondents had "high work–home satisfaction," whereas home was viewed as a haven for another 40 percent plus.

The next chapter examines communication and managing conflict in families, skills that can smooth the negotiation of work–family roles.

Summary

- We look at men's and women's participation in the labor force. Traditionally, the husband's job was as provider, the wife's as homemaker. These roles changed as more and more women entered the workforce. Women remain segregated occupationally, and they earn lower incomes than men, on average.
- We have seen that paid work is not usually structured to allow time for household responsibilities and that women, more than men, continue to adjust their time to accomplish both paid and unpaid work. Many wives would prefer shared roles, and negotiation and tension over this issue can cast a shadow on a marriage. An incomplete transition to equality at work and at home affects family life profoundly. However, in recent years, men have been increasing their share of the housework, and men and women now have a balance in total work hours.
- Household work and child care are pressure points as women enter the labor force and the two-earner marriage becomes the norm. To make it work, either the structure of work must be changed, social policy must support working families, or women and men must change their household role patterns—very probably all three.
- We have emphasized that both cultural expectations and public policy affect people's options. As individuals come to realize this, we can expect pressure on public officials and corporations to meet the needs of working families by providing supportive policies: parental leave, child care, and flextime.
- To be successful, two-earner marriages will require social policy support and workplace flexibility. But there are some things couples themselves can do to better manage a working-couple family. Recognition of both positive and negative feelings and open communication between partners can help working couples cope with an imperfect social world.

Questions for Review and Reflection

1. Discuss to what extent distinctions between husbands' and wives' work are disappearing.
2. What do you see as the advantages and disadvantages of men being househusbands? Discuss this from the points of view of both men and women.
3. What are some advantages and disadvantages of home-based work?
4. What work–family conflicts do you see around you? Interview some married or single-parent friends of yours for concrete examples and for some suggestions for resolving such conflicts.
5. **Policy Question.** What family-friendly workplace policies would you like to see instituted? Which would you be likely to take advantage of?

Key Terms

attachment 307
center care 305
child care 304
commuter marriage 304
elder care 310
family child care 305
family-friendly workplace policies 311
family leave 310
flexible scheduling 310
flextime 310
good provider role 288
househusband 290
in-home caregiver 305
job sharing 310
labor force 282
leisure gap 297
market approach to child care 305
motherhood penalty 285
mothering approach to child care 305
nanny 291
neotraditional families 287
occupational segregation 283
opting out 286
parenting approach to child care 305
second shift 295
self-care 305
shift work 291
stay-at-home dad 290
trailing spouse 303
two-career marriage 291
two-earner marriage 290
unpaid family work 294
wage gap 284

Online Resources

Sociology CourseMate

www.CengageBrain.com

Access an integrated eBook, chapter-specific interactive learning tools, including flash cards, quizzes, videos, and more in your Sociology CourseMate, accessed through CengageBrain.com.

www.CengageBrain.com

Want to maximize your online study time? Take this easy-to-use study system's diagnostic pre-test, and it will create a personalized study plan for you. By helping you identify the topics that you need to understand better and then directing you to valuable online resources, it can speed up your chapter review. CengageNOW even provides a post-test so you can confirm that you are ready for an exam.

12

Communication in Relationships, Marriages, and Families

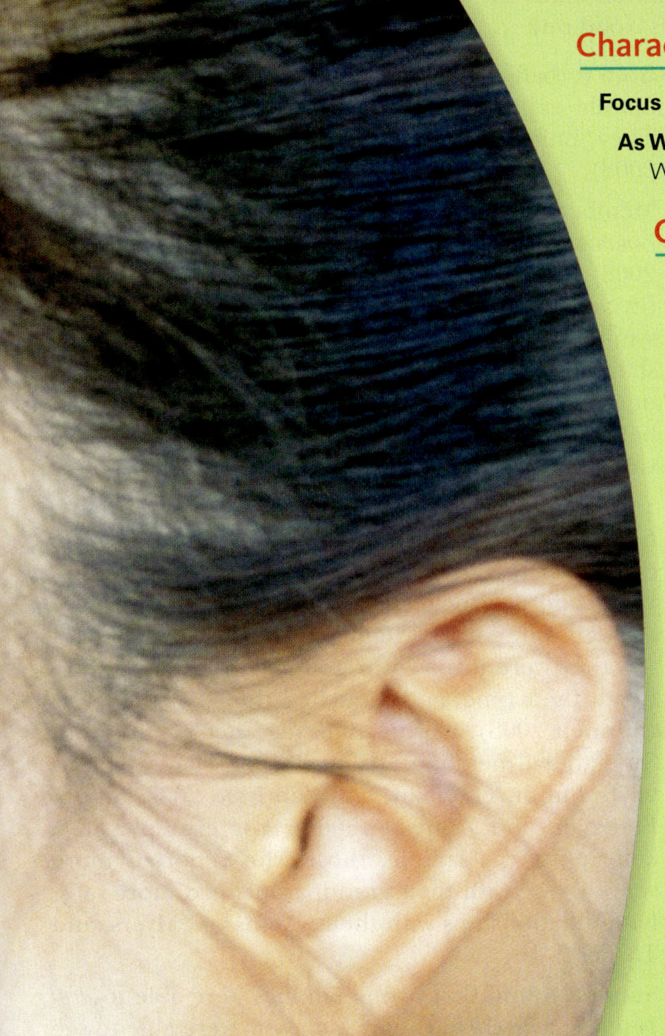

Providing emotional security is an important function of today's families. Moreover, families are powerful environments. Virtually nowhere else in our society is there such capacity to support, hurt, comfort, denigrate, reassure, ridicule, hate, and love. Research from a variety of samples and pertaining to a variety of family situations overwhelmingly supports what may be intuitively obvious: Conveying affection for one's partner and other family members is a very important determinant of relationship and family happiness, as well as each family member's psychological well-being (Fagan 2009; Soliz, Thorson, and Rittenour 2009). And although conflict is a natural part of every relationship, developing positive communication skills can help family members to resolve conflicts in positive ways.

This chapter will address the importance of communicating affection as well as addressing conflict in positive ways. We'll examine the relationship between communication and relationship satisfaction. We'll discuss gender differences with regard to couple and family communication. We will review ten guidelines suggested for addressing family and couple conflicts. To begin, we'll look at characteristics of cohesive families.

Characteristics of Cohesive Families

Family cohesion, or "togetherness," is defined as "the emotional bonding that couples and family members have toward one another" (Olson and Gorall 2003, p. 516). A couple or family can have too much cohesion (an *enmeshed* couple or family) or too little (a *disengaged* or *disconnected* couple or family). Experts advise a *balanced level of cohesion*—one that combines a reasonable and mutually satisfying degree of emotional bonding with individual family members' need for autonomy. In this chapter, we will use the term *family cohesion* to refer to a balanced degree of cohesion—neither enmeshed nor disengaged.

Before going further, we should recognize that for different families—and for families of different race/ethnicities—the definition of *balance* with regard to family cohesion varies. "If a couple's/family's expectations or subcultural group norms support more extreme [cohesion levels], families can function well as long as all family members desire the family to function [at that level]" (Olson and Gorall 2003, p. 522). For instance, in Mexican American families, a relatively high level of family cohesion has been related to positive outcomes for adolescents (Behnke et al. 2008; Martyn et al. 2009).

To find out what makes families cohesive, social scientist Nick Stinnett researched 130 "strong families" in rural and urban areas throughout Oklahoma (Stinnett 1985, 2008). Obviously, this limited sample, selected with help from home economics extension agents, has no claim to representativeness. Furthermore, the concept *strong family* is subjective. Various individuals or groups have their own ideas about just what a strong family is. But Stinnett's research helped to advance ideas about what makes for couple and/or family cohesion. In general, Stinnett's families constructed their lives in ways that enhance family relationships. Instead of drifting into relationship habits by default, they made knowledgeable choices, each member playing an active part in carrying out family commitments. When Stinnett made his observations, the following six qualities stood out:

1. Both verbally and nonverbally, family members often openly expressed their *appreciation for one another.* They "built each other up psychologically" (Stinnett 2008).
2. Members of cohesive families had a *high degree of commitment* to the family group as a whole (Stinnett 2008). Families like this create a shared family identity and reality (Rueter and Koerner 2008).[1] From a symbolic interactionist perspective, families create a shared reality through frequent, spontaneous, and unconstrained conversations that allow family members to participate together in defining family beliefs, values, situations, events, and rituals.
3. Stinnett found that, on a regular basis, family members *arranged their personal schedules* so that they could do things together. They invested in their family. When life got so hectic that members didn't have enough time for their families, they listed the activities they were involved in, found those that weren't worth their time, and scratched them off their lists (Stinnett 2008). Leisure time together is important for family members (Clayton and Perry-Jenkins 2008; Smith, Freeman, and Zabriskie 2009; Smith, Freeman, and Zabriskie 2009). For example, in a college-student sample, those who reported more shared time with their grandparents had more satisfying relationships with them (Mansson, Myers, and Turner 2010).
4. Stinnett found that strong families were able to *deal positively with crises.* Family members were able to see something good in bad situations, even if it was just gratitude that they had each other and could face the crisis together (Stinnett 2008). Chapter 14 addresses dealing creatively with stress and crises.
5. Many of the families that Stinnett studied had a *spiritual orientation.* Although they were not necessarily

[1] Some family structures may have an easier time of this than others. For instance, many same-sex couples and their children must create a family identity in the absence of full cultural legitimacy. Then too, "Genetically related family members likely share a sense of belonging based on physical appearance, blood ties, and shared social attitudes or cognitions based in genetic inheritance. All these shared characteristics facilitate their ability to create a shared reality" (Rueter and Koerner 2008).

members of any organized religion, they did have a sense of some power and purpose greater than themselves and typically evidenced a "hopeful attitude toward life" (DeFrain 2002).

6. These families had *positive communication* patterns. Members of families like these talk with and listen to one another, conveying respect and interest (Schrodt 2009). They confirm, validate, and accept each other (Dailey 2009). One study of college-aged daughters found that they were happier with their father-daughter relationship when it involved higher levels of ordinary and reciprocal conversation (Punyanunt-Carter 2008).

In addition to the previously mentioned, cohesive families and supportive couple relationships involve some "old-fashioned" virtues such as prudence, humility, tolerance, gratitude, justice, charity, and forgiveness (Fincham, Stanley, and Beach 2007). How do children benefit from family cohesiveness?

Children, Family Cohesion, and Unresolved Conflict

Regardless of family structure, a family characterized by warmth, cohesion, and generally supportive communication is better for children (Hillaker et al. 2008; Lindsey et al. 2009; Matiasko, Grunden, and Ernst 2007). Furthermore, parental values are more readily passed on to children when the family atmosphere is generally cohesive (Roest, Dubas, and Gerris 2009).

Conversely, a home characterized by significant, unresolved, and ongoing conflict negatively impacts children (Schoppe-Sullivan, Schermerhorn, and Cummings 2007). Meanwhile, contrary to the idea that couple conflicts in the home are necessarily detrimental to children, conflicts can end in constructive ways from the children's perspective.

> We posit that children's positive response to conflict resolution is an indication of enhanced emotional security. That is, children feel an increased sense of well-being resulting from the confidence of knowing that although their parents disagree, their relationship is safe and will endure. (Goeke-Morey, Cummings, and Papp 2007, p. 751)

However, a climate of *unresolved* marital conflict, especially when accompanied by parental depression, which it often is, correlates with children's emotional insecurity (Kouros, Merrilees, and Cummings 2008). A Hong Kong study of children's responses to ongoing parental conflict found that the children felt anxious over the future of their parents' relationship as well as feeling that they had to mediate the conflict (Lee et al. 2010).

Research shows a link between unresolved parental conflict and children's behavior problems (Feinberg, Kan, and Hetherington 2007; Teachman 2009). One study (Buehler et al. 1998) sampled 337 sixth through eighth graders. Three-quarters were non-Hispanic white, 12 percent were Hispanic, and 13 percent represented other racial/ethnic groups. The parents of 87 percent of the children in the sample were married. The parents' average education level was somewhere between high school graduate and some college.

The students were asked to fill out questionnaires that assessed their behavior and any conflict between their parents. *Externalizing behavior problems* (associated with "acting out," aggression toward others, or rule breaking) were measured by students' agreeing or disagreeing with statements such as "I cheat a lot" or "I tease others a lot." *Internalizing behavior problems* (those associated with emotional or psychological problems) were measured by students' agreeing or disagreeing with statements such as "I am unhappy a lot" or "I worry a lot." The children were also asked about their parents' conflict. Negative *overt parental conflict styles* involved such things as the parents' calling each other names, telling each other to shut up, or threatening each other in front of the child. Negative *covert parental conflict styles* included such things as trying to get the child to side with one parent and asking the child to relay a message from one parent to the other because the parents refused to speak to each other.

The researchers found that conflict between parents was not the only cause of children's behavior problems. Nevertheless, for both girls and boys, a strong correlation existed between interparental

Among other things, cohesive families have high levels of commitment and positive communication patterns. Making time to be together, they build one another up psychologically.

As We Make Choices

Communicating with Children—How to Talk So Kids Will Listen and Listen So Kids Will Talk

There are more and less effective ways to communicate with children, and a knowledgeable choice would involve more effective ways. What are some of these methods?

Helping Children Deal with Their Feelings

Children—including adult children—need to have their feelings accepted and respected.

1. *You can listen quietly and attentively.*
2. *You can acknowledge their feelings with a word.* "Oh . . . mmm . . . I see. . . ."
3. *You can give the feeling a name.* "That sounds frustrating!"
4. *You can note that all feelings are accepted, but certain actions must be limited.* "I can see how angry you are at your brother. Tell him what you want with words, not fists."

Engaging a Child's Cooperation

1. *Describe what you see, or describe the problem.* "There's a wet towel on the bed."
2. *Give information.* "The towel is getting my blanket wet."
3. *Describe what you feel.* "I don't like sleeping in a wet bed!"
4. *Write a note* (above towel rack): Please put me back so I can dry. Thanks! Your Towel

Instead of Punishment

1. *Express your feelings strongly—without attacking character.* "I'm furious that my saw was left outside to rust in the rain!"
2. *State your expectations.* "I expect my tools to be returned after they've been borrowed."
3. *Show the child how to make amends.* "What this saw needs now is a little steel wool and a lot of elbow grease."
4. *Give the child a choice.* "You can borrow my tools and return them, or you can give up the privilege of using them. You decide."

Encouraging Autonomy

1. *Let children make choices.* "Are you in the mood for your gray pants today or your red pants?"
2. *Show respect for a child's struggle.* "A jar can be hard to open."
3. *Don't ask too many questions.* "Glad to see you. Welcome home."

conflict and behavior problems. When parents used an overtly negative style, the youth were more likely to report externalizing behavior problems. When parents used a covert, negative style, the youth were more likely to report internalizing behavior problems.

In another study of fifty-five Caucasian middle- and upper-middle-class five-year-olds and their married mothers, the mothers completed questionnaires on parent–child relations and interparental arguing that were mailed to them at home. Later, the mothers took their children to be observed in a university laboratory setting. The researchers found that marital discord was positively related to children's externalizing and internalizing behavior problems. However, this research also showed that the interparental conflict influenced a child's behavior *indirectly:* Marital discord negatively affected parental discipline and the parent-child relationship more generally. This situation then negatively affected the child's behavior.[2]

The researchers concluded that "if parents are able to maintain good relations with children in the face of marital conflict, the children may be buffered from the potential emotional fallout of the conflict" (Harrist and Ainslie 1998, p. 156; see also Lindsey, Caldera, and Tankersley 2009; Schoppe-Sullivan, Schermerhorn, and Cummings 2007; Schrodt, Witt, and Messersmith 2008). Recent research has investigated the effects of parental and general family conflict on sibling relationships.

Unresolved Family Conflict and Sibling Relationships One interesting study of mothers, fathers, and adolescents from 200 middle- and working-class, mostly European American families found parental conflict to be causally associated with parents' differential treatment of their children. A possible reason is because ongoing, unresolved parental conflict encourages a parent to form a parent-child alliance with one sibling—a situation that leaves other siblings out. Perceived differential treatment among siblings leads to sibling conflict and underlying resentments that can linger into adulthood (Kan, McHale, and Crouter 2008).

Another study looked at a racially and ethnically diverse sample of elderly mothers with at least two adult children and found that a mother's perceived favoritism while the children were growing up reduced siblings' closeness in adulthood. "Further, mothers' favoritism appeared to reduce closeness regardless of which child

[2] A recent study from the biosocial theoretical perspective (see Chapter 2) sampled mothers and found that a mother's high level of cortisol, a chemical associated with being stressed, "spilled over" after having been secreted during parental conflict to subsequently have a negative effect on her parenting behaviors (Sturge-Apple et al. 2009). Interestingly, other research shows that an individual's ingesting the hormone oxytocin—see footnote #11—reduces cortisol levels during couple conflict and also increases positive communication behaviors (Ditzen et al. 2009; see also Ellison and Gray 2009; Priem, McLaren, and Solomon 2010).

4. *Don't rush to answer questions.* "That's an interesting question. What do you think?"
5. *Encourage children to use sources outside the home.* "Maybe the pet shop owner would have a suggestion."
6. *Don't take away hope.* "So you're thinking of trying out for the play! That should be an experience."

Praise and Self-Esteem

Instead of evaluating, describe.

1. *Describe what you see.* "I see your car parked exactly where we agreed it would be."
2. *Describe what you feel.* "It's a pleasure to walk into this room!"
3. *Sum up the child's praiseworthy behavior with a word.* "You sorted out your pencils, crayons, and pens, and put them in separate boxes. That's what I call *organization*!"

Freeing Children from Playing Roles

1. *Look for opportunities to show the child a new picture of himself or herself.* "You've had that toy since you were three, and it looks almost like new!"
2. *Put children in situations in which they can see themselves differently.* "Sara, would you take the screwdriver and tighten the pulls on these drawers?"
3. *Let children overhear you say something positive about them.* "He held his arm steady even though the shot hurt."
4. *Model the behavior you'd like to see.* "It's hard to lose, but I'll try to be a sport about it. Congratulations!"
5. *Be a storehouse for your child's special moments.* "I remember the time you. . . ."

Critical Thinking

What bit of advice given here might you choose to practice when communicating with the child(ren) in your life? Why is it important to encourage children to talk? Why is it important to listen to children? Why does how we talk to children matter?

Source: Excerpts from Rawson Associates/Scribner, an imprint of Simon & Schuster, from *How to Talk So Kids Will Listen and Listen So Kids Will Talk,* by Adele Faber and Elaine Mazlish. Copyright © 1980 by Adele Faber and Elaine Mazlish. Also see Faber and Mazlish (2006) as well as the Faber Mazlish website, www.fabermazlish.com, and the Mental Health America website, www.mentalhealthamerica.net.

was favored, suggesting that siblings' relationships are shaped . . . by principles of equity" (Suitor et al. 2009, p. 1032).[3] However, a different study found that, in childhood and adolescence, the sibling who felt slighted was likely to be depressed (Shanahan et al. 2008). Meanwhile a study of 246 two-parent Mexican American families found that adolescents in families with a solution-oriented conflict management style, rather than ongoing unresolved conflict, had better sibling relationships (Killoren, Thayer, and Updegraff 2008).

Of course, children's behavior also depends on how the parents communicate with the children themselves, even when family conflict exists (Schrodt et al. 2009). "As We Make Choices: Communicating with Children—How to Talk So Kids Will Listen and Listen So Kids Will Talk" describes some effective ways to communicate with children.

By now you may have surmised that in families headed by coupled partners, family communication tends to be influenced by the degree of supportiveness or negativity in the couple relationship itself (Doohan et al. 2009). Distressed couples tend toward negative exchanges that put family relationships on a downward spiral (Driver and Gottman 2004). Partners who communicate mutual affection create a positive "spiraling effect" so that the atmosphere becomes one of emotional support (L. White 1999).

Communication and Couple Satisfaction

Couples demonstrate different **relationship ideologies**—expectations for closeness and/or distance as well as ideas about how partners should play their roles. A pivotal task for all couples is to balance each partner's need for autonomy with the simultaneous need for intimacy, togetherness, and support (Brock and Lawrence 2009; Lavy et al. 2009).

Couples also differ in their attitudes toward conflict. Some expect to engage in conflict only over big issues. Others argue more often. Still others expect a relationship that largely avoids not only conflict but also demonstrations of affection (Fitzpatrick 1995). All of these couple types can be happy with their relationship. What matters is whether the partners' actual interaction matches their ideology.

Meanwhile, unhappy relationships have some common features: less positive and more negative verbal and nonverbal communication, together with more reciprocity of negative—but not of positive—messages (Noller and Fitzpatrick 1991; Gottman and Levenson 2000).

[3] According to linguist Deborah Tannen (2006), many grown daughters continue to feel rejected because their mothers persist in showing preference to their brothers.

An important characteristic of happy couples involves disclosure of feelings and showing affection for one another. Meanwhile, even the happiest couples experience conflicts. Whether and how a couple resolves interpersonal conflicts creates a "spiraling effect" that positively or negatively influences communication throughout the family.

Regarding married couples, Huston and Melz (2004) found that after the honeymoon stage, there is a "coming down to earth" stage in a marriage. Interestingly, however, in the years after "the honeymoon's over," couples did not necessarily argue more. Instead, their marriages showed a decline in signs of love and affection. "One year into marriage, the average spouse says 'I love you,' hugs and kisses their partner, makes their partner laugh, and has sexual intercourse about half as often as when they were newly wed." Although marriages do not necessarily "become more antagonistic as time passes, the unpleasant exchanges that *do* occur are embedded in a less affectionate context, and thus, the spouses are likely to come to feel that their marriage is less of 'a haven in a heartless world'" (p. 951).

Having gathered data on married couples, researchers Ted Huston and Heidi Melz (2004) classified relationships into four types: *warm*, or friendly; *tempestuous*, or stormy; *bland*, or empty shell; and *hostile*, or distressed (p. 951).[4] As indicated in Figure 12.1, warm relationships are high on showing signs of love and affection while low on antagonism. Tempestuous unions are high on both affection and antagonism. Bland marriages are low on showing signs of affection as well as on antagonism. Hostile marriages are low on love and affection but high on antagonism.

We can assume that warm and friendly relationships best fill the family function of providing emotional security. We can also conclude that hostile ones are undesirable. Huston and Melz called both bland and tempestuous unions "mixed blessing" relationships because these two types evidenced only one of two desirable attributes. Although bland relationships have little antagonism, they lack displays of affection. And although tempestuous couples intermittently show affection, they deal with conflicts in aggressive, or antagonistic, ways.

> If our goal is to identify the early signs of a marital rupture, our research suggests that we look to the loss of love and affection early in marriage as symptomatic. . . . This loss of good feelings, rather than the emergence of conflict early in marriage, seems to be what sends relationships into a downward spiral, no doubt eventually leading to increased bickering and fighting and, ultimately, to the collapse of the union. (Huston and Melz 2004, pp. 951–52)

This situation helps to explain the general finding, discussed in Chapter 7, that for many couples the early years of marriage are the happiest. Of course, partners can change this by making knowledgeable decisions about communicating intimacy.

Other research, conducted by widely recognized communication psychologist, John Gottman and his colleagues, found that "[t]he absence of positive affect and not the presence of negative affect . . . was most predictive of later divorcing" (Gottman and Levenson 2000, p. 743). **Positive affect** involves the verbal or nonverbal expression of affection. Gottman further argued that, at least for the middle-class couples in his sample, he could predict a married couple's later divorce by examining how well the spouses showed that they were interested in each other:

> In a careful viewing of the videotapes, we noticed that there were critical moments during the events-of-the-day conversation that could be called either "requited"

[4] This research by Huston and Metz (2004) studied heterosexual, married couples only. The extent to which their findings and conclusions apply to otherwise committed couples, such as cohabiting or same-sex partners, is unknown. Increasingly, researchers are making the point that correlates of relationship satisfaction need to be studied among other than heterosexually married couples, and researchers are beginning to do this (e.g., Lincoln, Taylor, and Jackson 2008).

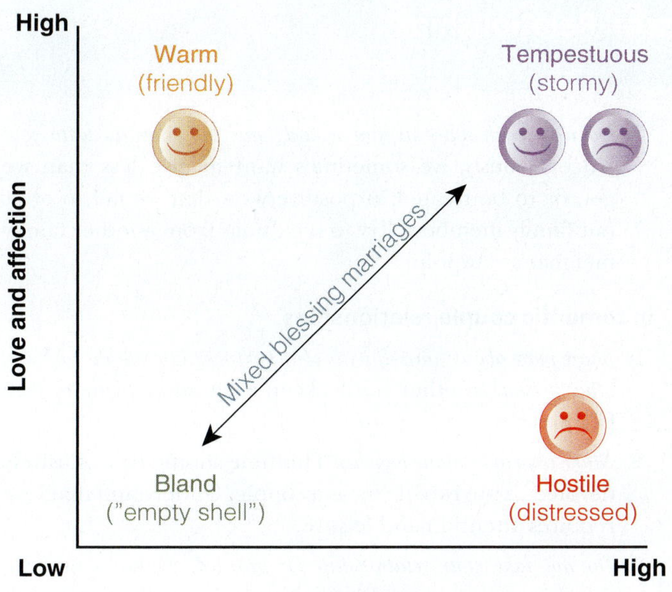

Figure 12.1 The emotional climates of committed relationships. This figure depicts the classification of emotional climates along two dimensions: (1) love and affection, and (2) antagonism. Warm relationships are high on love and affection while low on antagonism. Tempestuous unions are high on love and affection but also on antagonism. Bland relationships are low on love and affection as well as on antagonism. Hostile relationships are low on love and affection but high on antagonism. Why do you think that the tempestuous and bland types are called "mixed blessings"?

Source: From Huston and Melz 2004. Reprinted by permission of Blackwell Publishing. See footnote #2 in this chapter.

> [returned, acknowledged, or reciprocated] or "unrequited" interest and excitement. For example, in one couple, the wife reported excitedly about something their young son had done that day, but she was met with her husband's disinterest. After a time of talking about errands that needed doing, he talked excitedly about something important that happened to him that day at work, but she responded with disinterest and irritation. No doubt this kind of interaction pattern carried over into the rest of their interaction, forming a pattern for "turning away" from one another. (Gottman and Levenson 2000, p. 744)

Relatedly, UCLA psychologist Shelly Gable studied how one partner responds when something positive happens to the other one, such as a promotion at work (Gable et al. 2004). A partner might respond enthusiastically ("That's wonderful, and it's because you've had so many good ideas in the past few months."). But he or she could instead respond in a less-than-enthusiastic manner ("Hmmm, that's nice."), seem uninterested ("Did you see the score of the Yankees game?"), or point out the downsides ("I suppose it's good news, but it wasn't much of a raise."). According to Gable's research, the only "correct" reaction—the response that's correlated with intimacy, satisfaction, trust, and continued commitment—is the first response: the enthusiastic, active one (Lawson 2004a).

"As We Make Choices: Ten Rules for Successful Relationships" presents ideas on how to show positive affect. But even the happiest couples have conflicts, and how they are addressed has much to do with maintaining supportive relationships.

"It worries me that you keep referring to our honeymoon as our 'honeymoon period.'"

As We Make Choices

Ten Rules for Successful Relationships

Psychologists Nathaniel Branden and Robert Sternberg have developed some rules for nourishing relationships. Here are ten. The first seven can be applied to all family relationships. The final three pertain to romantic couple relationships.

In all family relationships

1. *Express your love verbally.* Say "I love you."
2. *Be physically affectionate. Offer (and accept) a touch or hug that says, "I care," "I'm sorry," or "I understand."*
3. *Express your appreciation.* Tell your loved ones what you like, enjoy, and admire about one another. Listen with interest.
4. *Help the relationship or family to become an emotional support system.* Be there for each other in times of illness, difficulty, and crisis; be generally helpful and nurturing—devoted to each other's well-being.
5. *Express your affection in material ways.* Send cards or give presents on more than just expected occasions. Lighten a family member's burden once in a while by doing more than your agreed-upon share of the chores.
6. *Accept your family members' shortcomings.* We are not talking about putting up with physical or verbal abuse here. But harmless shortcomings are part of every relationship. Love your family members, not an unattainable idealization of them.
7. *Do unto each other as you would have the other do unto you.* Unconsciously, we sometimes want to give less than we get, or to be treated in positive ways that we fail to offer our family members. Try to see things from another family member's viewpoint.

In romantic couple relationships

1. *Share more about yourself with your partner than you do with any other person.* In other words, keep each other primary (see Chapter 7).
2. *Make time to be alone together.* This time should be exclusively devoted to the two of you as a couple. Understand that love requires attention and leisure.
3. *Do not take your relationship for granted.* Make your relationship your first priority and actively seek to meet each other's needs.

Critical Thinking

Often, we read a list like the previous one and think about whether our partner or other family members are doing them, not whether we ourselves are. How many of the items on this list do you yourself do? Which two or three items might you begin to incorporate into a relationship?

Sources: Branden 1988, pp. 225–28; Sternberg 1988b, pp. 272–77; see also Gottman and Silver 1999; Gottman and DeClaire 2001; Mackey, Diemer, and O'Brien 2000; Markman, Stanley, and Blumberg 2001.

Conflict in Relationships

Couples argue about their children, money, household chores, in-laws, how to allocate their time, other relatives, and irritating little habits that one of them has. Another common topic for arguments involves the couple's communication itself, often with each partner feeling that the other is not paying attention or understanding (Papp, Cummings, and Goeke-Morey 2009). Anger and conflict are challenges to be met rather than avoided (Schechtman and Schechtman 2003).

Sociologist Judith Wallerstein (Wallerstein and Blakeslee 1995) conducted lengthy interviews with fifty predominantly white, middle-class married couples in northern California. The shortest marriage was ten years and the longest forty years. To participate, both husband and wife had to define their marriage as happy. When discussing what she found, Wallerstein wrote this:

> [E]very married person knows that "conflict-free marriage" is an oxymoron. In reality it is neither possible nor desirable. . . . [I]n a contemporary marriage it is expected that husbands and wives will have different opinions. More important, they can't avoid having serious collisions on big issues that defy compromise. (p. 143)

The couples in Wallerstein's research quarreled:

> In one marriage the husband and wife sat in the car to argue, to avoid upsetting the children. She told him that passive smoke was a proven carcinogen, and while the children were young he could not smoke in their home. He could do what he wanted outside. The man admitted that the request was reasonable, but he was furious. He punished her by not talking to her except when absolutely necessary for three months. Then he accepted the injunction on his smoking and they resumed their customary relationship. (p. 148)

Wallerstein concluded that

> [t]he happily married couples I spoke with were frank in acknowledging their serious differences over the years. . . . What emerged from these interviews was not only that conflict is ubiquitous but that these couples considered learning to disagree and to stand one's ground one of the gifts of a good marriage. (p. 144)

Counselors generally advise that an important aspect of learning to disagree involves expressing anger directly, a skill explored later in this chapter. Here we turn to an examination of *indirect* expressions of anger.

Indirect Expressions of Anger

Many of us may feel uncomfortable about expressing our anger directly. As a result, we can find ourselves engaging in **passive-aggression**—that is, expressing anger indirectly. Chronic criticism, nagging, nitpicking, and sarcasm are all forms of passive-aggression. Procrastination, especially when you have promised a partner that you will do something, may be a form of passive-aggression (Ferrari and Emmons 1994). These behaviors create unnecessary distance and pain in relationships. Most people who use sarcasm do so unthinkingly, unaware of its hurtful consequences. But being the target of sarcastic or otherwise hurtful remarks can result in partners feeling alienated from each other (Murphy and Oberlin 2006). Then too, sex and other expressions of intimacy become arenas for ongoing conflict when partners passive-aggressively withhold them. For example, a partner makes a disparaging comment in front of company. The hurt spouse says nothing at the time but rejects the other's sexual advances later.

Other forms of indirect anger include sabotage and displacement. **Sabotage,** a means of getting revenge, or "payback" (Boon, Deveau, and Alibhal 2009), involves one partner's attempts to spoil or undermine some activity that the other has planned. For example, the partner who is angry because the other invited friends over when he or she wanted to relax may sabotage the evening by acting bored. In **displacement**, a person directs anger at people or things that the other cherishes. An individual who is angry with a partner for spending too much time on a career may hate the partner's expensive car.

Typically, individuals express anger indirectly because they are afraid of conflict, either generally or with reference to a specific person or persons (Murphy and Oberlin 2006; Oyamot, Fuglestad, and Snyder 2010). Advising partners to express anger directly rests on assumptions of equitable power and feelings of security in a relationship (Knobloch and Knobloch-Fedders 2010; Knudson-Martin and Mahoney 2009). Nevertheless, partners and family members who do not express their anger directly risk emotional and/or sexual detachment (Gottman and Levenson 2000). Of course, it is important to recognize that direct expressions of anger can go too far, resulting in domestic violence (Rehman et al. 2009), discussed in Chapter 13. We turn now to what an important research team has to say about conflict management.

Learning to express anger and dealing with conflict early in a relationship are challenges to be met rather than avoided. Acknowledging and resolving conflict is painful, but it often strengthens the couple's union in the long run. A key to effective conflict management is to share everyday—and positive—events in friendly, supportive ways so that arguments occur within an overall context of couple satisfaction and mutual trust.

John Gottman's Research on Couple Communication and Conflict Management

Social psychologist John Gottman (1979, 1994, 1996; Gottman et al. 1998; Gottman and DeClaire 2001; Gottman and Notarius 2000, 2003) has made his reputation in the field of marital communication.[5] In the 1970s, applying an interactionist perspective to partner communication, he began studying newly married couples in a university lab while they talked casually, discussed issues that they disagreed about, or tried to solve problems. Video cameras recorded the spouses' gestures, facial expressions, and verbal pitch and tone. After he began this research, Gottman kept in contact with more than 650 of the couples, some for as many as fourteen years. Typically, the couples were videotaped intermittently. Some couples volunteered for laboratory observation that monitored shifts in their heart rate and chemical stress indicators in their blood and urine as a result of their communicating with each other (Gottman 1996).

Studying marital communication in this detail, Gottman and his colleagues were able to chart the

[5] As explored in "Issues for Thought: A Look Behind the Scenes at Communication Research," the extent to which Gottman and colleagues' findings apply to other than heterosexually married couples has been questioned.

Issues for Thought

A Look Behind the Scenes at Communication Research

An important scientific norm requires that research findings be critically reviewed by others to help ensure that they are accurate. One way to follow this norm is for subsequent studies to try to reproduce, or *replicate,* the findings of an earlier researcher—that is, follow the first researcher's design and methods over again to discern whether the same findings emerge. If a study replicates well (the same findings show up), we can be better assured that the research is to be taken seriously. If the study does not replicate (the same findings do not emerge in both studies), then we cannot be certain what to think until even more studies are done.

In 2007, a team of researchers (Kim, Capaldi, and Crosby 2007) sought to reproduce findings from the much publicized earlier research of well-known and highly respected social psychologist John Gottman and his colleagues. The research that sought to reproduce Gottman's findings used observation methods similar to Gottman's. However, the sample Kim and colleagues used was purposefully different. Gottman had used a sample of newlyweds who had been married for the first time within the previous six months and who answered media ads that requested their participation. Most of these couples were middle-class college graduates. Kim, Capaldi, and Crosby (2007) used a sample of young adults who had grown up in poor neighborhoods and who, by their twenties, were unlikely to have graduated from college. Furthermore, Kim and colleagues' sample included both married and cohabiting couples. Kim and colleagues used a different sample to discern whether Gottman's findings could be applied to couples other than middle-class marrieds.

One thing that Gottman and his colleagues had found was that a serious communication problem faced by couples occurs when the wife raises complaints to her husband in ways that he perceives as abrasive or attacking. The husband then withdraws and apparently ignores her—the *female-demand/male-withdraw communication* pattern. Based on their findings, Gottman and his colleagues advised therapists to focus on gender differences when counseling (heterosexual) couples' communication. Therapists were encouraged to help wives to raise issues more gently and husbands to be more willing to be influenced by their wives (Gottman et al. 1998).

The later researchers pointed out that Gottman and his colleagues had published advice to therapists without the qualification that it might only apply to middle-class, married couples. Therefore, they argued that Gottman's research needed to be further examined to see whether his findings applied to couples who were not middle class and/or were not married, but cohabiting.

This story might not be news if Kim and colleagues had successfully reproduced Gottman's findings. However, this was not the case. For one thing, the later researchers' findings did not support the female-demand/male-withdraw pattern. In a published response, Gottman argued, among other things, that his research was not necessarily meant to apply to cohabiting couples (Coan and Gottman 2007). Nevertheless, Kim and colleagues agued that their failure to replicate Gottman's findings

> calls into question the extent to which [Gottman and his colleagues'] findings . . . should be used as a basis for recommendation for therapy and interventions with young couples and in general provides a caution against translating empirical findings to treatment recommendations without replication. (Kim, Capaldi, and Crosby 2007, p. 66)

When researchers fail to replicate another's findings, "it is often difficult for readers to know what to conclude." Therefore, we need to be "cautious with initial findings until they are replicated" (Heyman and Hunt 2007, p. 84) and tested in many different samples.

Critical Thinking

Given Kim, Capaldi, and Crosby's (2007) failure to reproduce the findings of Gottman et al. (1998) in a sample that was not primarily middle-class and included cohabiting couples, what do you think about the generalizability of Gottman's suggestions to therapists? How might yet another research team further investigate Gottman's findings?

effects of small gestures. For example, early in his career he reported that when a spouse—particularly the wife—rolled her eyes while the other was talking, divorce was likely to follow sometime in the future, even if the couple was not thinking about divorce at the time (Gottman and Krotkoff 1989). Gottman's research has been challenged and may apply only to middle-class, married couples (see "Issues for Thought: A Look Behind the Scenes at Communication Research"). Recognizing the need for continued research in this area, we present Gottman's highly influential findings here.

The Four Horsemen of the Apocalypse

Gottman's research (1994) showed that conflict and anger themselves did not predict divorce, but processes that he called the **Four Horsemen of the Apocalypse** did.[6] The Four Horsemen of the Apocalypse are contempt, criticism, defensiveness, and stonewalling. Rolling

[6] The word *apocalypse* refers to the biblical idea that the world is soon to end, being destroyed by fire. The Four Horsemen are allegorical figures representing war, famine, and death, with the fourth uncertain (*Concise Columbia Encyclopedia* 1994, p. 309). Gottman used the phrase to indicate attitudes and behaviors that foreshadow impending divorce.

one's eyes indicates **contempt**, a feeling that one's spouse is inferior or undesirable. **Criticism** involves making disapproving judgments or evaluations of one's partner. **Defensiveness** means preparing to defend oneself against what one presumes is an upcoming attack. **Stonewalling** involves resistance—refusing to take a partner's complaints seriously.[7] In several of Gottman's studies, these behaviors identified those who would divorce, with an unusually high accuracy of about 90 percent.

Later, after more research, Gottman added **belligerence**, a behavior that challenges the other's power or authority (for example, "What can you do if I do go drinking with Dave? What are you going to do about it?") (Gottman et al. 1998, p. 6). Still later, Gottman and his colleagues identified similar patterns among gay and lesbian couples (Gottman et al. 2003; see also Houts and Horne 2008). To illustrate how Gottman's horsemen make their ways into communication, consider the following exchange:

PARTNER A: I can't find my cell phone.

PARTNER B: Don't accuse me of taking it. It's never on when I call you anyway.

PARTNER A: What's that got to do with anything?

PARTNER B: So look for it.

PARTNER A: So help me.

PARTNER B: You're just like your dad—always expecting somebody to do things for you.

PARTNER A: Jerk!

In this scenario, *Partner A* mentions having misplaced a cell phone, and an argument develops, illustrating contempt, defensiveness, and belligerence. When *Partner A* announces the need for the cell phone, *Partner B* becomes defensive: "Don't accuse me of taking it." At this point, *B* raises a complaint: "It's never on when I try to call you anyway." In a less-distressed couple, *A* might respond to *B*'s complaint. However, *A* fails to de-escalate the interchange and does not acknowledge *B*'s complaint. Less distressed couples might stop this negative spiral with shared humor or some sign of affection. However, *Partner A* subsequently requests that *B* help look for the cell phone. *Partner B*'s reply is contemptuous and critical: "You're just like your dad—always expecting somebody to do things for you." Again, the couple fails to de-escalate the negative affect. This time *A* calls *B* a jerk. Name-calling is contemptuous.

It appears the couple has forgotten what the fight is about. In fact, one wonders whether they ever knew what the fight was about. Counselors point out that distressed couples, like the couple depicted here, may unconsciously allow trivial issues to become decoys so that they evade the real area of conflict and leave it unresolved. In sum, contempt, criticism, defensiveness, stonewalling, and belligerence characterize unhappy marriages and may signal impending divorce (Gottman and Levenson 2002). Gottman, like other researchers, found that communicating positive feelings for a partner characterized happier, more stable unions.

Positive versus Negative Affect Gottman and his colleagues videotaped 130 newlywed couples as they discussed a problem that caused ongoing disagreement in their marriage for fifteen minutes (Gottman et al. 1998). Each couple's communication was coded in one-second sequences, and then synchronized with each spouse's heart rate data, which was being collected at the same time. The heart rate data would indicate each partner's physiological stress.

The researchers examined all the interaction sequences in which one partner first expressed **negative affect**: anger, sadness, whining, disgust, tension and fear, belligerence, contempt, or defensiveness. Belligerence, contempt, and defensiveness (three of Gottman's indicators of impending divorce) were coded as *high-intensity, negative affect.* The other emotions listed previously (anger, sadness, whining, and so on) were coded as *low-intensity negative affect.*

Next, the researchers watched what happened immediately after a partner had expressed negative affect or raised a complaint. Sometimes the partner reciprocated with negative affect in kind, either low or high intensity. As examples, *Partner A* whines, and *Partner B* whines back; *A* expresses anger, and *B* responds with tension and fear; or *A* is contemptuous, and *B* immediately becomes defensive.

At other times, one partner's first negative expression was reciprocated with an escalation of the negativity. As examples, *Partner A* whines, and *Partner B* grows belligerent; or *A* expresses anger, and *B* becomes defensive. Gottman and his colleagues called this kind of interchange *refusing-to-accept influence,* because the spouse on the receiving end of the other's complaint refuses to consider it and, instead, escalates the fight. Negative escalation is evidenced in the previous cell phone conflict.

Meanwhile, still other couples were likely to communicate with positive affect, responding to each other warmly with interest, affection, or shared (not mean or contemptuous) humor. Positive affect typically de-escalated conflict (Gottman and Levenson 2000, 2002). Gottman and his colleagues found that "[t]he only variable that predicted both marital stability and marital

[7] Stonewallers react to their partner's attempts to raise tension-producing issues by refusing to entertain them. Avoiding or evading an argument is an example of stonewalling. Argument evaders use several tactics to avoid fighting, such as vacating the scene when an argument threatens; turning sullen and refusing to talk; declaring, "I can't take it when you yell at me"; using the hit-and-run tactic of filing a complaint, then leaving no time for an answer or resolution; saying "OK, you win" without meaning it.

happiness among stable couples was the amount of positive affect in the conflict" (1998, p. 17). In stable, happy couples, shared humor and expressions of warmth, interest, and affection were apparent even in conflict situations and, therefore, de-escalated the argument.

The researchers "found no evidence . . . to support the [idea that] anger is the destructive emotion in marriages" (1998, p. 16). Instead, they found that contempt, belligerence, and defensiveness were the destructive attitudes and behaviors. Furthermore, Gottman and his colleagues concluded that the interaction pattern best predicting (heterosexual) divorce was a wife's raising a complaint, followed by her husband's refusing-to-accept influence, followed, in turn, by the wife's reciprocating her husband's escalated negativity, and the absence of any de-escalation by means of positive affect. Despite changing gender roles (see Chapter 4), researchers continue to observe gender differences in communication patterns.

Gender Differences and Communication

Before the nineteenth century, men's and women's domestic activities involved economic production, not personal intimacy. With the development of separate gender spheres in industrializing societies during the nineteenth century, expressions of emotion became the domain of middle-class women, whereas work was defined as more appropriate to masculinity. As a result of this historical legacy, we have come to see men as less well equipped than women for emotional relatedness (Real 2002).

Sociologist Francesca Cancian (1987) has expanded on these points to argue that men are equally loving, but women, not men, are made to feel primarily responsible for love's endurance or success. Furthermore, expressions of love are defined and perceived mostly on feminine terms—that is, verbally—and women are the more verbal sex. Expressions of love that men may make, such as doing favors or reducing their partners' burdens, are not credited as love (Cancian 1985). Recent research appears to support Cancian's analysis. For instance, a study with 453 heterosexual couples drawn from a national representative survey looked at changes that women would like in their partners, compared with changes that men would like. The women were more likely than the men to want increases in a partner's demonstrations of positive emo-tion (Heyman et al. 2009).

In Cancian's analysis, "The consequences of love would be more positive if love were the responsibility of men as well as women and if love were defined more broadly to include instrumental help as well as emotional expression" (1985, p. 262). Cancian has also argued that a more balanced view of how love is to be expressed—one that includes masculine as well as feminine elements—would find men equally loving and emotionally profound.

Meanwhile, Deborah Tannen's book *You Just Don't Understand* (1990) suggests that men typically engage in **report talk**, conversation aimed mainly at conveying information. Women, on the other hand, are likely to engage in **rapport talk**, speaking to gain or reinforce intimacy or connection with others. Men are likely to bring up problems, for instance, only when hoping to trigger suggestions for solution. Women, on the other hand, are likely to talk about problems simply to share or foster rapport. These gendered differences

> lead to an imbalance in many families. If the mother is telling about troubles she confronted during her day but the father is not, the result is that mothers come across as more problem-ridden and insecure than fathers. And many men, because they don't tend to talk in this way, understandably assume that a woman who recounts a problem must be seeking help solving it; why else would she talk about

"Sometimes I wonder what life would be like with you."

> it? That's why they generously provide solutions. So the woman's conversational gambit ends up being refracted through the man's point of view. This misunderstanding of women's rapport-talk often results in mothers appearing to their families as less confident, or even less competent, than their husbands. (Tannen 2006, pp. 83–84)

Moreover, some researchers speculate that women, being more expressive and attuned to the emotional quality of a relationship, are more likely than men to bring conflict into the open, sometimes in an attention-getting negative tone (Cui et al. 2005). Men try to minimize the impending conflict either by conciliatory gestures or by stonewalling. The male's minimization of conflict may appear to the female as failure to recognize her emotional needs (Noller and Fitzpatrick 1991; Canary and Dindia 1998). In the following, a husband describes this situation:

> The more I try to be cool and calm her the worse it gets. I swear, I can't figure her out, I'll keep trying to tell her not to get so excited, but there's nothing I can do. Anything I say just makes it worse. So then I try to keep quiet, but . . . wow the explosion is like crazy, just nuts. (in Rubin 2007, p. 323)

We might compare this to a wife, who told her interviewers that,

> I can't stand that he's so damned unemotional and expects me to be the same. He lives in his head all of [the] time, and he acts like anything that's emotional isn't worth dealing with. (in Rubin 2007, pv. 322)

Reviews of research on couple communication in the 1990s (Gottman and Notarius 2000; Bradbury, Fincham, and Beach 2000) concluded that men and women differ in their responses to negative affect in close relationships. When faced with a complaint from a partner, men tend to withdraw emotionally whereas women do not. Researchers have found this pattern to be common enough that some call it the *female-demand/male-withdraw communication pattern* (Gottman and Levenson 2000). In distressed marriages, this pattern becomes a repeated cycle of negative verbal expression by one partner and withdrawal by the other (Bradbury, Fincham, and Beach 2000).

Many researchers and therapists agree that generally there is a female-demand/male-withdraw pattern (Miller and Roloff 2005; Weger 2005). However, an alternative view argues that "it is not gender per se but the nature of the marital discussion—for example, whether it is the wife or the husband who desires a change—that may determine who is demanding and who is withdrawing" (Roberts 2000, p. 702; also see Kim, Capaldi, and Crosby 2007). Research on same-sex couples has found the same pattern—that is, one partner demands while the other withdraws (Parker-Pope 2008). And research in stepfamilies suggests that neither partner is likely to demand as much as in high-risk, first marriages, and both are more likely to withdraw from a conflict (Halford, Nicholson, and Sanders 2007).

Obviously, the **female-demand/male-withdraw interaction pattern** leads to both partners feeling misunderstood, thereby decreasing marital satisfaction (Weger 2005). Gottman and his colleagues (1998) concluded that wives and husbands have different goals when they disagree:

> The wife wants to resolve the disagreement so that she feels closer to the husband and respected by him. The husband, though, just wants to avoid a blowup. The husband doesn't see the disagreement as an opportunity for closeness, but for trouble. (p. 17)

In one husband's words, "I just got mad and I'd take off—go out with the guys and have a few beers or something. When I'd get back, things would be even worse." From his wife's perspective, "The more I screamed, the more he'd withdraw, until finally I'd go kind of crazy. Then he'd leave and not come back until two or three in the morning sometimes" (Rubin 1976, pp. 77, 79).

Gottman and his colleagues sought to better understand this pattern. You'll recall that the researchers monitored spouses' heart rates as indicators of physiological stress during conflict. They hypothesized that, "it is likely that the biological, stress-related response of men is more rapid and recovery is slower than that of women, and that this response is related to the greater emotional withdrawal of men than women in distressed families" (Gottman et al. 1998, p. 19). That is, when confronted with conflict from an intimate, men may experience more intense and uncomfortable physical symptoms of stress than women do. Therefore, men are more likely than women to withdraw emotionally and/or physically.

An alternative—or complementary—view is that men have been socialized to withdraw. The cultural options for masculinity include "no 'sissy' stuff," according to which men are expected to distance themselves from anything considered feminine. We guess this could include a wife's complaints. In two books on men and communication, the first called *I Don't Want to Talk About It,* therapist Terrence Real (1997, 2002) attributes males' withdrawal to a "secret legacy of depression," brought on by men's traditional socialization, particularly society's refusal to let them grieve over losses (e.g., "Don't cry over nothing"). It is possible that physiology and culture interact to create a female-demand/male-withdraw pattern.

What Couples Can Do The general conclusion of Gottman's research on couple communication and conflict management is as follows. Both partners:

1. need to try to be gentle when they raise complaints;
2. can help to reduce anxiety in their mate by communicating care and affection, hence reducing physical stress symptoms;

3. can learn techniques for reducing anxiety in oneself—for example, taking a time-out or saying that "I just can't talk about it now, but I will later" (and meaning it);
4. need to be willing to accept influence from each other;
5. need to do what they can—perhaps using authentic, shared humor, kindness, and other signs of affection—to de-escalate the argument. It is important to recognize that this does not mean avoiding the issue altogether.

Finally, Gottman and his colleagues (1998) suggest that, as we have already seen, it is important for couples to think about communicating with positive affect more often in their daily living and not just during times of conflict (Gottman and DeClaire 2001). "As We Make Choices: Ten Rules for Successful Relationships" suggests ways to do this. Then too, as we have seen, cohesive families have arguments. But the argument ends; conflicts are resolved. We turn to some guidelines for accomplishing this.

Working Through Conflicts in Positive Ways—Ten Guidelines

Different cultural groups vary in their endorsement of openly expressing emotion and directly expressing conflicts (see, for example, Hirsch 2003). We need to recognize that preferred standards for communication vary culturally (Matsunaga and Imahori 2009) and that the guidelines suggested in this chapter, which accent direct communication styles, may be ethno- or Eurocentric.[8] Nevertheless, counselors do advise that there are better (and not-so-good) ways that virtually all couples and family members can resolve differences.

Before going further, we want to point out that not all negative facts and feelings need to be communicated. Before voicing a complaint, we might ask ourselves, "How important is it?" (Sanford 2006). Counselors suggest that if, after giving it some time and thought, we believe that raising a particular grievance is important, then we should do so. Similarly, when offering negative information, it is important to ask ourselves why we want to do so and whether the other person really needs to know. We turn now to ten specific guidelines for constructive conflict management.

[8] Deborah Tannen's (1990) book *You Just Don't Understand,* which drew wide attention for its comparison of men's and women's communication styles, also points out cultural communication differences among, for example, New Yorkers, Californians, New Englanders, and Midwesterners, and among Scandinavians, Canada's native peoples, and Greeks. Interpersonal communication differences are evidenced by other race/ethnicities as well (Matsunaga and Imahori 2009).

Guideline 1: Express Anger Directly and with Kindness

Family members may have the false belief that their intimates automatically know—or should know—what they think and how they feel. This incorrect idea is detrimental to relationships (Hamamci 2005). When complaints are not addressed directly, conflict goes unresolved, with lingering grievances sparked again and again by "subtle triggers." Consider the following family situation:

> An ongoing point of contention in this family is the mother's belief that her teenage daughter, Joyce, spends too much money on clothes and makeup, which she buys in upscale stores rather than more economical stores, like Wal-Mart. So when the father, who is scanning a newspaper, remarks, "I see Wal-Mart set a record for sales yesterday," the seed is planted for an argument to sprout. (Tannen 2006, p. 123)
>
> The underlying conflict is voiced as follows:
>
> **Mom:** So? We don't shop at Wal-Mart, so what's the point?
>
> **Dad:** Okay.
>
> **Joyce:** What does that have to do with anything?
>
> **Mom:** Okay, I'm just saying—
>
> **Joyce:** Saying what?
>
> **Mom:** Yeah, so what's the point?
>
> **Joyce:** What point, Mom? You don't shop there either, Mom.
>
> **Mom:** Yes, I do. You could shop there for toiletries.
>
> **Joyce:** For clothes you shop there, Mom?
>
> **Mom:** No.
>
> **Joyce:** See, so why should we go shopping there for toiletries? . . . I don't go shopping for toiletries anywhere because you buy them for me.
>
> **Mom:** No, but you buy makeup.
>
> **Dad:** Well, this year we can do all our Christmas shopping at Wal-Mart. (Tannen 2006, pp. 123–25)

Tension and conflict go unresolved.

Counselors advise expressing anger directly because doing so makes way for resolution (Bernstein and Magee 2004). For example, the mother might say, "I feel that you've been spending more than we can afford on makeup." Counselors further advise that a grievance will be less threatening to the receiver when positive feelings are conveyed at the same time that the grievance is voiced.

© Noel Hedrickson/Getty Images/Digital Vision

Chronic stonewallers may fear rejection or retaliation and therefore hesitate to acknowledge their own or their partner's angry emotions. Examples of stonewalling include saying things like, "I can't take it when you yell at me," or turning sullen and refusing to talk. It may sound impossible to fight more fairly when you're angry, but "practice makes better." Using "I" statements, avoiding mixed messages, focusing your anger on specific issues, and being willing to change are some guidelines worth trying.

> If you're angry and resentful, requests for change will be met with resistance and countercharge efforts: "It's not my problem; it's your problem." But if you learn to approach each other with acceptance and empathy, you can create a collaborative context, and often people will make spontaneous changes. ("Loving Your Partner" 2000)

So, even better, the mother might say, "You always look nice, and I like the way that you choose to wear your makeup, but I feel that you're spending more than we can afford on it." Being direct is not the same as being unnecessarily critical.

Guideline 2: Check Out Your Interpretation of Others' Behaviors

Because family members and partners in distressed relationships seldom understand each other as well as they think they do, a good habit is to ask for feedback by a process of *checking it out:* asking the other person whether your perception of her or his feelings or of the present situation is accurate. Checking it out often helps to avoid unnecessary hurt feelings or imagining trouble that may not exist, as the following example illustrates:

> **Family Member A:** I think you're mad about something. *(checking it out)* Is it because it's my class night and I haven't made dinner?
>
> **Family Member B:** No, I'm irritated because I was tied up in traffic an extra half hour on my way home.

Guideline 3: To Avoid Attacks, Use "I" Statements

Attacks, sometimes interpreted as blame, involve insults or assaults on another's character or self-esteem. Needless to say, attacks do not help to bond a couple (Sinclair and Monk 2004). A rule in avoiding attack is to use the word, *I* rather than *you* or *why*. For example, instead of declaring, "You're late," or asking "Why are you late?"—both of which can smack of blame—a statement such as, "I was worried because you hadn't arrived" may allow for more positive dialogue. The receiver is more likely to perceive "I" statements as an attempt to recognize and communicate feelings; "you" and "why" statements are more likely to be perceived as attacks, even when not intended as such.

Of course, making "I" statements may be too much to ask in the heat of an argument. One social psychologist has admitted what many of us may have experienced: "It is impossible to make an 'I-statement' when you are in the . . . 'wanting-revenge, feeling-stung-and-needing-to-sting-back' state of mind" (quoted in Gottman et al. 1998, p. 18). Of course, this is partly the point. Keeping in mind the possibility of expressing a complaint—at least *beginning* a confrontation—with an "I" statement can discourage family members from getting to that wanting-revenge state of mind in the first place.

Guideline 4: Avoid Mixed, or Double Messages

Mixed, or double messages contradict each other. Contradictory messages may be verbal, or one may be verbal and one nonverbal. For example, a family member offers to take the family to a movie yet sighs and says that he or she is exhausted after a really hard day at work. Or a partner insists, "Of course I love you" while picking an invisible speck from his or her sleeve in a gesture of indifference.

Senders of mixed messages may not be aware of what they are doing, and mixed messages can be very subtle. They sometimes result from simultaneously wanting to recognize and to deny conflict or tension. A classic example is the *silent treatment.* One partner becomes aware that she or he has said or done something upsetting and asks what's wrong. "Oh, nothing," the other replies without much feeling, but everything about the partner's face, body, attitude, and posture suggests that something is indeed wrong (Lerner 2001).

Moreover, communication involves both a sender and a receiver. Just as the sender gives both an overt message and an underlying *meta-message*,[9] so also does a receiver give cues about how seriously she or he is taking the message. For example, listening while continuing to do chores sends the nonverbal message that what is being heard is not very important.

Guideline 5: When You Can, Choose the Time and Place Carefully

Arguments are less likely to be constructive if the complainant raises grievances at the wrong time. One partner may be ready to argue about an issue when the other is almost asleep or working on an important assignment, for instance. At such times, the person who picked the fight may get more—or less—than he or she had expected.

Family members might negotiate a time and place for addressing issues. Arguing "by appointment" may sound silly and be difficult to arrange, but doing so has advantages. For one thing, complainants can organize their thoughts and feelings more calmly and deliberately, increasing the likelihood that they will be heard. Also, recipients of complaints have time before the argument to prepare themselves to hear some criticism.[10]

Guideline 6: Address a Specific Issue, Ask for a Specific Change, and Be Open to Compromise

Constructive relationships aim at resolving current, specific problems. Recipients of complaints need to feel that they can do something specific to help resolve the problem raised. This will be difficult if they feel overwhelmed by old gripes. Furthermore, complainants should be ready to propose one or more solutions. Recipients might come up with possible solutions themselves. When family members can entertain potential solutions to a definite problem at hand, they are better able to negotiate alternatives.

John Gottman found that happily married couples reached agreement rather quickly. Either one partner gave in to the other without resentment, or the two compromised. Unhappily married couples continued in a cycle of stubbornness and hostility (Gottman and Krotkoff 1989; see also Busby and Holman 2009).

Guideline 7: Be Willing to Change Yourself

The principle that couples or family members should accept each other as they are sometimes merges with the idea that individuals should be exactly what they choose to be. The result is an erroneous assumption that if someone loves you, he or she will accept you just as you are and not ask for even minor changes. In truth, partners need to be willing to be influenced by their loved ones and to change themselves (Lerner 2001).

Therapists note that, in some relationships, each person expects the other one to do the changing: "You have to understand, she's [or he's] impossible to live with" (Ball and Kivisto 2006, p. 155). One counselor team (Christensen and Jacobson 1999) has suggested "acceptance therapy," helping individuals accept their partners and other family members as they are instead of demanding change—although these counselors also suggest that, paradoxically, showing acceptance can lead to a partner's changing behavior. We need to balance acceptance of another against not being a doormat, but being willing to change ourselves is key.

Guideline 8: Don't Try to Win

Counselors encourage us to recognize that there are probably several ways to solve a particular problem, and backing others into a corner with ultimatums and counter-ultimatums is not negotiation but attack. Moreover, wanting to win a dispute with a loved one typically encourages us to use unnecessarily hurtful language, which nonproductively increases the recipient's stress (Priem, McLaren, and Solomon 2010). We're reminded that recipients of painful messages typically see them as more hurtful than do the senders (Zhang 2009). How we say things impacts how others perceive them (Young 2010). Even hurtful information can be conveyed with sensitivity.

Societies that emphasize competition, such as ours does, encourage people to see almost everything they do in terms of winning or losing (Fromm 1956). Yet research clearly indicates that for same-sex and heterosexual couples, the tactics associated with winning in a particular conflict are also those associated with lower relationship satisfaction (Clunis and Green 2005; Heene, Buysse, and Van Oost 2007; Houts and Horne 2008). Losing lessens a person's self-esteem, increases resentment, and adds strain to the relationship. On the

[9] Communication scholars and counselors point out that there are two major aspects of any communication: *what* is said (the verbal message) and *how* it is said or interpreted (the nonverbal "meta-message"). The meta-message depends on tone of voice, inflection, and body language, as well as on the receiver (Nierenberg and Calero 1973). In a mixed message, the verbal message does not correspond with the meta-message.

[10] A qualitative British study of teenagers and their parents found that some parents and teens use mobile phones to raise sensitive issues that they intend to later pursue face to face. One teen said, "Well, I think mobiles can be really good if you've got something you don't wanna tell straight away," and another young respondent said, "I'd maybe text if it's something that I can't, I dunno, something I can't get across [face to face] and stuff" (in Devitt and Roker 2009, p. 192).

other hand, everyone wins when family members mutually agree on solutions to their differences (Carroll, Badger, and Yang 2006).

Guideline 9: Be Willing to Forgive

A growing number of therapists suggest that being willing to forgive is critical to ongoing happy relationships (Fincham, Hall, and Beach 2006). Forgiveness "is the idea of a change whereby one becomes less motivated to think, feel, and behave negatively (e.g., retaliate, withdraw) in regard to the offender." Forgiveness is not something to which the offender is necessarily entitled, but it is granted nevertheless.

Contrary to what many individuals believe, however, forgiveness does not require that the offended partner minimize or condone the offense. Rather, "an individual forgives despite the wrongful nature of the offense and the fact that the offender is not entitled to forgiveness." Further, "forgiveness is distinct from denial (an unwillingness to perceive the injury) . . . or forgetting (removes awareness of offence from consciousness)" (Fincham, Hall, and Beach 2006, p. 416).

Forgiveness is often a process that takes time, rather than one specific decision or act of the will. Being willing to forgive has been associated in research with marital satisfaction, lessened ambivalence toward a partner, conflict resolution, enhanced commitment, and greater empathy (Fincham, Hall, and Beach 2006).

Guideline 10: End the Argument

Ending the argument is important. Sometimes when individuals are too hurt to continue, they need to stop arguing before they reach a resolution. A family member may signal that he or she feels too distressed to go on by calling for a time-out. Or it could help to bargain about whether the fight should continue at all.

As pointed out earlier in this chapter, the happily married couples that Gottman and his colleagues, as well as Wallerstein, interviewed knew how and when to stop fighting. Arguments can end with compromise, apology, submission, or agreement to disagree (Goeke-Morey, Cummings, and Papp 2007). Ideally, a fight ends when there has been a mutually satisfactory airing of each partner's views.

Toward Better Couple and Family Communication

Keeping a loving relationship or creating a cohesive family is not automatic. Doing so requires working on ourselves as well as on our relationships. A first step involves consciously recognizing how important the relationship is to us. A second step is to set realistic expectations about the relationship (Cloud and Townsend 2005). As one married woman put it,

> You just have this idealized version of getting married, you know, everybody plays it up as so romantic and so wonderful and sweet. Now that I am married and now that I have gotten older and hit the real world I'm kind of like . . . It's a lot more hands-on, you know, getting stuff done . . . than it is that idealized romantic notion that you get as a girl. (in Fairchild 2006, p. 13)

A third step involves improving our own (1) **emotional intelligence**—awareness of what we're feeling so that we can express our feelings more authentically; (2) ability and willingness to repair our moods, not unnecessarily nursing our hurt feelings; (3) healthy balance between controlling rash impulses and being candid and spontaneous; and (4) sensitivity to the feelings and needs of others (Keaten and Kelly 2008). We can develop greater flexibility of thought, learning to think of several alternative workable solutions to problems and to have several ways of responding to a situation, not just one that habitually comes up by default (Koesten, Schrodt, and Ford 2009). Support is mutually reinforcing. When we can support others, they are more likely to be supportive (Priem, Solomon, and Steuber 2009).

With regard to the relationship itself, counselors encourage making time for play and incorporating new activities into relationships (Lawson 2004b; Smith, Freeman, and Zabriskie 2009).[11] Social psychologist John

[11] An intriguing area of research from the biosocial theoretical perspective (see Chapter 2) suggests that brain chemistry helps to explain why shared new activities enhance romantic relationships (Gottlieb 2006; Slater 2006). This research points to two hormones. The first, dopamine, is a chemical naturally produced in our brains. Although dopamine has many functions, its importance to love is that it acts upon the pleasure center in our brains, giving us powerful feelings of enjoyment and motivating us to do whatever we're doing that is so pleasurable over and over again (Berridge and Robinson 1998). Dopamine helps to explain why we have a second helping of a really tasty dessert, for example. Furthermore, dopamine is associated with new or novel pleasurable experiences and activities. Research shows that when people are newly in love, they tend to have higher brain levels of dopamine (Slater 2006). Dopamine makes you "high on" your partner. The second hormone relevant here is oxytocin, also produced naturally in our brains. Some researchers have nicknamed oxytocin the "love" or "cuddle" hormone (Barker n.d.; Bosse 1999).

Like dopamine, oxytocin has several functions (inducing labor and stimulating breast milk production in females, for example). Research in mammals has long demonstrated that oxytocin facilitates more general maternal, nurturing behaviors ("Oxytocin" 1997). In addition, oxytocin seems to be related to human feelings of deep friendship, trust, sexuality, love, bonding, and commitment ("Biology of Social Bonds" 1999; Bosse 1999; see also Ditzen et al. 2009). Hormones affect feelings and behavior, but the reverse is also true: Behaviors can stimulate hormone production. Doing novel things together and engaging in supportive touch, including sex, stimulate the production of dopamine and oxytocin, respectively (Slater 2006; see also Ellison and Gray 2009). All this gives a somewhat new slant to the phrase "making love," doesn't it?

Crosby points out that people may misinterpret the idea of "working at" committed relationships: Instead of working *at* relationships, "we may, with all good intentions, end up making work *of*" them (Crosby 1991, p. 287).

Some of us have grown up with poor role modeling on the part of our parents (Ledbetter 2009; Rovers 2006; Schrodt et al. 2009; Zimmerman and Thayer 2003). Regardless of how our parents behaved, we can choose to change how we communicate (Braithwaite and Baxter 2006; Turner and West 2006; Wright 2006b).

Training programs in couple and family communication, often conducted by counseling psychologists, have proven effective in helping to change negative communication patterns (Blanchard et al. 2009; Bodenmann, Bradbury, and Pihet 2009; Sevier et al. 2008; Yalcin and Karaban 2007). One program for married and cohabiting couples is ENRICH, originally developed by social psychologist David Olson at the University of Minnesota. A similar program is PREP (the Prevention and Relationship Enhancement Program), developed by marital communication psychologists Scott Stanley and Howard Markman, with the overall aim of strengthening marriages and preventing divorce (Markman, Stanley, and Blumberg 2001; Schilling et al. 2003). Marriage Encounter and similar organizations offer weekend workshops, designed for mostly satisfied marrieds who want to improve their relationship (Yalcin and Karaban 2007). Advertising "psychological care for the whole family," the Family Success Consortium offers programs for all couples, whether or not married (www.familysuccessconsortium.com).

Some programs have been designed for same-sex couples (Heffner, 2003; Unitarian Universalist Association nd.). Men's groups aimed at encouraging their expressions of emotional intimacy have been shown to enhance couple and family relationships (Garfield 2010). Some conflict management programs have been developed for young and adolescent siblings (Kennedy and Kramer 2008; Thomas and Roberts 2009) and/or for families of particular race/ethnicities (e.g., Soll, McHale, and Feinberg 2009). As mentioned in Chapter 10, some parenting enhancement programs incorporate anger management components (Fetsch, Yang, and Pettit 2008).

Couples or family members who want to work for change on their own might practice the previously mentioned guidelines for conflict resolution. As partners and family members grow accustomed to voicing grievances regularly and in more respectful or caring ways, their disagreements less often become full-fledged fights: Family members gradually learn to incorporate many irritations and requests into their normal conversations, arguing in normal tones of voice and even with humor.

Although these suggestions may help, learning to fight fair is not easy. Sometimes couples and families feel that they need outside help, and they may decide to engage a counselor. See "Facts about Families: Relationship and Family Counseling" for a discussion of this alternative.

Then too, a number of books and Internet resources are available that could help. As examples, there are books on overcoming passive-aggressive behavior (Murphy and Oberlin 2006), recognizing how we sabotage our relationships (Matta 2006), and changing habits that can thwart a satisfying life in general (Kagan and Einbund 2008). Some books, such as *Person to Person: Positive Relationships Don't Just Happen* (Hanna, Suggett, and Radtke 2008) focus on both individual self-improvement and couple communication. Susan Halpern's *Finding the Words: Candid Conversations with Loved Ones* (2009) covers topics such as cultivating conscious conversations as a couple, communicating in ways that might lessen the disruptive effects of divorce, and improving communication between parents and their adult children. There are books on communication designed specifically for same-sex couples (Clunis and Green 2005). And, of course, there are university courses and textbooks

Couples can change their fighting habits. The key to staying happily together is to make knowledgeable choices—about not avoiding conflict but dealing with it openly, or directly, and in supportive ways. Doing so involves listening—without judgment, without formulating a response while the other talks, and without interrupting. The goal isn't necessarily agreement, but acknowledgment, insight, and understanding.

Facts about Families

Relationship and Family Counseling

Relationship and family counseling is a professional service having two goals: (1) helping individuals, couples, and families gain insight into the actually or potentially troublesome dynamics of their relationship(s); and (2) teaching clients more effective and supportive communication techniques. According to the American Association for Marriage and Family Therapy (AAMFT), this type of counseling is meant to be "solution-focused; specific, with attainable therapeutic goals; [and] designed with the 'end in mind'" ("What Is Marriage and Family Therapy?" 2005; Clinton and Trent 2009).

Experts advise couples or families to visit a counselor when communication is typically hostile or conflict goes unresolved, when they cannot figure out how to resolve a family problem themselves, or when a partner is thinking of leaving a committed relationship. However, counseling is also appropriate—and perhaps more effective—as a preventive technique, undertaken at the onset of family stress or when a couple or family sees a potentially troublesome transition ahead.

People go to counselors for help in working through premarital and engagement issues, as well as cultural clashes, same-sex couple, cohabitation, infidelity, divorce, substance abuse, finances, unemployment, co-parenting conflict, infertility, sexual difficulties, and changing roles such as with retirement, remarriage, and stepfamily issues, among others (Clinton and Laaser 2010; Mayo Clinic Staff 2005).

Qualifications of Counselors

The qualifications of counselors vary. A counselor who is a member of the American Association for Marriage and Family Therapy (AAMFT) has a graduate degree and at least three years of clinical training under a senior counselor's supervision. The safest way to choose a qualified counselor is to select one who belongs to the AAMFT. To do so, check the organization's website, www.aamft.org. Personal recommendations from family members or friends or both may also be helpful.

It is important to have a counselor whom you like and trust and who empathizes with you. It is also important that the counselor respect your religious and personal values. Even well-trained counselors can be capable of unintentional bias that may get in the way of productive therapy (Charles, Thomas, and Thornton 2005; Knudson-Martin and Laughlin 2005). If after three or four sessions you do not feel comfortable with the counselor or don't believe the counselor is effective, it might be a good idea to try someone else. Experts advise interviewing a prospective counselor before beginning therapy. The Mayo Clinic Staff (2005) advises asking lots of questions, including the following:

- Are you a clinical member of the AAMFT or licensed by the state, or both?
- What is your educational and training background?
- What is your experience with my type of problem?
- How much do you charge?
- Are your services covered by my health insurance?
- Where is your office and what are your hours?
- How long is each session?
- How often are sessions scheduled?
- How many sessions should I expect to have?
- What is your policy on canceled sessions?
- How can I contact you if I have an emergency?

Will Counseling Save a Relationship?

Despite its substantiated benefits, the extent to which counseling "saves" a relationship is difficult to measure (Corliss and Steptoe 2004; Sprenkle 2003). Counseling is based on the presumption that partners are willing to cooperate, and it is possible that one's partner may not be willing. No counselor can or will attempt to change a person to a partner's liking without active cooperation from all involved (Rasheed, Rasheed, and Marley 2010). To read—or participate in—an online discussion of ordinary people's opinions on whether counseling "saved" their relationship, you might want to visit the Berkeley Parents Network webpage, "Does Couples Counseling Work?" on the University of California, Berkeley website (parents.berkeley.edu).

Critical Thinking

Can you think of a specific example from your own experience when couple or family counseling was helpful? When it could have been helpful? Can you think of examples when couple or family counseling might be less than helpful?

on interpersonal communication and relationships (e.g., Knapp and Vangelisti 2009; Verderber, Verderber, and Berryman-Fink 2010). In addition, there is a vast number of good (and perhaps not-so-good, so be selective) Internet resources (e.g., Robinson 2009; Von Rosenvinge n.d.; and see Gilkey, Carey, and Wade 2009).

Family relationships are dynamic and can change for the better. For example, an adult woman told

Many observers strongly criticize the way that American culture tends to equate love with infatuation, or chemistry. "Every pop-cultural medium portrays the heights of adult intimacy as the moment when two attractive people who don't know a thing about each other tumble into bed and have passionate sex." But infatuation "merely brings the players together" (Lewis, Amini, and Lannon 2000, pp. 206–07). "Relationships live on time" (Lewis, Amini, and Lannon 2000, p. 205). We need to move from infatuation to "the deep connection that is the hallmark and destination of true love" (Love 2001, p. xi). Positive communication is critical to this process.

this story about her improving relationship with her sister:

> [We] spent some time together. . . . We hadn't done that in 3 or 4 years. . . . It was . . . getting to the point where . . . we could just continue to stick our head in the sand or we could . . . try this again. Because this is the only family. . . . So [now, after beginning to repair the relationship], it's sort of inching along like that. A little better, a little better. (in Connidis 2007, p. 489)

The Myth of Conflict-Free Conflict

By now, enough attention has been devoted to conflict resolution techniques that it may seem as if conflict itself can be free of conflict. It can't. Even the fairest fighters hit below the belt once in a while, and just about all fighting involves some degree of frustration and hurt feelings. Moreover, some individuals have a partner who chooses not to learn to face conflict positively. In relationships where one wants to change and the other doesn't, sometimes much can be gained if just one partner begins to communicate more positively. Other times, however, positive changes in one individual do not spur growth in the other. Situations like this may end in alienation, separation, or divorce.

Then too, even when both partners develop constructive habits, all their problems will not necessarily be resolved (Booth, Crouter, and Clements 2001; Driver and Gottman 2004). Although a complainant may feel that he or she is being fair in bringing up a grievance and discussing it openly and calmly, the recipient may view the complaint as critical and punitive, and may not want to bargain about the issue.

Not every conflict can be resolved, even between the fairest and most mature individuals. If an unresolved conflict is not crucial, then the two may simply have to accept their inability to resolve that particular issue. Family cohesiveness, as well as supportive couple relationships, has much to do with commitment, gentleness, and humor, and on letting our loved ones know how much we care about and appreciate them—a task largely accomplished by little gestures such as a touch or hug, and also by sharing ourselves and listening with genuine interest (Love and Stosny 2007).

Summary

- Members of cohesive families express their appreciation for each other, have a high level of commitment to the family group as a whole, do things together, know how to deal positively with stress or crises, and evidence positive communication patterns.
- There is evidence that a family's having a spiritual orientation is positively related to cohesiveness.
- Research on couple communication indicates the importance to relationships of both positive communication and the avoidance of a spiral of negativity.
- Although some family communication patterns may reach the point of pathology, family conflict itself is an inevitable part of normal family life.
- Although arguing is a normal part of the most loving relationships, there are better and worse ways of managing conflict.
- Alienating practices, such as belligerence and the Four Horsemen of the Apocalypse—contempt, criticism, defensiveness, and stonewalling—should be avoided.
- Constructive arguing habits may not only resolve issues but also bring participants closer together.
- Constructive arguments are characterized by efforts to be gentle and by de-escalation of negativity. No one loses.
- There is no such thing as conflict-free conflict.

Questions for Review and Reflection

1. Explain why families are powerful environments. What are the advantages and disadvantages of such power in family interaction?
2. Explain the interactionist theoretical perspective on families, and show how John Gottman's research illustrates this perspective.
3. Describe the Four Horsemen of the Apocalypse. If someone you care for treated you this way in a disagreement, how would you feel? Do you ever treat others with one or more of the "four horsemen"?
4. Discuss your reactions to each of the ten guidelines proposed in this chapter for constructive arguing. What would you add—or subtract?
5. **Policy Question.** Besides the suggestions in "As We Make Choices: Ten Rules for a Successful Relationship," what *society-wide* ideas might you offer for maintaining loving relationships?

Key Terms

belligerence 327
contempt 326
criticism 326
defensiveness 326
demand/withdraw interaction pattern 329
displacement 325
emotional intelligence 333
family cohesion 318
Four Horsemen of the Apocalypse 326
mixed, or double, messages 331
negative affect 327
passive-aggression 324
positive affect 327
rapport talk 328
relationship ideologies 321
report talk 328
sabotage 325
stonewalling 326

Online Resources

Sociology CourseMate

www.CengageBrain.com

Access an integrated eBook, chapter-specific interactive learning tools, including flash cards, quizzes, videos, and more in your Sociology CourseMate, accessed through CengageBrain.com.

www.CengageBrain.com

Want to maximize your online study time? Take this easy-to-use study system's diagnostic pre-test, and it will create a personalized study plan for you. By helping you identify the topics that you need to understand better and then directing you to valuable online resources, it can speed up your chapter review. CengageNOW even provides a post-test so you can confirm that you are ready for an exam.

13

Power and Violence in Families

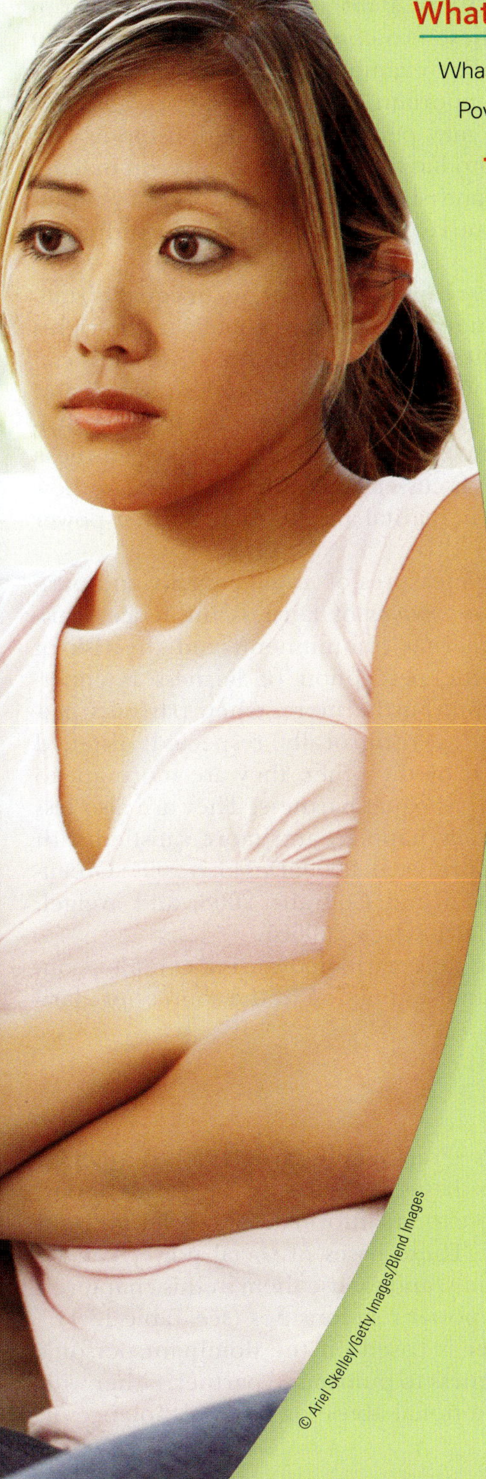

© Ariel Skelley/Getty Images/Blend Images

- Sarah gets a chance for a promotion at work, but accepting it will mean moving to another city; Sarah's spouse does not want to relocate.
- Antonio wants a new stereo for his truck; his partner would prefer to spend the money on ski equipment.
- Marietta would like to talk to her husband about what he does (and doesn't do) around the house, but he is always too busy to discuss the issue.
- Greg feels that he gives more and is more committed to his marriage than his wife is.

This chapter examines power in relationships, particularly marriage and intimate partner relationships. We will discuss some classic studies of marital decision making and look at what contemporary social scientists say about marital power. We will discuss why playing power politics is harmful to intimacy and explore an alternative. Finally, we will explore one tragic result of the abuse of power in families—family violence between intimate partners and violence involving children. We begin by defining power.

What Is Power?

Power may be defined as the ability to exercise one's will. There are many kinds of power. Power exercised over oneself is *personal power,* or autonomy. Having a comfortable degree of personal power is important to self-development. *Social power* is the ability of people to exercise their wills over the wills of others. Social power may be exerted in different realms, including within the family. Parental power, for instance, operates between parents and children. (In this chapter, we focus more on the general dynamics of power in *couple* relationships, rather than parent–child relationships, but we do include child abuse and neglect in the section on family violence.)

The analysis of power in couples originally focused on marriage, but it has been extended to include couples who are not married, both heterosexual cohabitors and same-sex partners. We will use the term **intimate partner power** in referring to unmarried couples or to unmarried *and* married couples, when discussing both together. But because much research on relationship power still focuses on married couples, we will often be discussing **marital power,** with the partners described as husbands and wives.

What Does Marital Power Involve?

Marital power is complex and has several components. First, marital power involves *decision making:* Who gets to make decisions about everything from where the couple will live to how they will spend their leisure time? Second, marital power involves the *division of labor:* Who earns money? Who does the work around the house? A third arena of marital power is the *allocation of money* earned by either or both partners. Who controls spending for the household? Who has access to personal spending money? Finally, marital power involves a partner's *sense of empowerment, being able to influence* one's partner and feeling free to raise complaints to one's spouse about the relationship.

In addition to the components of marital power, the concept involves both *objective measures of power* (who actually makes more—or more important—decisions, and so on) and a *subjective measure of fairness* in the marriage. These two concepts may be related, but not necessarily. For example, a husband who makes virtually all the important decisions and does relatively little housework may perceive the relationship as fair, whereas a wife who has a larger role in decision making and whose husband shares the housework may nevertheless feel that the relationship is unfair, depending on her expectations.

Judging fairness can be grounded in an **equality** standard—both partners should share equally in the rights and responsibilities of the relationship. Or fairness can be thought of in terms of **equity**—are the rewards and privileges of the relationship proportional to the contributions of the partners? The difference between these concepts will be discussed later, when we analyze how gender plays out in marital and intimate partner power relationships.

Both objective measures of *actual* equality and partners' subjective *perceptions* of fairness influence marital satisfaction, marital commitment, and the risk of disruption, but the perception of fairness is generally more powerful. Furthermore, when partners perceive themselves as reciprocally respected, listened to, and supported by the other, they are more apt to define themselves as equal partners. They are also less depressed, generally happier, and more satisfied with their marriage (Corra et al. 2009; DeMaris 2007; Greenstein 2009; Sullivan and Coltrane 2008; and Weigel, Bennett, and Ballard-Reisch 2006b).

Understanding that marital power is a complex concept, we turn to an examination of the sources of marital power.

Power Bases

Two psychologists (French and Raven 1959) developed a typology of six bases, or sources, of social power: coercive, reward, expert, informational, referent, and legitimate power. These bases of social power can be applied to the family, and we use them in this chapter in analyzing couple power relationships (see Table 13.1).

Coercive power is based on the dominant person's ability and willingness to punish the partner, either with psychological–emotional abuse or physical violence or,

Table 13.1 Bases of Social Power as Applied to the Family

Type of Power	Source of Power	Example
Coercive Power	Ability and willingness to punish the partner	Partner sulks, refuses to talk, and withholds sex; physical violence
Reward Power	Ability and willingness to give partner material or nonmaterial gifts and favors	Partner gives affection, attention, praise, and respect to partner, and assists him or her in realizing goals; takes over unpleasant tasks; gives material gifts
Expert Power	Knowledge, ability, judgment	Savings and investment decisions shaped by partner with more education or experience in financial matters
Informational Power	Knows more about a consumer item, child rearing, travel destination, housing market, health issue	Persuades other parent about most effective mode of child discipline, citing experts' books
Referent Power	Emotional identification with partner	Partner agrees to purchase of house or travel plans preferred by the other because she or he wants to make partner happy
Legitimate Power	Society and culture authorize the power of one or the other partner, or both	In traditional marriage, husband has final authority as "head" of household; current ideal is that of equal partners

Source: Typology of power concepts from French and Raven (1959). Specific wording of definitions and the examples are the authors' (Lamanna/Riedmann).

more subtly, by withholding favors or affection (Davies, Ford-Gilboe, and Hammerton 2009, p. 28). Slapping a mate and spanking a child are examples of *coercive power*, so is refusing to talk to the other person—the silent treatment. **Reward power** is based on an individual's ability to give material or nonmaterial gifts and favors, ranging from emotional support and attention to financial support or recreational travel.

Expert power stems from the dominant person's superior judgment, knowledge, or ability. Although this is certainly changing, our society traditionally attributed expertise in such important matters as finances to men, while women were attributed special knowledge of children and expertise in the domestic sphere. **Informational power** is based on the persuasive content of what the dominant person tells another individual. A husband may be persuaded to stop smoking by his wife's giving him information on smoking's health dangers.

Referent power is based on a person's emotional identification with the partner. In feeling part of a couple or group, such as a family, whose members share a common identity, an individual gets emotional satisfaction from thinking as the more dominant person does. Alternatively, *referent power* might be a source of influence for the partner who is generally less dominant, for the dominant partner may gain satisfaction in behaving as the "referent" to individual wishes. A husband who attends a social function when he'd rather not "because my wife wanted to go and so I wanted to go too" has been swayed by *referent power*. In happy relationships, *referent power* increases as partners grow older together (Raven, Centers, and Rodrigues 1975; Pyke and Adams 2010).

Finally, **legitimate power** stems from the dominant individual's ability to claim authority, or the right to request compliance. *Legitimate power* in traditional marriages involves acceptance by both partners of the husband's role as head of the family. Although this is not the case for all families in the United States, the current ideal in mainstream culture is an egalitarian couple partnership (Gerson 2010, pp. 106–07).

Throughout this chapter, we will see the various power bases at work. The consistent research finding, for instance, that the economic dependence of one partner on the other results in the dependent partner's being less powerful may be explained by understanding the interplay of both *reward power* and *coercive power*. If I can reward you with financial support—or threaten to take it away—then I am more able to exert power over you.

Native Man and Woman by unidentified Native artist, Chukotka Peninsula, Russia. Artist workshop, Uelen.

The Dynamics of Marital Power

We turn now to look more specifically at research on marital power and the theoretical perspectives used to explain couple power relationships.

Classical Perspectives on Marital Power

Research on marital power began in the 1950s. At that time—before the feminist movement of the 1970s—interest in marital power was more academic than political. Social scientists Robert Blood and Donald Wolfe were curious about how married couples made decisions. Their book *Husbands and Wives: The Dynamics of Married Living* (1960) was based on interviews with wives only. Nevertheless, it was a significant piece of research and shaped thinking on marital power for many years.

Egalitarian Power and the Resource Hypothesis Blood and Wolfe began with the assumption that although the American family's forebears were patriarchal, "the predominance of the male has been so thoroughly undermined that we no longer live in a patriarchal system" (pp. 18–19). They reasoned that the relative power of wives and husbands results from their relative resources. The **resource hypothesis** holds that the spouse with more resources has more power in marriage. Resources include education and earnings; within marriage, a spouse's most valuable resource would be the ability to provide money. Another resource would be good judgment, probably enhanced by education and experience. (Note that the resource hypothesis is a variation on *exchange theory,* presented in Chapter 2.)

To test their resource hypothesis, Blood and Wolfe interviewed about 900 wives in Greater Detroit and asked who made the final decision in eight areas, such as what job the husband should take, what car to buy, whether the wife should work, and how much money the family could afford to spend per week on food. From their interviews, they drew the conclusion that most families (72 percent) had a "relatively egalitarian" decision-making structure (that is, the spouses held roughly equal power, whether that involved separate areas of decision making or joint decisions). However, there were families in which the husband made the most decisions (25 percent), and a few wife-dominated families (3 percent).

The resource hypothesis was supported by the finding that the relative resources of wives and husbands were important in determining which partner made more decisions. Wage and salary earnings or other individual income was a major source of decision-making power. Older spouses and those with more education also made more decisions. Blood and Wolfe also found the relative power of a wife to be greater after she no longer had young children (and was less dependent on her husband) or when she worked outside the home and thereby gained wage-earning resources for herself.

The Blood and Wolfe study had the effect of encouraging people to see marital power as shared rather than patriarchal and resting on their individual attributes or resources rather than on social roles. But this study was strongly criticized, particularly because it tended to ignore the nuances of hidden power—the power of gender expectations and roles that most of us are socialized into.

Criticism of the Resource Hypothesis One criticism concerns Blood and Wolfe's criteria for attributing power to husbands or wives. The decisions wives made (such as how much to spend on food) were generally less important than those that husbands typically made (such as which city the couple should live in): "Having the power to make trivial decisions is not the same as having the power to make important ones" (Brehm et al. 2002, p. 321). And there were important areas of family life that were not included in the Blood and Wolfe study—such as sexual life, how many children to have, and how much freedom partners might have for same- or opposite-sex friendships.

Critics stated that power between spouses involves far more than which partner makes the most *final* decisions—deciding what *alternatives* are going to be considered may be the real decision. Moreover, the person who seems to be making a decision may in fact be acting on a delegation of power from the other partner (Safilios-Rothschild 1970). For example, a husband might ask his wife to make vacation arrangements, specifying that it be a skiing vacation.

Another criticism of the resource hypothesis concerns its narrow focus—on individuals' background characteristics and abilities—but does not take into account their personalities and the way they interact (Brehm et al. 2002). And finally, marital power is more than decision making; it also implies the relative autonomy of wives and husbands, along with the division of labor in marriages (Safilios-Rothschild 1970; Tichenor 2010, p. 419).

Blood and Wolfe came under heaviest fire for their conclusion that a patriarchal power structure had been replaced by egalitarian marriages.

Resource and Gender Feminist Dair Gillespie (1971) pointed out that power-giving resources tend to be unevenly distributed between the sexes. Husbands usually earn more money even when wives work, so husbands have access to more economic *resources.* Husbands are often older (and at the time of the study were often better educated than their wives). So husbands are more likely to have more status, and they may be more knowledgeable, or seem to be (*expert* or *informational power*).

Even their greater physical strength may be an important resource (*coercive power;* Collins and Coltrane 1995), although it can be a destructive one, as we will see later in this chapter.

Women are likely to have fewer alternatives to the marriage than their husbands, especially if wives cannot support themselves or are responsible for the care of young children. Moreover, men can remarry more readily than women. Consequently, according to Gillespie, the resource hypothesis, which presents resources as neutral and power as gender-free, is simply "rationalizing the preponderance of the male sex." Marriage is hardly a "free contract between equals" (p. 449; see also Komter 1989 and Tichenor 2010).

Current research tends to support Gillespie's insight that American marriages continue to be inegalitarian even though they are no longer traditional, although younger marrieds are working toward more egalitarian relationships (Gerson 2010; Rosenbluth, Steil, and Whitcomb 1998; Spade and Valentine 2010; Wilkie, Ferree, and Ratcliff 1998). True, resources make a difference, and an important factor in marital power is whether or not a wife is employed. Wage-earning wives have more to say in important decisions and in the division of household labor, but gendered divisions remain nonetheless (Johnston 2007).

One way in which women come to have fewer resources is through their reproductive roles and resulting economic dependence. Just after marriage, the relationship is apt to be relatively egalitarian, with the husband only moderately more powerful than the wife—if at all. Often at this point, the wife has considerable economic power in relation to her husband because she is employed and may even have a well-paying career. But relationships tend to become less egalitarian with the first pregnancy and birth (Coltrane and Ishii-Kuntz 1992).

During the childbearing years of the marriage, the practical need to be married is felt especially strongly by women, who are more often than not the primary caregivers as well as bearers of children (Johnson and Huston 1998). A divorce would likely mean that the woman must parent and support small children alone. Women engaged in reproduction and child rearing may have less energy to resist dominance attempts. On the other hand, a mother may exert power over her husband by threatening to leave and take the infant with her (LaRossa 1979).

As we noted, working contributes to marital power. But working for wages or even outearning a husband does not necessarily give a wife full status as an equal partner (Coltrane 2000; Teachman 2010; Tichenor 2005). Even though a working wife is, in theory, less obliged to defer to her husband and has greater authority in making family decisions, she does not necessarily participate equally in decision making in fact, and she is still unequally burdened with housekeeping and child rearing.

Resource Theory Researchers have come to realize that resource theory does not fully explain marital power. Although women's employment rates, occupational status, and income have increased in recent decades, their share of household work has not declined to a similar degree (Cooke 2006; Hall and MacDermid 2009; Sullivan and Coltrane 2009). This "failure of resource and exchange perspectives to explain marital power dynamics in two earner couples" (Tichenor 1999, pp. 638–39; 2005) has led scholars to turn to other theoretical perspectives.

Resources in Cultural Context Studies comparing traditional societies with more modern ones suggest that in a traditional society, norms of patriarchal authority may be so strong that they override personal resources and give considerable power to all husbands (Safilios-Rothschild 1967; Blumberg and Coleman 1989). Put another way, in a traditional society, male authority is *legitimate power*. This perspective, termed **resources in cultural context**, stresses the idea that resources are not effective in conferring marital power in traditional societies that legitimate male dominance with a patriarchal norm.

This situation may be especially true for immigrant families from traditional societies, such as in Asia or Central and South America, at least for those who are newly arrived. However, subsequent generations may be expected to adopt the more common American pattern. The generation born in the United States has moved to a **transitional egalitarian situation** regarding marital power, typical of the rest of the country, in which "husband–wife relationships are more flexible and negotiated . . . [and] socioeconomic achievements become the basis for negotiation within the family" (Cooney et al. 1982, p. 622).

Even among native-born Americans, however, we must recognize the continuing salience of tradition and the assumption that it is legitimate to some degree for husbands to wield authority in the family (Nock, Sanchez, and Wright 2008; Komter 1989). The continued importance of the legitimation of husbands' authority is apparent in religious groups that accept the principle of male headship of the family (Meyers 2005; Wilcox 2004). Although egalitarianism is undoubtedly the most sought after mode among American couples generally, whether an **egalitarian norm** of marital power is fully realized in any sector of American society is a question we will discuss throughout this chapter. Presently it seems those most likely to have attained this idea are lesbian couples, in which the resources, for example, that each brings to the relationship do not affect each person's power (Jeong and Horne 2009).

In sum, the cultural context conditions resource theory explains marital power only when there is no overriding egalitarian norm or **patriarchal norm of marital power**. Put another way, if traditional norms of male authority are strong, husbands will almost inevitably dominate regardless of personal resources. Similarly, if an egalitarian norm of marriage were completely accepted, then a husband's superior economic achievements would be irrelevant to his decision-making power because both spouses would have equal power. It is only in the present transitional egalitarian situation, in which neither patriarchal norms nor egalitarian norms are firmly entrenched, that marital power is negotiated by individual couples, and the power of husbands and wives may be a consequence of their resources (Stevenson and Wolfers 2006).

Love, Need, and Power Some have argued that a primarily economic analysis does not do justice to the complexities of marital power. Perhaps a wife has considerable power through her husband's love for her, what we have termed *referent power*. Generally, however, the wife holds the less-powerful position even in this reckoning. In our society, women value close emotional relationships more than men do (Lois 2010). They are encouraged to express their feelings, whereas men are less likely to articulate their feelings for their partners. Overt dependency affects power: "A woman gains power over her husband if he clearly places a high value on her company or if he expresses a high demand or need for what she supplies. . . . If his need for her and high evaluation of her remain covert and unexpressed, her power will be low" (Cancian 1985, p. 258).

But another way of looking at it is that men are less relatively powerful in the private, intimate sphere than they are in the public world because the private world is more likely to give priority to *referent power*. Therapists and mass media, and, to an increasing degree, the public, support women's desire for more expression of feelings. Men have been much influenced by the expectation that they should respond favorably to wives' influence (Connell 2005). They are encouraged to engage in "emotion work," "to express emotion to their wives, to be attentive to the dynamics of their relationship and the needs of their wives, [and] . . . to set aside time for activities focused especially on the relationship" (Wilcox and Nock 2006, p. 1,322).

We have spent some time on earlier theory and research because these lead to issues of marital power that are still current.

Current Research on Marital Power

The first research on marital power by Blood and Wolfe focused solely on decision making. A later research project by sociologists Philip Blumstein and Pepper Schwartz (1983) covered other aspects of couple relationships—money and sex, for example—and it compared married couples to heterosexual cohabiting couples and gay male and lesbian couples. As a major step forward in the study of couple relationships, this study is still cited (Gilbert and Rader 2008; Moore 2008; Pinto and Coltrane 2009).

One reason for its longevity may be that social scientists had seemed to lose interest for a time in researching "marital power." Instead, they pursued marital and partner equality issues indirectly, by examining women's expanding entry into the labor force and related issues of who does the unpaid labor of household and child care. Recently, however, the word *power* has begun to reappear in journal articles and books examining couples' allocation of money, their capacity to influence each other and to raise touchy issues, and, still, the question of fairness (or not) in the division of household labor (Vogler, Lyonette, and Wiggins 2008).

Equality, *equity*, and *gender* and their interrelationship are themes of current thinking about marital and other intimate partner power. Are men and women now equal in their family relationships? If not, why not?

Although an older generation may hold to traditional patriarchal power, the next generation may renegotiate and consciously change those roles, especially as women assume more autonomy and make gains in the workplace. In this photo, the classic card game of Hwoa-tu and the Chinese vase and screen in the background suggest a world of traditional authority, a man's *legitimate power* as head of the family. The posture and clothing of the younger family members suggest more casual and democratic family relations.

© Steve Skjold/PhotoEdit

Gay and lesbian couples are more likely to share domestic duties than are heterosexual couples, although attainment of an egalitarian ideal eludes many gay/lesbian couples as well. In marriages, men's participation in housework has increased, although wives continue to do more.

Social scientists generally agree that the cultural ideal today is one of spousal and partner equality and of shared work and family roles. According to the resource hypothesis, as wives entered the labor force and began earning substantial income, they would be able to bargain for equality at home based on their resources. By and large, this vision of equality has not been attained in a number of respects:

> Feminists and scholars assumed that women's moving into the labor force and becoming important co-breadwinners would increase their power in the family—especially in terms of control over money management and decision making. However, the marital power literature over the last several decades has not borne this assumption out. Women's power in decision-making has increased somewhat, but not to a degree commensurate with the level of income many of them have been earning. In short, their income does not seem to buy them the same . . . power that men have typically enjoyed. (Tichenor 2005, p. 91; see also Vogler, Lyonette, and Wiggins 2008)

We examine the complexities of partner equality by looking at current research on couples and their unpaid household work, control over money, decision making, and the expression of grievances and management of emotions. We draw on a number of studies (research reviews, quantitative and qualitative studies) of varying methodologies, sample sizes, and social locations.[1] We then look at where things stand regarding gender equality in the family and consider the future of family power.

Household Work and Leisure Time Virtually all research indicates that women's satisfaction with the fairness of their partners' contributions to household work is strongly associated with women's (and sometimes men's) relationship happiness, marital commitment, and depression and with the risk of marital disruption. Where women have more egalitarian expectations than men fulfill, there is often marital conflict (DeMaris 2007; Gerson 2010; Greenstein 2009; Sullivan and Coltrane 2009).

Fairness of the division of household labor is not usually evaluated on a 50–50 standard. What's "fair" to a man may be less than half, while a woman has to be doing all or almost all the housework to find it "unfair" (Kendall 2007). "[U]nequal divisions of labor are accepted as normal" (Coltrane 2000, p. 1,223).

Women whose husbands work more hours are less apt to see the division of household labor as unfair (Kendall 2007). So are more traditional women, perhaps because their expectations are shaped by a religious doctrine of separate spheres and male headship (Myers 2006; Nock, Sanchez, and Wright 2008). Still, even in evangelical couples, there is an implicit acknowledgment of a norm of equality in the attention given by evangelical men to expressing great appreciation for their wives' doing the preponderant share of housework. In the context of a societal egalitarian ideal, the additional domestic work of evangelical wives becomes a "gift," which is reciprocated by the husband's emotional work of expressed appreciation in an "economy of gratitude" (Vaaler, Ellison, and Powers 2009; Wilcox 2004, p. 154, referencing Hochschild 1989).

In American society more generally, there has been a significant increase in men's share of housework (Eckel 2010; Gilbert 2008; Kelleher 2007; Sullivan and Coltrane 2008). Although that share still does not approach equality, the increase since 1965 is quite dramatic. In 1965, women did seven hours of housework for every hour that men put in; in 2005, it was nearly one and a half hours (see Figure 13.1).

Social scientists now tend to use housework as one criterion of power (on the assumption that no one really

[1] In this limited space, it becomes impossible to discuss the details of the research methodology of each source cited. For more detail, consult the original sources.

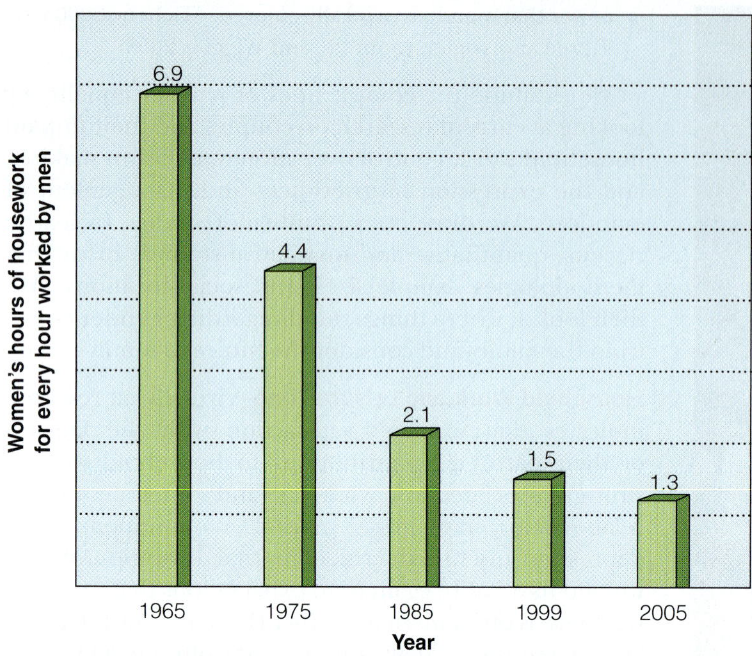

Figure 13.1 Trends in average weekly housework[a] hours for women and men (ages twenty-five through fifty-four), 1965–2005 (ratio of women's hours to men's hours)

[a]"Housework" includes "core housework" (cooking meals, meal cleanup, housecleaning, laundry, and ironing) as well as "other housework" (outdoor chores, repairs, gardening, animal care, bills, other financial).

Source: Adapted from Sayer, Cohen, and Casper 2004, Table 3; Mixon 2008.

wants to do it). The current situation—women do one and one half times what men do in housework—can be seen as a metaphor for their relative marital power. Women have gained men's participation in housework—and gained in power—but have not achieved absolute equality.

There also continues to be a "leisure gap." Although in formal terms, women have only one-half hour less of leisure time than men have, what is labeled "leisure" for women is often indirectly child care and household management (Bianchi, Robinson, and Milkie 2006; Gerson 2010).

Some women see their greater responsibility in household work as enabling the acquisition of some measure of power at the practical level (Tichenor 2005):

> As wives gather information in preparation for having some kind of discussion, they often form opinions about what . . . they would prefer to happen. They are then free to present the information . . . in such a way that makes what they want to do seem like the . . . most reasonable course of action. . . .
>
> [This] suggests that information is an important source of power in these relationships. While women carry a tremendous burden in terms of managing household responsibilities, that work . . . gives women access to knowledge that either gives them direct control or sometimes allows them an extra measure of influence in joint decision making. Most important is that women are often completely aware of this power and use it consciously to their advantage. (Tichenor 2005, p. 96)

Thus, women's *informational power* can offset men's *resource* or *legitimate power* or enable them to have the influence that their own *resource power* apparently does not. Of course, it must be exercised clandestinely.

Control Over Money Research on couples' **allocation systems**—whether they pool their money and who controls pooled or separate money—is relatively recent. British social policy scholar Jan Pahl (1989; see also Kenney 2006 and Vogler 2005 for recent research using this typology) developed a typology of allocation systems that subsequent researchers have used or adapted.

In the industrial era, a family's allocation system was typically one of complete control of his earnings by the male breadwinner, who doled out a housekeeping allowance to his homemaker wife. The allowance was often rather skimpy, while the husband was privileged to take money "off the top" for personal spending and recreation.

Even before the emergence of feminism, this system began to be seen as inappropriate to a companionate model of marriage in which men and women were seen as equal, though with different family roles. To resolve the tension between a theoretical equality of men and women in the family, but their much different worth in the market economy, the typical marital allocation system became one of pooled resources. The husband's earnings were deposited into an account maintained in both names and controlled jointly by the spouses—at least, that was the theory. Given male dominance in decision making in this era, the husband usually controlled the pooled account. Moreover, nonearning women typically felt uncomfortable making decisions about "his" earnings. In reality, the joint account was not jointly controlled.

Feminists began to criticize the joint pool system. Women were now earning money as well. Separate financial accounts and control began to be seen as a favored alternative, with each spouse or partner making equal contributions to running the household. But in another iteration, scholars and feminists have pointed out that equal household contributions may not be equitable when women typically earn less than men—their contribution to household expenses represents a larger proportion of their earnings (Kenney 2006; Tichenor 2005; Vogler, Lyonette, and Wiggins 2008).

A variety of allocation systems operate in American (and European) marriages at present, involving two dimensions: whether to pool and who controls—man,

© Comstock Images/Jupiterimages

This couple seems to be sharing control over their money on an equal basis.

woman, or both?. There continues to be a tension in many marriages and other partner relationships between the communal values of the couple relationship and the individualism of the market, in which each person may have a very different level of earned income (Vogler 2005). Cohabitants and those who have been previously divorced are especially likely to maintain separate money (Kenney 2006).

Gender still plays a strong role, and men seem to retain more control over the family's income no matter who earns it. They are especially likely to retain personal spending money and/or to feel free to spend the family's income on personal and recreational desires without consulting their partner. Women may spend some of their "personal" money on household needs. And even otherwise egalitarian men may assume they have "veto power" over major decisions (Tichenor 2005; Vogler, Lyonette, and Wiggins 2008; Vogler, Brockmann, and Wiggins 2008). This would seem to be an example of traditional *legitimate power* ascribed to a male, overriding the wife's *resource power.*

Power and Decision Making Here, we look at decision making and marital power in general terms rather than in the specific domains of spending and housework. Using a national sample survey to compare decision making in 1980 and 2000, Amato, Johnson, Booth, and Rogers found that, in 2000, "respondents were significantly more likely to report equal-decision-making" (2003, p. 9). Even wives in evangelical families often have more decision-making power than their formal submission to the male family head would indicate. In fact, some research shows that "co-parenting and joint decision-making are more common in evangelical homes than in secular and mainline religious households" (Bartkowski and Read 2003, p. 88; Bartkowski 2001; Vaaler, Ellison, and Powers 2009).

Power asymmetry was found more often among dissatisfied couples. Men's power may not be visible, as they may have the ability to suppress issues so that they never arise overtly (Tichenor 2005, p. 25). "The spouse with less power [usually the wife] typically spends more time aligning emotions with [the spouse's] expectations" (Coltrane 1998) rather than risking confrontation. This increases emotional pressure. Coltrane notes that some men may *feel* powerless despite their greater power:

> Men's subjective sense of powerlessness—of lost or slipping privilege—is often a precursor to wife-beating or sexual abuse. . . . This does not mean that these men are less powerful than their wives. . . . This contradictory co-existence of felt powerlessness and actual (if latent) power is quite common for men. (Coltrane 1998, p. 201)

Women, on the other hand, may fear appearing too powerful. "For some women, expressing or exercising power seems threatening either to their relationships or to their gender identities. Some wives speak openly of the danger that power poses for them" (Tichenor 2005, p. 110). They are concerned about their husbands' sense of masculinity, as well as their gender identity (p. 114). In fact, many women attempt to "preserve their husbands' masculinity by backing away from power . . . deferring to husbands and adopting various strategies to make it look as if husbands were in control" (Vogler, Lyonette, and Wiggins 2008, p. 131).

Bases of Marital Power To sum up, in these discussions of marital power and decision making, we see the interplay of three bases of social power: *resource power, legitimate power,* and *informational power.*

Resource power traditionally gave provider husbands greatest power in marital decision making, including the capacity to keep troubling issues and decisions from even arising. But the equation of resources (that is, earnings) with power hasn't worked in the same way for women. A study of wives who earn more than their husbands suggests that "the gender structure exerts an influence that is independent of breadwinning or relative financial contributions" (Tichenor 2005, p. 117). A residual sense of the propriety of traditional male privilege—that is, *legitimate power*—ascribed more authority to men even in situations where they lacked *resource power.* "Just as women's income does not buy them either relief from domestic labor or greater financial power . . . , it does not give them dominion in decision making" (p. 117).

In an interesting twist, women can sometimes gain power from their greater knowledge of the household. They can use this *informational power* to shape decisions about purchases and household arrangements, as we noted earlier.

Equality, Equity, and Gender Spouses are usually aware of imbalances in marital power. Wives typically have a greater sense of unfairness because they are so often disadvantaged (DeMaris 2007, p. 192). From 1980 to 2000, there has been a "shift toward more egalitarian marital relations" (Amato et al. 2003, p. 9; see also Gerson 2010, pp. 117, 122–23). At the same time, wives seem to have gained in average marital happiness. "Wives were less happy than husbands in both surveys, but the gap between husbands and wives grew smaller between 1980–2000. The narrowing of the gender gap in happiness may be attributable to more egalitarian marital relations" (p. 11; see also Corra et al. 2009).

The Future of Marital Power

Power disparities discourage intimacy, which is based on honesty, sharing, and mutual respect. For most, therefore, attainment of the American ideal of equality in marriage would seem to support the development of intimacy in marital relationships.

Yet the United States is a pluralistic society, and so we may expect to find varied visions of the future of marital power. Whether or not they reflect an egalitarian ideal, they generally take into account an egalitarian norm of marital power. We first sketch out this diversity, and then look at some of the specific marriage models scholars envision as they ponder the direction of change.

The Road to the Future One way to bring varied visions of the future together is to imagine couples driving along an interstate highway that leads to gender equality. Some couples are committed to getting there fast, and they take the express lane directly to shared and equal roles and power.

Most of the couples remain on the main interstate and are not completely sure if they want to travel all the way to the end. They keep consulting their maps to see if there is a stopping point they would like better, a mix of equality and gender identity.

A few couples exit the interstate, looking for a setting, perhaps a small town, where they can reproduce the more differentiated gender roles of the mid-twentieth century, though with some respect for equality in the relationship.

Some couples pull into a rest stop to continue the quarrel that has sprung up—she prefers a greater degree of sharing of power and household work than he does. After some negotiation, they reach at least a temporary compromise and continue on their way.

Finally, some couples have a complete breakdown and are waiting along the road for assistance, to return home and then move into separate lives.

Mutually Economically Dependent Spouses or Other Egalitarian Relationships Sociologist Steven Nock sees the future as one of *mutually economically dependent spouses*. "What I propose [as] . . . the emerging

© Pixland/Jupiter Images

This family is having breakfast in a household where roles may be somewhat differentiated by gender, but there is no sharp difference in status and power between the adults.

form of American marriage [is] a relationship in which couples are equally dependent on one another's earnings" (2001, p. 755). He defines *MEDS,* or **mutually economically dependent spouses**, as dual-earner couples in which each spouse earns between 40 and 59 percent of the family's income. Examining data from the 1999 Current Population Survey, he finds that presently just under one-third of all dual earners (some 20 percent of all couples) are mutually economically dependent. This pattern occurs at all economic levels (Nock 2001; see also Amato and Hohmann-Marriott 2007).

Nock not only sees equality in this arrangement but also finds it less threatening to marriage than one might think. True, an independent income increases the risk of divorce on the part of wives who are dissatisfied with household contributions of their husbands (Stevenson and Wolfers 2006). At the same time, in a MEDS marriage, the two would become equally dependent financially, which could strengthen commitment if husbands change to contribute more household work.

This is a complex argument and rests on the thought that a marriage would be grounded in "extensive dependencies by both partners," as was the case in traditional society. As Nock sees it, the decline in divorce rates since the early 1980s may reflect "the gradual working out of the gender issues first confronted in the 1960s. If so, this implies that young men and women are forming new types of marriages that are based on a new understanding of gender ideals" (Nock 2001, p. 774). Men growing up today, often with working mothers, are more likely to adapt to changing gender roles. "We are still at the early stages of a fundamental realignment of gender in our society" (p. 773).

Another possibility is that *norms of equality* may come to be so strong that men and women will have equal power in marriage regardless of resources. *Legitimate power* would endorse women's equality with men in the family. Pepper Schwartz's research on *peer marriage* (also referred to in the literature as "post-gender" or "equal sharer") offers an example of a strong equality norm at work (1994; 2001; see also Hall and MacDermid 2009). She studied couples who attempt to make their marriage according to this ideal. "As We Make Choices: Peer Marriage" describes this research.

Neotraditional Families In a pluralistic society, there are alternative visions of the family model. Among evangelical Christians and other conservative religious sectors, a gendered division of labor, formal male dominance in decision making, and an egalitarian spirit combine in the **neotraditional family** (see Chapter 11 for more discussion on this type of family).

Although a husband's dominant power is legitimated in this milieu, marital power in practice is often negotiated. First "articulated by evangelical feminists," the "mutual submission" (of husband and wife to each other) has become increasingly popular because it justifies the shared decision making that characterizes many evangelical marriages (Dolan 2008; p. 32; Bartkowski and Read 2003; Bartkowski 2001; Vaaler, Ellison, and Powers 2009). Another way in which a norm of equality is represented in these ostensibly husband-dominant marriages is in the emotional "economy of gratitude" (Pugh 2009, p. 6; Wilcox 2004, p. 154), as husbands display appreciation for their wives' "gift" of household work. Evangelical couples *are* committed to a headship model of marital power, yet this has an "enchanted" quality, symbolic of the religious commitment of the couple (Wilkins 2009, p. 363). In many ways, then, the edges of difference and dominance are softened in the neotraditional family, as the title of sociologist Bradford Wilcox's book—*Soft Patriarchs*—suggests.

A Gender Model of Marriage Writing from a perspective somewhat different than Nock's MEDS vision, Wilcox and Nock (2006) suggest that the egalitarian, equal-resource model of marriage does not represent what most couples want, at least at present, or what makes them happy with their marriage. Instead, they construct a **gender model of marriage**.

Wilcox and Nock see the egalitarian definition of marital power as circumscribed by the symbolic importance of maintaining gender boundaries. Couples want to construct conventional relationships and marriages in which they are comfortable. Compromise with an egalitarian ideal occurs "as spouses work together to construct appropriate gender identities and maintain viable marriages" (Tichenor 2005, p. 32).

> Because wives—even wives with egalitarian attitudes—have been socialized to value gender-typical patterns of behavior, wives will be happier in marriages with gender-typical practices in the division of household labor, work outside the home, and earnings. Because husbands—even husbands with egalitarian attitudes—have been socialized to value gender-typical patterns of behavior, husbands will be happier in marriages that produce gender-typical patterns and will be more inclined to invest themselves emotionally in their marriages than husbands organized along more egalitarian lines. (Wilcox and Nock 2006, p. 1,328)

In their study of over 5,000 couples drawn from the second wave of the National Survey of Families and Households (1992–94), Wilcox and Nock did find support for the hypothesis that "the gendered character of marriage seems to remain sufficiently powerful as a tacit ideal among women to impact women's marital quality" (pp. 1,339–40). Nevertheless, when men's household work departed from the expectations of more egalitarian wives, marital quality was also affected. "'Her' marriage is happiest when it combines elements of the new and old" (p. 1,321).

As We Make Choices

Peer Marriage

A piece of research by Pepper Schwartz paints a picture of couples who have developed egalitarian marriages, or tried to. Schwartz followed up her earlier research on couples with an exploration of the factors that facilitate **peer marriage** (1994, 2001): "I began looking for couples who had worked out no worse than a 60–40 split on child rearing, housework, and control of discretionary funds, and who considered themselves to have 'equal' status or standing in the relationship" (2001, p. 182). The study was based on fifty-seven egalitarian couples, with some additional interviews with couples considered **near peers** and **traditionals** for comparison.

Near peers believed in equality, but the combination of the arrival of children and the desire to maximize income meant that the husband did not participate as much as the couple's egalitarian ideals required. *Traditionals* were those marriages in which males dominated decision making except regarding children, but both parties were OK with this—the wife did not seek equality.

Peer marriages did not necessarily stem from a feminist ideology. Only 40 percent of women and 20 percent of men in peer marriages cited feminism as a motive. The rest gave other reasons for wanting a peer marriage: a rejection of negative parental models (women resented their father's dominance of their mothers; men wished for more involvement as parents); a desire to undertake co-parenting; and, in some cases, a period of serious tension in the marriage that required renegotiation of roles. However, for men especially, partner's preference was what led their marriage in an egalitarian direction. In an interesting twist on the expressive role of women, "[m]any of these men told me they had always expected a woman to be the emotional architect of a relationship and were predisposed to let her set the rules" (p. 183).

There was "no single blueprint" (p. 189), nor were these peer marriage couples high-earning "yuppies" or academics with flexible schedules. Peer marriage seemed, in the long run, to require an intense desire to have such a marriage and a persistent willingness to forgo male career advancement and income. Everyday responsibilities also had to be constantly monitored and renegotiated. Over time, the peer marriage couples evolved strong egalitarian norms that override the surrounding structure and typical power processes, much as Blumstein and Schwartz had earlier found in their lesbian couples (and sociologist Barbara Risman [1998] found in her research on "fair" marriages). The couple's respect for each other as described in Schwartz's study of peer marriage is essentially a "no-power" relationship.

Critical Thinking

Do you see peer marriages as an ideal for yourself, or not? How common do you think peer marriages will become in the future?

Source: Pepper Schwartz 1994.

Power Politics versus No-Power Relationships

Marriage and other intimate partner relationships that partners find fair and equitable are generally more apt to be stable and satisfying. Social scientist Peter Blau terms this situation *no-power.* **No-power** does not mean that one partner exerts little or no power; it means that each partner has the ability to mutually and reciprocally influence and be influenced by the other (Gottman et al. 1998; Schwartz 1994). We turn now to a discussion of the process of changing power relationships in marriage.

A fair division of household labor is not the only standard by which women and men judge the equality or lack of equality in their marriage. The respect one has for the other's views is extremely important; that is a central element in a no-power conceptualization of marriage and other partner relations. As we use the term, *no-power* also implies that partners do not seek to exercise their relative power over each other. No-power partners seek to negotiate and compromise, not to win (see Chapter 12). They are able to avoid **power politics**.

Power Politics in Marriage

As gender norms move from traditional toward egalitarian, all family members' interests and preferences gain legitimacy, not only or primarily those of the husband or husband/father. For example, the man's occupation is no longer the sole determining factor in where the family will live or how the wife will spend her time. This means that decisions formerly made automatically, or by spontaneous consensus, must now be consciously negotiated. A possible outcome of such conscious negotiating, of course, is greater intimacy; another is locking into power politics and conflict.

In the worst case, both equal and unequal partners may engage in a cycle of devitalizing power politics. Partners come to know where their own power lies, along with the particular weaknesses of the other. They may alternate in acting sulky, sloppy, critical, or distant, or even hint at leaving the marriage (Blumberg and Coleman 1989;

"I'm trying to look at it from my point of view."

Chafetz 1989). The sulking partner carries on this behavior until she or he fears the mate will "stop dancing" if it goes on much longer; then it's the other partner's turn. This kind of seesawing may continue indefinitely, with partners taking turns manipulating each other. However, the cumulative effect of such power politics is to create distance and loneliness for both spouses.

New research into marital power politics in immigrants examines the changes that take place in immigrant marriages once these couples integrate into the American culture. The findings suggest similar patterns of tension, resistance, and acceptance to shifts in power as seen in marriages of native-born Americans. The reason for this, the researchers suggest, is that patterns of gendered power evolve over time—no couple's relationship is static. Because human beings and their relationships are dynamic, patterns of power will also change, regardless of consciousness and social context (Falicov 2007; Maciel, Van Putten, and Knudson-Martin 2009). Few couples knowingly choose power politics, but this is an aspect of marriage in which choosing by default may occur. Our discussion of power in marriage is designed to help partners become sensitive to these issues so that they can avoid such a power spiral, or reverse one if it has already started.

Alternatives to Power Politics

There are alternatives to this kind of power struggle. Robert Blood and Donald Wolfe (1960) proposed one in which partners grow increasingly separate in their decision making; that is, they take charge of separate domains: one buying the car, perhaps the other taking charge of disciplining their children. This alternative is a poor one for partners who seek intimacy, however, for it enforces separateness rather than the sharing of important decisions.

A second, more viable alternative to perpetuating an endless cycle of power politics is for one partner to disengage from power struggles, as described in "As We Make Choices: Disengaging from Power Struggles." This includes a third, perhaps best, alternative, which is for the more powerful partner to consciously relinquish some power in order to save or enhance the marriage. We saw in Chapter 12, for instance, that marriage communication expert John Gottman and his colleagues (Gottman et al. 1998) advise husbands to be willing to share power with their wives if they want happy, stable marriages, something he says can be difficult for men who had difficult childhoods (pp. 18–19; Coan and Gottman 2007).

The Importance of Communication As we've noted earlier, partners who see themselves as mutually respected, equally committed, and listened to when they raise concerns are more likely to see their relationship as egalitarian and are more satisfied overall with their relationship.

Meanwhile, unequal relationships discourage closeness between partners: Exchange of confidences between unequals may be difficult, especially when self-disclosure is seen to indicate weakness. Men more than women have been socialized not to reveal their emotions (Hoyt 2009; Panayiotou and Papageorgiou 2007; Rudman and Glick 2008; Spade and Valentine 2010). Women, feeling less powerful and more vulnerable, may resort to pretense and the withholding of sexual and emotional response. In fact, because the female partner in a heterosexual relationship is the only socially acceptable outlet for a male to express his vulnerabilities, when the woman leaves the relationship, the effect is a "greater emotional cost" for the man than for the woman (Rudman and Glick 2008, p. 223).

Nevertheless, trying to change the balance of marital power may bring the risk of devitalizing a relationship, depending on how partners go about it. Mates who try to disengage from power struggles, without explaining what they are doing and why, risk estrangement. The reason is that dominant partners may have taken a mate's compliance as evidence of love rather than fear. If this deference is withdrawn, a dominant partner may conclude that "she (or he) doesn't love me anymore" and escalate efforts at control, contributing to a spiral of alienation and estrangement that is not acknowledged or discussed openly.

The Change at a No-Power Relationship Changing power patterns can be difficult, even for couples who talk about it, because these patterns usually have been established from the earliest days of the relationship. From the interactionist perspective, certain behaviors come not only to be expected but also to have symbolic meaning. In addition, sociologist William Goode had an insight that continues to be relevant for many couples. He wrote about the important change in men's position as women gain equality in society and in the family. According to Goode:

As We Make Choices

Disengaging from Power Struggles

The late Carlfred Broderick, sociologist and marriage counselor, offered the following exercise to help people disengage from power struggles. The object of this exercise is to get you out of the business of monitoring everyone else's behavior and free you from the unrewarding power struggles resulting from that assignment. Here is the exercise:

1. Think of as many things as you can that your spouse or children should do, ought to do, and would do if they really cared, but don't do (or do only grudgingly because you are always after them). Write them down in a list.
2. From your list, choose three or four items that are especially troublesome right now. Write each one at the head of a sheet of blank paper. These are the issues that you, considerably more than your spouse, want to resolve (even though he or she, by rights, should be the one to see the need for resolution). Right now you are locked in a power struggle over each one, leading to more resentment and less satisfaction all around.
3. In this step you'll consider, one by one, optional ways of dealing with these issues without provoking a power struggle. Place an A, B, C, and D on each sheet of paper at appropriate intervals to represent the four options listed below. Depending on the nature of the issue, some of these options will work better than others, but for a start, write a sentence or paragraph indicating how each one might be applied in your case. Even if you feel like rejecting a particular approach out of hand, be sure to write something as positive as possible about it.

Option A: Resign the Crown

Swallow your pride and cut your losses by delegating to the other person full control and responsibility for his or her own life in this area. Let your partner reap his or her own harvest, whatever it is. In many cases, your partner will rise to the occasion, but if this doesn't happen, resign yourself to suffering the consequences.

Option B: Do It Yourself

There's an old saying: "If you want something done right, do it yourself." Accordingly, if you want something done, and if the person you feel should do it doesn't want to, it makes sense to do it yourself the way you'd like to have it done. After all, who ever said someone should do something he or she doesn't want to do just because you want him or her to do it?

Option C: Make an Offer Your Partner Can't Refuse

Too many interpret this, at first, as including threats of what will happen if the partner doesn't shape up. The real point, however, if you select this approach, is to find out what your partner would really like and then offer it in exchange for what you want him or her to do. After all, it's your want, not your spouse's, that is involved. Why shouldn't you take the responsibility for making it worth your spouse's while?

Option D: Join with Joy

Often the most resisted task can become pleasant if one's partner shares in it, especially if an atmosphere of play or warmth can be established. This calls for imagination and goodwill, but it can also be effective in putting an end to established power struggles.

Critical Thinking

Have you ever tried any of these in a couple situation? If so, how did it work out? Would these principles be useful, do you think, in other relationships, such as with children, extended family, or coworkers?

Source: Broderick 1979a, pp. 117–23.

> Men have always taken for granted that what they were doing was more important than what the other sex was doing, that where they were, was where the action was. Men occupied the center of the stage, and women's attention was focused on them. . . . [But] the center of attention shifts to women more now than in the past. I believe that this shift troubles men far more, and creates more of their resistance, than the women's demand for equal opportunity and pay in employment. (Goode 1982, p. 140)

One small study of twelve fairly equal newlywed couples found that some of them either consciously or unconsciously avoided issues about marital power and developed a "myth of equality" (Knudson-Martin and Mahoney 1998). Sometimes this seems to work—but only for a while. The best way to work through power changes is to openly discuss power and to fight about it fairly, using the techniques and cooperative attitudes we describe in Chapter 12. The partner who feels more uncomfortable can bring up the subject, sharing his or her anger and desire for change but also stressing that he or she still loves the other. Indeed, research suggests that spouses think of their marital relationship as fair when they feel listened to and emotionally supported (Gudmunson 2009; Rudman and Glick 2008; Soliz, Thorson, and Rittenour 2009).

Meanwhile, partners need to remember that managing conflict about power in a positive way is easier said than done. Attempts at communication—and open communication itself—do not solve all marital

Doing laundry does not seem to have become the site of a power struggle for this couple, but rather it is just something that needs to be done. Partners in a no-power relationship work at doing things on equal terms and seek to negotiate and compromise, thus avoiding deadly power games.

problems. Changing a power relationship is a challenge to any marriage. It can be painful for both partners, though promising a more rewarding relationship in the long run. One option for handling power and gender role change is to seek the help of a qualified marriage counselor or counselor team.

The Role That Marriage Counselors Can Play

Today, many marriage counselors are committed to viewing couples as two human beings who need to relate to each other as equals. In other words, they are committed to helping couples develop no-power relationships. They realize that once both spouses admit—to themselves and to each other—that they do in fact love and need each other, the basis for power politics is gone. On this assumption, counselors help spouses learn to respect each other as people and not to engage in coercive withdrawal.

Couples need to be aware that, like everybody in society, marriage counselors have internalized their own perspectives on gender roles—and these may not match the goals of the couple. There may be issues concerning potential racial and cultural bias on the part of therapists (Sluzki 2008) or simple lack of awareness of cultural differences in communication style or other matters. Choosing (or retaining) an appropriate counselor should involve an assessment of the counselor's sensitivity to the values, goals, and needs of the couple (Soliz, Thorson, and Rittenour 2009).

The counselor's gender may be an issue for some couples as they explore power and gender issues. A dominant husband, fearful that "it's going to be two against one," may feel threatened by a female counselor. On the other hand, a wife may fear that a male counselor will be too traditional or unable to relate to her. In this situation, counselors sometimes work as a team, woman and man. In any case, it is important that both partners feel comfortable with a counselor or counseling team from the beginning.

Whether on their own or with the help of counselors, partners can choose to emphasize no-power over the politics of power. No marriage—indeed, no relationship of any kind—is entirely free of power politics. But as Chapter 12 points out, the politics of love requires managing conflict in such a way that both partners win.

When, on the other hand, power politics triumphs over no-power, one result may be family violence—psychological (emotional) and/or physical.

Family Violence

The use of physical violence to gain or demonstrate power in a family relationship has occurred throughout history, but only in the last fifty years has violence been labeled a social problem.[2]

The identification of child abuse as a social problem in the 1960s was followed in the 1970s by attention to wife abuse. With the 1980s came concern about elder abuse, as well as husband abuse. More recently, attention has been given to youth dating violence, to violence in adult dating and cohabiting relationships, including

[2] Dr. C. Henry Kempe and his colleagues are credited with the "discovery" of child abuse. They published an article on the "battered child syndrome" based on their observation of hidden injuries to children revealed by X-rays (Kempe et al. 1962). Social scientists took note, and then pursued their interest in child abuse and other forms of family violence. The discovery of child abuse was somewhat like Columbus's discovery of America in that the phenomenon was always there but had not been noticed or taken seriously by academics or authorities.

same-sex relationships, sexual coercion in marital and nonmarital relationships, sibling violence, and child-to-parent violence. We discuss many of these forms of violence in this chapter; dating violence and acquaintance rape are discussed in Chapter 6 and elder abuse and neglect in Chapter 17.

Major Sources of Data on Family Violence

There are several major sources of current data on family violence. Probably the best for our purposes is the National Crime Victimization Survey (NCVS), conducted every two years by the Bureau of Justice Statistics (BJS). This is a national sample survey that asks respondents about all violence they have experienced, their relationship if any to the perpetrator, and whether the violence was reported to the police. Violent acts covered by the survey include assault and rape/sexual assault, as well as other crimes not relevant to family violence. Although murder is obviously not included in the victimization survey, other data on homicides are included in Bureau of Justice Statistics reports on **intimate partner violence**. Spouses, ex-spouses, and current or former boyfriends or girlfriends, including same-sex partners, are considered *intimate partners.*

Other relevant government data include the Uniform Crime Reports of the FBI based on the National Incident-Based Reporting System (NIBRS). Data on criminal incidents reported to the police are compiled from records submitted by many (though not all) local law enforcement agencies (Durose et al. 2005; Catalano 2007). A weakness of these data is that many crimes are not reported to the police, including an estimated one-half of intimate partner violent crimes (Groves and Cork 2008). However, because most homicides are reported, the homicide data are more valid (e.g., Fox and Zawitz 2004; Loftin, McDowall, and Fetzer 2008). The BJS uses these data to supplement the NCVS in producing its report series, *Intimate Partner Violence in the United States.*

A third major source of data on family violence is the National Violence Against Women Survey (NVAWS) (Chen and Ullman 2010), commissioned by the National Institute of Justice and the Centers for Disease Control and Prevention and conducted between 1995 and 1996. The survey employed a modified version of Murray Straus's Conflict Tactics Scale rather than asking about "crimes." While this survey remains the most important tool in understanding violence against women, it is not problem-free, and it is important to acknowledge those problems. Social researchers Yingyu Chen and Sarah E. Ullman recently analyzed the survey and noted that the NVAWS used "random-digit dialing methods to select the sample, which excluded women without telephones and those who were homeless or institutionalized" (2010, p. 275). Also, the survey interviews were done over the telephone, but topics such as rape and sexual assault are very sensitive and are best done in person, thus the findings could be impacted by the way the survey was administered. Additionally, research into post-assault psychological outcomes shows that women who receive assistance from others after they've been assaulted are more likely to report sexual assaults, but the NVAWS did not account for those differences (Chen and Ullman 2010). Despite the limitations, the study is an invaluable resource on violence against women.

The work of Murray Straus, Richard Gelles, and their colleagues in their National Family Violence Surveys pioneered the scientific study of family violence. Before we examine current patterns of family violence, let us look at the work of this early research group.[3]

The National Family Violence Surveys The early and continuing research of Straus, Gelles, and their colleagues shaped the social science study of family violence. This research group undertook a household survey in 1975, followed by a 1985 telephone survey; together, the surveys produced data from more than 8,000 husbands, wives, and cohabiting individuals (Straus, Gelles, and Steinmetz 1980; Straus and Gelles 1986, 1988, 1995; Gelles and Straus 1988).

The authors defined violence as "an act carried out with the intention, or perceived intention, of causing physical pain or injury to another person." This definition is synonymous with the legal concept of assault.

Researchers developed a measure of family violence termed the **Conflict Tactics Scale**. Respondents were asked about the following acts: threw something at the other; pushed, grabbed, or shoved; slapped or spanked; kicked, bit, or hit with a fist; hit or tried to hit with something; beat up the other; burned or scalded (children) or choked (spouses); threatened with a knife or gun; and used a knife or gun (Straus and Gelles 1988, p. 15). *Severe violence* was defined as acts that have a relatively high probability of causing an injury: kicking, biting, punching, hitting with an object, choking, beating, threatening with a knife or gun, using a knife or gun—and, for violence by parents against children, burning or scalding the child (Straus and Gelles 1988, p. 16). Later modified somewhat (Straus et al. 1996), the Conflict Tactics Scale is different from and broader than the crime categories of assault and homicide that form the basis of criminal justice system statistics. Many other family violence researchers have used the scale.

The 1975 and 1985 National Family Violence Surveys found that, in 16 percent of the couples surveyed, at least one of the partners had engaged in a violent act

[3] Murray Straus still leads the Family Violence Research Program at the University of New Hampshire's Family Research Laboratory. Many of the colleagues he has copublished with are there. Richard Gelles is now at the University of Pennsylvania.

against the other during the previous year. Considering the entire length of the marriage rather than just the previous year, respondent reports indicated that a violent act occurred in 28 percent of couples. National Family Violence Survey data also yielded information on violence directed toward children by parents and siblings. The National Family Violence Surveys explored social variation in family violence and some of the circumstances thought to be associated with family violence, such as stress and alcohol use.

Having presented some major sources of data on family violence, we examine the circumstances and outcomes of spouse or partner abuse in more detail in the next sections.

Intimate Partner Violence

Intimate partner violence—the physical or emotional abuse of spouses, cohabiting or noncohabiting relationship partners, or former spouses or intimate partners—is a serious and significant problem. First identified in terms of *wife abuse,* the growing practice of cohabitation places many unmarried women in similar situations. Husbands or male partners may also be subject to abuse from intimate partners as may same-sex partners of gay males and lesbians. Employing the term *intimate partner violence,* the federal government now includes all these forms of couple violence in its reports on domestic violence.

We will focus primarily on marital violence in analyzing the dynamics of intimate partner violence, but it is worth noting that the rate of violence between cohabiting partners is higher than that of spouses (Magdol et al. 1998). As the proportion of cohabiting couples in the population increases, this setting becomes of greater importance in an overall perspective on domestic violence. That is, if cohabiting couples have higher rates of domestic violence and if there come to be more of them, theories of domestic violence may need to be modified to take this group into greater account.

We focus on physical abuse, but verbal abuse (such as name-calling, demeaning verbal attacks), and other kinds of emotional abuse (such as threats to take away children, threats to the victim's extended family or friends, and threats or attacks on pets) virtually always occur along with physical aggression (Johnson 2008, p. 88; McCue 2008) and may be part of a pattern of control and domination.

Intimate partner violence can indeed result in serious injuries. National Crime Victimization Survey data indicate that, for the period between 1993 and 2005, 5 percent of female victims of intimate partner abuse and 4 percent of male victims were seriously injured. More women (44 percent) than men (36 percent) had minor injuries (Catalano 2007). Another source of injury data is the Study of Injured Victims of Violence (SIVV), which is a count of emergency room admissions

Local advocacy groups draw attention to efforts to prevent domestic violence and to the need for more resources. In many localities, there are still not enough shelters to meet the needs of battered women and their children.

attributable to family or nonfamily violence. In 1994, there were more emergency room admissions due to serious family violence (not only intimate partner violence) than reported in the National Crime Victimization Survey. However, the emergency room study was small and the two data sources are not truly comparable (Durose et al. 2005, p. 72).

Who Are the Victims of Intimate Partner Violence?

According to a report based on the National Crime Victimization Survey, there were over 615,000 "victimizations" by intimate partners in 2005. One-third of these were serious violent crimes: rapes, sexual assaults, and aggravated assaults, and/or crimes involving serious injuries, weapons, or sexual offenses. The other two-thirds were lesser offenses, mostly simple assaults (Catalano 2007).

Women are the primary victims of intimate partner violence reported in the National Crime Victimization Survey. A much larger proportion of non-fatal violent victimizations of women are perpetrated by intimate partners: 22 percent compared with only 4 percent of the violent victimizations of men, who are more at risk of violence from others than from intimate partners.

The rate of non-fatal violent victimization of women by intimate partners is over four times that of men. In every racial/ethnic category (see Figure 13.2), women have higher rates of victimization than men. Although intimate partners commit only 5 percent of murders of men, they account for 30 percent of homicides of women (Catalano 2007).

Younger women (twenty through twenty-four) are more likely to have experienced intimate partner victimization, as are those women who are separated or divorced (Catalano 2007), although some experts question the lower rates of marital violence, arguing that married women are simply less likely to acknowledge their victimization ("Domestic Violence Decline" 2006).

Although the data suggests that the rates of intimate partner violence have dropped for all racial groups since 2004, as Figure 13.2 indicates, rates of intimate partner violence vary greatly by race/ethnicity. Victimization rates are strikingly higher (11.1 per 1,000) for Native American women. Black women's rates are high (5.0), but still less than one-half the rate for Native American women. White and Hispanic females have moderate rates (4.0 and 4.3, respectively), whereas Asian females, as well as Asian males, have very low rates of intimate partner violence victimization (1.4 and > 0.1, respectively). White, black, and Hispanic male victimization rates are also low, whereas those of Native American men are relatively high (Catalano 2007).

Multiple studies have demonstrated that cohabiting partners have higher rates of *situational couple* violence (violence that arises out of a quarrel and is often mutual), but married women are more likely to be the target of *intimate terrorism* (a systematic pattern of violence employed by a man to intimidate and control his partner) (Brownridge and Halli 2002; Johnson 2010; Leone, Johnson, Cohan 2007). These concepts will be developed in more detail later in the chapter. A variety of explanations have been offered, but none conclusively

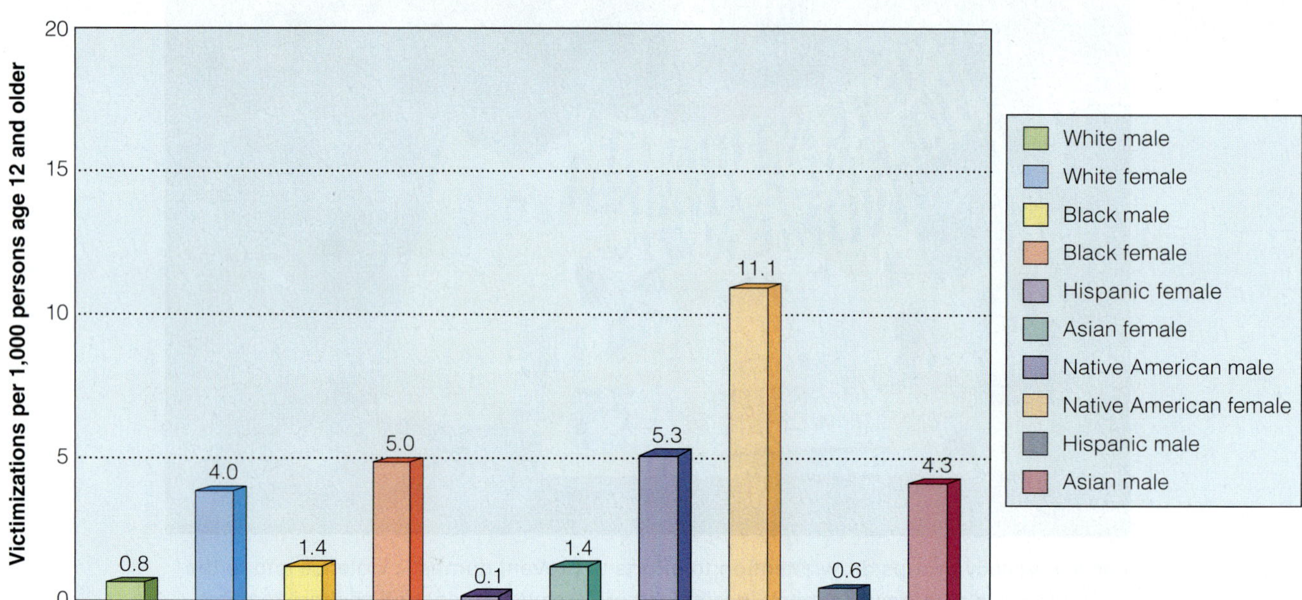

Figure 13.2 Intimate partner victimization rate (nonfatal) by gender, race, and Hispanic origin, 1993–2005
Source: Catalano 2007.

proven. Overall, cohabitors are younger, less integrated into family and community, and more likely to have psychobehavioral problems such as depression and alcohol abuse—all factors associated with family violence (Stets 1991). Another possibility is that there is less institutional control over cohabiting relationships than over marriage (Ellis 2006; Nock 1995). Still another thesis is that the less-violent cohabiting couples end up getting married whereas more-violent married couples get divorced, sharpening the difference between the two groups (Kenney and McLanahan 2006).

Several recent studies have reported that pregnancy increased the likelihood of physical violence by intimate partners (Cox 2008; Burch and Gallup 2004; S. Martin et al. 2004). None of these studies used a representative sample. Earlier studies using national samples found that when age was controlled, there was no increased risk with pregnancy. Still, the many studies, however imperfect, that have found an association between pregnancy and violence have kept this hypothesis alive, along with a possible explanation—jealousy, specifically that the new baby would interfere with the wife's attention to and care of the man. What is known with more certainty is that those pregnant women who are abused seek medical care later in pregnancy and are more likely to have preterm and low-birth-weight babies (Janssen et al. 2003; Sarkar 2008).

Substance abuse, especially of alcohol, is often cited as a factor in male violence against women. That seems to be true of heavy use of alcohol and binge drinking, though not necessarily for other patterns of alcohol use. Alcohol is implicated in violence through cognitive impairment, impulsivity, and a tendency to perceive threats, particularly in married-couple relationships where research finds an association between alcohol and "more severe forms of intimate partner violence" (Catalano 2007; Kaukinen 2004; Wiersma et al. 2010, p. 372). Drinking may also serve as a rationalization and excuse for violence that would have occurred in any case (Gelles 1974).

Marital Rape Wife and female partner abuse may take the form of sexual abuse and rape. Estimates are that between 10 and 14 percent of women experience marital rape (Ferro, Cermele, and Saltzman 2008, p. 765; Bergen 2006). These sexual assaults often involve other violence as well.

The issue of **marital rape** arose as a feminist one in the 1970s, and as such was conceptualized in terms of the law of *marriage*. Under traditional common law, a husband's sexual assault or forceful coercion of his wife was not considered rape because marriage meant the husband was entitled to unlimited sexual access. The legal situation has improved since the 1970s, as a result of feminist political activity. As of 1993, all states have provisions against marital rape in their legal codes[4] (McMahon-Howard, Clay-Warner, and Renzulli 2009, p. 507). More research is needed in this area; the "lack of empirical and theoretical attention to sexual assault and coercion in marriage . . . is striking" (Christopher and Sprecher 2000, p. 1,007). Data on sexual assault of women intimate partners, married or nonmarried, are collected as part of the federal government's documentation of intimate partner violence.

Intimate Partner Violence is Declining The preceding data show us how significant the problem of intimate partner violence still is. Yet, the direction of change gives us some indication that efforts to combat domestic violence are paying off. Intimate partner violence declined dramatically from 1993 to 2005, as Figures 13.3 and 13.4 indicate. The rate of nonfatal victimization declined nearly 44 percent for men and over 63 percent for women. Intimate partner homicide rates declined 48 percent for men and 24 percent for women (Catalano 2007; Pastore and Maguire 2007, Tables 3.131.2005, 3.132.2005).

Shannan Catalano, author of the Bureau of Justice Statistics intimate partner violence study, cites experts' opinions that stronger law enforcement, increased education, and expanded services for battered partners have led to this decline. A cautious note is also sounded: "[T]he apparent decline could [also] mean that women are choosing to suffer in silence rather than seek help ("Domestic Violence Decline" 2006).

As we go on to explore gender issues in intimate partner violence, we will consider why women may not seek

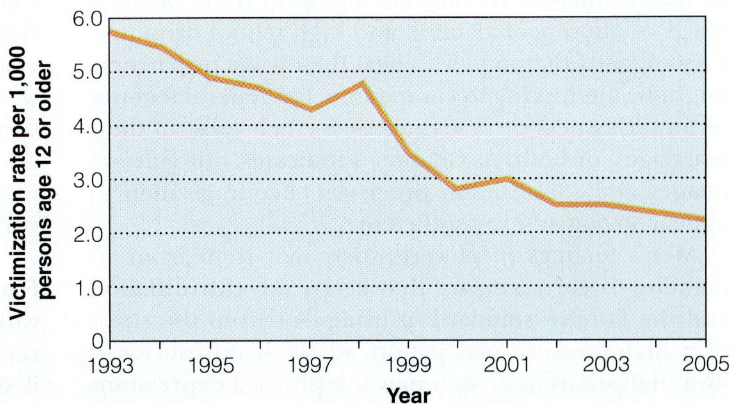

Figure 13.3 Intimate partner victimization rate (nonfatal), 1993–2005

Source: Catalano 2007.

[4] There are some exemptions in the laws of thirty of the states. One common example is that if a wife is asleep or unconscious, thus legally unable to consent, a husband may be exempt from prosecution (National Clearinghouse on Marital and Date Rape 2005).

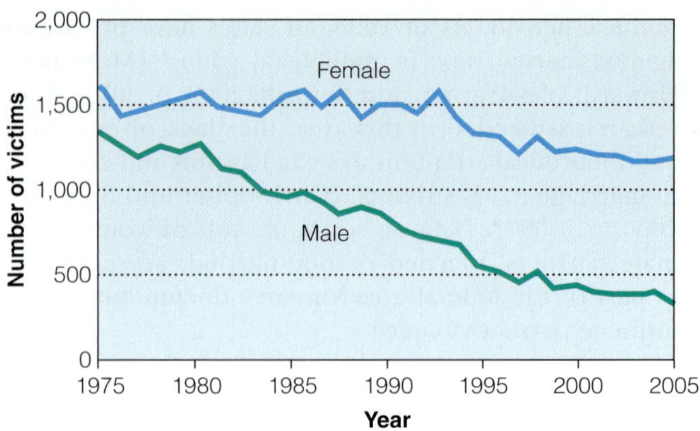

Figure 13.4 Homicides of intimates by gender of victim, 1976–2005

Source: Catalano 2007.

help or leave their marital or other relationships—and why and how they do. We'll also consider whether men are equally victims of domestic violence.

Gender Issues in Intimate Partner Violence

Three questions arise regarding gender and intimate partner violence: Why do men beat their wives and partners? Why do women live with it? And what about husband or male partner abuse?

Why Do Men Do It? From data in the National Crime Victimization Survey, we find that about 96 percent of females experiencing nonfatal intimate partner violence were victimized by a male (Catalano 2007).

Richard Gelles (1994, 1997) lists "risk factors" for men who abuse women: those who are between eighteen and thirty years old; unemployed; users of illicit drugs or abusers of alcohol; and high school dropouts. This suggests that men who beat their wives or partners might be attempting to compensate for general feelings of powerlessness or inadequacy—in their jobs, in their marriages, or both. As Chapter 4 indicates, our cultural images and socialization processes encourage men to appear strong and self-sufficient.

Men's feelings of powerlessness may stem from an inability to earn a salary that keeps up with inflation and the family's standard of living—or from the stress of a high-pressure occupation, which is not necessarily a high-status one. Men may use physical expressions of supremacy to compensate for their lack of occupational success, prestige, or satisfaction (K. Anderson 1997). Research using the National Survey of Families and Households found that financial adequacy reduced the risk of couple violence. Employment in low-status and unpleasant jobs that increased irritability, on the other hand, was associated with man-to-woman violence, a stress explanation of family violence (Fox et al. 2002; "Promoting Respectful" 2009). The husband's unemployment is also associated with domestic violence (Condon 2010; Lauby and Else 2008).

In terms of relative status, a woman's risk of experiencing severe violence is greatest when she is employed and her husband is not. Much research has found violence associated more generally with status reversal, where the woman is superior in some way to the man in terms of employment, earnings, or education (Kaukinen 2004). A man's loss of status upon immigration—when jobs commensurate with education or expectations do not measure up, economic hardship is the family's lot, and wives, children, and people in general do not accord a male the respect he is accustomed to in a more hierarchical society—can lead to family conflict and violence (Min 2002).

Absent a *reward power* base for family power, some men resort to *coercive power:* "[V]iolence will be invoked by a person who lacks other resources to serve as a basis for power—it is the "ultimate resource" (Goode 1971, p. 628; see also Allen and Straus 1980, p. 190, in Fox et al. 2002). Men may use violence to attempt to maintain control over wives or partners trying to become independent of the relationship (Dutton and Browning 1988). Figure 13.5, developed by staff members of a program for male batterers in Duluth, Minnesota (Pence and Paymar 1993), illustrates how a male partner's need for power and control may result in both psychoemotional and physical violence. This type of family violence has been called *intimate terrorism* (M. Johnson 2008) and will be discussed along with other types of intimate partner violence in a subsequent section of this chapter.

Why Do Women Continue to Live With It? Women do not like to get beaten up. However, they may stay married to husbands or remain with violent male partners who beat them repeatedly. For the most part, battered wives leave and/or seek divorce only after a long history of severe violence and repeated conciliation. There are several reasons for this, and they all point to those women's lack of personal resources with which to take control of their own lives.

Fear Battered women's lack of personal power begins with fear (DeMaris and Swinford 1996). "First of all," reports social scientist Richard Gelles, "the wife figures if she calls police or files for divorce, her husband will kill her—literally" (Gelles, quoted in C. Booth 1977, p. 7). This fear is not unfounded. An estimated 74 percent of murders of women by their male partners occurred in response to the woman's attempt to leave the relationship (Seager 2009, p. 2287). Husbands or ex-husbands have shown enormous persistence in stalking, pursuing, and beating or killing women who try to leave an abusive situation (Snider et al. 2009). Fear of reprisals by the batterer continues to be a barrier to

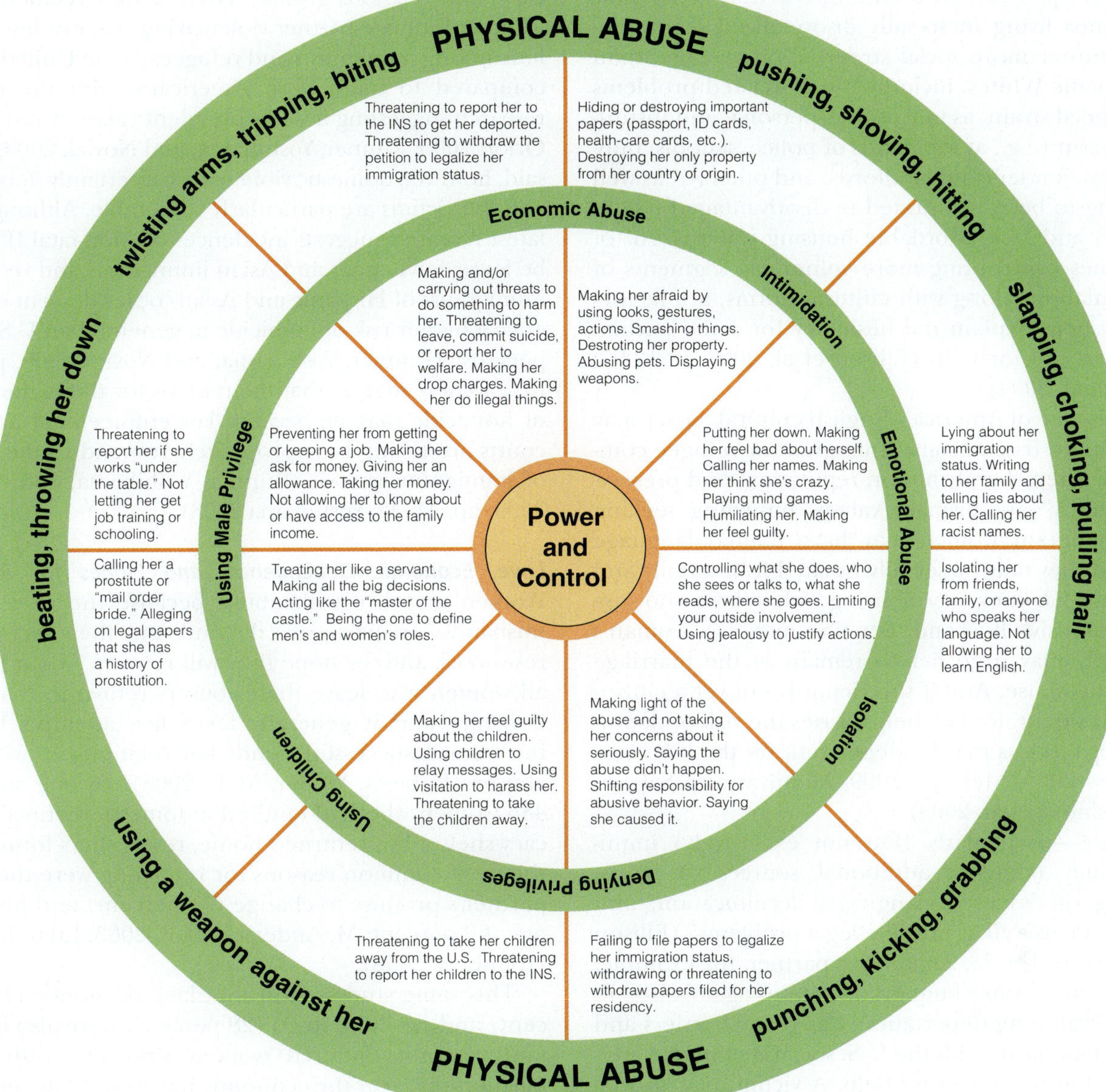

Figure 13.5 The power and control wheel for immigrant and native born: behaviors that some male partners use for coercive power and control

Source: Immigrant Battered Women Power and Control Wheel, produced and distributed by National Center on Domestic and Sexual Violence, Austin, TX, available at www.endingviolence.org/files/uploads/ImmigrantWomenPCwheel.pdf and adapted from the original wheel by Domestic Abuse Intervention Project, Duluth, MN.

seeking police intervention, according to recent studies (M. Anderson et al. 2003; Wolf et al. 2003). In addition to the immediate concerns of injury and death, women who live with violent partners exhibit greater "adverse health conditions and health risk behaviors" than the general population (Black and Breiding 2008, p. 116 Table 2; Breiding, Black, and Ryan 2008). Women with disabilities suffer greater rates of intimate partner violence than the general population (Black and Breiding 2008; Brownridge 2006).

Cultural Norms Historically, women were encouraged to put up with abuse. English common law, the basis of the American legal structure, asserted that a husband had the right to physically "chastise" an errant wife. Although the legal right to physically abuse women has long since disappeared, our cultural heritage continues to have an influence on seeking help and getting it (Ellison et al. 2007). For some women of color, hesitancy to call the police may derive from historic tensions between racial/ethnic communities and the police force (Wolf et al. 2003, p. 124). In addition, "African Americans and Latinos living in socially disorganized communities encounter more social stressors, on average, than non-Hispanic Whites, including work-related problems and financial strain, as well as interpersonal and institutional racism (e.g., at the hands of police, schools, public officials, lenders and landlords, and others)," as well as tending to be concentrated in disadvantaged neighborhoods and lack affordable housing options. All of these issues confronting more vulnerable segments of our population, along with cultural norms, are factors that may help explain the hesitancy for some women of color to call for help (Ellison et al. 2007, p. 1,097; Benson et al. 2004).

What is true of America's English cultural legacy may be even more true of some immigrant or refugee communities, when "family honor, reputation, and preserving harmony" are primary values, impeding seeking help. Immigrant women may have limited language skills, and they may be socially isolated from family and community. Or they may be living with in-laws who support the abusive husband. For that matter, a woman's own family may urge her to remain in the marriage despite the abuse. And if the victim is not yet a citizen or legal resident, to seek help carries the risk of deportation; legal status may be dependent on the marriage (Childress 2003; Mehrota 1999; Menjívar and Salcido 2002; Yoshioka et al. 2003).

"Latinos—particularly (but not exclusively) immigrants—may confront additional sources of stress, centering on issues of language, acculturation, and assimilation, as well as possible legal problems" (Ellison et al. 2007, p. 1,097). An abusive partner, for example, "may use the victim's immigration status against her, in effect, threatening deportation. Language barriers and a lack of familiarity with the U.S. social system may prevent a victim from seeking help. A victim may also be afraid that if she reports violence to the authorities, she and/or her partner will be treated with insensitivity, hostility, and/or discrimination. That fear may be justified; mainstream organizations may lack sociocultural understanding and/or may have discriminatory or insensitive attitudes toward immigrants and refugees," as can be seen in newspaper reports of immigrant domestic violence issues (Runner, Yoshihama, and Novick 2009, pp. 4, 11; Yoshihama 2008).

Programs are beginning to emerge to assist immigrant women (Abraham 1995, 2000). Moreover, there is evidence for changed attitudes in some settings. An article about Jewish immigrants from Central Asia living in New York reported that the "word has spread" that wife abuse (and harsh physical discipline of children) is not the way things are "done in America" ("Old Ways" 2003).

Of course, domestic violence issues are clearly an American problem that crosses all generational, social, cultural, class, and religious groups. There is disagreement as to whether intimate partner violence is greater or less prevalent among immigrants and refugees in the United States compared to native-born Americans, with the newest research suggesting it is less prevalent (Hass, Ammar, and Orloff 2006; Runner, Yoshihama, and Novick 2009). This said, however, domestic violence most certainly does exist, and the victims are particularly vulnerable. Although the latest research suggests incidences of "non-fatal IPV may be lower for Latinas and Asian immigrants and refugees, immigrants of Hispanic and Asian/other descent experience a higher risk of homicide in general than U.S.-born persons" (Runner, Yoshihama, and Novick 2009, p. 11). Researchers suggest that the reasons for the higher rates of homicide may be because law enforcement and the courts are failing to appropriately respond to the needs of immigrant women (Runner, Yoshihama, and Novick 2009, pp. 41–42; Yoshihama 2008).

Love, Economic Dependence, and Hopes for Reform

Women may live with abuse because they love their husbands or partners, depend on their economic resources, and/or hope they will reform. About half of all women who leave their abusers return to that relationship, and it generally takes five attempts before the woman successfully ends her relationship with her abuser (Roberts, Wolfer, Mele 2008). In one study of 485 women who had entered a domestic victims' advocacy shelter but returned home, researchers found that the most common reasons for returning were the male partner's promise to change (71 percent) and his apology (60 percent; M. Anderson et al. 2003; Enander and Holmberg 2008).

This same study found that lack of money (40 percent) and nowhere to go (28 percent) were also important reasons. Battered women who stay with their partners may fear the economic hardship or uncertainty that will result if they leave. They hesitate to summon police or to press charges not only out of fear of retaliation but also because of the loss of income or damage to a husband's professional reputation that could result from his incarceration. Fear of economic hardship is heightened when children are involved. For a mother, leaving requires being financially able to take along her children and support them—or leaving them behind, where they may also be in danger.

A new wrinkle in economic dependency has emerged with the passage of welfare reform legislation in 1996. Studies show that 20 to 30 percent of women on welfare are in situations of risk for domestic violence. Some men become abusive when the woman gets a job, which may threaten his control. Abusive men inhibit a woman's economic independence in many ways, for example, physical restraint, harassment on the job (including calling a woman's supervisor or coworkers), stalking, and destroying her work clothes (Kimerling et al. 2009).

Compliance with the requirement to report paternity of children may also trigger retaliation by a man, who now will be pursued for child support. Although the law contains a waiver provision directed at exactly these problems, it is not certain that women are being informed or that the provision is implemented. Some women will find it difficult to comply with welfare requirements because of the objections and control tactics of men in their lives (Riger, Staggs, and Schewe 2004, p. 812; see also Handler and Hasenfeld 2006, p. 304). Cut off from welfare, they become even more dependent on violent men.

Apart from such special circumstances, it is possible that though a dramatic rise in women's employment and earnings may prove threatening to low-earning husbands in the short run, in the long run, mutual awareness of a woman's potential economic independence may deter wife abuse by changing the family power dynamic (Yakushko and Espin 2010).

Gendered Socialization Another factor that helps perpetuate abuse is the cultural mandate that it is primarily a woman's responsibility to keep a marriage or relationship from failing. Believing this, wives are often convinced that their emotional support may lead husbands to reform. Thus, wives often return to violent mates after leaving them (Roberts, Wolfer, and Mele 2008).

Childhood Experiences Research suggests that people who experience violence in their parents' home while growing up may regard beatings as part of married life, and this is another factor associated with women's living with abuse. Men, as well as women, are more likely to be victims of intimate partner violence as adults if they were exposed to child abuse or witnessed parental interpersonal violence as children (Brown and Bulanda 2008; Pettit et al. 2010).

Low Self-Esteem Finally, unusually low self-esteem interacts with fear, depression, confusion, anxiety, feelings of self-blame (Walker 2009, pp. 155–165), and loss of a sense of personal control (Umberson et al. 1998) to create the *battered woman syndrome,* in which a wife cannot see a way out of her situation (Walker et al. 2009).

A Way Out: Shelters and Domestic Violence Programs

A woman in such a position needs to redefine her situation before she can deal with her problem, and she needs to forge some links with the outside world to alter her circumstances. This usually occurs over time, with some unsuccessful attempts to leave as part of the process.

Although there are not enough of them, a network of shelters for battered women provides a woman and her children with temporary housing, food, and clothing to alleviate the problems of economic dependency and physical safety. These organizations also provide counseling to encourage a stronger self-concept so that the woman can view herself as worthy of better treatment and capable of making her way alone in the outside world if need be. Finally, shelters provide guidance in obtaining employment, legal assistance, family counseling, or whatever practical assistance is required for a more permanent solution.

This last service provided by shelters—obtaining help toward longer-range solutions—is important. Two face-to-face interviews with the same 155 wife-battery victims (a "two-wave panel study") were conducted within eighteen months during 1982 and 1983 in Santa Barbara, California. Each of the women interviewed had sought refuge in a shelter. Findings showed that victims who were also taking other measures (for example, calling the police, trying to get a restraining order, seeking personal counseling or legal help) were more likely to benefit from their shelter experience: "Otherwise, shelters may have no impact or perhaps even trigger retaliation (from husbands) for disobedience" (Berk, Newton, and Berk 1986, p. 488). As the researchers conclude,

> The possibility of perverse shelter effects for certain kinds of women poses a troubling policy dilemma. On the one hand, it is difficult to be enthusiastic about an intervention that places battered victims at further risk. On the other hand, a shelter stay may for many women be one important step in a lengthy process toward freedom, even though there may also be genuine short-run dangers. (p. 488)

As with some other decisions discussed in this text, social scientists have applied *exchange theory* to an abused woman's decision to stay or leave (McDonough 2010). As Figure 13.6 illustrates, an abused wife weighs such things as her investment in the relationship, her (dis) satisfaction with the relationship, the quality of her alternatives, and her beliefs about whether it is appropriate for her to leave ("subjective norm") against such questions as whether she will be better off if she leaves (might her husband retaliate, for example?) and whether she can actually do it. The woman's personal resources along with community (structural) resources, such as whether shelters or other forms of assistance are available, further affect her decision. Personal barriers might involve not having either a job with adequate pay or an extended family that could help. Structural barriers might include the lack of community systems for practical help.

Michael Johnson and Kathleen Ferraro (2000) answer the question "Why do they stay?" with: "The truth is, they don't stay." Instead, abused women went "through a process of leaving and returning, each time gaining more psychological and social resources . . . until they escaped from the web" (pp. 956–57).

Men as Victims of Intimate Partner Abuse Both women and men sometimes resort to violence. A major question regarding family violence is whether female-to-male violence is trivial in numbers and effects or should be regarded as a serious social problem.

The early National Family Violence Surveys reported approximately equal amounts of both minor and serious partner violence on the part of men and women. Researcher Murray Straus and his colleagues continue to point to data indicating comparable levels of male and female intimate partner violence. In fact, "IPV by men, but not by women has been decreasing since the mid 1970s but assaults by women on male partners have stayed about the same" (Straus 1999b; 2005; 2008; Straus and Ramirez 2007, p. 9). A number of other studies and research reviews also find that comparable numbers of males and females have engaged in physical violence (Dutton and Nicholls 2005; Medeiros and Straus 2006).

As with most social research, there are debates as to the methodological validity of the sample and the study itself. This holds true for research into intimate partner violence—particularly the research into intimate partner violence against males. Although the National Family Violence Survey is a national sample survey, many of the other studies cited as evidence for gender symmetry are convenience samples, studies of college students, or clinical samples of couples who have sought help for their marital problems—in other words, some might argue these other studies are not so strong methodologically. On the other hand, metadata analysis of seventeen large-scale studies suggests gender symmetry in intimate partner violence (Cook 2009, pp. 14–15, Tables 1.3, 1.4). In addition, critiques of relevant studies (e.g., Were women asked about perpetration of violence, or only of victimization?) suggest there has been a bias toward an assumption of women as victims of male violence, thus skewing the surveys themselves in favor of the preconception (Straus and Scott, forthcoming).

Crime victimization data, including large-sample surveys, indicate that women are overwhelmingly the victims of intimate partner violence. These conflicting reports set off a dispute, still not resolved, as to whether intimate partner violence is *asymmetrical*—with women primarily victims of male aggression—or whether couple violence is *symmetrical*—both men and women engage in intimate partner violence and at similar rates.

The first assumption—that males primarily perpetrate violence against partners—underlies policy directed toward providing resources for women victims; it is a strongly held feminist perspective. If, on the contrary, women are as likely as men to perpetrate intimate partner violence, then they begin to look less like victims and more like aggressors.

Differences in conclusions may simply arise from methodological differences. Critics of the National Crime Victimization Survey (which finds *asymmetric* violence) point out that "crime" terminology may dampen reports of less-serious female-to-male violence because those acts may not seem to be crimes to those interviewed. Questions on the Conflict Tactics Scale (CTS) include a broader range of actions that may be characterized by the survey respondent as family conflict and violence, but not criminal victimization (Dutton and Nicholls 2005; Medeiros and Straus 2006; Straus 1999b, 2005; 2008; Straus and Ramirez 2007). A key problem with the Conflict Tactics Scale (used in many studies that find *symmetric violence*), however, is that sexual assault, a substantial part of male-to-female violence, was not included in the first version of the CTS used in the 1975/1985 National Family Violence Surveys. (The later modification of the CTS does include sexual assault [Straus et al. 1996].)

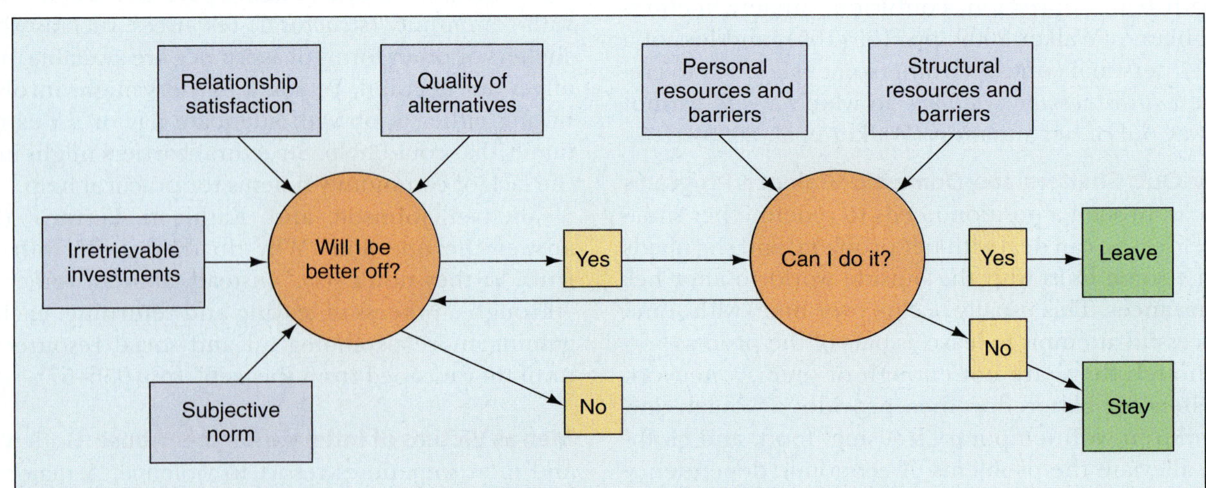

Figure 13.6 Conceptual model of abused women's stay/leave decision-making process

Source: Choice and Lamke 1997, p. 295.

The Conflict Tactics Scale, used by many researchers and most associated with findings of gender-balanced violence, has been widely criticized for lack of context. In reporting lifetime or annual incidence of violence, a single, never-repeated act could be equated with a marriage-long pattern of abuse. Feminist critics assert that the context of violence is ignored in simple counts of male and female violence: Where does a particular violent act fit into the couple relationship? Who initiated the violence? Was it in self-defense? (Carney, Buttell, and Dutton 2007; Hines, Brown, and Dunning 2007; Loseke and Kurz 2005); at the same time, other critics assert that all violence against partners must be examined fully through the lens of science rather than through the lens of ideology (Hines and Douglas 2009).

Recent reviewers of the literature have tried to make distinctions that might explain the contradictory conclusions about who is violent. Definitions and measurements of violence continue to be relevant, as does whether a survey asks about victimization only or also asks whether the respondent has been a perpetrator of violence (Hines and Douglas 2009; Straus and Scott in press). The most convincing explanations for contradictory findings—that men are the more violent sex (asymmetrical violence) or that men and women are both violent (symmetrical violence)—are (1) sample differences, (2) measures, and (3) typologies of intimate partner violence (to be discussed momentarily).

Studies and research reviews that are dominated by samples of younger people show "that among violent adolescent relationships, the percentage of relationships in which there was reciprocal partner violence ranged from 45% to 75%." Moreover, a "recent meta-analysis found that a woman's perpetration of violence in a youthful relationship was the strongest predictor of her being a victim of partner violence." The focus on research into adolescent and young adult relationship violence is important because youthful relationship violence is a strong predictor of adult relationship violence (Stith et al. 2004; Whitaker et al. 2007, p. 941).

The question of whether wives' violence toward husbands is mostly in self-defense, as feminist violence researchers argue, is part of the debate about gender differences in domestic violence perpetration. Demie Kurz (Kurz 1993; Loseke and Kurz 2005) offers evidence that intimate partner violence by women is largely in self-defense or at least retaliation rather than the initiation of a violent attack. Sociologist Murray Straus claims that better data indicate that wives often strike out first and that the data do "not support the hypothesis that assaults by wives are primarily acts of self-defense or retaliation" (Straus 1993, p. 76; 2008; Straus and Ramirez 2007). Moreover, he argues that though women's violence produces fewer serious injuries and deaths than men's, these are substantial enough in numbers to challenge any minimization of women's intimate partner violence (Dutton and Nicholls 2005; Medeiros and Straus 2006; Straus 2005; 2008). A substantial number of researchers have argued that couple violence is gender symmetrical, despite the criticism they have received from feminists who argue that male intimate partner violence is simply a "means for men to systematically dominate, control, and devalue women" (Dutton and Nicholls 2005, p. 684).

Other researchers examining the issue suggest that the root explanation for contradictory research results may be that there are two primary forms of heterosexual violence against women—"intimate terrorism" (formerly termed "patriarchal terrorism") and "situational couple violence" (formerly termed "common couple violence") (M. Johnson 1995; 2008).[5] **Intimate terrorism** refers specifically to abuse that is almost entirely male and that is oriented to controlling the partner through fear and intimidation. Physical abuse is but one of the tools a terrorist uses; emotional abuse is frequent as well. Intimate terroristic violence is not focused on a particular matter of dispute between the partners, but is intended to establish a general pattern of dominance in the relationship. This form of intimate partner violence occurs more often in marriage than in cohabitation. It includes more incidents, is likely to escalate, and is more likely to produce serious injury.

Situational couple violence refers to mutual violence between partners that often occurs in conjunction with a specific argument. It involves fewer instances, is not likely to escalate, and tends to be less severe in terms of injuries (M. Johnson 2008; Johnson and Ferraro 2000). Situational couple violence appears to be perpetrated by women as well as men and may be more common than intimate terrorism, producing the gender-balanced rates found in some studies (M. Johnson 2008, pp. 60–71).

Some researchers argue that there is "compelling evidence that men's and women's experiences with violence at the hands of marital and cohabiting partners differ greatly" (Tjaden and Thoennes 2000, p. 156). The problem with such analysis is that other analyses of the same data suggest it contains serious problems. For example, psychologist John Archer (2000) takes issue with Tjaden and Thoennes (2000) because the NWAWS "was presented to respondents as a study of victimization

[5] Johnson's typology of domestic violence includes additional types that reflect a pattern of violent resistance to a partner's violence, sometimes mutual violent resistance to each other's violence. Although an important consideration, Johnson's conceptualization of violent resistance has changed somewhat in a short time (2006; 2008). For the moment it seems most useful to emphasize his two primary types of violence, while including some research on the topic of violent resistance in the chapter.

of women, it contained 'filters' or demand characteristics that would make men less likely to report their own victimization" (cited in Dutton and Nicholls 2005). Also, other studies show that, as with immigrant women abuse discussed earlier in the chapter, the police appear ill-equipped to deal with female abuse of males, going so far as to downplay violence against men even when they're called to the scene (Brown 2004).

A good deal of research shows that there is an overwhelming victimization of women shown by crime victimization data, including data on homicides, which suggests that women are victims of the most serious violence. Unfortunately, however, when research shows comparable rates of violence between the genders, oftentimes "female-perpetrated abuse is minimized and understood as either defensive or situational in nature, an isolated expression of frustration in communicating with an unsympathetic partner, in contrast to the presumably intentional, pervasive, and generally controlling behaviors exhibited by men" (Hamel and Nicholls 2006, p. xxxix; M. Johnson & Leone 2005).

American society socializes men to believe they are the "strong" ones. In fact, the image of men (discussed in Chapter 4) that is presented to society is that of a successful and strong "man," who is confident, self-reliant, and even aggressive; and who can physically outwit and defeat any opponent (Sullivan and McHugh 2009; Katz 2006). Given the socialization of both men and women in our modern society, some researchers question if it is scientifically appropriate to assume that males socialized into this cultural milieu would acknowledge on surveys or in interviews that they had been battered by the "weaker" sex—their female companions, given the internalized self-concepts males in the United States are socialized to believe (Brown 2004; Dutton and Nicholls 2006).

There is a need for programmatic support for male victims of spouse abuse: "Compassion for victims of violence is not a zero sum game.... Reasonable people would rationally want to extend compassion, support, and intervention to all victims of violence" (Kimmel 2002, p. 1,354). Indeed, the male victim of violence has few resources and often little sympathy (Cook 2009, p. 41).

Abuse among Same Gender, Bisexual, and Transgender Couples

We discuss gay male, lesbian, and bisexual intimate partner violence apart from our discussion of married-couple and heterosexual cohabitants violence because the analysis of heterosexual intimate partner violence is largely based on gender *difference*. In fact, it was initially assumed that the likely greater similarity in power of same-sex couples would deter couple violence—unfortunately not. Rates of same-sex intimate partner violence (SSIPV) are "comparable to rates of heterosexual domestic violence, with approximately one quarter to one half of all same-sex intimate relationships demonstrating abusive dynamics," and upwards of half of all transgendered people reporting intimate partner victimization (Murray and Mobley 2009, p. 361; Bornstein et al. 2006, p. 162).

Same-sex intimate partner violence has long been shrouded in silence in lesbian and gay communities (Murray and Mobley 2009). Lesbians may have effectively denied the issue through a lack of conceptualizing lesbian intimate partner violence as domestic violence (particularly because domestic violence has long had a connotation of male-perpetrated violence in the research community). As for violence in the relationships of gay men, there may be even more silence and denial, as there is a very real fear (as is for immigrant women and some women of color discussed earlier in this chapter) of being victimized by the system (Island and Letellier 1991).

Research on lesbian, gay male, bisexual, and transgendered relationship violence was initially scanty, but more research and service-oriented articles and books have appeared in the last few years. Studies done to date suggest that violence between same-sex partners occurs at the same or greater rate as in heterosexual relationships (Kulkin et al. 2008; Little and Terrance 2010; Murray and Mobley 2009). One large-sample study of 499 couples found that 9 percent reported physical violence in current couple relationships, and 32 percent in past relationships (Brown 2008; Kulkin et al. 2008; Little and Terrance 2010; Turell 2000).

As is also true for straights, domestic violence may be found in all racial/ethnic categories, social classes, education levels, and age groups. Among lesbians, neither "butch/femme" roles nor the women's physical size has been found to figure into violence (Obejas 1994).

Some of the relationship dynamics in same-sex abusive partnerships are similar to those in abusive straight relationships (Kurdek 1994), and because of this, the Violence Against Women Act was expanded in April 2010, to include same-gender couples under its criminal provisions (Barron 2010; Savage 2010). As with heterosexual intimate partner violence, batterers may use drugs or alcohol or have a history of childhood exposure to violence, justifying and excusing attacks on his or her partner. The abusive partner uses violence or threats of violence to keep the partner from leaving. Also like heterosexuals involved in domestic violence, the gay or lesbian couple is likely to deny or minimize the violence, along with believing that the violence is at least partly the victim's fault (Kulkin et al. 2008).

A special problem for lesbian and gay male domestic-violence victims is that few resources exist to serve their needs. The availability of legal protection is problematic in many states, although as of 2007, seventeen states and many municipalities now have legal protections for sexual minorities (Saxe 2007, p. 58). Although some states specifically exclude same-sex couples from domestic violence laws, the federal government has expanded the criminal provisions under the Violence Against Women Act to include sexual minority intimate partner violence (Barron 2010; Savage 2010). Still, a real lack of resources are available for lesbian and gay male domestic-violence victims, often because of the stigmatization of sexual minorities.

Such social stigmatization exacerbates the problem because it sometimes leads sexual minorities to suffer from **minority stress**. Lesbians and bisexual women, in particular, are subject to "a double risk of minority stress due to their social status as both women and sexual minorities. Lesbian women of color often experience what is known as 'triple jeopardy,' that is, they experience minority stress threefold, gender, race, and sexual preference" (Balsam and Szymanski 2005; Brown 2008, p. 459). Gay men of color also face a double risk of minority stress because they are both sexual and racial minorities.

Such external stressors are an important component in domestic abuse issues. As has been discussed elsewhere in this text, vulnerable families, such as those living in economic deprivation, who face discrimination, and so on, tend to have greater rates of domestic distress. Hate crimes, discrimination, internalized homophobia, fear of being "outed," are all stressors that can impact homosexual and bisexual relationships. For sexual minorities, these minority stresses are directly correlated with intimate partner violence. Because gays, lesbians, bisexuals, and transgendered people are sexual minorities, there is a real fear of a negative response by police, domestic abuse shelters, courts, and other services responding to homosexuals and bisexuals involved in domestic abuse (Brown 2008; Fountain et al. 2009).

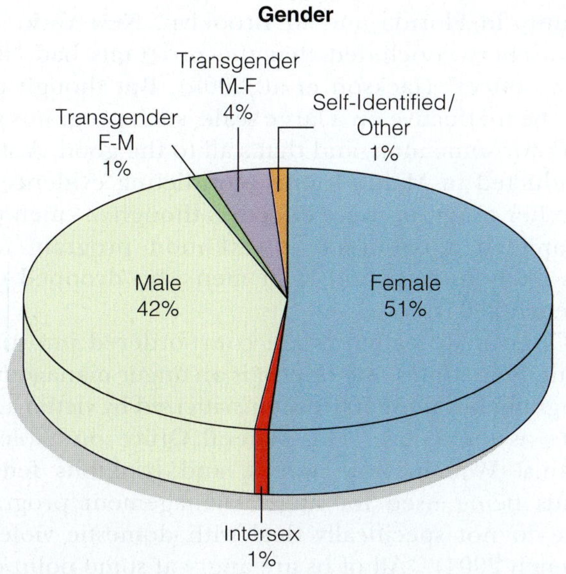

Figure 13.7 Gender Identity of Victims and Survivors. Data are from 2989 cases in which sexual orientation was known.

Source: Fountain et al. 2009.

Gay/lesbian/bisexual individuals may be afraid to go to the police—or to use any domestic violence intervention services—for fear of having their gay identity revealed or receiving a hostile response. In fact, although sexual minorities experience all of the same threats as heterosexual victims, they have an additional concern—the abusive partner can threaten to "out" a person to employers, family members, and friends (Brown 2008). When victims finally do call the police, some lesbians, for example, will describe their batterers as male because they fear being "outed," as well as discrimination on the part of first responders, hospitals, and the courts (Simpson and Helfrich, 2005).

Reporting by member organizations of The National Coalition of Anti-Violence Programs (see Figure 13.7) show that women callers to their domestic violence hotlines were 51 percent, which is "similar to the percentage reported in 2007. Those identifying as male represented the next largest category (42%), signifying a slight decrease in reports (10%). Callers identifying as intersex rose from 7 to 19 (171% increase). Reports from transgender men dropped 14% and those from transgender women rose 1%" (Fountain et al. 2009, p. 20). The reduction in calls from transgendered men is of concern because transgendered men experience the greatest amounts of social stigma from the broader society, and have the greatest risk of all sexual minority groups for hostility and discrimination from police and service providers when facing intimate partner violence (IPV).

An important obstacle for gay men is the fear of being feminized if they seek help. The dominant ideology in American society is that men are strong, so, just like heterosexual male IPV victims, to acknowledge abuse is to acknowledge weakness. This means gay men, like heterosexual men, not only suffer the abuse, but struggle with their own masculine identities. Although lesbians do seek help from the same services as heterosexual women, they find friends, counselors, and relatives the most helpful sources of support. Gay men find friends, counselors, and support groups of greatest help. Domestic violence services oriented to gay men, lesbians, bisexuals, and transgendered people are now somewhat available in larger cities with substantial gay/lesbian communities (Fountain et al. 2009).

Immigrants include gay men, lesbians, bisexuals, and transgendered people, but little research has been done on these particular segments of the immigrant population who, like heterosexual immigrant spouses, face a far different set of difficulties than native-born citizens when dealing with IPV. Sexual minority immigrants are particularly vulnerable in American society (because of immigration policies that favor heterosexuals), and tend to remain invisible to the broader society. Even still, according to research done by the National Coalition of Anti-Violence Programs, intimate partner violence in sexual minority immigrant communities is being reported at an increasing rate. "Striking increases [in domestic violence calls] were seen in a relatively new category of immigration, especially people with recent visas (1700%), refugees and asylees (900%), and people who are undocumented (250%)," particularly high are immigrants from East Africa (Fountain et al. 2009, pp. 24, 57).

The wide variety of research into the issues raised by domestic violence tells us is that "perpetrators and survivors of abuse, regardless of sexual orientation were more aggressive, hostile, more distressed, had more substance abuse problems, and reported being less satisfied with their relationships than those not in abusive relationships" (Brown 2008, p. 459).

Stopping Relationship Violence

The debate over whether women are as violent as men—or not—may be resolved at the practical level by noting that the interests of men as a group converge with those of women in curbing spousal violence—not only in hopes of having viable relationships but simply for survival. Even though men kill wives and girlfriends at a much higher rate than women kill husbands and boyfriends, some victimized women do murder or seriously injure their male partners. Progress in stopping intimate partner violence will benefit both sexes.

We have already discussed the shelter movement. Other approaches involve (1) counseling and group therapy directed toward abusive male partners (or the couple), and (2) the criminal justice system.

Counseling and Group Therapy Counseling and group therapy were earlier thought to be ineffective for male abusers. That may have been partly due to the inapplicability of general programs to this specific problem.

A number of male batterer intervention (or treatment) programs have now been developed. Many abusing husbands and male partners have difficulty controlling their response to anger and frustration, dealing with problems, and relinquishing their excessive control over their partner. Many men have a sincere desire to stop abusing their partners, even though abusers are difficult to reach and may drop out of treatment. However, data from therapists suggest that supportive and therapeutic-style group therapy reduces dropout rates because it promotes change in "abuse-supporting attitudes" in such a way as to reduce stigma and provide a setting in which abusers can learn more-constructive ways of both coping with anger and balancing autonomy and intimacy. In other words, supportive group therapy focuses on "psychological targets" such as emotion regulation (that is, anger management and stress tolerance), sobriety, and psychopathology (depression, anxiety, and so on), as opposed to "re-education" (Dutton 2006; Scott 2004; Straus and Scott, forthcoming, p. 34).

Although there is ongoing debate about the number of women who batter their spouses, the debate does not reduce the importance of treatment for these offenders. Research suggests that, like male abusers, women are at risk for re-offending unless provided appropriate and adequate therapy and counseling. Findings suggest that, like male abusers, female abusers must learn to regulate their emotions, deal with substance abuse issues, take responsibility for their behavior, and learn how to peacefully resolve familial conflicts (Carney and Buttell 2006; Carney, Buttell, and Dutton 2007; Dowd, Leisring, and Rosenbaum 2005).

Approximately 25 percent of male abusers engage in repeat intimate partner violence (Straus and Scott, forthcoming, p. 35). It is difficult to evaluate the level of success of male batterer intervention programs because of design problems, low response rates, and high program dropout rates and because programs do not always follow the research protocol (Jackson et al. 2003). Two recent and rigorously designed evaluations sponsored by the National Institute of Justice were conducted on intervention programs in Broward County in Florida and in Brooklyn, New York. The researchers concluded that the programs had "little or no effect" (Jackson et al. 2003). But though they may be ineffective on a large scale, such programs may work for some men, and that's all to the good. A study conducted in Maine found "conflicting evidence on whether programs were effective, though . . . men who completed a batterers' intervention program were less likely to re-offend than men who dropped out" (Hench 2004).

Often male batterers are court-ordered into treatment. Sometimes one option is an anger management program, but these have been criticized by victim advocates as ineffective. The Federal Office on Violence Against Women now agrees, and prohibits federal funds being used for anger management programs that do not specifically deal with domestic violence (Hench 2004). "All of us are angry at some point during our day; violence, on the other hand, is very different. It's an action," says one director of a program that offers both kinds of treatment to varied clients. Another says, "The issue regarding domestic violence is power and control. The offender is likely to beat or abuse the victim whether or not he or she is angry" (in Hench 2004).

In the past two decades, some couples' therapy programs have emerged to treat wife abuse. Typically, these programs counsel husbands and wives—or just husbands—separately over a period of up to six months. After this first treatment phase, couples are counseled together and are taught anger management techniques, along with communication, problem-solving, and conflict-resolution skills. Research has shown that spirituality is important to many people who have experienced IPV, and religious communities are strengthening their domestic violence counseling for couples in an effort to reduce incidences of re-battering (Ellison et al. 2007; Gillum, Sullivan, and Bybee 2006).

Couples' therapy programs designed to stop domestic violence are somewhat controversial because they proceed from the premise that a couple's staying together without violence after an abusive past is possible. Feminist scholars have expressed concern that therapists underestimate the danger that women face in violent relationships. There is some evidence that negative social sanctions from either partner's relatives or friends may help stop wife abuse.

Same-gender couple IPV also includes many of the components found in heterosexual couple violence counseling and therapy, but this poses some problems as well as solutions. For example, individual therapists may not take IPV as seriously and begin the couple in counseling (rather than suggesting police intervention and shelter services) where abuse can become even more pronounced (Helfrich and Simpson 2005; Kulkin et al. 2008).

The Criminal Justice Response There was little legal protection for battered women in the past. The street wisdom among police, as well as those who worked with battered women, was that calling the police was an ineffective strategy and posed some risk to the woman. Arresting an abusive partner or pressing charges would only aggravate the situation and result in escalating violence later. Officers also felt themselves to be at risk in responding to domestic violence calls.

Police officers typically avoided making arrests for assault that would be automatic if the man and woman involved were not married. The laws themselves contributed to police reluctance: Statutes might require a police officer to witness the act before making an arrest at the scene, or more severe injury might be required for prosecution for battery. In some cases, restraining orders required additional court action before they could be enforced.

A sociological experiment in Minneapolis in the 1980s obtained results indicating that mandatory arrest could be an effective deterrent to future violence (Sherman and Berk 1984),[6] although caution must be used when assigning causality to such laws because it is possible that the changes could also be the result of "increased efforts of the battered women's and shelter movement over the past several decades which have aided women in safely exiting violent relationships" (Leisenring 2008, p. 462). As a consequence of this experiment, laws have been changed to make arrests for domestic violence more feasible, and some states or jurisdictions have policies that mandate arrest in certain situations involving family violence.

Most subsequent replications of the arrest experiment did not get the same result. In fact, according to the National Institute of Justice, "policies and services designed to help victims of domestic violence appear to have two possible and opposing effects: either they decrease the abuse and risk of homicide, or they have the unintended consequence of increasing them." (Dugan, Nagin, and Rosenfeld 2004, p. 21; Leisenring 2008). It now appears that arrest will deter future violence only on the part of men who are employed and married, men with a "stake in conformity." Other men, those who are unemployed and/or not married to the woman they abused, may react to arrest by *increased* violence (Dugan, Nagin, and Rosenfeld 2004).

An even more serious problem of the arrest strategy has been that a literal reading of a mandatory arrest law has resulted in the arrest of victims, along with perpetrators, when the victim has resisted with violent force. Women also fear that reporting domestic violence to the police will risk contact with Child Protective Services and the removal of their children from the home. Some women who did contact police reported that the batterer was not arrested, as they had expected, and that the police sometimes trivialized their situation. In some cases, women claimed that the exchange between the perpetrator and the police officer was characterized by "male bonding," in which the perpetrator's story overrode the woman's complaint of violence.

Some women reported positive and protective experiences to researchers: "[S]o when the police did intervene that night, they made it pretty clear that I didn't deserve it (the abuse). . . . [T]hey talked to me and I filed a report . . . and that's the last I saw of my husband" (M. Wolf et al. 2003).

This seems a good time to remind ourselves of the good news that appears in recent reports. Both fatal

[6] In the Minneapolis experiment, officers were randomly assigned to respond by arresting the (presumably male) perpetrator, by counseling the parties, or simply by separating them for a cooling-off period. A six-month follow-up by telephone and an examination of police call records indicated that arrest was the most effective response in deterring subsequent violence (Sherman and Berk 1984).

and nonfatal violence against intimate partners has declined since 1993, and that may well be a consequence of the support and treatment programs we have described.

The drop in the male homicide rate is attributed to the greater availability of options for abused women. When women kill a partner, it is usually out of desperation to exit a violent relationship. The shelter programs and other resources that now exist have given battered women escape routes so that they are less likely to kill spouses or partners in an attempt to stop the violence (Dugan, Nagin, and Rosenfeld 2004; Leisenring 2008).

Shelter options, women's increased ability to support themselves, a cultural change that takes domestic violence seriously and endorses women's taking self-protective actions, and increased interest in and understanding of domestic violence on the part of law enforcement agencies are all developments that may account for the decrease in fatal and nonfatal violence against women by their intimate partners.

We turn now to another type of family violence in which the more powerful abuse the less powerful—child abuse.

Violence Against Children

Perceptions of what constitutes child abuse or neglect have differed throughout history and in various cultures.[7] Practices that we now consider abusive were accepted in the past as the normal exercise of parental rights or as appropriate discipline.

Even today, standards of acceptable child care vary according to culture and social class. What some groups consider mild abuse, others consider right and proper discipline. In 1974, however, Congress provided a legal definition of *child maltreatment* in the Child Abuse Prevention and Treatment Act. (The federal government and some researchers use the umbrella term *child maltreatment* to cover both abuse and neglect.)

The act defines child abuse and neglect as the "physical or mental injury, sexual abuse, or negligent treatment of a child under the age of 18 by a person who is responsible for the child's welfare under circumstances that indicate that the child's health or welfare is harmed or threatened" (U.S. Department of Health, Education, and Welfare 1975, p. 3).

Child Abuse and Neglect People use the term **child abuse** to refer to overt acts of aggression—excessive verbal derogation (emotional child abuse) or physical child abuse such as beating, whipping, punching, kicking, hitting with a heavy object, burning or scalding, or threatening with or using a knife or gun. (By current American standards, spanking or hitting a child with a paddle, stick, or hairbrush is not "abuse," although it is in Sweden and several other countries [Straus and Donnelly 2001]; and see Chapter 10 of this text.) Data collected by the federal government between the years of 1992 and 2007 show a 52 percent decline in physical abuse. Fatalities of children from abuse and neglect, however, increased 15 percent from 2006 to 2007 (U.S. Department of Health and Human Services 2010, pp. 55, 94). The number of child fatalities due to neglect and abuse has been increasing in the past few years.

Courtesy of Against Child Abuse Agency, Hong Kong

Child abuse is not specific to the United States. This pamphlet was produced by social service agencies in Hong Kong.

[7] A dramatic example of cultural difference in defining child abuse is the controversy surrounding *female genital mutilation (FGM)*. Some sub-Saharan African and Muslim cultures practice FGM, which is the surgical removal of the clitoris and other external female genital organs, and suturing of the vaginal opening until marriage. In those cultures, FGM is an important rite of passage for young girls and considered necessary to make them eligible to marry. (It does not seem to be a Muslim religious teaching, however.) FGM has been brought to the United States by some immigrants as part of their cultural heritage. It has been outlawed in the United States since 1996, and is now prohibited in some African countries. FGM is still practiced clandestinely here (Renteln 2004, pp. 51–53).

Some of the increase can be attributed to improvements in data collection.

Child Neglect In 2008, nearly 24 percent of investigations or assessments by child protective services agencies "determined at least one child to be a victim of abuse or neglect," with 70 percent of them suffering neglect (U.S. Department of Health and Human Services 2010, pp. xii, xiii). Child neglect includes acts of omission—failing to provide adequate physical or emotional care. Physically neglected children often show signs of malnutrition, lack immunization against childhood disease, lack proper clothing, attend school irregularly, and need medical attention for such conditions as poor eyesight or bad teeth. Often these conditions are grounded in parents' or guardians' economic problems, mental health issues, lack of parenting skills, a history of childhood abuse, and so on (Currie and Widom 2010; Daniel, Taylor, and Scott 2010). Research into the differences between child neglect and child abuse suggests that the largest cases of child neglect are found in children from birth to age three, and are associated with larger families with low incomes. Children twelve and older are the most frequent victims of physical and sexual abuse (Bundy-Fazioli, Winokur, and DeLong-Hamilton 2009; U.S. Department of Health and Human Services 2010, p. 47, Table 3-12).

Emotional child abuse or neglect involves a parent's often being overly harsh and critical, failing to provide guidance, or being uninterested in a child's needs. Emotional child abuse might also include allowing children to witness violence between parents—there were children in residence in 35.2 percent of households where intimate partner violence took place (Catalano 2007). Although emotional abuse may occur without physical abuse, physical abuse results in emotional abuse as well.

Child Sexual Abuse Another form of child abuse is **sexual abuse**: a child's being forced, tricked, or coerced, by an older person, into sexual behavior—exposure, unwanted kissing, fondling of sexual organs, intercourse, rape, incest, prostitution, and pornography—for purposes of sexual gratification or financial gain (Goldman et al. 2003; U.S. Department of Health and Human Services 2010, p. 115). Nine percent of abused children (of all ages) in a national sample survey were sexually abused in 2008 (U.S. Department of Health and Human Services 2010, p. 45, Table 3-10). Data collected between 1992 and 2007 show that child sexual abuse has declined 53 percent (U.S. Department of Health and Human Services 2010, p. 94).

Incest involves sexual relations between related individuals. The most common forms are sibling incest followed by father–daughter incest. The definition of child sexual abuse *excludes* mutually desired sex play between or among siblings close in age, but coerced sex by strong and/or older brothers is sexual abuse and is more widespread than parent–child incest (Bass et al. 2006; Carlson, Maciol, and Schneider 2006; Kiselica and Morrill-Richards 2007; Thompson 2009). Incest is the most emotionally charged form of sexual abuse; it is also the most difficult to detect. Incest appears to be in the background of a variety of sexual, emotional, and physical problems among adults who were abused as children (Brand and Alexander 2003; Carlson, Maciol, and Schneider 2006; Schlesinger 2006).

We see occasional media stories about female sex abusers, but research indicates that sexual abuse is almost entirely perpetrated by males (Peter 2009). Data on sexual exploitation indicate that 47 percent of sexual assaults on children were by relatives; 49 percent by others such as teachers, coaches, or neighbors; and only 4 percent by strangers (Hernandez 2001). Sexual abuse by paid caregivers and by mentors such as teachers, coaches, youth program directors, and clergy is a problem being addressed by policy makers and child care professionals. Sexual exploitation of homeless children is yet another abuse problem (Tyler and Cauce 2002).

Research by social psychologists finds lower self-esteem and greater incidences of depression among adults who have been victims of child abuse (Banyard et al. 2009; Sachs-Ericsson et al. 2010). A study of nearly 43,000 adolescents found that those who had been physically and/or sexually abused were more prone to binge drinking and thoughts of suicide. However, high levels of supportive interest and monitoring from at least one parent decreased the risk for these outcomes among sexually abused adolescents (Luster and Small 1997).

Sibling violence is not "kid stuff." This under-the-radar form of violence is rather frequent and can be quite injurious.

Sibling Violence **Sibling violence** is often overlooked and rarely studied (K. Butler 2006a; Finkelhor et al. 2005), even though the early National Family Violence Survey found it to be the most pervasive form of family violence (Straus, Gelles, and Steinmetz 1980).

Nor is it only of the "harmless" teasing variety ("UF Study" 2004). A national sample study found that 35 percent of children had been hit or attacked by siblings in the previous year. Fourteen percent were repeatedly attacked, 5 percent hard enough to have injuries such as bruises, cuts, chipped teeth, and sometimes broken bones. Two percent were hit with rocks, toys, broom handles, shovels, or knives (K. Butler 2006a).

Child psychologist John Caffaro (in K. Butler 2006a) sees sibling abuse as situational, not personality driven. When parents are frequently physically or emotionally absent from the home, or when they have their own problems, sibling violence is more apt to occur. Failure to intervene effectively also plays a part, as does parental favoritism of one child over another. Trauma, anxiety, and depression are likely to result from experiencing sibling violence, as well as an increased likelihood to perpetrate violence as an adult and to have relationship problems (K. Butler 2006a; Hoffman and Edwards 2004; Noland et al. 2004).

Perpetrators of sibling violence are more likely than others to become perpetrators of dating violence, according to a study of more than 500 men and women at a Florida community college. "Siblings learn violence as a form of sibling manipulation and control as they compete with each other for family resources. . . . They carry these bullying behaviors into dating, the next peer relationship in which they have an emotional investment" (researcher Virginia Noland in "UF Study" 2004; Noland et al. 2004). Yet sibling violence has received comparatively little research attention and even less attention has been given to preventive or therapeutic responses. Noland recommends that sibling violence be taken more seriously and that anger management programs be implemented while these violent individuals are still kids ("UF Study" 2004).

How Extensive is Child Abuse? As noted earlier in this chapter, rates of child physical abuse and child sexual abuse declined in the 1990s, and in the early years of the twenty-first century (Finkelhor and Jones 2004, 2006; U.S. Department of Health and Human Services 2010).

Current estimates from the federal report *Child Maltreatment 2010* are based on state reports of child abuse. Of the reported cases of child maltreatment, 71.1 percent are of neglect; 16.1 percent, of physical abuse; 9.1 percent, of sexual abuse; 7.3 percent, of psychological mistreatment; and 2.2 percent, of medical neglect. (The remainder are cases that include multiple factors or unspecified maltreatment.)[8] An estimated 1,740 children died from abuse or neglect in 2008, with nearly 80 percent under the age of four (U.S. Department of Health and Human Services 2010, pp. 27, 55, Figure 3-5).

Abused children live in families of all socioeconomic levels, races, nationalities, and religious groups, although child abuse is reported more frequently among poor and nonwhite families than among middle- and upper-class white families. Families below the poverty line have three times the rate of severe violence to children. Differences in rates may be partly due to differences in reporting—children of the poor are more apt to be seen in the emergency room or by social welfare authorities (Gelles and Cavanaugh 2005). Another reason may be unconscious racial discrimination on the part of physicians and others who report abuse and neglect (Lane et al. 2002). Experts believe there are also real differences, however (Gelles and Cavanaugh 2005), and a stress explanation is often offered.

In 2008, according to government data, 45.1 percent of the victims of child maltreatment were white, 21.9 percent were African American, 20.8 percent were Hispanic, 1.2 percent were American Indian/Alaska Native, and less than 1 percent were Asian. When the size of each racial/ethnic group is taken into account, it appears that African American, American Indian, and Pacific Islander children had the highest victimization rates; Hispanics and whites had moderate levels of victimization; and Asian American children had low rates of child maltreatment (U.S. Department of Health and Human Services 2010, pp. 42–43, Table 3-9).

The percentages of male (48.3 percent) and female (51.3 percent) victims were not very different. The youngest children (through age three) were more

[8] A controversy has arisen over accusations of child sexual and other abuse in the context of a child custody dispute. On the one hand, parents alleging child abuse (usually mothers) have been accused of fabricating the charge to gain an advantage in the custody determination (Childress 2006). On the other, those parents have claimed that their intent is to protect the child from real abuse by the other parent (usually fathers).

A study of over 9,000 contested divorces found that only 1 to 8 percent involved allegations of child abuse (Goldstein and Tyler 1998; McDonald 1998; citing Thoennes and Tjaden 1990). Half the allegations were considered "founded," that is, found to be true. In 33 percent of the cases, no abuse was found, and in 17 percent, it could not be determined if child abuse had occurred or not.

The key point about fraudulent reports is that only 14 percent were "deliberate false accusations" (Goldstein and Tyler 1998, p. 1). The remainder of the "unfounded" cases were sincerely made reports that were later found to be in error, typically due to misunderstandings of children's behavior or statements.

vulnerable than older children (U.S. Department of Health and Human Services 2010, p. 26). A child faces the greatest risk of becoming a victim of homicide during the first year of life (Collymore 2002).

Eighty-four percent of abused children were mistreated by at least one parent: by mother only in 38.3 percent of cases; by father only in 18 percent of cases; and by both mother and father in nearly 18 percent of cases. In 10 percent of cases, children were mistreated by other caregivers: foster parents or legal guardians, day care workers, or unmarried partners of a parent (U.S. Department of Health and Human Services 2010, pp. 28, 51, Table 3-15).

Abuse versus "Normal" Child Rearing It is too easy for parents to go beyond reasonable limits when angry or distraught or to include as "discipline" what most observers would define as abuse (Baumrind, Larzelere, and Cowan 2002; Feigelman et al. 2009). Hence, child abuse must be seen as a potential behavior in many families—even those we think of as "normal" (Feigelman et al. 2009).

Immigrant families may come from cultures where rather severe physical punishment is considered necessary for good child rearing. Those parents may not be aware that what they are doing by way of parental discipline is illegal in this country. They may instead view themselves as very responsible parents (Renteln 2004, pp. 54–57).[9]

Risk Factors for Child Abuse Consider the following society-wide beliefs and conditions that, when exaggerated, may encourage even well-intentioned parents to mistreat their children:

- A belief in physical punishment is a contributing (but not sufficient) factor in child abuse. Abusive parents have learned—probably in their own childhood—to view children as requiring physical punishment (Milner et al. 2010, p. 335).
- Parents may have unrealistic expectations about what the child is capable of; often, they lack awareness and knowledge of the child's physical and emotional needs and abilities (Letarte, Normandeau, and Allard 2010, p. 254). For example, slapping a bawling toddler to stop her or his crying is completely unrealistic, as is too-early toilet training.
- Parents who abuse their children were often abused or neglected themselves as children. Violent parents are likely to have experienced and thereby learned violence as children. Whether victims of child abuse or witnesses of adult interpersonal violence, those exposed to family violence in childhood are more likely than others to abuse their own children, and their spouses as well (Heyman and Slep 2002; Milner et al. 2010; Zielinski 2009). This does not mean that abused children are predestined to be abusive parents or partners. Gelles and Cavanaugh (2005) report an intergenerational transmission rate of 30 percent. That is much higher than the general average of 2 to 4 percent; nevertheless, "[t]he most typical outcome for individuals exposed to violence in their families of origin is to be nonviolent in their adult families. This is the case for both men and women" (Heyman and Slep 2002, p. 870).
- Parental stress and feelings of helplessness play a significant part in child abuse (Milner 2010). "Economic adversity and worries about money pervade the typical violent home" (Gelles and Straus 1988, p. 85; Zielinski 2009). Overload, often related to family problems, also creates stress that may lead to child abuse. Other causes of parental stress are children's misbehavior, changing lifestyles and standards of living, and a parent's feeling pressure to do a good job but being perplexed about how to do it.
- Families have become more private and less dependent on kinship and neighborhood relationships. Hence, parents are alone with their children, shut off at home from the "watchful eyes and sharp tongues that regulate parent–child relations in other cultures" (Skolnick 1978, p. 82). In neighborhoods that have support systems and tight social networks of community-related friends—where other adults are somewhat involved in the activities of the family—child abuse and neglect are much more likely to be noticed and stopped (Falconer et al. 2008).
- Other circumstances that are statistically related to child maltreatment include parental youth and inexperience, marital discord and divorce, and unusually demanding or otherwise difficult children (Milner et al. 2010). Other risk factors involve parental abuse of alcohol or other substances (Milner et al. 2010); a mother's cohabiting with her boyfriend (who could potentially abuse the child; Crary 2007); and having a stepfather (because stepfathers are as likely as biological fathers to abuse their children; Crary 2007). Still, it is important to remember that 80 percent of people who commit child abuse

[9] Immigrant parents may be mistakenly identified as having abused children because of certain cultural practices not initially understood in this country. There are healing practices in certain cultures that can produce what looks like evidence of injuries to an American doctor or social service worker. Southeast Asians employ a practice known as "coining" whereby they rub the edge of a coin along the skin. This leaves marks that can appear to be those of a whip (Child Abuse Prevention Council of Sacramento n.d.). Similarly, Asian children may have "Mongolian spots" on their skin, a natural phenomenon, but one that appears as bruising to an unaware health practitioner (Families with Children from China 1999).

are the children's own biological parents, whereas cohabitants and stepparents make up just 4.4 percent each (U.S. Department of Health and Human Services 2010, p. 66).

Combating Child Abuse Three major approaches to combating child abuse and willful neglect are the punitive approach, which views abuse and neglect as crimes for which parents should be punished; the therapeutic approach, which views abuse as a family problem requiring treatment; and the social welfare approach, which looks to stress factors and the family's social context.

The Criminal Justice Approach Those who favor the punitive approach believe that one or both parents should be held legally responsible for abusing a child.

A complicated issue emerging with regard to this approach involves holding battered women criminally responsible for "failing to act" to prevent such abuse at the hands of their male partners. Feminist legal advocates have begun to question whether the law should hold a battered woman responsible for failing to prevent harm to her children when, as a battered woman, she cannot even defend herself: "When the law punishes a battered woman for failing to protect her child against a batterer, it may be punishing her for failing to do something she was incapable of doing. . . . She is then being punished for the crime of the person who has victimized her" (Erickson 1991, pp. 208–9). Legal experts note that fathers are typically *not* held accountable for child abuse committed by female partners (Liptak 2002).

The courts are starting to recognize this paradox. The Illinois Supreme Court overturned such a mother's conviction in 2002, and courts have ruled in favor of mothers who lost custody or had children removed from the home, citing the mothers' domestic violence victimization (Liptak 2002; *Nicholson v. Scopetta* 2004; Nordwall and Leavitt 2004).

The Therapeutic Approach All states have criminal laws against child abuse. But the approach to child protection has gradually shifted from punitive to therapeutic. Not all who work with abused children are happy with this shift. These critics prefer to hold one or both parents clearly responsible. They reject the family system approach to therapy because it implies distribution of responsibility for change to all family members (M. Stewart 1984). Nevertheless, social workers and clinicians—rather than the police and the court system—increasingly investigate and treat abusive or neglectful parents.

The therapeutic approach involves two interrelated strategies: (1) increasing parents' self-esteem and their knowledge about children, and (2) involving the community in child rearing (Goldstein, Keller, and Erne 1985). A typical voluntary program holds regular meetings to enhance self-esteem and educate abusive parents. Programs may attempt to reach stressed parents before they hurt their children, and many operate a twenty-four-hour hotline for parents under stress. High school classes on family life, child development, and parenting are now virtually universal and are thought to reduce child abuse by giving future parents an understanding of what they can expect from children at different ages.

Involving the community means getting people other than parents to help with child rearing. There are options such as *supplemental mothers,* who are available to babysit regularly with potentially abused children. Another community resource is the *crisis nursery,* where parents may take their children when they need to get away for a few hours. Ideally, crisis nurseries are open twenty-four hours a day and accept children at any hour without prearrangement.

One form of protection for abused or neglected children is to remove them from their parents' homes and place them in foster care. This practice is controversial, as foster parents have been abusive in some cases, and there are not enough foster parents to go around in many regions of the country. Moreover, removal from the home can be quite traumatic to children, who are often very attached to their parents despite the abuse (Kaufman 2006). They may blame themselves for the breaking up of the family (Gelles and Cavanaugh 2005).

An alternative is **family preservation**, whereby a Child Protective Services worker is able to "leave the child with an impoverished or troubled family and provide support in the form of housekeeping help or drug treatment, and then visit frequently to monitor progress" (Kaufman 2006, p. A12). The family preservation approach would not be appropriate if harm to the child appears imminent. Family preservation is a controversial strategy (Gelles 2005; Wexler, 2005), but both removal of the child from the home and a family preservation approach carry risk.[10]

The Social Welfare Approach The social welfare approach overlaps with the therapeutic approach but takes note of the social, cultural, and economic context of child maltreatment to provide services and parent education that may make child abuse less likely. Housing assistance and subsidized child care, for example, might prevent a low-income or socially isolated parent from taking the risk of leaving children alone while working.

[10] For detailed discussions of this controversy see articles by Richard Wexler (2005; "Family Preservation Is the Safest Way to Protect Most Children") and Richard Gelles (2005; "Protecting Children Is More Important Than Preserving Families") in Loseke, Gelles, and Cavanaugh (2005).

Parent education directed toward new immigrant parents might mitigate the development of situations that end in removal of children from the home. For example, if some immigrant families do not realize that their traditional disciplinary practices constitute criminal child abuse in the United States, parent education offered through refugee service centers could anticipate that problem. The same is true regarding leaving children alone at home. This may be customary and perfectly safe in a small tribal village but not so safe in the United States; moreover, it is illegal (Gonzalez and O'Connor 2002; Renteln 2004, pp. 54–58).

Commercial Sexual Exploitation of Children We close this section on child maltreatment with a look at a form of child abuse that is not, strictly speaking, family violence, but which is often set in motion by developments in seriously troubled families—that is the commercial sexual exploitation of children. Researchers Richard J. Estes and Neil Weiner of the University of Pennsylvania go beyond family violence per se to look at society-wide organized sexual exploitation of children. Their study was based on interviews with victims and child welfare workers in twenty-eight cities in the United States, Mexico, and Canada (Estes and Weiner 2002; Hernandez 2001; Memmott 2001). Based on this research, they estimate that as many as 300,000 to 400,000 children a year are molested or used in pornography or prostitution. The National Institute of Justice supports this estimate, noting as many hotline tips regarding child exploitation (National Institute of Justice 2007).

Family dynamics often place children in harm's way. Typically, victims of organized sexual exploitation are runaways, "throwaways" (children who have been kicked out of the home by parents), or other homeless children who trade or sell sex to meet their basic survival needs. Some sexually exploited children live at home but are offered for sexual purposes by their families in exchange for money, drugs, or other benefits (*Domestic Sex Trafficking of Minors* n.d.; Harris 2009).

We are much more aware of parents' abuse of children than we are of children's abuse of parents, but it does happen. Sometimes it is an outgrowth of earlier child abuse. We turn now to the topic of child-to-parent abuse.

Child-to-Parent Abuse

The discussion of **child-to-parent abuse** is brief because not much research has been done (Cottrell and Monk 2004). Yet, like other forms of family violence, child-to-parent abuse has been there all along.

This section relies heavily on a review article by Cottrell and Monk (2004). Data suggest that 9 to 14 percent of parents have been abused by adolescent children, with injuries that include bruises, cuts, and broken bones. Types of assaults have included kicking, punching, biting, and weapons. Mothers, especially single mothers, and elderly parents of youth are the most frequent victims.

Adolescent boys are the most frequent perpetrators, and their growth in size and strength is associated with increases in violence. Although there are no clear findings of differences in race/ethnicity or social class, poverty and other family stressors are associated with this form of violence.

Abusive children may exhibit diminished emotional attachments to parents. The child may have been abused by the parent or witnessed intimate partner abuse in the household. Overly permissive parents and those who abandon their authority in response to the violence tend to see more of it. Parents whose child-rearing styles contradict each other are also at risk. Drug use by the adolescent may play a role.

Parents who are victims of assaults by their adolescent children often engage in denial. Unfortunately, at the moment, few if any support services exist, and the criminal justice system has not responded systematically (Cottrell and Monk 2004).

Generally, we see any form of family violence as more likely to occur in situations of unequal rather than equal power. We close this chapter with a reminder of everyone's basic right to be respected—and not to be physically, emotionally, or sexually abused—in any relationship. And we end on an optimistic note, as most forms of family violence show evidence of declining rather than increasing.

Summary

- Power, the ability to exercise one's will, may rest on cultural authority, on economic and personal resources that are gender-based and/or involve love and emotional dependence, on interpersonal dynamics, or on physical violence.
- Marital power or power in other intimate partner relationships includes decision making, control over money, the division of household labor, and a sense of empowerment in the relationship. American marriages experience a tension between egalitarianism on the one hand and, on the other, gender identities that in effect preserve male authority.
- The relative power of a husband and wife within a marriage or other intimate partnership varies by education, social class, religion, race/ethnicity, age, immigration status, and other factors. It varies by whether or not the woman works and with the presence and age of children. Studies of married couples,

cohabiting couples, and gay and lesbian couples illustrate the significance of economically based power and of norms about who should have power.

- Couples can consciously work toward more egalitarian marriages or intimate partner relationships and relinquish "power politics." Changing gender roles, as they affect marital and intimate relationship power, necessitate negotiation and communication.
- Physical violence is most commonly used in the absence of other resources.
- Researchers do not agree on whether intimate partner violence is primarily perpetrated by males or whether males and females are equally likely to abuse their partners. The effects of intimate partner violence indicate that victimization of women is the more crucial social problem, and it has received the most programmatic attention. Recently, some programs have been developed for male abusers. Studies suggesting that arrest is *sometimes* a deterrent to further wife abuse illustrate the importance of public policies in this area.
- Economic hardships and other stress factors (among parents of all social classes and races) can lead to physical and/or emotional child abuse as can lack of understanding of children's developmental needs and abilities. One difficulty in eliminating child abuse is drawing a clear distinction between "normal" child rearing and abuse.
- Physical, verbal, and emotional abuse, as well as sexual abuse and child neglect, are forms of violence against children. Sibling violence is an often overlooked form of child abuse.
- Criminal justice, therapeutic, and social welfare approaches are ways of addressing the problem of child maltreatment.
- Child-to-parent abuse is a recently "discovered" form of family violence. It may grow out of previous abuse of a child.

Questions for Review and Reflection

1. How is gender related to power in marriage? How do you think ongoing social change will affect power in marriage?
2. Do you think that power in a marriage or other couple relationship depends on who earns how much money? Or does it depend on emotions? Is it possible for a couple to develop a no-power relationship?
3. Looking at domestic violence, why might women remain with the men who batter them? Do you think that shelters provide an adequate way out for these women? What about arresting the abuser? Should intimate partner violence against men receive more attention in the form of social programs? Why or why not?
4. What factors might play a role when well-intentioned parents abuse their children?
5. **Policy Question.** What can we as a society do to combat child neglect that is really due to family poverty?

Key Terms

allocation systems 346
child abuse 368
child-to-parent abuse 373
coercive power 340
Conflict Tactics Scale 354
egalitarian norm (of marital power) 343
emotional child abuse or neglect 369
equality 340
equity 340
expert power 341
family preservation 372
gender model of marriage 349
incest 369
informational power 341
intimate partner power 340
intimate partner violence 354
intimate terrorism 363
legitimate power 341
marital power 340
marital rape 357
minority stress 365
mutually economically dependent spouses (MEDS) 349
near peers (Schwartz's typology) 350
neotraditional family 349
no-power 350
patriarchal norm (of marital power) 343

peer marriage (Schwartz's typology) 350
power 340
power politics 350
referent power 341
resource hypothesis 342
resources in cultural context 343
reward power 341
sexual abuse 369
sibling violence 370
situational couple violence 363
traditionals (Schwartz's typology) 350
transitional egalitarian situation (of marital power) 343

Online Resources

Sociology CourseMate

www.CengageBrain.com

Access an integrated eBook, chapter-specific interactive learning tools, including flash cards, quizzes, videos, and more in your Sociology CourseMate, accessed through CengageBrain.com.

www.CengageBrain.com

Want to maximize your online study time? Take this easy-to-use study system's diagnostic pre-test, and it will create a personalized study plan for you. By helping you identify the topics that you need to understand better and then directing you to valuable online resources, it can speed up your chapter review. CengageNOW even provides a post-test so you can confirm that you are ready for an exam.

15

Divorce: Before and After

All marriages end—either in death or divorce. Divorce has become a common experience in the United States for all social classes, age categories, and religious and ethnic groups. Over 40 percent of recent first marriages are likely to end in divorce (Teachman, Tedrow, and Hall 2006).[1] In this chapter, we'll examine factors that affect people's decisions to divorce, the experience itself, and ways the experience may be made less painful and become the prelude to the future, alone or in a new marriage. We'll also analyze why so many couples in our society decide to divorce and examine the debate over whether a divorce should be harder to get than it is today. We'll begin by looking at divorce rates in the United States, which are among the highest in the world.

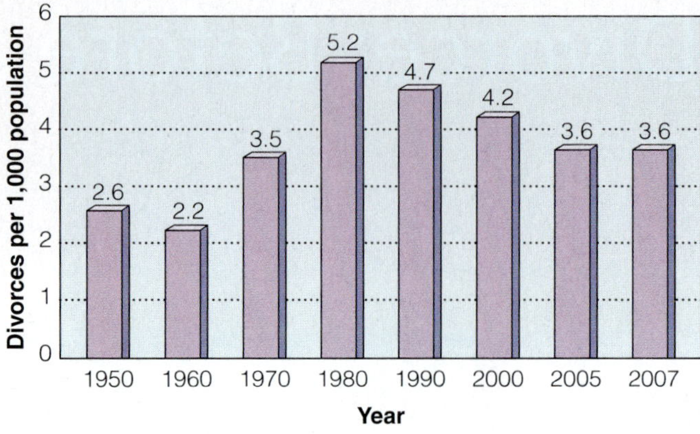

FIGURE 15.2 Divorces per 1,000 population, 1950 to 2007 (crude divorce rate).

Source: Adapted from U.S. Census Bureau 2010b, Table 78; U.S. National Center for Health Statistics 2006, Table A.

Today's High U.S. Divorce Rate

The divorce rate started its upward swing in the nineteenth century (Amato and Irving 2006; Teachman, Tedrow, and Hall 2006, Figure 4.1).[2] The frequency of divorce increased throughout most of the twentieth century, as Figure 15.1 shows, with dips and upswings surrounding historical events such as the Great Depression, Great Recession of 2007, and major wars. Between 1960 and its peak in 1979, the **refined divorce rate** more than doubled. The *refined divorce rate* declined throughout the nineties (Wilcox and Marquardt 2009, p. 75, Table 5).

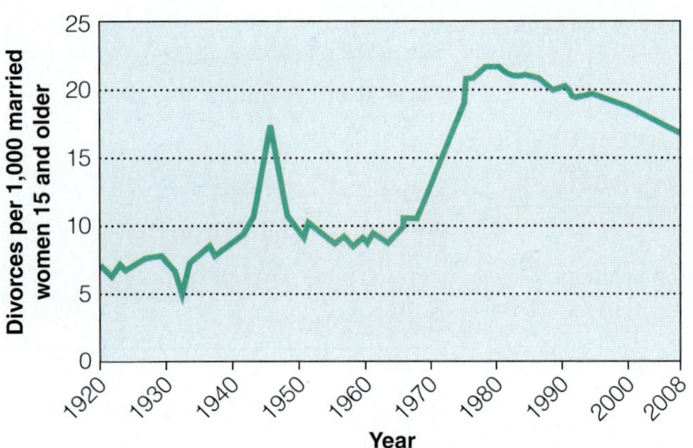

FIGURE 15.1 Divorces per 1,000 married women age fifteen and older in the United States, 1920–2008. This includes the latest data available for the refined divorce rate.

Source: U.S. National Center for Health Statistics 1990a, 1998, p. 3; Wilcox and Marquardt 2009, p. 76, Figure 5.

We can extend the time line to 2005, if we use the **crude divorce rate** (see Figure 15.2). The crude divorce rate has declined almost 30 percent since 1979, and has not been so low since around 1970 (Stevenson and Wolfers 2007; U.S. Census Bureau 2010b, Table 78).[3]

The decline in divorce rates varies by social category. It has declined dramatically for women college graduates, whereas less-educated women have experienced virtually stable divorce rates (S. Martin 2006; Martin and Parashar 2006). This has produced what sociologist Steven Martin calls the **divorce divide** (in Hurley 2005; Ono 2009). Predictions are that only 25 percent of college women who married in the early 1990s will divorce, whereas over 50 percent of less-educated women will experience a divorce.

Divorces occur relatively early in marriage. The median length of a first marriage that ends in divorce

[1] For years estimates were that as many as 50 percent of first marriages would end in divorce. Experts now think marital dissolutions never reached 50 percent and likely never will (Hurley 2005, citing Rose Kreider of the U.S. Census Bureau). As of 2001 (the most recent available data), the estimated percentages of marriages ending in divorce for men and women now in their fifties were 41 percent for men and 39 percent for women (Kreider 2005).

[2] See Paul. R. Amato and Shelley Irving's chapter in *Handbook of Divorce and Relationship Dissolution* (2006) for a presentation of divorce rates, divorce law, and attitudes toward divorce in various eras of American history.

[3] The *refined divorce rate* is the number of divorces per 1,000 married women. The refined divorce rate compares the number of divorces to the number of women at risk of divorce (that is, married women). It is a more valid indicator of the rate at which marriages are dissolved than the crude divorce rate.

The *crude divorce rate* is the number of divorces per 1,000 population. This rate includes portions of the population—children and the unmarried—who are not at risk for divorce. Despite its limitations, the crude divorce rate is used for comparisons over time because these data are the only long-term annual data available. The federal government discontinued compilation of the refined divorce rate in the mid-nineties (Broome 1995).

In lieu of detailed government data, we also rely on national-sample surveys—including the Census Bureau's Current Population Survey—for individuals' reports of their current or cumulative experience of divorce. These divorce data are *not* collected annually, but less frequently.

Facts about Families

The Rise of the "Silver Divorce"

They are high-school sweethearts who seemed happily married for 40 years after raising four children. But the announcement that Al and Tipper Gore were splitting up was not a surprise to researchers who study the most divorcing cohort in American history. Al is 61 and Tipper is 62, which means they came of age in the 1960s and '70s, an era when even the most intimate relationships were radically altered by huge social upheaval. "This is the generation that weathered a lot of changes that didn't match their expectations when they walked down the aisle," says Betsey Stevenson, an assistant professor of business and public policy at the University of Pennsylvania who studies marriage trends. "In some respects, it's a miracle how many of them stayed together."

Marriage researchers have long known that the rockiest years are the early ones, and, generally speaking, the longer a couple is married, the less likely they are to divorce. That's still true, says Stevenson, but "silver divorce" is no longer rare, and that's particularly true for the baby-boom generation, born between 1946 and 1964. In the 1950s, many couples married just past age 20, but only 8 percent were divorced at the 10-year mark. After 20 years, just 19 percent had split; after 30 years, 26 percent were divorced; and after 40 years, only 30 percent were no longer together.

The Gores married in 1970, when divorce rates had just begun a dramatic spike upward. Their contemporaries had much less stable marriages. Within 10 years, 27 percent of their unions had broken up. And after 30 years together, more than half were divorced. As those couples now start to hit the 40-year mark, the rate is slowing down, but some continue to divorce.

"If you look at every single year of marriage, they have the highest divorce rates of anyone born before or after them," Stevenson says. In fact, she adds, this group of baby boomers is most responsible for the commonly heard statistic that one out of every two first marriages will eventually end in divorce. Based on their track record to date, however, baby boomers' divorce rates will clearly end up being higher than that. About 4 percent of divorces every year now involve those married 40 years or more, she says.

The increase in silver divorces is not strictly an American phenomenon. The rate of divorce among those 55 and older is also creeping up in Britain, France, Canada, and Japan, even though divorce rates on the whole are inching down. "I keep hearing people say that this is rare or unusual, but it's not," Stevenson says.

Ironically, it's the fact that the '70s cohort was also the most marrying generation that set them up to be the most likely to divorce. After all, you have to be married to get divorced. And because they tended to marry in their early 20s and are expected to live into their 80s or 90s, theirs may be the generation that lives the most years as married couples, especially if you include people who remarry. "A couple like the Gores, if they had stayed together, had the prospect of being married for seventy years before one of them was likely to die," Stevenson says. "That's a long time."

And the years of social turbulence for these couples are far from over, she says. In the early years of their marriages, these couples were the first to confront the challenges of juggling two careers and balancing family and work. Now, as they face retirement, there are likely to be more battles over whether to keep working or start a new, slower-paced way of life. "They're not only trying to figure out what to do with the years ahead, but who they want to do it with," Stevenson says. "They're blazing a new way to live their lives past sixty, and they're figuring it out right now.

"Some will decide they have a lot of living left to do, and they may want to stop and reevaluate whether their marriage will continue to work for them over the next two decades," she says. "Some may make different choices about how to live the rest of their lives than they would if they thought they would die in a few years."

Rather than assuming divorces like the Gores' represent failure, it may make sense to cast their relationship as more than 35 years of success. "There is no way of knowing when things stopped working well for the Gores," Stevenson says, thinking back on the couple's famous kiss at the 2000 Democratic convention. "But none of us has any reason to believe it wasn't a good marriage for thirty or more years. I don't think we should look at a marriage that ends after forty years as a failure because it didn't make it to sixty or seventy years. It doesn't mean that most of those years weren't as special as we thought they were."

In any case, they are definitely a sign of what's to come. As the newlyweds of the '70s continue to age, we'll likely see record numbers of silver anniversaries reached, as well as a record number of silver divorces. Once again, the Gores will be trendsetters.

Source: Wingert and Kantrowitz 2010.

is about eight years. The proportion of divorces for couples married twenty years or more has increased. This "'silver divorce' is no longer rare, and that's particularly true for the baby-boom generation, born between 1946 and 1964," where more than half of all couples married in the 1970s were divorced by the time of their thirty-year anniversary (Kreider 2005; Wingert and Kantrowitz 2010, n.p.). These statistics need to be contextualized. The baby-boom generation is one of the largest in history, and subsequently, is the generation with the largest number of marriages. It is also the generation with the greatest rate of marriage. With that many people getting married, it's not surprising that we would find a high divorce rate as well. A recent *Newsweek* article discusses this in the Facts about Families box.

Most observers (though not all)[4] conclude that the divorce rate has stabilized, and even declined, for the time being (Teachman 2008a). Probably the most significant reason is the rise in the age at marriage. Fewer people are marrying at the vulnerable younger ages. Those who wait are likely to make better choices and to have the maturity and commitment to work through problems (Heaton 2002; Teachman, Tedrow, and Hall 2006).

Another reason is that better-educated and better-off working couples have had the economic tide in their favor. According to public policy professor Andrew Cherlin, "Families with two earners with good jobs have seen an improvement in their standard of living, which leads to less tension at home and lower probability of divorce," so long as the wife does not earn more than her husband. This is particularly true in white marriages, where the greater a woman's income, compared to her husband's, destabilizes the marriage (in "Divorce Rate" 2007; Teachman 2008, p. 16; Wilcox and Marquardt 2009, p. 44). Also, some societal adjustment to women's employment and dual-earner families now seems to have occurred (Teachman, Tedrow, and Hall 2006; Teachman 2008). Spouses "are learning how to negotiate marriages based on less rigid gender roles than in the past" (historian Stephanie Coontz in "Divorce Rate" 2007).

Some credit marriage education programs funded by the federal government for falling divorce rates. For poorer families, who could not afford family counseling on their own, the programs may have helped couples manage their marital relationships (Crary 2007b; "Divorce Rate" 2007). Moreover, some observers noted an increased determination on the part of children of a divorcing generation to make their own marriages work (Crary 2007b; Teachman, Tedrow, and Hall 2006).

[4] See Schoen and Canudas-Romo 2006; Teachman, Tedrow, and Hall 2006; and a comment by sociologist Andrew Cherlin in Hurley 2005, p. A7.

On a less enthusiastic note, demographers point out that divorce rates may have stabilized or declined because cohabitation has increased—if riskier relationships never become marriages, they never become divorces either. The fact remains that, since around 1980, there has been an unanticipated decline in divorce rates. Nevertheless, divorce rates remain high by historical standards.

Historians also point to the fact that marriage can be dissolved by death as well as divorce. The longer life span attained in the twentieth century gives people who remain married more time together. Married couples are now much more likely to reach their fortieth anniversary than they were at the beginning of the twentieth century, and children are more likely to be raised by both parents. In fact, couples who married "in the 1980s were less likely to part ways" than those who married during the 1970s, "and those marrying in the 1990s

Deciding to divorce is difficult. Couples struggle with concerns about the impact on children and feelings about their past hopes and current unhappiness.

and 2000s have been even more reluctant to divorce" (Stevenson 2010, n.p.).

Still, the continuation of a high incidence of divorce contributes to the increased prevalence of single-parent families. Children's living arrangements vary greatly by race and ethnicity, as Figure 15.3 indicates. Based on the most recent available data, we find that Asian and non-Hispanic white children are most apt to be living in two-parent families (with biological parents or a parent and stepparent). A majority of Hispanic, American Indian/Alaska Native, and Hawaiian/Pacific Islander children live with two parents, whereas just under a majority of black children are living in a single-mother household (Lugaila and Overturf 2004). There are many reasons why so many African American children live in single-mother households. We have discussed these reasons in previous chapters, and will continue to shed light on the issue in the next chapters of this book.

In summing up the statistics, we need to note that a high divorce rate does not mean that Americans have given up on marriage. It means that they find an unhappy marriage intolerable and hope to replace it with a happier one. But a consequence of remarriages—which have higher divorce rates than first marriages—is an emerging trend of **redivorce.** Many who divorce—and their children—can expect several emotionally significant transitions in family structure and lifestyle (Teachman 2008). (The stability of remarriages is addressed in greater detail in Chapter 16.)

In a context of a high though declining divorce rate, along with a positive view of marriage, why is it that married couples do divorce?

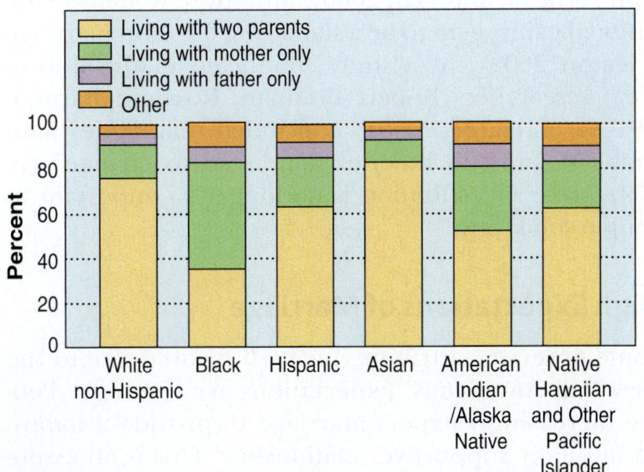

FIGURE 15.3 Living arrangements of children under eighteen by race/ethnicity, 2000. *Other* includes children who are living in the homes of relatives, in foster homes, or with other nonrelatives, or who are heads of their own households.

Source: Adapted from Lugaila and Overturf 2004, Table PHC-T-30b.

Why Are Couples Divorcing or Dissolving Their Unions?[5]

Various factors can bind married couples together: economic interdependence; legal, social, and moral constraints; and the spouses' relationship itself. Yet the binding strength of some of these factors has lessened. "[A]ll Western [and some non-Western] countries have been moving toward a less familistic set of attitudes and toward greater individual investments in self, career, and . . . personal growth and goals" (Goode 1993, p. 81; see also Gubernskaya 2010 for similar research findings).

Economic Factors

Traditionally, as we've seen, the family was a self-sufficient productive unit. Survival was far more difficult outside of families, so members remained economically bound to one another. But today, because family members no longer need one another for basic necessities, they are freer to divorce than they once were (Davis 2010).

Families are still somewhat interdependent economically. Even though marriage "has become less economically necessary . . . it remains economically advantageous in most cases" (Wilcox and Marquardt 2009, p. 42). As long as marriage continues to offer practical benefits, economic interdependence will help hold marriages together. The economic practicality of marriages varies according to several conditions.

Divorce and Social Class The higher the social class as defined in terms of education, income, and home ownership, the less likely a couple is to divorce. Income loss has been found to increase the likelihood of divorce, especially when it is the male who loses his income (Wilcox and Marquardt 2009, pp. 19, 34). Both the stress of living with inadequate finances and the failure to meet expectations for economic or educational attainment seem to contribute to marital instability (Rampell 2009a). This so concerns researchers that the general sense is that "the deep economic downturn of the last two years seems likely to pose a threat to the long-term health of working class marriage" (Wilcox and Marquardt 2009, p. 20). This situation, together with the tendency of low-income groups to marry relatively early, helps explain why less well-off families have the highest rates of marital disruption, including divorce, separation, and desertion; and why more advantaged groups, taking longer to marry, tend to have lower rates of marital disruption (Sassler, Cunningham, and Lichter 2009, p. 772).

[5] Although this research is specific to marriage, we think many of the dynamics apply to breakups of committed nonmarital relationships.

Some groups traditionally associated with a lower social class appear to have lower rates of divorce, even though they fit the general patterns of those in the lower strata of society. Latinos, for example, have lower rates of divorce. Researchers, however, have found that Latinos are more likely to separate but not divorce (Umaña-Taylor and Alfaro 2006), thus while Latinos may have divorce rates on par with whites, this hides the fact that many more Latinos may no longer be living as married couples.

Wives in the Labor Force The upward trend of divorce and the upward trend of women in the labor force have accompanied each other historically. But are they causally connected?

Much research, though not all, indicates that wives' employment in itself makes no difference in marital quality (Sayer and Bianchi 2000; Schoen, Rogers, and Amato 2006). As Chapter 11 points out, whether husbands are supportive of their wives' employment and share in housework *does* relate to wives' marital satisfaction. *Conflict theorists* hypothesize and research confirms that marital conflict may increase if women go into the job market but their husbands do not take over an equitable share of the domestic tasks. Symbolic interactionist research suggests this as well. For example, Arlie Hochschild's research on the "second shift" (discussed in Chapter 11) shows that even though women's employment, thus pay, has become an equally important component in the family income, the burden of household duties continues to be borne by working women, leading to marital conflict, and increasing the chances of divorce.

Although it may not affect marital quality, employment might nevertheless contribute to a divorce by giving an unhappily married woman the economic power, the increased independence, and the self-confidence to help her decide on divorce—called the **independence effect** (Sayer and Bianchi 2000; Teachman 2010). Some economists and sociologists posit that marriages are most stable and cohesive when husbands and wives have different and complementary roles—the husband the primary earner, while the wife bears and rears children and is the family's domestic and emotional specialist. Drawing on *exchange theory*, they assert that economic interdependency in marriage is a strong bond holding a marriage together (Becker 1981/1991; Oppenheimer 1997; Springer 2010). But this comes at a cost. New research into this issue finds that men who most strongly internalize the ideology of being the primary earner suffer greater physical and mental health issues because, as you have read elsewhere in this chapter and in this book, it is extremely difficult to thrive as a family on just the male income in our modern American economy. This promotes stress and feelings of impotence in men who adhere strongly to the male breadwinner ideology, ultimately leading, in many cases, to poor health outcomes for those men as they age (Springer 2010).

Most research does *not* support the premise that specialized roles and economic interdependence are necessary to marital stability. Moreover, there is an **income effect** to women's employment. Among low-income couples, a wife's earnings may actually help to hold the marriage together by counteracting the negative effects of poverty and economic insecurity on marital stability (Sayer and Bianchi 2000; Schoen, Rogers, and Amato 2006).

The effects of women's employment on marriage may depend on gender ideology. "[T]he sharp rise in the rates of divorce between 1965 and 1980 may have been at least partly a function of disjuncture between the expectations of spouses [at the time] and the reality of wives' labor market activities" (Teachman, Tedrow, and Hall 2006, p. 71). But for couples today, expectations of role sharing are common. To explore whether wives' employment has positive or negative effects on divorce proneness, researchers Sayer and Bianchi (2000) analyzed a national sample survey based on 3,339 female respondents interviewed around 1988 and again around 1994. When gender ideology and other variables related to likelihood of divorce were taken into account, there was no direct effect of women's employment on divorce. The desirability of the marriage relationship was a much more important factor in predicting divorce.

It is probably the case that there is considerable variety in the impact of women's employment and earnings on a marriage. It is also likely that the effect of wives' employment on marital stability is in transition (Teachman, Tedrow, and Hall 2006). Moreover, women's educational gains seem to be a stabilizing factor in marriage (Heaton 2002). In a study conducted in the Boston area, researchers Robert Brennan, Rosalind Barnett, and Karen Gareis (2001) concluded that "times have changed and the theories may need to change" (p. 179)—role specialization is no longer so important to couple solidarity.

High Expectations of Marriage

Some observers attribute our high divorce rate to the view that Americans' expectations are too high. People increasingly expect marriage to provide a happy, emotionally supportive relationship. This is an essential family function, yet too-high expectations for intimacy between spouses may push the divorce rate upward (Demo and Fine 2010). Research has found that couples whose expectations are more practical are more satisfied with their marriages than are those who expect completely loving and expressive relationships (Demo and Fine 2010; Plotnick 2007; see also

Oberlander et al. 2010 for a discussion of racial differences and marital expectation). Although many couples part for serious and specific reasons, others may do so because of unrealized expectations and general discontent.

Decreased Social, Legal, and Moral Constraints

"**Barriers to divorce** function to keep marriages intact even when attractiveness of the marital relationship is low and the attractiveness of alternatives to the relationship is high" (Knoester and Booth 2000, p. 81). But the social constraints that once kept unhappy partners from separating operate less strongly now.

The official posture of many—though not all—religions in the United States has become less critical of divorce than in the past. **No-fault divorce** laws, which exist in all fifty states,[6] have eliminated legal concepts of guilt and are a symbolic representation of how our society now views divorce. But it does not appear that changes in the law have themselves led to more divorce—in fact, divorces have actually fallen from "23 divorces per 1,000 married couples in 1979 to under 17 per 1,000 in 2005" (Coontz 2010a, p. A29; Wolfers 2006). Rather, legal change seems to have followed the trajectory of cultural attitudes and behavioral practice regarding divorce.[7]

To say that societal constraints against divorce no longer exist would be an overstatement; nevertheless, barriers have weakened. Knoester and Booth (2000) go so far as to conclude that "perhaps the concept of barriers has outlived its usefulness" (p. 98).

Attitudes toward Marriage Virtually no respondents in a study of marital cohesion mentioned stigma or disapproval as a barrier to divorce (Amato and Hohmann-Marriott 2007; Previti and Amato 2003). Emphasis on the emotional relationship over the institutional benefits of marriage results in marriage being viewed as not necessarily permanent (Cherlin 2004; Demo and Fine 2010). Friedrich Engels, a colleague of Karl Marx and an early family theorist, noted: "If only the marriage based on love is moral, then also only the marriage in which love continues" (1942 [1884], p. 73). The changing nature of marriage is a worldwide phenomenon as far as the industrialized world is concerned (Giddens 2007).

Self-Fulfilling Prophesy Defining marriage as semi-permanent can become a self-fulfilling prophecy, says Joshua Goldstein, a Princeton professor of sociology and public affairs: "Expectations of high divorce rates are in some ways self-fulfilling. . . . [T]hat's a partial explanation for why the rates went up in the 1970s." If partners behave as if their marriage could end, it is more likely that it will. But "as word gets out that rates have tempered or even begun to fall, '[i]t could lead to a self-fulfilling prophecy in the other direction'" (in Hurley 2005; see also Goldstein 1999).

Marital Conversation—More Struggle and Less Chitchat If barriers can no longer be counted on to preserve marital stability, the quality of the relationship becomes central to the survival of a marriage (Bodenmann, Ledermann, and Bradbury 2007; Ledermann, et al. 2010). That will "heighten the need for individuals to be committed to the union and the need to make a good marital match—with someone with whom it is possible to negotiate the details of everyday life without relying on the structural constraints generated by a highly gendered division of labor" (Teachman, Tedrow, and Hall 2006, p. 71). No longer are the normative role prescriptions for wives, husbands, or children taken for granted. Consequently, marriage entails continual negotiation and renegotiation among members about trivial matters as well as important ones. As one divorced woman put it,

> It had taken Howard and me only about ten minutes to pronounce the "I do's," but we would spend the next ten years trying to figure out who, exactly, was supposed to do what: Who was responsible for providing child care, finding babysitters and tutors, driving car pools, for which periods and where? (Blakely 1995, p. 37)

Intergenerational Transmission of Divorce

As discussed in Chapter 6, having parents who divorced increases the likelihood of divorcing (Amato and DeBoer 2001; Teachman, Tedrow, and Hall 2006). Researchers are not certain of the reasons for this. It is possible that (1) divorcing parents are models of divorce as a solution to marital problems, or (2) children of divorced parents are more likely to exhibit

[6] Some authorities say that "most states" have no-fault divorce laws (Buehler 1995; Stevenson and Wolfers 2007), whereas others cite all fifty states (Nakonezny, Shull, and Rodgers 1995). There is a gray area in that some "no-fault" divorce laws may require a specific period of separation rather than just a declaration by one of the parties that the marriage is over (Hakim 2006). Moreover, some states have retained fault divorce alongside no-fault. In those states, a spouse may choose to file for divorce under a fault provision, alleging that the other partner has committed whatever statutory faults are relevant to the state's marital dissolution laws.

[7] Nakonezny, Shull, and Rodgers (1995) published an article purporting to prove that no-fault divorce laws have played a causative role in increasing divorce rates. Sociologist Norval Glenn (1997) responded with an effective critique of their methodology, concluding that "the adoption of no-fault divorce in itself had very little direct effect on divorce rates" (p. 1,023; and see the response of Rodgers, Nakonezny, and Shull 1997). Further research supports the view that the passage of "unilateral" divorce laws does not account for divorce trends (Wolfers 2006).

personal behaviors that interfere with maintaining a happy marriage. There is also evidence that children of divorced parents marry at younger ages and are more likely to experience premarital cohabitation and births; these factors are associated with higher divorce rates (Heaton 2002; Teachman 2002a).

In a test of the two major hypotheses about **intergenerational transmission of divorce**, using longitudinal data, Amato and DeBoer (2001) found support for the *commitment to marriage* hypothesis. When parents remained married, they served as models of optimism about solving marital problems. A hypothesis about the importance of *parents as models of relationship skills and interpersonal behavior* was not supported in this study (although there is other evidence for it—e.g., Amato 1996). The conclusion of Amato and DeBoer's study is that "it is actual termination of the marriage rather than the disturbed family relationships that affects children. Divorce, rather than conflict, undermines children's faith in marriage" (p. 1,049).

As more parents divorce, more offspring would seem to be vulnerable to the intergenerational transmission of divorce. Yet research spanning the period between 1973 and 1996 finds a decline of almost 50 percent in the rate of intergenerational transmission of divorce. It may be that acceptance of divorce is now so widespread that having parental models is less significant for marital stability (Wolfinger 1999; see Li and Wu 2008 for their critique of this study). It would be nice to conclude on that hopeful note. But analysis of data from the Marital Instability Over the Life Course study suggests that "divorce has consequences for subsequent generations, including individuals not yet born at the time of the original divorce" (Amato and Cheadle 2005, p. 191). Problems evident in the grandchildren of the original divorcing couple include less education, more marital conflict, and poorer relationships with their parents.

On the other hand, research by Li and Wu, analyzing data from the National Survey of Families and Households found no evidence that parent's marital status impacted their children's marital commitment. This study does not deny that children of divorced parents are themselves more likely to divorce, but it demands caution in assuming causality (in the way Wolfinger does). Rather, the findings suggest simply that the longer couples are married, the greater their opportunity for conflict and divorce (Li and Wu 2008). Research on Swedish couples whose parents had divorced and remarried had similar findings, that is, no impact on children's divorce risk (Lyngstad and Engelhardt 2009).

Other Factors Associated with Divorce

Thus far in this section, we have looked at sociohistorical, cultural, and intrafamilial factors that encourage high divorce rates. Another way to think about divorce is to recognize that certain demographic and behavioral factors might be related to divorce rates. These include the following:

- *Remarried mates are more likely to divorce.*
- *Premarital sex and cohabitation before marriage increase the likelihood of divorce, but only when these take place with someone other than the future marital partner* (Heaton 2002; Teachman 2003). "There is evidence that the relationship between premarital cohabitation and divorce is waning" (Teachman, Tedrow, and Hall 2006, p. 74).
- *Premarital pregnancy and childbearing usually increase the risk of divorce in a subsequent marriage* (Heaton 2002; Teachman 2002b). However, if the biological parents marry, and especially if the birth occurred during cohabitation, "it might simply represent the continued evolution of the process of mate selection" (Teachman, Tedrow, and Hall 2006, p. 75).
- Young children stabilize marriage (Hetherington 2003). Hence, *remaining childfree is associated with a higher likelihood of divorce.*
- *Race and ethnicity are differentially associated with the chances of divorcing.* But "racial differences in dissolution are not well understood . . . and we know little about the underlying processes that may generate differences in divorce rates among racial and ethnic groups" (Teachman, Tedrow, and Hall 2006, p. 76).

A government survey reported that, as of 2001 (latest detailed data), the duration of marriage to particular anniversary dates was lower for black, Asian, and Hispanic women than for non-Hispanic whites. If, on the other hand, you look at lifetime experience of divorce for those over age fifteen (see Table 15.1), blacks have a relatively low percentage of "ever divorced," while that of whites is the highest (Kreider 2005, p. 12 and Appendix Table 1).

This discrepancy results from several patterns. Asian and Latino populations are relatively young, so they have not been married and at risk of divorce for as long. Their ultimate divorce rates are difficult to predict.

The black population is also younger than the white non-Hispanic population. But the percentage of blacks who have "ever divorced" is low in large part because of the black "retreat from marriage." "Blacks who marry are an increasingly select subgroup of all blacks . . . who are committed to marriage and therefore less likely to divorce" (Teachman 2002b, p. 345; see also Stevenson and Wolfers 2007). Economic and educational factors seem to play a much more significant role in marital stability among African Americans than in other racial/ethnic groups (Sweeney and Phillips 2004).

- Not surprisingly, *when marital partners are emotionally mature and possess good interpersonal communication skills, "they are better able to deal with the bumps along the road to marital survival"* (Hetherington 2003, p. 322).

The preceding are the connections scholars have made between divorce and other factors. Marital complaints given by the divorced themselves include the partner's infidelity, alcoholism, drug abuse, jealousy, moodiness, violence, low levels of trust, and, much less often, homosexuality, as well as perceived incompatibility and growing apart (Amato 2010; Fincham and Beach 2010). Counselors suggest that some common complaints—about money, sex, and in-laws, for example—are really arenas for acting out deeper conflicts, such as who will be the more powerful partner, how much autonomy each partner should have, and how emotions are expressed (Amato 2010; Amato and Hohmann-Marriot 2007). A general conclusion to be drawn from research is that deficiencies in the emotional quality of the marriage lead to divorce. "In Western cultures, happiness and satisfaction are integral to relationships and are thought to guide decisions regarding their future" (Rodrigues, Hall, and Fincham 2006, p. 97). The personal decision about divorce involves a process of balancing alternatives against the practical and emotional satisfactions of one's present union.

Gay and Lesbian Divorce

In 2005, Carolyn Conrad filed for dissolution of her civil union from Kathleen Peterson—what is noteworthy about this couple, is that they were in the first same-sex marriage in the State of Vermont (Barlow 2005). Like heterosexual relationships that end, the phenomenon of homosexual breakups have been around for a very long time, but some states are now allowing same-sex marriage, and some of those will end in divorce. Same-sex divorce is one of the benefits of same-sex marriage (where it exists) in that it provides for a formal, clearly recognized way to address couple breakup issues regarding property, child custody, and so on.

Currently, six states and the District of Columbia allow same-gender marriage, and three other states recognize the marriages from those six states. The 2007 American Community Survey showed approximately 340,000 married same-sex couples (Sherman 2009). The United States is beginning to see a smattering of divorce in states where same-sex marriage is legal. For example, in 2008, Massachusetts had 10,000 same-sex married couples, and "more than 100 gay divorces had been granted," while around 2 percent of the 8,666 civil unions in Vermont had been dissolved (Henry 2008, n.p.).

Table 15.1 Percentage of Men and Women (Fifteen Years and Older) Ever Divorced, by Race/Ethnicity and Gender, 2001

Race/Ethnicity	Men	Women[a]
White, non-Hispanic	23.3%	25.4%
Black[b]	18.8	20.1
Asian	8.8	10.4
Hispanic	12.7	15.9

[a]Women's rates of divorce are higher because they have usually married younger and so are at greater risk of experiencing a divorce than are men of the same ages.

[b]Over 40 percent of black men and women have never married, so are not at risk of divorce.

Source: Adapted from Kreider 2005, Table 1.

Thinking about Divorce: Weighing the Alternatives

Not everyone who thinks about divorce actually gets one. As divorce becomes a more available option, spouses may compare the benefits of their union to the projected consequences of not being married.

Marital Happiness, Barriers to Divorce, and Alternatives to the Marriage

One model of deciding about divorce, derived from exchange theory (see Chapter 2) by social psychologist George Levinger, posits that spouses assess their marriage in terms of the *rewards* of marriage, *alternatives* to the marriage (possibilities for remarriage or fashioning a satisfying single life), and *barriers* to divorce (Levinger 1965, 1976). Here we look at **Levinger's model of divorce decisions** from the perspective of the person considering divorce.

Respondents to the Marital Instability Over the Life Course surveys named children, along with religion and lack of financial resources, as *barriers* to divorce in open-ended interviews (Previti and Amato 2003). Indeed, another study found that both mothers and fathers anticipated that "divorce would worsen their economic situation and their abilities to fulfill the responsibilities of being a parent" (Poortman and Seltzer 2007, p. 265). However, when researchers Chris Knoester and Alan Booth (2000) examined *quantitative data* from these Marital Instability Over the Life Course surveys, they found that only three of nine barriers studied were associated with a lower likelihood of divorce: (1) when the wife's income was a smaller percentage of the family income, (2) when church attendance was high, or (3) when the couple had a new child.

When parents consider divorce, they often think about the potential impact on their children—and that is a barrier to divorce.

Other research evidence shows that young children do serve as a barrier to divorce, especially when one of the children is a boy (Leonhardt 2003). Anticipated economic loss was not as important as parenting concerns. Affection for their children and concern about the children's welfare after divorce discourage some parents from dissolving their marriage. This concern sometimes leads to delaying an intended divorce (Furstenberg and Kiernan 2001; Heaton 2002; Poortman and Seltzer 2007).

Long marriages are less likely to end in divorce. One reason for this, in addition to the marital bond itself, is that common economic interests and friendship networks increase over time and help stabilize the marriage at times of tension (Brown, Orbuch, and Maharaj 2010). When divorce does occur in a longer marriage, it may be partly related to dissatisfaction with one's marital relationship at the onset of the empty nest. After all, people are living longer and are "not only trying to figure out what to do with the years ahead, but who they want to do it with" (Wingert and Kantrowitz 2010, n.p.).

Although some barriers do seem to have an impact on decisions to divorce, it is the *rewards* of marriage—love, respect, friendship, and good communication—that are most effective in keeping marriages together. "Generally, marriages that have built up positive emotional bank accounts through respect, mutual support, and affirmation of each person's worth are more likely to survive" (Hetherington 2003, p. 322).

"Would I Be Happier?"

Alternatives, the third element of Levinger's theory, was found to be the least important in decisions to divorce (Previti and Amato 2003). Yet, some married people may ask themselves whether they would be happier if they were to divorce. This is not an easy question to answer. Some people may prefer to stay single after divorce, but many partners probably weigh their chances for a remarriage.

Some research finds that leaving a bad marriage may have a positive outcome regardless of whether the individual remarries. A British study found people to be less happy one year after separation, but by one year after the divorce, both men and women were happier than they had been while married (Gardner and Oswald 2006).

A study of 1,755 whites in Detroit found that higher levels of depression among the divorced were not apparent among those who saw themselves as escaping marriages with serious, long-term problems (Aseltine and Kessler 1993). Other research (Ross 1995) used data from a national sample of 2,031 adults to compare depression levels among those with no partners and those in relationships of varying quality; still other research, the Health and Retirement Study, shows a wide variety of chronic mental and physical health conditions associated with people who were divorced (Hughes and Waite 2009).

Additionally, researchers compared data from the waves of the National Survey of Families and Households and found, like the other studies, that emotional well-being declines after divorce. What was most interesting about this study, however, are the findings that suggest well-being declines (and improves little) after a divorce regardless of the unhappiness or even violence associated with the now-dissolved marriage. They note,

> our results do not support the hypothesis that disruption of a marriage rated as unhappy, even among those who experienced violence in their marriage, leads to improvements in emotional well-being. In no case did those who divorced or separated show higher well-being than those who remained married, and on some measures they show lower well-being.
>
> We would expect the largest improvements in well-being, should they appear, among those who ended a marriage that they thought was unhappy and entered another. However, on none of the dimensions of well-being that we examined do we see improvements in emotional well-being for those who ended one marriage and formed another, compared to those who remained married. Clearly, if one of the goals of ending a marriage with which one is unhappy is to improve one's emotional well-being, this goal is not typically reached. (Waite, Luo, and Lewin 2009, p. 209)

It is a paradox—people without a partner are likely to be depressed—but those in unhappy relationships are likely to be even more depressed. Marriage can and often does provide emotional support, sexual gratification, companionship, and economic and practical benefits, including better health. But unhappy marriages do not provide these benefits and may be a factor in poorer health (Elias 2004). "[I]t appears that at any particular point in time most marriages are 'good marriages' and that such marriages have a strong positive effect on well-being and that 'bad marriages' have a strong negative effect on well-being" (Gove, Style, and Hughes 1990, p. 14).

Can This Marriage Be Saved? In some cases, partners might be happier trying to improve their relationship rather than divorcing. "Can This Marriage Be Saved?" is the title of a series that ran in the Ladies Home Journal beginning in the 1950s—articles about couples in troubled marriages who were counseled about how to save their marriages. In this spirit, sociologist Linda Waite reports that couples may be in the lowest grouping on marital satisfaction, yet, if they don't divorce, five years later, two-thirds of the unhappily married couples she and her colleagues studied described themselves as "very happy." Those who divorce do not report themselves as very happy later: "If you are playing the odds in favor of happiness, . . . 'staying married is the better bet'" (Waite, quoted in Peterson 2001, p. 8D).

A recently completed ten-year longitudinal study of newly married couples shows that early support in a young couple's life enhanced their marital satisfaction and helped reduce conflict and marital dissolution (Verhofstadt, Ickes, and Buysse 2010; Sullivan et al. 2010). The kinds of support in the form of social support and individual communication behaviors toward one another is key. The researchers note that "how spouses respond to one another's everyday disclosures and requests for support may be more consequential than how they negotiate their differences of opinion in producing behavioral changes that foreshadow later marital satisfaction and stability" (Sullivan et al. 2010, p. 640). The researcher noted specifically that social support is the most important predictor of long-term marital satisfaction. The kinds of support needed for long-term marital satisfaction include, for example, asking for and offering validation of feelings, and asking for and offering understanding and compassion rather than anger and contempt when disagreements arise (Sullivan et al. 2010, p. 641).

Improvements in those marriages came about through the passage of time (children got older, jobs or other problems improved); because partners' efforts to work on problems, make changes, and communicate better were effective; or because individual partners made personal changes (travel, work, hobbies, or emotional disengagement) that enabled them to live relatively happily despite an unsatisfying marriage. In fact, a new study suggests that people who remain in an unsatisfying marriage are less depressed than those who leave their marriages. These unhappily marrieds also tend to have healthier emotional lives than even those who divorce and eventually remarry (Waite et al. 2002; Waite, Luo, and Lewin 2009, p. 205).

One must decide, then, whether divorce represents a healthy step away from an unhappy relationship that cannot be satisfactorily improved or is an illusory way to solve what in reality are personal problems. Going to a marriage counselor may help partners become more aware of the consequences of divorce so that they can make this decision more knowledgeably and not by default.

Marital Separation Nearly two and a half percent of married couples in the United States were separated in 2008 (U.S. Census Bureau 2010b, Table 66). Some marital partners who have separated do make efforts to reconcile. Little research has been done on marital separation. But "each year [it appears] that a substantial number of separated women try to save their marriage" (Wineberg 1996, p. 308). Wineberg's study, using a sample of white women from the 1987 National Survey of Families and Households, found that 44 percent of the separated women attempted reconciliation. Half of the resumptions of marriage that followed took place within a month, suggesting that those separations may have been impulsive and soon regretted. Virtually no marriages were resumed after eight months of separation.

Only one-third of the reconciliations "took"—that is, resulted in a continued marriage (Wineberg 1996). For a majority of individuals, first separation from the spouse denoted permanent dissolution (Binstock and Thornton 2003). Researcher Howard Wineberg cautions that "not all separated couples should be encouraged to reconcile since a reconciliation does not ensure a happy marriage or that the couple will be married for very long" (p. 308).

Stable Unhappy Marriages From time to time, researchers have taken up the question of what happens to couples who are distanced, unhappy, or in conflict if they don't divorce (e.g., Waite, Luo, and Lewin 2009). It is, however, "surprising" that "long-term low-quality marriage . . . has received relatively little attention" (Hawkins and Booth 2005, p. 451). Contradicting other research noted elsewhere in this chapter, Hawkins and Booth's study followed unhappy marriages for twelve years and compared people in unhappy marriages to divorced single and remarried individuals. "Divorced individuals who remarry have greater overall happiness, and those who divorce and remain unmarried have greater levels of life satisfaction, self-esteem, and overall health than unhappily married people. . . . We suggest that unhappily married people who dissolve low-quality marriages likely have greater odds of improving their well-being than those remaining in such unions" (p. 468). The differences in findings you are reading in these sections are useful learning opportunities. What the seemingly contradictory findings remind us of is that social scientists asking different questions to different people at different times in their life may elicit vastly different findings than other social scientists doing the same kind of research. This is good scholarship because it encourages us to critically examine the methodologies used in each study so that we can find where those differences in outcomes might lie.

Is Divorce a Temporary Crisis or a Permanent Stress?

Initially, studies portrayed divorce as a temporary crisis, with adjustment completed in two to four years. Some scholars now consider divorce to be a lifetime chronic stress for both children and adults (Hughes and Waite 2009; Waite, Luo, and Lewin 2009). Although outcomes vary, divorce researcher E. Mavis Hetherington maintains that 70 percent of those who obtain a divorce have a "good enough" postdivorce adjustment (Hetherington and Kelly 2002). In fact, 20 percent of women in this study embraced their new autonomy, developing self-confidence and working toward enhancing their lives (Demo and Fine 2010, p. 114). "Most men, women, and children adapt to their new lives reasonably well within 2–3 years if they are not confronted with continued or additional stresses" (Hetherington 2003, p. 322).

It appears likely that both temporary crisis and chronic stress are outcomes of divorce—some divorced people are rather permanently derailed from an economically and emotionally comfortable life, whereas others are mostly recovered after several years. Of the latter—those who may be considered "recovered"—some have diminished well-being in some respects, whereas others arrive at a higher level of life satisfaction (Amato 2000, 2003; 2010; Hetherington and Kelly 2002). Difficulties and adjustments don't seem to vary much by race or ethnicity (Amato 2000; 2010). They do vary by whether or not the couple are parents. "Generally . . . [for childless couples] recovery is almost always rather swift" (Braver, Shapiro, and Goodman 2006, p. 313).

Getting the Divorce

One of the reasons it feels so good to be engaged and newly married "is the rewarding sensation that out of the whole world, you have been selected. One of the reasons that divorce feels so awful is that you have been de-selected" (Bohannan 1970, p. 33). Anthropologist Paul Bohannan analyzed the divorce experience in terms of six different facets, or "stations": the emotional, the legal, the community, the psychic, the economic, and the co-parental divorce. Experience in each of these realms varies from one individual to another; some stations, such as the co-parental, do not characterize every divorce. Yet the six stations capture the complexity of the divorce experience. In this section, we will examine the first three stations just listed; we will explore the economic and co-parental aspects of divorce in greater detail later in this chapter, and then make brief mention of the psychic divorce.

The Emotional Divorce

Emotional divorce involves withholding positive emotions and communications from the relationship (Vaughan 1986; Dupuis 2009), typically replacing these with alienating actions and words. Partners no longer reinforce but, rather, undermine each other's self-esteem through endless large and small betrayals: responding with blame rather than comfort to a spouse's disastrous day, for instance, or refusing to go to a party given by the spouse's family, friends, or colleagues. As emotional divorce intensifies, betrayals become greater.

In a failing marriage, both spouses feel profoundly disappointed, misunderstood, and rejected (Brodie 1999). The couple may want the marriage to continue for many reasons—continued attachment, fear of being alone, obligations to children, the determination to be faithful to marriage vows—yet they may hurt each other as they communicate their frustration by look, posture, and tone of voice.

Not all divorced people wanted or were ready to end their marriage, of course. It may have been their spouse's choice. Initiating and noninitiating partners tend to talk about their reasons in different terms. The initiator of the divorce typically invokes a "vocabulary of individual needs" while the noninitiating partner speaks in terms of "familial commitment" (Hopper 1993).[8]

Women are more often the initiators of a divorce, regardless of how long the marriage has endured (Brinig and Allen 2000; Coontz 2010b). The initiator describes many and ongoing complaints that essentially reprise the issues and events described in this chapter and others: conflict over sharing domestic work; infidelity, physical and emotional abuse; alcoholism; political and recreational differences; sexual tensions, disagreements about children; and so on. Whatever the specifics, the initiator decides that the marriage will never be what she or he wants: "'My needs were not being met'; 'I wasn't being fulfilled'" (Hopper 1993, p. 807). The noninitiating partner, who may have been fairly ambivalent

[8] This analysis references sociologist C. Wright Mills's (1940) *vocabularies of motive*, a concept that students of sociology or communication may have encountered before. The idea is that individuals construct accounts to justify their actions. These are not necessarily their actual motives, of which they may be somewhat unaware, but narratives of explanation.

and uncertain about the marriage as well, begins to point to the good in the marriage: "'You need to do something to keep this relationship going'; 'you tell someone you're going to be there forever, then you're going to work on it'" (p. 809).

Not surprisingly, research shows that the degree of trauma a divorcing person suffers usually depends on whether that person or the spouse wanted the dissolution because the one feeling "left" experiences a greater loss of control and has much mourning yet to do—the divorce-seeking spouse may have already worked through his or her sadness and distress (Amato 2000; Braver, Shapiro, and Goodman 2006). Even for those who actively choose to divorce, however, divorce and its aftermath may be unexpectedly painful.

The Legal Divorce

A **legal divorce** is the dissolution of the marriage by the state through a court order terminating the marriage. The principal purpose of the legal divorce is to dissolve the marriage contract so that emotionally divorced spouses can conduct economically separate lives and be free to remarry.

Two aspects of the legal divorce make marital breakup painful. First, divorce, like death, creates the need to grieve. But the usual divorce in court is a rational, unceremonial exchange that takes only a few minutes. Divorcing individuals may feel frustrated by their lack of control over a process in which the lawyers are the principals. In one study of divorced women, virtually all had complaints about their lawyers and the legal system (Arendell 1986). A myriad of websites are dedicated to women discussing those complaints (for example, divorcedwomenonline.com; womensenews.org).

A second aspect of the legal divorce that aggravates conflict and misery is the adversary system. Under our judicial system, lawyers advocate their client's interest only and are eager to "get the most for my client" and "protect my client's rights." Opposing attorneys are not trained to and ethically are not even supposed to balance the interests of the parties and strive for the outcome that promises most mutual benefit.

No-Fault Divorce A major change in the legal process of divorce has been the introduction of no-fault divorce. This revision of divorce law was intended to reduce the hostility of the partners and to permit an individual to end a failed marriage readily. Before the 1970s, the fault system predominated. Parties seeking divorce had to prove that they had "grounds" for divorce, such as the spouse's adultery, mental cruelty, or desertion. Obtaining a divorce might require falsifying these facts.

A fault divorce required a legal determination that one party was guilty and the other innocent. The one judged guilty rarely received custody of the children, and the judgment largely influenced property settlement and alimony awards, as well as the opinions of friends and family (Coontz 2010a; Stevenson and Wolfers 2007; Vlosky and Monroe 2002). Such a protracted legal battle of adversaries increased hostility and diminished chances for a civil postdivorce relationship and successful co-parenting.

Some researchers suggest that the no-fault system of divorce began in Oklahoma in 1953. The reason for concluding 1953 as the date is the way the law was written. The 1953 Oklahoma law allows for a divorce if one party believed there was "irretrievable breakdown and/or irreconcilable differences and/or incompatibility" in the marriage, regardless of what the other person believes or wants (Vlosky and Monroe 2002; Nakonezny, Shull, and Rodgers 1995; Sepler 1981). Other research posits the beginning of no-fault divorce in California as 1970, and continuing until all states passed no-fault legislation. Divorce was redefined as "marital dissolution" and no longer required a legal finding of a "guilty" party and an innocent one. Instead, a marriage became legally dissolvable when one or both partners declared it to be "irretrievably broken" or characterized by "irreconcilable differences." No-fault divorce is sometimes termed **unilateral divorce** because one partner can secure the divorce even if the other wants to continue the marriage.

A final note on the legal divorce is that, by definition, it applies only to marriage. There is no legal forum in which cohabitants, whether heterosexual or gay/lesbian, may obtain a divorce. Some couples may be cohabiting precisely to avoid the prospect of going to court should their relationship sour. However, they are likely to find that the absence of a venue in which to resolve separation-related disputes in a standardized way is also a problem. (The legal side of living together is discussed in more detail in Chapter 8.)

Courts in some states are beginning to grant orders of legal separation or orders of dissolution of civil unions to the nonmarried (Hartocollis 2007; "Iowa Supreme Court" 2007). These may apply the same principles of property arrangements, child custody, and child support to nonmarital cohabiting relationships (Hartocollis 2007). Cohabiting couples may also avail themselves of mediation services.

Divorce Mediation **Divorce mediation** is an alternative, nonadversarial means of dispute resolution by which a couple, with the assistance of a mediator or mediators (frequently a lawyer–therapist team), negotiate the settlement of their custody, support, property, and visitation issues. In the process, it is hoped that they learn a pattern of dealing with each other that will enable them to resolve future disputes. Mediation is recommended or mandatory in all states for child custody and visitation disputes before litigation can be commenced (Comerford 2006).

Early research indicated that couples who use divorce mediation have less relitigation, feel more satisfied with the process and the results, and report better relationships with ex-spouses and children (Bailey and McCarty 2009; Holtzworth-Munroe, Applegate, and D'Onofrio 2009). Recent research summaries are less enthusiastic: "Overall, the corpus of available research does not indicate that mediation (relative to more traditional litigation) serves to either increase or decrease general psychological distress or . . . improve co-parenting relations." However, people were more satisfied with mediation than litigation in child custody cases: "Your feelings were understood" and "Your rights were protected" (Sbarra and Emery 2006, pp. 556–57).

There are arguments for and against mediation in child custody. Women's advocacy groups have claimed that mediation may be biased against females in that they may be less assertive in negotiations. It is also argued that mediators take insufficient account of prior domestic violence (Comerford 2006; Freeman 2008, note 16). Judith Wallerstein believes that the positive effects of divorce mediation for children may be overstated, but new practitioners are attempting to level the field (2003, p. 80; see also Freeman 2008 for a discussion on positive and negative qualities of mediation). Yet it does seem that "[m]ediation produces higher levels of compliance [with court decisions] and lower relitigation rates than litigation or attorney-negotiated settlement." It is less costly and generally less time-consuming than litigation (Comerford 2006; Crary 2007a).

The Community Divorce

Marriage is a public anno-uncement to the community that two individuals have joined their lives. Marriage usually also joins extended families and friendship networks and simultaneously removes individuals from the world of dating and mate seeking. The **community divorce** refers to ruptures of relationships and changes in social networks that come about as a result of divorce. At the same time, divorce provides the opportunity for forming new ties.

Kin No More? Given the frequency of divorce, most extended families find themselves touched by it. Grandparents fear losing touch with grandchildren, and this does happen. In response, all fifty states have passed grandparent visitation laws. However, a Supreme Court decision struck down Washington's law (*Troxel v. Granville* 2000) because it was considered to interfere with parents' rights to determine how their children are to be raised. The status of other states' laws is uncertain; some courts have allowed grandparents visitation rights in certain circumstances (Dao 2005; Henderson and Moran 2001; Hsia 2002; Stoddard 2006).

In favorable circumstances, grandparents very commonly become closer to grandchildren, as adult children turn to grandparents for help or grandchildren seek emotional support (Henderson et al. 2009; Ruiz and Silverstein 2007). Researchers and therapists have concluded that

> these relationships work best when family members do not take sides in the divorce and make their primary commitment to the children. Grandparents can play a particular role, especially if their marriages are intact: symbolic generational continuity and living proof to children that relationships can be lasting, reliable, and dependable. Grandparents also convey a sense of tradition and a special commitment to the young. . . . Their encouragement, friendship, and affection has special meaning for children of divorce; it specifically counteracts the children's sense that all relationships are unhappy and transient. (Wallerstein and Blakeslee 1989, p. 111; see also Henderson et al. 2009 for a discussion on the importance of grandmother/grandchild relationships and adolescent postdivorce psychological adjustment)

Divorce affects the extended family as well as the nuclear one. In some families, grandparents may lose touch with grandchildren, whereas in others, they may become more central figures of support and stability.

Indeed, children who were close to their grandparents had fewer problems adjusting to their parents' divorce (Connidis 2009; Ruiz and Silverstein 2007).

Of course, more and more grandparents' own marriages are not intact today. Nevertheless, one can assume that even a loving, divorced grandparent could add to the support system of a grandchild of divorce.

Women are more likely than men to retain in-law relationships after divorce, particularly if they had been in close contact before the divorce and if the in-law approves of the divorce (Connidis 2009). Relationships between former in-laws are more likely to continue when children are involved. In any event, grandchildren were most likely to remain closest to maternal grandparents, as mothers typically grew closer to and relied more on their parents after divorce (Connidis 2009; Henderson et al. 2009).

Divorce and remarriage tend to connect chains of people in complex kinship systems. One study looked at the general character of postdivorce extended-kin relationships. This study found that in half the cases, the kinship system included **relatives of divorce** and *relatives of remarriage* (C. Johnson 1988, p. 168). These would be familial connections established through networks of marriage and remarriage: grandparents of half siblings, for example. A photo in this chapter portrays a young boy with his *eight* grandparents, all in attendance at his basketball game (Harmon 2005a).

After divorce, adult children's relationships with their own parents may change. According to one study:

> Members of both generations had to revise their expectations of the other, and members of the older generation found themselves in a situation of having to give more of themselves to a child than they had expected to do at their stage of life. They were often forced into a parenting role, and this greater involvement provided more opportunity to observe and comment on their adult child's life. . . . Adult children were more likely to feel that parents should be available to help them with their emotional problems than their parents felt was appropriate. Divorcing children did not want their parents to interfere in child rearing or offer unsolicited advice, while their parents felt they could voice their concerns. (C. Johnson 1988, pp. 190–91)

There was considerable variation in these relationships within the sample of fifty-two adult–child dyads followed over several years in Johnson's study. But most older parents espoused "modern values of personal freedom and self-fulfillment" (p. 191); that is, they did not criticize the decision to divorce from a traditional perspective.

Friends No More? A change in marital status is likely to mean changes in one's community of friends. Divorced people may feel uncomfortable with their friends who are still married because activities are done in pairs; the newly single person may also feel awkward. Couple friends may fear becoming involved in a conflict over allegiances, and they may experience their own sense of loss. Moreover, if married friends have some ambivalence about their own marriages, a divorce in their social circle may cause them to feel anxious and uncomfortable. A common outcome is a mutual withdrawal.

Like many newly married people, those who are newly divorced must find new communities to replace old friendships that are no longer mutually satisfying. The initiative for change may in fact come not only from rejection or awkwardness in old friendships but also from the divorced person's finding friends who share with him or her the new concerns and emotions of the divorce experience. Priority may also go to new relationships with people of the opposite sex; for the majority of divorced and widowed people, building a new community involves dating again.

Deciding knowledgeably whether to divorce means weighing what we know about the consequences of divorce. The next section examines the economic consequences of divorce.

The Economic Consequences of Divorce

Social scientists and policy makers worry about the economic consequences of divorce, especially for children, but also for women and men.

Divorce, Single-Parent Families, and Poverty

Figure 15.4 displays the proportions of children who were living in poverty in 2007, for the largest racial/ethnic groups, comparing poverty rates by family type. As you can see, 43 percent of all children who reside in mother-only, single-parent families live in poverty. This compares to 9 percent of those living in married-couple families. The relationship between family type and poverty is consistent across racial/ethnic categories.

Another consistent research finding is that divorce is related to a woman's and sometimes a man's lowered economic status. "Divorce carr[ies] economic costs" (Sayer 2006, p. 392).

Husbands, Wives, and Economic Divorce

Upon divorce, a couple undergoes an **economic divorce** in which they become distinct economic units, each with its own property, income, control of expenditures, and responsibility for taxes, debts, and so on.

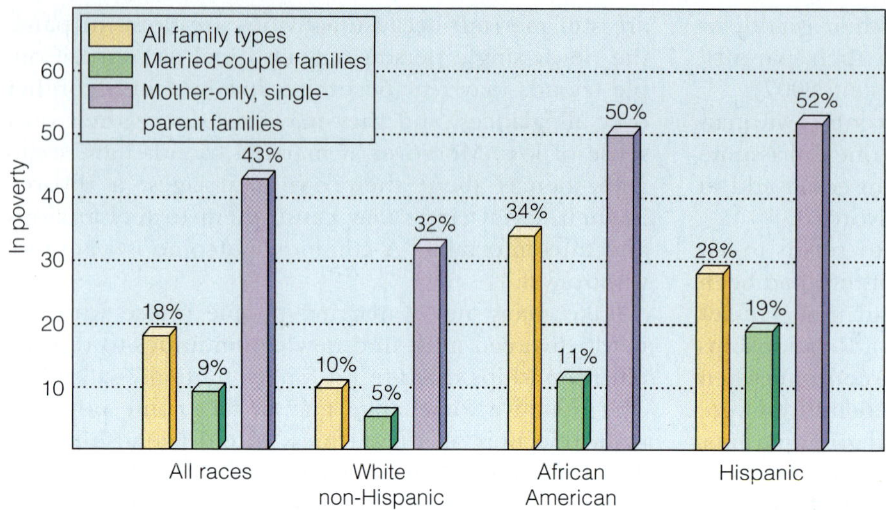

FIGURE 15.4 Poverty status of families with children under eighteen by race/ethnicity and type of family, 2007 (percentage of families with incomes below the poverty level).

Source: Adapted from U.S. Federal Interagency Forum on Child and Family Statistics 2009, Table ECON1A.

Women Lose Financially in Divorce Sociologist Lenore Weitzman addressed the financial plight of divorced women and their children in her landmark book *The Divorce Revolution* (1985). She compared the postdivorce economic decline of women with children to the improved standard of living of ex-husbands.[9] Women and their children experience declines in family income of between 27 percent and 51 percent (depending on the research study). An even more telling statistic is the **income-to-needs ratio**—that is, how well income meets financial needs. Women and their children experience a decline of 20 to 36 percent in their income-to-needs ratio (Meadows, McLanahan, and Knab 2009; Sayer 2006).

A study that compared former spouses in terms of their postdivorce economic situations found that wives with custody of children had only 56 percent of the income relative to needs that noncustodial fathers had (Bianchi, Subaiya, and Kahn 1999). Another study, which differentiated between income quintiles, found that mothers whose income was in the top two quintiles suffered little income loss (with some experiencing economic gains) after the divorce, whereas mothers in the bottom three economic quintiles experienced large losses after the divorce (Ananat and Michaels 2007). Additionally, Braver, Shapiro, and Goodman (2006) contend that the differences in income and taxation rates between custodial and noncustodial parents generally lead to better financial circumstances for custodial mothers than noncustodial fathers. Regardless of the fineness with which social researchers split the proverbial hair, there remain important differences between male and female outcomes of a divorce.

A fundamental reason for the income disparity between ex-husbands and their former wives is men's and women's unequal wages and different work patterns (Hartmann, English, and Hayes 2010; Oldham 2008a). Despite women's greater participation in the labor force, any reduction in employment during childbearing and child-raising years means they have forgone opportunities for career development. "[A]lthough women are moving toward greater equality with men in the labor market, they remain more economically vulnerable when marriages end" (Bianchi, Subaiya, and Kahn 1999, p. 196).

It is also the case that women who are custodial parents must depend on child support from the other parent to meet their new single-parent family's expenses. Child support amounts are set relatively low, and much child support remains unpaid (as discussed in a later section of this chapter).

A third reason has to do with the typical division of property in divorce. Most state laws require a division of property that is specified as "equitable" (Oldham 2008b). Behind the idea of a fair property settlement run two legal assumptions: The first is that marriage is an economic partnership. A man could not earn the money he earns without the moral support and domestic work of his wife, whether or not she was employed during the marriage. A minority of states have community property laws based on the premise that family property belongs equally to both partners. The remaining states, the majority, have laws promising a divorced wife either an equitable (fair) or an equal (exactly the same) share of the marital property.

A second assumption is that property consists of such tangible items as a house or money in the bank, or other investments. Yet, except for very wealthy people, the valuable "new property" (Glendon 1981) in today's society is the earning power of a professional degree, a business or managerial position, work experience, a skilled trade, or other human capital. When property is divided in divorce, the wife may get an equal share of tangible property, such as a house or savings, but usually that does not put her on an equal footing with

[9] Weitzman's book brought attention to the different economic outcomes of divorce for men and women. Her specific figures were later proven to be erroneous, but a reanalysis of her data still showed a substantial loss for divorced women compared to a slight gain for men (R. Peterson 1996).

© Jeff Greenberg/ PhotoEdit

Women and their children experience a substantial decline in their standard of living after a divorce. They may need to move to less-expensive—and less-desirable—housing and away from their former neighborhood, school, and friends. Many men also experience a decline in standard of living.

her former husband for the future. An even split of the marital property may not be truly equitable if one partner has stronger earning power and benefits than the other, and if the parent with custody of the children has a heavier child support burden in actuality (even paid-up child support is typically not adequate to meet children's expenses). Put another way, dividing property may be easy compared to ensuring that both partners and their children will have enough to live on comfortably after divorce or at least will be on a similar financial footing. "Most women would have to make heroic leaps in the labor or marriage market to keep their losses as small as the losses experienced by the men from whom they separate" (McManus and DiPrete 2001, p. 266).

In part, this situation results from the assumption of legislators and the courts that women and men would come to have equal earning power. When divorce laws were reformed in the 1970s, self-support for both parties was presumed. Some financially dependent spouses have been awarded short-term **spousal support** or *maintenance*[10] in the form of *rehabilitative alimony*, in which the ex-husband pays his ex-wife maintenance for a few years while she prepares to reenter the job market. In many, perhaps most, cases, this is not truly enough to enable the woman to reestablish herself financially, and it is not that commonly awarded in any case (Oldham 2008a).

Some activists have argued that wives who left the labor force to raise children or to help with their husband's career deserve not alimony but an *entitlement*, the equivalent of severance pay for the work they did at home during the length of a marriage (Weitzman 1985). (Social Security provisions do allow an ex-wife who had been married at least ten years to collect 50 percent of the amount paid her ex-husband.) Given the risk of divorce, a recent spate of books have warned today's career women not to "opt out" of the labor force to nurture small children, but to maintain employability (Bennetts 2007; Hirschman 2006). In the future, more women who are divorced *will* have a history of almost continual employment and a current job, although they are still likely to have the heavier expenses of a custodial parent.

Anticipating the difference that the stronger labor force attachment and likely higher earnings of younger women may make, one review article takes the position that the long-term divorce disadvantage for women compared to men is, or at least will be, less striking than it now appears (Braver, Shapiro, and Goodman 2006). These authors argue that more research using long-term data is needed and should include custodial and noncustodial parents' differences in tax status and a father's expenses during visitation. They argue that "[i]t is premature to say exactly how the two parents compare in [postdivorce] economic well-being" (p. 324).

Some Men Win, Most Lose Financially in Divorce In fact, the postdivorce economic situation of men has undergone some rethinking. Circumstances have changed since the 1970s, and men and women are both likely to be family earners now. A study covering the years between 1980 and 1993 (McManus and DiPrete 2001) found that most men lose economically in divorce (or in a separation from a cohabiting union). The chief reason for their declining standard of living is the loss of the partner's income. Depending on the study, married men experience a decline in *family income* of from 8 percent to 41 percent; cohabiting men's drop in income is comparable (Sayer 2006). Additional studies examining child support, income, and taxes, suggest that fathers actually suffer significant financial losses in a divorce. The analysis suggests that the financial loss has less to do with a

[10] These terms have replaced *alimony* to describe a former spouse's support payment to his or her ex-spouse following divorce. Historically, alimony was a payment of husband to wife resting on the assumption that the contract of marriage included a husband's lifetime obligation to support his wife and children. Traditionally, of course, the wife had not been employed, but instead had primary responsibility for making a home and bearing and raising children. Popular myth had it that ex-wives lived comfortably on high alimony awards. But in reality, courts awarded alimony to only a small minority of wives.

In 1979, the U.S. Supreme Court determined that laws against sex discrimination should make alimony gender-neutral—in essence, transforming the basis for spousal support from the common-law tradition of husbands' and wives' specialized roles into an economic partnership model. Along with this and other reforms of divorce law came a presumption that spouses should be self-supporting after divorce (Buehler 1995, pp. 102–11).

decline due to loss of a partner's income, and more to do with taxation rates for noncustodial parents—usually fathers. The argument is that the custodial parent is taxed differently (taxed at lower rates), and, coupled with child support, receives benefits that increase financial benefits, whereas the noncustodial parent is now taxed at a much higher rate because (usually) he has no dependents to claim (Braver, Shapiro, and Goodman 2006).

However, though family income drops for a man when he is no longer part of a couple, so do his expenses; his household is now smaller. Consequently, his *income-to-needs ratio* rises anywhere from 8 percent to 41 percent, even taking child support into account (Sayer 2006). But usually, that is not enough to maintain his previous standard of living and quality of material life.

To sum up, though there are no women "winners" in divorce, a majority of men lose, too. Only men who had contributed at least 80 percent of their family's predivorce income in a traditional marriage gain economically in divorce. Still, to continue the gender comparison, "[s]tudies that focus on women's outcomes have yet to unearth any comparable core of women who gain financially following union dissolution" (McManus and DiPrete 2001, p. 266).

Child Support

Child support involves money paid by the noncustodial to the custodial parent to support the children of a now-ended marital, cohabiting, or sexual relationship. Because mothers retain custody in the preponderance of cases, the vast majority of those ordered to pay child support are fathers.

For many years, the child support awarded to the **custodial parent** was often not paid, and states made little effort to collect it on the parent's behalf. Policy makers' concerns about poverty, the economic consequences of divorce for women, and, in particular, welfare and social services costs led to a series of federal laws that have changed that situation considerably.[11] In recent years, government authorities have been more successful at securing payment, and at standardized amounts that are often higher than previously. With better child support enforcement, the poverty of custodial parents and their children dropped from 33 percent in 1993 to 24.6 percent in 2007.

Nevertheless, child support awards have historically been and continue to be small. In 2008, 54 percent of custodial parents had child support awards, and three-fourths of those received payments. Only 46.8 percent received full payment of what was due, however, and the amounts involved are not very impressive, averaging less than $3,500. Some noncustodial parents do make additional contributions in the form of gifts, clothes, food, medical costs (beyond health insurance), and camp or child care.

Because psychologists and sociologists have understood for some time that noncustodial parents' involvement in their children's lives is beneficial to not only the children, but also to the psychological and emotional health of the parents as well (Schindler 2010), the question is therefore asked: Why do some parents not pay their child support obligations? Some research suggests that the principal reason for a noncustodial parent's failure to pay is unemployment or underemployment (Sorensen 2010). Among families in which the absent parent has been employed during the entire previous year, payment rates are 80 percent or more. Not so when unemployment is involved. "The key to reducing poverty [among single-parent families] thus appears to be the old and unglamorous one, of solving un- and underemployment, both for the fathers and the mothers" (Braver, Fitzpatrick, and Bay 1991, pp. 184–85).

Some noncustodial fathers provide support in ways other than money (Garasky et al. 2007, p. 4,401), such as child care: "In some cases attempts to locate and require payments from such fathers may result in severing these ties" (Peterson and Nord 1990, p. 539). Compliance may be related to the noncustodial parent's involvement in the child's life. Seventy-eight percent are in compliance when they have either joint custody or visitation arrangements; only 67 percent are in compliance when the parent has neither.

Two suggested solutions to the problem of nonpayment of child support are guaranteed child support and a children's allowance. Both are based on the principle of society-wide responsibility for all children. With **guaranteed child support**, a policy adopted in France and Sweden, the government sends to the custodial parent the full amount of support awarded to the child. It then becomes the government's task to collect the money from the parent who owes it. A second alternative, a **children's allowance**, provides a government grant to all families—married or single-parent, regardless of income—based on the number of children they have. All industrialized countries except the United States

[11] The Child Support Enforcement Amendments (1984) to the Social Security Act, the Family Support Act (1988), and the child support provisions of the Personal Responsibility and Work Opportunity Reconciliation Act (1996) did the following: (1) encouraged the establishment of paternity and consequent child support awards, (2) required states to develop numerical guidelines for determining child support amounts, (3) required periodic review of award levels to amend them for inflation and to ensure that the noncustodial parent continued to pay an appropriate share of his or her income, and (4) enforced payments through locator services to find nonpaying noncustodial parents. States were required to implement automatic wage withholding of child support, and some states imposed penalties such as revoking a driver's license, seizing a delinquent payer's assets, or garnishing his or her wages ("Child Support Collected" 1995; Garfinkel, Meyer, and McLanahan 1998; Pirog-Good and Amerson 1997). Perhaps the most interesting collection device is that of the state of Maine, where child support must be paid before worm digging or moose hunting licenses will be issued (Koch 2006).

have some version of a children's allowance. In the present political and economic climate in the United States, it seems unlikely that such measures would be adopted.

As another approach to securing payment of child support, some states have begun experimenting with "responsible fatherhood" programs, often supported by government grants. Low-income fathers are typically expected to pay a higher portion of their income in child support than are middle-class fathers, resulting in a spiral of expanded debt and often withdrawal from their children (Huang, Mincy, and Garfinkle 2005). Recognizing that there are low-income fathers who want to provide support for their children but lack the income to do so, these multifaceted programs provide employment services, family support, and mediation services. Results thus far are only modest. Some increase in child support payments has occurred, though not yet enough to produce the dramatic improvement in the lives of men and their children that program designers had hoped for (Sorenson 2010).

We have been speaking of child support in the context of marriage and divorce, but some courts have awarded child support when same-sex couples who have been raising children together break up (Graham 2008; Kravets 2005; "State Court Orders" 2005). California courts provide an insight into the legal thinking behind child support decisions when same-sex couples break up or dissolve their marriages or civil unions.

The "California Supreme Court confirms the rights of a lesbian mother to have the legal rights of a natural mother" (Graham 2008, p. 1022). It does this using the Uniform Parentage Act to hold the noncustodial parent responsible for child support. According to section 7611 of the Act, the way "a man can be presumed to be the natural father of a child is if he receives the child into his home and openly holds out the child as his natural child. The court construed this statute to apply to mothers who . . . entered into a lesbian partnership and committed to a relationship with children born to their lesbian partner" (Graham 2008, pp. 1,023–24).

We turn now from the economics of postdivorce family support to a broader examination of the aftermath of divorce for children.

Divorce and Children

More than half of all divorces involve children under eighteen, and about 40 percent of children born to married parents will experience marital disruption (Amato 2000). How do separation and divorce affect children? There is strong disagreement on the answer to this question. One research review spoke of the "polemical nature of divorce scholarship" (Amato 2000, p. 1,270).

Outcomes for children depend a great deal on the circumstances before and after the divorce (Amato 2010). Although the divorce experience is psychologically stressful and, in most cases, financially disadvantageous for children, children in high-conflict marriages seem to benefit from a divorce. Living in an intact family characterized by unresolved tension and alienating conflict can cause as great or greater emotional stress and a lower sense of self-worth in children than living in a supportive single-parent family (Barber and Demo 2006). When the conflict level in the home has been low, however, children have poorer postdivorce outcomes. They are likely surprised by a divorce and seem to suffer more emotional damage. Among other things, it is difficult for them to see the divorce as necessary in this situation (Stevenson and Wolfers 2007).

The Various Stresses for Children of Divorce

We begin this section with the research of Judith Wallerstein and her colleagues. This group's research has been very influential in defining the situation of children of divorce for both professionals and the public.

The Wallerstein Research In their longitudinal study of children's postdivorce adjustment, psychologists Judith Wallerstein and Joan Kelly interviewed all of the members of some sixty families with one or more children who had entered counseling at the time of the parents' separation in 1971. Wallerstein and her colleagues reinterviewed children at one year, two years, five years, ten years, and, in some cases, fifteen years later and finally again at the twenty-five-year point (Wallerstein and Lewis 2007, 2008).

In the initial aftermath of the divorce, children appeared worst in terms of their psychological adjustment at one year after separation. By two years postdivorce, households had generally stabilized. At five years, many of the 131 children seemed to have come through the experience fairly well: 34 percent "coped well"; 29 percent were in a middle range of adequate, though uneven, functioning; and 37 percent were not coping well, with anger playing a significant part in the emotional life of many of them (Wallerstein and Kelly 1980). If the middle group is considered to be well enough adjusted, one can say that two-thirds of these children emerged from the divorce intact.

Wallerstein and Lewis performed a twenty-five-year follow-up with fifty-two of the families and found four different types of adult–child and father relations. Their Group A, representing 29 percent of the fathers in the study, had no contact with their adult children. Group B made up 27 percent of the study's fathers. This is the group who seldom or sporadically saw their children, and had very limited contact with them as adults. The third group, Group C, composed 23 percent of the fathers in the study, and this group had good relations with their children postdivorce, which continued on into their children's adulthood. Finally, Group D had varied relationships with their adult children. This group appeared to exhibit some form of preferential treatment to some children—providing economic resources for their preferred adult children but not to the others (Wallerstein and Lewis 2007).

Children whose parents have divorced will more than likely have less money available for their needs. This is especially significant because some of the negative impact of divorce can be attributed to economic deprivation (Strohschein 2005; Wallerstein and Lewis 2007).

Wallerstein found considerable deprivation among even middle-class children compared to what they could have expected had their parents remained married. Because divorce settlements seldom include arrangements to pay for children's college education[12] and family savings are often eroded by divorce, financing higher education is especially problematic. Wallerstein, who followed her sample into young adulthood, was surprised at the extent of their educational downward mobility. Sixty percent of the children in the study were likely to receive less education than their fathers; 45 percent were likely to receive less than their mothers. Even divorced fathers who had retained close ties, who had the money or could save it, and who ascribed importance to education seemed to feel less obligated to support their children through college (Wallerstein and Blakeslee 1989; Wallerstein and Lewis 2007, 2008).

After following their sample of children of divorce for ten years, Wallerstein and her colleagues found the majority to be approaching economic self-sufficiency, to be enrolled in educational programs, and, in general, to be responsible young adults. Even so, the overall impression left by the Wallerstein research is one of loss. In their examination of the impact of divorce on the relationship between children and their fathers, Wallerstein and Lewis eloquently noted that the "twists and turns of the postdivorce father–child relationship, its high vulnerability to change, satisfactions laced with disappointments, and undercurrent of love, longing, and anxiety all call attention to the complexity of building a lasting father-child relationship outside the marriage" (Wallerstein and Lewis 2008, n.p.).

Children may lose fathers, who become uninterested and detached; they may lose mothers, who are overwhelmed by the task of supporting the family and managing a household alone and who either see little chance of happiness for themselves or are busy pursuing their "second chance." Children of divorce experience the loss of daily interaction with one of their parents. Boys, especially, seem to find it difficult to establish themselves educationally, occupationally, or maritally (Wallerstein and Blakeslee 1989; Wallerstein and Lewis 2007). Wallerstein found that half of the children in her study had experienced a second divorce of one or both parents. ("My Family: How It Feels When Parents Divorce" illustrates many points raised in this section.)

The Wallerstein study has methodological problems: it was a small, unrepresentative sample recruited by offering free counseling to the family; it lacked a control group; and there was difficulty separating family troubles and mental health concerns that predate the separation and divorce from those that might be effects of divorce. It has also been challenged by studies with more representative samples. These studies reach less-negative conclusions. Some critics have also noted that, when the study began in the early 1970s, women were less likely to be in the labor force. The need for an inexperienced mother to enter the labor force created an adjustment problem in the 1970s that would be less of a stress now.

Another methodological problem, although one shared by other longitudinal studies, is that continual interviewing of children about the impact of the divorce might create a mind-set in which any problems are given a divorce-generated interpretation (Ahrons 1994; Cherlin 1999, 2000; Coontz 1997a). As with all research that studies human behavior, the methodological weakness of this study is important, but so too is the qualitative data that a study of this sort provides. True, a large quantitative study provides an important snapshot into various moments in time, but the in-depth interviews found in this study provide rich details and allow for the subjects to be reflective about their own life histories and trajectories. It has allowed social researchers to see something they cannot see in quantitative data—the divergent experiences individuals have, and the impact divorce has had on each of the individual's lives.

Still, other researchers have come to think, like Wallerstein, that divorce has long-term effects (Amato 2010; Conger, Conger, and Martin 2010; Frisco, Muller, and Frank 2007). Divorce is a "risk factor for multiple problems in adulthood" (Amato 2000, p. 1,279). Children of divorce continue to have lower outcomes than children from intact families in the areas of academic success, conduct, psychological adjustment, social competence, and self-concept, and they have more troubled marriages and weaker ties to parents, especially fathers (Amato 2010; Kreider and Elliott 2009b; Magnuson and Berger 2009). See Chapters 7, 8, and 10 for additional discussions on marriage and better child outcomes.

Reasons for Negative Effects of Divorce on Children Researchers and theorists offer a variety of explanations for why and how divorce could adversely affect children. Amato (1993) has summarized five

[12] Some divorce agreements provide for support of children through college, provided they are doing well and advancing toward the goal of graduation. It has happened occasionally, but rarely, that courts have ordered such support against the wishes of a parent.

theoretical perspectives concerning the reasons for negative outcomes. We present his typology, along with some relevant research by others. Then we introduce an additional theoretical perspective.

1. The **life stress perspective** assumes that, just as divorce is known to be a stressful life event for adults, it must also be so for children. Furthermore, divorce is not one single event but a process of associated events that may include moving—often to a poorer neighborhood—changing schools, giving up pets, and losing contact with grandparents and other relatives (Benner and Kim 2010; Burrell and Roosa 2009; Jackson, Choi, and Bentler 2009; Teachman 2009; White et al. 2009). This perspective holds that an accumulation of negative stressors results in problems for children of divorce.
2. The **parental loss perspective** assumes that a family with both parents living in the same household is the optimal environment for children's development. Both parents are important resources, providing children love, emotional support, practical assistance, information, guidance, and supervision, as well as modeling social skills such as cooperation, negotiation, and compromise. Accordingly, the absence of a parent from the household is problematic for children's socialization.
3. The **parental adjustment perspective** notes the importance of the custodial parent's psychological adjustment and the quality of parenting. Supportive and appropriately disciplining parents facilitate their children's well-being. However, the stress of divorce and related problems and adjustments may impair a parent's child-raising skills, with probably negative consequences for children. Divorced parents do spend less time with children. Compared to married parents, divorced parents are "less supportive, have fewer rules, dispense harsher discipline, provide less supervision, and engage in more conflict with their children" (Amato 2000, p. 1,279; see also Schoppe-Sullivan, Schermerhorn, and Cummings 2007).
4. The **economic hardship perspective** assumes that economic hardship brought about by marital dissolution is primarily responsible for the problems faced by children whose parents divorce (Amato 2010). Indeed, economic circumstances do condition diverse outcomes for children—perhaps accounting for one-half the differences between children in divorced compared to intact two-parent families. Differences in outcomes exist *within* social class groupings, however. Children in better-off remarried or single-parent families still lag behind children from two-parent families on various outcome indicators (Amato 2010; Kreider and Elliott 2009b; Magnuson and Berger 2009; Waite, Luo, and Lewin 2009).
5. The **interparental conflict perspective** holds that conflict between parents is responsible for the lowered well-being of children of divorce. Many studies, including that of Wallerstein, indicate that some negative results for children may not be simply the result of divorce per se, but are also generated by exposure to parental conflict prior to, during, and subsequent to the divorce (Barber and Demo 2006; Benner and Kim 2010; Burrell and Roosa 2009; Jackson, Choi, and Bentler 2009; Teachman 2009; White et al. 2009).

   Visitation is one frequent arena of postdivorce parental disputes. The child isn't ready to go when visitation time starts, or the visiting parent brings the child home late. Child support is another. The Stanford Child Custody Project, which followed over one thousand parents and children, found that a quarter of parents had a conflicted co-parenting relationship three and a half years after the divorce (M-Y. Lee 2002).

The factors that seem to affect co-parenting success are rather straightforward: a previous good co-parenting relationship during the marriage; a mediated rather than hostile divorce process; a reasonably good post-divorce relationship between ex-spouses; and length of time since the divorce. Research on the relationship between good co-parenting and type of custody is inconclusive except that a joint custody arrangement chosen by the parents is much more conducive to good co-parenting than one imposed by the courts. Research on the effect of remarriage on co-parenting is not sufficiently developed for conclusions to be drawn (Adamsons and Pasley 2006).

Multiple Transitions and Children's Outcomes The **family instability perspective** is an additional theory of children's negative outcomes of divorce that has emerged since Amato's original article. The **instability hypothesis** stresses that *transitions* in and out of various family settings are the key to children's adjustment (Barber and Demo 2006; Hetherington 2005). The logic of the instability hypothesis is this:

> Transitions may include parents' separation; a cohabiting romantic partner's move into, or out of, the home of a single parent; the remarriage of a single (noncohabiting) parent[;] or the disruption of a remarriage. The underlying assumption is that children and their parents, whether single or partnered, form a functioning family system and that repeated disruption of this system may be more distressing than its long-term continuation. . . . Stable single-parent households or stepfamilies, in contrast, do not require that children readjust repeatedly to the loss of coresident parents and parent-figures or the introduction of cohabiting parents and stepparents. (Fomby and Cherlin 2007, p. 182)

My Family

How It Feels When Parents Divorce

In the following excerpts, four children of divorce tell their own stories. As you will see, they talk about issues raised in this chapter.

Zach, Age 13

Even though I live with my Dad and my sister lives with my Mom, my parents have joint custody, which means we can switch around if we feel like it. I think that's the best possible arrangement because if they ever fought over us, I know I would have felt I was like a check in a restaurant—you know, the way it is at the end of a meal when two people are finished eating and they both grab for the check . . . but secretly neither one really wants it, they just go on pretending until someone finally grabs it, and then that one's stuck. . . .

My parents knew they couldn't live together, but they also knew it was nobody's fault. It was as if they were magnets—as if when you turn them the opposite way they can't touch. . . . Neither of them ever blamed the other person, so they worked it out the best they could—for their sakes and ours, too.

Nevertheless, it's very sad and confusing when your parents are divorced. I think I was five when they separated. . . .

When my parents first split up, it affected me a lot. . . . I got real fat and my grades went way down, so I went to a psychologist. She made me do a lot of things which seemed dumb at the time—like draw pictures and answer lots of silly questions. . . . My school work suffered because I was so distracted thinking about my situation that I couldn't listen very well, and for a long time I didn't work nearly as hard as I should have. Everyone told me I was an underachiever, and my parents tell me I still am, but I don't think so. What I do think is that I am a lot more independent—a go-out-and-do-it-yourself person. . . .

I've heard about kids who are having all these problems because their parents are getting divorced, but I can't understand what the big deal is. I mean, it's upsetting, sure, but just because your parents are separated it doesn't mean you're going to lose anybody. . . . It's not something I talk about very much. Most of my friends would rather talk about MTV than talk about divorce.

FIGURE 15.5.a and FIGURE 15.5.b Professional counselors often use art to gain insight into children's feelings about how divorce affects their family. The first drawing reveals the creative coping of a child whose parents are divorcing. She has figured out a way to *include* her father while keeping within the bounds of reality as she knows it. Her sister, on the other hand, used a jagged line to *separate* her father from the rest of the family.

Source: From *The Difficult Divorce: Therapy for Children and Families,* by Marla Beth Isaacs, Braulio Montalvo, and David Abelsohn. Copyright © 1986 by Basic Books, Inc. Reprinted by permission of Basic Books, a member of Perseus Books, L.L.C.

Ari, Age 14

When my parents were married, I hardly ever saw my Dad because he was always busy working. Now that they're divorced, I've gotten to know him more because I'm with him every weekend. And I really look forward to the weekends because it's kind of like a break—it's like going to Disneyland because there's no set schedule, no "Be home by five-thirty" kind of stuff. It's open. It's free. And my father is always buying me presents.

My mom got remarried and divorced again, so I've gone through two divorces so far. And my father's also gotten remarried—to someone I don't get along with all that well. It's all made me feel that people shouldn't get married—they should just live together and make their own agreement. Then, if things get bad, they don't have to get divorced and hire lawyers and sue each other. And, even more important, they don't have to end up hating each other.

I'd say that the worst part of the divorce is the money problem. It's been hard on my Mom because lots of times she can't pay her bills, and it makes her angry when I stay with my father and he buys me things. She gets mad and says things like, "If he can buy you things like this, then he should be able to pay me." And I feel caught in the middle for two reasons: First, I can't really enjoy whatever my Dad does get for me, and second, I don't know who to believe. My Dad's saying, "I don't really owe her any money," and my Mom's saying he does. Sometimes I fight for my Mom and sometimes I fight for my Dad, but I wish they'd leave me out of it completely.

Caleb, Age 7

My parents aren't actually divorced yet. But they're getting one soon. They stopped living together when I was one and a half, and my Dad moved next door. Then, when I was five, he moved to Chicago, and that hurt my feelings because I realized he was really leaving and I wouldn't be able to see him every day. My father's an artist, and when he lived next door to us in New York, I used to go to his studio every day and watch him when he was welding. I had my own goggles and tools, and we would spend many an hour together. I remember when I first heard the bad news that he was moving away, because I almost flipped my lid. My father said he would be divorcing my Mom but that he wouldn't be divorcing me and we'd still see each other a lot—but not as often. I started crying then and there, and ever since then I've been hoping every single second that he'd move back to New York and we'd all live together again. I don't cry much anymore because I hold it back, but I feel sad all the same.

I get to visit my father quite often. And Shaun. He's my collie. My cat lives in New York with me and Mom. Whenever I talk with Daddy on the phone I can hear Shaun barking in the background. The hardest thing for me about visiting my father is when I have to leave, and that makes me feel bad—and mad—inside. I still wish I could see him every day like I did when I was little. It's hard to live with just one person, because you don't have enough company, though my Mom has lots of great babysitters and that helps a little.

Tito, Age 11

It seems like my parents were always fighting. The biggest fight happened one night when we were at a friend's house. Mommy was inside the house crying, and Daddy was out on the sidewalk yelling and telling my mother to come down, and my little sister, Melinda, and I were outside with a friend of my father's. We were both crying because we were so frightened. Then Daddy tried to break the door down, so Mommy came downstairs. And then the police cars came and Daddy begged Mommy to stay quiet and not say anything and to give him another chance, but she was so unhappy that she got into one of the cars. I was only four but I remember everything. We stayed with our cousin for about two months, and during this time I saw my father whenever he visited us at my grandmother's house. . . . I was always happy to see him, but sometimes it made me feel sad, too, because I would look forward to our visits so much, and then when we were together it could never be as perfect as I was hoping it would be. He was still so angry at Mommy's leaving him that it was hard for him to feel anything else for anybody. . . .

About the time of the divorce I started to get into fights with other kids, and my mother got worried. She thought I must be feeling very angry and having a hard time expressing my feelings, so she took me to a therapist. . . . We got really close and he'd talk to me about my problems with my Dad. This went on for about two years, and during that time he helped me realize that the divorce was better for me in the long run because our home was more relaxed and there wasn't so much tension in the air.

The other thing that happened around this time was that my mother found out about an organization called Big Brothers, where I could have another male figure in my life. . . . They paired me off with a guy named Pat Kelly, and we've been getting together every weekend for a couple of years. . . . Pat and I do a lot of things like play baseball or video games and eat hot dogs. But the best thing we do is talk—like when I do something good in school I can tell him, and if I feel sad I can talk about that, too. His parents got divorced when he was twelve, and so we have a lot of the same feelings.

Critical Thinking

Overall, do you see these stories as hopeful, dismaying, or both? Why? Were there any particular points that you found surprising or interesting? What do these stories suggest to divorcing parents about how they might help their children cope with divorce?

Source: Excerpts from *How It Feels When Parents Divorce,* by Jill Krementz.

Andrew Cherlin develops this perspective in a book appropriately titled, *The Marriage-Go-Round.* He contrasts the American practice of movement in and out of marriage and relationships with the more stable family patterns of European and Oceanic nations, whether or not these are anchored in marriage (Cherlin 2009a). Cherlin and his colleague Paula Fomby tested the instability hypothesis, as well as a competing *selection hypothesis,* to assess whether the number of transitions produces lower cognitive (academic) outcomes or behavior problems or whether preexisting characteristics of the mother explain both household instability and the effects of that instability on children. They used the National Longitudinal Survey of Youth waves between 1979 and 2000, and a supplemental survey of the original respondents' children.

Multiple transitions did not seem to impact black children. The researchers were not able to determine why from the data they had, but speculate that black children may have more support from the extended family. It may also be the case that other stresses on many black families are so overwhelming as to overshadow changes in family structure.

Multiple transitions did not seem the key to explaining white children's *academic outcomes.* But the number of transitions *did* seem related to white children's *behavioral problems.* Even so, multiple transitions did not seem so powerful a negative influence as living in a single-parent, mother-only family in a child's early years.

A More Optimistic Look at Children in Divorce Having considered reasons for the negative effects of divorce on children, we now try to assess just how important divorce is in the lives of affected children. We've given considerable attention to the research of Wallerstein and her colleagues because it has been very influential. "Judith Wallerstein's research on the long-term effects of divorce on children has had a profound effect on scholarly work, clinical practice, social policy, and the general public's views of divorce" (Amato 2003, p. 332). In fact, this is not a definitive study, and the strongly negative conclusions about divorce that Wallerstein presents seem overstated. "Many of Wallerstein's conclusions about the long-term consequences of dissolution on children are more pessimistic than the evidence warrants" (Amato 2003, p. 332).

Nevertheless, concern that children of divorce are disadvantaged does not rest solely on Wallerstein's research and what many see as her exaggerated presentation of the dangers of divorce (Cherlin 1999). A "persuasive body of evidence supports a moderate version of [her] thesis" (Amato 2003, pp. 338–39; Hetherington 2005). The remaining question, then, is this: *How much* does divorce affect children?

E. Mavis Hetherington has been studying divorcing families for about the same length of time as Judith Wallerstein, and she has a much more optimistic view of the outcomes for children—and adults. Starting in 1974 in Virginia with parents of four-year-olds, forty-eight divorced and forty-eight married-couple families, her research ultimately included 1,400 stable and dissolved marriages and the children of those marriages, some followed for almost thirty years. Hetherington found that 25 percent of these children of divorced parents had long-term social, emotional, or psychological problems, compared to 10 percent of those whose parents had not divorced. However, in assessing the impact of divorce, she would emphasize the 75 to 80 percent of children who are coping reasonably well (Hetherington and Kelly 2002).

> Researchers have clearly demonstrated that, on average, children benefit from being raised in two biological or adoptive parent families rather than separated; divorced; or never married single-parent households. . . . But . . . there is considerable variability, and the differences between groups, while significant, are relatively small. Indeed, despite the well-documented risks associated with separation and divorce, the majority of divorced children as young adults enjoy average or better social and emotional adjustment. (Kelly and Lamb 2003, p. 195, citations omitted; see also Kelly and Emery 2003)

Other scholars agree: "On average, parental divorce and remarriage have only a small negative impact on the well-being of children" (Barber and Demo 2006, p. 291; see also Demo, Aquilino, and Fine 2005, p. 125). All in all, divorce researchers seem to be moving to a middle ground in which they acknowledge that children of divorce are disadvantaged compared to those of married parents—and that those whose parents were not engaged in serious marital conflict have especially lost the advantage of an intact parental home. But many have moved away from simplistic or overly negative views of the outcomes of divorce. A theme that runs through virtually all studies on the impact of marriage and divorce on the well-being of children is socialization. At the end of the day, both negative and positive outcomes for children in both married and divorced households suggest that the behavior of the parents has the greatest impact on their children's well-being. If there is significant discord between married parents, that chronic discord will lead to poor outcomes for their children. If a divorced couple continues to have a relationship that is fraught with conflict, the outcomes for their children will be negative. If children of married, cohabitating, divorced, remarried, or single parents feel nurtured, loved, and supported by parents and families who engage in conflict resolution and work hard at getting along with one another, the outcomes for those children tend to be positive.

In fact, studies that reach different conclusions about overall outcomes show we can still learn much that is potentially useful about what postdivorce circumstances are most beneficial to children's development and what pitfalls to avoid. A good mother–child (or custodial parent–child) bond and competent parenting by the custodial parent seem to be the most significant factors (Amato and Cheadle 2008). Another highly important factor in children's adjustment to divorce is the divorced parents' relationship with each other (Ahrons 2004; Barber and Demo 2006; Freeman 2008). And good nonresident parental relationships are also a positive influence on outcomes (Demo and Fine 2010; Guzzo 2009c).

We now turn to issues of custody, the setting in which children will live after the divorce.

"So what's your custody deal?"

Custody Issues

A basic issue in a divorce of parents is the determination of which parent will take **custody**—that is, assume primary responsibility for caring for the children and making decisions about their upbringing and general welfare.

Custody after Divorce As formalized in divorce decrees, child custody is most commonly an extension of traditional gender roles. Divorced fathers typically have legal responsibility for financial support, while divorced mothers continue the physical, day-to-day care of their children. Eighty-three percent of custodial parents are mothers; 17 percent are fathers. (Not all "custodial mothers" in these government statistics have been divorced; 34 percent were never married.)

Custody patterns and preferences in law have changed over time. As part of a patriarchal legal system, fathers were automatically given custody until the mid-nineteenth century. Then the first wave of the women's movement made mothers' parental rights an issue. Emerging theories of child development also lent support to a presumption that mother custody was virtually always in the child's best interest, the so-called "tender years" doctrine (Artis 2004).

In the 1970s, states' reforms of divorce law incorporated new ideas about men, women, and parenthood; custody criteria were made gender neutral. Under current laws, a father and a mother who want to retain custody have theoretically equal chances. Judges try to assess the relationship between parents and children on a case-by-case basis. But because mothers are typically the ones who have physically cared for the child, and because many judges still have traditional attitudes about gender, some courts continue to give preference to mothers (Demos and Fine 2010). The "best interests of the child" or the more recent "primary caretaker" standard was often assumed by judges to signal a choice of the mother (Artis 2004).[13]

When both parents seek custody, the odds of father custody are slightly higher when the children are older (Fox and Kelly 1995). Judges may have become more favorable to father custody, but there are no definitive studies on whether fathers are now winning more contested custody cases. One study found that, by 1995, court decisions were almost equalized, with 45 percent of mothers and 42 percent of fathers awarded sole custody and 9 percent sharing custody in disputed cases (Mason and Quirk 1997). Other data, taking as a starting point the original hope of each parent, found that "fathers get

[13] Several new legal approaches have appeared in recent child custody cases. One is the *friendly parent* concept, the idea that custody should favor the parent who is more likely to grant access to the child and foster the child's relationship with the other parent. Many states have incorporated the friendly parent doctrine into their statutory standards for custody as one factor among many or as the determining factor.

"There is, however, a small but growing movement to reject the friendly parent statute or limit its application" (Dore 2004, p. 43). This is because in practice it has generated hostility and litigation, as competing parents denigrate each other and sometimes try to provoke the other parent into behavior that will look bad in court. It has also made parents hesitant to raise legitimate child abuse or domestic violence allegations for fear of appearing critical of the other parent. Some courts have rejected the friendly parent doctrine, and some states are modifying their laws (W. Davis 2001; Dore 2004).

A second concept is that of *parental alienation syndrome*, originated by psychiatrist Richard Gardner. This is the idea that one parent has turned the child against the other parent without cause and that a parent may raise false allegations of child abuse (Lavietes 2003). This concept is most often introduced by fathers seeking custody.

Parental alienation syndrome has not received legal acceptance nor is it accepted by the American Psychiatric Association, the American Medical Association, or the American Psychological Association (American Psychological Association 2005b; Lavietes 2003). Courts have not to date permitted it to enter into consideration (e.g., *People v. Michael Fortin* 2000).

the arrangement they prefer less often than mothers do" (Braver, Shapiro, and Goodman 2006, p. 317).

It may be the case that mothers have become less inclined to insist on sole custody. Fatherhood scholar James Levine thinks that "[w]e're seeing some weakening of the constraints on women to feel they can only be successful if they are successful mothers," so they are more willing to concede custody to willing fathers (quoted in Fritsch 2001, p. 4). As with mothers, not all custodial fathers are or were married; in 2003, 21 percent were never married.

Generally, studies have found nothing to preclude father custody or to prefer it (Buchanan, Maccoby, and Dornbusch 1996; Luepnitz 1982). Neither does it seem to make a difference in a child's adjustment whether the custodial parent is the same sex as the child (Powell and Downey 1997).

Noncustodial Mothers With unpromising economic prospects and in the context of changing attitudes about gender roles, some mothers are relinquishing custody. There are more than two million noncustodial mothers (Sousa and Sorensen 2006), concentrated in the twenty-five to forty-five age range and lower- to middle-class economic level. Some of those mothers have lost custody of children due to their abuse or neglect, whereas others have voluntarily surrendered custody or lost a custody contest to the other parent (Eicher-Catt 2004b).

In an earlier study of noncustodial mothers based on interviews with more than 500 mostly white women in forty-four states, only 9 percent reported losing their children in a court battle or ceding custody to avoid a custody fight. The others voluntarily agreed to father custody and gave the following as reasons: money (30 percent); child's choice (21 percent); difficulty in handling the children (12 percent); avoidance of moving the children (11 percent); and self-reported instability or problems (11 percent; Greif and Pabst 1988, p. 88; see also Depner 1993).

More than 90 percent of mothers in the Greif and Pabst study reported that the experience of becoming the noncustodial parent was stressful. So was maintaining a relationship with the child. Deborah Eicher-Catt's qualitative study of noncustodial mothers (2004b) found that the minority of mothers whose custody was abrogated by the courts were restricted in their contact, perhaps permitted only supervised visitation with their children. The larger group who voluntarily relinquished custody found it hard to achieve a workable relationship with the child as well. They were unable to be traditional mothers, but found a "mother-as-friend" role insufficient and uncomfortable. Eicher-Catt advises noncustodial mothers to focus on building a relationship, rather than thinking in terms of the traditional maternal role. "A Closer Look at Family Diversity: A Noncustodial Mother Tells Her Story" describes one mother's struggle to perform the mother role in this challenging context.

Judith Fisher, who also studied noncustodial mothers, believes that women should not relinquish custody just because they feel inadequate in comparison to their successful husbands. At the same time, she strongly supports the freedom of men and women to make choices about custody—including the woman's choice to live apart from her children—without guilt or stigma. She urges

> the negation of the unflattering stereotypes of noncustody mothers; . . . supportiveness of the woman's choice when it appears to have been well thought out; and . . . [not] blaming the mother when others (the children, the children's father, the courts) decide that the children should live apart from her. (1983, p. 357)

The Visiting Parent To date, most research and discussion on visiting parents has been about fathers, but one study did compare the two sexes. Nonresidential mothers were more apt to telephone and to engage in extended visits with children. But nonresidential mothers and fathers had essentially similar levels of visitation in terms of frequency and activities during the visit. Both were more likely to engage in only leisure activities with their children rather than spending time helping with homework or going to school activities. In reality, less frequent and more recreational visitation seem to be a result of structural factors: distance from the child's home; the difficulty of finding an appropriate setting for the visit; and the wish not to engage in conflict or disciplinary actions in the limited time spent with the child (S. Stewart 1999).[14]

Noncustodial fathers, like noncustodial mothers, find it difficult to construct a satisfying parent–child relationship. During the marriage, a father's authority in the family gave weight to his parental role, but this vanishes in a nonresidential situation. Geographical distance and conflict with the mother may also be barriers to frequent contact. Custodial mothers are effectively gatekeepers, facilitating, or not, the noncustodial father's relationship with his children (Adamsons and Pasley 2006; Sano, Richards, and Zvonkovic 2008).

[14] There are some special situations of visitation. In some communities, courts and social workers have developed programs to offer *supervised visitation* between a noncustodial parent and his or her offspring. In this situation, parent–child contact occurs only in the presence of a third party, such as a social worker or a court employee. Supervised visitation is often mandated in situations of alleged domestic violence, drug abuse, long absenteeism, or past imprisonment. Although no doubt a warranted precaution in many cases, supervision is also a hardship on the parent, who must not only visit in a strained situation but also cover the financial cost. Some fathers must forgo visits they desire because they lack money to pay the typical $100 a visit (Kaufman 2007).

A Closer Look at Family Diversity

A Noncustodial Mother Tells Her Story

As I fold the last batch of warm clothes from the dryer, I glance over at the kitchen clock on the wall. Oh dear . . . it's almost four-thirty. . . . It's Sunday and I need to get the guys ready to go home to their dad's. . . .

Nowadays, I live [in a room] in someone else's house, see my kids every other weekend, and pay child support. How can I continue to call myself a mother when I no longer provide their regular care and nurturance? Unlike some mothers . . . who lose custody of their children . . . I voluntarily chose my status. . . . With little money coming in as a full time student, I am unable to provide adequately for them. Like other mothers I've interviewed, making the difficult decision to leave the care of my children to someone else because I deemed it "in their best interest" is not a decision reached lightly. . . . I suddenly realize that it's awfully quiet in the house. "Ty . . . Zachary," I call out, with the basket of clothes now resting on one hip. No response. All I hear is the low drone of a televised basketball game coming from the . . . living room. That's odd, I wonder where they could be. . . . I'm sure they were here just a minute ago.

Have I been too involved in cleaning up our breakfast mess or doing laundry to notice that they'd disappeared? It is a rarity that my boys, Ty, age ten, and Zac, age six, would be unaccounted for during a weekend visit. After all, I consider our time together precious time, although very much punctuated and measured according to planned activities and events. Granted, I have been daydreaming about how good this weekend with them has been. I think I've managed to keep them sufficiently "entertained. . . ." I know that's not my only goal while they're with me, but I do want them to enjoy coming to see me.

Yes, let's see. Friday night we went to the movies. Yesterday afternoon I took them roller skating. . . . We stayed up late last night and watched a rented movie. Dare I say it felt like "family time," if only temporarily? This morning our time together was more improvised. . . . Zac talked me into making waffles for breakfast. How long has it been since I did that? Seldom do I cook anymore.

[After breakfast] I helped Ty finish some homework and talked with him about dealing with his math teacher, whom he hates. I must admit the "down time" with them has been nice. . . . It's the routine patterns of being together, the sense of everydayness, that we miss the most. . . .

Muffled voices outside my window bring me back from my thoughts. They must be outside. . . . "Mom, come here, quick!" Ty yells excitedly . . . [and Zac explains]: "[W]e're building a fort!"

"Well, that sounds pretty good guys, but it's almost time to go and you still haven't packed up yet. Your dad's expecting you for dinner, remember?" "Ah, Mom, can't we stay a little longer," Ty insists, "we just got started." "I know, honey, but this project will be here when you come to visit next time. . . . " I hear myself reluctantly saying. . . . I'm immediately filled with mixed emotions. Although I'm happy to see them finally comfortable enough to make some aspect of this experience their own, I have to begin the departure process. . . . If I don't get them moving now, I won't keep my agreed-on visitation schedule with their dad.

We've entered the kitchen and the door slams behind us, as if to punctuate my words and mark the beginning of our "departure routine." The three of us take the cue and scatter to make preparations.

Source: Adapted from Eicher-Catt 2004a. Deborah Eicher-Catt is assistant professor of Communication Arts and Sciences at Pennsylvania State University.

A related issue is **interference with visitation**, discussed earlier in conjunction with conflict between parents. Such a situation can be very frustrating for fathers who want to maintain close contact with their children (Perrine 2006). In 1998, Congress passed the Visitation Rights Enforcement Act, which requires states to recognize and enforce visitation orders of another state. The earlier Family Support Act of 1988 authorized court intervention programs such as intensive case supervision, mediation, parent education and so on, but so far experimental programs to address interference with visitation have had disappointing results (Pearson and Anhalt 1994; Turkat 1997). As a last resort, courts can order a change of custody.

A new marriage or cohabiting relationship was not itself a factor in decreasing visitation, but the presence of children in a new family, particularly biological children, did lead to a decline. Fathers seemed to find it difficult to parent their children across two families (Guzzo 2009c; Juby et al. 2007; Swiss and Le Bourdais 2009). Be that as it may, the situation of noncustodial fathers seems to have improved since earlier research found that many had detached from their children. "Although the incidence of joint physical custody has remained low, between 35% and 60% of children now have at least weekly contacts with their fathers in many locations, most often a brief midweek visit or overnight" (Kelly 2007). In Ahrons's longitudinal study of postdivorce families, 62 percent of now-adult children reported that their relationships with their father got better or at least stayed the same over the twenty years since the divorce. "Those children whose relationships got better or stayed the same benefited from significantly more father involvement during the first 5 years postdivorce, whereas low father involvement was associated with reports that their relationships with their fathers got worse" (Ahrons 2007, p. 59; Ahrons and Tanner 2003).

A father's minimal or decreased visiting may be painful for children, and so are visits that alienate rather than bond the child and the noncustodial parent. In one example, described in the Wallerstein study,

> [a]lmost always, there would be other adults around or adult activities planned. Carl watched hundreds of hours of television at his father's house, feeling more and more alone and removed from his earlier visions of family life. (Wallerstein and Blakeslee 1989, p. 79)

Children often forgave geographically distant fathers who did not appear frequently, but were very hurt by those nearby fathers who rarely visited. Recent works by Judith Wallerstein and Julia Lewis, and Liam Swiss and Céline Le Bourdais, discuss the complicated nature of these relationships between geographically close fathers who are distant in their relationships with their children.

Wallerstein and Lewis (2008) point out the complex array of hurt feelings, new relationships, trust issues, and other emotional factors that set postdivorce families and their relationships on trajectories that lead to a child's emotional distress. For example, in interviews with Wallerstein and Lewis, fathers spoke of their discomfort with having their adolescent daughters stay overnight with them, while the adolescent daughters of these fathers were themselves anxious about staying with their father if he lived alone. "Several spoke of their embarrassment about experiencing their early menstruation in the father's home" (p. 228). Swiss and Le Bourdais (2009) discuss the material conditions that impact the noncustodial father's relationship negatively. For example, they point out that working-class fathers, especially those who earn "lower incomes are more likely to be working in low-paying, part-time, or shift-oriented work where they may not be available to their children when the latter are free, that is, in the evenings and weekends" (p. 644).

The visitation of fathers does not always affect children positively (Marsiglio et al. 2000). In extreme cases—where there is verbal, physical, or sexual abuse—father contact may actually be damaging to children (King 1994). We've seen that some divorces are precipitated by alcoholism, drug abuse, or domestic violence; in such cases, visitation is not necessarily in the best interest of a child.

When the father enacts an authoritative parenting style (see Chapter 10) and when the visit does not lead to conflict between the parents, it has a favorable impact on the child's adjustment. The most recent studies do show a higher level of paternal parenting skills, so perhaps younger divorced fathers have been more involved with children in the marriage and have a better mastery of parenting during visitation.

Good relationships with noncustodial fathers foster better outcomes for children (Carlson 2006; White and Gilbreth 2001). Contact is a threshold requirement for a father's positive influence. Relationship quality and responsive parenting (that fathers consider the child's point of view and explain decisions) were found to have a positive effect regarding adolescents' "internalizing" (depression) and "externalizing" (aggressive and antisocial behavior) problems. Adolescents' relationships with their mothers were a more powerful influence on well-being, however. Noteworthy is that if an adolescent had a poor relationship with his or her mother, a good one with a nonresidential father seemed to make a difference. Adolescents with poor relationships with both custodial mothers and nonresidential fathers were, not surprisingly, at greatest disadvantage in terms of adjustment (King and Sobolewski 2006; Sobolewski and King 2005).

A custodial parent's moving away has become a significant postdivorce visitation issue, to be discussed later in this section. In some moving cases, as well as others, judges have ordered "electronic communication" or "virtual visits," by video conferencing, instant messaging, webcam setups, and the like. Although they can be costly, these virtual visits allow the noncustodial parent to talk, play chess, view art projects or at-home dance or music performances, and the like over the Internet. On the whole, such electronic communication enhances contact between parents and children. There is some concern that courts will come to rely on electronic visitation rather than the real thing: "'You can't virtually hug your child'" (Clemetson 2006c).

Child Abduction At the other extreme from dissociating from children is kidnapping one's children from the other parent. A study sponsored by the Justice Department reports that over 350,000 children were abducted by family members in 1999. Biological fathers were the most often to abduct their children, but 43 percent were abducted by biological mothers, and 14 percent by grandparents, with the rest by siblings, aunts, uncles, or mothers' boyfriends. Younger children (under six) are most apt to be abducted; there is no difference in the numbers of boys or girls. Most of the children abducted by family members were returned or located (Miller et al. 2008, p. 527).

Child snatching is frightening and confusing for the child, may be physically dangerous, and is usually detrimental to the child's psychological development. Yet for years, the abduction of a child by a biological parent (without custody) was not legally considered kidnapping—or at least not prosecuted as such. Now, however, due to the passage of the Uniform Child-Custody Jurisdiction and Enforcement Act and the Parental Kidnapping Prevention Act, states must recognize out-of-state custody decrees and do more to find the child and prosecute offenders (Fass 2003).

Another form of child snatching is international abduction, increasingly common when cross-cultural marriages fail and a parent has transnational ties. Of the 350,000 child abductions in the United States, it is estimated that 10,000 of them are "held in foreign countries by a parent of a different nationality" (Slota 2009, p. 73). Retrieving a child from another country is very difficult, despite the Hague Convention on the Civil Aspects of International Child Abduction (an international treaty that requires countries to recognize original custody determinations), and is very costly—upwards of $100,000 with no guarantee of retrieval. Advocates argue that the U.S. government has not been sufficiently aggressive in pursuing such cases, and parents often turn to private services that attempt re-abduction of the child back to the parent in the United States (Alanen 2007; Alvarez 2003; Sapone 2000; Slota 2009).

Child abduction is an extreme act, but it points up the frustration involved in arrangements regarding sole custody, or, in some cases, a lack of attention to the noncustodial parent's allegations of child abuse. For example, "50 percent claimed that their children were being abused, neglected or subjected to an unhealthy home environment by the other parent; 42 percent blamed unfair custody terms" (Alanen 2007, p. 12).

Joint Custody California was the first state to enact a statute on joint custody. "Currently joint custody is either recognized, presumed, or mandated in most states [and] provinces of the United States and Canada" (M-Y. Lee 2002, p. 672).

In **joint custody**, both divorced parents continue to take equal responsibility for important decisions regarding the child's general upbringing. When parents live close to each other and when both are committed, joint custody can bring the experiences of the two parents closer together, providing advantages to each. Both parents may feel they have the opportunity to pass their own beliefs and values on to their children. In addition, neither parent is overloaded with sole custodial responsibility. Joint custody gives each parent some downtime from parenting (M-Y. Lee 2002).

Joint custody agreements have two variations. One is *joint legal and physical custody,* in which parents or children move periodically so that the child resides with each parent in turn on a substantially equal basis. The second variation is *joint legal custody*—in which both parents have the right to participate in important decisions and retain a symbolically important legal authority—with physical custody (that is, residential care of the child) going to just one parent (Siebel 2006). Parents with higher incomes and education are more likely to have joint custody, and "[f]athers with higher levels of education and better financial resources were more likely to request, negotiate, and have shared physical custody" (Kelly 2007, p. 37).

Table 15.2 lists advantages and disadvantages of joint custody from a father's perspective. Shared custody gives children the chance for a more realistic and normal relationship with each parent (Arditti and Keith 1993). It results in more father involvement and in closer relationships with both parents (Kelly 2007). The parents of Zach, whose story is included in "My Family: How It Feels When Parents Divorce," have joint custody; this may be one reason for his conclusion that "just because your parents are separated it doesn't mean you're going to lose anybody."

The high rate of geographic mobility in the United States can make joint physical custody difficult. Even without that, some children who have experienced joint custody report feeling "torn apart," particularly as they get older. Although some youngsters appreciate the contact with both parents and even the "change of pace" (Krementz 1984, p. 53), others don't. The following account from eleven-year-old Heather shows both sides of a joint physical custody arrangement:

> The way it works now is we switch houses every seven days—on Friday night at five-thirty. . . . [E]ach of our parents likes to help us with our homework and when we stay with them for a week at a time it's easier for them to keep up with what we're doing. . . . And as long as they're divorced, I don't see any alternative because it wouldn't seem right to live with either parent a hundred percent of the time and only see the other one on weekends. But switching is definitely the biggest drag in my life. . . . My rooms are so ugly because I never take the time to decorate them—I can't afford enough posters and I don't bother to set up my hair stuff in a special way because I know that I'll have to take it right back down and bring it to the next house. Now I'm thinking that I'll try to make one room my real room and have the other one like camping out. I can't buy two of everything, so I might as well have one good room that's really mine. (quoted in Krementz 1984, pp. 76–78)

Joint custody is expensive. Each parent must maintain housing, equipment, toys, and often a separate set of clothes for the children and must sometimes pay for travel between homes if they are geographically distant. Mothers, more than fathers, would find it difficult to maintain a family household without child support, which is often not awarded when custody is shared.

Table 15.2 Advantages and Disadvantages of Joint Custody from a Father's Perspective

Advantages	Disadvantages
Fathers can have more influence on the child's growth and development—a benefit for men and children alike. Fathers are more involved and experience more self-satisfaction as parents. Parents experience less stress than sole-custody parents. Parents do not feel as overburdened as sole-custody parents. Generally, fathers and mothers report more friendly and cooperative interaction in joint custody than in visitation arrangements, mostly because the time with children is evenly balanced and agreement exists on the rules of the system. Joint custody provides more free social time for each single parent. Relationships with children are stronger and more meaningful for fathers. Parental power and decision making are equally divided, so there is less need to use children to barter for more.	Children lack a stable and permanent environment, which can affect them emotionally. Children are prevented from having a relationship with a "psychological parent" as a result of being shifted from one environment to another. Children have difficulty gaining control over and understanding their lives. Children have trouble forming and maintaining peer relationships. Long-term consequences of joint custody arrangements have not been systematically studied.

Source: Adapted from Robinson and Barret 1986, p. 89. Copyright © 1986 Guilford Publications. Adapted by permission.

There may be situations—an abusive parent, other domestic violence, or extremely high levels of parental conflict, for example—where sole custody is preferable (Hardesty and Chung 2006).

Research does not consistently support the presumption that joint custody is always best for children of divorced parents. The Stanford Child Custody Study (Maccoby and Mnookin 1992) found that children in mother custody did as well as those in joint custody: "'[T]he welfare of kids following a divorce did not depend on who got custody, but on how the household was managed and how the parents cooperated'" (psychologist Eleanor Maccoby in Kimmel 2000, p. 141; see also Barber and Demo 2006; Freeman 2008). One reviewer of the research literature concluded that there is "no consistent evidence of the superiority of one arrangement over another" (M-Y. Lee 2002, p. 673).

Another review of thirty-three studies of joint and sole custody (Bauserman 2002) did find that children in joint custody arrangements had superior adjustment. In fact, "joint custody and intact family children did not differ in adjustment" in terms of general adjustment, family relationships, self-esteem, emotional and behavioral adjustment, and divorce-specific adjustment (p. 98). This finding of the advantages of joint custody applies to *legal joint custody* as well as to *legal and physical joint custody*. Sole custody was not necessarily bad, but joint custody was simply better in terms of child outcomes.

When a Custodial Parent Wants to Move The desire of a joint custodian or a parent with sole custody to move and take the children "is the hottest issue in the divorce courts at the moment," according to Judith Wallerstein (in Eaton 2004, p. A-1). Some divorce decrees mandate judicial consent and/or the consent of the other parent for a move to another locality. Other cases have gone to court as a result of a parent's initiating legal action to prevent a move.

In deciding these cases, judges tend to demand that the "custodial parent demonstrate that the move serves the best interests of the child" (Glennon 2008, p. 57). States tend to employ two tests to these cases: The first, the relocation doctrine "require[s] custodial parents who wish to relocate to provide notice of the proposed relocation to the other parent 60 days before the move" (Glennon 2008, p. 58). If the noncustodial parent does not give consent, the custodial parent must ask the court for permission to relocate.

These relocation doctrines prohibit custodial parents from moving if they want to retain custody or share joint custody (Cooper 2004; *Navarro v. LaMusga* 2004). "As a result, women have been torn between their wish to remarry or otherwise rebuild their lives and their wish to have their children reside in their homes at least part-time. . . . In checking with legal experts, I found no instance where the father's wish to move was contested" (Wallerstein and Blakeslee 2003, p. 201).

Some judges do see a constitutional issue in the right to move, especially in this "highly mobile society" (Elrod and Spector 2002, p. 595). This is the custody modification approach in which the courts assume that "as long as the parent has a legitimate reason to relocate . . . [it is the court's duty to simply] determine what custody arrangement is in the best interests of the child upon relocation" (Glennon 2008, p. 59). Courts are now more inclined to permit moves for remarriage or economic reasons than they were in the 1980s and 1990s (Kelly and Lamb 2003).

Judith Wallerstein has appeared in court in support of relocating parents, and her opinion has proven very influential. She takes the position that the well-being of the custodial parent and that parent's relationship with the child are the most important factors in adjustment, trumping the question of contact with the other parent. Another divorce researcher, Richard Warshak, presents the opposite point of view in advocating that attention be paid to the importance of a child's maintaining contact with each parent (Eaton 2004). There is little research to date on the issue of parental relocation and none yet on the adjustment of young children to parental relocation.

Parent Education for Co-Parenting Ex-Spouses

Forty-six states have begun to offer or require parent education for divorcing parents, with twenty-six of them making program attendance mandatory (Kelly 2007; Pollet and Lombreglia 2008, p. 375). In some communities, the children also meet in groups with a teacher or mental health professional (Pollet and Lombreglia 2008). The idea is that parents will continue to raise their children as **co-parents,** and they are likely to need help in meeting this new challenge. Evaluation forms completed after the sessions have shown predominantly positive responses. But "there has been no evaluation of whether the information provided is actively employed by parents in their relationship with each other or with the child or whether, indeed, there is any change in the child's well-being" (Wallerstein 2003, p. 86).

Parents in many states are now required to negotiate a "parenting plan" before their divorce is approved (McGough 2005). Again, we have no research yet as to the effectiveness of this requirement in facilitating cooperative postdivorce parenting.

This discussion of mothers' and fathers' custody, visitation, and child support issues suggests that being divorced is in many ways a very different experience for men and women.

His and Her Divorce

Perhaps nowhere is this difference more evident than in the debate over which partner—the ex-wife or the ex-husband—is the primary victim of divorce. Both are affected by the divorce, but often in different ways.

The first year after divorce is especially stressful for both ex-spouses. Divorce wields a blow to each one's self-esteem. Both feel they have failed as spouses and, if there are children, as parents (Demo and Fine 2010). They may question their ability to get along well in a remarriage. Yet each has particular difficulties that are related to the sometimes different circumstances of men and women. In this discussion, we are primarily speaking of divorced men and women who are parents.

Her Divorce

Women who were married longer, particularly those oriented to traditional gender roles, lose the identity associated with their husband's status. Getting back on their feet may be particularly difficult for older women, who usually have few opportunities for meaningful career development and limited opportunities to remarry (Yin 2008). Women of the baby boom generation and later have usually had significant work experience, so they may find it easier to reenter the work world, if they are not already there.

Divorced mothers who retain sole custody of their children often experience severe overload as they attempt to provide not only for financial self-support but also for the day-to-day care of their children. Monitoring and supervising children as a single parent is especially difficult (Braver, Shapiro, and Goodman 2006). Mothers' difficulties are aggravated by lingering gender discrimination in employment, promotion, and salaries and by the high cost of child care. They may have less education and work experience than their ex-husbands. All in all, custodial mothers frequently feel alone as they struggle with money, scheduling, and discipline problems. Objective difficulties are reflected in decreased psychological well-being (Doherty, Su, and Needle 1989; Ross 1995). An encouraging note, though, is that the poverty rate of single custodial mothers dropped significantly between 1993 and 2007, although at 27 percent, it remains higher than that of custodial fathers.

Although those experiencing marital dissolution are less happy than those who are married, another comparison gives us a picture of "her" divorce that is a bit brighter. A majority of women respondents to the National Survey of Families and Households (1992–1993) who

"Her" divorce often involves financial worries and task and emotional overload as she tries to be the complete parent for the children.

compared their lives before and after marital separation perceived improvement in overall happiness, home life, social life, and parenting, although not in finances or job opportunities (Furstenberg 2003, p. 172, Figure 1). Women, compared to men, are more likely to have built social support networks, and they do show greater emotional adjustment and recovery than men (Braver, Shapiro, and Goodman 2006).

His Divorce

Divorced men miss having daily contact with their children and are concerned about possible qualitative changes in their parent–child relationships as well (Braver, Shapiro, and Goodman 2006). In some ways, divorced noncustodial fathers have more radical readjustments to make in their lifestyles than do custodial mothers. In return for the responsibilities and loss of freedom associated with single parenthood, custodial mothers escape much of the loneliness that divorce might otherwise cause and are rewarded by social approval for raising their children (Demo and Fine 2010; Wallerstein and Lewis 2008). Many children of divorce, especially daughters, developed closer relationships with their mothers after the divorce (Wallerstein and Lewis 2007).

Custodial fathers, like custodial mothers, are under financial stress. Noncustodial fathers often retain the financial obligations of fatherhood while experiencing few of its joys. Whether it takes place in the children's home, the father's residence, or at some neutral spot, visitation is typically awkward and superficial. The man may worry that if his ex-wife remarries, he will lose even more influence over his children's upbringing. For many individuals, parenthood plays an important role in adult development: "Removed from regular contact with their children after divorce, many men stagnate" (Wallerstein and Blakeslee 1989, p. 143; Swiss and Le Bourdais 2009).

Ex-husbands' anger, grief, and loneliness may be aggravated by the traditional male gender role, which discourages them from sharing their pain with other men. Sociologist Catherine Ross (1995) compared levels of psychological distress for men and women in four different categories: marrieds, cohabitors, those who were dating, and those with no partner. Ross found that divorced men had the lowest levels of emotional support of any group, whereas emotional support among divorced women was "not that much lower than married women's" (p. 138). In situations of isolation and depression, men are more likely than women to be vulnerable to substance abuse and alcoholism (Braver, Shapiro, and Goodman 2006). Yet in most cases, men still hold the keys to economic security, and ex-wives suffer financially more than do ex-husbands.

The fact is that both men's and women's postdivorce situations would be somewhat alleviated by eliminating the economic discrimination faced by women, especially women reentering the labor force, by strong child support enforcement, and by constructing co-parenting relationships that give fathers the sense of continuing involvement as parents that most would like.

Monkey Business Images/Shutterstock

"His" divorce involves loss of time with children, as well as a more general loneliness. Being the "visiting parent" is often difficult, but maintaining the father–child bond is significant in a child's adjustment to divorce.

Some Positive Outcomes?

First came *Creative Divorce.* As divorce rates rose steeply in the 1960s and into the 1970s, many were heartened by Mel Krantzler's 1973 book, which offered the hope that some good would come of this painful experience.

The eighties and nineties saw an accounting of the all-too-real problems of divorce for children and adults. "Creative divorce" seemed not only ironic but almost maliciously misleading to those making the difficult decision of whether to divorce.

Another swing of the pendulum seems to be taking place. Researchers have begun to explore positive outcomes of divorce. Scholars and clinicians have begun to talk about

Facts about Families

Postdivorce Pathways

Not all divorces have the same outcomes, as research by E. Mavis Hetherington and her colleagues demonstrates. These researchers developed a typology to describe the adjustment to divorce of 238 divorced women and 216 men whom they had interviewed regularly over a ten-year period in the Virginia Longitudinal Study of Divorce and Remarriage. The variability of outcomes is striking.

The Virginia researchers developed a typology based on a cluster analysis of eleven adjustment measures: neuroticism, antisocial behavior, social maturity/responsibility, health, achievement, well-being and satisfaction, self-efficacy, autonomy, parenting competence, social relations, and self-esteem. Six patterns of adjustment emerged from the analysis: Figure 16.7 presents the percentages of men and women in each category at the ten-year point.

Enhancers composed 20 percent of the sample, with more women than men in the group. These individuals "grew more competent, well adjusted, and fulfilled" (Hetherington 2003, p. 324) and had good success at work, in social relations, as parents, and often in remarriages. Some had had a good start in terms of their predivorce qualities, while others were "women who looked ordinary until the stresses of divorce and the challenges of being a single parent activated competencies or forced them to seek out additional resources" (p. 324).

Goodenoughs "had some vulnerabilities, some strengths, some successes, and some problems. They fell in the middle on most personal characteristics.... Ten years after divorce, the goodenoughs' postdivorce life looked like their old predivorced life" (p. 324). At 40 percent, the Goodenoughs were the largest group, almost equally divided between men and women.

Seekers were those who "were eager to find a new mate as quickly as possible." They are hard to quantify because they dropped out of this category once they repartnered. Seekers had less self-esteem and independence, and the men "required a great deal of affirmation.... [If not remarried, Seeker men] succumbed to anxiety, depression, and sometimes sexual dysfunction" (p. 324). They were very dependent on their partners, both old and new. Haste to remarry meant that they sometimes did not make good choices in remarriage partners.

Swingers were a predominantly male group that also declined in numbers over time as the attraction of a libertine lifestyle waned. At the ten-year point, fewer than 10 percent of the divorced people studied were Swingers.

More women than men were *Competent Loners.* "Healthy, well-adjusted, self-sufficient, and socially skilled, competent loners often had gratifying careers, active social lives, and a wide range of hobbies and interests.... [They] were often involved [in] intimate relationships, but these relationships were not enduring ... [as competent loners] had little interest in permanently committing to share their lives with anyone" (p. 325). Hetherington characterizes Competent Loners, along with Enhancers, as "divorce winners" (p. 325).

Defeated individuals, a little over 10 percent of the divorced group at the ten-year point, had low social responsibility and self-esteem and high depression and antisocial behavior. In essence, they did not have satisfying lives.

Hetherington remarks that in analyzing divorce, many commentators assume that the "defeated" type is the "standard outcome of a marital breakup"—but this is not the case (p. 325). "When marriages dissolve, there is no one adaptive pathway adults follow. Some pathways may be destructive, others may be constructive and enhancing" (p. 329).

Critical Thinking

Hetherington and her colleagues have provided us with a set of types. How well do these types of postdivorce adjustment apply to situations that you may have witnessed or personally experienced?

Source: Hetherington 2003.

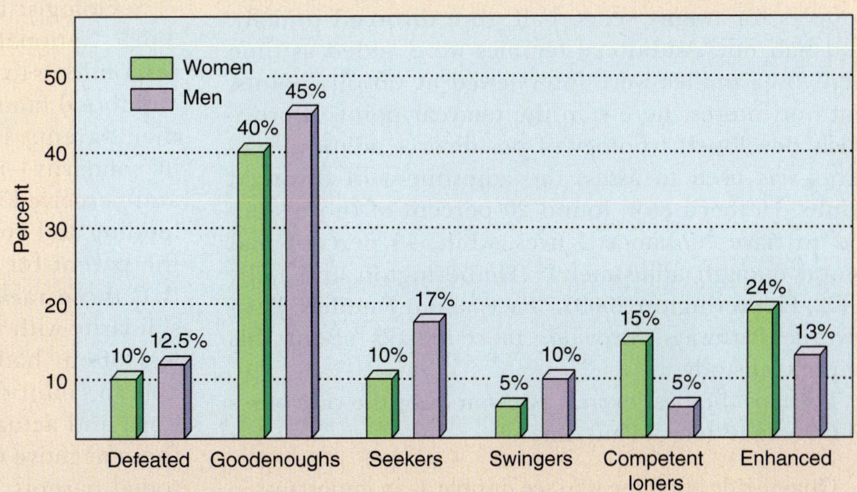

Figure 15.6 Postdivorce adaptive patterns of 216 men and 238 women at the ten-year point: Virginia Longitudinal Study of Divorce and Remarriage.

Source: From Hetherington 2003, pp. 318–331, Figure 3. Reprinted by permission of Blackwell Publishing.

stress-related growth (for children as well as adults). There is now more emphasis on the diversity of outcomes of divorce.

Those studying positive outcomes have connected this line of research to other research on stress-related growth. Stress-related growth can take different paths. A *crisis-related pathway* is marked when a traumatic event generates an ultimate result that makes the person stronger. (See Chapter 14, "Family Stress, Crisis, and Resilience," for a more general discussion of these ideas as applied to the family.) A *stress-relief pathway* occurs, when, for example, the end of a marriage and its problems brings relief to one or both of the partners. Kinds of growth include growth in the self; growth in interpersonal relationships (closer to family and friends); and growth or change in philosophy of life. The specifics are as yet a little vague, and more research is needed. Yet, scholars reviewing the literature conclude that

> [r]esearch on stress-related growth indicates that most individuals who have experienced traumatic events report positive life changes. . . . One thing that is clear from the existing research . . . is that it is at least as common to experience positive outcomes following divorce as negative one[s], and that positive outcomes can coexist with even substantial pain and stress. (Tashiro, Frazier, and Berman 2006, pp. 362, 364)

Another way of looking at stress-related growth—as well as less happy outcomes—comes from E. Mavis Hetherington's Virginia Longitudinal Study of Divorce and Remarriage. She and her colleagues followed 144 couples for twenty years; half were divorced initially, and half not. Additional families were added as time went by. Families were interviewed at various points, but our interest here is in the ten-year point. A previously developed typology of postdivorce adaptive patterns was used to assess the adjustment of divorced adults. Hetherington found 20 percent of those studied to have "enhanced" lives, while 40 percent had "good enough adjustment" (Hetherington and Kelly 2002; Hetherington 2003). "Facts about Families: Postdivorce Pathways" provides more details about this important study.

Perhaps the best overall assessment of the outcomes of divorce is that of Paul Amato:

> On one side are those who see divorce as an important contributor to many social problems. On the other side are those who see divorce as a largely benign force that provides adults with a second chance for happiness and rescues children from dysfunctional and aversive home environments. . . . Based on . . . research . . . it is reasonable to conclude that . . . [d]ivorce benefits some individuals, leads others to experience temporary decrements in well-being that improve over time, and forces others on a downward cycle from which they might never fully recover. (Amato 2000, p. 1,282)

Adult Children of Divorced Parents and Intergenerational Relationships

We have talked about the general effect of divorce on children, but what do we specifically know about how a parental divorce affects adult children's married and family lives? Marital stability for adult children of divorce is discussed earlier in this chapter, as well as in Chapter 6. Here we address the topic of the quality of intergenerational relationships between adult children and their divorced parents.

There is evidence that adult children of divorced parents have probably come to accept their parents' divorce as a desirable alternative to ongoing family conflict (Ahrons 2004; Ahrons 2007; Wallerstein and Lewis 2007). Nevertheless, a number of studies point to one conclusion: Ties between adult children and their parents are generally weaker (less close, less supportive) when the parents are divorced (Ahrons 2007; Connidis 2009; Kelly 2007). The effect for divorced parents is stronger for fathers, usually the noncustodial parent, but the relationship has been found for mothers as well.

Sociologist Lynn White (1994) analyzed data from 3,625 National Survey of Families and Households respondents to examine the long-term consequences of childhood family divorce for adults' relationships with their parents. Using a broad array of indicators of family solidarity—relationship quality, contact frequency, and perceived and actual social support (doing favors, lending and giving money, feeling that one can call on the parent for help in an emergency)—White found that those raised by single parents reported lowered solidarity with them. As adults, they saw their parents less often, had poorer-quality relationships, felt less able to count on parents for help and emotional support, and actually received less support. White found these negative effects to be stronger regarding noncustodial parents (usually the father) but not limited to them.

In another study, sociologist William Aquilino (1994a) analyzed National Survey of Families and Households data from 3,281 young adults between ages nineteen and thirty-four. All grew up in intact families and had therefore lived with both biological parents from birth to age eighteen, but in about 20 percent of the sample, their parents had subsequently divorced. Aquilino found that even when parents divorce after the child is eighteen, the divorce seems to negatively affect the quality of their relationship. Children of divorced parents were in contact with their parents less often and reported lower relationship quality overall. These findings applied to both mothers and fathers, although the effect was much stronger for fathers.

Generally, evidence suggests that adult children of divorced parents feel less obligation to remain in contact with them and are less likely to receive help from them or to provide help to them. Social scientists (Lye et al. 1995) have posited four reasons for these findings:

1. Children raised in divorced, single-parent families may have received fewer resources from their custodial parent than did their friends in intact families, and thus they may feel less obliged to reciprocate.
2. Strain in single-parent families, deriving from the single parent's emotional stress or economic hardship or both, may weaken subsequent relations between adult children and their parents.
3. The reciprocal obligations of family members in different generations may be less clear in single-parent, postdivorce families.
4. Adult children raised in divorced, single-parent families may still be angry, feeling that their parents failed to provide a stable, two-parent household.

Remarriage and stepfamily relationships may generate similar tensions (remarriage and stepfamilies are discussed in Chapter 16).

Should Divorce Be Harder to Get?

In reviewing the process of divorce and its effects, this question arises: Should divorce be harder to get? Some Americans and some family scholars and policy makers think so. At the same time, the American public holds somewhat ambivalent attitudes about divorce. In one poll, one-half of those surveyed thought divorce should be harder to get (Stokes and Ellison 2010, p. 13, Table 1). It also appears that some unhappily married individuals postponed divorce until their children were older (Foster 2006; Schwartz 2010). Yet one poll found most people saying that they do want divorce laws to be tougher—but not when the divorce is their own ("The Divorce Dilemma" 1996).

Some family scholars argue that our high divorce rate signals the decline of the American family (see Chapter 1). To address this situation, policy makers have proposed changes in state divorce laws so that divorces would be more difficult to get than they have been since the 1970s. As noted earlier, with no-fault divorce laws, a marriage can be dissolved simply by *one* spouse's testifying in court that the couple has "irreconcilable differences" or that the marriage has suffered an "irretrievable breakdown."

Concerned about the sanctity of marriage, the impact on children of marital impermanence, and what seems to some a lack of fairness toward the spouse who would like to preserve the marriage, some states have developed—or at least considered—laws and policies that would make divorce harder to obtain. Three states—Louisiana (in 1997), Arizona (in 1998), and Arkansas (in 2001)—have enacted covenant marriage laws. Such laws have been proposed in a number of other states but not enacted (Nock, Sanchez, and Wright 2008).

Covenant marriage, also discussed in Chapter 7, is an alternative to standard marriage that couples may select at the time of marriage or later. It is essentially a return to fault-based divorce because it requires spouses to prove fault (adultery, physical or sexual abuse, imprisonment for a felony, or abandonment) or to live apart for a substantial length of time to obtain a divorce or to do both. Premarital counseling and counseling directed toward saving the marriage are also required. Although polls indicate that some Americans support covenant marriage (Covenant Marriage: A Fact Sheet 2010), only a small minority of couples have chosen this option—less than 2 percent in Louisiana (Nock, Sanchez, and Wright 2008). "Overall, covenant marriage has not proved as popular as supporters have hoped" (Zurcher 2004, p. 288), although those who have chosen covenant marriage are very satisfied (Nock et al. 2003). Most likely, this is because covenant marriage appeals more to highly religious couples who see it as a "symbol of their belief in a Christian marriage and as a public manifestation of their commitment to God" (Baker et al. 2009, p. 166). Chapter 7 discusses covenant marriage and other marriage support programs in detail.

Those who believe divorce is too readily available have proposed other restrictions on divorce or postdivorce arrangements. These have included the restoration of fault for all divorces; a waiting period of as long as five years; a two-tier divorce process, with a more extensive process for divorces involving children; prioritization of children's needs in postdivorce financial arrangements; requirement of a "parenting plan" to be negotiated prior to granting a divorce; and publicizing research that would convince the public of the risks of divorce (Stokes and Ellison 2010; Wilcox 2009). Many states and cities have established premarital counseling, marriage education, marriage counseling, or some combination of the three as either required or elective for couples planning to marry. Some locales require divorcing parents to attend a parent education program. Few object to such programs when voluntary, though some have objected to their being required. Research is lacking on their effectiveness in preventing divorce; however, research shows these kinds of programs are useful in addressing the needs of separating and divorcing couples, and improving the postdivorce lives of families (Belluck 2000; Pollet and Lombreglia 2008).

Opposition to restrictions on divorce centers around various points. First, divorce is not always or necessarily bad for children. Second, some marriages—those involving physical violence or overt conflict or both—are harmful to children and to one or both spouses. Divorce provides an escape from marital behaviors that may be more harmful than divorce itself, such as a parent's alcoholism or drug abuse (Coontz 1997a). An interesting study by economists Betsey Stevenson and Justin Wolfers (2004; 2007) found that no-fault divorce was associated with a decline in suicide rates for women, as well as a decline in domestic violence against both men and women, and a decline in intimate partner homicides of women. The existence of an escape route seems to change the balance of power and reduce violence.

It also appears that staying married would not necessarily provide economic stability for women and children. Those women who obtain divorces would be better off economically if they remained married, but they would not be as well off as that portion of the population that has not divorced; there are differences between the two groups in economic resources quite apart from divorce (Braver, Shapiro, and Goodman 2006; Stevenson and Wolfers 2007).

Those who oppose restoration of fault divorce point to the fraudulent practices that characterized the divorce process under fault statutes. Seldom was either party truly "innocent" of contributing to the marital difficulties, although one party had to pose as such. "Mental cruelty" was the most easily proven grounds for divorce, but the "evidence" for this was often exaggerated at best and completely trumped up at worst. In New York State—where adultery was the only grounds for divorce—"adultery" was often staged, in a drama organized by lawyers and colluded in by both spouses.

Is Divorce Necessarily Bad for Children?

Having thoroughly reviewed the literature and conducted longitudinal research on the subject, sociologists Paul Amato and Alan Booth (1997) conclude that children whose parents were continuously and happily married are indeed the most successful in adulthood. Children of divorce or those whose parents remained unhappily married were less successful. Amato and Booth note the significant role that level of parental conflict plays in conclusions about benefit or harm to children from divorce. They divide divorce outcomes into two classes: In one-third of the cases, marital conflict is so serious and so affects children that they are much better off if the parents divorce. But in two-thirds of the cases—in these researchers' opinion—conflict is low-level and not very visible to children. Then the children seem better off if the parents remain married. Amato and Booth present their conclusions as informative, not as advocacy for legal restrictions on divorce.

Is Making Divorce Harder to Get a Realistic Idea?

Noting that divorce is "an American tradition" that began in colonial times and has grown more prevalent with industrialization and urbanization, historian Glenda Riley, among others, argues that making divorce harder to get will not change this trend (Riley 1991; Wolfers 2006).

Given the likelihood that the restrictions on divorce that some reformers would like to see put in place are unlikely to become law, what may be done to address the negative consequences of divorce for children and to help postdivorce families more generally?

Surviving Divorce

Studies in other countries suggest that policy remedies can make divorce less fraught with hardship. And there is research on "the good divorce," one that promotes a workable family in the aftermath of divorce.

Social Policy Support for Children of Divorce

A cross-cultural study gives insight into what the wider U.S. society might do to help. Sociologists Sharon Houseknecht and Jaya Sastry (1996) examined the relationship between "family decline" and child well-being in four industrialized countries: Sweden, the United States, the former West Germany, and Italy. These researchers' measures of family decline included nonmarital birth and divorce rates, the proportion of one-parent households with children, and the percentage of employed mothers with children under three years old. Child well-being was measured by six factors: educational performance, the percentage of children in poverty, infant deaths from child abuse, teenage suicide rates, juvenile delinquency rates, and juvenile drug offense rates. The researchers found that "Sweden, which has the highest family decline score, does not demonstrate a high level of negative outcomes for children compared with other countries with lower levels of family decline. It looks much better than the U.S., which ranks the lowest on child well-being" (p. 736).

What makes the difference between child well-being in the United States and in Sweden? Sweden's welfare policies are "egalitarian and generous" when compared to those of the United States (p. 737). Sweden's society-wide willingness to support children's needs by paying relatively high taxes translates into significantly less child poverty, fewer working hours for parents, and more family support programs, such as paid parental leave. This situation results in relatively high levels of child well-being despite high proportions of nonmarital births, mother employment, divorces, and single-parent households. A review of policies and outcomes in Nordic countries by sociologist William Goode reached similar conclusions (Goode 1993).

The Good Divorce

Is there such a thing as a "good divorce"? That depends on expectations. Against the assumption that divorce is a disaster and solidifies a lasting enmity between the partners to the detriment of their children, one can indeed find a different pattern, whereby couples maintain civility and cooperative parenting, and perhaps even spend some holidays together with their children (Scelfo 2004). "My Family: The Postdivorce Family as a Child-Raising Institution" describes a couple that continued to parent their children together after divorce, with the assistance of a counselor and after some turmoil.

The Binuclear Family Study The Binuclear Family Study, led by sociologist Constance Ahrons (1994), interviewed ninety-eight divorcing couples approximately one year after their divorce. Ninety percent of them were followed to the five-year point, in a total of three interviews each. These were primarily white, middle-class couples from one Wisconsin county.

At the one-year point, 50 percent of the ex-spouses had amicable relations whereas the other 50 percent did not. In half the cases, the divorce was a bad one and harmful to family members; in the other half, the divorcing spouses had "preserved family ties and provided children with two parents and healthy families" (p. 16):

> In a good divorce a family with children remains a family. The family undergoes dramatic and unsettling changes in structure and size, but its functions remain the same. The parents—as they did when they were married—continue to be responsible for the emotional, economic, and physical needs of their children. (Ahrons 1994, p. 3; see also Kelly 2007 and Ahrons 2007 for additional discussion of positive co-parenting)

The ninety-eight couples represented a broad range of postdivorce relationships. In 12 percent of the cases, couples were what Ahrons termed *perfect pals*—friends who called each other often and brought their common

When divorcing parents continue to engage in conflict and especially when children are drawn into it, a child's adjustment is poorer. Interparental conflict does tend to diminish with the passage of time.

My Family

The Postdivorce Family as a Child-Raising Institution

Jo Ann is thirty-eight and has been divorced for six years. She has five children. Gary, nineteen, her oldest, lives with his father, Richard. At the time of this interview, Jo Ann and Richard and their children had recently begun family counseling. The purpose, Jo Ann explained, was to create for their children a more cooperative and supportive atmosphere. Jo Ann and Richard do not want to renew an intimate relationship, but they and their children are still in many ways a family fulfilling traditional family functions.

We've been going to family counseling about twice a month now. The whole family goes—all five kids, Richard, and me. The counselor wants to have a videotaping session. He says it would help us gain insights into how we act together. The two older girls don't want any part of it, but the rest of us decided it might be really good for Joey to see how he acts. [Joey's] the reason we're going in the first place. At the first counseling sessions, he sat with his coat over his head. . . .

Joey's always been a problem. He's used to getting his own way. Some people want all the attention. They will do anything to get it. I guess I never knew how to deal with this. . . . He drives us nuts at home. He calls me and the girls names. . . . He was disrupting class and yelling at the teacher. And finally they expelled him. . . . Joey gets anger and frustration built up in him.

So I took him to a psychologist, and the psychologist said he'd like the whole family to come in, including Richard. Well, Richard still lives in this city and sees all the kids, so I asked him about it. And he said okay. . . .

In between sessions, the counselor wants us to have family conferences with the seven of us together. One day I called Richard and asked him over for supper. In the back of my mind I thought maybe we could get this family conferencing started.

Well, after dinner Joey, our eleven-year-old, started acting up. So I went for a walk with him. We must have walked a mile and a half, and Joey was angry the whole time. He told me I never listen to him; I never spend time with him. Then he started telling me about how he was mad at his dad because his dad won't listen to him.

He said his dad tells all these dumb jokes that are just so old, but he just keeps telling them and telling them. So when we got home, I saw Richard was still there, and I asked Joey, "Would you like to have a family conference? Maybe tell your dad some of the things that are bothering you?" And he said, "Could we?" . . . [During the conference] Joey talked first. Then everybody had a chance to say something. There was one time I was afraid it was going to get out of hand. Everybody was interrupting everybody else. But the counselor had told me you have to set up ground rules. This is where we learned that we got some neat kids because when I said "Let somebody else talk," everybody did! So it went real well. . . . And then finally Richard said, "I think it's time for us to come to a conclusion." I said, "Well, you're right."

Critical Thinking

How might this divorced family differ from the same family before divorce? How is it the same? Even though Jo Ann and Richard's family is no longer intact, what functions does it continue to perform for its members? For society?

children and new families together on holidays or for outings or other activities. This was a minority pattern among the "good divorces." More often (38 percent), the couples were *cooperative colleagues,* who worked well together as co-parents but did not attempt to share holidays or be in constant touch—occasionally, they might share children's important events such as birthdays. Ex-spouses might talk about extended family, friends, or work. They still had areas of conflict but were able to compartmentalize them and keep them out of the collaboration that they wanted to maintain for their children (Ahrons 1994; 2007). "As We Make Choices: Ten Keys to Successful Co-Parenting" provides some general guidelines for divorcing parents who want to cooperate in parenting their children.

Other divorcing couples were the *angry associates* (25 percent) or *fiery foes* (25 percent) that we often think of in conjunction with divorce. Over time, one-quarter of the "cooperative colleagues" drifted into one of these more antagonistic categories.[15]

Ahrons's overall point is that the "good divorce" does not end a family but instead produces a **binuclear family**—two households, one family. She argues that we must "recognize families of divorce as legitimate." She notes that it is "important to provide parents with some hope and some goals by informing them that it is never too late to improve their relationship and have a good divorce" (2007, p. 62). To encourage more "good divorces," it is

[15] Ahrons (1994; 2007) identified a fifth type of postdivorce couple relationship, the *dissolved duo.* These are couples who have completely lost touch with each other. Because Ahrons's specification of her sample required that a divorced couple have children and be in touch, there were no instances of "dissolved duos" in her sample.

As We Make Choices

Ten Keys to Successful Co-Parenting

Melinda Blau, author of *Families Apart: Ten Keys to Successful Co-parenting*, observes that "[d]ivorce ends a marriage—it does not end a family; we got divorced; our children didn't" (1993, p. 16). Here are her general guidelines for those who hope to accomplish the "heroic feat" of co-parenting after divorce (pp. 16–17):

- Key #1: . . . get on with your life without leaning on your kids.
- Key #2: . . . care for your kids and . . . act in their best interest.
- Key #3: Listen to your children; understand their needs.
- Key #4: Respect each other's competence as parents and love for the children.
- Key #5: Divide parenting time . . . so that the children feel they still have two parents.
- Key #6: Accept each other's differences. . . .
- Key#7: Communicate about (and with) the children directly, not *through* them.
- Key #8: Step out of traditional gender roles. . . .
- Key #9: Recognize and accept that change is inevitable and therefore can be anticipated.
- Key #10: Know that co-parenting is forever; be prepared to handle holidays, birthdays, graduations, and other milestones in your children's lives with a minimum of stress and encourage your respective extended families to do the same.

Critical Thinking

Do you agree or disagree with the advice presented here?

Source: Blau 1993.

important to dispel the "myth that only in a nuclear family can we raise healthy children" (1994, p. 4). People often find what they expect, and social models of a functional postdivorce family have been lacking.

Ahrons (2004, 2007) reinterviewed 173 children from eighty-nine of the original families in her Binuclear Family Study. Now averaging thirty-one years of age, they had been six through fifteen at the time of the

© Michael Newman/PhotoEdit

These divorced parents have both come to meet with their child's teacher. When parents work together to co-parent their children, they continue to have a sense of "family."

marital separation. At present—twenty years later—79 percent think that their parents' decision to divorce was a good one, and 78 percent feel that they are either better off than they would have been, or else not that affected. Twenty percent, however, did not do so well, with "emotional scars that didn't heal" (p. 44). Ahrons judges that the prime factor affecting outcomes was how the parents related to each other in terms of avoiding conflict. The title of Ahrons's most recent book—*We're Still Family* (2004)—characterizes the positive outcomes of divorce that she has found among many of the families she studied.

There is a legal trend that seems to be in tandem with Ahrons's findings and suggestions. This trend is called collaborative divorce. It centers on the idea that divorcing couples will forego litigation and work together—compromising on issues as they proceed—including property divisions and child custody. According to an article by law professor Marsha B. Freeman (2008), collaborative law requires the divorcing couple and their attorneys to "attempt to reach a more amicable, or at least more workable, settlement. Where traditional litigation methods themselves promote anger between the parties and may harm family relationships, collaborative law provides for a more economical and hopefully less hostile way to reach a resolution" (p. 222). In this style of divorce process, the court system does not act as a decision-making body, but instead supports the couple by acting in an advisory capacity, and formalizing the divorce agreement. This style of divorce emphasizes outcomes that are similar to the more collaborative postdivorce relationships Constance Ahrons advocated.

Attachment between Former Partners A more controversial outcome of the "good divorce," and perhaps even some bad ones, is continuing attachment between ex-spouses. One of Paul Bohannon's "stations of divorce" is the psychic divorce, marking the end of the divorce process. **Psychic divorce** refers to the regaining of psychological autonomy through emotional separation from the personality and influence of the former spouse. In Bohannon's view, one must distance oneself from the still-loved aspects of the spouse, from the hated aspects, and "from the baleful presence that led to depression and loss of self-esteem" (Bohannan 1970, p. 53).

By this standard, attachment between former spouses had been seen as a failure of adjustment. But now, clinicians and social scientists are beginning to rethink this stance. "[A]ttachment may be a natural outcome of shared parenting" (Madden-Derdich and Arditti 1999, p. 243). Ahrons and others have written favorably about continuing attachment in the context of co-parenting and maintenance of a family identity and activities (Ahrons 2007).

But what about the postdivorce partner bond as an end in itself? Not only has it been "underacknowledged" but "the nonparenting aspect of ex-spousal relationships has been considered synonymous to psychological maladjustment" (Masuda 2006, pp. 114, 117).

Taking a positive view of former partners who redefine their relationship as friendship, Masahiro Masuda points out that there can be other than parenting elements in a continued attachment. Exploratory research found some interesting themes that point to good reasons ex-partners might maintain a degree of attachment. What these ex-partners, now friends, talked about was that he or she is "part of my life." They had shared experiences with the former partner that they did not want to consign to limbo. They also claimed to have had a "clean breakup" and that "we're different now." In other words, there were boundary markers that would make sure the past relationship did not prevent formation of new serious relationships despite the continuation of a friendship.

Masuda studied young people and had a sample of limited size—thirty-four college students. But journalists have reported on later-life playing out of postdivorce couple attachments. It appears that it is not unusual for one divorced spouse to provide assistance to the other who needs it at the end of life:

> Hospice workers, academics, and doctors say they are seeing more such cases. . . . Often a person feels deep ties to a former husband or wife or feels a responsibility born of common experience and child rearing. . . . "They are acting more like a brother or sister, or cousin, or extended family member" [said the CEO of a public policy hospice group]. (Richtel 2005, p. ST1-2)

The Divorce-Extended Family A continued post-divorce partner connection can result in a much expanded family. Ahrons, author of *The Good Divorce*, offers a number of suggestions that she believes would contribute to good divorce outcomes and successful binuclear families. One suggestion is that the parent "accept that your child's family will expand to include nonbiological kin" (1994, p. 252). She adds that there is an added benefit to the acceptance of nonbiological kin, saying that the "relationships formed when a parent remarries also tend to be more rewarding for the children as their kinship system expands rather than contracts" (2007, p. 64). Indeed, divorce and the new relationships that follow can produce a **divorce-extended family**.

A surprising phenomenon encountered by those who do research on divorced families is the expansion of the kinship system that is produced by links between ex-spouses and their new spouses and significant others and beyond to *their* extended kin. Sociologist Judith Stacey (1990) speaks of a divorce-extended family (p. 61) and quotes writer Delia Ephron's apt observation:

© Lori Waselchuk/The New York Times/ Redux

These eight grandparents, all connected to the young basketball player by marriage, divorce, and remarriage, come together to cheer him on and enjoy his game.

> It occurred to me . . . that the extended family is in our lives again. . . . Your basic extended family today includes your ex-husband or -wife, your ex's new mate, your new mate, possibly your new mate's ex, and any new mate that your new mate's ex has acquired. It consists entirely of people who are not related by blood, many of whom can't stand each other. (Ephron 1988, front leaf)

Ephron's version may be out of date in one respect. Some postdivorce extended families find they can enjoy and benefit from connections to one another even when there had earlier been conflict and old tensions sometimes resurface (Kleinfield 2003). "Letting go of old resentments, whether between ex-spouses, parent and child, or stepparent and child, is the most challenging part of" creating divorce-extended families, but to do so presents additional resources, friendship, and love to individuals and families (A. Bernstein 2007, p. 74). Bernstein suggests that in order to create these beneficial connections, families must unlearn the unfavorable conclusions they have made about the members of the new extended family, and create a basis for mutual respect and understanding.

Therapists claim to see "a new norm" of rapport and social contact among the divorce-extended family that is "becoming part of the culture" (Dr. Harvey Ruben, professor of clinical psychiatry at Yale School of Medicine, quoted in Kuczynski 2001, pp. 9-1, 9-6; see also A. Bernstein 2007). In this spirit, "[n]o longer are the names of exes unmentioned at the dinner table. No longer are the details of passing children between homes confined to emotionless email messages. Family therapists, sociologists, and journalists note that 'family members who 25 years ago might not have had anything to do with one another are finding it desirable to stay connected'" (Kuczynski 2001, p. 9-1).

To the extent that relationships between ex-spouses are cordial and the ties of a divorce-extended family come to seem natural, tension for children moving between families should be reduced. Familial occasions such as graduations and weddings that bring everyone together should be less strained. New research finds that good relationships between children and noncustodial fathers *and* residential stepfathers make independent contributions to good child outcomes (Connidis 2009; Wallerstein and Lewis 2007). If the therapists are right about "new norms," what we could see in the future would be an institutionalization of the "good divorce"—perhaps not attainable for all, but recognized as "normal" for those who do.

That change involves incorporating remarriage bonds into the original family. In Chapter 16, we turn to a consideration of that common step for many divorced people: remarrying.

Summary

- Divorce rates rose sharply in the twentieth century, and divorce rates in the United States are now among the highest in the world. Since around 1980, however, they have declined substantially.
- Among the reasons divorce rates have increased to the present level are changes in society. Economic interdependence and legal, moral, and social constraints are lessening. Expectations for intimacy have risen, while expectations of permanence are declining.
- People's personal decisions to divorce involve weighing the advantages of the marriage against marital complaints in a context of weakening barriers to divorce and an assessment of the possible consequences of divorce.
- Two consequences that receive a great deal of consideration are how a divorce will affect any children and whether it will cause serious financial difficulties.
- Bohannan has identified six "stations of divorce," or aspects of the divorce process and adjustment to divorce. These are the emotional divorce, the legal

divorce, the community divorce, the psychic divorce, the economic divorce, and the co-parental divorce.

- The economic divorce is typically more damaging for women than for men, and this is especially so for custodial mothers. Over the past twenty-five years, child support policies have undergone sweeping changes. The results appear to be positive, with more child support being collected. Fathers' chief concern is maintaining a relationship with their children, so visitation, joint custody, and the moving away of custodial mothers are their chief legal and policy issues.
- Researchers have proposed six possible theories to explain negative effects of divorce on children. These include the life stress perspective, the parental loss perspective, the parental adjustment perspective, the economic hardship perspective, the interparental conflict perspective, and the family instability perspective.
- Husbands' and wives' divorce experiences are typically different. Both the task overload and financial decline that characterize the wife's divorce and the loneliness that often accompanies the husband's might be mitigated by less-gender-differentiated postdivorce arrangements. Joint custody offers the opportunity of greater involvement by both parents, although there are some concerns about joint custody as a universal remedy.
- Debate continues among family scholars and policy makers concerning how important a threat of divorce is to children today. Some call for return to a fault system of divorce or other restrictions on divorce. Others see divorce as part of a set of broad social changes, the implications of which must be addressed in ways other than turning back the clock. Now there is also a centrist view of the impact of divorce on children: Yes, there is some disadvantage; no, divorce is not the most powerful influence on children's lives.
- New norms and new forms of the postdivorce family seem to be developing. Some postdivorce families can share family occasions and attachments and work together civilly and realistically to foster a "good divorce" and a binuclear family.

Questions for Review and Reflection

1. What factors bind marriages and families together? How have these factors changed, and how has the divorce rate been affected?
2. How is "his" divorce different from "her" divorce? How are these differences related to society's gender expectations? In your observation, are the descriptions given in this chapter accurate assessments of divorce outcomes for men and women today?
3. In what situation(s), in your opinion, would divorce be the best option for a family and its children?
4. Do you think couples are too quick to divorce? What are your reasons for thinking so?
5. **Policy Question**. Should divorced parents with children be required to remain in the same community? Permitted to move only by court authorization? Be free to choose whether to be geographically mobile?

Key Terms

barriers to divorce 407
binuclear family 438
child support 418
children's allowance 419
community divorce 414
co-parents, co-parenting 431
covenant marriage 435
crude divorce rate 402
custodial parent 418
custody 425
divorce divide 402
divorce-extended family 440
divorce mediation 413
economic divorce 416
economic hardship perspective (on children's adjustment to divorce) 421
emotional divorce 412
family instability perspective (on children's adjustment to divorce) 421
guaranteed child support 419

Online Resources

Sociology CourseMate

www.CengageBrain.com

Access an integrated eBook, chapter-specific interactive learning tools, including flash cards, quizzes, videos, and more in your Sociology CourseMate, accessed through CengageBrain.com.

www.CengageBrain.com

Want to maximize your online study time? Take this easy-to-use study system's diagnostic pre-test, and it will create a personalized study plan for you. By helping you identify the topics that you need to understand better and then directing you to valuable online resources, it can speed up your chapter review. CengageNOW even provides a post-test so you can confirm that you are ready for an exam.

Appendix A

Human Sexual Anatomy

If you are to understand sexual relations between individuals, you need to be aware of both the anatomy and physiology of sex and the attitudes and emotions that shape people's feelings about their own sexuality and that of others. In Appendix A we will consider the first of these elements, the anatomy and physiology of sex. We will look at female and male sexual anatomy and describe the genitalia, or external reproductive parts, and the internal reproductive systems of each sex.

Female Genital Structures

The external genitalia of a woman are technically referred to as the **vulva.** The vulva is composed of the following structures:

- the **mons veneris,** or pubic mound: an area of fatty tissue above the pubic bone
- the **labia majora** (Latin for "greater lips"): two rounded folds of skin and, within them, the labia minora (or "lesser lips")
- the **prepuce,** or clitoral hood: a fold of skin that covers the clitoris when it is not erect and that is formed where the labia minora join.
- the **clitoris,** which consists of an internal shaft composed of **erectile tissue**—tissue that becomes engorged with blood during arousal, causing it to increase in size—and a **glans,** a highly sensitive tip, about the size of a pea
- the **urethra,** the opening through which urine passes from the bladder to the outside
- the **vestibule,** or entryway to the vagina
- the **perineum,** the area between the vestibule and the anus (the opening from the rectum and bowel)
- the **hymen,** a ring of tissue that partially covers the vaginal opening. The hymen contains small blood vessels that may bleed the first time the tissue is broken: at first intercourse, first insertion of a tampon, during masturbation, or as a result of some accidental injury.

The main internal structures of the female reproductive system are the vagina, the cervix, the uterus, the fallopian tubes, and the ovaries (see Figure A.1).

The **vagina** is the passageway from the uterus to the external genitalia. It is a potential space within a woman's body. Usually, the vaginal walls touch one another, but the vagina is elastic and capable of opening wide enough to allow a baby to pass through during birth. Such stretching would be extremely painful if the vagina had the same number of nerve endings as many of the structures of the vulva. Therefore, the vagina is not so sensitive to feeling.

At the top of the vagina is the **cervix:** the neck of the uterus (cervix means "neck" in Latin). The **uterus,** or womb, is a cavity the purpose of which is to cradle a fetus until birth. Leading from the uterus are two passageways, called **fallopian tubes,** that connect a woman's uterus to her ovaries.

Ovaries are female **gonads,** or sex glands. Women have two ovaries, one on each side of their bodies. They produce reproductive cells (**ova,** or eggs) and two female sex hormones: estrogen and progesterone. Ordinarily, the ovaries alternate in producing one **ovum** per month, in a process called **ovulation.**[1] The egg released in ovulation then travels along the fallopian tubes to the uterus.

1. Sometimes women produce more than one egg at a time. This is one way that twins or higher multiples are conceived.

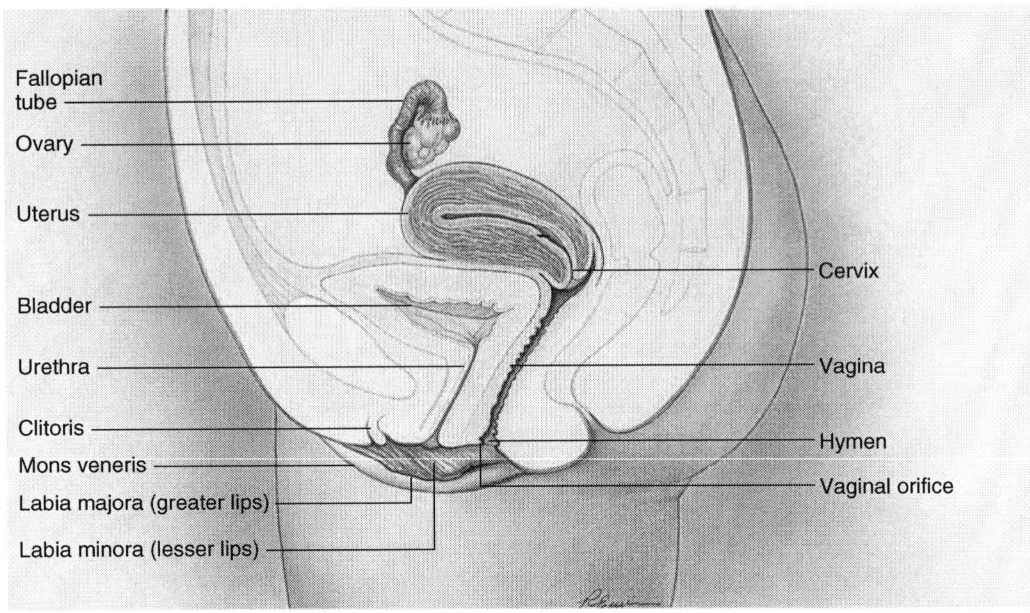

Figure A.1 Female urogenital system.

In preparing to receive the egg, the lining of the uterus, called the **endometrium,** thickens with a layer of tissue and blood (see Figure A.2). This tissue can nourish an embryo during the early stages of pregnancy if the egg becomes fertilized during its passage from the ovaries. When fertilization does not occur, the egg and the unused endometrial tissue and blood are discarded during **menstruation.**[2]

Male Genital Structures

The external male genitalia are the **penis** and the scrotum (see Figure A.3). Like the female clitoris, the penis is composed of an erectile shaft and a sensitive tip, or **glans.** The glans is especially sensitive to touch at the **corona:** a crownlike ridge at its base. If a male has not been circumcised, the glans is covered by a thin membrane, the **foreskin,** when his penis is not erect. In **circumcision,** this foreskin is removed.[3] On the side of the penis, which rests against the scrotum, is the **frenum,** the place where the foreskin is or was connected to the penis. The frenum, even more than the corona, is sensitive to tactile stimulation.

When a man is not sexually aroused, his penis is flaccid. When erect, penises vary somewhat in size and are usually about six inches in length and about an inch and a half in diameter. The **urethra** runs through the penis

2. Menstruation occurs in monthly cycles, ranging from about twenty-one to thirty-five days. Travel, anxiety, illness, extreme athletic activity, or change in diet can make menstrual periods more or less frequent.

3. Circumcision is commonly performed in the United States. The procedure is done shortly after a male baby's birth. For some—particularly Jews and Muslims—circumcision is an important religious or cultural ritual.

Conclusions about whether there are significant health or hygiene benefits to circumcision have varied over the years. Current thinking is that "the medical benefits aren't as compelling as once believed" (Blecher 2001). Also, beginning in the 1970s, the circumcision of male babies has been challenged by those who argue—with some research evidence—that there is enough pain to pose a psychological trauma to the infant (Greenberg, Bruess, and Haffner 2002, pp.142–45; Blecher 2001).

In 1999, the American Academy of Pediatrics (AAP) ceased recommending circumcision as a medically advantageous routine procedure and has adopted a neutral position. It is AAP policy that parents should determine what is in the best interest of the child. Parents should be given accurate information and then make an individual decision based on their assessment of the advantages and disadvantages of circumcision. "It is legitimate for the parents to take into account cultural, religious, and ethnic traditions, in addition to medical factors, when making this choice" (American Academy of Pediatrics 1999).

As circumcision has become less routine, rates have declined. In 1999, only 65 percent of male infants were circumcised, compared to 90 percent in the 1970s. White rates, which had been much higher than those of other racial/ethnic groups, have almost converged with black rates now (66 percent of white baby boys and 64 percent of black babies were circumcised in 1999). Circumcision is less common for Latino or Asian babies (Blecher 2001; Rubin 2001; U.S. National Center for Health Statistics 2002). Some Jews have adopted a substitute circumcision ritual in which there is no actual surgery performed (Blecher 2001).

Recently, the U.S. Centers for Disease Control and Prevention (2007) has reported some research suggesting that circumcision may reduce the risk of HIV infection, including the risk to women of male-to-female transmission through heterosexual intercourse. This development may influence future decision making about infant circumcision.

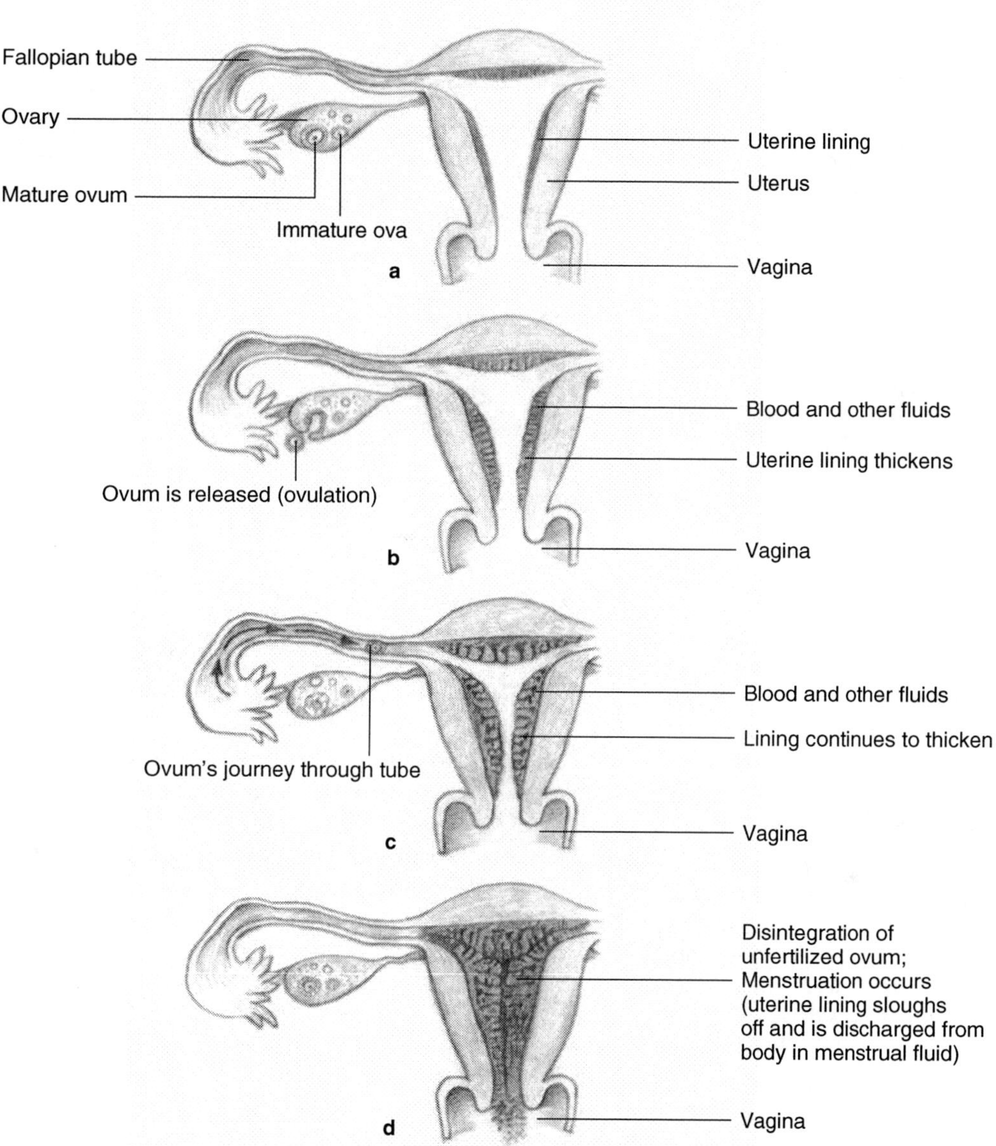

Figure A.2 The menstrual cycle: (a) During the early part of the cycle, an ovum matures in an ovary; the endometrium, or uterine lining, begins to thicken. (b) About fourteen days after the onset of the last menstruation, a mature ovum is released; the endometrium is thick and spongy. (c) The ovum travels through one of the fallopian tubes; blood and other fluids engorge the uterine lining. (d) If the ovum is not fertilized, the endometrium breaks down and sloughs off in a form of bleeding (menstruation).

and carries male reproductive cells and urine, though never at the same time.[4] This opening at the tip of the penis is called the **meatus,** Latin for "passage." Behind the penis hangs a sac, the **scrotum,** which holds the two male gonads, the **testicles.** One testicle is usually lower than the other. Testicles, sometimes called *testes,* are the male counterpart to the female ovaries. They produce the male reproductive cells, called **sperm,** as well as male hormones such as testosterone. Unlike ovaries,

4. A man's urethra cannot carry urine while the penis is erect because erection automatically blocks the opening from the bladder to the urethra.

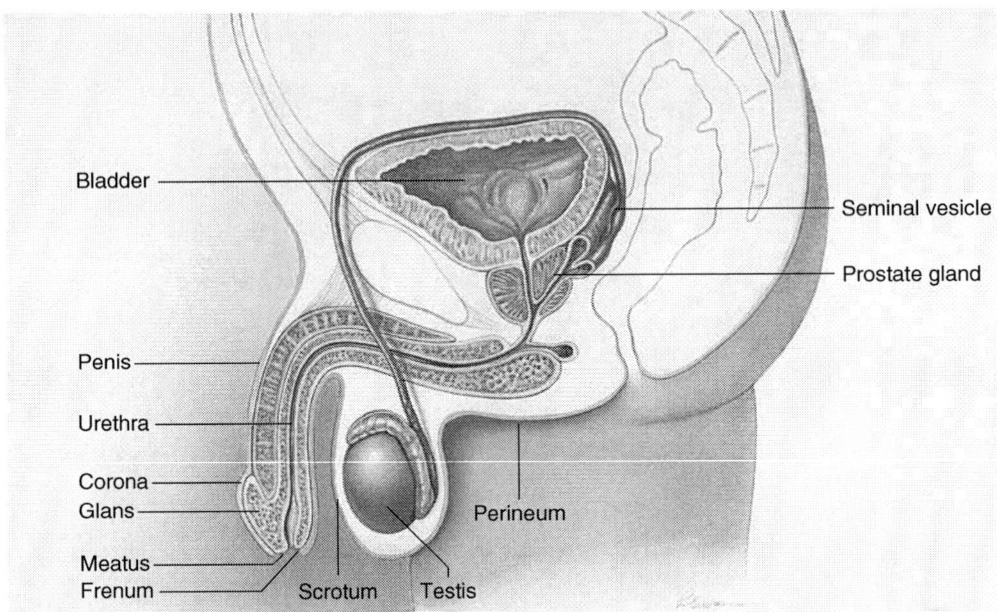

Figure A.3 Male urogenital system.

however, testicles are external structures. That is because they must be maintained at a temperature lower than the body temperature in order to produce living sperm. Between the scrotum and the anal opening is an area called the **perineum.** As in women, this area is sensitive to the touch.

The internal male reproductive structures are also shown in Figure A.3. Above the testicles, near the internal surface of the rectal walls, are two glands, the **seminal vesicles** and the **prostate.** These glands produce **semen,** the milky fluid that carries the sperm through the urethra and out the meatus at **ejaculation.** There are usually between 200 million and 500 million sperm in a teaspoonful of semen. Sperm are ejaculated, or ejected, during the rhythmic contractions of **orgasm.**

If they are ejected into a woman's vagina, sperm move toward her fallopian tubes. Sperm can live in the fallopian tubes from two to five days. If a sperm cell fuses with a female's egg, fertilization occurs, and a fetus is conceived. There are a number of methods that may be used to prevent conception, and these are discussed in Appendix F.

The structures just described make up the male and female reproductive systems. Their reproductive functions are discussed in Appendix E. Appendix B describes the physiology of human sexual response and sexual expression. (See also the Boston Women's Health Book Collective, Our Bodies, Ourselves for the New Century [New York: Simon and Schuster, 1998].)

References

American Academy of Pediatrics. 1999. "Circumcision Policy Statement." *Pediatrics* 103:686–93. Retrieved July 1, 2007 (www.pediatrics.org).

Blecher, Michele. 2001. "Cutting to the Point on Circumcision." WebMD Medical News. September 26. Retrieved July 3, 2006 (www.webmd.com).

Greenberg, Jerrold S., Clint E. Bruess, and Debra W. Haffner. 2002. *Exploring the Dimensions of Human Sexuality.* Sudbury, MA: Jones and Bartlett.

Rubin, Rita. 2001. "Circumcision Rate Increases in Midwest, Drops in West." USA Today, August 21.

U.S. Centers for Disease Control and Prevention. 2007. "Male Circumcision and Risk for HIV Transmission: Implications for the United States." Fact Sheet. Atlanta, GA: U.S. Centers for Disease Control and Prevention. March. Retrieved July 2, 2007 (www.cdc.gov).

U.S. National Center for Health Statistics. 2002. "Trends in Circumcision among Newborns." Press Release. Hyattsville, MD: National Center for Health Statistics. June 21.

Glossary

cervix At the top of the vagina in the female, the neck of the uterus.
circumcision Surgical removal of the foreskin, a membrane that covers the glans of the penis.
clitoris Part of the female genitalia: female erectile tissue, consisting of an internal shaft and a tip, or glans, that contains concentrations of nerve endings and is highly sensitive.
corona A crownlike ridge at the base of the glans on the penis.
ejaculation The rhythmic discharge of seminal fluid containing sperm from the penis during orgasm.
endometrium The lining of the uterus, which thickens with a layer of tissue and blood in order to nourish an embryo should an egg become fertilized. If no egg is fertilized, the endometrial tissue and blood are discarded during menstruation.
erectile tissue Genital tissue that becomes engorged with blood during sexual arousal, causing it to increase in size. In women, erectile tissue composes the clitoris; in men, it composes the penis.
fallopian tubes The tubes that connect a female's uterus with her ovaries. Named after sixteenth-century Italian anatomist Gabriel Fallopius, who first described them.
foreskin A thin membrane that covers the glans of the penis at birth and is sometimes removed by circumcision.
frenum The place where the foreskin is or was connected to the penis.
glans The sensitive tip at the end of the clitoris in women and of the penis in men.
gonads Sex glands—that is, glands secreting sex hormones: the ovaries in women, the testicles in men.
hymen In the female, a ring of tissue that partly covers the vaginal opening.
labia majora Two rounded folds of skin, the external lips in the female genitalia.
labia minora Latin for "lesser lips"; two folds of tissue within the labia majora in the female genitalia.
meatus The opening at the tip of the penis.
menstruation The monthly (approximately) process of discarding an unfertilized ovum and unused tissue and blood through the vaginal opening when no pregnancy takes place.
mons veneris The female pubic mound, an area of fatty tissue above the pubic bone.
orgasm The climax in human sexual response during which sexual tension reaches its peak and is suddenly discharged. In men, ejaculation almost always accompanies orgasm.
ova Plural of ovum.
ovaries Two female gonads, or sex glands, that produce reproductive cells called ova, or eggs.
ovulation The process by which the ovary produces an ovum, or egg.
ovum An egg produced by the ovary. Usually the two ovaries alternate in producing one ovum each month in a process called ovulation.
penis The penis and the scrotum together make up the external male genitalia. The penis is composed of an erective shaft and a sensitive tip, or glans.
perineum In the female, the area between the vestibule and the vagina and the anus. In the male, the area between the scrotum and the anus.
prepuce Part of the female genitalia. The fold of skin that sometimes covers the clitoris, formed where the labia minora join; the clitoral hood.
prostate A male internal reproductive organ that, along with the seminal vesicles, produces semen.
scrotum A sac behind the penis that holds the two male gonads, or sex glands, the testicles.
semen The milky fluid that carries the sperm through the urethra and out the meatus.
seminal vesicles Internal male reproductive glands that, with the prostate, produce semen.
sperm Male reproductive cells present in semen.
testicles Male gonads, or sex glands, that hang in the scrotum behind the penis and produce male reproductive cells (sperm) and the hormone testosterone.
urethra The opening in women and men through which urine passes from the bladder to the outside.
uterus A cavity inside the female in which a fetus grows until birth; also called womb.
vagina The passageway in the female from the uterus to the outside. The vagina is the site of sexual intercourse, which occurs when the male inserts his penis in the female's vagina. The vagina is also the birth canal.
vestibule Entryway to the vagina.
vulva The female external genitalia.

Appendix B

Human Sexual Response

Appendix A describes human sexual anatomy; in Appendix B we examine the physiology of sexual response.

The Four Stages of Human Sexual Response

Through carefully controlled laboratory observation over a period of eleven years, sex researchers William Masters and Virginia Johnson (1966) recorded in detail the bodily changes that take place as a consequence of sexual arousal: the awakening, stirring up, or excitement of sexual desires and feelings in either oneself or others. Masters and Johnson described four phases of human sexual response: excitement, plateau, orgasm, and resolution. These phases characterize both men's and women's responses and take place in sex with partners of the same or the opposite sex. Specific stimulation and sexual movements may vary with the presence or absence of a partner and the sex of the partner, as well as with individual preference and spontaneity on any given occasion. However, the underlying physiological response is the same.[1]

Excitement

When people begin to feel sexually aroused, they enter the **excitement phase** of sexual response. Many forms of stimuli—fantasy, sights, sounds, smells, touches—can cause sexual excitement. Women and men share several responses during the excitement phase, including an increase in blood pressure and pulse rate, and faster breathing. There is a heightened feeling in and awareness of the genitals. This is caused by engorgement, or **congestion,** of the genital blood vessels, which causes the affected tissue to swell and, often, coloration to deepen. Another effect of excitement is **mytonia:** increased muscle tension, especially in the abdominal region and in the long muscles of the arms and legs. A rash or reddening of the skin, called a **sex flush,** appears on the abdomen and chest in about 75 percent of sexually excited women and 25 percent of aroused men.

In women, sexual excitement is marked by the onset of vaginal lubrication, or "sweating" of fluid from the inner walls of the vagina. In men, sexual excitement is characterized by erection of the penis, caused by congestion.

The excitement phase can be stopped intentionally by removing the sexual stimulus. It can also be stopped or interrupted unintentionally through distractions, such as babies crying, phones ringing, changes in lighting and temperature, or feelings of anxiety or guilt. Though interrupted, the excitement phase can be resumed.

Plateau

The **plateau phase** involves an intensification of processes begun during the excitement phase, with several marked bodily changes. The color of the penile glans and the labia minora becomes a deeper red or reddish-purple. There is increased tension in both involuntary and voluntary muscles. Pelvic thrusting, which begins voluntarily when **intercourse** (the insertion of the penis into the vagina) commences, grows more rapid and becomes involuntary, especially among men. Heart rates may nearly double, and blood pressure continues to rise. If the sex flush appeared on a woman during the excitement phase, much of her body will now be flushed. A man may now show the first signs of a sex

1. For a detailed review of men's and women's responses to sexual stimulation, see the Boston Women's Health Book Collective (1998).

flush, which begins under his rib cage and spreads over his chest, neck, and face.

In men, the corona becomes more swollen. Several drops of fluid, which is not semen but which may contain some sperm cells, may emerge from the meatus.[2] Late in this phase, a woman's clitoris pulls deeply underneath the clitoral hood. This, along with the marked change in color in the labia minora, is evidence of her impending orgasm.

The plateau phase may be intentionally prolonged by decreasing the stimulation, returning to the excitement phase, and then increasing stimulation. If stimulation is withdrawn and not restored, sexual tensions will decrease only very gradually. This can be an uncomfortable process, with feelings of fullness and pressure in the pelvis, cramps, lower back pain (Masters and Johnson 1973, p. 119), and general physical and emotional frustration.

Orgasm

In **orgasm,** or climax, sexual tension reaches its peak and is suddenly discharged. This extremely pleasurable and totally involuntary response, the **orgasmic phase,** lasts a few seconds and is accompanied by pronounced physiological changes. Heart and pulse rates peak. Breathing becomes deeper and faster than in the plateau phase, so an individual may sometimes momentarily experience a shortage of oxygen. The senses of smell, taste, hearing, sight, and feeling (except for genital sensation) are temporarily diminished. The sex flush is brightest at this point. Muscles in the neck, legs, arms, buttocks, and abdomen may contract spasmodically, and hand and foot muscles often contract strongly. Involuntary rhythmic contractions in the vagina and penis also occur, though their strength varies from person to person and from orgasm to orgasm. In adult men, orgasm is almost always accompanied by **ejaculation,** the rhythmic discharge of seminal fluid containing sperm. Once these contractions begin, a man cannot voluntarily stop ejaculation. Men normally experience a single orgasm; however, women can be **multiorgasmic,** experiencing several orgasms successively during one sexual encounter. About 15 percent of women regularly have multiple orgasms (McCary 1979, p. 109). In women who experience multiple orgasms, each successive orgasm is often more intense than the preceding one.

2. If this fluid is discharged while the penis is in the vagina, a woman can be impregnated. Thus, interrupting intercourse before ejaculation (*coitus interruptus*) is not a reliable birth control method.

Resolution

During the **resolution phase** of sexual activity, partners' bodies return to their unstimulated state. The genitals resume normal size and color, the sex flush disappears, muscles relax, and erect nipples soften. Heart rate, blood pressure, and respiratory rates revert to normal.

Return of the penis to its flaccid state begins quickly, then proceeds more slowly. During this stage, men experience a **refractory period:** a time during which they cannot become sexually aroused. The refractory period usually lasts at least twenty minutes and may be considerably longer, particularly as a man grows older. For women, the resolution phase lasts about ten to fifteen minutes and occasionally as long as a half hour. During this time, women may remain sexually aroused and, with continued or renewed stimulation, can experience subsequent orgasms.

References

Boston Women's Health Book Collective. 1998. *Our Bodies, Ourselves for the New Century.* New York: Touchstone/Simon and Schuster.

Masters, William H. and Virginia E. Johnson. 1966. *Human Sexual Response.* Boston, MA: Little, Brown.

———. 1973. "Orgasm, Anatomy of the Female." In *Encyclopedia of Sexual Behavior,* edited by Albert Ellis and Albert Abarbanel. New York: Aronson.

McCary, James Leslie. 1979. *Human Sexuality.* 2nd ed. New York: Van Nostrand.

Glossary

congestion The engorgement of blood vessels, which causes the affected tissues to swell. Occurs to the genitals during the excitement phase of sexual response.

ejaculation The rhythmic discharge of seminal fluid containing sperm from the penis during orgasm.

excitement phase One of the four phases of human sexual response described by Masters and Johnson. The excitement phase begins when people begin to feel sexually aroused and is characterized by increased breathing, increased blood pressure and pulse rates, vasocongestion of the penis and clitoris, and vaginal lubrication in women.

intercourse The insertion of the penis into the vagina, also called *coitus.*

multiorgasmic Capable of experiencing several successive orgasms during one sexual encounter.

mytonia Increased muscle tension, which can occur as a result of sexual arousal.

orgasm The climax in human sexual response during which sexual tension reaches its peak and is suddenly discharged. In men, ejaculation almost always accompanies orgasm.

orgasmic phase The third of four progressive phases of human sexual response described by Masters and Johnson. The orgasmic phase is characterized by extremely pleasurable sexual sensations and by involuntary rhythmic contractions in the penis and vagina.

plateau phase The second phase of human sexual response, during which the bodily changes begun during the excitement phase intensify, and pelvic thrusting, which begins voluntarily, grows more rapid and becomes involuntary, especially among men.

refractory period A time after orgasm during which a man cannot become sexually aroused. It usually lasts at least twenty minutes and may be considerably longer, particularly in older men.

resolution phase The final phase of human sexual response described by Masters and Johnson, during which bodies return to their previous unstimulated state.

sex flush A rash or reddening of the skin that appears during sexual arousal; especially common in women.

sexual arousal The process of awakening, stirring up, or exciting sexual desires and feelings in oneself or others.

Appendix C

Sexually Transmitted Diseases

Because HIV/AIDs has taken center stage, we sometimes overlook other **sexually transmitted diseases (STDs)** and **sexually related diseases (SRDs)**[1] that also threaten comfort, health, reproductive capacity, and sometimes life. Public health officials have become very aware of the serious impact of some STDs that were previously unknown or thought to be relatively trivial. The effects of STDs may extend to infants born to infected mothers. Not including HIV/AIDS, around 19 million Americans become infected with a sexually transmitted disease each year; almost half are youth between the ages of fifteen and twenty-four (U.S. Centers for Disease Control and Prevention 2004l).

STDs are named according to the bacterium or virus (e.g., syphilis or herpes) that produces them, or they may be defined by their symptomatic effects. Such terms as *vaginitis* and *pelvic inflammatory disease,* for example, refer to inflammations or infections of the vagina or reproductive organs.

We'll first describe some common sexually transmitted diseases (not including HIV/AIDS), then talk about protective practices, and conclude by discussing the connections between HIV/AIDS and other sexually transmitted diseases.

1. *Sexually related diseases* are "diseases of the reproductive tract that occur in both sexually active and sexually abstinent individuals. These can be caused by organisms that live in the healthy body, but under certain conditions, such as stress, diabetes, drug use, and other health-related problems, affect the delicate chemical balance of the body and cause disease conditions of the sexual organs. . . . A sexually related disease can sometimes be transmitted to a sexual partner" (Greenberg, Bruess, and Haffner 2002, p. 462). *Cytomegalovirus* (*CMV*) and *Hepatitis B* are examples of sexually related diseases.

Sexually related diseases are often grouped with sexually transmitted diseases—as we have done here—in order to inform sexually active individuals about disease conditions associated with sexual activity. When tissue becomes irritated or broken or germs are transferred from their normal site in the body to elsewhere in the reproductive, urinary, or digestive systems, an infection can occur that is not strictly speaking a sexually transmitted disease, but which is produced by or related to sexual activity.

Common Sexually Transmitted Diseases

Table C.1 describes the nature, symptoms, complications, and treatment of STDs other than HIV/AIDS. These include: syphilis, gonorrhea, chlamydia, human papillomavirus (HPV), genital herpes, cytomegalovirus (CMV), chancroid, Hepatitis B, pelvic inflammatory disease (PID), and bacterial vaginosis and trichomoniasis.

Syphilis

Rates of *syphilis,* a bacterial disease, peaked in 1990 and then began to decline. By 2000, they were the lowest since reporting began in 1941. In 2001, syphilis rates began to increase again, especially among men, including men who have sex with men. Rates among women began to increase in 2005. Rates have decreased among African Americans while rising among white men. Still, African American men have rates of syphilis that are five times as high as those of white men (U.S. Centers for Disease Control and Prevention 2006).

Gonorrhea

Gonorrhea is also a bacterial disease. Gonorrhea rates have declined among African American men and women, while rising among whites; nevertheless they remain higher among African Americans. Currently, women have higher rates of gonorrhea than men do. African

Table C.1 Sexually Tranmitted Diseases

Disease	Nature, Symptoms, and Complications	Treatment
Chancroid	Bacterial infection that causes genital ulcers sometimes accompanied by enlarged, painful lymph nodes in the groin. Screening for chancroid is technically difficult, but the disease has now become relatively rare.	Antibiotics
Chlamydia	Genitourinary tract bacterial infection. Chlamydia can cause pelvic inflammatory disease in women, which can lead to infertility and is potentially life threatening. Can also lead to infertility in men. Can cause prematurity, eye disease, and pneumonia in infants born to infected mothers. Frequently asymptomatic, so screening is important. Screening is recommended for women under the age of twenty-six and for older women who are with a new partner or who have multiple sexual partners. A test now exists for screening men.	Antibiotics
Cytomegalovirus (CMV)	A virus that is part of the herpes family. It produces mononucleosis-like symptoms in an active infection. CMV can be transmitted through sexual contact, but in other ways as well. This virus is present in a majority of the American population, but is usually latent; that is, no symptoms are manifested. For people with impaired immunological systems, the effects of CMV are more severe and include gastrointestinal problems or blindness. When a newly acquired infection is transferred to a fetus during pregnancy, especially when it is a first infection for the mother, a possible result is retardation or death.	Contact CDC for latest developments. Immunosuppressed adults with serious symptoms are treated with antiviral drugs.
Genital Herpes	A viral disease that produces lesions on the genitals that are similar to cold sores that appear on the mouth. May be asymptomatic, but symptoms often take the form of a general malaise (tiredness, depression, low energy, not feeling right). Frequently recurs, but the first episode is usually the worst. Genital herpes can be transmitted to sex partners or infants even when symptomless. Can cause blindness, hearing problems, or death of infants born to infected mothers, although this last is a rare occurrence.	Antiviral drugs such as acyclovir can control outbreaks of symptoms, although the infection cannot be cured. Taking care of general health and avoiding stress may help prevent outbreaks.
Gonorrhea	Gonorrhea is a bacterial disease, transmitted through sexual contact, including oral contact. It can also be transmitted from mother to child during delivery. Symptoms include genital irritation, discharge, and painful urination, although gonorrhea in women may be symptomless. Gonorrhea can lead to pelvic inflammatory disease in women, which can, in turn, lead to infertility. Infertility is possible in men also. Newborns of infected, untreated mothers are at risk of serious complications. In adults gonorrhea may spread to the blood and joints and become life threatening.	Penicillin or other antibiotics. There are now penicillin-resistant strains, making gonorrhea riskier than it had been and turning treatment into a search for the right antibiotic. At-risk people should be tested routinely, and certainly if they detect possible symptoms.
Hepatitis B (HBV)	This viral disease, contracted primarily through sexual contact or infected blood or needles, is a liver disease similar to other forms of hepatitis. Symptoms are general, such as nausea, vomiting, pain, malaise, loss of appetite, and jaundice, but HBV can be asymptomatic. HBV can cause short-term liver inflammation that subsides after the active phase, or chronic infections that can lead to such life-threatening conditions as cirrhosis and liver cancer. It can also be passed from mother to child during birth.	Treatment consists of certain medications used to prevent or retard liver damage. There is now a vaccine for hepatitis B, recommended for individuals at high risk in terms of their sexual behavior or exposure to the disease in their household or work and routinely given to children. Also recommended for overseas travelers to countries where HBV is prevalent.
Human Papillomavirus (HPV)	Also termed genital warts because one possible symptom of this viral disease is warts—sometimes painful—on genital organs or rectum. Can increase the risk for cervical cancer and, more rarely, for penile and anal cancer. HPV is often symptomless, and this viral infection usually resolves on its own. But serious complications are possible, notably cervical cancer. Pap smears can detect precancerous or cancerous lesions caused by HPV, and these can be treated. Genital warts can be removed surgically, chemically, or cryogenically (freezing of tissue).	A vaccine against HPV is now available. To provide most prevention, it needs to be administered before a young woman becomes sexually active. It is approved for women 9–26 but has not yet been tested in an older age group.

Table C.1 Sexually Tranmitted Diseases—*Continued*

Disease	Nature, Symptoms, and Complications	Treatment
Pelvic Inflammatory Disease (PID)	A condition that may develop when other STDs go untreated. Can result in chronic pelvic pain in women and/or harm to the reproductive organs—such as damage to the fallopian tubes—that causes infertility.	Treat the causal STD with antibiotics before PID develops. Sex partners should also be treated to prevent reinfection.
Syphilis	A bacterial disease that is transmitted through vaginal, anal, or oral sex; transmission through oral sex is increasingly common. Syphilis develops in stages. In the first stage, a genital sore appears. It disappears but is followed in a few weeks by fever, swollen lymph nodes, and rash, which also recede. May be in remission for some years, but arrival of the last stage involves damage to heart, nervous system, brain, and other organs. In infected pregnant women, can cause stillbirth or birth defects.	Syphilis is diagnosed by a blood test. Early diagnosis is important because syphilis can be cured by antibiotics if caught early enough. Syphilis can sometimes be asymptomatic, so it is important that people at risk be regularly screened. Later-stage syphilis cannot be successfully treated.
Trichomoniasis, Bacterial Vaginosis, and Vaginitis	Bacteria, fungi, and other infectious organisms, allergens, or physical irritation can cause inflammation, discharge, and itching of the vagina and genital area. *Trichomoniasis* is caused by a microscopic parasite, while *bacterial vaginosis* may or may not be sexually transmitted. *Vaginitis* is the term used for nonspecific vaginal and genital irritations of uncertain cause. Male sex partners may develop urethritis (inflammation of the urinary tract) or penile lesions. Vaginitis from some causes can result in an oral infection in newborn infants and trichomoniasis and bacterial vaginosis are associated with premature or low-birth-weight babies.	Various prescription and over-the-counter medications are used to treat these common—and often persistent—conditions. Male sex partners—who may be asymptomatic—also need to be treated to avoid reinfection. Women's health books such as *Our Bodies, Ourselves: A New Edition for a New Era* (Boston Women's Health Book Collective 2005) provide useful advice on diet, clothing, hygiene, and so on, which can help prevent some forms of vaginitis or prevent recurrences.

Sources: (U.S. Centers for Disease Control and Prevention. 2001; 2002; 2003; 2004a, b, c, d, e, f, g, h, i, j, k, l, m; 2006; 2007a, b, c).

American females fifteen to nineteen have the highest rates of any racial/ethnic/gender category. A current concern is the growing resistance of gonorrhea to antibiotic drugs that were previously effective in curing the disease ("Gonorrhea Is Now a Superbug" 2007; U.S. Centers for Disease Control and Prevention 2006).

Chlamydia

Although syphilis and gonorrhea have long been known and regarded as serious health threats, some more recently identified STDs, *chlamydia* and *human papillomavirus (HPV),* are the most commonly occurring STDs today. Chlamydia is a risk factor for pelvic inflammatory disease, a significant cause of infertility. *PID (pelvic inflammatory disease)* can be life threatening as well.

Reported cases of chlamydia have increased in recent years, but some of the apparent increase is due to better reporting after screening programs were introduced in the 1980s. Chlamydia is asymptomatic and often not recognized. Thus, it is important for sexually active women under twenty-six and older women at risk—those with new or multiple partners—to be tested periodically. Men can now be tested for chlamydia as well (U.S. Centers for Disease Control and Prevention 2004b, 2006). A test used for diagnosis of chlamydia can also be used to detect *lymphogranuloma venereum (LGV),* a related disease (U.S. Centers for Disease Control and Prevention 2007c).

Human Papillomavirus (HPV)

Human papillomavirus (HPV) is the most common STD, affecting at least 50 percent of sexually active men and women at some point in their lives. Most will not have symptoms, and in many instances the disease will recede on its own. But HPV is a family of viruses. Some strains are "high risk," implicated as a causal factor in cancer of the cervix and, more rarely, other cancers of the genital area, including penile and anal cancers in men. "Low-risk" HPV viruses can produce genital warts (Brody 2007; U.S. Centers for Disease Control and Prevention 2004d).

A vaccine has now become available to protect against many variations of the HPV virus, reducing the risk of cervical cancer (Brody 2007). For full effectiveness, the vaccine needs to be administered before sexual activity occurs. It has been recommended that it be given to eleven- to twelve-year-old girls, and it is approved for the age range nine through twenty-six. (Tests have not yet commenced on women over twenty-six). Nevertheless, more than half of U.S. pediatricians surveyed have expressed reluctance to recommend it to their young patients ("Many Pediatricians" 2007).

Proponents argue that virtually the only drawback is the cost (Brody 2007). The governor of Texas ordered mandatory vaccination of eleven- to twelve-year-old girls, but quickly rescinded the order in the face of objections from legislators, conservative groups, and members of the public (Blumenthal 2007). Whether the vaccine will be widely accepted remains to be seen.

Pelvic Inflammatory Disease (PID)

Pelvic inflammatory disease (PID) is an infection of the reproductive organs (uterus or fallopian tubes) that symptomatically causes abdominal pain but may also be symptomless. PID often occurs as a complication of such sexually transmitted diseases as chlamydia or gonorrhea, although it may also be caused by other infections that invade the reproductive organs through the vagina and cervix. More than a million women have an episode of pelvic inflammatory disease each year, and 100,000 cases of infertility are attributed to PID annually (U.S. Centers for Disease Control and Prevention 2004i).

Genital Herpes and Chanchroid

Genital herpes is a viral disease transmitted through genital or oral sex. Genital herpes increased 30 percent from the 1970s to the 1990s, but declined 17 percent in the 1990s, perhaps as a consequence of the decline in risky sexual behavior among teens. Still, approximately 20 percent of American adolescents and adults are infected. Women have slightly higher rates of infection, while African Americans have rates of genital herpes that are substantially higher than those of whites. In part, this has to do with differential reporting. But part of the difference is real, attributed to poverty, drug use, and sexual networks in which STDs are prevalent, as well as less access to health care (Altman 2004; Rosenthal 2003; U.S. Centers for Disease Control and Prevention 2001, 2004c).

Chancroid is a bacterial STD similar to genital herpes, found primarily in men. However, from a high point of around five thousand cases in 1987, chancroid has declined to almost the point of extinction; only fifty-four cases were reported in 2003 (Rosenthal 2003; U.S. Centers for Disease Control and Prevention 2004j).

Cytomegalovirus (CMV)

Cytomegalovirus (CMV) is a viral STD that infects a majority of adults by the time they reach age forty. Symptoms of active CMV resemble mononucleosis. In most individuals the disease is latent, with no symptoms or health effects. However, immunosuppressed adults and infants exposed during their mother's pregnancy are at risk of serious health damage if they become infected with CMV. There is no treatment for fetuses in utero, and post-birth drug treatment for hearing problems has such severe side effects that it is not recommended. Work is in progress on a vaccine (U.S. Centers for Disease Control and Prevention 2002, 2007c).

Hepatitis B

Hepatitis B is a liver disease caused by infection with the hepatitis B virus (HBV). It is spread from one person to another by contact with blood, semen, or vaginal fluids, most commonly through vaginal, oral, or anal sexual contact. There is now a vaccine for HBV that is routinely administered to children. New infections have decreased from about a quarter of a million annually in the 1980s to fewer than eighty thousand today (U.S. Centers for Disease Control and Prevention 2004f).

Trichomoniasis, Bacterial Vaginosis, and Vaginitis

Trichomoniasis, bacterial vaginosis, and *vaginitis* are grouped together because their symptoms are similar—vaginal discharge and itching—and so are their complications. These diseases increase the risk of transmission of HIV and other sexually transmitted diseases, and they are associated with premature delivery and low-birth-weight babies (U.S. Centers for Disease Control and Prevention 2004a, m). But they do differ as to nature and cause.

Bacterial vaginosis is a sexually related disease of women that results from a disruption of the normal balance of bacteria in the vagina. The specific cause of bacterial vaginosis is not well understood. Having multiple sex partners does seem to increase the risk, and an argument can be made that it is a sexually transmitted disease ("Evidence Supporting" 2005; U.S. Centers for Disease Control and Prevention 2004a).

Trichomoniasis is clearly a sexually transmitted disease, caused by parasites. Both men and women can get trichomoniasis, though it is more common among women and the itching/discharge symptomology is more pronounced in women (U.S. Centers for Disease Control and Prevention 2004m).

Vaginitis, sometimes termed *candidiasis,* is a nonspecific irritation or infection of the female genital tract.

Protective Practices and Treatment

Because many STDs can be asymptomatic—that is, have no visible symptoms to indicate the presence of the disease—it is important for people at risk to have frequent screening for STDs. **"At risk"** in this context includes anyone with multiple sex partners or a partner who has a history of multiple partners. Individuals whose general health makes them vulnerable to infection are also at risk. In truth, any sexual relationship that is not long term and not known to be monogamous should be considered risky. Sexually active individuals, particularly women who have regular gynecological checkups, might wish to make *STD screening* a normal part of their health care.

As We Make Choices HIV/AIDS —Some Precautions

AIDS has changed the context of sex, relationships, and life choices. You will want to keep updating your information, but here are some precautions that at present seem reasonable:

1. **Safer sex** (no precautions can make sex completely risk-free). For sexually active individuals who are not in long-term, securely monogamous relationships, this means the use of latex condoms (sheathed by a plastic condom for those who are allergic to latex). *Do not use* animal skin because it is permeable and will permit transmission of the HIV virus.

    > Unless it is possible to know with *absolute certainty* that neither you nor your sexual partner is carrying the HIV/AIDS virus you must use protective behavior. *Absolute certainty* means not only that you and your partner have maintained a mutually faithful monogamous sexual relationship, but it means that neither you nor your partner has used illegal intravenous drugs. (Koop n.d., p. 16)

2. For heterosexuals as well as those in the gay community, safer sex also means the limiting of partners in number and selectivity. It would be prudent to confine sexual activity and relationships to those worth the risk. This can mean decisions about individuals, or it can mean categorical decisions about multiple partners or sex with members of high-risk groups such as men who have sex with men, individuals who have multiple partners, intravenous drug users, or people known to have AIDS or HIV.

    Inquiring about a potential sex partner's health, HIV status, and previous partners is useful. However, it is entirely possible that a prospective partner will not be honest. "Large proportions of men and women with HIV have sex without telling partners that they are infected" ("Large Proportions" 2003, p. 235). Many people are unaware and untested (Altman 2002). It is also the case that antibodies to HIV do not develop for up to six months or longer after infection with the virus, so an infected person may appear virus-free in early tests and may report the possibly erroneous results in good faith. Consequently, experts argue that the use of latex condoms with any partner is the most protective approach.

3. Deciding to take risks may involve others: your current or future sex partners, your children, and your family. A responsible sexually active individual concerned about risk to others will be voluntarily tested and, if the test is positive, will either refrain from sex or inform the partner beforehand and use condoms during sex. Responsible sex also includes telling prospective sex partners about past sexual activity with infected or high-risk individuals.

4. Women planning to become pregnant or not taking precautions against pregnancy should be sure that they are free of HIV by being tested and perhaps retested over a six-month period. If they are infected and become pregnant, they should seek medical help; with that, they are likely to prevent passage of the HIV virus to their child.

5. Health care workers should take the precautions recommended by guidelines for their occupation.

6. Citizens should support sex education designed to prevent the spread of AIDS. Appropriate AIDS education should be encouraged for children (because even young children can be exposed to AIDS through sexual abuse), as well as for teenagers and adults. Videotapes intended for home viewing are available from schools, libraries, public health departments, and commercial sources.

    Keep yourself informed by consulting your local public health department, physicians, clinics, reproductive health services, student health services, churches, gay/lesbian activist groups, and/or media sources. A good source for comprehensive and updated information and links to other websites is the National Library of Medicine MedlinePlus website: http://medlineplus.gov. The Centers for Disease Control and Prevention website is also an important resource: www.cdc.gov.

Latex condoms[2] provide some but not absolute protection from STDs. Condoms are clearly effective in the prevention of HIV infection, gonorrhea, chlamydia, and trichomoniasis. These are "discharge STDs," spread by the discharge of semen or vaginal secretions, and condoms prevent these fluids from entering the body. Condoms provide some unknown degree of protection from genital herpes, syphilis, and chancroid and from human papillomavirus (Brody 2006; "Consistent Condom Use" 2006; "Frequent Male Condom" 2006; U.S. Centers for Disease Control and Prevention 2003).

To be effective, condoms must be used always, and used correctly. A survey of 1,155 adults eighteen through thirty-five years old conducted by the American Social Health Association found that one-quarter of single, sexually active individuals said they never use condoms in vaginal sex, and 71 percent never use them in oral sex (Oglesby 2004).

2. Only latex condoms have been shown to be effective against HIV. Polyurethane (plastic) condoms are available for people allergic to latex, but they need to be used in combination with latex condoms. Condoms made out of lambskin, or other "natural" materials, are known to be ineffective (Brody 2003, 2006).

Many mistakes are made by users. A study of 158 male students at Indiana University found that 43 percent waited too long, putting the condom on after sex began; 30 percent put the condom on upside down; and 15 percent removed it before the sex act was completed.

Broken or slipped condoms were also reported (Webster 2002). A study of almost 800 sexually active young women between the ages of eighteen and twenty-four found that 44 percent of the women who used condoms in a sexual encounter waited too long (after first penetration). Another study of 243 sexually active women found inconsistent use (Brody 2003, 2006). Condom users should check condoms for intactness and currency (not past expiration date) and should carefully read directions about usage, best done beforehand.

Vaccines exist for Hepatitis B (U.S. Centers for Disease Control and Prevention 2004f) and for human papillomavirus (Brody 2007). Efforts are under way to develop vaccines for some other STDs.

Early treatment can often prevent the most severe outcomes of STDs. CDC guidelines recommend these principles regardless of the STD being treated:

1. Refrain from sex while infectious and while under treatment.
2. Inform sex partners so they can be treated.
3. Continue treatment as long as recommended and return for follow-up visits.
4. Use condoms to minimize future transmission, as many STDs tend to recur. Successful treatment of STDs may require a great deal of trial and error on the physician's part and considerable patience from the patient.
5. Seek the advice of a physician before becoming pregnant.

AIDS and Other Sexually Transmitted Diseases

Sexually transmitted diseases other than HIV/AIDS are important health risks in their own right. But many STDs are also significant risk factors for transmission of HIV/AIDS. Genital ulcers (open sores) or other bodily vulnerabilities produced by STDs make infection by the HIV virus much more likely. In fact, many HIV-infected people are found to have other STDs as well (Kaiser Family Foundation 2003; U.S. Centers for Disease Control and Prevention 2007b).

Although HIV/AIDS is in a class by itself in terms of threat to life and health, precautionary guidelines against the risk of HIV/AIDS are also useful for sexually active individuals who wish to avoid other sexually transmitted diseases. See "As We Make Choices: HIV/AIDS—Some Precautions" for a discussion of guidelines.

The Division of Sexually Transmitted Diseases at the Centers for Disease Control and Prevention (CDC) in Atlanta is a central resource for information and research on HIV/AIDS and other STDs. The CDC website is http://www.cdc.gov. You can find material on sexually transmitted diseases by clicking on Diseases and Conditions on the home page and then choosing HIV/AIDS or Sexually Transmitted Diseases. Alternatively, go to Health Topics A–Z, and find HIV/ AIDS and Sexually Transmitted Diseases, or search for a particular STD.

References

Altman, Lawrence K. 2002. "Many Americans with H.I.V. Don't Know It or Don't Seek Care, Study Shows." New York Times, *February 26.*

———. 2004. "Genital Herpes Decline 17% Surveys Show." *New York Times.* March 9.

Blumenthal, Ralph. 2007. "Texas Governor Is First to Require Cancer Shots for Schoolgirls." New York Times, February 3.

Boston Women's Health Book Collective. 2005. *Our Bodies, Ourselves: A New Edition for a New Era.* New York: Simon and Schuster.

Brody, Jane. 2003. "Facts of Life: Condoms Can Keep Disease at Bay." *New York Times,* January 23.

———. 2006. "Condoms Stay Faithful When Prevention Is the Goal." *New York Times,* August 22.

———. 2007. "HPV Vaccine: Few Risks, Many Benefits." *New York Times,* May 15.

"Consistent Condom Use Reduces the Risk of Type 2 Herpes Virus." 2006. *Perspectives on Sexual and Reproductive Health* 38(1):54–55.

"Evidence Supporting the Notion That Bacterial Vaginosis Can Be Transmitted Sexually Continues to Accumulate." 2005. *Perspectives on Sexual and Reproductive Health* 37(4):206.

"Frequent Male Condom Use Decreases Women's Risk of HPV Infection." 2006. *Perspectives on Sexual and Reproductive Health* 38(4):228–29.

"Gonorrhea Is Now a Superbug." 2007. Perspectives on Sexual and Reproductive Health39(2):73.

Greenberg, Jerrold S., Clint E. Bruess, and Debra W. Haffner. 2002. *Exploring the Dimensions of Human Sexuality.* Sudbury, MA: Jones and Bartlett.

Kaiser Family Foundation. 2003. "Sexually Transmitted Diseases in the U.S." Fact Sheet. Menlo Park, CA: Kaiser Family Foundation. June (www.kff.org).

Koop, C. Everett. N.d. *Surgeon General's Report on Acquired Immune Deficiency Syndrome.* Washington, DC: U.S. Dept. of Health and Human Services.

"Large Proportions of Men and Women with HIV Have Sex Without Telling Partners They Are Infected." 2003 *Perspectives on Sexual and Reproductive Health* 35:235–36.

"Many Pediatricians Are Reluctant to Vaccinate Young Females Against Human Papilloma Virus." 2007. *Perspectives on Sexual and Reproductive Health* 39(2):121–22.

Oglesby, Christy. 2004. "Survey: Adults Still Skip Condom Use." April 6 (www.cnn.com).

Rosenthal, M. Sara. 2003. *The Gynecological Sourcebook.* 4th ed. New York: McGraw-Hill.

U.S. Centers for Disease Control and Prevention. 2001. *Tracking the Hidden Epidemics: Trends in STDs in the United States: 2000.* Atlanta, GA: U.S. Centers for Disease Control and Prevention (www.cdc.gov).

———. 2002. "Cytomegalovirus (CMV) Infection." Atlanta, GA: U.S. Centers for Disease Control and Prevention (www.cdc.gov).

———. 2003. "Male Latex Condoms and Sexually Transmitted Diseases." Atlanta, GA: U.S. Centers for Disease Control and Prevention. January 23.

———. 2004a. *Bacterial Vaginosis Fact Sheet.* Atlanta, GA: U.S. Centers for Disease Control and Prevention. May 2004.

———. 2004b. *Chlamydia Fact Sheet.* Atlanta, GA: U.S. Centers for Disease Control and Prevention. May 2004.

———. 2004c. *Genital Herpes Fact Sheet.* Atlanta, GA: U.S. Centers for Disease Control and Prevention. May 2004.

———. 2004d. *Genital HPV Infection Fact Sheet.* Atlanta, GA: U.S. Centers for Disease Control and Prevention. May 2004.

———. 2004e. *Gonorrhea Fact Sheet.* Atlanta, GA: U.S. Centers for Disease Control and Prevention. May 2004.

———. 2004f. *Hepatitis B Fact Sheet.* Atlanta, GA: U.S. Centers for Disease Control and Prevention. May 2004.

———. 2004g. *HIV/AIDS Surveillance Report.* Vol. 15. Atlanta, GA: U.S. Centers for Disease Control and Prevention.

———. 2004h. *HIV/AIDS Surveillance Supplementary Report* 10(1). Atlanta, GA: U.S. Centers for Disease Control and Prevention.

———. 2004i. *Pelvic Inflammatory Disease Fact Sheet.* Atlanta, GA: U.S. Centers for Disease Control and Prevention. May 2004.

———. 2004j. *STD Surveillance 2003.* Atlanta, GA: U.S. Centers for Disease Control and Prevention. November 15.

———. 2004k. *Syphilis Fact Sheet.* Atlanta, GA: U.S. Centers for Disease Control and Prevention. May 2004.

———. 2004l. "Trends in Reportable Sexually Transmitted Diseases in the United States, 2003." Press Release. Atlanta, GA: U.S. Centers for Disease Control and Prevention. November 15.

———. 2004m. *Trichomoniasis Fact Sheet.* Atlanta, GA: U.S. Centers for Disease Control and Prevention. May 2004.

———. 2006. "Sexually Transmitted Disease Surveillance 2005." Atlanta, GA: U.S. Centers for Disease Control and Prevention. November. Retrieved May 20, 2007 (www.cdc.org/std).

———. 2007a. "HPV Questions and Answers." Atlanta, GA: U.S. Centers for Disease Control and Prevention. Retrieved June 20, 2007 (www.cdc.gov).

———. 2007b. "The Role of STD Detection and Treatment in HIV Prevention." Atlanta, GA: U.S. Centers for Disease Control and Prevention. Retrieved June 20, 2007 (www.cdc.gov).

———. 2007c. "Sexually Transmitted Diseases: Treatment Guidelines." Atlanta, GA: U.S. Centers for Disease Control and Prevention. July 13. Retrieved July 27, 2007 (www.cdc.gov/std).

Webster, Tia. 2002. "Condom Error Common among College Men." *Emory Report.* September 10 (www.emory.edu).

Glossary

"at risk" (for STDs) *"At risk"* in this context includes anyone with multiple sex partners or a partner who has a history of multiple partners. Individuals whose general health makes them vulnerable to infection are also at risk. In truth, any sexual relationship that is not long term and not known to be monogamous should be considered risky.

safer sex Use of protective methods (such as latex condoms) or strategies (careful selection of partners) in sexual activity. Use of the term *safer sex* rather than *safe sex* points to the risk of sexually transmitted disease that remains even when these methods and strategies are used.

sexually related diseases (SRDs) Diseases or conditions that may be transmitted through or in conjunction with sexual activity, although they may also be acquired in other ways.

sexually transmitted diseases (STDs) Contagious diseases transmitted from one person to another through sexual contact. They are also termed *sexually transmitted infections (STIs).*

Appendix D

Sexual Dysfunctions and Therapy

A sexual dysfunction may be defined as "a specific chronic disorder involving sexual performance" (Greenberg, Bruess, and Haffner 2002, p. 515). But the concept of sexual dysfunction has been rethought in recent years, to give priority to whether or not an individual or couple finds a particular condition or situation to be troublesome. In these terms, a sexual dysfunction is a "chronic inability to respond sexually in a way one finds satisfying" (p. 515). Research indicates that 43 percent of women and 32 percent of men report that they experience sexual problems (Laumann, Paik, and Rosen 1999).

Sexual dysfunctions identified by sexuality experts include: premature ejaculation, delayed ejaculation, and erectile dysfunction in men; female sexual arousal disorder, female orgasmic dysfunction, and vaginismus among women; and dyspareunia as a sexual dysfunction that may be experienced by either men or women (Kaplan 1974; Greenberg, Bruess, and Haffner 2002). See Table D.1 for an outline of common sexual dysfunctions, their symptoms, and treatment.[1]

In addition, there are situations of absent or minimal sexual desire that are not considered sexual dysfunctions per se, but that indicate a sexual life that an individual is not happy with and wishes to change. Technical terms are *inhibited sexual desire, dissatisfaction with sexual activity frequency,* and *sexual aversion.*

Inhibited sexual desire references lack of sexual interest or sexual unresponsiveness that occurs only in the context of particular relationships or situations (such as lack of privacy). *Dissatisfaction with sexual frequency* is very common. Partners as individuals often differ in their preferences, and men typically prefer more frequent sexual activity than do women.

Sexual aversion refers to a general distaste for sex that can have varying origins: parents who were very negative about sex; a traumatic experience of rape or abuse; too much pressure from partners; or gender confusion (Kaplan 1995; Greenberg, Bruess, and Haffner 2002).

It may be hard to determine in measurable terms whether or not a person has a sexual dysfunction. For one thing, virtually all sexually active people will have some instances of unsatisfactory sexual experience or nonperformance. Moreover, couples and individuals vary in their expectations of sex. It is for this reason that therapists would rather rely on the individual's or couple's definition of the situation in considering the need for treatment (Greenberg, Bruess, and Haffner 2002).

Sexual dysfunction, along with the more general situation of decreased sexual desire, may result from certain physical disabilities and chronic diseases such as diabetes and heart and vascular diseases. Thus, the first step in sex therapy needs to be a medical review and examination. Some surgical and chemotherapy treatments for cancer can cause sexual dysfunction. Various medications are related to sexual difficulties: drugs for hypertension and some heart conditions, antidepressants, antianxiety drugs, and street narcotics, for example (Forman, Gilmour-White, and Forman 2005; Hellstrom 1997; Kaplan 1974; "Mental Health: Male Sexual Problems" 2005).

Some 40 percent to 90 percent of sexual problems have psychological aspects—if that term is broadly defined to include relational and cultural issues (Greenberg, Bruess, and Haffner 2002, pp. 515, 529). Women with female sexual arousal disorder and men with erectile dysfunction, for example, were more likely to be generally unhappy with their lives than those not reporting sexual problems. Of course, what is cause and what

1. General information on sexual dysfunction has been presented in most sources in the context of heterosexual relationships, often presuming marriage. There are now sources, as well as therapists, who give attention to same-sex relationships.

Table D.1 Common Sexual Dysfunctions

Dysfunction	Symptoms	Usual Treatment[a]
Premature Ejaculation	Inability of a man to control ejaculatory reflex or if one or both partners are dissatisfied with length of intercourse.	Repeated stimulation to the point just before ejaculation. Pharmaceutical remedies are being explored by drug companies.
Delayed Ejaculation (also termed Retarded Ejaculation)	Inability of a man to trigger orgasm; may be situational or a general dysfunction.	Sexual exercises combined with therapeutic counseling; temporary avoidance of intercourse and use of other means to elicit ejaculation.
Erectile Dysfunction	Inability of a man to produce or maintain an erection.	For medical conditions or other erectile dysfunction, pills such as Viagra, Levitra, or Cialis stimulate erection (new drugs may come on the market). Alternatives include another drug, which is injected into the penis, or penile implant or vacuum pump. For psychosocial factors, sexual exercises combined with therapeutic counseling, with focus shifted away from performance aspect of sexual interaction.
Female Sexual Arousal Disorder	Sexual unresponsiveness; inability of a woman to derive erotic pleasure from sexual stimulation.	Education about arousal techniques, creation of relaxed, sensuous environment free from pressure to have intercourse. Efforts to find a pharmaceutical treatment for female sexual arousal disorder or other female sexual dysfunction have thus far proven unsuccessful.
Female Orgasmic Dysfunction	Difficulty of a woman in reaching orgasm.	Focus on helping woman learn to reach climax by herself, then with partner in sexual exercises not initially aimed at intercourse.
Vaginismus	Involuntary contraction of vaginal walls that prevents intercourse.	Correction of possible physical conditions; counseling plus exercises to recondition muscles.
Dyspareunia	Painful sexual intercourse	Treatment of any relevant medical conditions; education about hygiene. For women, education of self/partner about stimulation in foreplay, similar to therapy for orgasmic difficulties.

Sources: Kaplan 1974, 1995; Greenberg, Bruess, and Haffner 2002.
[a] Treatment of sexual dysfunction should be preceded by a complete physical examination to identify any physiological causes for the disturbance.

is effect are often unclear (Laumann, Paik, and Rosen 1999); sexual difficulties *would* be likely to dampen one's life satisfaction.

The general state of a couple's relationship will interact with their sexual relations. Typically, women's sexual problems are more closely tied to relationship issues than are men's (Bancroft, Loftus, and Long 2003). Married men and women have fewer sexual problems than nonmarried individuals. The highly educated have fewer sexual problems, and people experience more sexual dysfunction or disinterest as they age (Laumann, Paik, and Rosen 1999).

The cultural climate regarding sex is relevant to sexual attitudes and experiences. Women in a culture that maintains a double standard may be less free sexually, while men's gender-related cultural issues would typically center on performance pressure (Greenberg, Bruess, and Haffner 2002, p. 527).

Sexual Dysfunctions[2]

Premature Ejaculation

Inability to control the ejaculatory reflex, termed **premature ejaculation,** is one of the most common male sexual complaints, reported by around 30 percent of men (Laumann, Paik, and Rosen 1999). A man might ejaculate after several minutes of foreplay or just after entering his partner's vagina. In contrast, a man who has good ejaculatory control can continue to engage in sex play while in a highly aroused state.

The expectations of the man and woman play a role in defining whether there is a premature ejaculation problem. Some sexuality experts, especially in the past,

2. Rather than presenting sexual dysfunction terms in a separate glossary, we refer you to Table D.1.

would look at the actual time a man can maintain sexual thrusting without ejaculation. More recently, partners' satisfaction is used as a diagnostic criterion by some therapists, while others would focus on the man's inability to control ejaculation (Berger 2005; "Study Seeks Standard" 2005).

One way therapists deal with premature ejaculation is to teach a couple an exercise through which the man can gradually learn to control his orgasm. Therapists report that in most cases they have treated, premature ejaculation eventually ceases to be a problem (Mulcahy 1997).

Numbing creams have been used since the 1940s. Several drug companies are working on more sophisticated pharmaceutical remedies. Some medical experts believe the extent of premature ejaculation has been exaggerated and that pharmaceutical remedies are not the solution. "Sex is highly individualized and cannot be medicalized" (Berger 2005). "'Why would you want to take a drug the rest of your life when . . . your problem might well respond to some short-term therapy?'" (Dr. Sidney Wolfe, director of a nonprofit advocacy organization, Public Citizens Health Research, in Berger 2005). At the same time, it is now recognized that *delayed ejaculation* is sufficiently troubling to some men that this problem needs to be recognized rather than dismissed (Berger 2005).

Delayed Ejaculation

A man experiencing **delayed ejaculation** (sometimes termed **retarded ejaculation** or *ejaculatory inhibition*), cannot trigger orgasm. Less than 10 percent of men report this dysfunction (Laumann, Paik, and Rosen 1999), although it may be more prevalent as an occasional experience. In mild form, ejaculatory inhibition is confined to specific anxiety-producing situations, such as when a man is with a new partner or when he feels guilty about the sexual encounter. In more severe cases, a man may seldom experience orgasm during intercourse but may be able to achieve it by masturbation or by a partner's fondling or oral stimulation.

Once physical or drug-related causes are ruled out, treatment consists of couple counseling sessions along with a series of progressive sexual exercises designed to relieve the man of his latent fears about intercourse. The rate of success with therapy is fairly high (Mulcahy 1997; Hellstrom 1997).

Erectile Dysfunction

A man who experiences erectile dysfunction is unable to produce or maintain an erection.[3] Although he may become aroused in a sexual encounter and want to have intercourse, he cannot. Virtually all men of whatever age occasionally experience an episode of erectile dysfunction—perhaps in response to excessive consumption of alcohol or circumstances in which either the environment or feelings about the partner are not conducive to good sex. As a more chronic condition, estimates are that some 30 million American men experience erectile dysfunction, a problem that increases with age: 7 percent of younger men experience erectile dysfunction, while rates among older men range from 10 percent of men in their sixties to over half of men in their nineties (Greenberg, Bruess, and Haffner 2002; Laumann, Paik, and Rosen 1999).

Physicians estimate that 70 to 80 percent of the erectile dysfunction cases they see have at least partial physical causes. Diabetes, certain medications, spinal cord injury, and nerve damage from prostate cancer or other surgery are just a few of the many health conditions that may affect a man's erection (Greenberg, Bruess, and Haffner 2002). Today, there are several medical treatments for chronic erectile dysfunction, including Viagra and other medications designed to sustain an erection. Surgical insertion of an inflatable implant into the penis is another option (Leland 1997), although somewhat displaced now by pharmaceutical treatment. Newer drugs have been developed to assist men who do not respond well to Viagra.

Nonmedical factors that may affect erectile function are usually situational rather than deeper psychological problems: fear of sexual failure, pressures created by an excessively demanding partner, or guilt. Because our society tends to equate the capacity to have an erection with adult masculinity, even transient erectile dysfunction may cause a man to feel anxious. As with other sexual dysfunctions, the anxiety produced by one otherwise insignificant and transitory failure may initiate a downward spiral in which anxiety retards sexual responsiveness, leading to more anxiety about performance, less sexual success, and so on.

Depression or relationship discord may accompany erectile dysfunction, and, if so, these symptoms must be at least somewhat relieved before a therapist can treat the sexual dysfunction itself. Therefore, therapists combine sexual exercises at home with therapeutic counseling. The exercises are designed to free the man from pressures to perform and let him simply enjoy his sexual feelings. Essentially, the couple is instructed to caress each other during sexual play but not to have intercourse. Permission to enjoy himself without having to perform allows the man to relax without worrying whether his body will respond. Paradoxically, the more he relaxes, the more likely his body is to respond.

This same philosophy lies behind much of the treatment for *female sexual dysfunction*. The term female sex-

3. *Impotence* is the term by which erectile dysfunction was known until very recently. Sex therapists now reject the term because of its implication of a more general powerlessness.

ual dysfunction is often used as an umbrella term for a variety of problems, sometimes given more specific definitions.[4]

Female Sexual Arousal Disorder

Women who experience **female sexual arousal disorder**[5] derive little if any erotic pleasure from sexual stimulation and do not evidence such physiological responses as vaginal lubrication. About 30 percent of women (compared to 15 percent of men) report that they lack interest in sex (Laumann, Paik, and Rosen 1999). Some women have never experienced erotic pleasure; others have at one time but no longer do. Often they enjoyed petting before marriage but became unable to respond when intercourse was the expected form of sex.

Besides giving couples basic information, therapists encourage them to create a relaxed, sensuous atmosphere at home, one that allows for the natural unfolding of sexual responses. In one exercise, the individuals take turns caressing each other, but they do not progress to sexual intercourse and orgasm. Freed from the pressure to have intercourse, a woman can often experience erotic sensations, and the couple can gradually build on this sensation of pleasure until they are eventually ready for intercourse.

Female Orgasmic Dysfunction

About a quarter of women have difficulty in reaching orgasm, termed **female orgasmic dysfunction** (Laumann, Paik, and Rosen 1999). A few women cannot reach a climax under any circumstances. More often, a woman can reach orgasm, but only under specific conditions.

Many women with this dysfunction enjoy sex; they just "get stuck" at the plateau phase and cannot proceed to a climax (Masters and Johnson 1970; Masters, Johnson, and Kolodny 1994). As in erectile dysfunction, anxiety about performance may feed back to further inhibit a woman's sexual responsiveness. Only about 5 percent of orgasmic dysfunction is believed to have organic causes (Greenberg, Bruess, and Haffner 2002).

Treatment for women who have never experienced orgasm usually begins by focusing on the woman. The therapist asks her to masturbate at home alone, stressing that the environment should be free from distractions and interruptions. Another approach for women who have never experienced orgasm is group education. Women meet together to learn about their bodies; they are then encouraged to masturbate at home until they become familiar and confident with their own response cycles (Masters, Johnson, and Kolodny 1994). Research confirms the effectiveness of both masturbation and various forms of talk therapy, including general couple therapy (Konner 1990; Kaplan 1974, 1995).

Once a woman can stimulate herself to climax, her partner enters the treatment program. The couple is told to make love as usual, except that after the man ejaculates, he stimulates his partner to orgasm. The woman is told to be utterly selfish, not to monitor her progress toward orgasm but to simply enjoy her sensations. Women are cautioned that watching their own responses to see if they are "right"—that is, headed toward orgasm—tends to inhibit physical responsiveness and to contribute to tension that sometimes develops into long-term sexual problems (Masters and Johnson 1970; Masters, Johnson, and Kolodny 1994). Instead, each partner is to enjoy the pleasurable sensations produced by the caresses of the partner.

This treatment is helpful in letting couples see beyond the myth of the simultaneous orgasm—the erroneous idea that true love or really great sex means that both partners must always reach orgasm at the same time. Sometimes partners do climax simultaneously, but not usually. The belief that they *should* can leave the woman, who is typically slower to become aroused, frustrated; it may even encourage her to fake it. It may be better to take turns in being pleasured to orgasm.

Direct Clitoral Versus Vaginal Stimulation One reason that it may be better to take turns is that many women report they do not reach orgasm through vaginal stimulation in intercourse. As Appendix A points out, there is a much greater concentration of nerve endings in the clitoris than in the vagina itself. One possible pattern is for the husband

4. In 1998, pharmaceutical companies organized the Consensus Development Conference to work out a classification system for *female sexual dysfunctions*. In this system, there are four categories of sexual dysfunction: *desire disorder, arousal disorder, orgasm disorder,* and *pain disorder* (as defined, this last category must cause personal distress).

There is some overlap between this typology and the categorization presented in this textbook appendix. However, we do not adopt it because it has been criticized by medical professionals, psychologists, and feminists on several points: It is considered too subjective, with the result that some objective experiences would sometimes be classified as sexual disorders and sometimes not. (We do note that subjective elements do appear in our definition of *premature* or *delayed ejaculation*).

Another criticism is that the categories are too broad, especially as subjective definitions. By these standards, that include transient as well as more stable dysfunctions, a majority of American women would be classified as having *female sexual dysfunction*.

Critics note that this typology, developed by pharmaceutical companies, would tend to connect vaguely defined sexual problems to pharmaceutical remedies. We discuss the **medicalization of sexuality** later in this appendix (Savoie 2007).

5. *Frigidity* has been replaced as a term for female sexual dysfunction because of its negative aura and the implication that a woman who has a sexual response problem is emotionally "cold" or hostile to her partner.

to stimulate his wife's clitoris until she reaches orgasm and then to enter her vagina to attain his own climax.

Research indicates that of those women who experience orgasm, only about 30 to 44 percent do so without clitoral stimulation (Greenberg, Bruess, and Haffner 2002, p. 522). Most experts and therapists see the need for direct clitoral stimulation as normal to female sexuality. The best strategy, it would seem, would be for the individual woman to be aware of and make her partner aware of her own response pattern.

Some women never achieve orgasm with a partner even with direct clitoral stimulation, although they are able to climax by masturbating. Typically, this situation reflects a woman's anxiety, ambivalence, or anger about the relationship. Treating this type of inorgasm typically involves individual or marital therapy or both.

Vaginismus

Vaginismus is relatively rare. A woman with this dysfunction is anatomically normal, but whenever her partner attempts to penetrate her vagina, the vaginal muscles involuntarily contract so that intercourse is impossible. Typically, vaginismic women are, at least unconsciously, afraid of vaginal penetration and intercourse.

After any physical conditions have been corrected, therapists treat vaginismus by seeking to uncover through counseling the basis for the woman's fear of vaginal entry. Then progressive exercises are used to recondition the muscles at the entrance to the vagina.

The length of the treatment varies, but therapists report excellent results (Kaplan 1974).

Dyspareunia

The recurrent pain that men or women may experience during sexual activity is termed **dyspareunia.** For men, pain may localize in the penis or testes or be felt internally. For women, pain may take the form of burning or cramping felt in the vagina or pelvis. Around 1 to 2 percent of women experience dyspareunia, which is more common among younger than older women (Greenberg, Bruess, and Haffner 2002).

There are a variety of possible physical causes for dyspareunia in either men or women, and these call for appropriate medical treatment or improved hygienic practices. Women may experience pain during intercourse if the vagina has not become sufficiently lubricated before penile insertion. Here the solution seems to be education about sexual anatomy and response, and changed practices regarding foreplay—as well as ensuring the most anxiety-free setting for intercourse. If relationship issues underlie problems in physical responsiveness, they need to be addressed.

Sex Therapy

In all the dysfunctions we have described, a common thread is the emotional climate of a couple's relationship. As therapists help a couple to overcome their immediate sexual difficulties, they also try to help partners recognize and avoid alienating practices that may become obstacles to mutually pleasurable sex. Maintaining and enhancing the total couple relationship is an important part of the therapeutic process.

The number of people seeking treatment for sexual dysfunction has increased in recent years. This is probably due to increased openness about sexuality and willingness to admit a problem—perhaps former Senator Bob Dole has led the way in his acknowledgment of erectile difficulties in advertisements for Viagra (Hitt 2000). Viagra exemplifies the development of more effective sex therapies in recent years, whether medical or involving new forms of psychological or relationship therapy (Greenberg, Bruess, and Haffner 2002).

In traditional approaches to treating sexual dysfunction, therapists looked for subtle and profound psychological sources, such as unresolved emotional conflicts from childhood or severe marital power struggles. These causes and therapies still exist, but today most therapists focus on more immediate and obvious reasons for the dysfunction. These include not only health conditions (in a population whose median age is increasing) but also anxieties about sexual failure or the partner's satisfaction. These fears can create various sexual defenses and inhibit people from abandoning themselves to the experience.

One important feature of Masters and Johnson's therapy is its attempt to remove performance pressure by insisting that the couple not strive for orgasm or even have intercourse but rather focus on allover body pleasure and pleasuring. Masters and Johnson laid down some ground rules for sex therapy in their book *Human Sexual Inadequacy* (1970). They said that therapists should work in male–female teams and with both partners in the relationship. They stressed that the team should be comfortable with their own sexuality and nonjudgmental about the full range of human sexual activity. Since then, some respected therapists—Helen Singer Kaplan, for example—have successfully treated couples without a co-therapist (Kaplan 1974). Many contemporary therapists continue to follow the Masters and Johnson guidelines, however.

Therapy normally begins with a physical and psychological examination of both partners. Recent years have witnessed a significant return to a consideration of medical problems and physical treatments for male sexual dysfunction. New hormonal products are also sought for the treatment of female sexual dysfunction (Angier 2007; "'Female Viagra'" 2004; Sweeney 2005).

A legitimate therapist will give a couple a clear picture of what to expect during treatment and will probably make a therapeutic contract with them that clearly establishes the couple's responsibility for their treatment. They will also scrupulously follow professional ethical guidelines that prohibit therapists' becoming sexually involved with clients. Sensitivity to racial/ethnic cultural differences and religiously based values is also important.

One way to check sex therapists' qualifications is to find out whether they belong to a professional association. An important national organization is the American Association of Sexuality Educators, Counselors, and Therapists. This group publishes the *Journal of Sex Education and Therapy* and maintains a website that offers a state-by-state listing of certified sex therapists. A sex therapists' code of ethics is posted on the website http://www.aasect.org.

There are also regional professional associations. In the absence of membership in a professional association, therapists are more likely to be legitimate if they are accountable to a community agency, teaching hospital, medical school, or university. Some states license or certify therapeutic professionals of various kinds. One might also seek recommendations from trusted friends who have had experience with sex therapists.

A choice for couples is to recognize that sexual problems often reflect their relationship and to seek help from a qualified marriage or relationship counselor. Individuals might also address sexual problems in a general therapeutic context. A woman's group approach to sex therapy is another option (Barbach 1980, 1991 [1975]). For more information, see Jerrold S. Greenberg, Clint E. Bruess, and Debra W. Haffner, *Exploring the Dimensions of Human Sexuality* (2002); Kamal Hanash, *Perfect Lover: Understanding and Overcoming Sexual Dysfunction* (1994); Judith Heiman and Joseph Lopiccolo, *Becoming Orgasmic: A Sexual and Personal Growth Program for Women* (1992); Helen Singer Kaplan, *The Sexual Desire Disorders: Dysfunctional Regulation of Sexual Motivation* (1995); Bernie Zilbergeld, *The New Male Sexuality* (1999); and the *Journal of Sex Research*. There are also books available in bookstores and libraries that address sexual dysfunctions associated with various health and disability conditions or that address sexual problems in gay and lesbian relationships. In evaluating books on sexual dysfunction, check the credentials and affiliation of the author as one would do in choosing a therapist.

The Medicalization of Sexuality

A sharp departure from the model of relationship-oriented sex therapy is a growing tendency to focus solely on medical solutions to sexual dysfunctions or sexual dissatisfaction. The merits and drawbacks of this shift are currently being debated.

Medical Treatment of Sexual Dysfunction

The acceptance of Viagra and its success in remedying many men's erectile dysfunction problems has set off a search for a pharmaceutical cure for other sexual dysfunctions, including those affecting women.

Research and development for a female equivalent of Viagra to treat female sexual arousal disorder has been in progress for almost ten years—with little success, however. "Women, the maker of Viagra has found, are a lot more complicated than men. . . . The problem . . . is that men and women have a fundamentally different relationship between arousal and desire" (Harris 2004, p. C-1). "'There is a disconnect in many women between genital changes and mental changes,' said Mitra Boolel, leader of Pfizer's sex research team" (p. C-1). Pfizer has given up on marketing Viagra to women because company researchers have found that when physiological arousal is stimulated by drugs, that does not lead to a woman's desire, or even willingness, to have sex. Viagra may, however, help women whose sexual desire levels were previously normal, but have fallen because of medications such as antidepressant pills.

The Food and Drug Administration has refused to approve another approach, a testosterone patch, concluding that long-term studies are needed to rule out the risk of cancer or other harms ("'Female Viagra'" 2004; Pollack 2004). Pfizer has explored yet another approach—changing focus from "a woman's genitals to her head" (i.e., drugs that might affect brain chemistry). As one professor of clinical medicine at Columbia University put it, facetiously, "'What we need to do is to find a pill for engendering the perception of intimacy'" (in Harris 2004, p. C-1).

A "New View" of Female Sexual Disorder

The point is that women's sexual feelings are very much connected to relationships, and they are shaped by the cultural climate as well. Daily pressures are another factor affecting women's sexual desire: "[A]nyone affected by FSD [female sexual dysfunction] might do better to claim some leisure in her life and work on rekindling the romance" (Ehrenreich 2004, p. 154).

A more formal reconceptualization of female sexual dysfunction has been developed by a working group of psychiatrists, sex therapists, feminists, and social scientists: **a new view of female sexual disorder** (Kaschak and Tiefer 2002; The Working Group on a New View of Women's Sexual Problems 2003). Their manifesto categorizes female sexual dysfunction in terms of "sociocultural, political, or economic factors"; "sexual problems relating to partner and relationship"; "sexual problems due to psychological factors"; and "sexual problems due to medical factors." The New View group is opposed to the assumptions behind the development of pharmaceutical treatments. They argue that this approach labels women as sexually deficient, does not address women's real problems, and may pose medical risks.

This "new view" of female sexual issues is supported by current research on heterosexual women's sexual response (Bancroft, Loftus, and Long 2003). John Bancroft, director of the Kinsey Institute, resists labeling women dysfunctional if they lack desire or fail to have orgasms. "'Dysfunctional for whom?'" Bancroft asks. If a woman is stressed or has children and a job, "'she might put sex on the back burner for good reason. It could be adaptive for her. . . . It doesn't mean there's anything wrong with her response system or that she's dysfunctional'" (in Elias 2003, p. A-1).

Medicalization and Men

The shift of focus regarding men's sexual problems to the physiological realm has been widely accepted (Leland 1999). That model has given men Viagra. Although Viagra is not effective for all men and has some drawbacks in terms of lack of spontaneity, newer drugs have been added to the pharmaceutical roster, and many men have seen their sex lives resume or improve. It is still the case that medical considerations prevent use of these erectile dysfunction drugs by some men, or that they are deterred by side effects.

Now some sexuality professionals and activists are questioning whether the tight link between drugs and sexual performance has gone beyond remedying specific medical/sexual problems that have impaired sexual satisfaction and is redefining all men's (and women's) sexuality in almost entirely physiological terms (Savoie 2007). "[T]here's something deeply creepy about the medicalization of sexuality, male and female," says social critic Barbara Ehrenreich (2004, p. 154).

Concern has also been expressed that drugs intended for men who have sexual problems due to surgery or health conditions are being used by men who have no sexual dysfunction, but who believe the pills will enhance sexual experience, or perhaps provide insurance against the occasional failure to achieve erection. Some ads for erectile dysfunction drugs now emphasize their recreational use (Kirby 2004; "Younger Men" 2004).

There are several ways to think about this. Ehrenreich would prefer to see individual choice in the use of sex-enhancing erectile drugs rather than a sharp distinction between recreational and therapeutic use. The latter would require labeling individuals as either sexually functional or dysfunctional.

Some sex therapists are concerned about the disappearance of the partner and of the psychological context of sexual expression when the focus is entirely on producing an erection. Physicians in the field of sexual medicine believe a trend that ignores the psychological and relational factors that also enter into sexual satisfaction is not ultimately conducive to sexual happiness. "'Individual psychology and couple factors remain important causes'" [of sexual dysfunction or satisfaction], says an article, "Viagra and Broken Hearts," in the *Canadian Family Physician* (quoted in Stamler 2004, p. 10).

We see that new issues have emerged out of the medicalization of sexual dysfunction, including that of the essential meaning of sex. Discussion appears to have just begun.

References

Angier, Natalie. 2007. "The Search for the Female Equivalent of Viagra." *New York Times,* April 10.

Bancroft, John, Jeni Loftus, and J. Scott Long. 2003. "Distress about Sex: A National Survey of Women in Heterosexual Relationships." *Archives of Sexual Behavior* 32:193–208.

Barbach, Lonnie. 1980. *Women Discover Orgasm: A Therapists Guide to a New Treatment Approach.* New York: Free Press.

_____. 1991 [1975]. *For Yourself: The Fulfillment of Female Sexuality.* New York: New American Library.

Berger, Leslie. 2005. "The Definition of the Problem Depends on a Stopwatch." *New York Times,* June 20.

Ehrenreich, Barbara. 2004. "Do Women Need a Viagra? *Time,* January 19, p. 154.

Elias, Marilyn. 2003. "Women's Sex Problems May Be Overstated." *USA Today,* November 15.

"'Female Viagra' Fails to Win FDA Panel's Approval." 2004. *USA Today,* December 3.

Forman, Robert, Susanna K. Gilmour-White, and Hathalie H. Forman. 2005. *Drug Induced Infertility and Sexual Dysfunction.* New ed. New York: Cambridge University Press.

Greenberg, Jerrold S., Clint E. Bruess, and Debra W. Haffner. 2002. *Exploring the Dimensions of Human Sexuality.* Sudbury, MA: Jones and Bartlett.

Hanash, Kamal A. 1994. *Perfect Lover: Understanding and Overcoming Sexual Dysfunction.* New York: SPI.

Harris, Gardiner. 2004. "Pfizer Gives Up Testing Viagra on Women." *New York Times,* February 28.

Heiman, Julia R. and Joseph Lopiccolo. 1992. *Becoming Orgasmic: A Sexual and Personal Growth Program for Women.* New York: Simon and Schuster.

Hellstrom, Wayne J. G. 1997. *Male Infertility and Sexual Dysfunction.* New York: Springer.

Hitt, Jack. 2000. "The Second Sexual Revolution." New York Times Magazine, February 20, pp. 34ff.

Kaplan, Helen Singer. 1974. *The New Sex Therapy: Active Treatment of Sexual Dysfunction.* New York: Brunner/Mazel.

———. 1995. *The Sexual Desire Disorders: Dysfunctional Regulation of Sexual Motivation.* New York: Brunner/Mazel.

Kaschak, Ellyn and Leonore Tiefer, eds. 2002. *A New View of Women's Sexual Problems.* Binghamton, NY: Haworth.

Kirby, David. 2004. "Party Favors: Pill Popping as Insurance." *New York Times,* June 21.

Konner, Melvin. 1990. "Women and Sexuality." *New York Times Magazine,* April 29, pp. 24, 26.

Laumann, Edward, Anthony Paik, and Raymond C. Rosen. 1999. "Sexual Dysfunction in the United States: Prevalence and Predictors." *Journal of the American Medical Association* 281:537–44.

Leland, John. 1997. "A Pill for Impotence?" *Newsweek.* Nov. 17: 62-68.

_____. 1999. "Bad News in the Bedroom." *Newsweek.* Feb. 22: 47.

Masters, William H. and Virginia E. Johnson. 1970. *Human Sexual Inadequacy.* Boston, MA: Little, Brown.

Masters, William H., Virginia E. Johnson, and Robert C. Kolodny. 1994. *Heterosexuality.* New York: HarperCollins.

"Mental Health: Male Sexual Problems." 2005. WebMD. Retrieved July 3, 2007 (www.webmd.com).

Mulcahy, John J. 1997. *Diagnosis and Management of Male Sexual Dysfunction.* New York: Igaku-Shoin.

Pollack, Andrew. 2004. "More Data Sought on Drug for Sex Drive." *New York Times,* December 3.

Savoie, Keely. 2007. "Female Sexual Dysfunction." New York: Planned Parenthood Foundation of America. November 11, 2005; updated July 26, 2007. Retrieved July 27, 2007 (www.plannedparenthood.org).

Stamler, Bernard. 2004. "Now That There Are Choices, How to Choose?" *New York Times,* June 21.

"Study Seeks Standard for Sexual Disorder." 2005. CNN.com. April 14. Retrieved April 14, 2005 (www.cnn.com).

Sweeney, Camille. 2005. "Not Tonight." *New York Times,* June 3.

Working Group on a New View of Women's Sexual Problems. 2003. *The Manifesto: A New View of Women's Sexual Problems.* Retrieved February 15, 2004 (www.fsd-alert.org).

"Younger Men Turning to Sex Drugs." 2004. ATT Worldnet. December 5. Retrieved December 6, 2004 (www.att.net).

Zilbergeld, Bernie. 1999. *The New Male Sexuality.* Rev. ed. New York: Bantam.

Glossary

medicalization of sexuality The assumptions that sexual behavior and sexual problems are a product of biology rather than human agency and that sexual dysfunction can best be addressed by prescribing pharmaceuticals.

new view of female sexual disorder The thesis that women's (and men's) sexual feelings, behavior, and dysfunction are connected to relationship issues and cultural climate.

Appendix E

Conception, Pregnancy, and Childbirth

In Appendix E, we present some of the basic facts of conception, pregnancy, and childbirth, as well as some issues in the management of pregnancy and birth.

Conception

The process of conception begins with **ovulation.** A woman's **ovaries** alternate in releasing one egg, or **ovum,** each month. Ovulation takes place about fourteen days before a menstrual period; thus, a woman's most fertile time is usually midway between menstrual periods, when the ovum is traveling through the **fallopian tubes** to the uterus.

When **sperm** enter a female's vagina during sexual intercourse, they move into the fallopian tubes and can live there from two to five days. **Conception** takes place upon **fertilization,** or the joining of the sperm cell with the ovum. If this takes place in the fallopian tubes, the fertilized egg, or **zygote,** moves down to the **uterus,** where it embeds itself in the thickened lining, or **endometrium** (see Figure E.1), a process called **implantation.** Until an umbilical cord is formed during about the fifth week, the endometrial tissue provides nourishment for the developing fetus.

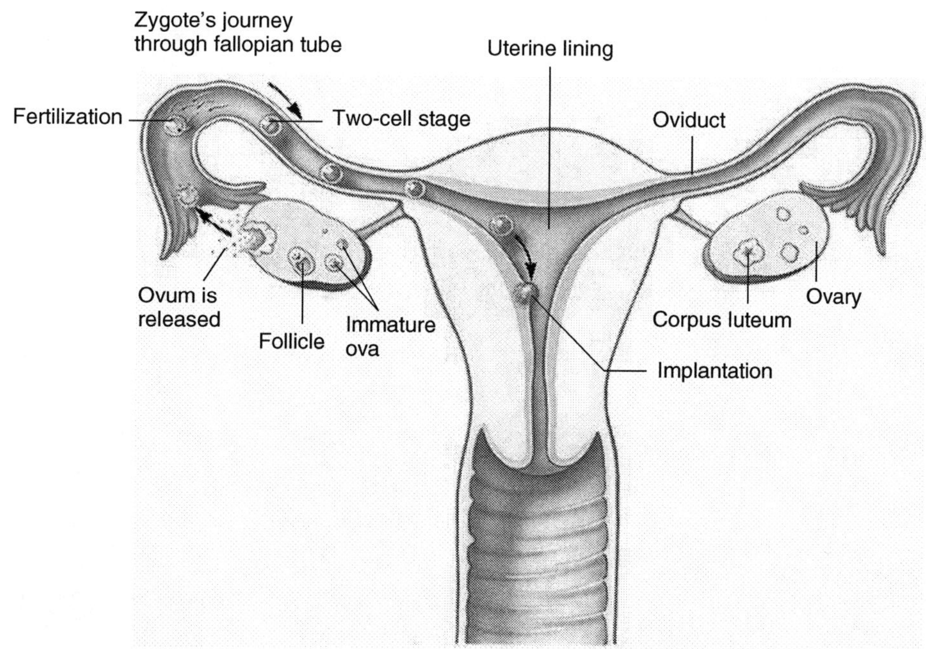

Figure E-1 Ovulation, fertilization, and the germinal period of pregnancy.

Pregnancy

The fertilization and implantation processes just described take place during the **germinal period,** or first two weeks of pregnancy.[1] During this early period, the woman usually isn't aware that she is pregnant. By the fourth week, however, she may begin to notice some changes.

The Germinal Stage

The first signs a woman often notices are a cessation of menstruation (because the endometrial tissue will not be sloughed off), nausea (a physical reaction to the zygote's embedding itself in the uterine wall), changes in the size and fullness of the breasts, darkened coloration of the **areolae** around the nipples, fatigue, and frequency of urination, a result of pressure on the bladder from the expanding uterus. Not all these signs, including nausea and cessation of menstruation, are always present, so a woman who suspects she is pregnant should have a pregnancy test even if she does not detect all these indicators of pregnancy.

The Embryonic Stage

The **embryonic stage** of pregnancy lasts from the second until about the eighth week. During this stage, the head, skeletal system, heart, and digestive system begin to form. Also during this time, a sac of salty, watery fluid called **amniotic fluid** surrounds the fetus to cushion and protect it. In later stages of pregnancy, doctors can detect some fetal defects by withdrawing a tiny portion of this amniotic fluid through the mother's abdomen with a syringe and testing it in a laboratory. During this period, the **placenta** develops inside the uterus. It is an organ that holds the fetus in place and provides nourishment and oxygen through the **umbilical cord,** which links the fetus to the mother; waste is expelled through the cord. (The placenta will be discharged in the final stage of childbirth.)

The Fetal Stage

The **fetal period** of development lasts from about eight weeks until birth. During the fetal period, the organs and structural system that budded during the embryonic stage refine themselves and grow. Some of the changes that take place up to fifteen weeks are illustrated in Figure E.2.

In the third month, the facial features become differentiated. The lips take shape, the nose begins to stand out, and the eyelids are formed, although they remain fused. The fingers and toes are well developed, and fingernails and toenails are forming.

During the fourth month, most of the fetus's bones have formed, although they are still soft cartilage and will not be completely hardened into bone until after birth.

In the fifth month, the fetal heartbeat can be heard through a stethoscope. Around this time, too, the **quickening**—the first fetal movements apparent to the mother herself—progresses from a mild fluttering to solid kicks against the side of the mother's abdomen. Any nausea that the mother may have experienced usually disappears by now, and she is in the most comfortable period of her pregnancy.

In the sixth month, the fetus grows to a foot in length and about twenty ounces in weight. The fetus now has eyelashes, it can open and close its eyes, and it may even learn to suck its thumb. By the end of this month, its essential anatomy and physiology are almost complete; further development consists largely of an increase in size and refinement and stabilization of the organs' functions. A fetus born or aborted at this time is likely to emerge alive and may live several hours. Survival beyond that will require constant medical attention, and the chances for survival are slim.[2]

By seven months, the fetus weighs about two and a half pounds. If born now, it will have a substantial chance of survival with the aid of specialized attention and equipment. A baby born in the eighth month of pregnancy has a very good chance of survival because its development is virtually complete.

In the eighth and ninth months of pregnancy, the fetus grows very rapidly, gaining an average of a half pound per week. At this time, the mother is likely to feel generally healthy but may also be uncomfortable because of the crowding in her expanding uterus and because weight increases may disrupt her equilibrium and her ability to get around. Toward the end of pregnancy, the fetus usually changes its position so that the head is in the

1. Pregnancy is commonly thought of in terms of three 3-month trimesters, but those do not correspond to the obstetrical identification of germinal, embryonic, and fetal periods. The embryonic and germinal periods take place in the first trimester; the fetal period of development begins in the first trimester and continues through the second and third trimesters.

2. The survival of very small babies is not unknown and is becoming more common. An infant weighing only 8.6 ounces at birth is thought to be the smallest surviving baby. She was born in 2004 at Loyola Hospital in Chicago, which has cared for some 1,700 newborns weighing less than two pounds. Ninety percent of babies born at Loyola who are of twenty-eight weeks' gestation have survived; the normal length of pregnancy is forty weeks ("World's Smallest Baby" 2004). Loyola's record is unusual, however; 41 percent of babies who are premature at twenty-eight weeks or fewer do not survive the first year (Martin et al. 2003).

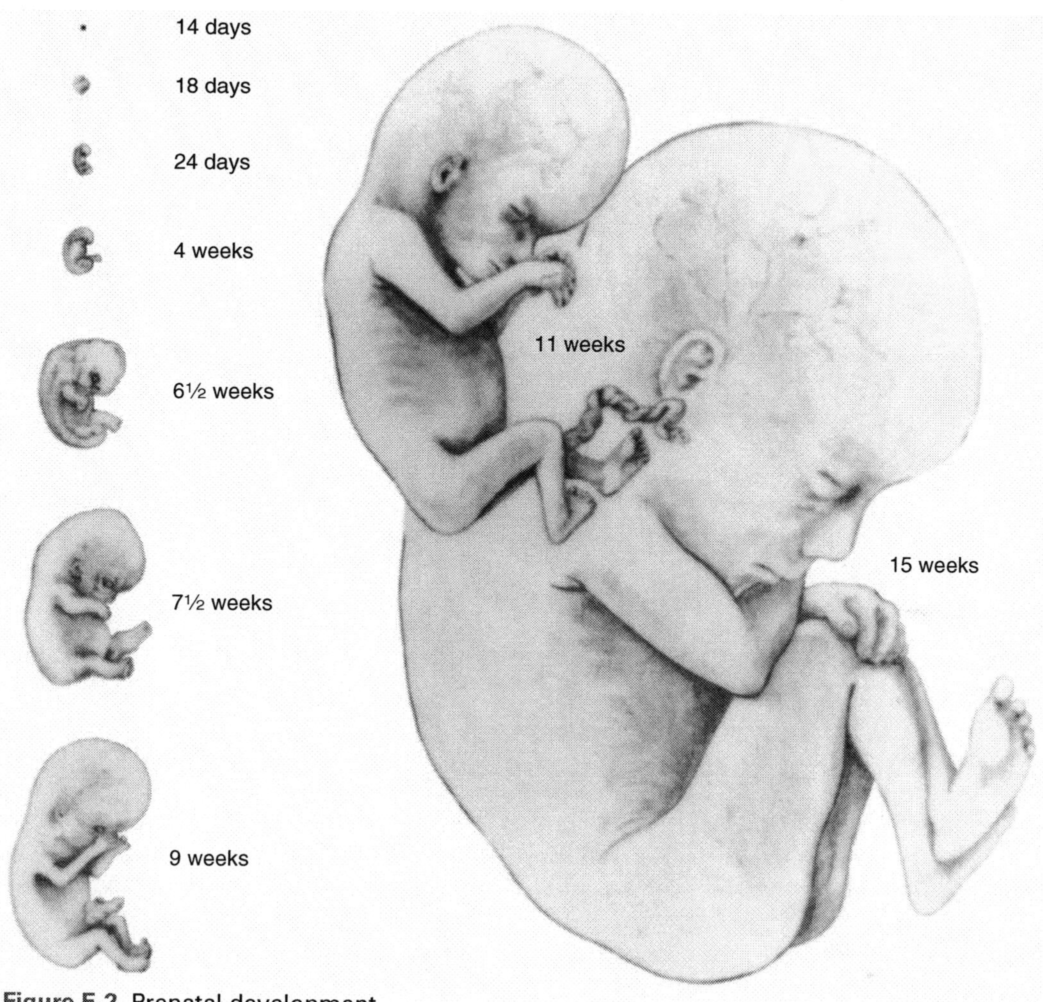

Figure E-2 Prenatal development.

lower part of the uterus. This marks the beginning of preparation for birth. The normal length of **gestation,** or development of a pregnancy into a full-term baby, is forty weeks.

Monitoring Fetal Development

Recent years have seen extraordinary scientific advances in monitoring fetal development. Here we look at several such advances—ultrasound, amniocentesis, chorionic villus sampling, and the newer blood screening techniques used to assess a fetus's risk of abnormality.

Ultrasound

In **ultrasound,** sound waves are bounced off the abdomen of the pregnant woman to determine the shape and position of the fetus. Ultrasound is now widely and routinely used; ultrasound monitoring was used in the pregnancies of 68 percent of the women who gave birth in 2002 (Martin et al. 2003). Doctors say that it helps to predict the date of birth within two weeks, that it can detect twins 90 percent of the time, and that it shows whether the fetus is maturing as it should. Ultrasound can also reveal several different kinds of birth defects—especially malformations of the skeleton—early enough for a legal abortion if parents choose to have one. In other cases, defects or problems revealed by ultrasound have led to corrective surgery that takes place before birth (Jones 2001).

The use of ultrasound has implications beyond diagnosis, however. Sonograms permit prospective parents to do something they have never been able to do before—observe the fetus. They are often given pictures or videotapes of the fetus to take home. This technology is pushing back parental bonds to before birth: "You just feel like you already know him'" (in Kempley 2003, p. C-01).[3]

Amniocentesis, Chorionic Villus Sampling, and Other Prenatal Testing

Although ultrasound can assess the overall structural normality of a fetus, amniocentesis and other prenatal testing provide more information to parents about their risk of having a child with a birth defect[4]—that is, a condition substantially lowering the quality of life or leading to premature illness and death. Common concerns of parents are Down syndrome and spina bifida, a neural-tube defect in which the spinal covering fails to close, which may lead to severe mental and physical disability and early death. Cystic fibrosis is another health condition that is testable prenatally. The risk of genetically or gender-linked diseases such as Tay-Sachs disease or hemophilia may be assessed through such testing. In some cases, there is the potential of fetal surgery to correct problems discovered by prenatal testing.

In *amniocentesis,* a physician inserts a needle through the abdominal wall into the uterus, withdrawing a small amount of amniotic fluid. Cells and other substances that the fetus has cast off float in this fluid, which technicians can examine for clues to fetal health and the presence of the most common birth defects. When doctors suspect that a woman might give birth to a child with a particular disorder—often because she carries a recessive gene for this disorder or because she has already given birth to a child with the disorder—scientists can examine the fluid for those conditions, including nearly one hundred rare genetic diseases. As women postpone childbearing to older ages, they are more concerned about the risk of birth defects; the risk of Down syndrome, for example, increases with age. Pregnant women over thirty-five are usually advised to have amniocentesis or chorionic villus sampling.

When performed by experienced medical personnel, amniocentesis appears reasonably safe, but the technique is not without risks. Hazards include spontaneous abortion (miscarriage) and risk of premature birth, with fetal damage occurring in 0.5 percent of cases ("Amniocentesis" 2004)—a slight risk, but one that concerns parents. Moreover, amniocentesis cannot take place until the second trimester, when sufficient amniotic fluid is present. This timing is a major drawback. The prospect of a second-trimester abortion is more emotionally troubling, and a later abortion heightens the physical risk to the woman. Amniocentesis is also costly.

Chorionic villus sampling (CVS) can provide information earlier in pregnancy by testing tissue from the fetal membrane. This technique carries some risk and uncertainty as well. CVS seems to cause miscarriages in 0.5 percent to 1.0 percent of cases ("Chorionic Villus Sampling" 2004). Moreover, CVS cannot detect neural-tube defects.

The use of amniocentesis and CVS declined 50 percent between 1991 and 2002, as many women now have *blood screening* instead. This kind of testing can be performed in the first trimester for the detection of Down syndrome and brain, spinal, or abdominal wall defects. Initial screening is done by use of a formula that combines tests for certain substances that reveal the presence of a fetal problem with a sonogram, taking into account the mother's age. Only if tests suggest the possibility of a fetal deformity are CVS and amniocentesis done as a follow-up (Brody 2004, 2005; Weise 2003).

Social scientists working in this field find parents to be troubled when testing reveals the likelihood of a serious problem. Virtually all testing programs include genetic counselors who can advise parents as to the significance of their test results and help them work through their decisions and their emotions. Because detection of an abnormal fetus gives prospective parents the chance to knowledgeably choose abortion, antiabortion groups have objected strenuously to prenatal screening and genetic counseling. Some advocates for Down syndrome children "see expanded testing as a step toward a society where children like theirs would be unwelcome" (Harmon 2007). But some parents who would reject abortion under any circumstances have undertaken prenatal screening with the thought that should testing reveal an abnormality, they would have time to prepare to care for their infant. Prenatal testing and the accompanying abortion decision remain ethically and personally difficult choices.

We turn now to the childbirth process.

3. Some commercial firms now offer elective ultrasound, not for medical diagnosis but to provide an early baby picture for the parents. These firms use 3-D machines that produce very realistic images. This type of ultrasound is controversial, with the FDA (Food and Drug Administration) and some physicians' groups opposed to what they see as an unnecessary use of expensive technology that might carry some unknown risk. But the FDA has not prohibited these practices, and some doctors believe such ultrasounds are a harmless concession to those parents who want them (Lubell 2004).

4. Parents of children with Down syndrome are beginning to dispute the "birth defect" label, arguing that these and other children so labeled may have good quality of life in many cases. A key to that is acceptance by their social networks. Parents and advocates argue for a general rethinking of attempts to select only "normal" fetuses, anticipating that social support for children with developmental disabilities and their families would decline in a world in which only relatively perfect children find acceptance (Harmon 2007).

Childbirth

The process of childbirth takes place in three stages: labor, delivery, and afterbirth (Figure E.3).

Labor

Labor is the process by which the baby is propelled from the mother's body through a series of contractions of the muscles of the uterus. Labor usually begins with mild contractions, at intervals of about fifteen to twenty minutes. The contractions increase steadily over the first phase of labor (usually from six to eighteen hours for the first birth, shorter for subsequent births). They also increase in intensity and duration until by the end of labor each contraction lasts a minute or more.

During labor, some other changes usually take place. The **cervix** dilates from its normal size (about one-eighth inch) to approximately four inches in preparation for the baby's passage. A second occurrence is the expulsion of a bloody plug (sometimes called *show*) from the base of the uterus through the vagina. During pregnancy, the plug helped prevent infectious bacteria from entering the uterus through the cervix. And third, the amniotic membrane (often called the *bag of waters*) ruptures, and amniotic fluid flows from the vagina. Show and breakage of waters are usually signs of imminent delivery. Together with these, full dilation of the cervix marks the beginning of the second, or delivery, stage of childbirth.

Delivery

The second phase of childbirth is the **delivery** of the baby. This phase extends from the time the cervix is completely dilated until the fetus is expelled—a process that may last from fewer than twenty minutes to (rarely) more than ninety minutes.

The mother can often speed the birth process at this stage by tightening the muscles in her diaphragm, abdomen, and back so that the uterine muscles are aided in pushing the baby through the cervix. Her active participation at this point may also help reduce pain. Childbirth preparation classes, offered by many hospitals, provide information and practice in these techniques. What husbands or other birthing partners can do to support the mother during labor and delivery is typically a part of childbirth education.

When the baby appears at the vaginal opening (*crowning*), its head usually turns so that the back of its skull emerges first, as is shown in Figure E.3a. After the head emerges, the infant usually turns again to find the path of least resistance. This kind of delivery, in which the baby's skull emerges first, is termed **vertex presentation** and occurs in about 95 percent of births. The remaining 5 percent of deliveries are more difficult: If the baby's buttocks, shoulder, foot, or face emerge first (**breech presentation**), the baby will not be able to take as compact a shape as it passes through the vagina.

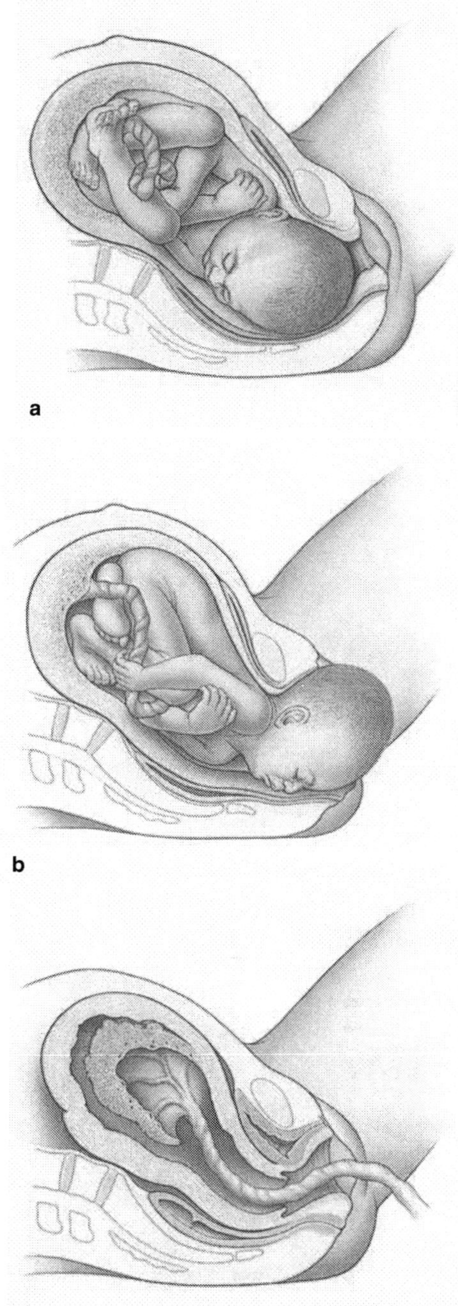

Figure E-3 Events in the childbirth process: (a) early stages of labor—cervix is dilating, baby's head starts to turn; (b) baby's head begins to emerge; (c) afterbirth.

Oversized babies (the average newborn weighs 7.5 pounds) can also cause problems because the baby's head must pass between the bones of the mother's pelvic arch. If the baby is too large, or if the mother's or baby's physical condition makes the stress of childbirth dangerous, a physician may decide to deliver the child by cesarean (or Caesarean) section, so called after Julius Caesar, who was supposedly born in this way. A **cesarean section** is a surgical operation in which a physician makes an incision in the mother's abdomen and uterine wall to remove the infant.

Another source of complications may be weak uterine contractions (perhaps caused by anesthesia). If contractions are not strong enough to expel the baby, a physician may use forceps—tongs that fit around the baby's head—to draw the baby out through the vagina. However, this procedure is risky, for the inaccurate placement of forceps, along with the force necessary to pull the infant free, may cause disfigurement or brain damage. There is a newer process using vacuum-assisted delivery devices, which also carries some risk (Gilbert 1998).

Afterbirth

The third and final stage of childbirth takes place between two and twenty minutes after delivery. It consists of the expulsion of the **afterbirth:** the placenta, the amniotic sac, and the remainder of the umbilical cord. The cord must be cut and tied to complete the baby's separation from the mother.

Issues in Pregnancy and Childbirth

Important policy issues and personal decisions center on pregnancy and childbirth, as societies and families reproduce the next generation. These include: access to prenatal care, natural childbirth versus the medicalization of childbirth (electronic fetal monitoring, induced labor, and cesarean section), midwives as birth attendants, and preterm delivery and low-birth-weight babies.

Prenatal Care

Early prenatal care has become more widespread for pregnant women in the last ten years. Eighty-four percent of pregnant women had medical care in the first trimester of pregnancy in 2004. Although black, American Indian, and Hispanic women are less likely than non-Hispanic white women or Asians to see a physician in the early months of pregnancy, there were increases in early prenatal care for all racial/ethnic groups from 1990 to 2003, although not since. Tobacco use in pregnancy has declined over the years (Martin et al. 2006).

Greater access to prenatal care, hospital delivery, and a doctor's assistance in childbirth contributed greatly to the sharp decrease in infant and maternal death during childbirth throughout the twentieth century. The overwhelming majority of babies (99 percent) are now born in hospitals. In 2004, 92 percent of births were attended by physicians, and 8 percent by midwives, mostly certified nurse-midwives (Martin et al. 2006).

Natural Childbirth

The reliance on hospitals and doctors that developed in the latter half of the twentieth century gave rise to a countertrend toward natural childbirth. Reaction against the treatment of childbirth as a medical problem rather than a natural event (Rothman 1982, 1989) included criticism of the usual practices of mid-twentieth-century pregnancy and birth: heavy anesthesia, the authority of the doctor (not the mother) in management of pregnancy and birth, barring the father from the labor and delivery rooms, electronic fetal monitoring throughout labor, the limited contact of mothers with their newborn infants, and lack of encouragement for breastfeeding. Infants born under heavy sedation are less responsive and alert; they also have somewhat reduced chances for surviving a medical emergency. When infants are kept in sterile isolation, the parent–child bond is less easily established.

Things began to change as parents—and health care providers—came to value a more natural childbirth process. Beginning in the 1950s and gaining momentum in the 1960s and 1970s, the **natural childbirth** movement came to influence not only parents' preferences but also physician and hospital practices regarding birth. The underlying philosophy of the movement was that natural methods of delivery are more emotionally satisfying to both mother and father and are often better for the infant (Korte 1995).

Educational and support groups provided training for parents so that mothers might deliver with minimal anesthesia and fathers could assist them in the labor room. Physicians, nurses, and expectant mothers accepted a labor process that was not artificially hurried by incising vaginal tissues (**episiotomy**) or by the use of forceps, or by a too-quick decision to do a cesarean section. In natural childbirth, the baby may be given to the mother for nursing or affectionate contact even before the umbilical cord is tied. These practices are now virtually standard practice in birthing, except that anesthesia is not precluded.

Cesarean-Section Births and Induced Labor

Concerns about the medicalization of childbirth include the trend toward **induced labor**—administering certain drugs to the mother that will cause the birthing process to begin—and more frequent delivery of babies by cesarean section. Public health concerns led the U.S. Department of Health and Human Services to set a goal of reducing cesarean sections to no more than 15 percent of births by 2000 (Gilbert 1998). Instead, there has been a 46 percent rise in cesarean births since 1996; they now comprise 30 percent of all births (Hamilton, Martin, and Ventura 2006).

Reasons offered for this high rate include the now common practice of fetal monitoring (done in 85 percent of labors in 2002 [Martin et al. 2003]), which may trigger unnecessary intervention. Physicians' and hospitals' fears about liability—if they fail to intervene surgically and the infant suffers some damage—are also thought to be a factor in the increase (Gilbert 1998). Also, vaginal births after a cesarean have declined dramatically since 1996 (Bakalar 2005; Martin et al. 2006).[5]

A study suggests that at least one-quarter of the increase in cesareans is due to the performance of cesareans in situations of no indicated medical risk (Declercq, Menacker, and MacDorman 2004). Of course, difficult births may require surgical intervention, and there is no question that cesareans are often lifesaving procedures for both mothers and infants. But experts express alarm at the high rates of cesarean births because they are riskier for mothers and infants (Bakalar 2005; 2006). A cesarean section also deprives a mother of the experience of normal childbirth. Cost is also a factor, as it costs much more than a normal vaginal delivery.[6]

Mothers and Medicalized Childbirth

Ironically, a major reason for the increase in cesareans has been a change in the views of pregnant women about how they want to do childbirth. Against the recommendations of the public health establishment and their own physicians, women are asserting a right to control over the birth process. What many women seem to be demanding is a movement away from natural childbirth.

Birthing mothers are requesting more pain medication than in the past. In larger hospitals in the late 1990s, 66 percent of mothers giving birth received spinal or epidural injections, compared to 22 percent in the 1980s (Chivers 1999; Talbot 1999). There are also more elective cesarean births and inductions of labor (instead of waiting for birth to occur naturally, a woman is given a drug that will make labor begin). In 2004, 21 percent of births were induced, a rate that has more than doubled since 1990 (Martin et al. 2006). "The latest trend is to book your induction or your caesarean months ahead, a strategy that seems just right . . . for two-career parents—and doctors—who don't want nature to disrupt their busy schedules" (comments of nurse-midwife Penny Simkin, summarized in Brockman 2000).

Mothers seek control over the birth process now, not to enhance birthing as a life experience, but to get through it with minimal discomfort and inconvenience (Springen 2000). They are rejecting what is seen to be an ideological invocation of pain as a moral experience or character test (Talbot 1999), focusing on the parenthood that follows birth rather than the birthing experience. Moreover, some women who have been through childbirth argue that pain kept them from an awareness of the birth process anyway. Dr. Frederic Frigoletto, head of obstetrics at Massachusetts General Hospital, says, "I think there's a trend away from the culture of a few years past, when natural childbirth was important to women. . . . [Now patients] don't want pain with their baby" (quoted in Pan 1999, p. 106; see also Brockman 2000).

There is some medical support for these choices. Some physicians are themselves coming to think that natural childbirth may have been oversold. In part, anesthesia has now evolved so that dosage is much smaller and wears off quickly, so it has less effect on the newborn. There are medical arguments to be made for elective cesarean section. Although the risk of an infection for mother or child is higher with a cesarean, as is the risk of death (though small), vaginal births carry a risk of damage to pelvic tissue that may compromise bladder control and sexual responsiveness (research on this point is contradictory; Rubin 2005). There is a risk of cerebral palsy for the child, however small (Gilbert 1998; Springen 2000). Some experts would argue that a vaginal delivery using vacuum extraction might not be superior to a cesarean section in its risks and effects.

The American College of Obstetricians and Gynecologists has declared that elective C-sections are ethical if they are the best choice in the judgment of the physician. Reasons for an elective cesarean might be pragmatic, for example, a substantial distance from the patient's home to the hospital or her tendency to deliver quickly, which would make it difficult to reach a hospital when labor begins. Or, a physician may believe that she or he can do the best job when time of delivery is chosen rather than occurring in the middle of the night after a long day of medical practice.

Still, the risk–benefit balance is seen to favor vaginal birth where there is no apparent medical indication for

5. Public health officials encouraged women who had had cesarean births to try a vaginal delivery in subsequent pregnancies. Some research indicates that vaginal birth after cesarean (VBAC) is riskier than another cesarean (Stolberg 2001). The most recent research suggests that the risk is minimal (Rubin 2004). However, some hospitals will not accept patients who plan to have a VBAC, so those women do not have that option (Grady 2004).

6. Although cesarean births are more expensive than uncomplicated vaginal births, lengthy vaginal births are also costly.

a cesarean. There is much concern about the high cesarean rate and especially about elective C-sections (Brody 2003; Stein 2003; Villarosa 2002). "Obstetrics has become very consumer-driven," commented one physician (in Brody 2003, p. D-7).

Midwives and Home Births

At the same time that natural childbirth is receding in popularity and practice, the use of midwives is growing. Midwives delivered 8 percent of babies in 2004 compared to less than 1 percent in 1975 (Martin et al. 2006). This trend seems also to be driven by the preferences of parents.

A **midwife** is a birth attendant who is not a physician. Midwives may be *nurse-midwives*—nurses with additional specialized training, who are credentialed as CNMs—or certified nurse-midwives. Or, they may be *direct-entry midwives,* who are not nurses but who may be *certified professional midwives* or *certified midwives* (Pew Health 1999). A third category is the **doula,** a birthing coach without medical claims, operating in a long folk tradition of laywomen who assist at birth: "Part mentor, part coach, all-around handholder and advocate" (Wilgoren 2005, p. A-11). Doulas have now become professionalized. There were five thousand registered doulas in 2004. Some women may combine a physician-managed pregnancy with the presence of a midwife or doula at birth (Liptak 2006). The legal status of these birthing choices and state supervision of these professions vary by state.[7]

Some women may have home births in conjunction with a midwifery approach to childbirth (Hartocollis 2005). The vast majority (97 percent) of certified nurse-midwife–attended births took place in hospitals in 2004, while 56 percent of births attended by other midwives took place in the home (Martin et al. 2006, Table 27).

Nurse-midwives attend births much more frequently in European countries—which have very low rates of maternal and infant mortality. Midwives provide emotional support as well as professional expertise, and they recognize that the baby belongs to the family, not the medical establishment (Korte 1995):

> The midwifery model of care views childbirth and well-woman care as normal processes that do not require medical intervention unless there are signs of pathology or deviations from the normal. . . . The midwifery model of care includes observational (nontechnological) monitoring of the physical, psychological, and social well-being of the mother throughout the childbearing cycle; providing the mother with individualized education . . . and prenatal care; continuous hands-on assistance during labor and delivery, and post-partum support; minimizing technological intervention; [but] referring women who require [a physician's] obstetrical attention. . . . This effective collaboration between the midwife and the physician, where the expertise of both professions is valued, is the key to ensuring optimal outcomes for women and their infants. (Pew Health 1999, pp. 5–6)

To summarize this section regarding pregnancy and childbirth in the United States at the beginning of the twenty-first century, we see a dominant preference for medicalized childbirth, with a "vocal minority" (Dr. David Birnbach, in Chivers 1999) committed to natural childbirth or midwifery or both. Both groups are able to exercise more choice and control over the birthing process than in the past.

Some Concerns: Premature Births and Low-Birth-Weight Babies

There are some concerns about the welfare of babies despite the increased use of prenatal care and improved infant mortality. The rate of preterm births has risen 20 percent since 1990. Premature birth (fewer than thirty-seven weeks' gestation) is a leading cause of infant deaths and of almost half of congenital neurological disabilities such as cerebral palsy. Low birth weight (fewer than 2,500 grams, or about five and a half pounds) is a related predictor of mortality and disability. There has been a 20 percent increase in low-birth-weight babies since the mid-1980s; in 2005 the percentage of low-birth-weight babies reached its highest level since 1968. The reasons for these trends are not clear, save for the recent increase in multiple births, which are more likely to be premature and low birth weight (Hamilton, Martin, and Ventura 2006; Martin et al. 2006).

Premature and low-birth-weight babies are at risk of physical and learning disabilities, but the latest research has found better than expected outcomes. Premature babies are almost as likely to complete high school as full-term babies. And they engage in *less* risky behavior

7. State laws vary as to the training, certification, and physician affiliation required of a practicing midwife, and regarding the legal status of home births. The American College of Nurse-Midwives maintains a website (www.midwife.org) that provides information and a registry of approved nurse-midwives in each state.

The Midwives' Alliance of North America site, www.mana.org, is sponsored by an organization of direct-entry midwives. The Doulas of North America website is www.dona.org.

An important and comprehensive source of information on midwifery is *The Future of Midwifery,* a report of the Taskforce on Midwifery, a joint venture of the Pew Health Professions Commission and the University of California, San Francisco Center for the Health Professions (Pew Health 1999): http://futurehealth.ucsf.edu.

Health plans vary in whether or not they will pay for a midwife-assisted delivery (Dower 1999).

in adolescence and young adulthood. Researchers have also found that the cognitive abilities of these at-risk children improve from infancy to middle childhood. It may be that worried parents become more involved with their children in a way that offsets their physiological disadvantage (Stolberg 2002; "Verbal and IQ Scores" 2003).

For a more detailed treatment of conception, pregnancy, and childbirth, see the Boston Women's Health Book Collective, *Our Bodies, Ourselves: A New Edition for a New Era* (2005) and Greenberg, Bruess, and Haffner 2002, Chapter 9.

References

"Amniocentesis." 2004. WebMD (www.webmd.com).

Bakalar, Nicholas. 2005. "Premature Births Increase Along with C-sections." *New York Times,* November 22.

2006. "Voluntary C-sections Result in More Baby Deaths." *New York Times,* November 22.

Boston Women's Health Book Collective. 2005. *Our Bodies, Ourselves: A New Edition for a New Era.* New York: Simon and Schuster.

Brockman, Erin Schoen. 2000. "The Baby and the Bathwater: Birth Methods Then and Now." *New York Times,* June 25.

Brody, Jane E. 2003. "As Cases of Induced Labor Rise, So Do Experts' Concerns." New York Times, January 14.

———. 2004. "Prenatal Tests: More Information, Less Risk." *New York Times,* July 27.

———. 2005. "35 and Pregnant? Assessing Risk Becomes Easier." *New York Times,* December 27.

Chivers, C. J. 1999. "Fighting Trend, Women Choose to Bear with Pain." *New York Times,* October 18.

"Chorionic Villus Sampling." 2004. WebMD (www.webmd.com).

Declercq, Eugene, Fay Menacker, and Marian MacDorman. 2004. "Rise in 'No Indicated Risk' Primary Caesareans in the United States, 1991–2001: Cross-Sectional Analysis." *British Medical Journal* (doi:10.1136/bmj.38279.705336OB). On-line First BMJ.com. November 19.

Dower, Catherine. 1999. "Task Force Urges Inclusion of Midwifery in Managed Care Plans" (www.futurehealth.ucsd.edu/press_releases/midwifery.html).

Gilbert, Susan. 1998. "Doctors Report Rise in Elective Cesareans." *New York Times,* Sept. 22.

Grady, Denise. 2004. "Trying to Avoid Second Caesarean, Many Find Choice Isn't Theirs." *New York Times,* November 29.

Greenberg, Jerrold S., Clint E. Bruess, and Debra W. Haffner. 2002. *Exploring the Dimensions of Human Sexuality.* Sudbury, MA: Jones and Bartlett.

Hamilton, Brady E., Joyce A. Martin, and Stephanie J. Ventura. 2006. "Births: Preliminary Data for 2005." *National Vital Statistics Reports* 55(11). Hyattsville, MD: National Center for Health Statistics. December 28.

Harmon, Amy. 2007. "Prenatal Test Puts Down Syndrome in Hard Focus." *New York Times,* May 9.

Hartocollis, Anemona. 2005. "Home Delivery Is Available." *New York Times,* June 2.

Jones, Maggie. 2001. "A Miracle—and Yet." *New York Times Magazine,* July 5, pp. 39–43.

Kempley, Rita. 2003. "The Grin before They Bear It: Peek-a-Boo Prenatal Portraits for the Ultrasound Set." *Washington Post,* August 9.

Korte, Diana. 1995. "Midwives on Trial." Mothering(Fall):52–63.

Liptak, Adam. 2006. "Prosecution of Midwife Casts Light on Home Births." *New York Times,* April 3.

Lubell, Sam. 2004. "The Womb as Photo Studio." *New York Times,* September 30.

Martin, Joyce A., Brady E. Hamilton, Paul D. Sutton, Stephanie J. Ventura, Fay Menacker, and Sharon Kirmeyer. 2006. "Births: Final Data for 2004." *National Vital Statistics Reports* 55(1). Hyattsville, MD: National Center for Health Statistics. September 29.

Martin, Joyce A., Brady E. Hamilton, Paul D. Sutton, Stephanie J. Ventura, Fay Menacker, and Martha Munson. 2003. "Births: Final Data for 2002." *National Vital Statistics Reports* 52(10). Hyattsville, MD: National Center for Health Statistics. December 17.

Pan, Esther. 1999. "Not Mother Nature's Way." *Newsweek,* November 29.

Pew Health Professions Commission and the University of California, San Francisco Center for the Health Professions. 1999. *The Future of Midwifery.* San Francisco, CA: The Center for the Health Professions, University of California. April.

Rothman, Barbara Katz. 1982. *In Labor: Women and Power in the Birthplace.* New York: Norton.

———. 1989. *Recreating Motherhood: Ideology and Technology in a Patriarchal Society.* New York: Norton.

Rubin, Rita. 2004. "Birthing Study Reexamines Risks." USA Today, December 15.

———. 2005. "Studies on Incontinence in Mothers Differ on Role C-sections Play." *USA Today,* December 1.

Springen, Karen. 2000. "The Right to Choose." *Newsweek,* December 4, p. 7.

Stein, Rob. 2003. "Elective Caesarians Are Judged Ethical." *Washington Post,* October 30.

Stolberg, Sheryl Gay. 2001. "A Risk Is Found in Natural Birth after Caesarean." *New York Times,* July 5.

———. 2002. "Study Says Premature Babies Fare Better Than Expected." *New York Times,* January 17.

Talbot, Margaret. 1999. "Pay on Delivery." *New York Times Magazine,* October 31, pp. 19–20.

"Verbal and IQ Scores Improve as Premature Infants Grow, Yale Researchers Report." 2003. Yale News Release. February 11 (www.yale.edu/opa).

Villarosa, Linda. 2002. "Making an Appointment with the Stork." *New York Times,* June 23.

Weise, Elizabeth. 2003. "Science Peers behind the Veil of the Unborn." *USA Today,* March 3.

Wilgoren, Jodi. 2005. "'Mothering the Mother' with Childbirth Support." *New York Times,* May 9.

"World's Smallest Baby Ready to Go Home." 2004. *USA Today,* December 21.

Glossary

afterbirth The placenta, amniotic sac, and the remainder of the umbilical cord, all of which are expelled during delivery after the birth of the baby.
amniotic fluid Salty, watery fluid that surrounds the developing fetus within the mother's uterus, cushioning and protecting it.
areolae The pigmented areas of the breasts surrounding the nipples.
breech presentation In childbirth, a delivery in which the baby's buttocks, shoulder, foot, or face emerge first. This makes for a more difficult delivery than the vertex presentation.
cervix At the top of the vagina in the female, the neck of the uterus. Must be dilated during labor so that the baby can pass from the uterus into the vagina and emerge from the mother's body.
cesarean section Childbirth by means of a surgical operation in which a physician makes an incision in the mother's abdomen and uterine wall to remove the infant. Named after Julius Caesar, who was supposedly delivered this way. Sometimes the term is shortened to cesarean.
conception The joining of an ovum (egg) with a sperm cell to begin the development of a zygote, to become an embryo, then a fetus, then a baby, if development is uninterrupted.
delivery The second phase (after labor) of childbirth, lasting from the time the cervix is completely dilated until the baby is expelled.
doula A lay birth attendant whose skills and attention reflect a folk tradition of lay midwifery.
embryonic stage The period of pregnancy after the first two weeks (germinal period) until about eight weeks, during which the fetal head, skeletal system, heart, and digestive system begin to form. The developing infant is termed an embryo (not a fetus) during this period.
endometrium The endometrium is the lining of the uterus, which thickens with a layer of tissue and blood in order to nourish an embryo should an egg become fertilized. If no egg is fertilized, the endometrial tissue and blood are discarded during menstruation.
episiotomy A surgical incision of the perineum (the skin between the vaginal opening and the anus) thought to facilitate the emergence of the baby from the uterus and prevent tearing of the skin.
fallopian tubes Tubes connecting each ovary to the uterus. After ovulation the egg travels through the fallopian tubes to the uterus and may be fertilized by a sperm during this time.
fertilization The joining of an ovum with a sperm cell.
fetal period The period of pregnancy lasting from about eight weeks until birth.
germinal period The first two weeks of pregnancy.
gestation The entire period of pregnancy during which the fertilized egg develops into the baby that will be born.
implantation The process in which the fertilized egg, or zygote, embeds itself in the thickened lining of the uterus.
induced labor Administration of drugs to a pregnant woman to start the birth process, rather than waiting for it to begin naturally.
labor In childbirth, the process in which the cervix dilates to permit passage of the baby, who is propelled from the mother's body by contractions of the uterus.
midwife A birth attendant who is not a physician, but who supports the mother and monitors and facilitates childbirth, drawing on a tradition of lay assistance at childbirth. In modern times, many midwives are medically trained professionals, who offer an emotionally supportive and personalized birth experience to the mother in addition to their professional skills.
natural childbirth Management of childbirth to minimize medical and technological intervention. Usually involves minimization of anesthesia, no electronic monitoring or use of such medical interventions as forceps delivery or surgical episiotomy. Usually includes pre-birth training and the presence of the husband or other labor partner in the delivery room.
ovaries Two female gonads, or sex glands, that produce reproductive cells called ova, or eggs.
ovulation The process by which an ovary produces an ovum, or egg. Usually the ovaries alternate so that only one ovulates each month.
ovum An egg produced by the female ovary. The plural form is ova.
placenta Tissue and membrane that hold the fetus in place inside the uterus and connect the mother to the fetus through the umbilical cord for the purpose of delivering nourishment and oxygen and removing waste.
quickening The first fetal movement apparent to the pregnant woman. Not a technical term, but an important indicator of fetal development in an era before the existence of medical monitoring technology—and often a marker of some emotional importance to the mother.
sperm Male reproductive cells present in semen (male ejaculate).
umbilical cord Tube that connects the abdomen of a fetus to the placenta inside the mother's uterus. Serves to channel nourishment to the fetus and remove waste.
uterus A cavity inside the female in which a fetus grows until birth; also called womb.
vertex presentation In childbirth, a delivery in which the baby's skull emerges first. This is the most common and most advantageous form of delivery.
zygote A fertilized ovum (egg).

Glossary

ABC-X model A model of family crisis in which A (the stressor event) interacts with B (the family's resources for meeting a crisis) and with C (the definition the family formulates of the event) to produce X (the crisis).

abortion See **induced abortion.**

abstinence The standard that maintains that nonmarital intercourse is wrong or inadvisable for both women and men regardless of the circumstances. Many religions espouse abstinence as a moral imperative, while some individuals are abstinent as a temporary or permanent personal choice.

acculturation The process whereby immigrant groups adopt the beliefs, values, and norms of their new culture and lose their traditional values and practices.

acquaintance rape Forced or unwanted sexual contact between people who know each other, often—although not necessarily—taking place on a date. See also **date rape**.

active life expectancy The period of life free of disability in activities of daily living, after which may follow a period of being at least somewhat disabled.

agape The love style that emphasizes unselfish concern for a beloved, in which one attempts to fulfill the other's needs even when that means some personal sacrifice. See also **eros, ludus, mania, pragma,** and **storge**.

agentic (instrumental) character traits Traits such as confidence, assertiveness, and ambition that enable a person to accomplish difficult tasks or goals.

AIDS See **HIV/AIDS.**

allocation systems The arrangements couples make for handling their income, wealth, and expenditures. Allocation systems may involve pooling partners' resources or keeping them separate. Who controls pooled resources is another dimension of an allocation system.

arranged marriage Unions in which parents choose their children's marriage partners.

asexual, asexuality A person who is asexual does not experience sexual desire. This is different from abstinence or celibacy, which is a choice to not engage in sexual activity despite feelings of sexual desire. Asexuality may be considered a sexual orientation.

assisted reproductive technology (ART) Advanced reproductive technology, such as artificial insemination, in vitro fertilization, or embryo transplantation, that enables infertile couples or individuals, including gay and lesbian couples, to have children.

assortative mating Social psychological filtering process in which individuals gradually filter out those among their pool of eligible individuals they believe would not make the best spouse.

attachment "An active, affective, enduring, and reciprocal bond between two individuals that is believed to be established through repeated action over time" (Coleman and Watson 2000, p. 297, citing Ainsworth et al. 1978).

attachment disorder An emotional disorder in which a person defensively shuts off the willingness or ability to make emotional attachments to anyone.

attachment theory A psychological theory that holds that, during infancy and childhood, a young person develops a general style of attaching to others; once an individual's attachment style is established, she or he unconsciously applies that style to later, adult relationships. The three basic styles are **secure, insecure/anxious**, and **avoidant**.

authoritarian parenting style All decision making is in parents' hands, and the emphasis is on compliance with rules and directives. Parents are more punitive than supportive, and use of physical punishment is likely.

authoritative parenting style Parents accept the child's personality and talents and are emotionally supportive. At the same time, they consciously set and enforce rules and limits, whose rationale is usually explained to the child. Parents provide guidance and direction and state expectations for the child's behavior. Parents are in charge, but the child is given responsibility and must take the initiative in completing schoolwork and other tasks and in solving child-level problems.

avoidant attachment style One of three attachment styles in **attachment theory,** this style avoids intimacy either by evading relationships altogether or by establishing considerable distance in intimate situations.

baby boom The unusually large cohort of U.S. children born after the end of World War II, between 1946 and 1964.

barriers to divorce Impediments to a decision to divorce, such as concern about children, religiously grounded objections to divorce, or financial concerns or dependencies.

belligerence A negative communication/relationship behavior that challenges the partner's power and authority.

bereavement A period of mourning after the death of a loved one.

binational family An immigrant family in which some members are citizens or legal residents of the country they migrate to, while others are **undocumented**—that is, they are not legal residents.

binuclear family One family in two household units. A term created to describe a postdivorce family in which both parents remain involved and children are at home in both households.

biosocial perspective Theoretical perspective based on concepts linking psychosocial factors to anatomy, physiology, genetics, and/or hormones as shaped by evolution.

bisexuals People who are sexually attracted to both males and females.

borderwork Interaction rituals that are based on and reaffirm boundaries and differences between girls and boys.

boundary ambiguity When applied to a family, a situation in which it is unclear who is in and who is out of the family.

bride price Money or property that a future groom pays a future bride's family so that he can marry her.

caregiver model of elder abuse and neglect A view of elder abuse or neglect that highlights stress on the caregiver as important to the understanding of abusive behavior.

caregiving "Assistance provided to persons who cannot, for whatever reason, perform the basic activities or instrumental activities of daily living for themselves" (Cherlin 1996, p. 762).

caregiving trajectory The process through which eldercare proceeds, according to which, first, the caregiver becomes concerned about an aging family member, then later begins to give advice to the older family member, and still later takes action to provide needed services.

case study A written summary and analysis of data obtained by psychologists, psychiatrists, counselors, and social workers when working directly with individuals and families in clinical practice. Case studies may be used as sources in scientific investigation and have played a role in the development of certain family theories.

center care Group child care provided in day-care centers for a relatively large number of children.

child abuse Overt acts of aggression against a child, such as beating or inflicting physical injury or excessive verbal derogation. Sexual abuse is a form of physical child abuse. See also **emotional child abuse or neglect.**

child care The care and education of children by people other than their parents. Child care may include before- and after-school care for older children and overnight care when employed parents must travel, as well as day care for preschool children.

child neglect Failure to provide adequate physical or emotional care for a child. See also **emotional child abuse or neglect.**

child support Money paid by the noncustodial parent to the custodial parent to financially support children of a former marital, cohabiting, or sexual relationship.

child-to-parent abuse A form of family violence involving a child's (especially an adolescent's) physical and emotional abuse of a parent.

children's allowance A type of child support that provides a government grant to all families—married or single-parent, regardless of income—based on the number of children they have.

choosing by default Making semiconscious or unconscious choices when one is not aware of all the possible alternatives or when one pursues the path of least resistance. From this perspective, doing nothing about a problem or issue, or making no choice, is making a choice—the choice to do nothing.

choosing knowledgeably Making choices and decisions after (1) recognizing as many options or alternatives as possible, (2) recognizing the social pressures that can influence personal choices, (3) considering the consequences of each alternative, and (4) becoming aware of one's own values.

civil union Legislation that allows any two single adults—including same-sex partners or blood relatives, such as siblings or a parent and adult child—to have access to virtually all marriage rights and benefits on the state level, but none on the federal level. Designed to give same-sex couples many of the legal benefits of marriage while denying them the right to legally marry.

coercive power One of the six power bases, or sources of power. This power is based on the dominant person's ability and willingness to punish the partner either with psychological–emotional or physical abuse or with more subtle methods of withholding affection.

cohabitation Living together in an intimate, sexual relationship without traditional, legal marriage. Sometimes referred to as *living together* or *marriage without marriage,* cohabitation can be a courtship process or an alternative to legal marriage, depending on how partners view it.

collectivist society A society in which people identify with and conform to the expectations of their relatives or clan, who look after their interests in return for their loyalty. The group has priority over the individual. A synonym is *communal society.*

commitment (to intimacy) The determination to develop relationships in which experiences cover many areas of personality, problems are worked through, conflict is expected and seen as a normal part of the growth process, and there is an expectation that the relationship is basically viable and worthwhile.

commitment (Sternberg's triangular theory of love) The short-term decision that one loves someone and the long-term commitment to maintain that love; one dimension of the triangular theory of love.

common law marriage A legal concept whereby cohabiting partners are considered legally married if certain requirements are met, such as showing intent to enter into a marriage and living together as husband and wife for a certain period. Most states have dropped common law marriage, but cohabiting relationships may sometimes have a similar effect on property ownership and custody rights.

communal (expressive) character traits Traits that foster relationships with others, such as warmth, sensitivity, the ability to express tender feelings, and the desire to place concern about others' welfare above self-interest.

communal society See **collectivist society.**

communes Groups of adults and perhaps children who live together, sharing aspects of their lives. Some communes are group marriages, in which members share sex; others are communal families, with several monogamous couples, who share everything except sexual relations and their children.

community-based resources Characteristics, competencies, and means of people, groups, and institutions outside the family that the family may call upon, access, and use to meet their demands.

community divorce Ruptures of relationships and changes in social networks that come about because of divorce.

commuter marriage A marriage in which the two partners live in different locations and commute to spend time together.

companionate marriage The single-earner, breadwinner–homemaker marriage that flourished in the 1950s. Although husbands and wives in the companionate marriage usually adhered to a sharp division of labor, they were supposed to be each other's companion—friends, lovers—in a realization of trends beginning in the 1920s.

concerted cultivation The parenting model, or style, according to which parents often praise and converse with their children, engage them in extracurricular activities, take them on outings, and so on, with the goal of cultivating their child's talents and abilities.

conflict perspective Theoretical perspective that emphasizes social conflict in a society and within families. Power and dominance are important themes.

Conflict Tactics Scale A scale developed by sociologist Murray Straus to assess how couples handle conflict. Includes detailed items on various forms of physical violence.

Confucian training doctrine Concept used to describe Asian and Asian American parenting philosophy that emphasizes blending parental love, concern, involvement, and physical closeness with strict and firm control.

consensual marriages Heterosexual, conjugal unions that have not gone through a legal marriage ceremony.

consummate love A complete love, in terms of Sternberg's triangular theory of love, in which the components of passion, intimacy, and commitment come together.

contempt One of the **Four Horsemen of the Apocalypse** (which see), in which a partner feels that his or her spouse is inferior or undesirable.

co-parenting, co-parents Shared decision making and parental supervision in such areas as discipline and schoolwork or shared holidays and recreation. Can refer to parents working together in a marriage or other ongoing relationship or after divorce or separation.

courtly love Popular during the twelfth century and later, courtly love is the intense longing for someone other than one's marital partner—a passionate and sexual longing that ideally goes unfulfilled. The assumptions of courtly love influence our modern ideas about romantic love.

courtship The process whereby a couple develops a mutual commitment to marriage.

covenant marriage A type of legal marriage in which the bride and groom agree to be bound by a marriage contract that will not let them get divorced as easily as is allowed under no-fault divorce laws.

criticism One of the **Four Horsemen of the Apocalypse** (which see) that involves making disapproving judgments or evaluations of one's partner.

cross-national marriages Marriages in which spouses are from different countries.

crude divorce rate The number of divorces per 1,000 population. See also **refined divorce rate.**

cultural script Set of socially prescribed and understood guidelines for relating to others or for defining role responsibilities and obligations.

culture war Deep cultural conflict, often buttressed by religious belief systems, over matters concerning human sexuality and gender.

custodial grandparent A parent of a divorced, custodial parent.

custodial parent The parent who has legal responsibility for a child after parents divorce or separate. In sole custody, the child resides with the custodial parent. In joint custody, the child may reside primarily with one parent or may live part of the time with each.

custody Primary responsibility for making decisions about a child's upbringing and general welfare.

cyberadultery Marital infidelity or adultery on the Internet.

data collection techniques Ways that data are gathered when doing research; these include interviews and questionnaires, naturalistic observation, focus groups, experiments and laboratory observation, and case studies, among others.

date rape Forced or unwanted sexual contact between people who are on a date. See also **acquaintance rape.**

Defense of Marriage Act (DOMA) Federal statute declaring marriage to be a "legal union of one man and one woman," denying gay couples many of the civil advantages of marriage and relieving states of the obligation to grant reciprocity, or "full faith and credit," to marriages performed in another state.

defensiveness One of the **Four Horsemen of the Apocalypse** (which see) that means preparing to defend oneself against what one presumes is an upcoming attack.

deinstitutionalization of marriage A situation in which time-honored family definitions are changing and family-related social norms are weakening so that they "count for far less" than in the past.

displacement A passive-aggressive behavior in which a person expresses anger with another by being angry at or damaging people or things the other cherishes. See also **passive-aggression.**

divorce divide The gap in divorce rates between college-educated and less-educated women. The divorce rate has declined substantially for college-educated women, but not for less-educated women.

divorce-extended family Kinship ties that form in the wake of a divorce. May include former in-laws, new spouses of one's ex-spouse, and that person's children and kin as part of one kinship system.

divorce mediation A nonadversarial means of dispute resolution by which the couple, with the assistance of a mediator or mediators (frequently a lawyer–therapist team), negotiate the terms of their settlement of custody, support, property, and visitation issues.

domestic partners Partners in an unmarried couple who have registered their partnership with a civil authority and then enjoy some (although not necessarily all) rights, benefits, and entitlements that have traditionally been reserved for marrieds.

domestic violence model of elder abuse and neglect A model that conceptualizes elder abuse as a form of family violence.

double message See **mixed message.**

double remarriage A remarriage in which both partners were previously married.

double standard The standard according to which nonmarital sex or multiple partners are more acceptable for males than for females.

dowry A sum of money or property brought to the marriage by the female.

economic divorce The aspect of divorce that divides the couple into separate economic units, each with its own property, income, control of expenditures, and responsibility for taxes, debts, and so on.

economic hardship perspective (on children's adjustment to divorce) One of the theoretical perspectives concerning the negative outcomes among children of divorced parents. From this perspective, it is the economic hardship brought about by marital dissolution that is primarily responsible for problems faced by children.

egalitarian norm (of marital power) The norm (cultural rule) that husband and wife should have equal power in a marriage.

elder abuse Overt acts of aggression toward the elderly, in which the victim may be physically assaulted, emotionally humiliated, purposefully isolated, or materially exploited.

elder neglect Acts of omission in the care and treatment of the elderly.

elder care Care provided to older generations.

emerging adulthood The youth and young adult stage of life, which is a period of frequent change and exploration.

emotion A strong feeling arising without conscious mental or rational effort, such as joy, reverence, anger, fear, love, or hate. Emotions are neither bad nor good and should be accepted as natural. People can and should learn to control what they do about their emotions.

emotion labor The display of certain emotions that one believes is expected in a given situation, regardless of whether one feels those emotions.

emotional child abuse or neglect A parent or other caregiver's being overly harsh and critical, failing to provide guidance, or being uninterested in a child's needs.

emotional divorce Withdrawing bonding emotions and communication from the marital or other relationship, typically replacing these with alienating feelings and behavior.

emotional intelligence (1) Awareness of what we're feeling so that we can express our feelings more authentically; (2) ability and willingness to repair our moods, not unnecessarily nursing our hurt feelings; (3) healthy balance between controlling rash impulses and being candid and spontaneous; and (4) sensitivity to the feelings and needs of others.

endogamy Marrying within one's own social group. See also **exogamy.**

equality Power or resources divided between partners so that each has the same amount.

equity A standard for distribution of power or resources of partners according to the contribution each person has made to the unit. Another way of characterizing an equitable result is that it is "fair."

eros The love style characterized by intense emotional attachment and powerful sexual feelings or desires. See also **agape, ludus, mania, pragma**, and **storge.**

ethnicity A group's identity based on a sense of a common culture and language.

Euro-American families Families whose members are of European ethnic background.

evolutionary heritage In the biosocial perspective, human behavior is encoded in genetic or other biological features that come to us as members of a species.

exchange balance Balance of rewards and costs in a relationship.

exchange theory Theoretical perspective that sees relationships as determined by the exchange of resources and the reward–cost balance of that exchange. This theory predicts that people tend to marry others whose social class, education, physical attractiveness, and even self-esteem are similar to their own.

exogamy Marrying a partner from outside one's own social group. See also **endogamy**.

expectations of permanence One component of the marriage premise, according to which individuals enter marriage expecting that mutual affection and commitment will be lasting.

expectations of sexual exclusivity The cultural ideal according to which spouses promise to have sexual relations with only each other.

experience hypothesis The idea that the independent variable in a hypothesis is responsible for changes to a dependent variable. With regard to marriage, the experience hypothesis holds that something about the experience of being married itself causes certain results for spouses. See also the antonym, **selection hypothesis.**

experiential reality Knowledge based on personal experience.

experiment One tool of scientific investigation, in which behaviors are carefully monitored or measured under controlled conditions. Participants are randomly assigned to treatment or control groups.

expert power One of the six power bases, or sources of power. This power stems from the dominant person's superior judgment, knowledge, or ability.

expressive sexuality The view of human sexuality in which sexuality is basic to the humanness of both women and men, all individuals are free to express their sexual selves, and there is no one-sided sense of ownership.

expressive traits See **communal (expressive) character traits.**

extended family Family including relatives besides parents and children, such as aunts or uncles. See also **nuclear family.**

extrusion "[I]ndividuals' being 'pushed out' of their households earlier than normal for members of their cultural group, either because they are forced to leave or because remaining in their households is so stressful that they 'choose' to leave" (Crosbie-Burnett et al. 2005, p. 213).

facilitation of natural growth parenting model Parenting model, or style, in which the parent defines his/her role as allowing the child's abilities to develop naturally, rather than being consciously cultivated.

familistic (communal) values Values that focus on the family group as a whole and on maintaining family identity and cohesiveness.

family Any sexually expressive or parent-child or other kin relationship in which people live together with a commitment in an intimate interpersonal relationship. Family members see their identity as importantly attached to the group, which has an identity of its own. Families today take several forms: single-parent, remarried, dual-career, communal, homosexual, traditional, and so forth. See also **extended family, nuclear family.**

family boundaries Family members' understandings of who is and who is not in the family. Markers, whether material (e.g., doors, fences, communication devices) or social (e.g., symbols of identity, conversational styles and content, time spent together), indicate the boundaries of the family.

"family change" perspective See **"family decline," "family change" perspectives.**

family child care Child care provided in a caregiver's home.

family cohesion That intangible emotional quality that holds groups together and gives members a sense of common identity.

family crisis A situation (resulting from a stressor) in which the family's usual behavior patterns are ineffective and new ones are called for.

"family decline," "family change" perspectives Some family scholars and policy makers characterize late-twentieth-century developments in the family as "decline," while others describe "change." Those who take the "family decline" perspective view such changes as increases in the age at first marriage, divorce, cohabitation, and nonmarital births and the decline in fertility as disastrous for the family as a major social institution. "Family change" scholars and policy makers consider that the family has varied over time. They argue that the family can adapt to recent changes and continue to play a strong role in society.

family development perspective Theoretical perspective that gives attention to changes in the family over time.

family ecology perspective Theoretical perspective that explores how a family influences and is influenced by the environments that surround it. A family is interdependent first with its neighborhood, then with its social–cultural environment, and ultimately with the human-built and physical–biological environments. All parts of the model are interrelated and influence one another.

family foster care Foster care that takes place in a trained and licensed foster parent's home.

family-friendly workplace policies Workplace policies that are supportive of employee efforts to combine family and work commitments.

family function Activities performed by families for the benefit of society and of family members.

family identity Ideas and feelings about the uniqueness and value of one's family unit.

family instability perspective (on children's adjustment to divorce) The thesis that a negative impact of divorce on children is primarily caused by the number of changes in family structure, not by any particular family form. A stable single-parent family may be less harmful to children than a divorce followed by a single-parent family followed by cohabitation, then remarriage, and perhaps a redivorce.

family leave A leave of absence from work granted to family members to care for new infants, newly adopted children, ill children, or aging parents, or to meet similar family needs or emergencies.

family life course development framework Theoretical perspective that follows families through fairly typical stages in the life course, such as through marriage, childbirth, stages of raising children, adult children's leaving home, retirement, and possible widowhood.

family life cycle Stages of family development defined by the addition and subtraction of family members, children's ages, and changes in the family's connection with other social systems.

family of orientation The family in which an individual grows up. Also called *family of origin.*

family of procreation The family that is formed when an individual marries and has children.

family policy All the actions, procedures, regulations, attitudes, and goals of government that affect families.

family preservation A program of support for families in which children have been abused. The support is intended to enable the child to remain in the home safely rather than being placed in foster care.

family stress State of tension that arises when demands tax a family's resources.

family structure The form a family takes, such as nuclear family, extended family, single-parent family, stepfamily, and the like.

family systems theory An umbrella term for a wide range of specific theories. This theoretical perspective examines the family as a whole. It looks to the patterns of behavior and relationships within the family, in which each member is affected by the behavior of others. Systems tend toward equilibrium and will react to change in one part by seeking equilibrium either by restoring the old system or by creating a new one.

family transitions Expected or predictable changes in the course of family life that often precipitate family stress and can result in a family crisis.

family values See **familistic (communal) values.**

fecundity Reproductive capacity; biological capability to have children.

demand/withdraw interaction pattern A cycle of negative verbal expression by one partner, followed by the other partner's withdrawal in the face of the other's demands.

femininities Culturally defined ways of being a woman. The plural conveys the idea that there are varied models of appropriate behavior.

feminist theory Feminist theories are conflict theories. The primary focus of the feminist perspective is male dominance in families and society as oppressive to women. The mission of this perspective is to end this oppression of women (or related pattern of subordination based on social class, race/ethnicity, age, or sexual orientation) by developing knowledge and action that confront this disparity. See also **conflict perspective.**

fertility Births to a woman or category of women (actual births, not reproductive capacity).

fictive kin Family-like relationships that are not based on blood or marriage but on close friendship ties.

filial responsibility A child's obligation to a parent.

flexible scheduling A type of employment scheduling that includes scheduling options such as **job sharing** or **flextime**.

flextime A policy that permits an employee some flexibility to adjust working hours to suit family needs or personal preference.

formal kinship care Out-of-home placement with biological relatives of children who are in the custody of the state.

foster care Care provided to children by other than their parents as a result of state intervention.

Four Horsemen of the Apocalypse Contempt, criticism, defensiveness, and stonewalling—marital communication behaviors delineated by John Gottman that often indicate a couple's future divorce.

free-choice culture Culture or society in which individuals choose their own marriage partners, a choice usually based at least somewhat on romance.

friends with benefits Sexual activity between friends or acquaintances with no expectation of romance or emotional attachment; typically practiced by unattached people who want to have a sexual outlet without "complications."

gay A person whose sexual attraction is to people of the same sex. Used especially for males, but may include both sexes. This term is usually used rather than *homosexual.*

gender Attitudes and behavior associated with and expected of the two sexes. The term sex denotes biology, while *gender* refers to social role. See also **gendered**.

gender model of marriage [13]

gender role Prescription for masculine or feminine behavior. The masculine gender role demands instrumental character traits and behavior, whereas the feminine gender role specifies expressive character traits and behavior.

gender schema theory of gender socialization A framework of knowledge and beliefs about differences or similarities between males and females. Gender schema shape socialization into gender roles.

gender similarities hypothesis Assertion—backed by research—that there are few gender differences in characteristics and abilities.

gendered The way that aspects of people's lives and relationships are influenced by gender.

geographic availability Traditionally known in the marriage and family literature as propinquity or proximity and referring to the fact that people tend to meet potential mates who are present in their regional environment.

gerontologists Social scientists who study aging and the elderly.

GLBT An acronym for gay, lesbian, bisexual, or transgendered; a term commonly used when discussing sexual minorities.

globalization The interdependency of people, organizations, economies, or governments across national borders.

good provider role A specialized masculine role that emerged in this country around the 1830s and that emphasized the husband as the only or primary economic provider for his family. The good provider role had disappeared as an expected masculine role by the 1970s. See also **provider role.**

grandfamilies Families headed by grandparents.

grandparent families Families in which a grandparent acts as primary parent to grandchildren.

group home One type of foster-care setting in which several children are cared for around-the-clock by paid professionals who work in shifts and live elsewhere.

guaranteed child support Type of child support (provided in France and Sweden, for example) in which the government sends to the custodial parent the full amount of support awarded to the child and assumes responsibility for collecting what is owed by the noncustodial parent.

habituation The decreased interest in sex over time that results from the increased accessibility of a sexual partner and the predictability of sexual behavior with that partner.

habituation hypothesis Hypothesis that the decline in sexual frequency over a marriage results from habituation.

Healthy Marriage Initiative (HMI). Federal program initiated in 2004 and targeted to TANF ("welfare") recipients, consisting of workshops on listening, communication, and problem-solving skills, as well as presentations on the value of marriage.

hermaphrodite See **intersexual.**

heterogamy Marriage between partners who differ in race, age, education, religious background, or social class. Compare with **homogamy**.

heterosexism The taken-for-granted system of beliefs, values, and customs that places superior value on heterosexual behavior (as opposed to homosexual) and denies or stigmatizes nonheterosexual relations. This tendency also sees the heterosexual family as standard.

heterosexuals People who prefer sexual partners of the opposite sex.

hierarchical compensatory model of caregiving The idea that elderly people prefer their caregivers in ranked order as follows: an available spouse, adult children, siblings, grandchildren, nieces and nephews, friends, neighbors, and, finally, a formal service provider.

hierarchical parenting Concept used to describe a Hispanic parenting philosophy that blends warm emotional support for children with demand for significant respect for parents and other authority figures, including older extended-family members.

HIV/AIDS HIV is *human immunodeficiency virus*, the virus that causes AIDS, or *acquired immune deficiency syndrome.* AIDS is a sexually transmitted disease involving breakdown of the immune system defense against viruses, bacteria, fungi, and other diseases.

homogamy Marriage between partners of similar race, age, education, religious background, and social class. See also **heterogamy**.

homophobia Fear, dread, aversion to, and often hatred of homosexuals.

homosexuals People who are sexually attracted to people of the same sex. Preferred terms are *gay* or *gay man* for men and *lesbian* for women. See also **gay** and **lesbian**.

hooking up A sexual encounter between young people with the understanding that there is no obligation to see each other again or to endow the sexual activity with emotional meaning. Usually there is a group or network context for hooking up; that is, the individuals meet at a social event or have common acquaintances. On some college campuses and elsewhere, hooking up has replaced dating, which is courtship-oriented socializing and sexual activity.

hormonal processes Chemical processes within the body regulated by such hormones as testosterone (a "male" hormone) and estrogen (a "female" hormone). Hormonal processes are thought to shape behavior, as well as physical development and reproductive functions, although experts disagree as to their impact on behavior.

hormones Chemical substances secreted into the bloodstream by the endocrine glands.

household As a Census Bureau category, a household is any group of people residing together.

househusbands Men who take a full-time family care role, rather than being employed; male counterparts to housewives.

hyperparenting The situation in which parents are excessively involved in their children's lives.

impaired fertility Describes the situation of a woman who is not able to succeed in having a child due to a physical barrier or an inability to carry a pregnancy to full term.

incest Sexual relations between closely related individuals.

income effect Occurs when an increase in income contributes to the stability of a marriage by giving it a more adequate financial basis.

income-to-needs ratio An assessment of income as to the degree it meets the needs of the individual, family, or household.

incomplete institution Cherlin's description of a remarried family due to cultural ambiguity.

independence effect Occurs when an increase in income leads to marital dissolution because the partners are better able to afford to live separately.

individualism The cultural milieu that emerged in Europe with industrialization and that values personal self-actualization and happiness along with individual freedom.

individualistic society Society in which the main concern is with one's own interests (which may or may not include those of one's immediate family).

individualistic (self-fulfillment) values Values that encourage self-fulfillment, personal growth, autonomy, and independence over commitment to family or other communal needs.

individualized marriage Concept associated with the argument that contemporary marriage in the United States and other fully industrialized Western societies is no longer institutionalized. Four interrelated characteristics distinguish individualized marriage: (1) it is optional; (2) spouses' roles are flexible—negotiable and renegotiable; (3) its expected rewards involve love, communication, and emotional intimacy; and (4) it exists in conjunction with a vast diversity of family forms.

induced abortion The scientific term for what is commonly termed *abortion.* The removal of the fetus from the uterus is "induced"; that is, it requires a deliberate surgical or pharmaceutical act. What we commonly call "miscarriage" is termed *spontaneous abortion* in scientific language because it happens without any initiative on the part of individuals or medical personnel and, in fact, is usually not desired.

informal adoption Children are taken into a home and considered to be children of the parents, although the "adoption" is not legally formalized.

informal caregiving Unpaid caregiving, provided personally by a family member.

informational power One of the six power bases, or sources of power. This power is based on the persuasive content of what the dominant person tells another individual.

informed consent A requirement of research involving human subjects; before agreeing to participate, subjects are told the purpose of the research and the procedure and whether any risk is involved in participation. The process of obtaining informed consent is supervised by an *institutional review board.*

in-home caregiver A caregiver who provides child care in the child's home, either coming in by the day or as a live-in caregiver.

insecure/anxious attachment style One of three attachment styles in attachment theory, this style entails concern that the beloved will disappear, a situation often characterized as "fear of abandonment."

instability hypothesis The idea that the instability of postdivorce family structure(s) can be damaging to children. According to this hypothesis, a stable single-parent family might be better for a child than a single-parent family succeeded by a remarried family.

institution See **social institution.**

institutional marriage Marriage as a social institution based on dutiful adherence to the time-honored *marriage premise* (which see), particularly the norm of permanence. "Once ensconced in societal mandates for permanence and monogamous sexual exclusivity, the institutionalized marriage in the United States was centered on economic production, kinship network, community connections, the father's authority, and marriage as a functional partnership rather than a romantic relationship. . . . Family tradition, loyalty, and solidarity were more important than individual goals and romantic interest" (Doherty 1992, p. 33). Also referred to as *institutionalized marriage.*

institutional review board (IRB) A local body of experts and community representatives established by a university or research organization to scrutinize research proposals for adherence to professional ethical standards for the protection of human subjects.

instrumental traits See **agentic (instrumental) character traits.**

interaction–constructionist perspective Theoretical perspective that focuses on internal family dynamics; the ongoing action among and response to one another of family members.

interactionist perspective on human sexuality A perspective, derived from symbolic interaction theory, which holds that sexual activities and relationships are shaped by the sexual scripts available in a culture.

interethnic marriages Marriages between spouses who are not defined as of different races but do belong to different ethnic groups.

interference with visitation A legal term for actions of a custodial parent that hinder the noncustodial parent's scheduled visitation with a child. Such interference may consist of alleging (falsely) that the child is too ill to visit, has other plans, is not at home at the pickup time, and the like. Some states have legislated penalties for interference with visitation, whereas others make little effort to enforce the noncustodial parent's right to contact with her or his child. Often allegations of interference with visitation are difficult to evaluate.

intergenerational transmission of divorce risk The tendency for children of divorced parents to have a greater propensity to divorce than children from intact families.

internalize Make a part of oneself. Often refers to the socialization process by which children learn their parents' norms and values to the point that they become the child's own views.

interparental conflict perspective (on children's adjustment to divorce) One of the theoretical perspectives concerning the negative outcomes among children of divorced parents. From the interparental conflict perspective, the conflict between parents before, during, and after the divorce is responsible for the lowered well-being of the children of divorce.

interpersonal exchange model of sexual satisfaction A view of sexual relations, derived from exchange theory, that sees sexual satisfaction as shaped by the costs, rewards, and expectations of a relationship and the alternatives to it.

interracial marriages Marriages of a partner of one (socially defined) race to someone of a different race.

intersexual A person whose genitalia, secondary sex characteristics, hormones, or other physiological features are not unambiguously male or female.

intimacy (Sternberg's triangular theory of love) Committing oneself to a particular other and honoring that commitment in spite of some personal sacrifices while sharing one's inner self with the other. Intimacy requires interdependence.

intimate partner power Power in a relationship, whether of married or unmarried intimate partners.

intimate partner violence Violence against current or former spouses, cohabitants, or sexual or relationship partners.

intimate terrorism Abuse that is almost entirely male and that is oriented to controlling the partner through fear and intimidation.

intimate terrorism A man's systematic use of verbal or physical violence to gain or maintain control over his female partner.

involuntary infertility Situation of a couple or individual who would like to have a baby but cannot. Involuntary infertility is medically diagnosed when a woman has tried for twelve months to become pregnant without success.

job sharing Two people sharing one job.

joint custody A situation in which both divorced parents continue to take equal responsibility for important decisions regarding their child's general upbringing.

kin Parents and other relatives, such as in-laws, grandparents, aunts and uncles, and cousins. See also **extended family.**

labor force A social invention that arose with the industrialization of the nineteenth century, when people characteristically became wage earners, hiring out their labor to someone else.

laboratory observation Observation of behavior, including verbal behavior, in an environment controlled by the researcher. For example, a researcher may ask a father, a mother, and an adolescent to discuss an issue, solve a problem, or play a game and observe their responses and interactions, which may be audio- or video-recorded.

laissez-faire parenting style Overly permissive parenting. Children set their own standards for behavior, with little or no parental guidance or authority. Parents are indulgent but not necessarily involved in a supportive way with the child's everyday activities and problems.

latent kin matrix "A web of continually shifting linkages that provide the potential for activating and intensifying close kin relationships" (Riley 1983, p. 441).

legal divorce The dissolution of a marriage by the state through a court order terminating the marriage.

legitimate power One of the six power bases, or sources of power. Legitimate power stems from the more dominant individual's ability to claim authority, or the right to request compliance.

leisure gap Men enjoy more free time to spend engaged in activities of their own choosing than do women.

lesbian A woman who is sexually attracted to other women. This term is usually used rather than *homosexual*.

leveling Being transparent, authentic, and explicit about how one truly feels, especially concerning the more conflictive or hurtful aspects of an intimate relationship. Among other things, leveling between intimates implies self-disclosure and commitment (to intimacy).

Levinger's model of divorce decisions This model, derived from exchange theory, presents a decision to divorce as involving a calculus of the *barriers* to divorce (e.g., concerns about children and finances; religious prohibitions), the *rewards* of the marriage, and *alternatives* to the marriage (e.g., can the divorced person anticipate a new relationship, career development, or a single life that will be more rewarding and less stressful than the marriage?).

life chances The opportunities that exist for a social group or an individual to pursue education and economic advancement, to secure medical care and preserve health, to marry and have children, to have material goods and housing of desired quality, and so forth.

life stress perspective (on children's adjustment to divorce) One of the theoretical perspectives concerning the negative outcomes among children of divorced parents. From the life stress perspective, divorce involves the same stress for children as for adults. Divorce is not one single event but a process of stressful events—moving, changing schools, and so on.

limerence A psycho-emotional situation in which one obsesses about another person (the "limerent object") and yearns for reciprocation but has little, if any, concern for the other person's well-being. Not to be confused with love or the early, anxious stage of discovering love.

longitudinal study One technique of scientific investigation in which researchers study the same individuals or groups over an extended period, usually with periodic surveys.

looking-glass self The concept that people gradually come to accept and adopt as their own the evaluations, definitions, and judgments of themselves that they see reflected in the faces, words, and gestures of those around them.

love A deep and vital emotion resulting from significant need for satisfaction, coupled with a caring for and acceptance of the beloved, and resulting in an intimate relationship. Love may make the world go 'round, but it's a lot of work, too.

love style A distinctive characteristic or personality that loving or lovelike relationships can take. One social scientist has distinguished six: **agape, eros, ludus, mania, pragma,** and **storge.**

ludus The love style that focuses on love as play and on enjoying many sexual partners rather than searching for one serious relationship. This love style emphasizes the recreational aspect of sexuality. See also **agape, eros, mania, pragma,** and **storge.**

male dominance The cultural idea of masculine superiority; the idea that men should and do exercise the most control and influence over society's members.

mania The love style that combines strong sexual attraction and emotional intensity with extreme jealousy and moodiness, in which manic partners alternate between euphoria and depression. See also **agape, eros, ludus, pragma,** and **storge.**

manipulating Seeking to control the feelings, attitudes, and behavior of one's partner or partners in underhanded ways rather than by assertively stating one's case.

marital power Power exercised between spouses.

marital rape A husband's forcing a wife to submit to sexual contact that she does not want or that she finds offensive.

marital stability The quality or situation of remaining married.

market approach to child care Child-care arrangement of working parents; other people are hired to care for children while parents are at their jobs.

marriage market The sociological concept that potential mates take stock of their personal and social characteristics and then comparison shop or bargain for the best buy (mate) they can get.

marriage premise By getting married, partners accept the responsibility to keep each other primary in their lives and to work hard to ensure that their relationship continues.

martyring Doing all one can for others while ignoring one's own legitimate needs. Martyrs often punish the person to whom they are martyring by letting the person know "just how much I put up with."

masculinities Culturally defined ways of being a man. The plural conveys the idea that there are varied models of appropriate behavior.

mate selection risk The idea that children of divorce may be likely to select spouses who are unlikely to make good marriage partners.

Miller's typology of urban Native American families

- **bicultural:** Families that develop a successful blend of native beliefs and practices with those adaptive to living in urban settings.
- **marginal:** Urban families that have become alienated from both Indian and mainstream American cultures.
- **traditional:** Families that retain primarily Indian ways in their urban environment.
- **transitional:** Families that are tending to assimilate to the white working class.

minority stress The negative consequences of chronic stress that result from minority-group stigmatization such as discrimination and prejudice. Outcomes include suffering from psychological disorders and increased health risks. Manifestations include self-loathing, fear of attacks, substance abuse, and so on.

mixed message Two simultaneous messages that contradict each other; also called a *double message*. For example, society gives us mixed messages regarding family values and individualistic values and about premarital sex. People, too, can send mixed messages, as when a partner says, "Of course I always like to talk with you" while turning up the TV.

modern sexism Sexism that takes the form of (a) denial of the existence of discrimination against women, (b) resentment of complaints about discrimination, and (c) resentment of "special favors" for women.

motherhood penalty Negative lifetime impact on earnings for women who raise children.

mothering approach to child care A family's child care arrangement that gives preference to the mother's caregiving role. A couple balances nonemployment of the mother with extra jobs or hours for the father, or, if the mother must work to maintain the family economically, her employment role is minimized.

multipartnered fertility Having children in more than one marriage or relationship.

mutually economically dependent spouses (MEDS) Describes a dual-earner marriage in which each partner earns between 40 and 59 percent of the family income.

nadir of family disorganization Low point of family disorganization when a family is going through a family crisis.

nanny An in-home child care worker who cares for a family's children either on a live-in basis or by the day; may include traveling with the family.

naturalistic observation A technique of scientific investigation in which a researcher lives with a family or social group or spends extensive time with them, carefully recording their activities, conversations, gestures, and other aspects of everyday life.

near peer marriage (Schwartz's typology) Couples who believe in partner equality but fall short of a 60–40 division of household labor, usually because of the need for the husband's higher earnings.

negative affect Showing emotion(s) defined as negative, such as anger, sadness, whining, disgust, tension, fear, and/or belligerence.

neo-sexism Same as **modern sexism.**

neotraditional families Families that value traditional gender roles and organize their family life in these terms as far as practicable. Formal male dominance is softened by an egalitarian spirit.

no-fault divorce The legal situation in which a partner seeking a divorce no longer has to prove "fault" according to a state's legal definition but only needs to assert "irretrievable breakdown" or "irreconcilable differences." Sometimes termed **unilateral divorce.**

noncustodial grandparent A parent of a divorced, noncustodial parent.

no-power A situation in which partners are equally able to influence each other and, at the same time, are not concerned about their relative power vis-à-vis each other. No-power partners negotiate and compromise instead of trying to win.

normative order hypothesis The thesis that to proceed through the family life cycle "on time" provides the best chance for a good adjustment in each family stage. Applies as well to the sequencing of education, job, marriage, and parenthood.

nuclear family A family group comprising only the wife, the husband, and their children. See also **extended family.**

nuclear-family model monopoly The cultural assumption that the first-marriage family is the "real" model of family living, with all other family forms viewed as deficient.

occupational segregation The distribution of men and women into substantially different occupations. Women are overrepresented in clerical and service work, for example, whereas men dominate the higher professions and the upper levels of management.

occupations Employment—that is, work for pay—as contrasted with unpaid household work.

"on-time" transition Moving from one family life cycle stage to another according to the most common cultural pattern.

opportunity costs (of children) The economic opportunities for wage earning and investments that parents forgo when raising children.

opting out A woman's leaving the labor force, permanently or temporarily, in order to devote full time to child-raising.

para-parent An unrelated adult who informally plays a parentlike role for a child.

parental adjustment perspective (on children's adjustment to divorce) One of the theoretical perspectives concerning the negative outcomes among children of divorced parents. From the parental adjustment perspective, the parent's child-raising skills are impaired as a result of the divorce, with probable negative consequences for the children.

parental loss perspective (on children's adjustment to divorce) One of the theoretical perspectives concerning the negative outcomes among children of divorced parents. From the parental loss perspective, divorce involves the absence of a parent from the household, which deprives children of the optimal environment for their emotional, practical, and social support.

parenting alliance The degree to which partners agree with and support each other as parents.

parenting approach to child care In this approach, child care is shared by the parents on as equal a basis as possible. Working parents try to restructure their employment arrangements to make this possible.

parenting style A general manner of relating to and disciplining children.

passion (Sternberg's triangular theory of love) The drives that lead to romance, physical attraction, sexual consummation, and so on in a loving relationship; one dimension of the triangular theory of love.

passive-aggression Expressing anger at some person or situation indirectly, through nagging, nitpicking, or sarcasm, for example, rather than directly and openly. See also **displacement, sabotage.**

patriarchal norm (of marital power) The norm (cultural rule) that the man should be dominant in a marital relationship.

patriarchal sexuality The view of human sexuality in which men own everything in the society, including women and women's sexuality. Males' sexual needs are emphasized while females' needs are minimized.

patriarchy A social system in which males are dominant.

peer marriage (Schwartz's typology) Couples who have a close-to-equal split of household chores and money management and who consider themselves to have equal status in the marriage or cohabiting union.

period of family disorganization That period in a family crisis, after the stressor event has occurred, during which family morale and organization slump and habitual roles and routines become nebulous.

permissiveness with affection The standard that permits nonmarital sex for women and men equally, provided they have a fairly stable, affectionate relationship.

permissiveness without affection The standard that allows nonmarital sex for women and men regardless of how much stability or affection exists in their relationship. Also called the *recreational standard.*

permissive parenting style One of three parenting styles in this schema, permissive parenting gives children little parental guidance.

pileup (stressor overload) Concept from family stress and crisis theory that refers to the accumulation of family stressors and prior hardships.

pleasure bond The idea, from Masters and Johnson's book by the same name, that sexual expression between intimates is one way of expressing and strengthening the emotional bond between them.

pluralistic family Term used to designate the contemporary family, characterized by "tolerance and diversity, rather than a single family ideal" (Doherty 1992, p. 35). Taking many forms, the pluralistic family is also referred to as the *postmodern family*.

polyamory A marriage system in which one or both spouses retain the option to sexually love others in addition to their spouses.

polyandry A marriage system in which a woman has more than one spouse.

polygamy A marriage system in which a person takes more than one spouse.

polygyny A marriage system in which one man has multiple wives; a marriage of a woman with plural husbands is termed **polyandry**.

pool of eligibles A group of individuals who, by virtue of background or social status, are most likely to be considered eligible to make culturally compatible marriage partners.

positive affect The expression, either verbal or nonverbal, of one's feelings of affection toward another.

postmodern family Term used to describe the situation in which (1) families today exhibit multiple forms, and (2) new or altered family forms continue to emerge or develop.

postmodern theory Theoretical perspective that largely analyzes social interaction (discourse or narrative) in order to demonstrate that a phenomenon is socially constructed.

power The ability to exercise one's will. *Personal power*, or *autonomy*, is power exercised over oneself. *Social power* is the ability to exercise one's will over others.

power politics Power struggles between spouses in which each seeks to gain a power advantage over the other; the opposite of a **no-power** relationship.

pragma The love style that emphasizes the practical, or pragmatic, element in human relationships and involves the rational assessment of a potential (or actual) partner's assets and liabilities. See also **agape, eros, ludus, mania,** and **storge.**

primary group A group, usually relatively small, in which there are close, face-to-face relationships or equivalent ties that are technologically mediated. The family and a friendship group are primary groups. See also **secondary group.**

primary parent Parent who takes full responsibility for meeting the child's physical and emotional needs by providing the major part of the child's care directly or by managing the child's care by others or by doing both.

principle of least interest The postulate that the partner with the least interest in the relationship is the one who is more apt to control the relationship and to exploit the other.

private face of family The aspect of the family that provides individuals with intimacy, emotional support, and love.

private safety net Social support from family and friends, rather than from public sources.

pronatalist bias A cultural attitude that takes having children for granted.

provider role A term for the family role involving wage work to support the family. May be carried out by one spouse or partner only or by both.

psychic divorce Regaining psychological autonomy after divorce; emotionally separating oneself from the personality and influence of the former spouse.

psychic intimacy The sharing of people's minds and feelings. Psychic intimacy may or may not involve sexual intimacy.

psychological control Control over others by use of manipulative strategies, such as inducing guilt or withdrawing signs of affection.

psychological parent The parent, usually but not necessarily the mother, who assumes principal responsibility for raising the child.

public face of family The aspect of the family that produces public goods and services.

race A group or category thought of as representing a distinct biological heritage. In reality, there is only one human race. "Racial" categories are social constructs; the so-called races do not differ significantly in terms of basic biological makeup. But "racial" designations nevertheless have social and economic effects and cultural meanings.

race socialization The socialization process that involves developing a child's pride in his or her cultural heritage while warning and preparing him or her about the possibilities of encountering discrimination.

rape myths Beliefs about rape that function to blame the victim and exonerate the rapist.

rapport talk In Deborah Tannen's terms, this is conversation engaged in by women aimed primarily at gaining or reinforcing rapport or intimacy. See also **report talk.**

redivorce An emerging trend in U.S. society. Redivorces take place more rapidly than first divorces so that many who divorce (and their children) can expect several rapid and emotionally significant transitions in lifestyle and family unit.

referent power One of the six power bases, or sources of power. In a marriage or relationship, this form of power is based on one partner's emotional identification with the other and his or her willingness to agree to the other's decisions or preferences.

refined divorce rate Number of divorces per 1,000 married women over age fifteen. See also **crude divorce rate.**

relationship ideologies Expectations for closeness and/or distance as well as ideas about how partners should play their roles.

relatives of divorce Kinship ties established by marriage but retained after the marriage is dissolved—for example, the relationship of a former mother-in-law and daughter-in-law.

remarriages Marriages in which at least one partner has already been divorced or widowed. Remarriages are becoming increasingly common for Americans.

replacement level (of fertility) The average number of births per woman (a total fertility rate of 2.1) necessary to replace the population.

report talk In Deborah Tannen's terms, this is conversation engaged in by men aimed primarily at conveying information. See also **rapport talk.**

resilience The ability to recover from challenging situations.

resilient families Families that emphasize mutual acceptance, respect, and shared values; members rely on one another for emotional support.

resilient individuals Individuals with the capacity to recover from or rise above adverse situations and events.

resource hypothesis Hypothesis (originated by Robert Blood and Donald Wolfe) that the relative power between wives and husbands results from their relative resources as individuals.

resources In exchange theory or intimate partner power analysis, the assets an individual can bring to the relationship. Resources can be material (e.g., income, gifts) or nonmaterial (e.g., emotional support, practical assistance, personality qualities).

resources in cultural context The effect of resources on marital power depends on the cultural context. In a traditional society, norms of patriarchal authority may override personal resources. In a fully egalitarian society, a norm of intimate partner and marital equality may override personal resources. It is in a transitional society that the resource hypothesis is most likely to shape marital power relations.

reward power One of the six power bases, or sources of power. With regard to marriage or partner relationships, this power is based on an individual's ability to give material or nonmaterial gifts and favors to the partner.

rewards and costs In exchange theory or related theoretical analyses, the benefits and disadvantages of a relationship.

role The expectations associated with a particular position in society or in a family. The mother role, for example, calls for its occupant to provide physical care, emotional nurturance, social guidance, and the like to her children.

role ambiguity The situation in which there are few clear guidelines regarding what responsibilities, behaviors, and emotions family members are expected to exhibit.

role-making Improvising a course of action as a way of enacting a role. In role-making, we may use our acts to alter the traditional expectations and obligations associated with a role. This concept emphasizes the variability in the ways different individuals enact a particular role.

role-taking Role-taking has two meanings. It can mean playing a role associated with a status one occupies, such as taking the mother role when one has a child. It can also mean acting out a role that is not, or not yet, one's own, as when children play "mommy" or "daddy" or "police officer."

sabotage A passive-aggressive action in which a person tries to spoil or undermine some activity another has planned. Sabotage is not always consciously planned. See also **passive-aggression.**

sandwich generation Middle-aged (or older) individuals, usually women, who are sandwiched between the simultaneous responsibilities of caring for their dependent children (sometimes young adults) and aging parents.

science "A logical system that bases knowledge on . . . systematic observation, empirical evidence, facts we verify with our senses" (Macionis 2006, p. 15).

scientific investigation In social science, the systematic gathering of information—using surveys, experiments, naturalistic observation, archival historical material, and case studies—from which it is often possible to generalize with a significant degree of predictability. Data collection and analysis are usually guided by theory or earlier scientific observations. They point to theory modification and a greater understanding of the phenomenon being studied.

second shift Sociologist Arlie Hochschild's term for the domestic work that employed women must perform after coming home from a day on the job.

secondary group A group, often large and geographically dispersed, characterized by distant, practical relationships. An impersonal society is characterized by secondary groups and relations. See also the opposite, **primary group.**

secure attachment style One of three attachment styles in attachment theory, this style involves trust that the relationship will provide necessary and ongoing emotional and social support.

segmented assimilation Assimilation may vary within an immigrant stream. Immigrants with professional education and skills or from favored national origin groups or both may do very well economically and socially and become culturally integrated. Other immigrants may not have the educational background or other human capital necessary to advance in the new environment and may even experience downward mobility.

selection hypothesis The idea that many of the changes found in a dependent variable, which might be assumed to be associated with the independent variable, are really due to sample selection. For instance, the selection hypothesis posits that many of the benefits associated with marriage—for example, higher income and wealth, along with better health—are not necessarily due to the fact of being married but, rather, to the personal characteristics of those who choose—or are selected into—marriage. Similarly, the selection hypothesis posits that many of the characteristics associated with cohabitation result not from the practice of cohabiting itself but from the personal characteristics of those who choose to cohabit. See also the antonym, **experience hypothesis.**

self-care An approach to child care for working parents in which the child is at home or out without an adult caretaker. Parents may be in touch by phone.

self-concept The basic feelings people have about themselves, their characteristics and abilities, and their worth; how people think of or view themselves.

self-disclosure Letting others see one as one really is. Self-disclosure demands authenticity. Also see **self-revelation.**

self-identification theory A theory of gender socialization, developed by psychologist Lawrence Kohlberg, that begins with a child's categorization of self as male or female. The child goes on to identify sex-appropriate behaviors in the family, media, and elsewhere and to adopt those behaviors.

self-revelation Gradually sharing intimate information about oneself. Also see **self-disclosure**.

self-worth Part of a person's self-concept that involves feelings about one's own value; also called *self-esteem.*

seven-stage model of stepfamily development Model of stepfamily progression that proceeds through the following stages: fantasy, immersion, awareness, mobilization, action, contact, and resolution.

sex Refers to biological characteristics—that is, male or female anatomy or physiology. The term **gender** refers to the social roles, attitudes, and behavior associated with males or females.

sex ratio The number of men per 100 women in a society. If the sex ratio is above 100, there are more men than women; if it is below 100, there are more women than men.

sexting Using cell phones to send sexually explicit images or messages to others.

sexual abuse A form of child abuse that involves forced, tricked, or coerced sexual behavior—exposure, unwanted kissing, fondling of sexual organs, intercourse, rape, and incest—between a minor and an older person.

sexual intimacy A level of interpersonal interaction in which partners have a sexual relationship. Sexual intimacy may or may not involve psychic intimacy.

sexual orientation The attraction an individual has for a sexual partner of the same or opposite sex.

sexual responsibility The assumption by each partner of responsibility for his or her own sexual response.

sexual scripts *Scripts* are culturally written patterns or "plots" for human behavior.

Sexual scripts offer reasons for having sex and designate who should take the sexual initiative, how long an encounter should last, what positions are acceptable, and so forth.

shared parenting Mother and father, or two same-sex parents, who both take full responsibility as parents.

shift work As defined by the Bureau of Labor Statistics, any work schedule in which more than half of an employee's hours are before 8 a.m. or after 4 p.m.

sibling violence Family violence that takes place between siblings (brothers and sisters).

single mothers by choice Women who intentionally become mothers, although they are not married or with a partner. They are typically older, with economic and educational resources that enable them to be self-supporting.

single mothers by circumstance Women who become single mothers in ways other than by purposeful choice.

situational couple violence Mutual violence between partners that often occurs in conjunction with a specific argument. It involves fewer instances, is not likely to escalate, and tends to be less severe in terms of injuries.

social capital perspective (on parenthood) Motivation for parenthood in anticipation of the links parenthood provides to social networks and their resources.

social class Position in the social hierarchy, such as *upper class, middle class, working class,* or *lower class.* Can be viewed in terms of such indicators as education, occupation, and income or analyzed in terms of status, respect, and lifestyle.

social fathers Males who are not a biological father but are performing the role of father, such as a stepfather.

social institution A system of patterned and predictable ways of thinking and behaving—beliefs, values, attitudes, and norms—concerning important aspects of people's lives in society. Examples of major social institutions are the family, religion, government, the economy, and education.

social learning theory (of gender socialization) According to this theory, children learn gender roles as they are taught or modeled by parents, schools, and the media.

socialization The process by which society influences members to internalize attitudes, beliefs, values, and expectations.

socioeconomic status One's position in society, measured by educational achievement, occupation, and/or income.

spectatoring A term Masters and Johnson coined to describe the practice of emotionally removing oneself from a sexual encounter in order to watch oneself and see how one is doing.

spousal support Economic support of a separated spouse or ex-spouse by the other spouse ordered by a court following separation or divorce.

status exchange hypothesis Regarding interracial/interethnic marriage, the argument that an individual might trade his or her socially defined superior racial/ethnic status for the economically or educationally superior status of a partner in a less-privileged racial/ethnic group.

stepmother trap The conflict between two views: Society sentimentalizes the stepmother's role and expects her to be unnaturally loving toward her stepchildren but at the same time views her as a wicked witch.

stonewalling One of the **Four Horsemen of the Apocalypse** (which see) that involves refusing to listen to a partner's complaints.

storge An affectionate, companionate style of loving. See also **agape, eros, ludus, mania,** and **pragma.**

stress model of parental effectiveness The idea that stress experienced by parents causes parental frustration, anger, and depression, increasing the likelihood of household conflict and leading to poorer parenting practices.

stressors Precipitating events that cause a crisis; they are often situations for which the family has had little or no preparation. See also **ABC-X model.**

stressor overload A situation in which an unrelenting series of small crises adds up to a major crisis.

stress-related growth Personal growth and maturity attained in the context of a stressful life experience such as divorce.

structural antinatalism The structural, or societal, conditions in which bearing and raising children is discouraged either overtly or—as may be the case in the United States—covertly through inadequate support for parenting.

structural constraints Economic and social forces that limit options and, hence, personal choices.

structure–functional perspective Theoretical perspective that looks to the functions that institutions perform for society and the structural form of the institution.

survey A technique of scientific investigation using questionnaires or brief face-to-face interviews or both. An example is the U.S. census.

swinging A marriage agreement in which couples exchange partners to engage in purely recreational sex.

symbolic interaction theory (of gender socialization) Uses the concepts of Charles Cooley (primary group, looking-glass self) and George Herbert Mead ("me" and "I," "play, the game, and the generalized other") to explain how children are socialized into culturally defined gender roles.

system A combination of elements or components that are interrelated and organized as a whole. The human body is a system, as is a family.

Temporary Assistance for Needy Families (TANF) Federal legislation that replaces Aid to Families with Dependent Children and whereby government welfare assistance to poor parents is limited to five years for most families, with most adult recipients required to find work within two years.

theoretical perspective A way of viewing reality, or a lens through which analysts organize and interpret what they observe. Researchers on the family identify those aspects of families that are of interest to them, based on their own theoretical perspective.

theory of complementary needs Theory developed by social scientist Robert Winch suggesting that we are attracted to partners whose needs complement our own. In the positive view of this theory, we are attracted to others whose strengths are harmonious with our own so that we are more effective as a couple than either of us would be alone.

total fertility rate For a given year, the number of births that women would have over their reproductive lifetimes if all women at each age had babies at the rate for each age group that year; can be calculated for social or age categories as well as for nations as a whole.

traditional sexism Beliefs that men and women are essentially different and should occupy different social roles, that women are not as fit as men to perform certain tasks and occupations, and that differential treatment of men and women is acceptable.

traditionals (Schwartz's typology) Marriages or domestic partnerships in which the man dominates all areas of decision making except children. He is the primary breadwinner and she is the primary homemaker, even if employed. In Schwartz's typology, both spouses favor this arrangement.

trailing spouse The spouse of a relocated employee who moves with the other spouse.

transgendered A person who has adopted a gender identity that differs from sex/gender as recorded at birth; a person who declines to identify as either male or female.

transition to parenthood The circumstances involved in assuming the parent role.

transitional egalitarian situation (of marital power) Marriages or domestic partnerships in which neither patriarchal nor egalitarian norms prevail. The couple negotiate relationship power, with the relative resources of each individual playing an important role in the outcome.

transnational family A family of immigrants or immigrant stock that maintains close ties with the sending country. Identity and behavior connect the immigrant family to the new country and the old, and their social networks cross national boundaries.

transsexual An individual who has begun life identified as a member of one sex, but later comes to believe he or she belongs to the other sex. The person may undertake surgical reconstruction to attain a body type closer to that of the desired sex.

triangular theory of love Robert Sternberg's theory that consummate love involves three components: intimacy, passion, and commitment.

two-career marriage Marriage in which both partners have a strong commitment to the lifetime development of both careers. Also called *dual-career couple* or *dual-career family*.

two-earner marriages Marriages in which the wife as well as the husband is employed, but her work is not viewed as a lifetime career. His may be viewed as a "job" rather than a career, as well. Sometimes termed *dual-earner marriage* or *two-paycheck marriage*.

undocumented immigrant The preferred term for "illegal" immigrants, those who are present in a country but are not citizens or legal residents. The implication of the term *undocumented* (compared to *illegal*) is that immigrants may or should have legitimate claims to asylum or residence even if these have not been formally recognized.

unilateral divorce A divorce can be obtained under the no-fault system by one partner even if the other partner objects. The term *unilateral divorce* emphasizes this feature of current divorce law. See also **no-fault divorce.**

unpaid family work The necessary tasks of attending to both the emotional needs of all family members and the practical needs of dependent members, such as children or elderly parents, and maintaining the family domicile.

value of children perspective (on parenthood) Motivation for parenthood because of the rewards, including symbolic rewards, that children bring to parents.

voluntary childlessness The deliberate choice not to become a parent.

vulnerable families Families that have a low sense of common purpose, feel in little control over what happens to them, and tend to cope with problems by showing diminished respect and/or understanding for each other.

wage gap The persistent difference in earnings between men and women.

wheel of love An idea developed by Ira Reiss in which love is seen as developing through a four-stage, circular process, including rapport, self-revelation, mutual dependence, and personality need fulfillment.

Subject Index